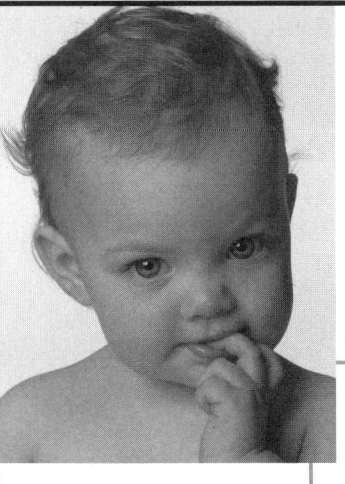

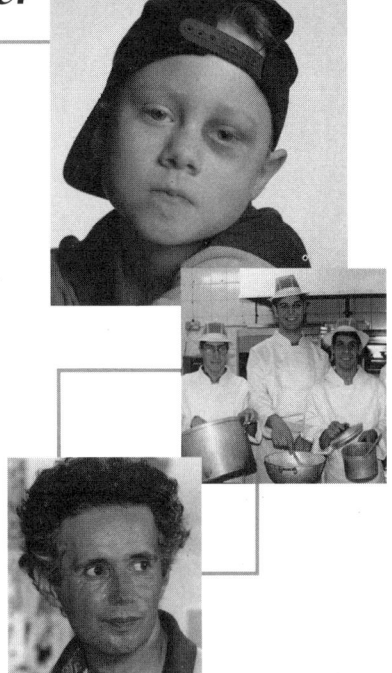

All your needs... one caring answer

- ✓ Community services
- ✓ Residential care
- ✓ Binoh – special education needs
- ✓ Fostering and adoption
- ✓ Respite care
- ✓ Day services
- ✓ Family centre
- ✓ Vocational training
- ✓ Koleinu – for young Jewish deaf
- ✓ **Family Information Link**
- ✓ Unity – integrated youth club for children
- ✓ Links – recreation for adults with learning disabilities
- ✓ **Association for Jewish Youth**
- ✓ Annie Lawson School

Norwood Ravenswood is Europe's largest Jewish family services charity, working with over 6,000 children, young people and adults, people of all ages with learning disabilities and their families every year. We provide local, lifelong family services from birth onwards for all those in need.

For more information please contact
Broadway House • 80-82 The Broadway
Stanmore • HA74HB • Telephone 0181 954 4555

Norwood Ravenswood is a company limited by guarantee registered in England under the number 3263519.
Registered Charities No 1059050

You can always judge a person by his Friends

EINSTEIN *SPIELBERG* *FREUD*

These 'Friends', both past and present, have chosen to link their names with the world renowned Hebrew University of Jerusalem. Add your name to these distinguished personalities and make new friends by promoting the outstanding achievements of Israel's largest basic research University.

Special Interest Groups

Young Friends/Alumni - Womens' Groups - The Jewish & National University Library Group - British Friends of YISSUM (commercialisation of HU research) Jerusalem Botanical Gardens - Legal - Medical - Anglo-Israel Archaeological Society

Regional Groups

Glasgow - Birmingham - Sheffield - Brighton & Hove - Leicester Bradford, Harrogate and Leeds - Ireland - Southport - Cardiff

For further information on our activities contact

0171 286 1176

This advertisement has been sponsored

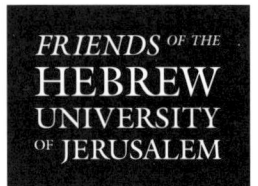

Registered Charity Number 209691

3 St. John's Wood Road London NW8 8RB. Tel: 0171 286 1176. Fax: 0171 289 5549.

British EMUNAH

WORKS TO STRENGTHEN THE FAMILY UNIT IN ISRAEL!

DAY CARE CENTRES

KINDERGARTENS

CHILDREN'S HOMES

VOCATIONAL HIGH SCHOOL

VOCATIONAL TRAINING SCHOOL
For Girls with Learning Disabilities

AFTER SCHOOL PROGRAMMES AND ACTIVITIES FOR DEPRIVED TEENAGERS

HOSTEL FOR TEENAGE GIRLS AT RISK

COMMUNITY CENTRES

WELFARE PROGRAMMES FOR VICTIMS OF FAMILY ABUSE

CARE FOR NEEDY FAMILIES AND THE ELDERLY

Head Office
British EMUNAH
Norwood House,
Harmony Way (off Victoria Road)
London NW4 2DR
Tel. 0181-203-6066
Fax 0181-203-6668

In aid of Child Resettlement Fund
Charities Reg. No. 215398

Bar Ilan University

An international campus of 23,000 students, and regional colleges serving Israel from north to south, pioneering research in the detection of cancer, male infertility, children's disabilities, information and technology, Jewish culture.

Bar Ilan University, Ramat Gan, Israel, for 40 years has brought together the religious and secular, and achieved academic excellence with tolerance and integrity.

For further information, please contact:

Friends of Bar Ilan University
16 Wigmore Street
London W1H 9DE
Tel: 0171 436 9706
Fax: 0171 436 2483

Charity Reg. No. 314139

OPERATION WHEELCHAIRS COMMITTEE

Our logo has changed, but the need for your support has not!

TERRORIST ATTACKS CONTINUE TO MAIM AND WOUND OUR ISRAELI SOLDIERS.

Please help us to provide vital rehabilitation and medical equipment

Donations to: Chairman: Anita Alexander-Passe
Operation Wheelchairs Committee
Box YB, 34/36 Maddox Street, London W1R 9PD
Telephone: 0171 495 8849
PLEASE REMEMBER US WHEN MAKING YOUR WILL
Charity No. 263089

Leo Baeck College
Rabbinic Programme:
Applications by 31st December

LEO BAECK COLLEGE

FOR THE STUDY OF JUDAISM AND THE TRAINING OF RABBIS AND TEACHERS

BA in Hebrew & Jewish Studies
Full Time   Part Time

MA in Hebrew & Jewish Studies
Full Time   Part Time

MA in Jewish Studies
Part Time   Evening
London   Manchester

Courses include: Qumran - Contemporary Jewish Theology - Midrash.

Please write to: The Registrar Leo Baeck College 80 East End Road, London N3 2SY Tel: 0181 349 4525 Fax: 0181 343 2558

TECHNION
the cradle of Israel's technology

For over seventy years the Technion has been Israel's primary technological university and largest centre of applied research. During that time more than 40,000 graduates have made indispensable contributions to Israel's agricultural and industrial development, economic growth and national security.

Today no less than 75% of all engineers and scientists working in Israel are Technion graduates. Twice as many will be required by the end of the decade to meet the needs of Israel's science-based industries.

Remembering TECHNION in your Will or a life-time donation enables you to play your part in ensuring that Israel meets this vital challenge.

British Technion Society
62 Grosvenor Street London W1X 9DA
Telephone: 0171-495 6824 Fax: 0171-355 1525.
Registered Charity No. 206922

"To save one life is as if one has saved the entire world"
Talmudic quote

BRITISH FRIENDS OF RAMBAM MEDICAL CENTRE

Why not save a life by giving a donation for the purchase of bone-marrow transpant equipment for sick children at the Rambam Medical Centre in Haifa, Israel.

Your donation WOULD make a difference between life and death.

Donations to: Director: Anita Alexander-Passe
BRITISH FRIENDS OF RAMBAM MEDICAL CENTRE
Box YB, 34/36 Maddox Street, London W1R 9PD
Telephone: 0171 495 8849
PLEASE REMEMBER US WHEN MAKING YOUR WILL
Charity No. 1028061

CENTRE FOR JEWISH EDUCATION

The Sternberg Centre for Judaism
80 East End Road, London N3 2SY
Tel: 0181 343 4303   Fax: 0181 349 0694
E-mail: cjeuk@compuserve.com
Website: www.knowledge.co.uk/cje/

The Centre for Jewish Education provides educational services for The Reform Synagogues of Great Britain, The Union of Liberal and Progressive Synagogues and the Leo Baeck College

Our aim is to bring about the development of life long Jewish Education in synagogues through:

- provision of education for all ages
- enhanced quality of education
- the setting of a higher priority for educational planning
- trained teachers, head teachers, rabbis and educational leaders
- innovative educational resources

We provide:

- training programmes
- educational courses and workshops
- curriculum materials in Hebrew and Jewish studies
- three learning and resource centres
- educational consultants
- family/community education training and programmes
- support for the development of education in communities

We seek to develop in individuals and communities the skills and vision to transmit a love of Judaism and a love of learning so that they become self-reliant and inspirational in the practice of Jewish Education

BEN-GURION UNIVERSITY OF THE NEGEV

"To build in Zion a scientific and teaching centre… a source of moral inspiration and courage…" DAVID BEN-GURION

Through academic excellence, commitment to the Negev and the community and to building bridges of peace to the world, BEN-GURION UNIVERSITY OF THE NEGEV (est. 1969) is fulfilling this prophecy…

- *Faculties:* Engineering Sciences, Health Sciences, Natural Sciences and Humanities/Social Sciences
- *Research Institutes:* Institutes for Applied Research, Jacob Blaustein Institute for Desert Research, Ben-Gurion Research Centre, Institute for Applied Bio-Sciences
- *Schools:* School of Management, Kreitman School of Advanced Graduate Studies
- *Student enrolment:* (1997–98) 12,500 at all degree levels

Please help this vital work with a donation or bequest

BEN-GURION UNIVERSITY FOUNDATION
21/22 Grosvenor Street, London W1X 9FE
Tel: 0171-499 2276. Fax: 0171-491 2649. Registered Charity No. 276203.

UJIA
UNITED JEWISH ISRAEL APPEAL

no contribution touches more lives

Head Office: Balfour House, 741 High Road London N12 0BQ
T: 0181 446 1477. **F**: 0181 446 1180

*The majority of work for which the UJIA is known is carried out by its associated charity the Joint Jewish Charitable Trust Charity Reg. No. 1060078.
A company limited by guarantee. Registered in England No. 3295115 Registered office as above.*

JEWISH TRAVEL GUIDE 1998
INTERNATIONAL EDITION

More Jews today, from a record number of countries, are travelling, be it for business, holiday pleasure or to explore and seek their roots. And as the world continues shrinking and more places are readily accessible, Jews are, like the rest of the world population, extending their travel horizons.

Where to pray if business calls you to Singapore or Hong Kong? Open this book and find out that not only do you have an option, you have a choice! We know there are many memorials and cemeteries in eastern Europe, but is there anywhere to eat? Yes, says the *Jewish Travel Guide International Edition*. How is Israel celebrating its fiftieth year of independence? Flip through these pages and your questions are answered.

In an effort to make this overload of data intelligible, the format has been revised for clarity, breaking the information into clearer categories.

Jewish Travel Guide International Edition. Don't leave home without it.

ISBN 0 85303 338 2   432 pages   £10.95/$14.95 paperback

Vallentine Mitchell
UK AND OVERSEAS ORDERS TO:
Vallentine Mitchell, Newbury House, 900 Eastern Avenue, London IG2 7HH, England
Tel: +44(0)181 599 8866   Fax: +44(0)181 599 0984   E-Mail: info@vmbooks.com
US AND NORTH AMERICA ORDERS:
c/o ISBS, 5804 NE Hassalo Street, Portland, OR 97213-3644, USA
Tel: (503) 287-3093, (800) 944 6190   Fax: (503) 280-8832   E-mail: orders@isbs.com

The Jewish Year Book

Published in association with
the Jewish Chronicle, London

Founded 1896

1998
5758–5759

Edited by
STEPHEN W. MASSIL

VALLENTINE MITCHELL
LONDON

Published in 1998 in Great Britain by
VALLENTINE MITCHELL PUBLISHERS
Newbury House, 900 Eastern Avenue,
London IG2 7HH

and in the United States of America by
VALLENTINE MITCHELL PUBLISHERS
c/o ISBS, 5804 N.E. Hassalo Street, Portland, Oregon, 97213-3644
Website: http://www.vmbooks.com

Copyright © 1998 Vallentine Mitchell and The Jewish Chronicle

ISBN 0 85303 339 0
ISSN 0075 3769

All rights reserved. No part of this publication may be reproduced in any form or by any means, electronic, mechanical, photocopying, recording or otherwise, without the prior permission of Vallentine Mitchell and Company Limited.

Printed in Great Britain by Bookcraft (Bath) Ltd.

Contents

Preface	v
Essays	
Israel's Fiftieth Anniversary *Ezer Weizman*	ix
Is the Peace Process Irreversible? *Abba Eban*	x
The Israeli Diaspora: Yordim (Emigrants) are	
the Authentic Diaspora *Gabriel Sheffer*	xix
The Jewish Community in the United	
States *Donald Feldstein*	xxxii
Fragments of Anglo-Jewry *Stefan Reif*	lviii
Abbreviations	lxviii
Anglo-Jewish Institutions	
Representative Organisations	1
Jewish Press, Radio and Information Services	5
Religious Organisations	7
Welfare Organisations	13
Refugee Organisations	17
Organisations Concerned with	
the Jews of Eastern Europe	19
Zionist Organisations	20
Other Organisations Concerned with Israel	24
Educational and Cultural Organisations	35
University Centres and Organisations	43
Organisations Concerned with Jewish Youth	46
Libraries, Museums and Exhibitions	54
Professional Organisations	59
Miscellaneous Organisations	61
International Organisations	66
Local Organisations	
London	
Synagogues	76
Religious Organisations	87
Memorials, Cemeteries	88
Educational Organisations	89
Welfare Organisations	93
Clubs and Cultural Societies	98
Miscellaneous Organisations	100
The Regions	
England	102

Wales	129
Scotland	130
Northern Ireland	133
Isle of Man	133
Channel Islands	133
Ireland	134
Other Countries	135
Jewish Statistics	191
Historical Note on British Jewry	197
United Kingdom Legislation Concerning Jews	200
Listed Synagogues and Other Jewish Monuments in the UK	204
Privy Counsellors, Peers, MPs, etc	206
Who's Who	210
Obituaries 1996–1997	310
Events of 1997	312
Publications of 1996–1997 and Booksellers	314
Principal Festivals and Fasts	322
The Jewish Calendar	323
The Jewish Year	324
Abridged Calendar for 1998	325
Abridged Calendar for 1999	326
Hebrew and English Calendar	327
Evening and Twilight Variations for Regions	341
Sidrot and Haftarot for 1999	342
Marriage Regulations	344
Jewish Calendar for 30 years	346
Index	360

Preface

It has been a year of continuing divisions within the community and the issues where the fractures emerge are primarily those on pluralism, on unity and leadership, on conversion, and on the state of the peace process in Israel. The fact that British worshippers were among a group who were stoned at the Kotel in June only brings home what is clearly a world-wide controversy as regards pluralism within Jewry. Rumblings over the debates in the Knesset about conversions and missionary literature underline the stirrings of apprehension around the world's communities. In Britain, the controversy that flared over the Chief Rabbi's ambivalence about the funeral and memorial of Hugo Gryn and the terms and publication of his correspondence with Dayan Chanoch Padwa is symptomatic; the polarisation of opinion and concern over Israeli policy and engagement with the peace process is beginning to take concrete forms.

High turnover of rabbinical appointments at synagogues (of all sections) around the country and concern over the student chaplaincy service, one of the year's topics, suggest uncertainties beyond the normal phasing of change and adjustment. The United Synagogue announced a far-reaching review of Jews' College. The closure of Carmel College was the most graphic sign of changing times, although its possible rescue is currently under discussion.

Following the General Election, the tally of Jewish members remained at 21 but the names this time are predominantly of Labour members (and five of them are women, as opposed to three in the last Parliament); the new government benches in the Lords saw the early return to Westminster of Greville Janner after his retirement at the dissolution, and other new peers include Lord Levy, Lord Levine, Lord Putnam and Lord Jacobs. David Sumberg, after his defeat at the polls, secured the position of Chairman of the Anglo-Jewish Association. In Israel, Ehud Barak was elected Labour leader in succession to Shimon Peres.

Karen Phillips became Executive Director of the newly constituted Manchester Federation. The further process of the merging of Jewish Continuity and the IJA has been consolidated with the birth of the UJIA. Eldred Tabachnik was re-elected for a second term as President of the Board of Deputies. The Board voted to accede to the proposal for the inclusion of a question on religious affiliation in the Census of 2001.

The Great Garden Street Synagogue finally closed its doors, as did the Woolwich Synagogue, and, while the New West End unveiled its resplendent refurbishment, we have included for the first time a section on Listed Buildings to give a focus to the work of the Working Party on Jewish

Monuments in the UK and Ireland, whose recent bid for lottery funding was remarkably successful, and at a time when mergers and closures of synagogues are regularly being reported. Several of the buildings listed – Liverpool, Brighton – have had stars added to their status in recent months. Prospects for Singer's Hill, following agreement to the proposed merger of the (three) orthodox congregations in Birmingham at the Central Synagogue, will be of close interest in the coming months. The Jewish Historical Society considered evidence of recent excavations of medieval foundations in Guildford.

The Swiss banks published a list of 'dormant accounts', not without controversy, and a second is promised; there are plans for a conference on looted gold to be held shortly in London. At Drancy, the French Roman Catholic Church made a declaration of formal repentance of its silence during the Vichy period. The Spiro Institute included a visit to the village of Le Chambon in its summer touring programme.

The year's deaths include those of many notable women: Baroness Birk, Lady Sieff, Kitty Stein, Miriam Abramsky, Myra Janner and, among the centenarians, Marutha Menuhin. Sir Isaiah Berlin, doyen of the Order of Merit, died as I was completing my notes; Sir Georg Solti died in September; the former Lord Chief Justice, Lord Taylor, died a few months after his retirement; Victor Lucas, Jack Wolkind, Schneier Levenburg, Dayan Braceiner and the Rev. Solomon Bernstein were among the elders of the community leadership to go, and statesmen Chaim Herzog and Sir Joshua Hassan. Librarians Charles Burman and Dietrich Borchardt also died.

The Chief Rabbi and Eldred Tabachnik took up a formal stand on the route of the funeral of Diana, Princess of Wales, whose death brought forth Jewish sentiment along with that of the nation. Of poignant recollection for the community were the deaths of Esther Simpson and Lord Tonypandy.

Professor Geller was appointed to the Jewish Chronicle Chair at University College and Professor Bernard Jackson to the Alliance Chair at Manchester University. Graham Zellick became Vice-Chancellor of the University of London. Stephen Smith of the Beth Shalom Holocaust Centre was awarded the Pentland Jewish Care award and R.B. Kitaj, a tapestry of whose holocaust picture 'If not, not' has just been unveiled at the new British Library, was awarded the Wollaston Award at the Royal Academy. Dr Miriam Stoppard succeeded to Marjorie Proops's agonyship at the *Mirror*.

Frank Cass celebrated 40 years in publishing. Books of the year include: Lionel Kochan's *Beyond the Graven Image*; W.I. Massil's *Immigrant Furniture Workers in London 1881–1939*, a timely memoir of an industry at its heyday; Laurence Joffe's edition of the *Keesing's Guide to the Middle*

East; Claudia Roden's *Book of Jewish Food*; Grossman's *Zigzag*, among the Israeli novels in translation; Rubinstein's *Myth of Rescue* for controversial historiography; Sherman's *Mandate Days* for a timely re-appraisal; Bellow's *The Actual* and Anita Brookner's *Visitors* among the novels; Sufott's *China Diary*, among the curiosities; Selous Books have reprinted the *British Jewry Book of Honour 1914–1919*, compiled by Michael Adler in 1922; Arnold Wesker, whose *Chips with Everything* enjoyed a very successful revival at the National Theatre, published a diary of *The Birth of Shylock and the Death of Zero Mostel*; Chaim Herzog's *Living History* was launched at Jewish Book Week, only a few weeks before his death. Gerda Charles died. Joshua Sobol's *Kfar* toured the regional theatres. The performance of what was billed as the first Australian opera, *Don John of Austria*, by Byron's old friend Isaac Nathan and his librettist Jacob né Levy Montefiore (1847) was perhaps the most unlikely Jewish event of the year; the progress of the film *Shine* and public performances by its real-life hero were also of note.

The year 1998 sees the centenary of the Taylor–Schechter Genizah Collection at Cambridge University Library. Zola's 'J'accuse' was published on 13 January 1898 giving the long-drawn-out saga of the Dreyfus Affair its decisive turn.

In giving thanks once again to John Fischer for the calendar (and we have extended the 30-year calendar in this volume), we both wish to acknowledge the work of his predecessor, Dr Alexander Tobias, whose death was reported early in the year. Other thanks are due as usual to a wide range of people in correspondence and to the officers of organisations who ensure the fullness of these records. Thanks in particular are due: to Keith Pearce (Penzance), Joan Lozowitz, the Board of Deputies Communal Enquiry Desk, Lilian Bennett, Jo Greenfield and Phillippa Wainwright (House of Commons); to the new officers of the various parliamentary and party committees whose memberships underwent so thorough a shake-out at the General Election; and to those organisations in Britain and Israel, Kibbutz secretaries especially, who took special pains to make of their best for Israel's fiftieth anniversary, to which this volume is dedicated, published with a glossy jacket by way of celebration.

It is a measure of the change of editorial style over 50 years that in his preface to the 1949 Year Book, Albert Hyamson made but the barest mention of the establishment of the State in May 1948. Here, now, among the essays that we feature, we have a greeting from the President, whose state visit to Britain was the highlight of the year, a review of Israel's prospects for peace from one of her elder statesmen, and an account of that curious community, the 'Israeli diaspora' or Yordim, whose numbers over the years have been surprisingly large and whose presence is apparently pervasive throughout the established and not so established communities world wide. The contribution by Donald Feldstein brings home the amplitude of the American Jewish community with a substantive analysis of currents in American Jewry and an account of its organisation and, by way of anticipation, Stefan Reif marks the Genizah centenary with a review of the century's Anglo-Jewish scholarship.

Cambridge & London,
17 November 1997, 17th MarCheshvan 5758

SWM

Israel's Fiftieth Anniversary

Ezer Weizman
President of Israel

This year marks Israel's fiftieth anniversary. Much has been achieved during these 50 years. Millions of immigrants from the four corners of the earth have been successfully integrated into Israeli society. Israel stands at the forefront in science, technology and agriculture. Israel is recognised by most countries in the world, and their leaders are anxious to visit and learn from our experience.

All this must be borne in mind when considering the years of ongoing struggle for our very existence and for achieving peace with our neighbours. This past year has had its full share of great tragedies. No matter how severe and painful the losses incurred, we must not become victims to helplessness and despondency. We are in the midst of a very difficult and protracted process, with many painful contentions. However, just as peace treaties were concluded with Egypt and Jordan, I am convinced that, eventually, these, too, will be achieved with the Palestinians and our other neighbours.

The Diaspora was always proud when Israel fought and won its battles. Now Israel is strong and it warrants no less your continued pride and support. The stronger we are and the greater in number, the easier it will be to achieve our aims. I once again, call on you, our brothers and sisters in the diaspora, to join us in creating a nation, a light unto the nations.

We pray for better years to come, for peace and well-being and the values we wish to instil. Let us learn from the past but look ahead to a better future.

Is the Peace Process Irreversible?

Abba Eban

Wisdom is born only when illusions die. There could never have been any progress towards a peace settlement in the Middle East until Arabs and Israelis liberated themselves from two illusions. There was the illusion of the Arabs that they could get back their lost territories without making peace with Israel. And there was a parallel Israeli illusion, shared by significant sectors of Israeli opinion, that Israel could get peace or, at least, security, while retaining its rule over most of the territories occupied in the Six Day War of 1967. Either one of these illusions would have been sufficient to prevent a settlement; two of them together made progress to peace objectively impossible.

There are no serious Israelis who believe any longer that Israel can obtain peace while retaining most of the conquered territories and rejecting accords with the Palestinians on boundaries and security arrangements. The fact that Syria will never accept a settlement that leaves the Golan area in total Israeli possession is too self-evident to need supporting evidence. To renounce the Golan area voluntarily, Syria would have to become converted to a passionately fervent form of all Zionism. There is no evidence that such counsels exist in Damascus. The Syrian conviction that Golan is a province of Syria is shared by all the nations of the world, not excluding Israel, whose leaders acknowledged Syrian sovereignty in 1967 and again during Yitzhak Rabin's premiership between 1993 and 1996.

There are no precedents for a state to renounce territories which the entire international community recognises as its own national domain. Similarly, there are no Israelis who would consider a proposal for peace with Syria without a fundamental transformation in Syrian attitudes towards Israel's security and national identity.

The Middle Eastern peace process coincided with a much broader movement in the world diplomatic arena. Diplomacy, so often accused of traditionalism, is now being ventilated by fresh winds. This is the age of 'odd couples'; leaders of nations are now holding civilised discourse with adversaries whom they would have puritanically shunned a few years ago.

This tendency has already produced a thaw in some of the most obdurate international conflicts. Behind twin microphones stood F. W. De Klerk and Nelson Mandela, speeding apartheid in South Africa towards its overdue demise. Hardly had we rubbed our eyes at this spectacle when Yitzhak Rabin and Yassir Arafat took their places in a similar ritual, closely followed by King Hussein and Prime Minister Rabin, opening horizons towards a new Middle East. Next, the Vatican – author of the medieval expulsions, the Inquisition, and the humiliating ghetto system – sent its representatives to Jerusalem to mark its reconciliation with Israel, the state of the Jews. A long saga of Jewish suffering and gentile intolerance came to an official end. More recently, the prime ministers of the United Kingdom and Ireland have outlawed the bomb and gun, and virtually legitimised the IRA as a negotiating partner. All this only a few years after George Bush and Bill Clinton began to regard Mikhail Gorbachev and Boris Yeltsin not as sworn enemies but as partners in a journey towards international peace. And the agreements signed by Bosnia, Croatia and Serbia at Dayton, Ohio, in 1994 assured at least a temporary tranquillity in the Balkan area.

This is not yet the only norm of international conduct, and I am aware of the contrary examples which are still taking a tragic toll. But the strange encounters that I have evoked are more than individual episodes. The diplomatic discourse is liberating itself from entrenched routines. World opinion no longer tolerates the idea that rulers have the right to appoint their own representatives – and also those of their adversaries. The ANC, the PLO, and the IRA all have abrasive chapters in the resumés, but so do their more powerful interlocutors. It is deemed more fertile to confer with radicals who represent their constituencies than with amiable 'moderates' who do not.

It is against this background that Israelis, aware of a new ecumenical spirit in international relations, were electrified by the exchange of declarations of principle on the White House lawn in September 1993. Israel and the PLO were willing to conclude an accord in the following terms:

> The government of the State of Israel and the PLO team representing the Palestinian people, agree the time has come to put an end to decades of confrontation and conflict, recognize their mutual legitimate and political rights and strive to live in peaceful coexistence and mutual security and achieve a just, lasting and comprehensive peace settlement and historic reconciliation through the agreed political process.

Together with this change in the principle of discourse, the Rabin–Peres representatives witnessed a new approach to agendas. Negotiators used to fill their rhetoric with arguments about the origins of conflicts and the culpability for their eruption. In the new diplomacy, the question 'who provoked and who responded?' is marginalised. The issue now is how to quench the fires, not to hold interminable debate about who kindled them. Pragmatic compromises now usurp the pride of place hitherto occupied by reciprocal exchanges of self-righteousness. Even the United Nations is experiencing a new spasm of lucidity. International agencies previously allowed the issues of origins and culpability to monopolise their agendas and to exhaust the disputants. Today, the United Nations has joined, and may even claim to have inspired, the impulse and movement of the modern diplomatic age. The UN General Assembly has gone so far as to express contrition for its previous anti-Zionist frenzy. Its adoption of a joint Israeli/PLO resolution, legitimising the Mid-Eastern peace process, would have been inconceivable two or three years ago.

Diplomacy can only gain in public esteem by shaking off the intrinsically insoluble arguments about virtue and conscience and concentrating on more practical goals. Reciprocal self-interest is and should remain the central theme. Mankind has never had a single vision of justice, virtue, truth or legitimate pride, but nations have often been able to unite around themes of converging interest. Diplomacy should be judged by what it prevents, not only by what it initiates and creates. Much of it is a holding action designed to avoid explosion until the unifying forces of history take humanity into their embrace. The least that can be said of the new diplomatic age is that those who control the decisions are conducting the negotiations.

Another illusion now suffering eclipse is one that used to tell us that it is possible for one nation to rule over a foreign population without consent. A central law of the new diplomatic age is that coercive jurisdictions have disqualified themselves through experience and suffering. Some form of coexistence must take the place of military occupations. We Israelis are not colonial newcomers to the Middle East. Israel's roots in the region are older and deeper than the roots of any other people on any other soil. But Israel is undoubtedly alien to the Palestinian people over whom it has been exercising absolute rule for the last 25 years. What the British could not do any longer in India or the French in Algeria or the Dutch in Indonesia or the Belgians in Congo and Rwanda or the Soviet Union in Afghanistan or the United States in Vietnam and what the white Africans could no longer do in South Africa, despite their crushing, overwhelming power, has not become possible for Israel, despite the deep emotional roots that join Israel to what is now an arena of Palestinian self-government.

I am not very interested in the question whether an Arab mini-state that might well emerge from the current peace process will be democratic or not. The international system will always display a great diversity of social structures and orientations. We should not make the realisation of a stable regional order dependent on an impossible search for democratic perfection. What the peace process does offer is the chance for Israel to reassert its democratic identity. It is not in the nature of a modern

IS THE PEACE PROCESS IRREVERSIBLE?   xiii

democracy to rule over two million members of a different nation, without offering them either equal justice as citizens or a chance to establish their own separate jurisdiction. The initial debate about the future of Arabs and Jews in their common land was concerned with the principle of partition. The basic document about the future of our area was lucidly formulated by the United Nations General Assembly and its committees: 'The political unity of the Palestine area can only be maintained at the cost of rigorous repression.' The international judgment said simply that neither of the two nations could justly maintain its rule over the other, irrespective of whether it was the Palestinians, who then claimed the right to rule over the Jewish minority, or whether it was an Israeli state that found itself ruling over a large Palestinian Arab population for more than a quarter of the century.

The peace process reflected the central truth about our land. It is a land of two nations, two faiths, two tongues, two national sentiments, two historic experiences. Duality is written so deeply on the history and geography of this country that any subjection of one to the other would be morally fragile and inherently explosive. This means that sovereignty and territory must be shared by both peoples and not monopolised by either one of them. It was on the wings of the historic partition decision, in which the United States and the Soviet Union joined together, that Israel was able to put its flag into the winds of history.

The truth is that Israel was most vulnerable and insecure when it ruled the entire area between the Suez Canal and the Golan Heights. The map showing the full extent of that jurisdiction had a solid and reassuring look. In reality, we were greatly over extended. We were governing areas that had previously been parts of three other states. We could only continue to hold them by maintaining great armies in areas hundreds of miles apart from each other, and we were doing this without any context of regional or international consent.

I wish to reiterate my conviction that the Six Day War, during which Israel rose up against deadly peril, was a war of salvation for us. I take nothing back of what I then said in describing our danger. I used the following words:

> As righteous as the defence of freedom at Valley Forge, as just as the expulsion of Hitler's bombers from British skies, as noble as the protection of Stalingrad against the Nazi hordes, so was the defence of Israel's security and existence against those who sought our nation's destruction. Never have freedom, honour, justice, national interest, and international morality been so righteously protected.

But to say this is not to say that the same justice and logic would apply to the continued maintenance into the third decade of the military administration established in 1967. Israel's current leaders were not the first to understand the total inadmissibility of that condition. The first and decisive turning point came in 1977 to 1978. Prime Minister Menachem Begin decided that Israel should renounce all its assets and establishments in Sinai, and also make provision for the withdrawal of the Israeli civil and administrative administrations in order to make way for 'self-government' under which 'the inhabitants of the West Bank and Gaza should govern themselves'. It was clear even then that the continued maintenance of our conquests was not salvation; it was, in fact, fraught with disaster. Israelis justly mourn the dozens of individual recent tragedies that have taken a toll of precious life. But this must be understood against the background of the far greater number of those who would have been lost if the peace process had not been initiated.

It would be ridiculous to look back, with any sense of consolation, on the map that showed Israel ruling the whole area between Golan and Suez from 1967 to 1973. Two thousand five hundred Israeli dead to protect Israel's positions in Sinai in 1973. Over 750 Israelis lost in the effort to maintain Israeli positions along the canal against artillery bombardment. Seven hundred and thirty Israeli soldiers lost in Lebanon, including Beirut, in a war that was supposed to put an end to the action of Palestinian radical nationalists. All this, together with a high state of military preparedness, to withstand periodic outbursts of violence in the West Bank and Gaza.

The allegedly ideal boundaries of Israel, between 1967 and 1973, were maintained at a cost of life that would be equivalent to 200,000 Americans, in proportionate terms. Moreover, it was evident that, so long as Israel had its forces arrayed from Golan to Suez, war would eventually be inevitable and the only question would be when it would erupt.

The opponents of the current peace process in Israel and abroad denounce what they call the exchange of solid territory for 'pieces of paper'. Let me say a word about 'pieces of paper'. Since 1967, when Israel negotiated a disengagement agreement with Syria, with Henry Kissinger as mediator, no Israelis have lost their lives at the hands of the Syrian army. Was the disengagement agreement merely a 'piece of paper'? Since the signature of the peace treaty with Egypt, no Israeli lives have been lost through confrontation with Egyptian forces. To prefer the old and large map to the situation created after the disengagement agreement and the peace treaty is to prefer war and death to peace and life. It is false to assert that diplomatic pieces of paper are less effective in saving life than military occupation. Our experience points just to the contrary. Since the enactment of the two pieces of paper, our losses have been zero and war has become virtually inconceivable. Before the treaty, our losses were immense and war was inevitable. This is because the pieces of paper – as they are contemptuously called – do not depend for their viability on the mere signature of the Arab party or its will for peace. The documents signed with Syria and Egypt, as well as that concluded at Oslo with the Palestinians, reflect basic realities arising from the balance of power. Experience has taught us that pieces of paper that reflect concrete realities and situations of power are far more effective in protecting individual life and national existence than were the enforced jurisdictions that were in force before the signatures were affixed. Nevertheless, there was little that Israel could effectively do to change its regional context until the dramatic events of 1990 were enacted before the astonished gaze of the world.

First came the Desert War. This, of course, was not an Israeli enterprise; we were urgently persuaded by the United States as the leader of that great coalition, to adopt a policy of conspicuous unobtrusiveness. This is not a characteristic Israeli posture. But we understood that a military campaign that would blunt the force of Iraqi aggression for at least several years would be a more tangible gain for Israel than anything that could be achieved by action that would disrupt the anti-Iraqi coalition.

Second, there came an even more revolutionary event: the collapse of the communist empire. Suddenly, almost overnight, the vast weight and bulk of the Soviet Union and the East European countries were transferred from the negative scale to the positive scale of Israel's strategic balance. Without Soviet support, Soviet arms and the concentrated vigilance of Soviet policies, Israel would not have been in existential danger at any time. The Soviet Union is no longer the greater spoiler, no longer the saboteur of all peace initiatives, no longer the source of campaigns of calumny and defamation against Israel. The Soviet Union no longer bars Israel from access to international agencies, where for some decades it had been able to find no remedy. The Soviet Union, now personified by Russia, is a joint sponsor of the peace process, together with the United States. Its influence, such as it is, has been wielded for stability and peace, not for violence and war. When this great burden of antagonism, with its explosive consequences, was shifted from the negative to the positive scale, Israel's strategic balance underwent a vast transformation, the full extent and intensity of which have not yet been digested in our own country, let alone in the rest of the world.

This naturally brought about a chain reaction in the power balance. Let me recall that Syria had never thought of attacking Israel except on three conditions that no longer exist. The first condition was that Egypt would be attacking Israel from the other side. The second condition was that Syria had a Soviet safety net. Syria knew that if it got itself into trouble on the battlefield against Israel, which it often did, it could rely on the intimidation and pressure of the Soviet Union to halt any Israeli advance. Syria could, therefore, fight its wars with limited liability. Its attractive alternatives were to win or not to lose.

The third condition for Syrian military activism was that there would be a friendly and fraternal Iraq at Syria's side. Well, Syria no longer has an Egyptian alliance, it does not have a Soviet safety net, there is not much fraternity between Syria and Iraq, which fought on opposite sides in the Gulf War. Therefore, to believe that the Syrian leader might be interested in a peace negotiation is to believe not in his virtue or conscience, but simply in his sense of national self-interest.

It may be true, as some observers have said, that Syria wants peace with America more than it wants peace with Israel. There is nothing incongruous in that idea. What is certain is that Syria would not find anything like peace or stability if, after its alienation from the Soviet Union, it were to suffer crisis in its relations with the United States while Syrian policies are still distant from solutions acceptable to Israel.

The question whether to hold discussions with the mainstream Palestinian organisation agitated the Israeli political scene for many years. Unfortunately, there was an attempt, in large sectors of the Israeli establishment, to evade the central truth that peace treaties have to be negotiated with those who have once made war. Our first Prime Minister, David Ben Gurion, constantly insisted to me, 'Always look for abrasive interlocutors; don't look for amiable moderates'.

The eventual decision (in my opinion, belated) to accede to talk with the PLO was very interestingly connected with what I have called the era of odd couples. Israel has integrated itself into what has become the normative tradition of international life. What counts for your interlocutor is not his amiability but his representativity. Not whether it is agreeable to converse with him, but whether anybody else has any chance of accepting the principle of historic reconciliation.

It is true that Chairman Arafat is now weaker in his Arab and regional relationships than previously. The truth is, however disagreeable in terms of recent history, that it is a considerable achievement for Israel to be in a contractual relationship with the mainstream Palestinian organisation whose spokesmen are now dealing more effectively with the dissident terrorists than before. It remains, alas, painfully true that not even the powerful Israeli army, with its world-renowned intelligence services, has ever been able to ensure total individual security against individual Palestinians. Nor in areas under Israeli exclusive control has the plague of the suicide bombers been proved susceptible to easy treatment.

The Arab country on which the new moderating trends of policy exerted an immediate influence was Jordan. King Hussein has never pretended that he represents the leadership of the Arab world. It is, however, undeniable that projects of mutual co-operation are more feasible in the Israeli/Jordanian relationship than in any other. This arises from the proximity and reciprocal movement that have always characterised these two neighbours. It is not absurd that there should be two separate ports: one at Elat and one at Akaba, only a few kilometres apart. Should there not be joint authorities enabling both countries to exploit their access to East Africa and to the prosperous economies of the Pacific Rim? Is it really an enactment of history that the Dead Sea should always be dead, with Jordan and Israel each capable of preventing its neighbour from utilising what is still one of the great concentrations of pharmaceutical raw materials? Might there not be a real exuberance of fruitful contacts if those searching for the roots of Western civilisation could pass from the Israeli capital in Jerusalem across the river to Petra, seat of the old Nabatean civilisation, and thence southward to witness the glories of Egypt's pharoanic legacy? Something of this new accessibility is already in vogue between Israel, Jordan and Egypt. This does not mean that we are free of controversy. But we are exchanging words and arguments, not bombs and shells with Egypt, Syria, Jordan and the PLO.

Nor can we make the intermediate balance without reference to the general expansion of Israel's international network. Israel's strategic predominance and peace policies have enabled us to achieve dazzling diplomatic successes. We now have diplomatic relations, not with a mere 50, but with 160 other countries. Our flag now flies in Cairo, Oman, Tunisia and Morocco. There have been fruitful and promising contacts with many countries in the Gulf area. Even Saudi Arabia endorsed the Oslo peace process and has virtually eliminated the main pressures of the boycott. Instead of being the most isolated country in the world, Israel bids fair to become the least isolated country in the world. Israel is smaller in its area of rigorous jurisdiction, but it is larger than ever before in the pride and confidence of the world. When it comes to maps, big is not necessarily beautiful.

I do not say that the success of the peace process will lead to Utopia. I do, however, declare that the failure of the peace process would lead to an inferno of explosive antagonisms and volcanic hatreds. Generations might have to pass before anybody would attempt such a peace project again. So many currents of policy and interest had to converge to bring the peace process to birth. If it were to end in failure, peace itself and the very hope of it would probably be eclipsed.

I conclude with a particular tribute to the generation of Israel's founders who have very few spokesmen left to recall their achievements. We were vulnerable and fragile in those early days and our prospect of survival was a matter much more of faith than of reason. But we were sustained by a clear and lucid vision. We knew how to distinguish between reality and fantasy. We understood that our task was not only to assert our own rights, but also to bring those rights into harmony with the rights and interests of others. We had no illusion that we could live forever outside the universal human order in which the interaction of destinies mocks the pretensions of unilateral power.

We were inspired by our history without being enslaved by it. And we remembered. We remembered that our land had been twice ravaged and our people dispersed because our leaders sometimes gave free rein to a suicidal zealotry that did not give survival its due priority of concern. We took that history to heart. And during our first decades, we have given a new impulse and direction to the Jewish journey. We have set Israel on a path in which the opportunities transcend the dangers.

The Israeli Diaspora: Yordim (Emigrants) Are the Authentic Diaspora

Gabriel Sheffer

I

Like millions of people from other home countries all over the world, during the last 50 years Israelis have been migrating and permanently settling in various host countries. Yet, as is well known, both Israelis in the homeland and Jews in the Diaspora exhibit attitudes towards Israeli emigrants that are markedly different to those that other homeland societies have shown towards their emigrants. While in most other cases, emigration from the homeland has been regarded either as an understandable act of despair in view of hardship or as a normal private choice intended to improve the fortune of the emigrant, in the Israeli case emigration from the Land of Israel has had negative connotations (and, for that matter, immigration to the homeland still has noble meanings of a 'return', or of 'going up' to the homeland).

Thus, until recently, immigration to and emigration from Israel were not regarded as connected to the current world-wide phenomenon of migration. Rather, because of extraordinarily strong primordial ties to the Land of Israel, coupled with vivid memories of traumatic existence and suffering in dozens of host countries, Zionists and most Israelis regarded Jewish existence outside the holy land as nationally dangerous, intolerable and unforgivable.

Therefore, and again as is well known, in the case of the Jews, the term diaspora itself – which essentially and neutrally means a dispersion of an ethno-national group – acquired an utterly negative meaning and became synonymous with detested 'exile'. By the same token, immigration to the Land of Israel was regarded as a physical and spiritual imperative. Hence, it was termed Aliya, that is, 'going up' to the holy land. Consequently, the intertwined dreams of Diaspora Jews were a massive return, which would culminate in the ingathering of as many Jews as possible in the land of Israel, and the creation there of a secure basis for a sovereign nation. Jewish leaders and rank and file regarded such a development as the

---

Gabriel Sheffer is Professor of Political Science at the Hebrew University of Jerusalem.

ultimate personal and collective redemption. Furthermore, during their 'exile', many Jews regarded the return to the homeland not only as a religious and national cognitive imperative, but also as a highly emotional matter. Eventually, this cognitive imperative and charged emotional matter became the essential cornerstones of the Zionist movement and its creation – the Jewish state.

The other side of the same coin was that during the pre-state period in Palestine – the 'Yishuv (the Jewish community in Palestine during the pre-state era) period' – and in the four decades since Israel's establishment, voluntary emigration out of the Yishuv and Israel, and the eventual permanent settlement of these emigrants in various host countries have been regarded as desertion, and thus a betrayal of the most sacred tenets of Zionism and of the new Israeli ethos. So much so, that emigration was dubbed 'Yerida', that is, 'going down' from the holy land, and the emigrants 'Yordim' (Schweid, 1981; Mekel, 1982; Sobel, 1986).

Like developments in other spheres of Jewish and Israeli life, in the 1980s and especially in the 1990s Israelis have altered their attitudes towards Yerida and Yordim. Simultaneously, and probably for similar reasons, certain segments of the Jewish Diaspora have also modified their approach towards these former Israelis. In a sense, therefore, Israelis and Diaspora Jews now show symmetrical tolerance towards this phenomenon. Yet, it will be argued here that there is still a strong residual anti-Yerida sentiment, and a clear difference between the Yordim communities and the established Jewish Diaspora.

In any case, we have reached a time when there is a need to reassess the current state of the phenomenon, preferably within a comparative framework. This is the overall purpose of this essay. In order to do so, we will examine Israelis' motivations for emigration; their selection of host countries; their decision to settle permanently abroad; their identity, identification and loyalty; their social, economic and cultural activities in host countries; their organisational patterns in host countries; their relations with the local Jewish communities, on the one hand, and with Israel, on the other; and the emotionally and ideologically loaded issue of their return to Israel. These issues will be examined in light of the recent findings of diaspora studies (for example, Sheffer, 1986; Cohen, 1997). This perspective will facilitate drawing some theoretical conclusions of wider applicability from the Israeli case.

II

During each phase in the development of the Yishuv and Israel, the 'push' and 'pull' (on these notions see Fridberg, 1988) reasons for voluntary emigration out of the Land of Israel were evidently different. Thus, as far as it is now possible to ascertain, the reasons for the first relatively large wave of this emigration (the absolute numbers were small but the proportion to the total number of Jews in Palestine was high), which occurred between the end of the nineteenth century and the First World War, were the severe economic hardship, the Turkish authorities' anti-Zionist policies resulting in political persecution and expulsion, the clashes with the Palestinian Arabs, and the ideological and practical disappointment with various aspects of the emerging Yishuv. Thus, this first wave of emigration produced a recurrent pattern: there was no one predominant reason and motivation, but rather a combination of emotional, ideological, political, economic and what might be called 'environmental' pressures that pushed Jews to leave the Land of Israel (Gorni, 1970).

A somewhat different mix of reasons was behind the second wave of emigration, which, relatively, was probably the largest wave in the entire history of the Yishuv and Israel. It occurred during the social and economic crisis of 1924-27 in Palestine. During this period about 25 per cent of all the immigrants of the Third Aliya (1919-24) left Palestine. Since, during that period, the security situation in Palestine was more or less under control and tension between Jews and Arabs had temporarily abated, the security factor for emigration was secondary. It seems that among the 'push factors' that served as the main motivations for emigration, the environmental economic crisis was the most important. The other consequential factor was again the ideological disappointment at what was then expiring in the Yishuv (Giladi, 1977).

In the 1930s, because of the dramatic events in Europe in the latter part of the decade, the restrictions on immigration in the United States, and later because of the Second World War itself, Palestinian Jews stayed put during this period and emigration was insignificant. Hence, the main waves of emigration that eventually served as the basis for present-day Yordim communities occurred after the establishment of the state.

The first of these post-independence cycles occurred in the 1950s. By then the main 'push' reasons were again economic, together with difficulties in the integration of newcomers, especially those of European origin. Considerable dissatisfaction with unemployment, austerity regulations, lack of economic growth, severe housing shortages, and the generally low standard of living then prevailing in Israel were the main reasons for leaving the country. There is also evidence – probably for the first time – that during this period 'pull' factors began to play a role in the decision to emigrate, and that, consequently, Israelis preferred to join their relatives, especially those in Anglo-Saxon host countries (Cohen, 1989). Like other migrants of the same period, the migrants of this wave now have children and grandchildren living in the Diaspora.

The next wave of emigration occurred in the 1970s and early 1980s and it had two sub-phases. The first sub-phase took place after the initial euphoria following the 1967 War had evaporated, and especially against the backdrop of the War of Attrition and the debacle of the 1973 War. During this period, besides the economic factors, the depressed mood in view of the prolonged War of Attrition and the abysmal results of the 1973 War were among the chief reasons for Yerida. Although difficult to measure accurately, it seems that during this period the pull factors became no less significant than the push factors. The second sub-phase in this cycle occurred in the early 1980s. During this period, the sense of the existence of a security threat, low national morale after the debacles of the 1982 War and its aftermath, including the bloody Israeli occupation of southern Lebanon, were the main factors for Yerida (Sobel, 1986; Cohen, 1987; Desivilia, 1992). Moreover, because during that period more Israelis began touring various Western countries, the pull factors became more prevalent in the motivation for emigration (Kass and Lipset, 1982).

Towards the late 1980s and early 1990s – the period when enhanced global migration began and accelerated – one can discern two new developments as far as Israeli emigrants have been concerned. Since the peak of emigration of the mid- and late-1980s and in the first part of the 1990s, there has been a clear decline in the numbers of Yordim, and, as noted, both Israelis and Diaspora Jews began to alter their attitudes towards Yerida. This brings us to the present: now, as part of a social, political and economic liberalisation, the wider acceptance of pluralism and a greater openness, increasingly more Israelis tend to view Yerida as a 'normal phenomenon', similar to emigration from other homelands (compare, for example, Harsgor, 1987, and Galili, 1991).

A final note on the demographic aspect of Yerida: it is extremely difficult to determine the exact numbers of Yordim. This difficulty emanates from a number of facts: the lack of an exact definition of Yerida, that is, how long an Israeli citizen should live abroad to be included in this category and whether Israelis who regularly or occasionally visit Israel should be included; this is a long-term phenomenon, spreading over a period of more than 50 years; and we deal here with a highly dispersed group. (On the difficulty of determining the numbers see, for example, Elizur, 1974; Rabi, 1978; Plaut, 1982; Lamdani, 1982; Israeli Statistical Bureau, 1990, 1991, 1993, 1994.) In any case, the latest estimate of the Israeli government is that during the period May 1948–December 1993, 340,000 Israelis left the country and lived abroad for more than four years (Caspit, 1995). There are, however, other estimates that are closer to the real number. The highest of these is that more than 700,000 Israelis left the country from May 1948 to May 1989 (Alon, 1989). In addition, over the last decade or so there have been annual totals of some 10,000 Israeli students and academics living abroad, separate from the settled Yordim but contributing by their presence to that sense of an Israeli community amid the diaspora.

III

Similar to the difficulty in determining the number of Yordim, and closely connected to it, is the difficulty in determining the geographical dispersal of the Yordim. As a result of globalisation, ease of transport, an increase in the number of Israelis, especially of the younger generation, travelling to all continents and the porous borders of host countries, Israelis now migrate to and settle in numerous countries all over the globe. Their host countries also include the poorer and less developed countries, such as several South American and African states.

There are, however, new aspects to this growing dispersal. The first is that Israelis migrate to and settle in countries that until recently have been regarded as taboo for permanent residence. This applies to Germany, Spain, Portugal and a number of authoritarian states in Africa and South America. Although the number of Israeli emigrants in Spain and Portugal is not very high, yet there is a continuous, gradual but increasing inflow. The number of Israelis migrating to Germany is larger. It means that younger Israelis are immune to those troubling memories about the nearer and more remote past, and that like many other migrants they settle in countries wherever they can satisfy their needs and inclinations. Moreover, Israelis now migrate to and settle in countries whose cultures were totally alien barely a decade ago. Included in this category are various Asian countries, particularly Japan. All these trends considered, it means that, like all other present-day migrants, these Israelis are highly pragmatic in their choice of host countries. When considering possible future developments in this sphere it should be remembered that by settling in these remote countries the first Yordim create the basis and infrastructure to which additional Israeli migrants might be attracted.

This remarkable dispersal in numerous countries, however, is not even. Clearly, Yordim have preferred to emigrate to and settle in Anglo-Saxon countries. These include Great Britain (the estimate is that about 50,000 Israelis have settled there), Canada (about 15,000), Australia (about 15,000), South Africa (20,000), and, of course, the United States, where the largest Israeli community (about 500,000) prospers. Moreover, it is estimated that 50 to 60 per cent of all Yordim head for the US, and eventually settle there (Ben-Vered, 1990; Rosenthal, Kfir, Fridberg, 1994). In these and other host countries, Yordim tend to concentrate in larger cities, such as New York, Los Angeles, Chicago, London, Paris, Johannesburg, Sydney and Toronto. Again, like other migrants, in these big cities the Yordim concentrate in specific neighbourhoods.

The reasons for these preferences are pretty obvious: all these are liberal, democratic countries, generally showing reasonable tolerance towards migrants and aliens; in most of these countries immigration and naturalisation laws are relatively relaxed; their borders are porous; culturally these countries are not entirely strange to the Israeli; economically these states have been among the more prosperous countries throughout the post-Second World War era – these were regarded as the 'golden states' where 'the sky is the limit'; in some of these host countries there was a tradition of support to emigrants; to a lesser degree, the existence of well-established Jewish (and some Israeli) communities were regarded as a safety net for newcomers, and enhanced the 'contagion effect' that is attracting Yordim to specific cities and neighbourhoods (Danziger, 1984); communications with and transport to these countries were easy.

IV

Like most other migrants, immediately after their migration the majority of Israelis declare that they do not intend to settle in the host country. Although for various reasons – including guilt feelings about leaving the homeland that is still regarded as being under siege, a desire to maintain close relations with family and friends back in the homeland, an inclination to maintain homeland citizenship and other official contacts with it, and uncertainty about social and economic opportunities in the host country – the majority of these migrants state that their stay in the host country is only temporary, and that they intend to return to the homeland. Apparently these are not false or deceptive statements, for there is evidence that the majority of the migrants finally make up their mind about permanent settlement in the host country only after relatively long periods of sojourn in the host country, and as a result of complex considerations. The most important factors affecting their decision to settle permanently in host countries are the prospects of integration (not assimilation) in the host country; family considerations; and the general political and economic situation in the host country on the one hand, and the homeland on the other (Sheffer, 1995).

The recent return of various groups of migrants and members of diasporas to their respective homelands (for example, ethnic Germans and Greeks from the former Soviet Union, Russians from the former Soviet Republics, Jews from the former Soviet Union and other parts of the world, and Irish and Armenians from Western countries) has attracted the attention of those who follow developments in this sphere. Reviewing these movements it becomes clear that the return of large groups also depends on a number of factors, such as regime transformation, especially from a restrictive to an open regime that formerly prohibited emigration; difficult economic and political conditions in the host country on the one hand, and favourable conditions in the homeland on the other hand; and concerted activities by the homeland itself, directed at encouraging a return.

Because of the great sensitivity of the Yerida issue in Israel, return has been of major concern and interest to Israeli governments and citizenry (Damian, 1987; Fridberg and Kfir, 1992). Studies that were conducted in the 1980s suggested that Israelis who had left the country for educational purposes and to improve their personal economic position were among those who were better candidates for return; Israelis born of Ashkenazi origin were more inclined to return; most of the Yordim returnees were married, in their thirties, and owned a house or an apartment in Israel. A sense of strong connection to Israel on the one hand, and alienation towards the host countries on the other hand, constituted almost *sine qua non* motivational bases for a return. It is worth noting, however, that according to studies among Yordim who had emigrated to improve their economic status, that kind of connectedness to Israel was weaker (Fein, 1984).

The early 1990s signalled not only a noticeable reduction in the rate of emigration, but also a discernible tendency to return. Observers of this trend suggested that the main 'push' factor was the temporary economic slow-down in the United States and in other Western countries that had affected large concentrations of Israelis, such as those in the Silicon Valley and New York metropolitan areas. These studies showed that the main 'pull' factors were the expectation of better security conditions, hope for an improvement of the Israeli economy, and actual economic growth, especially in the field of high-tech industries (see, for example, Shafrir-Raanan, 1992; Arif and Damari, 1992; Natan, 1993; Rom, 1995).

V

Yordim stories in various host countries demonstrate that it is difficult to erase an ethno-national and religious identity. Thus a majority of first-generation Yordim (according to a recent study, about 70 per cent in the largest concentration outside Israel – New York – see Rosenthal, Kfir and Fridberg, 1994) regard their nationality as Israeli, and continue to hold this notion even after acquiring host country citizenship (for an earlier study of the identity question see Alias, 1984). According to informal information, most Israelis abroad indeed maintain their Israeli citizenship and use their Israeli passport when entering the homeland. Even if second generation Yordim might distance themselves from Israel, and declare that they are of the host country nationality, the third generation tends to show a renewed attachment to Israel and an inclination to identify as such. There are also other indications that the Israeli identity surfaces whenever the Jewish state faces a major crisis, especially in regard to its security.

There is a wide popular consensus that it is relatively easy to identify Israelis abroad: they maintain an 'Israeli accent', many have difficulties in mastering English or other local languages, they demonstrate a special body language, and they participate in pro-Israeli events (though mostly after a crisis in Israel, and mainly in closed sessions). As far as their self-identification is concerned, for example, 60 per cent of the first-generation participants in a survey conducted among Yordim in New York identified themselves as Israelis, 81 per cent thought that Hebrew should be spoken in their homes, and 78 per cent rejected the idea of adopting American names.

There are also ample indicators that many Yordim feel a sense of loyalty to their homeland. Ideologically, again like members of other diasporas, probably a majority of the Yordim support the rightist and religious nationalist parties in Israel. Moreover, many Yordim wanted to fly back to serve in the army during the 1973 and 1982 wars. Also, Yordim avowedly follow the news from and about Israel (according to figures pertaining to the 1980s, about 30 per cent listened to Israeli radio on a daily basis and about 46 per cent listened to Israeli radio once a week). Recently it has become easier to follow news about Israel, especially with the greater popularity of direct television coverage by networks such as the BBC and CNN, the expansion of cheaper telephone connections, the availability of Israeli newspapers now printed in certain host countries, regular radio transmissions and, of late, the Internet.

On the other hand, however, only a very few Yordim contribute to funds for Israel. They prefer to remit money to their families back in the homeland, though apparently the total sums of remittances are not consequential. Similarly, until recently, rich Yordim did not invest much in Israel. But there are some indications that the situation is changing in this respect. The reasons for this change are that over the years the number of rich Yordim has increased and, as a result of economic liberalisation, Israel has become a reasonable target country for investments. There are also signs that Yordim collaborate with Israeli secret services and industries in collecting information about various aspects of politics, economics and defence in their host countries.

VI

For various reasons that will be discussed later, most of the Yordim used to keep apart from the Jewish communities in their host countries. Observers disagreed about the reasons for this alienation: some alleged that because of their ideological and political socialisation, the Israelis exhibited a sense of superiority *vis à vis* Diaspora Jews, others suggested that the Yordim were immersed in solving their own problems, and yet others proposed that the cultural gap that existed between Diaspora Jews and Yordim was responsible for that distance. In any event, almost everybody agrees that this alienation was not one-sided, that is, Diaspora Jews were far from happy to welcome the Israelis and integrate them into their communities (Kass and Lipset, 1982).

Yet, since many Yordim, like most Israelis, are basically products of a collectivist social and political system where very strong communitarian inclinations prevailed, in their host countries the Yordim also show a tendency to create their own social networks. However, these networks have been limited in their depth of institutionalisation, as well as in their scope and purposes. Usually these were restricted to close friends and friends of friends. Their purpose was mainly social. Within these limited networks Yordim met and entertained, especially on Jewish and Israeli holidays. Since during the first four decades after the establishment of Israel, its government and public condemned Yerida, there were only minimal contacts between Yordim and Israeli legations abroad. And finally, only in rare cases did these networks serve as a basis for financial or business partnerships and co-operation.

Yordim are engaged in a great variety of occupations. Like other incipient diasporic groups, however, they prefer to find a living in certain characteristic fields, where they can use their actual or alleged qualifications. Thus, many among the Yordim are in commerce and finance (about 20 per cent); an equally large group are skilled workers, craftsmen and repairmen; a growing group of Yordim are technicians, engineers, programmers and similar high-tech specialists; and recently there has emerged a relatively large group of physicians and academics in various fields (Fein, 1983).

Studies in this area have been very partial and analyses do not go very deep, but as well as the white-collar occupations, Yordim have also engaged in blue-collar activities such as taxi driving, garage repair work, buildings maintenance and janitorships. There are those engaged in businesses (such as brokerage and real estate), trade (retail, weapons and military equipment, communications, diamonds), services (both Israeli and local banks, community services – as 'madrichim', 'schlichim' and teachers) and more recently in various branches of high-tech IT, in both hardware and software.

This great variety of occupations is not typical for any particular host country and applies throughout the Yordim communities in the western democratic countries. In Africa, Asia and South America there is a more obvious bias towards a variety of representation of private and government

Israeli firms, but there is no reliable survey of those working for Israel-based firms as compared with those in work for local companies.

In the relatively large urban concentrations of Yordim, such as London, Paris, New York, Los Angeles and Miami, a variety of cultural enterprises have proliferated and have attracted many Yordim and their Jewish and non-Jewish acquaintances and associates. Among these are television and radio stations, newspapers, numerous restaurants, special classes, support groups and concerts by famous Israeli performers. Tours by the Israeli Philharmonic Orchestra and Israeli theatres draw relatively large crowds of Yordim and Jews, and not only in the US. The same applies to the European, South American, South African and Australian communities.

One aspect of the activities that usually characterise established diasporas, that is, concerted political activities on the national level of host countries, is almost totally missing in this case. This lack of political activity is due to the ambivalent attitude shown by successive Israeli governments towards Yordim, and to the current stage of the development of these communities, which will be analysed later in this essay. On the other hand, and again like other diasporic groups, Yordim tend to exhibit nationalist rightist views as far as Israeli security and the peace process are concerned.

VII

Until the late 1980s, relations between the Yordim and most of the local Jewish communities were at best those of hostile coexistence, in many cases those of mutual alienation and disrespect, and at worst of total separation. As mentioned above, from the point of view of the Jewish communities, the reasons for these tense relations were ideological (connected to Zionist ideas about the need to concentrate the Jews in Israel and to oppose Yerida), emotional (in many cases these were responses to the Yordim sense of superiority), and practical (traditional suspicion towards large groups of immigrants even of the same origin).

There are indications that more recently, in many host countries, there are winds of change in this sphere – that is, Yordim are more welcomed by the local Jewish communities on the one hand, and more Yordim try to build bridges to these communities on the other. Moreover, there are clear signs of greater mutual acceptance. The reasons for this new trend are connected to the fact that many Israelis and Jews realise that the Israeli Diaspora is now a permanent feature in the nation's existence, along with the quest for 'normal' relations between the diaspora and the homeland, the legitimisation of pluralism of all kinds, and some concerted and deliberate attempts at reconciliation.

A similar change has occurred in Israel's relations with these groups.

The former denigrating attitude is being replaced by a new acceptance and a search for the means of establishing a fruitful dialogue for the mutual benefit of Israel and the Yordim. Thus, more Yordim attend the various functions that Israeli official delegations hold, there have been more attempts by Israeli leaders, politicians and officials to meet and conduct a dialogue with these former-Israelis, or persons who maintain Israeli passports, with calls in their direction to send their children to visit Israel. Moreover, Israeli representatives successfully try to effect reconciliation between local Jewish communities and Yordim.

The Yordim themselves are undergoing a transformation. They gain greater self-confidence, they are readier to maintain their Israeli identity and to identify as such. And probably the most important aspects of this new spirit are the first attempts to organise as a community and to act to promote their joint interests. In this they resemble other incipient diasporic communities (Weiner, 1986; Sheffer, 1995).

VIII

In conclusion, the analysis of Yerida presented in this essay draws attention to a number of significant features concerning the Yordim that are similar to those of other groups of migrants. Thus, Jewish diasporic communities are established as a result of voluntary emigration out of the homeland. Moreover, de-legitimisation of emigration and denigrating attitudes shown towards these persons and groups cannot stop this kind of migration. This became especially true after the opening up of many countries in various parts of the world in the 1990s. Subsequently, 'pull factors' rather than 'push factors' motivate them to leave Israel. In other words, these Israelis migrate to fulfil their personal inclinations and needs, they move to numerous countries, creating a vast dispersal, and they are pragmatic and rational in the selection of the host country where they settle. Like all other migrants, Yordim make the final decision to settle outside their homeland only after carefully considering and assessing the conditions prevailing in their target countries.

Liberalisation occurring as a result of Israel's growing integration in the global economy and the weakening of Zionist and collective ideology are the background factors slowly transforming Israel into a 'normal' state with regard to emigration (Yaar, 1987). Simultaneously, the Jewish Diaspora is also changing its attitude towards the Yordim, and in many places there are evident attempts at reconciliation and co-operation. It is not inconceivable that if the present processes of alienation between certain segments of the Jewish Diaspora and Israel continue, Yordim communities will eventually merge with the established Jewish Diaspora.

These developments notwithstanding, the fact that the Yordim still lack well-developed organisations (such as synagogues and benefit organisations) and elaborate trans-state networks, and continue to avoid massive political activity in their host countries, indicates that the Yordim are still only an incipient diaspora.

NOTE

This essay has greatly benefited from Dr Asher Fridberg's, *The Emigration from Israel: An Annotated Bibliography* (Jerusalem: The Jerusalem Center, 1996).

REFERENCES

Alias, N., 1984. 'Ethnic Identity of Israelis in the US: Generational Comparison', Dissertation Presented to the Faculty of Professional Psychology, University of California, Berkeley.
Alon, G., 1989. 'Since 1948. About 700,000 Persons Emigrated from Israel', *Haaretz* (Hebrew).
Arif, O., and Damari, H., 1992. 'The Return Home', *Yediot Aharonot*, 17 November (Hebrew).
Ben Vered, A., 1991. '800,000 Yordim in North America', *Haaretz*, 24 April (Hebrew).
Caspit, B., 1995. 'Decline in Emigration', *Maariv*, 3 October (Hebrew).
Cohen, R., 1997. *Global Diasporas* (London: UCL Press).
Cohen, Y., 1987. 'War and Social Integration: The Effects of the Arab–Israeli Conflict on Jewish Emigration From Israel', Discussion Paper 321, Golda Meir Institute for Social and Labour Research, Tel Aviv University (Hebrew).
Cohen, Y., 1989. 'Israelis in the US – Their Socio-Economic Status in Comparison to Israeli and American Citizens', Research Report, The Jerusalem Institute for the Study of Israel (Hebrew).
Damian, N., 1987. 'Israeli Public Attitudes Toward the Yerida Phenomenon, Israelis Abroad and the Policy for Encouraging Them to Return', Research Report, The Ministry of Immigration Absorption, Jerusalem (Hebrew).
Danziger, N., 1984. 'The Contagion Effect, an Additional Aspect in the Dynamics of Emigration: The Case of Israel', *International Migration Review*.
Desivilia, H., 1992. 'Motivations for Yerida – An Integration of Research Data', The Israeli Institute for Military Studies, Zichron Yaakov (Hebrew).
Elizur, D., and Elizur, M., 1974. *The Long Way Back* (Jerusalem: Applied Research Institute) (Hebrew).
Fein, A., 1978. *The Process of Migration – Israeli Emigration to the United States* (Cleveland, OH: School of Applied Social Science, Case Western Reserve University).
Fridberg, A., 1988. 'Yerida: The Pull and Push', *Forum*, 61, spring (Hebrew).
Fridberg, A., and Kfir, A., 1992. 'The Political Agenda and Policy-Making: The Case of Emigration From Israel', *International Journal of Public Administration*, Vol.15, No.7.
Galili, L., 1991. 'Land of No-Choice', *Haaretz*, 22 December (Hebrew).
Giladi, D., 1977. *The Yishuv in the Fourth Aliya Period* (Tel Aviv: Am Oved) (Hebrew).
Gorni, Y., 1970. 'Changes in the Social and Political Structure of the Second Aliya, 1904–1940', *Zionism*, Vol.1 (Hebrew).
Harsgor, M., 1987. 'Yerida: A National Catastrophe', *Hotam, Al Hamishmar*, 26 June (Hebrew).
Kass, D., and Lipset, M., 1982. 'Jewish Immigration to the US From 1967 to the Present: Israelis and Others', in M. Sklare (ed.), *Understanding American Jewry* (New Brunswick, NJ: Transaction).

Lamdani, R., 1982. 'Emigration from Israel', Discussion Paper No.82.08, Falk Institute, Jerusalem (Hebrew).
Mekel, A., 1982. 'Yerida and Yordim: Motivations, Trends and Consequences', Study Submitted to Columbia University.
Natan, R., 1993. 'The Weaklings Return Home', *Davar*, 9 June (Hebrew).
Plaut, S., 1982. *The Out Movement of Israelis*, Operations, Research, Statistics and Economics, Discussion Paper No.316 (Haifa: The Technion).
Rabi, Z., 1978. *Yerida From Israel, 1948–1977* (Jerusalem: Government of Israel, Central Bureau of Statistics (Hebrew).
Rosenthal, M., Kfir, A. and Fridberg, A., 1994. 'Israelis in New York', *Kivunim*, No.6, June (Hebrew).
Schweid, E., 1981. 'Yerida as a Process of Disintegration', *Maariv*, 7 June (Hebrew).
Shafrir-Raanan, R., 1992. 'There is no Choice: Returning Home', *Hadashot*, 2 February (Hebrew).
Sheffer, G., 1986. *Modern Diasporas in International Politics* (London: Croom Helm).
Sheffer, G., 1995. 'The emergence of New Ethno-national Diasporas', *Migration*, No.28.
Sobel, Z., 1986. *Migration from the Promised Land* (New Brunswick, NJ: Transaction Books).
The Government of Israel, Central Bureau of Statistics, 1990, 1991, 1993, 1994. *Indicators for the Number of Israeli Citizens Abroad* (Hebrew).
Yaar, E., 1987. 'There is nothing to do about it – Emigration from Israel as a Normal Phenomenon', *Politica*, No.16, August (Hebrew).

The Jewish Community in the United States

Donald Feldstein

THE BASIC CHARACTERISTICS OF THE ORGANISED JEWISH COMMUNITY IN THE UNITED STATES

The American Jewish community may be the best educated of any ethnic or religious population group in the United States and of any Jewish community in history. It is certainly one of the most influential communities among the ethnic groups in the United States. It is an ageing community, as is the general American population, but even more so among Jews.

The American Jewish population has traditionally been very highly concentrated in a number of metropolitan centres in the north-east. That is still where most Jews are to be found, but the pattern is shifting even as the American pattern has been shifting. Jews are spreading out from the north-east and Midwest into the 'edges', the rim of the United States from Atlanta south through Florida and up through the Pacific Coast into Oregon and the state of Washington. In fact, at this point there is approximately the same percentage of Jews in the West, about 20 per cent, as there are Americans in the West. There are several other general characteristics of the American Jewish population that may be worth noting.

Voluntarism

The Jewish population is intensely voluntaristic. There is no religious authority that all or even most Jews will follow, nor is there a secular authority or single organisation that can tell Jewish organisations and institutions how to act. In this regard, as well as in others, American Jews are like Americans, only more so. The voluntaristic bent was noted over

---

Dr Donald Feldstein is Associate Executive Vice-President (retired) of the Council of Jewish Federations in North America. He has had a distinguished career as social planner, Jewish communal service executive and social work educator. He has written or co-authored many articles and monographs on social welfare, social work education and Jewish communal service. His popular text *Understanding Social Welfare* has just been published in a fourth edition and *The National Jewish Population Study: Myths and Realities* was published by the American Jewish Congress in 1994.

(Parts of this essay were adapted from *The Organized Jewish Community in the United States: How It's Organized and How It Works* (Council of Jewish Federations, 1997) and 'The Jewish Federation in the United States: The First Hundred Years' (*Journal of Jewish Communal Service*, 1995).)

150 years ago by Alexis de Tocqueville. Americans are joiners and American Jews are even more that way. There are certain occasions when American Jews act with a great deal of consensus, so that Jews in Seattle may act on a crisis in Israel or to rescue Soviet Jews much as do Jews in Fort Lauderdale. However, each community insists that it is making its own determination with variations in the degree of response.

Localism

Just as Jews and Jewish organisations insist on their voluntaristic nature, so do they insist on their local autonomy. The approximately 200 Jewish Federations in the United States act with remarkable similarity, and yet each one will insist to a visitor and to the world at large that it is unique and that it will treasure its differences from the others however minor they may be. In recent years there has been some modification of this voluntarism and localism, as American Jews become aware of the degree to which there is one continental Jewish community in the United States and Canada. Some of these instances will be noted further on. In the main, however, American Jewish organisations and institutions continue to be essentially voluntary *and* local.

Americanism

At least since George Washington's famous 'to bigotry no sanction' letter, American Jews have engaged in a shameless love affair with the United States. They mimic American trends and American values. They follow closely behind American population and geographic trends. In some cases, such as in age distribution of the populations, they even anticipate trends, forming a kind of vanguard for developments in American life that will follow.

Purposes of the Enterprise

Towards what goals have organised Jewish efforts in the United States been directed? In the earliest Jewish settlements in New Amsterdam (New York) the community assumed responsibility for the welfare of fellow Jews and, for over 300 years until the late 1960s, the primary goals were:

- helping fellow Jews in the United States with their welfare, health and other needs;
- helping Jews to adjust to American society – in a sense helping them to assimilate;
- fighting persecution of Jews in other countries and discrimination against Jews in the United States;
- advocating for freer immigration into the United States for Jews and for others;

- contributing to a stronger democracy for all people.

This agenda began to change in the mid-1960s. Discrimination against Jews in academia and in industry was crumbling; Jews were prominent in literary circles; and attitudes towards Jews began to become more democratic and tolerant. The historian and rabbi Arthur Hertzberg has argued frequently that 'anti-anti-Semitism' has held too strong a place in the American pantheon, and is not a sufficient basis for Jewish continuity. A recent Op-Ed article by Professor Egon Mayer in the *New York Times* said, among other things, that 'For too long have we depended on the *un*kindness of strangers'. Since about 1967 there has been a gradual shifting away from 'anti-anti-Semitism' as the primary emphasis of the organised Jewish community to more interest and concern with the State of Israel – defending Israel and pride in Israel, Holocaust awareness and the determination that this terrible event must not be allowed to reoccur. A number of critics have argued that even pride in Israel and Holocaust awareness are not sufficient pillars for Jewish continuity.

A final shift in purpose has been a growing emphasis on Jewish education and support for Jewish education, formal and informal, including significant support for all-day Jewish schools as the best method of assuring and enhancing Jewish continuity and identity in the United States. Thus, while concern about anti-Semitism remains, there has been a basic change in the American Jewish enterprise. Today, the basis client is not the specific needy Jew; Judaism itself has become the client. Can Judaism thrive and grow, and, if so, how, in an atmosphere of freedom? How does the community deal, *can* it deal with a crippling 52 per cent rate of intermarriage? Barring a new crisis in Israel, the above will be the goals and purposes of the American Jewish community in the near future

CATEGORIES OF ORGANISATIONS IN THE JEWISH COMMUNITY

Jewish Religious Organisations

Traditionally, the American Jewish community has been known for having three denominations – Reform, Orthodox and Conservative. A fourth denomination, the Reconstructionist, is younger and smaller but has gradually developed basically the same kinds of institutions and organisations as have the other three. Each denomination maintains a major congregational body in which their synagogues maintain membership, and a rabbinical association and seminaries for the training and ordination of rabbis.

All told, about 38 per cent of American Jews indicate that they are affiliated with a particular synagogue of one of these denominations. This translates into 850,000 households and just over two million individuals. At some point during a lifetime, a much higher percentage of Jews affiliate with a synagogue. According to the 1990 National Jewish Population Survey (NJPS), a slight plurality expressed a preference for the Reform denomination, individually and as households. Yet the Conservative movement may still be the largest of actually affiliated individuals and households. Orthodoxy is a denomination of choice for about 8 per cent of American Jews. The denominations also invest in youth movements, trying to recruit and inspire young people to their brand of observance.

Basically, religious life is thriving, vigorous and evolving in the United States. What may have been the most commonly followed religious practices two generations ago are different from the ones most popular today, and the likelihood is that future changes await. Probably, today, the synagogue is the basic membership group for more Jews having face-to-face relationships with their peers than any other institution in American Jewish life.

Community Relations

Over 30 national Jewish organisations are primarily concerned with community relations or, as some of the organisations prefer to term it, human relations. Community relations is defined somewhat differently by different organizations; essentially, however, these are the organisations that are primarily concerned about promoting democracy in the United States, in working on intergroup relations and interreligious relations, creating a climate of tolerance and pluralism for all people in the United States, defending the rights of groups discriminated against and, particularly, defending Jewish interests and fighting anti-Semitism. Three large national organisations have been popularly accepted as being the leaders in community relations. In order of their age, these are the American Jewish Committee, the Anti-Defamation League of B'nai B'rith and the American Jewish Congress. A fourth national group, the Simon Wiesenthal Center, has grown in recent years and claims membership in that largest grouping. Its growth is related to its early use of direct mail marketing methods and the attraction of the name of Simon Wiesenthal.

At the same time, there is a network of well over 100 local community relations organisations, most of them affiliated with their local Jewish Federation. Sometimes these are committees or councils of the Federation; sometimes they are independent agencies receiving some support from the Federation, but they work on similar agendas, with local variations, and they vary greatly in their funding strength and their influence. It is safe to say that, for the foreseeable future, fighting anti-Semitism will continue to be an important priority among the large national community relations agencies mentioned above, albeit in slightly shrinking degrees as Jews in the United States feel more secure in their home. So these large national community relations agencies have begun to devote more resources to other activities – relationships with Israel and other countries, and certain specialised activities that each of the three largest groups have carved out for themselves. Community relations may no longer have the primary importance it once had in American Jewish life. Yet, the community relations agencies are a very important ingredient in the fabric and in the network of organised Jewish activity in the United States.

Zionist- and Israel-Related Organisations

Since the birth of the modern Zionist movement a century ago, most American Jews have been somewhat sympathetic to the aims of re-establishing a Jewish homeland in the Jewish people's ancient land. That sentiment was never unanimous, although support for Israel today is one of the most broadly supported issues in the American Jewish agenda. While Israel is supported today by a number of 'American Friends of' organisations related to each of the major universities, hospitals, and the like in Israel, the prime vehicle for raising funds for Israel and transmitting them to Israel via the Jewish Agency for Israel has been since its founding the United Jewish Appeal (UJA). Although some of these other organisations have grown more rapidly and have become rather large, none has reached anywhere near the proportions of the UJA–Federation movement in its activity of raising over $800 million per year in its campaigns and sending slightly less than half of that amount through the United Israel Appeal to the Jewish Agency for Israel and on to the services provided by the Jewish Agency for Israel.

Support for Israel also comes from a plethora of smaller organisations attached to the various movements and parties in Israel, and various special interests. The American Israel Political Affairs Committee (AIPAC) is well known as a group that eschews tax deductibility in order to lobby freely for Israeli interests in the United States. The Conference of Presidents of Major American Jewish Organisations is another umbrella group which carries a great deal of authority in speaking on behalf of Israel when addressing the United States and its government. We will see in a later section of this essay that, with Israel's GNP growing steadily and greater distance developing since the last major armed conflict in Israel, there is a great deal of pressure to devote a smaller percentage of the monies raised in the annual UJA–Federation appeals to Israel and to devote more money to local needs, and particularly to enhancing Jewish continuity and identity.

Jewish Education

In many ways, Jewish education in the United States and its organisation mirrors the organisation of the Jewish religious community. The religious denominations tend to have counterpart organisations for Jewish education. Within the Jewish community, in elementary and high schools, there are approximately one million young people. In the early 1980s, when a count was last made extensively, there were only 360,000 Jewish young people attending formal Jewish educational programmes. However, that is a snapshot, and over the course of life many more than that number attend Jewish educational programmes. About 85 per cent of Jewish young boys do have a Bar Mitzvah ceremony and, in most cases, that is not possible in a synagogue without some formal Jewish education. The growth area in the last 25 years has been in Jewish day schools, now enrolling approximately 135,000 students. One of every three Jewish young people who attends formal Jewish education at a given moment does so in a Jewish all-day school. That development would have been unbelievable had it been predicted in the 1950s. Virtually every Jewish community in the United States with a Jewish population of over 5,000 has a Jewish day school. The majority of Jewish day schools are under Orthodox auspices or leadership. A number are Conservative day schools, affiliated with the Solomon Schechter movement. A very small number of recently organised day schools are under Reform auspices.

Most of the larger Jewish communities in the United States have bureaux or boards of Jewish education co-ordinating services, educational materials, and so on, for students cross-denominationally. These bureaux or boards try to serve the day schools as well, with mixed degrees of success. There are also a number of national bodies serving or dealing with Jewish education. Not only the religious denominations but the American section of the World Zionist Organisation also sponsors its own commission or committee on Jewish education. In recent years, the national organisations involved in Jewish education have become increasingly concerned with the training of teachers and potential teachers for Jewish education, and funds have been made available for these purposes through some sizeable, specially earmarked grants.

Other Organised Jewish Agencies

A variety of other agencies also seek to touch and serve American Jews. The Hebrew Immigrant Aid Society (HIAS) brings Jewish refugees to the United States, where local agencies then take over. There are organisations affiliated with the various Zionist movements as well as the denominations of Jewish religious life and some others. There are also cultural agencies and, at this point, there are special groupings of those who are interested in or lead Holocaust memorial museums, Jewish museums, and the like. There are guilds for the Jewish arts, the Jewish blind, and almost any need that one might imagine, from Free Loan societies to Jewish music organisations.

There are well over 100 publications weekly or monthly that comprise the Anglo-Jewish press in the United States. These include slick cover magazines, expensive and well edited, weeklies with large circulations, some of which are independent while others, particularly in small cities, are published by the local Jewish Federation. The quality of these Anglo-Jewish publications varies considerably, from excellent to simple bulletin boards of coming events. But the Anglo-Jewish press is growing in importance and readership, and comprises an important part of the network of American Jewish organisations.

The Organisation of Jewish Lay Leadership in the United States

There are probably over 75,000 individuals who serve on boards or as active committee chair people or leaders of the congregational or Jewish Federation structures in the United States. This number has been described as very small and unrepresentative of the Jewish community, and has also been described as being remarkably large for a nation that is moving towards greater and greater anonymity all the time. So how involved American Jews are in the Jewish community continues to be a matter of debate. We know this at least: over 30 per cent of Jews have visited the State of Israel at least once (over 40 per cent of specific constituencies such as synagogue members, and perhaps over 60 per cent of Orthodox synagogue members). That fact can be grist for the mill of either point of view about Jewish involvement.

A smaller number of these tens of thousands of individuals – perhaps three or four thousand – are in the inner circle of leadership of the Federations and other major organisations of the Jewish community, meet each other often at meetings or on missions to Israel organised by UJA, recommend people from their circles of friends to be appointed to other leadership posts, and sometimes even have business connections with one another. While wealth is certainly a factor in upward mobility in the Jewish lay organisational community, it is not a necessary prerequisite, and a fair number of not poor but not extremely wealthy Jews have made it to top leadership levels.

The issue of the place of women is another one entirely. Women in the past decades have attained the presidency or chairpersonships of many of the major Jewish organisations in the United States. A number of Jewish Federations have appointed two or more women presidents during the last decade, and there is a feeling that while change is not fully adequate, it is happening. On the professional level matters are more grim. There have been no female chief executives ever in any of the largest community Jewish Federations in the United States, and almost none in other significant or major Jewish organisations. There is a good deal of female representation among executives of intermediate and small Federations in the United States and there is enough ferment in the Jewish community on this subject that one may expect that some significant changes will take place in the next decade or more.

Non-establishment and Anti-establishment Organisations

There have always been some organisations, albeit relatively small, that have taken a unique position. The American Council For Judaism with its strong anti-Zionist bias is a traditional example. In recent years there has been a proliferation of such groups and a number of leaders and thinkers in the Jewish community have predicted all kinds of dire results from their growth. Since the advent of the peace process in Israel, growth has accelerated of groups that are 'friends' of organisations for maintaining the settlements, achieving peace and harmony with Arabs, and so on. There are a handful of liberal or left-leaning organisations in American Jewish life. The New Israel Fund does appeal to a number of Jews, particularly younger ones, who seek to support various social causes in Israel that may differ from the things generally supported by the Jewish Agency for Israel. Jews for Justice has tried to become a kind of Jewish peace corps, doing good in areas of the United States and elsewhere where their help might be valuable and needed. Mazone is an organisation that has tried to interest Jews in donating three per cent of the normal costs of a major celebration, such as a Bar/Bat Mitzvah, to the fight against hunger. The Abraham Foundation seeks to work on a reconciliation between Jews and Arabs in Israel, as does Interns for Peace.

In spite of all the above, the most striking fact is that all of these organisations combined with the vastly larger fundraising efforts of the Israeli universities and hospitals and Israel Bonds has not really threatened thus far the primacy of the United Jewish Appeal as the major mechanism or conduit for aid from American Jews to the State of Israel. However, this may change in the years ahead as Israeli Jews themselves, and certainly American Jews, argue that with a growing economy Israel needs and should need less fiscal help from the United States, and because generally there is a decline in the percentage of monies raised in the United States from Jewish sources that are given to Israel in times of relative peace.

Will the Well Run Dry?

A popular article of 1979 argued that the sons and daughters of wealthy Jewish philanthropists were entering the professions rather than business or real estate where the 'big money is', that the Jewish community had to face the prospect of not being in a position to receive contributions in as large amounts and from as large a number people as had been the case in the past. More than 15 years later it is possible to assess this prediction and see in what ways it has come true and in what ways it has not:

1. The bottom line is that the Jewish Federations have been flat in their fundraising for a number of years and in terms of real dollars, allowing for inflation, the amounts raised are significantly down from what they were ten or 15 years ago; 1997 was the first time in several years that the campaign in the United States generally raised more increased money than the rate of inflation.
2. The number of donors has indeed decreased. There were about one million individual donors at the time of the Yom Kippur War. Today there are only about 800,000 and the number is probably still declining, again probably as a consequence of continued assimilation and intermarriage.
3. Jews continue to be as philanthropic as ever, probably the most philanthropic group in the United States except for the Mormons. Jews used to give at least two-thirds of their contributions to Jewish causes. Now they give about 50 per cent of their contributions to Jewish causes and 50 per cent to general causes. This is in part because Jews are so much more accepted in areas where they used to be excluded – boards of directors of museums, symphonies, and the like.

But the well is not running dry, for a number of reasons:

1. Just as the above-mentioned article was being written, Jews were becoming enamoured with receiving MBAs and more Jews are now in business, real estate, investment banking and other cutting-edge areas than ever. Jewish fortunes, as they are revealed, are constantly amazing Jews themselves. In terms of the well itself, it is certainly not running dry. It is only a question of how much of the well is being siphoned off for the Jewish establishment.
2. In the last two decades, the endowment funds of the Jewish Federations have grown to over four billion dollars and even though some of them are earmarked for special purposes, the income from the endowment funds is now producing 15–20 per cent of the income of the annual campaign of the Jewish Federations in the United States.
3. Recent years have seen the growth of giant Jewish private and family

foundations, from the Weinberg Foundation, which is one of the ten largest in the United States, to a number of others, whose exact number and the exact total of dollars they produce are not even known or accurately calculated. But all the above factors indicate that one may be optimistic that the well is not running dry at all. The flat campaigns mean that the well is running dry in the sense that the Jewish community has simply not been able to invent a moral equivalent of war and rescue, the issues which bring out Jewish contributions in great numbers.

There are two final points on this issue. For years the Jewish Federations dreamed of an annual campaign of one billion dollars but they never seemed to be able to achieve it. The campaign would fluctuate at around $800 million a year, sometimes slightly higher, sometimes lower. But for two years running, when Operation Exodus for the rescue of Jews from the Former Soviet Union was being conducted, the gross receipts from Operation Exodus and the regular campaign were $1.2 billion per year, and this was done without any damage to the wealth of the Jewish community, so the potential seems to be there. And when there is Jewish consensus, as there was in the march on Washington in 1989, 200,000 Jews or 4 per cent of all the Jewish men, women and children in the United States attended, showing the power of the Jewish community in the United States when there is strong consensus and when there is a strong will.

THE JEWISH FEDERATION

I have discussed the various categories of Jewish organisations in the United States in a very brief manner. The Jewish Federations, or the Human Service Agencies as they are sometimes termed, will be considered in greater detail because they do represent, in many cases as they try to, the central address of the Jewish community.

Introduction

For all we know, Jews may have accompanied Columbus on his voyages and most likely some Jews found their way to the New World during the sixteenth and the early seventeenth centuries. Yet, historians of the Jewish community in the United States generally commence with the first communal band of Jewish settlers in what was then New Amsterdam (New York) in 1654. The Governor, Peter Stuyvesant, did not want to receive these guests but was eventually overruled, and so the first organised Jewish settlement in North America began. For almost 250 years Jewish settlement continued and grew in what became the United States, and Jewish communities established synagogues, burial societies, credit unions and Hebrew youth organisations in dozens of cities before there was a single Federation. From the start, the Jewish community promised local governments that it would take care of its own people and that Jews would not become a burden to the community. This remains a basic tenet of Jewish Federations to this day. The first Jewish Federation in the United States was organised and founded in Boston in 1895. Another was organised in Cincinnati, Ohio, and within several years Federations had sprung up around the country wherever there were significant Jewish communities.

What is the Jewish Federation?

The Jewish Federations were founded primarily by secular Jews and the Federations never committed themselves to observance of the Torah and Jewish tradition. In spite of this, consciously or unconsciously, the Federations, their founding and their philanthropies were very deeply influenced by Jewish tradition and in some ways they were similar to the Kehillah, the communal organisation that had existed in many parts of eastern Europe. Federations were similar to the Kehillah in their attempt to be comprehensive and inclusive of Jewish organisations, and in their concern for meeting the welfare needs of Jews in their respective communities. But the Kehillah were usually formed by local government, were primarily subject to the authority of local government and were founded to collect taxes from the Jewish community to support the state or local government. The essential difference between the Kehillah and the Jewish Federation is that the latter was and is ultimately fully autonomous. Chesed (loving-kindness) was very much in the minds of the founders of Jewish Federations, although not always as a conscious primary purpose, at least not conscious that this was following in Jewish tradition. Thus, as God clothed Adam and Eve, Federations were concerned about clothing the naked; as Abraham cared for the strangers, Federations cared for strangers; as God buried Moses, Jewish Federations supported Jewish burial societies. The phenomenon of re-creation of a tradition is not unique. Anthropologists have taught us that certain native American tribes, generations removed from their tribal practices, once permitted to establish self-government sometimes reinvented or re-created certain activities and customs practised by their forebears generations earlier, of which they had no conscious memory. It just seemed like the right thing to do.

There is no single place where one can find a comprehensive history of the Jewish Federation in North America. (A bibliography is appended to this essay.) From the written pieces we have, a list of the principles and characteristics of the Jewish Federation in North America can be culled. Three – autonomy, localism and Americanism – have been discussed earlier. One should add, however, that too much localism has at times actually hurt the Jewish Federation movement in the United States and that a move away from localism seems to be one of the trends. This will be discussed later. The other characteristics of the Jewish Federation are listed below.

Communalism

Carmi Schwartz, former Chief Executive of the Council of Jewish Federations, has pointed out that Judaism may perhaps be unique among the great religions in making a commendment of the need to communalise or to form community. Almost from the beginning, the Federations saw their communities and the needs of the communities as their ultimate targets for service, rather than simply the needs of individual Jews. No one is exempt from contributing to the needs of the community, not even the very poor.

Joint Fundraising, Allocating and Central Budgeting

The idea is deceptively simple. As large Jewish communities began to develop a plethora of Jewish institutions to meet various needs, and each one had its own fundraising campaign, it appeared that it might be more efficient and successful to aid a variety of institutions in one appeal and to offer donors the opportunity to make one gift. Then the organisation could allocate funds to its member agencies in some equitable manner, and to the Federation itself for its own needs. The idea was so simple and successful that it was copied by many communities. Communities did, in fact, raise more money in a single campaign than had previously been raised in total. The first Federations were followed in 1913 by the first Community Chest in the United States, in Cleveland, Ohio, the forerunner of the contemporary United Way.

Community Planning

Although the fundraising and allocations were central to the Federation, the innovation was almost immediately followed by a desire to plan for the community's needs. Community planning has now become a central part of the Federation in the United States and in Canada.

Central Services

Federations vary widely in the amount of central services they provide for their agencies and for their communities. There are those that simply do some kind of bookkeeping beyond their own organisation for agencies, and those that provide research, demographic information, and statistical and central accounting data as well. Sometimes the Federation itself provides community relations services via a separate agency dealing with government relations and relations with the larger philanthropic community. Sometimes this is handled by a committee of the Federation itself rather than a separate agency.

Agency Benefits

Not only did the campaign provide more financial support to the agencies than they could have received separately but Federations also provide legitimacy and power through their reputation for doing good work.

Inclusion

Federations try to include services and agencies to meet emerging common needs. They aim to be inclusive rather than exclusive, even while trying to come to grips with the reality that no Federation can meet every possible need. Limitation and expansion are two pillars of the Federation concept of inclusiveness.

Governance

Federations differ in their governance structures but each one is accountable to the Jewish community through some kind of elected Board of Directors or Trustees who are ultimately responsible for the operations of the Federation. Further, all Federations now devote some resources and energy to locating, attracting and developing new or young lay leadership.

Leadership

At first, Federations were volunteer-led, but soon they needed to engage paid executive secretaries, financial officers and other staff. Before long, Federations became complex organisations with various departments and employing various skills. Between the 1930s and the 1960s, Federations developed a strong marriage bond between Jewish communal service and the emerging profession of social work. Federations and Jewish Community Centers (JCCs) vied with each other as to which employed the most MSWs, but always the major policy decisions of the Federations were, and are, made by volunteer citizens of the Jewish community.

Council of Jewish Federations (CJF) and other National Agencies

Since its inception in 1932, the Council of Jewish Federations (originally called the Council of Jewish Federations and Welfare Funds) has represented the Jewish Federations in the United States and Canada in a continental network. CJF was a leader in the efforts to help Federations secure public support for housing for the elderly (along with B'nai B'rith). CJF was also a keystone in the promotion of legislation to help to resettle Russian Jews in the United States, and hundreds of millions of dollars have gone to this purpose. Since the birth of Israel, the United Jewish Appeal has been a vital partner in the work of Federations. Local welfare funds and the United Jewish Appeal merged, locality by locality. Finally, CJF was instrumental in founding several national agencies to serve distinctive needs, such as the National Jewish Community Relations Advisory Council and the National Foundation for Jewish Culture. National agencies are now a small but essential part of the concerns of Jewish Federations.

Changes in Services

Jewish Federations are broadly based and therefore tend to be somewhat conservative and slow to change, but change is a constant. In the early twentieth century, Jewish orphanages were vital institutions. Now they have largely disappeared. On the other hand, publicly supported residential facilities for the elderly have grown up as a major service in most large and large–intermediate Jewish communities. These are just small examples of the way that the services of the Federations and their agencies have changed considerably over a century of development.

Public Social Policy

Public policy and advocacy (tax deductible groups avoid the word 'lobbying') have become increasingly important to Federations and to CJF. At this point, 15 states in the United States maintain associations of the Federations in their states, focusing on public policy issues in the state capital.

Community Chests

Almost since their inception, community chests, United Ways and other religious Federations have worked closely together with the Jewish Federations. The United Ways allocate over $15 million annually to the agencies of the Federations. This is but one example of the reality that Jewish Federations are concerned with and related to larger non-profit and community issues.

Unity

Broad representativeness is characteristic of the Jewish Federation and almost any constituency group can find representation on the Board of Directors. Occasionally, a group is seen as so far to the right or to the left that it is denied membership in the local Jewish Federation or Jewish Community Council. But, with rare exceptions, the Federation is committed to including every group and unifying on consensus issues.

Social Justice, Ethical Values

The Jewish community in the United States has never been solely concerned with Jewish issues. It has worked at promoting democracy for all, for freer immigration and for a just society. Writers debate how central the social justice agenda should be in the Jewish community, but it is certainly still there.

No institution can guarantee the ethical behaviour of every one of its members. Federations have noted the importance of individual ethical behaviour but have concentrated on ensuring the institutional behaviour of the organisation and its accountability to its community of contributors.

Creativity and Excellence

Almost from the start, Jewish Federations tried to demand that the agencies they supported be the finest. Federation agencies pioneered in residential child care, in developing professionalism in family agencies and in creating a wide array of services for the elderly. Some of the world's finest medical centres and nursing homes are Federation agencies.

Maximum Feasible Participation

Long before the above term was a slogan in the United States' war on poverty in the 1960s, it was a principle guiding the Jewish Federation, a commitment to plan *with* rather than *for* the members of the community.

Sanctity of Life and the Dignity of Each Person

These ancient elements of Jewish tradition were incorporated into Jewish Federation philosophy and practice, and continue to be part of the ethical framework of everything the Federation strives to do. The above characteristics are at the heart of what Federations do and inform the vast array of services that they provide. The above list should enhance our understanding of the history of the Jewish Federation in the United States.

HISTORY OF THE JEWISH FEDERATION

The history of the Jewish Federation may be divided into four periods.

1. Period of Jewish Integration, 1895–1945

The first half century of the Jewish Federation movement in the United States was largely devoted to what might be described as welfare – meeting the health, social and other needs of individual Jews. Federations expanded in number and in function as they served more people in the growing Jewish population in the United States. Most services were available to all Americans who wished to partake of them, although they were primarily addressed to the needs and interests of the Jewish community. (That condition, of being primarily interested in the Jewish community and tending to serve all people, is, to some degree, continuing to this day.) Federation agencies were and are clearly sectarian and, simultaneously, universal. It would not be far from the truth to say that the goal of the Jewish Federation and Jewish social service agencies during this period was actually assimilation, helping Jews integrate into the United States, learning its language, its culture and its values. That goal was expressed very frankly by the Jewish settlement houses in New York City and more subtly in other agency services. Nevertheless, the goal was to eliminate barriers to Jewish participation in America and to full Jewish participation in the American dream.

2. Period of Integration of Welfare and Israel, 1945–67

With the establishment of the modern State of Israel, many elements of the Federations changed dramatically. The United Jewish Appeal became a far more important institution nationally. Speakers from Israel were much in demand at major fundraising functions of the local Federation. Gradually, communities began to integrate their local welfare funds – which focused on social services in the local area – with the needs of the Jews in Israel and other places overseas. A symptom of this was the beginning of joint campaigns by the Federations for local and Israel/overseas needs. The entire American Jewish community was witnessing a very gradual and inevitable marriage between two major concerns: providing for the welfare of Jews in the United States and providing aid to Jews in the rest of the world and, in particular, in Israel.

3. Period of Israel-Centric and Holocaust-Centric Judaism, 1967–90

The Six-Day War in 1967 was a watershed event for Jews around the world and particularly in North America. After Israel's dramatic victory, simple pride in the Jewish state became a major foundation of Jewish identity in the United States. Similarly, after the capture and trial of Adolph Eichmann in Jerusalem, there was an awakening to the Holocaust. In fact, Holocaust awareness became a second pillar of Jewish faith, along with pride in Israel. That movement did not peak until the 1990s with the opening of the National Holocaust Museum in Washington, DC, devoted to education about the Holocaust.

Two other developments also characterised this period in Jewish Federation history. First, the integration of the local Federation and Welfare Funds with the United Jewish Appeal was completed. The last and largest community to effect this integration was the New York City area, which did so only in the mid-1980s. The second development was a major increase in funds allocated to Jewish education. Federations, in varying degrees, had always supported Jewish education. Larger Federations had boards or bureaux of Jewish education and some had colleges of Jewish studies supported by the Federation. A small amount of support from the Federations had even been given to specific Jewish educational institutions, but that support was minimal and most Jews believed that all-day Jewish schools were either somehow un-American or at least not worthy of specific support. This attitude, too, began to change dramatically after 1967. The year 1969 marked a student 'rebellion' at the CJF's General Assembly in Boston, where student activists demanded that Federations support Jewish education more directly and more fully. This set off a chain of small and large changes, from providing kosher food at General Assembly functions to making direct support of Jewish education the largest single component in local allocations in the Federations of North America (now about 25 per cent of Federation local allocations).

4. Period of Emphasis on the Future of Judaism, 1990 Onward

It was only several years after the National Jewish Population Survey (NJPS) of 1990 that the effects and findings of this study began to show. The year 1995 saw a major increase in the number of young Jews given the opportunity to make an extended visit to Israel, and the number is likely to increase even more in the years ahead. However, immediately after its release in 1990, the NJPS set off a wave of concerned meetings and follow-ups. These were stimulated by the realisation, shocking to most American Jews, that the intermarriage rate of 52 per cent threatened the Jewish future in the United States in the long term, and that even concerns for Israel and awareness of the Holocaust were not sufficient by themselves to guarantee Jewish continuity and survival. Since 1990 support has been increased for Jewish education, particularly among those who believe strongly that Jewish education for an extended period of years in all-day

Jewish schools is the best insurer of in-marriage. Others feel equally strongly that associational correlations, participation in the Hillel Foundation on campus, attendance at a Jewish summer camp, even taking a Jewish studies course while at college are the most important insurers of Jewish continuity and in-marriage. All of these responses are attempts to answer the fundamental question: Can the Jewish community, which has successfully survived and usually grown in atmospheres of persecution and discrimination, survive in a climate of complete freedom, autonomy and choice, where Jews are welcomed not only in medical schools and country clubs but also into the bosoms of the families of the larger general community? The answer to this question is being written and will be written in the coming years. By the time of the next National Jewish Population Study, it may even be possible to see whether certain specific programmes, such as visits to Israel, greater support for the Hillel Foundation and the like, do indeed have some positive effect on continuity. But the attempt to answer the question positively will go on well into the twenty-first century when it is likely that Israel will replace the United States as having the largest Jewish population of any country in the world.

WHAT DO FEDERATIONS DO AND WHAT SERVICES
DO THEY PROVIDE?

It would take at least a book to describe adequately the services provided by or supported by Jewish Federations. What can be offered here is only a brief summary of some of the major agencies and services. The title 'human services' is probably the best available for the package of activities described as Federation services, but they include social services to the poor, services to the ageing, resettlement services and a whole variety of services generally provided by or associated with the Jewish Federations of North America.

In recent years the largest single, local allocation, and one that is growing, is to Jewish education. This includes allocations to the boards or bureaux of Jewish education in the community, the day schools, the congregational schools, adult Jewish education in the Jewish Community Centre (JCC) or elsewhere, or other specialised programmes. These funds account for over 25 per cent of the domestic allocations from the Jewish Federations of the United States.

Close behind are the allocations to the local JCC or to JCCs in the larger cities. The JCCs have always faced the question of why the community should be supporting these institutions since they serve not only, or even primarily, the poor but a cross section of the population, including a number of people who could pay the full amount of an individual or family cost. JCCs do in fact try to recoup their costs, and they sometimes even succeed in specialised programmes such as health clubs and day care programmes. But, in order to survive, they do need the help of the organised Jewish community and the Jewish Federation.

Sometimes in third place, sometimes in second place in domestic allocations is the Jewish Family and Children's Service of the locality, providing a wide range of services to individuals, families and groups – counselling for troubled individuals, often highly specialised psychotherapeutic services and a variety of others. A few of the large cities also maintain group homes for child care. However, these child care institutions are decreasing. There seems to be a shrinking Jewish base for them and where they do continue they are increasingly dependent on public support.

There was a time when providing adoption services for prospective adoptive families was part of the basic operations and services of the Jewish Family and Children's Services, but this function has largely disappeared and has been transferred – where individuals make use of them at all – to attorneys. The Jewish demand for adoptive children is so disproportionate to its percentage in the total population that Jewish Family and Children's Service agencies in some communities have begun to reconstitute and rediscover adoption services and have learned, as the attorneys once learned, that such services can be provided and adoptive children can be found if the right methods are employed.

The Jewish Family and Children's Services, more often than not, are the institutions charged by the Jewish Federation to co-ordinate and lead local Jewish resettlement services. There was a time when this was a very small and insignificant service but in recent years 40,000 Jews from the Former Soviet Union have been admitted into the United States each year with some federal financial support, and providing resettlement services of all kinds for these people is a major undertaking and function of the agency.

Before the advent of Medicare and Medicaid in 1965, the largest domestic recipients of Jewish Federation funds in many of the larger cities were Jewish hospitals. Originally, these hospitals were created largely because Jews were not welcomed in medical schools, in internships and residencies, and because the medical profession was simply not open to people without quotas and without regard to religion. Jews have made such vast strides in the medical profession in recent decades that the very validity of any allocation to Jewish hospitals has come into question in some cities. The allocations are now a very small fraction of the total Jewish Federation allocation to its domestic agencies. In some cases, such as Pittsburgh, PA, a Jewish hospital was actually sold and in others, such as New York, Jewish hospitals have merged into general medical institutions. There continue to be major hospitals, very often leading hospitals, under Jewish auspices or sponsorship in some of the largest cities in the United

States, and the likelihood is that they will continue under this kind of sponsorship in the foreseeable future. But the allocations continue to become a smaller and smaller percentage of the total budget and the Jewish federations, where they do make allocations to Jewish hospitals, tend to do so for specific programmes or purposes.

Many Jewish communities and their Jewish federations also count among their member agencies a Jewish Home for the Aged, usually a skilled nursing facility, sometimes with an affiliated, less-intensive care unit. These homes include some of the finest nursing homes in the United States and are a source of great pride to the Jewish community. Perhaps equally as important are the large number of residences for the elderly built under Jewish auspices or with Jewish sponsorship, primarily from the Jewish federation system. B'nai B'rith International was also an early entrant into the effort to receive federal support for residences for the elderly. In the last 30 years or so, the federations have become by far the largest player in this field of Jewish communal service.

There are often a number of other Jewish social services provided by the federation, usually with a smaller allocation than those mentioned above. The federations have become major supporters of the B'nai B'rith Hillel Foundations in the United States, providing services for Jewish youth on the college campus. There may be a group home or homes for developmentally disabled or retarded young people or adults. A score or so of Jewish federations help to support a Jewish Vocational Services Agency, providing the services implied by the name and sometimes others. Some of these Vocational Service Agencies have melded into the general population as their clientele ceased to be primarily Jewish, but a number of them are large and important. There also tend to be special allocations made by the federation to some innovative service or to deal with a problem that the community has become aware of most recently and wishes to do something about. The large and growing endowment funds of the Jewish federations are usually the source of these particular grants and will be discussed further in the final section of this essay.

Some federations have among their members a Community Relations Council as a separate, independent agency. Other federations have a Community Relations Council or Committee as an arm of the federation. Either way, the vast majority of Jewish federations have some body which is charged with the concern for local Jewish community relations. These Community Relations Councils or Committees not only deal with outbreaks of anti-Semitism locally, as do the giant Community Relations agencies, but they also tend to support Jewish education about the Holocaust in their communities, sponsor interreligious or interracial committees promoting good will and democracy, and perform a number of other community relations tasks.

These services, a community newspaper and other small specialised services represent the bulk of what federations do and the kind of services they provide, but no document is available which gives an encyclopedic account of everything that the large federation undertakes today, and the above must suffice for the purposes of this review.

THE JEWISH FEDERATION IN THE FIRST PART OF THE TWENTY-FIRST CENTURY

One trend or characteristic in the organised Jewish community has already begun to appear – the emerging awareness of a continental Jewish community. The wealthy Jewish contributor in Scarsdale, New York, or Skokie, Illinois, has always been concerned for the poor Jew in the Bronx or the south side of Chicago. He or she has always been concerned for the poor, oppressed Jew in Russia or Ethiopia, or the poor Jew in Holon, Israel. Yet, traditionally, the same Jew has very little concern for the Jew in Albany, Georgia, or Albuquerque, New Mexico. The responsibility for that Jew was thought to rest in his or her community. However, there has been a sea change in the sense of Jewish community around continental issues as manifested by the following recent developments:

- The Jewish community taxed itself for the support of Jews from the Former Soviet Union coming to each community in the United States, in some proportional manner related to each community's Jewish population. Based on how many Jews were resettled in that community, the community either paid to or received funds from a central pool.
- In the same way, the Jewish communities through their federations taxed themselves to guarantee loans to Jews from the Former Soviet Union coming to Israel in a mini-version of the $10 billion Loan Guarantee Program from the United States government to Israel.
- The Jewish federations voted to accept a new governance structure for CJF in which certain decisions made by some kind of super-majority might be binding on the federations despite their tradition of autonomy.
- The Jewish federations are maintaining a fund for emergency disaster relief to be available to any community that might need it.
- Federations voted to develop a special fund to augment support for the Hillel Foundations in the United States and for Jews on the college campus.

Thus, the emergence of the awareness of the continental Jewish community, along with the growing emphasis on Jewish education and continuity are hallmarks of the current and future periods in the history of the Jewish federations and represent trends that are likely to continue for the next decade or two.

The federations will continue to augment and increase their support of programmes to strengthen Jewish identity and continuity in the United States. They will develop programmes and approaches to support formal Jewish education, primarily in day schools and for Jewish associational activities. In some cases, federations will strengthen their relationships and ties to synagogues, including even the funding of some staff members in particular synagogues. A somewhat different approach which is also gathering strength is increased outreach to marginally affiliated Jews and even to those individuals who are part of intermarried households. There is still little hard evidence that these approaches have produced significant results but the impetus is there to make the attempt, along with a counter-trend in some Jewish quarters to concentrate all or most activities on the Jews in the core.

There will certainly be continuing and growing attention given to fundraising efforts. On the one hand, contributions to the Federation/UJA system have generally not increased much in recent years and have not kept pace with inflation. On the other hand, as mentioned earlier, the growing endowment funds of the federations and the private or family foundations have presented a whole new opportunity for Jewish fundraising efforts. The emphasis in the next few years will be to try to make as much of those new funds as possible available to the kinds of programmes that federations would like to support.

The Jewish community has long been criticised for being over-organised, for proliferating organisations that often compete with one another for every need that emerges. There is also an important counter-trend that will be heard from in the future towards consolidation and merger in the organised Jewish community. Wealthy Jews in the United States have observed General Motors and IBM going from the red to the black after shrinking their work-forces, and there is some belief that the same could be done in the Jewish community. The only significant merger that has taken place in the last half-century in the Jewish community has been the gradual amalgamation, locality by locality, of the local federation welfare fund with the United Jewish Appeal or the major campaign for Israel and overseas. Other smaller mergers have taken place among federations, particularly in states where the federations are Balkanised, and this has produced some improvement in neatness in the federation map and structure. However, a new factor has come into play: the questioning of the traditional division of funds between local Jewish needs and the State of Israel and the Jewish Agency for Israel. UJA used to request a 50–50 split. Traditionally, the percentage allocated to Israel from the federation campaigns has gone up in times of war or crisis in Israel, and has gradually shrunk in years of relative peace. But at this point there is a growing Israeli GNP and a growing feeling from Israelis, as well as American Jews, that perhaps Israel could do just as well with less of or without the traditional philanthropic aid from the United States. A recent book, entitled *What Will Bind Us Now?*, laid out a half-dozen scenarios for different interrelationships between Israel and Diaspora Jewry. These developments and the desire of many American Jewish leaders to concentrate more of their limited resources on promoting Jewish continuity and identity, particularly in Jewish education, has put pressure on the allocation to Israel each year. Increasingly, federations are concentrating more on developing economic relationships with Israel among their leaders and in promoting state agencies to develop economic ties with Israel. Several state organisations exist, are funded by their states and are producing important results.

For all of these reasons, the Council of Jewish Federations and the United Jewish Appeal jointly appointed a high-level commission to analyse and recommend structures for continuing relationships in international philanthropy between the United States and Israel. This commission originally recommended a rather radical departure from the normally conservative and slow-moving Jewish establishment – the full merger of the UJA and the Council of Jewish Federations with the United Israel Appeal, to join that single-merged agency within a few years. Ultimately, that plan was rejected and, now, the Council of Jewish Federations and UJA have accepted the recommendations of an alternative plan. This plan calls for the consolidation or merging of certain services or departments, a lay group composed of representatives of both the Council of Jewish Federations and UJA, and co-location of the two giant agencies in one place. There are observers who believe that co-location is inevitably the forerunner of a full merger in several years time. This is certainly a possible trend to watch in the next decade.

As has been noted above and as has been the case in the general society, there has been a great increase in consciousness among Jewish women about achieving equality of opportunity in leadership of the Jewish federations and in the Jewish establishment generally. The progress that has been made has been noted above but one may also expect that in the next 15 years further important developments await in the emergence of female leadership, particularly on the professional level, in the organised Jewish community.

SUMMARY

Partly as a result of the frightening aspects of the 1990 NJPS findings, there is some feeling among a number of lay leaders in the Jewish community that a greater percentage of funds should be used for Jewish continuity, and therefore domestically, instead of going to Israel. Also, as Israel's GNP grows and if peace becomes more secure, there may need to be less emphasis on fundraising in the United States for Israel and the Jewish Agency and more emphasis on Israel's economic development. One conclusion is fairly certain. The Jewish federations are 100 years young and the organised Jewish community is almost 350 years young. The most important and most glorious chapters in the history of the Jewish community in the United States are yet to be written. Those of us who will be privileged to participate in the developments and changes that are in store are in for an exciting and fulfilling ride.

APPENDIX
WHAT HAPPENS TO A CONTRIBUTION FROM THE UNITED STATES?

Large Donor contributes $100,000 to local Federation/UJA	100,000
Local Federation deducts about 15% for overheads, administration, fundraising	15,000
	85,000
Local Federation adds similar amount from income of legacies and endowments	15,000
	100,000
Local Federation allocates 52% for local and national agencies	52,000
Balance is allocated to United Jewish Appeal	48,000
United Jewish Appeal deducts 4% for its costs	2,000
American Jewish Joint Distribution Committee receives 12%	5,000
New York Association for New Americans (resettles Jews in New York City area) deduct 5%	3,000
United Israel Appeal receives	38,000
To which is added income from United States Government Grants	6,000
Therefore Jewish Agency for Israel receives	44,000

JEWISH AGENCY FOR ISRAEL EXPENDS ITS FUNDS AS FOLLOWS:

Immigration, Absorption, Resettlement	45%
Youth Aliyah	19%
Rural and Urban Development	25%
Jewish/Zionist Education	9%
Special Grants and Allocations	2%
Total	100%

THE $52,000 ALLOCATED TO LOCAL AND NATIONAL AGENCIES IS DISTRIBUTED AS FOLLOWS:

Jewish Education	25%
Centres, Camps and Related Services	23%
Family Services and Resettlement	23%
Care of Aged	12%
Community Relations	4%
Campus	4%
Vocational Service	3%
Hospitals	3%
Community Newspaper	1%
National Agencies	2%
Total	100%

BIBLIOGRAPHY

Bernstein, Philip, *To Dwell in Unity* (Philadelphia: Jewish Publication Society, 1983).

Bernstein, Philip, *The Principles of Jewish Federations* (New York: Council of Jewish Federations, 1994).

Chanes, Jerome A., *The Voices of the American Jewish Community* (London: Survey of Jewish Affairs, 1989).

Elazar, Daniel J., *Community and Polity: The Organizational Dynamics of American Jewry* (Philadelphia: Jewish Publication Society of America, 1976).

Feldstein, Donald, 'The Jewish Federation: The First Hundred Years', *Journal of Jewish Communal Service* (1995).

Feldstein, Donald, *The Organization of the American Jewish Community: How It's Organized and How It Works* (New York: Council of Jewish Federations, 1997).

Jewish Education, Who, What, How? (New York: American Jewish Committee, 1983).

Maslow, Will, *The Structure and Functioning of the American Jewish Community* (New York: American Jewish Congress, 1974).

Miller, Charles, *An Introduction to the Jewish Federation* (New York: Council of Jewish Federations, 1985).

Norich, Sam, *What Will Bind Us Now?* (Washington, DC: Institute for the Middle East, 1995).

Fragments of Anglo-Jewry
Stefan Reif

The famous photograph showing Solomon Schechter assiduously sorting and identifying thousands of manuscript fragments in a special room set aside for the purpose at Cambridge University Library was taken exactly one hundred years ago. The Reader in Talmudic and Rabbinic Literature had visited Cairo between December 1896 and February 1897 and succeeded in persuading its Chief Rabbi and leading Jewish families to send him back to Cambridge laden with literary treasures. These items, many of them dating back to the eleventh and twelfth centuries, were a source of great excitement to Schechter and his research colleagues, and their identification and analysis were destined to change almost every theory previously proposed by historians of the Jewish Middle Ages. By the autumn of 1898, the remarkable range and importance of these unique documents had become clear and they were formally presented to the University of Cambridge in the names of Schechter, his non-Jewish friend and colleague Charles Taylor, Master of St John's College, who had sponsored and financed Schechter's trip, and the Cairene Jewish community. Given the role that the Taylor–Schechter Collection of Genizah manuscripts has played in rewriting Jewish history, it is appropriate that the centenary of the arrival in England of 140,000 of them, representing about two-thirds of what had survived after a thousand years of storage in the Ben Ezra Synagogue, is being marked around the world in a variety of ways.

The celebrations began in Jerusalem and Tel Aviv in December 1996, with a major international conference jointly sponsored by the Jewish National and University Library, the Hebrew University and Tel Aviv University. In the course of three days, more than 30 lectures were delivered by the world's specialists in different aspects of Genizah studies.

Dr Stefan Reif is Director of the Genizah Research Unit and Head of the Oriental Division at Cambridge University Library. His major fields of research are Jewish Liturgy and the Cairo Genizah and he is the author of six books and of over 200 scholarly articles. His most recent two volumes, both published by Cambridge University Press, are *Judaism and Hebrew Prayer*, which is a survey of Jewish liturgical history, and *Hebrew Manuscripts at Cambridge University Library*, in which he describes Cambridge's rich collection of over 1,000 Hebrew codices. He has recently completed a year in Israel as a Professorial Fellow of the Institute for Advanced Studies at the Hebrew University of Jerusalem. He is known not only for his research but also for his efforts over the years to make the contents of the Genizah known to the wider world.

They dealt with topics as varied as Hebrew poetry, Judaeo-Arabic language and literature, Jewish marriage customs, talmudic texts, and the story of the discovery itself, and will soon appear in a collective volume. Mrs Reuma Weizman, wife of Israel's President Ezer Weizman, attended one of the sessions and the presidential couple followed this up with a visit to Cambridge University Library in February 1997 to see some of the real thing. Accompanied by a large group of distinguished Israeli and British officials, they were shown an exhibit of the most outstanding Genizah items and it was explained how current technology can provide researchers around the world with images of these manuscripts on their personal computers. Mr Weizman was particularly excited by the relevance of the Genizah material to Jewish roots in the Holy Land and took home with him to Jerusalem facsimiles of a letter signed by Moses Maimonides over eight centuries ago and a lease relating to a Ramla synagogue from 1039.

President Weizman was examining Genizah fragments again in Jerusalem a few months later when he formally opened an historic exhibition at the Israel Museum entitled 'A Mosaic of Life'. Following almost two years of planning and organisation, some 50 fragments from Cambridge and six from the Jewish National and University Library went on display and attracted as many as 500 visitors a day during the exhibition's busiest period in the summer. The clearly labelled items covered the story of the discovery; examples of the handwriting of famous personalities including Maimonides, Judah Halevi and Joseph Karo; personal family letters; reports of business dealings, many in far-flung places; Jewish relations with their Muslim and Christian neighbours; the Karaites; and the communities of Eretz Yisrael and more distant lands. The international media attention that the exhibition attracted was unprecedented for an academic subject, and cultural and educational events, attached to the exhibition and often attended by VIPs, were numerous and crowded. A snappy 20-minute film, a 16-page newspaper, a souvenir brochure and access to the relevant Internet items were among the attractions. Later in the year, similar exhibitions were held at Cambridge University Library and at the Jewish Museum in New York.

That was by no means the end of the centenary celebrations. Newspapers, books and magazines, popular and scholarly, dealt with the Genizah theme and a joint project was launched by the Universities of Cambridge and Princeton that would provide computer images, together with transcriptions and annotated translations, of 100 specially selected Genizah documents. There was even a stamp issued to mark the Genizah centenary and the fiftieth jubilee of the discovery of the Dead Sea Scrolls. The Israel Philatelic Service issued a souvenir sheet on 29 May, featuring two stamps, created by the Dutch artist, Ad Vanooijen. The one commemorating Schechter's expedition included representations of the

Ben Ezra Synagogue, Schechter studying the fragments, and the Genizah manuscript of Ben Sira that inspired his trip. The semi-annual conference of the Society for Judaeo-Arabic Studies was centred on the Genizah and the World Congress of Jewish Studies, held every four years in Jerusalem, devoted a large number of lectures, as well as one plenary session, to the theme.

There is no doubt that a most distinguished English university has been glad to be a part of all these scholarly celebrations and that there has been an intense Jewish connection with such important academic pursuits. It is, of course, another story whether one can trace a consistency of enthusiasm on the part of either the University of Cambridge or the Anglo-Jewish world from 1897 until the present. The role of the former in the whole development of Hebrew studies over the centuries is a topic for another place and time. As far as the role of Jewish scholars in the UK in the unfolding of the Cambridge Genizah story is concerned, the suggestion is often made that the general intellectual atmosphere of Anglo-Jewry is a philistine one and that, as a result, little or no contribution to the historical study of Hebrew and Jewish sources has been made in these islands over the years. As we celebrate Schechter's retrieval of such a thrilling cache of texts, presentation of some of the evidence will clarify the degree to which the accusation is or is not justified, at least as far as the Taylor–Schechter Collection is concerned.

It should not be forgotten that it was Schechter's predecessor in his Cambridge academic post that created the intense interest in Jewish studies and in Hebrew manuscripts that ultimately led to the acquisition of the Genizah Collection. Solomon Marcus Schiller-Szinessy was one of the earliest in a long line of distinguished Hungarian scholars who combined the advantage of a western education with the best of traditional talmudic learning. In 1863, he came to Cambridge to earn his living, as many of his earlier co-religionists had done, by freelance teaching. Three years later, the University of Cambridge, at the prompting of some of its more liberal graduates and after no little controversy, formally appointed the Rabbi as Praeceptor in Rabbinic and Talmudic Literature. The removal of Jewish disabilities through the Test Act of 1871 gave the University the opportunity of granting him further recognition and, having been appointed Reader in Talmudic and Rabbinic literature in 1875, he was, in the following year, probably the first Jew to proceed to a conventional MA degree.

Schiller-Szinessy's controversialist bent led him into public disagreements with his fellow Anglo-Jewish academics, Adolf Neubauer and Solomon Schechter, in which vituperative accusations were hurled in both directions. Nevertheless, in his 27 years at Cambridge, he established rabbinic scholarship as an integral part of Oriental Studies and created a school of Hebraists who were to win distinction in the academic and ecclesiastical worlds, among them Charles Taylor. As far as his palaeographical skills are concerned, the University Library engaged him to compile 'a minute and elaborate catalogue' of the Library's Hebrew manuscripts. The first fruits of this endeavour appeared in 1876, and a second volume was printed but never formally published. During his Cambridge career, Schiller-Szinessy completed descriptions of about two-thirds of what had become a collection of about 800 manuscript works, and these, in the form of a handwritten catalogue of six bound volumes, remained, for many years, the most comprehensive guide to the collection. It was no doubt through his prompting that the Library purchased so many valuable Hebrew manuscripts, particularly from Jewish booksellers in Eastern Europe. When the rabbi died in 1890, the University had little doubt that it required a replacement, and Solomon Schechter was in post within a few months.

It hardly requires to be stated that Schechter's identification in 1896 of the first Genizah fragment of the Hebrew text of the Apocryphal book of Ben Sira did not occur in a scholarly vacuum. It is particularly interesting that there had already been considerable Jewish involvement in England in the controversy about the book's original language. The two major figures involved were Solomon Schechter and David Samuel Margoliouth. Schechter was raised in a Rumanian Hasidic family in the strained financial circumstances of Eastern European Jewry. He received an intensive rabbinic education but was also early inspired by a broader and more historical approach. He attended rabbinical seminaries in Vienna and Berlin, before making his way to London as the private tutor of the scholarly philanthropist, Claude Montefiore, and then to Cambridge in 1890 as its specialist in Talmudic and Rabbinic Literature. Though intellectually brilliant, enthusiastic and creative, he remained physically unkempt and socially unpolished, always the outsider in frustrated pursuit of somewhere he could call his spiritual home. He was a powerful supporter of traditional Judaism, both as ideology and way of life, an early advocate of Zionism, and an outstanding interpreter, editor and defender of rabbinic texts. He had little patience for Christian biblical critics.

Margoliouth, for his part, originated from a Jewish family that took a singularly different route from Eastern to Western European culture. His father, Ezekiel, and another relative, Moses, were converted to Anglican Christianity and became active missionaries among the Jews. David won a scholarship to the English public school, Winchester College, and carried off an assortment of university prizes as a student of classics at New College, Oxford, before turning his attention to oriental studies and winning election to the Laudian Chair of Arabic in 1889. With a deep voice, an 'exotic and vivid appearance' and an outstanding linguistic ability, Margoliouth was one of the great Oxford characters of his day. In matters academic, he delighted in adopting sceptical positions, such as when he denied the authenticity of the Elephantine Papyri and of pre-Islamic Arabic poetry, but in the Christian ecclesiastical context he remained thoroughly conservative. It would appear that not until his late years did he feel any special sympathy for the people from whom his family had stemmed.

One of Schechter's first publications after his appointment at Cambridge was an article on Ben Sira. Since talmudic and midrashic texts cite Hebrew verses from that work, it was obviously important to him to list, analyse and annotate these so that they could better be assessed in the context of 'solving the great Sirach difficulties'. Clearly he had at the back of his mind that he might at some later stage be able to argue for, if not prove an authentic Jewish transmission of the Hebrew text of Ben Sira, and he saw in the rabbinic texts a stage in that possible transmission. There can be little doubt about what constituted the immediate inspiration for his study. The inaugural lecture of the newly appointed Laudian Professor of Arabic in the University of Oxford had been published in the previous year and had dealt with the matter of the original Hebrew of Ben Sira. Having examined all the versions, Margoliouth had concluded that the most reliable evidence was to be found in the Greek and Syriac versions and proceeded to reconstruct a specimen Hebrew text based on their renderings. He was obviously of the view that the rabbinic testimony was of little consequence and indeed took the opportunity of a sideways swipe at the 'whole Rabbinic farrago' and of including a theologically tendentious statement about the 'grave of the Old-Hebrew and the old-Israel'.

Hebraists were not generally impressed with Margoliouth's reconstruction and a controversy got under way between him and the leading semiticists of the day. For Schechter, the matter appears to have called not only for a discussion concerning Semitic languages but also for a scholarly crusade(!) in defence of Jewish literary traditions. It was insufficient for him to claim that the Greek and Syriac versions were unlikely candidates for the role of authentic transmitters; more than that, they were no less than 'defaced caricatures of the real work of Sirach'. The battle lines had been drawn and the skirmishes continued for five years. Only then was a new weapon discovered that had the potential to settle the matter once and for all. In the spring of 1896, Mrs Agnes Smith Lewis and Mrs Margaret Dunlop Gibson brought home to Cambridge a haul of manuscripts from Jerusalem, the plain of Sharon and Cairo, and Schechter identified one as a Hebrew text of parts of Ben Sira 39–40 and he was convinced that it represented a reliable witness to the original language of the book. Now, surely, he must have thought, the scholarly controversy had been settled in his favour. But Margoliouth remained unconvinced; the opposing view to Schechter's was not finally to be refuted until discoveries by Yigael Yadin at Masada in 1964.

Schechter himself has little to say about which precise scholarly quest inspired him to undertake a trip to Cairo in the winter of 1896–97 in search of manuscripts. The undertaking was clearly important enough for him to cancel a previous intention of participating in Herbert Bentwich's Zionist pilgrimage to the land of Israel with the Maccabeans. It was surely his excitement about the Ben Sira fragment brought to him by Mrs Lewis that was a major factor in his decision to travel to Egypt rather than to Palestine, in pursuit of the source of such a precious item and in the expectation of discovering many more like it. He was doubtless eager to locate a goodly proportion of mediaeval Ben Sira texts, and to confirm his reputation as the Cambridge scholar who had restored its Hebrew text. But a Jewish colleague at the Bodleian Library in Oxford had other plans. Adolf Neubauer, expert in Jewish studies, assisted by Arthur Cowley, erudite semiticist, had, within five weeks of Mrs Lewis's letter appearing in the *Athenaeum*, located another nine leaves of the same manuscript of Ben Sira. It is possible that they were already working on such a project but more probable that Mrs Lewis was right when she later wrote that it was 'natural to think' that it was her letter of 13 May, published on 16 May, that had been 'of some assistance in guiding Messrs Neubauer and Cowley to this important result'. While Schechter was planning his trip to Cairo, his academic competitors in 'the other place' were losing no time in forging ahead in the scholarly race by preparing their texts for publication. Their volume, published by the Clarendon Press, was in the bookshops by January 1897, while Schechter was still ferreting around the various Cairo synagogues and checking whether they had any treasures to compare with those of the Ben Ezra.

The Lewis–Schechter fragment is included in the Neubauer–Cowley edition but the introduction covers much ground before it actually makes reference to that discovery on its fourth page, at which point it is also noted that Schechter's edition has been corrected by the writers. Even then there is something of a reluctance to set matters in an accurate chronological perspective. Far from clearly stating that they were inspired by Lewis and Schechter, the editors follow up their paragraph about Cambridge developments by reporting that 'almost simultaneously the Bodleian Library acquired, through Professor Sayce, a box of Hebrew and Arabic fragments' among which they had found other texts of Ben Sira. Schechter's personal and professional relations with Neubauer had never been quite as disastrous as those of his predecessor, Schiller-Szinessy, but they had nevertheless always been strained. News of Neubauer's work on Ben Sira could hardly have cheered Schechter up and he is on record during his 1897 visit to Cairo as having described his Oxford rival in German as a 'Lump', that is, nothing better than a scoundrel.

It was not only in the matter of the Ben Sira fragments that the Oxford Jewish scholar pre-empted his Cambridge colleague. It was also Neubauer who was the first to pay attention to Jewish liturgical fragments that had arrived in Oxford from the Cairo Genizah in the early 1890s. While preparing his monumental catalogue of the outstanding collection of Hebrew manuscripts at the Bodleian Library, Neubauer became aware that these fragments were of crucial importance to the history of Jewish prayer and Bible reading. He invited his nephew, Adolf Büchler, then in Vienna but later to become Principal of Jews' College in London, to co-operate with him in researching these items and Büchler worked with his uncle on this project between 1891 and 1893. Important as the description of the liturgical fragments undoubtedly was, the result of their endeavours extended beyond this. Through his study of the fragments, Büchler was able to identify the triennial cycle of synagogal readings that was current in the synagogue of the Palestinian Jews in Cairo almost a thousand years ago and to pave the way for many future studies of this phenomenon and of how it differed from the Babylonian annual cycle that ultimately predominated.

Three other scholars with connections in the Anglo-Jewish community also played significant roles in the story of the Genizah Collection during Schechter's period of residence in England, from 1882 until 1902. Without in any way undermining the key role of Schechter and his fellow Cambridge dons in arranging for the bulk of the contents of the Cairo Genizah to be brought to Cambridge University Library and for serious work to be undertaken on the conservation and identification of the fragments, today's historian must also recognise the pioneering efforts of earlier Genizah scholars, among them Elkan Nathan Adler, son of Chief Rabbi Nathan Marcus Adler and brother of his successor Hermann. Adler obtained access to the fragments for a second time a year before Schechter's visit and was content to remove one sackful and to leave the remainder. In Adler's own words, Neubauer rated him soundly 'for not carrying the whole lot away' and Schechter admired his continence 'but was not foolish enough to follow' his example. Adler's collection was, of course, sold to the Jewish Theological Seminary in 1923, when he was suffering the results of unwise financial investments.

Neither research nor the production of critical editions is possible without the initial industry of those who tackle the basic problems of decipherment, identification and description. In this connection, Herman Leonard Pass and Hartwig Hirschfeld played worthy roles. Pass was a student of Jews' College, the Orthodox London seminary, who continued his studies at Cambridge and, having there converted to Christianity, was ordained as an Anglican priest in 1916. He was on hand and ready to tackle the biblical items among the Genizah finds. He prepared an excellent summary of these and began work on a miscellany of apocryphal, pseudepigraphical and other literary pieces in Hebrew, Aramaic and Judaeo-Arabic that he identified in the Collection. Jews' College's contribution to the Genizah scholarship of the day is further represented by the work done by Hartwig Hirschfeld, its lecturer in Arabic and Syriac, who also taught at University College, London. It was Hirschfeld who was invited to examine and briefly describe the Arabic and Judaeo-Arabic parts of the Taylor–Schechter Collection. In 1901–2, he produced a preliminary survey of their contents, separating 255 'especially important' items and sorting the remainder into a number of cardboard boxes.

Though their primary interests did not lie in Genizah research, Schechter's two immediate successors in his Cambridge post, Israel Abrahams and Herbert Loewe, both of them actively involved in the Anglo-Jewish community though on different sides of the religious spectrum, made contributions to the field. While Schechter was still in Cambridge, he drew the attention of Abrahams to the fragments of the Passover Haggadah to be found in the Cambridge Genizah. This led to an article by the latter in which he published a number of texts which he correctly dated to the Geonic period and which contained most unusual versions of various parts of the Haggadah. Abrahams also acquired his own personal Genizah fragments, all of which are now housed at Cambridge University Library, and was instrumental in 1924 in persuading the Jewish Theological Seminary to restore to Cambridge a large collection of fragments borrowed by Schechter in 1902. Building on the foundations laid by earlier Cambridge Hebraists, Herbert Loewe completed a handlist of all the Hebrew manuscripts at Cambridge University Library in 1927, and those few Genizah fragments that had been acquired between 1890 and 1896, and were deemed numerically less daunting than the many thousands to be found in the other parts of its Genizah Collection, were included in the work.

Jacob Mann was a truly outstanding Genizah scholar who was also associated closely with Anglo-Jewry. Mann, born in Galicia (Austrian Poland), studied at Jews' College and the University of London between 1908 and 1915, and undoubtedly came under the influence of Adolf Büchler, who had earlier done some pioneering work on Genizah material. Mann's careful and brilliant analysis of the Cambridge Genizah fragments enabled him to rewrite the history of the Jewish communities in early mediaeval Egypt and Palestine. He continued Büchler's work on the Bible-reading traditions of the synagogue, as well as identifying many unknown Jewish Bible commentaries, and uncovering much of the prayer-book that had been used in pre-Crusader Eretz Yisrael. A host of his papers and books appeared between the world wars.

Between the end of the Second World War and the establishment of the Genizah Research Unit at Cambridge University Library in 1974, there were many Jewish scholars, particularly from Israel, and especially Shelomo Dov Goitein, who made a major impact on Genizah studies by their use of the Cambridge Collection. It is, however, the more local Jewish contribution that is occupying our attention. Naphtali Wieder, who lectured at Jews' College for a quarter of a century, brought to light some of the earliest versions of the Jewish prayer-book and Meir Wallenstein, who taught at the University of Manchester, did some similar work on liturgical poems. Jacob Teicher, then Lecturer in Rabbinics at Cambridge, did essential groundwork for the recovery of the first printed Hebraica on the basis of Genizah finds. He also played a major part in persuading the Faculty of Oriental Studies and the University Library to create an appointment that would be specifically devoted to the care and description of the Genizah material. In 1965, Henry Knopf, already employed to deal with the Hebrew printed books in the Library, was appointed as the first full-time librarian with responsibility for the Cambridge Genizah Collection and, as well as dealing with queries and visitors, began to catalogue the biblical fragments. During Knopf's term of office, which he resigned in 1972 to take up a library post at Bar-Ilan University in Israel, a number of important developments took place. A start was made on the cataloguing of the biblical fragments, additional boxes were appended to the New Series, the microfilming project made good progress, material was added to the Library's record of its published Genizah items, and the steady stream of researchers working on the Collection continued unabated. Even more importantly, a project was commenced to conserve the fragments in accordance with the latest techniques.

In the course of the last 24 years, with the encouragement and support of the Faculty of Oriental Studies and the Library Syndicate, a fully comprehensive programme of work on the Collection has been undertaken in the context of a newly created Genizah Research Unit. The remaining 32 crates of neglected material have been sorted under a variety of subject headings; the microfilming and conservation of all 140,000 fragments have been completed; over 40,000 fragments have been catalogued and some 50,000 published references to Cambridge Genizah items been located; ten volumes have been published in the *Genizah Series* handled by Cambridge University Press for Cambridge University Library; 14 visiting scholars (including E. J. Wiesenberg, after his retirement from a readership at University College, London) have been encouraged to play an active role in the description of the Collection and co-operative projects have been undertaken with the Israel Academy, Jewish National and University Library, Hebrew University and Jewish Theological Seminary of America; a team of young researchers has been a regular feature of the Unit and, after periods in the Unit, ten of them have found important posts in oriental faculties and libraries in various countries; over £1million has been raised from outside sources in support of the project; a serious attempt has been made, through a regular newsletter, *Genizah Fragments*, and various other publications and through the media, to bring the results of Genizah research to a wider public; and exhibitions of Hebraica around the world have often included Cambridge Genizah items. What is more, the progress made at Cambridge has contributed to an explosion of Genizah research throughout the field of Jewish studies and it is no longer possible even to attempt to list the hundreds of scholars outside Cambridge whose research is heavily dependent on the material that Schechter brought from Cairo one hundred years ago.

As even a cursory reading of the evidence makes clear, Anglo-Jewish scholars and philanthropists have been among those who have made all this possible. Through their respective contributions, they have ensured a local continuity for the work of Schechter and his successors. At the same time, it has to be acknowledged that the majority of Genizah scholars in Anglo-Jewry over the years have been born elsewhere, that some have abandoned Judaism, and that the philanthropic interest has not always been matched by a wider public enthusiasm. Perhaps the current excitement in Israel and the USA will leave its mark on those parts of Anglo-Jewry that are yet to be touched by what is undoubtedly one of the world's greatest literary discoveries.

Abbreviations Used

Ad. – Address
Admin. – Administrative; administration; administrator; administer
Adv. – Advisory; adviser
AJA – Anglo-Jewish Association
Ajex. – Association of Jewish Ex-Servicemen and Women
AJY – Association for Jewish Youth
Amer. – America; American
Assn. – Association
Asst. – Assistant
Auth. – Authority; author

B. – Born
Bd. – Board
BMA – British Medical Association
BoD – Board of Deputies
Br. – Branch
Brit. – British; Britain

C. – Council
CBF-WJR – Central British Fund for World Jewish Relief
CCJ – Council of Christians and Jews
C of E – Council of Europe
Cllr. – Councillor
Coll. – College
Com. – Communal; community; commission(er)
Comp. – Company
Cttee. – Committee

Dep. – Deputy
Dept. – Department
Dir. – Director
Distr. – District

Eccl. – Ecclesiastical
Edr. – Editor, Editorial
Educ. – Education; educationist; educational
Emer. – Emeritus
Exec. – Executive

Fdr. – Founder
Fed. – Federation; federal
Fel. – Fellow; Fellowship
Fin. – Finance; financial
Fom. – Former; formerly
Fr. – Friends

Gen. – General
Gov. – Governor; governing
Govt. – Government

H. – Honorary
Hist. – History; historical; historian
HM – Headmaster
HT – Head Teacher

IJPR– Institute for Jewish Policy Research
Instit. – Institute; institution(al)
Internat. – International

JBS – Jewish Blind Society
JEDT – Jewish Educational Development Trust
JIA – Joint Israel Appeal
JMC – Jewish Memorial Council

JNF – Jewish National Fund
JWB – Jewish Welfare Board

Lab. – Labour; laboratory
Lect. – Lecturer; lecture(ship)
Libr. – Librarian; library
Lit. – Literature
Lond. – London

M. – Minister
Man. – Manager; management; managing
Med – Medical; medicine
Min. – Ministry; ministerial
MEP – Member of European Parliament
MP – Member of Parliament

Nat. – National; nationalist; nation(s)

Off. – Officer; office
Org. – Organiser
ORT – Organisation for Resources and Technical Training

Parl. – Parliament; parliamentary
Pol. – Political; policy
Princ. – Principal
Prof. – Professor
Publ. – Publication; public; publicity; publishing

R. – Reader
Reg. – Registrar; Register(ed); region(al)
Rel. – Religion; religious; relation; relief
Rep. – Representative
Res. – Research; Residence
Ret. – Retired
RSGB – Reform Synagogues of Great Britain

Sch. – School; Scholar(ship)
SDP – Social Democratic Party
Sec. – Secretary
Soc. – Society; social; sociology
Sr. – Senior
Supt. – Superintendent
Syn. – Synagogue

T. – Treasurer
TAC – Trades Advisoy Council
Tech. – Technical; technology, -ical
Tr. – Trustee; trust

ULPS – Union of Liberal and Progressive Synagogues
Univ. – University
UK – United Kingdom
US – United Synagogue

V. – Vice
Vis. – Visitation; visitor; visiting
Vol. – Voluntary; volunteer; volume

W. – Warden
WIZO – Women's International Organisation
WJC – World Jewish Congress
WZO – World Zionist Organisation

Z. – Zionist; Zionism

ANGLO-JEWISH INSTITUTIONS

REPRESENTATIVE ORGANISATIONS

BOARD OF DEPUTIES OF BRITISH JEWS
5th Floor, Commonwealth House, 1-19 New Oxford St., WC1A 1NF.
☎ 0171-543 5400. Fax 0171-543 0010. Email bod@ort.org
 Founded in 1760 as a joint committee of the Sephardi and Ashkenazi communities in London, the Board of Deputies of British Jews has flourished in its role as the elected representative body of the British Jewish community. It has taken part in all movements affecting the political and civil rights of British Jewry and in many cases at times of crisis in affairs overseas. It conveys the views of the community to Government and other public bodies on political and legislative matters which affect British Jewry, and provides information about the Jewish community and Israel to the non-Jewish world. The Board examines legislative proposals in Britain and the European Union which may affect Jews, and ensures the political defence of the community. It collects statistical and demographic information and undertakes research on and for the community. It maintains contact with and provides support for Jewish communities around the world and promotes solidarity with Israel. It counters bias in the media and ensures that Jews enjoy the full rights of all British citizens.
 The basis of the Board's representation is primarily synagogal, although the body itself has no religious affiliations. All properly constituted synagogues in Great Britain are entitled to representation in addition to various communal organsiations, such as the Regional Representative Councils, youth organisations and others. The Board has recently introduced major changes in its structure, allowing it to confront the challenges of the Millennium and to continue promoting Jewish interests in this country with enhanced efficiency and effectiveness.
 President Eldred Tabachnik, Q.C.; *V. Presidents* Jo Wagerman, OBE, Henry Grunwald, Eric Moonman, OBE; *Tr.* Flo Kaufmann, JP; *Dir. Gen.* Neville Nagler.

The work of the Board is channelled through four new Divisional Boards, each chaired by an Honorary Officer and supported by a professional Director.

External Issues: *Chairman* Eric Moonman, OBE; *V. Chairman* June Jacobs; *Dir.* Jon Sacker.
Community Issues: *Chairman* Henry Grunwald; *V. Chairman* Robert Owen; *Dir.* Laurie Rosenberg.
Finance and Administration: *Chairman* Flo Kaufmann, JP; *V. Chairman* John Webber; *Dir.* Sandra Chippeck.
Defence Policy and Group Relations: *Chairman* Jo Wagerman, OBE; *V. Chairman* Elinor Lind, QC; *Dir.* Mike Whine, Jon Sacker.

Regional Council: *Chairman* Judith Tankel.
Community Research Unit: (Est. 1965) Compiles statistical data on various aspects of the community and prepares interpretative studies of trends. *Dir.* Marlene Schmool.
Yad Vashem Committee: *Chairman:* Ben Helfgott.
Trades Advisory Council: Affiliated to the Board of Deputies, the Council seeks to combat causes of friction in industry, trade and commerce, and discrimination in the workplace, where these threaten good relations in which Jews are concerned. The TAC offers arbitration and conciliation facilities in business disputes and

advice to employees who consider that they have suffered discrimination.
Central Enquiry Desk, Communal Diary, JCI: (Under the auspices of the Board of Deputies). Operated entirely by volunteers, the Desk provides factual information on all aspects of Jewish home and community life and indicates access to the appropriate authorities to members of the public requiring expert advice. The Desk provides the public access point for the community database created by Jewish Community Information (JCI). The Communal Diary is designed to avoid difficulties which often arise when dates and time of important meetings and functions clash. *Dir.* Lt.Col. Mordaunt Cohen, TD, DL. ☎ 0171 543 5421/5422.
All Aboard Shops Limited: (Est. 1988) To manage charity shops raising income for the Board and all British Jewish charities. ☎ 0171 543 5404/05/15; *Officers* Stella Lucas, Monique Landau, Trude Reiss, Jeffrey Pinnick; *Exec. Dir.* Rachel Arwas.

JEWISH REPRESENTATIVE COUNCILS

Representative Council of Birmingham & Midland Jewry. *President* Roland Diamond, 35 Hunstanton Avenue, B17 8SX. ☎ 0121-554 2170; *H.Sec.* L. Jacobs, 37 Wellington Road, Edgbaston, B15 2ES. ☎ 0121-236 1801. Fax: 0121-236 9906.
Bournemouth Jewish Representative Council. *Chairman* Mrs. H. Greene, 32 Alyth Rd., Talbot Woods, BH3 7DG; ☎ 01202 762101; *H. Sec.* Mrs. M. Perry. ☎ 01202-300 089. (The Southampton and adjacent area is also represented).
Brighton & Hove Jewish Representative Council. *Chairman* Dr. H. Sless. ☎ 01273-735632; *H.Sec.* Mrs. D. Levinson and Aubrey Milstein, P.O.B 2001, Hove, BN3 4RY. ☎ 01273 558559.
Bristol Jewish Liaison Committee. *Chairman* Bernard Barnett, 14 Tennyson Rd., Horfield, BS9 8SB. ☎ 0117-942 4837; *H. Sec.* Michael Romain, 7 College Fields, Clifton, BS8 3HP. ☎ 01435 845033 (office), 0117 9739312 (home). Fax: 01453 845004.
Cardiff Jewish Representative Council. *President* Prof. David Weitzman, 41 Hollybush Rd., Cardiff CF2 6SY; *H. Sec.* Mrs. J. Cotsen, 71 Cyncoed Road, Cyncoed, Cardiff, CF2 6AB. ☎ 01222 484999.
Glasgow Jewish Representative Council. 222, Fenwick Rd., Giffnock, Glasgow G46 6UE. ☎ 0141-620 1700. Fax: 0141-638 2100. E-mail: gjrc@ort.org *President* Dr K. Collins; *H. Sec.* Ephraim Borowski.
Hull Jewish Representative Council. *President* Mrs. Doreen Rose. ☎ 01482 655886; *H. Sec.* Mrs. A. Segelman, 251 Beverley Road, Kirkella, Hull HU10 7AG. ☎ 01482 650288.
Leeds Jewish Representative Council. *President* Tim Freedman, 151 Shadwell La., LS17 8DW. ☎ 01113 2697520. Fax: 01113 2370851; *Exec. Off.* B. Abis, JP. *Publ.* Year Book.
Jewish Representative Council of Greater Manchester & Region. *President* Isidore Fromson, Jewish Cultural Centre, Bury Old Road, M8 6FY. ☎ 0161-720 8721 (office). 0161-740 2024 (home). *H. Secs* Mrs M.R. Landsman, D. Arnold. *Publ.* Year Book.
Merseyside Jewish Representative Council. *President* Mrs S. Lander. *H. Sec.* Mrs A. Irvine, 433 Smithdown Road, L15 3JL. ☎ 0151-733 2292/3. Fax No.: 0151-734 0212. Publ. Year Book.
Representative Council of North East Jewry. *President* Mrs Susan Olsburgh; V. *Presidents* V. Gallant, G. Lurie; *Hon. Sec.* M. A. Levinson, 39 Kenton Road, Newcastle upon Tyne NE3 4NH. ☎ 0191-284 4647.
Nottingham Representative Council. *Chairman* M. Spungin, O.B.E.;. *Sec.* Mrs A. Lewis, 42 Weardale Rd., Sherwood, NG5 1DD. ☎ 01159-606 121.
Redbridge & District Jewish Community Council. *Chairman* Mrs. Angela Levene, Sinclair House, Woodford Bridge Road, Ilford, Essex, IG4 5LN. ☎ 0181-551 0017.
Sheffield Jewish Representative Council. *President* Selwyn M. Burchhardt; *H. Sec.*

ANGLO-JEWISH INSTITUTIONS   3

Tony Kay, 105 Bents Road, Sheffield S11 9RH. ☎ 0114 236 0970.
Southend & District Jewish Representative Council. *Chairman* Derek Baum, MBE; ☎ 01702 343789; *H. Sec.* J. Barcan, 22 2nd Avenue, Westcliff-on-Sea, Essex SS0 8HY. ☎ 01702-343192.
Southport Jewish Representative Council. *President* Mrs S. Abrahamson ☎ 01704 540704; *Hon. Sec.* I. Galkoff, Flat 18, Argyle Court, 5 Argyle Road, Hesketh Park, Southport. ☎ 01704 538119.

ANGLO-JEWISH ASSOCIATION
Commonwealth House, 1-19 New Oxford St., London W1A 1NF.
☎ 0171-404-2111.
The Anglo-Jewish Association was founded in 1871. Membership of the Association is open to all British Jews who accept as their guiding principle loyalty to their faith and their country. Its aims are: To promote the education of Jews in the United Kingdom and elsewhere; to instruct in Jewish affairs and matters relating to the Jewish religion or race; to collect and publish information relating to the religious and social conditions of Jews throughout the world; to encourage Jews in the UK to support Jewish charitable organisations by personal service and financial assistance; to join or promote any charitable society or body in the UK or elsewhere, in order to further any of its objects and people; to use its education cultural and political experience for the promotion of good will towards Israel.
President David Loewe; *T.* Warren S. Starr, FCA; *Gen. Sec.* Mrs. E. Salasnik. *Publ.* AJA Review.

ASSOCIATION OF JEWISH FRIENDSHIP CLUBS
26 Enford St., London W1H 2DD.
☎ 0171-724 8100. Fax 0171-706 1710.
(Est. 1949. Reg. Charity No. 211013) An umbrella organisation for men and women in the fifty plus age group, providing friendship with social and cultural activities. *Nat. Chairman* Mrs. Stella Harris. Full details may be obtained from the Association.

ASSOCIATION OF JEWISH WOMEN'S ORGANISATIONS IN THE UNITED KINGDOM
4th Floor, 24-32 Stephenson Way, London NW1 2JW.
☎ 0171-387 7688. Fax 0171-387 2110.
(Est. 1965.) To further communal understanding; to promote the achievement of unity among Jewish women of differing shades of opinion, belonging to autonomous organisations with different aims. *Member orgs.*: Assn. of US Women; B'nai B'rith First Women's Lodge; British Emunah; Brit. ORT Women's Div.; Fed. of Women Zionists (Brit Wizo); Frs. of the Hebrew Univ.; Jewish Women's Aid; Jewish Women's Network; JIA Women's Div.; League of Jewish Women; Na'amat UK; Reform Syn. Guilds; Sephardi Women's Assn.; 35's Women's Campaign for Soviet Jewry; ULPS; *H. President* V. Braynis; *Chairman* J. Conway; *V. Chairmen* I. Gee, S. Harris; *H. Sec.* S. Webber; *H. Tr.* J. Rose.

COUNCIL OF CHRISTIANS AND JEWS
Patron: Her Majesty the Queen.
Drayton House, 30 Gordon St., London WC1H 0AN.
☎ 0171-388 3322. Fax: 0171-388 3305. E-mail: ccjuk@aol.com
(Est. 1942. Reg. Charity No. 238005.) The Council brings together the Christian and Jewish Communities in a common effort to fight the evils of prejudice, intolerance and discrimination between people of different religions, races and colours, and to work for the betterment of human relations, based on mutual respect, understanding and goodwill. It is neither a missionary nor a political organisation.
Presidents The Archbishop of Canterbury; The Cardinal Archbishop of

Westminster; The Archbishop of Thyateira and Gt. Brit.; The Moderator of the Church of Scotland; The Chief Rabbi; *Chairman, Exec. Cttee.* The Rt. Revd. R. Harries; V. *Chairmen* The Rt. Revd. C. Henderson, V.G., K.C.H.S., Clive M. Marks, F.C.A.; *Jt. H. Ts.* Sir Michael Latham, D.L., M.A.; Roderick Wright, B.Sc., F.C.A.; *Jt. Hon. Secs.* Revd. Eric Allen, B.D. Rosalind Preston, O.B.E.; *Dir.* Paul Mendel; *Dep. Dir. Sr.* Margaret Shepherd nds, B.A., M.Th.; *Educ. Off.* The Revd Jonathan Gorsky, M.A.; *Asst. Educ. Off.* Jane Clements, B.D. *Publ.* Common Ground.

There are 60 local Councils. A list of these is obtainable from the central office.

LEAGUE OF JEWISH WOMEN
24-32 Stephenson Way, London NW1 2JW.
☎ 0171-387 7688. Fax 0171-387 2110.
(Est. 1943. Reg. Charity No. 261199) Vol. Service Org. to unite Jewish women of every shade of opinion who are resident in the United Kingdom to intensify in each Jewish woman her Jewish consciousness and her sense of responsibility to the Jewish community and the community generally: to stimulate her personal sense of civic duty and to encourage her to express it by increased service to the country. *President* Corinne Van Colle; *H. Sec.* Mrs. M. Herman.

Groups operate in the following centres:

London
Barnet; Bushey Heath; Chigwell & Hainault; Clissold; Coombe & District; Ealing; Elstree & Boreham Wood; Finchley; Hampstead Garden Suburb; Harrow & Kenton; Hendon; Ilford; Kingsbury; Kingston & Wimbledon; Loughton; Muswell Hill & Highgate; New Era; Newbury Park; North West End; Northwood; Oakwood & Winchmore Hill; Outer Limits; Pinner; Potters Bar & Brookman's Park; Radlett; Redbridge; Richmond Park; Ruislip & Ickenham; Southgate; Stanmore; Streatham; Totteridge & Whetstone; Watford; Wembley; Young Herts & Middlesex.

Outside London
Birmingham; Cardiff; Glasgow; Leicester; Maidenhead; Surrey; Thanet.

North Western Region (Centred at Manchester)
Bowdon & Hale; Brantwood; Broadway; Bury; Cheadle & Gatley; Didsbury; Fylde; Heaton Pk.; Higher Broughton & Polefield; Kingsway; Northenden Park; Prestwich; Sale & Altrincham; Southport; Sunningdale; Whitefield & Ringley; Windsor.

League Associate Division (Men)
Deja Vu (Men & Women, 22-36 years)

ORT HOUSE CONFERENCE CENTRE
126 Albert Street, London NW1 1NF.
☎ 0171-446 8509. Fax: 0171-446 8651. Website: www.ort.org
(Est. 1996) A Jewish conference centre with milk kitchen. Capacity 120. Suitable for business, community or social events. *Conference Centre Man.* Alison Hooper.

THE THREE FAITHS FORUM
The Sternberg Centre, The Manor House, 80 East End Road, London N3 2SY.
☎ 0171-485 2538. Fax: 0171-485 4512. E-mail: Strnberg@netcomuk.co.uk
(Est. 1997) To encourage friendship, goodwill and understanding amongst people of the 3 monotheistic faiths in the UK and elsewhere. (Muslim, Christian and Jewish). Basis of equality and exploring and enjoying those differences where appropriate. *Co-Chairman* Sir Sigmund Sternberg; Sheikh Dr Zaki Ma Badawi; *Coord.* Sidney L. Shipton.

WORKING PARTY ON JEWISH ARCHIVES IN THE UK AND IRELAND
Department of History, The University, Southampton SO7 1BJ.
☎ 01703 592211.
The working party was set up in 1988 to create awareness inside and outside the Jewish community of the need to locate, preserve and make available the records of British Jewry. It has the specific aim of carrying out a comprehensive survey of Jewish archive material in the UK which is currently in progress on a preliminary basis.
Chairman Dr. Tony Kushner; Representatives from Society of Archivists (Richard Potts); British Records Association (Peter Barber); British Library (Diana Rowland-Smith); Board of Deputies of British Jews (Sandra Chippeck); Anglo-Jewish Archives (Brian Diamond); *Historians* Tony Kushner, David Cesarani, Bill Williams, Geoffrey Alderman; JHSE (Edgar Samuel).

WORKING PARTY ON JEWISH MONUMENTS IN THE UK & IRELAND
c/o Jewish Memorial Council, 25 Enford St., W1H 2DD.
(Est. Dec. 1991. Reg. Charity No. 206565) For the preservation and documentation of Jewish Monuments of architectural and historical importance. (See listing p.204).
Chairman E. Jamilly (☎ 0171-839 5455); *Project Coord.:* Dr Sharman Kadish; *T.* Mr. A. Rosenzweig; *Sec.* Mrs. K. B. Green.

JEWISH PRESS, RADIO AND INFORMATION SERVICES
The following is a selection of the major national publications. The Representative Councils of Leeds, Manchester, Merseyside and the North East all publish yearbooks. Many synagogues and communal organisations throughout the country publish newsletters and magazines and these are referred to in the specific entries.

BRITISH-JEWISH PRESS

AJR Information, 1 Hampstead Gate, 1A Frognal, London NW3 6AL. ☎ 0171-431 6161. Fax 0171-431 8454. Monthly. *Edr.* Richard Grunberger.
BIMAH: The Platform of Welsh Jewry, 12 Birchwood Rd., Penylan, Cardiff, CF2 5LJ. ☎/Fax 01222 499565. Est. 1994. Quarterly. *Ed.* Mrs Stella J. Levey. *Ch.* Alan Schwartz. 1997 Communal Magazine of the Year.
Edinburgh Star, 9 Warriston Crescent, Edinburgh EH3 5LA. Est. 1989. 3 issues a year. *Edr.* Michael Adler; *Ch.* John Cosgrove, 14 Gordon Terrace, Edinburgh, EH16 5QR.
European Judaism, Leo Baeck College, 80 East End Rd., London N3 2SY. ☎ 0181-349 4525. Fax: 0181-343 2558. Est. 1966. Two issues a year. *Edr.* Rabbi Dr A. H. Friedlander, Rabbi Professor J. Magonet.
Hamaor, Federation of Synagogues, 65 Watford Way, London NW4 3AQ. Est. 1962. Two issues a year. *Edr.* Sarah M. Schleimer.
Jewish Book News and Reviews, PO Box 3786, London N8 7HZ. Est. 1986. (Reg. Charity No. 1032623.) Three issues a year. *Edr.* S. W. Massil and M. Daniels.
Jewish Chronicle, 25 Furnival St., London EC4A 1JT. ☎ 0171-415 1500. Fax: 0171-405-9040. Est. 1841. Weekly. *Chairman*: Lionel Gordon; *Edr.* Ned. Temko.
Jewish Community Pages (incorporating the Jewish Business Directory), Forum Publications Ltd., 2300 Northolt Rd., Harrow, Middx HA2 8DU. ☎ 0181-422 7086. Fax 0181-422 9175. *Edr.* B. King.
Jewish Journal of Sociology, 187 Gloucester Place, London W1A 1JR. ☎ 0171-262 8939. Fd. 1959. Published by Maurice Freedman Research Trust (Reg. Charity No. 326077) Semi-annual. *Edr.* Judith Freedman.
Jewish Quarterly, P.O. Box 2078, London W1A 1JR. ☎ 0171-629 5004. Fax:

0171-629 5110. Est. 1953. (Reg. Charity No. 268589.) *Edr.*
Jewish Review, Mizrachi-Hapoel Hamizrachi Fed. of Great Britain & Ireland: the voice of Religious Zionism; 2b Golders Green Rd., London NW11 8LH. ☎ 0181-455 2243. Fax: 0181-455-2244. Est. 1946. Quarterly. *Edr.* A. H. Handler.
Jewish Socialist: magazine of the Jewish Socialists' Group, BM3725, London WC1N 3XX. 1985. Quarterly. Edr. Cttee.
Jewish Telegraph, 11 Park Hill, Bury Old Rd., Prestwich, Manchester M25 0HH. ☎ 0161-740 9321. Fax: 0161-740-9325. Est. 1950. Weekly. (Published also in Leeds, Liverpool, the Midlands and Glasgow) *Edr.* P. Harris.
Jewish Travel Guide, Vallentine Mitchell, Newbury House, 890-900 Eastern Avenue, Ilford, Essex IG2 7HH. ☎ 0181-599-8866. Fax: 0181-599-0984. (Est. 1956. Formerly published by the Jewish Chronicle). Annual.
Jewish Tribune, 97 Stamford Hill, London N16 5DN. ☎ 0181-800 6688. Fax: 0181-800 5000. E-mail.: jtdcharedim@demon.co.uk. English & Yiddish. Est. 1962. Weekly. *Edr.* J. Bentov (Agudas Yisroel of Great Britain).
Jewish Year Book, Vallentine Mitchell, Newbury House, 890-900 Eastern Avenue, Newbury Park, Ilford, Essex IG2 7HH. ☎ 0181-599-8866. Fax: 0181-599-0984. (Est. 1896. Formerly published by the Jewish Chronicle). Annual. *Edr.* S. W. Massil.
Journal of Progressive Judaism, Two issues a year. *Edr.* Rabbi Dr S. D. Kunin, 46 Ebers Grove, Nottingham NG3 5EA.
Judaism Today, 1095/7 Finchley Rd., NW11 0PU. ☎ 0181-201 8772. Fax: 0181-201 8917. Est. 1995. *Edr.* Colin Shindler. (Masorti).
Le'Ela: a journal of Judaism today, Office of the Chief Rabbi & Jews' College, Albert Rd., London NW4 2SJ. ☎ 0181-203 6427, Fax: 0181-203-6420. Est. 1975. Two issues a year. *Edr.* Rabbi P. N. Ginsbury.
Manna, Sternberg Centre for Judaism, 80 East End Rd., London N3 2SY. ☎ 0181-346 2288/349 4731, Fax 0181-343-0901. Quarterly. *Edr.* Rabbi Tony Bayfield.
Mazel & Brocho, 168 Stamford Hill, 2nd Floor, N16 6QX. ☎ 0181-211-7876, Fax: 0181-211-7874. *Edr.* Sarah Schleimer.
New Moon: Jewish arts and listings monthly, 28 St. Albans Lane, London, NW11 7QE. ☎ 0181-731 8031 (Ed.); 0181-731 8088 (Adv); Fax: 0181-381 4033. Est. 1990. *Edr.* Simon Goodman. *Man. Dir.* Gary Stern.
Recorder, The Birmingham Jewish, 29 Salisbury Cl., Birmingham B13 8JX. ☎ 0121-449 0362. Monthly. Est. 1935. *Edr.* A. Chesses.
The Scribe: journal of Babylonian Jewry, 20 Queen's Gate Terrace, London SW7 5PF. Est. 1971. Two issues a year. *Edr.*
West Quest Magazine: the Jewish magazine for the West country. Two issues a year. *Edr.* Mrs. J.A. Samuel, 70 Cranwells Park, Weston, Bath BA1 2YE.

JEWISH RADIO PROGRAMMES

Greater London Radio: Contact: 'Jewish London', 35c Marylebone High St., W1A 4LG. Programmes at 19.00 hours, every Sunday evening on GLR 94.9FM. *Ed.* Gloria Abramoff ☎ 0171-224 2424, 0171-935 1026; *Prod.* Roma Felstein ☎ 0171-224 2424, 0181-446 0927 (home); *Res.* Osa Fowler ☎ 0171-224 2424, 0171-935 1696; *Presenter* Wendy Robbins ☎ 0717-224 2424.
Jewish Spectrum Radio, P.O. Box 12591, London NW2 2ZP. *Presenter* Piri Dunner. A daily two-hour programme of news, views and discussion. Weekly features include Rabbi Shmueley Boteach, Chazanut, Israeli Sports, Jewish music, live report from Israel, theatre, art and the Sedra. Broadcasts Sun. 12 noon-2 pm; Mon.-Fri. 1 pm-3.00 pm, 558 AM. ☎ 0181-905 5533. Phone-In: 0181-209 0055. Fax: 0181-209 1565. E-mail: PK57@dial.pipex.com
Radio Sussex Radio Shalom: *Presenters* Laurie Rosenberg, Maureen Kendlar. ☎ 01273 23714 or 0171-387 3952.

INFORMATION SERVICES

'It's Kosher' Produced by Ruth Kaitiff. Broadcast every Wednesday evening at 6.30pm-7.00pm. On G.M.R 95.1, FM. ☎ 0161 244-3050/3058. Write to 'It's Kosher', c/o BBC GMR, PO Box 951, New Broadcasting House, Oxford Road, Manchester M60 1SD.
'You don't have to be Jewish': Sun. (LBC): 7pm-8pm 97.3 FM; 1152 AM. *Contact* Michael Freedland: 0181-953 3000.

INFORMATION SERVICES

Brijnet
11, The Lindens, Prospect Hill, Waltham Forest, London E17 3EJ.
☎ 0181 520 3531. Email: rafi@brijnet.org
Provider of UK Jewish communal internet services. Creates awareness of the use and benefits of the Internet in the community through training and assistance with all Internet tools. Creates and maintains a useful quality communal electronic information database. Published electronic listings including: brijannounce, daf-hashavua, ujs-update. Web sites: http://shamash.org/ejin/brijnet/; http://www.brijnet.org *Dir.* Rafael Salasnik.

Jewish Community Information, Board of Deputies, Commonwealth House, 1-19 New Oxford Street, London WC1A 1NF. ☎ 0171-543 5423. Fax: 0171-543 0010. Email: Jci@ort.org *Prof. Off.* Craig Levison. (Est. 1996) is a cross-community initiative conceived by B'nai B'rith with support from the Board of Deputies and Jewish Continuity. JCI is an on-going, in-depth information service of Jewish activities and resources being made available to Communal Organisations to assist with future development and research. The information will be continually updated.

RELIGIOUS ORGANISATIONS

THE CHIEF RABBINATE

The Chief Rabbinate of Britain has developed from the position of the Rabbi of the Great Syn., London. From the early years of the 18th century until recently, he was acknowledged as the spiritual leader of the London Ashkenazi Com. and this recognition was also accepted in the provinces and overseas. Jonathan Sacks was inducted into office in 1991. Previous holders of the office were: Aaron Hart (1709-1756); Hart Lyon (1756-1764); David Tevele Schiff (1765-1792); Solomon Herschell (1802-1842); Nathan Marcus Adler (1845-1890); Hermann Adler (1891-1911); Joseph Herman Hertz (1913-1946); Israel Brodie (1948-1965); Immanuel Jakobovits (1967-1991).

To conform with the constitutional practice, the official designation (1845-1953) was 'Chief Rabbi of the United Hebrew Congregations of the British Commonwealth of Nations' and subsequently 'Chief Rabbi of the United Hebrew Congregations of the Commonwealth'.

Chief Rabbi Rabbi Dr. Jonathan Sacks, M.A.(Cantab), Ph.D. Office of the Chief Rabbi: 735 High Road, London N12 0US. ☎ 0181-343 6301. Fax 0181-343 6310. *Exec. Dir.*:

Chief Rabbinate Council: *Chairman* Elkan Levy; *Chief Exec.* J. M. Lew, B. Com., A.C.M.A. *Publ.*: Le'Ela. (See Jews' Coll., p.44)

BETH DIN (COURT OF THE CHIEF RABBI)

735 High Road, London N12 0US. ☎ 0181-343 6270. Fax 0181-343 6257. *Dayanim* Rabbis Chanoch Ehrentreu, Casriel David Kaplin, Menachem Gelley, Ivan Binstock BSc. *Asst. Registrar* Mrs F.B. Gottlieb.

The Beth Din fulfils the following functions for the orthodox community: (i) dispute arbitration and mediation, (ii) supervision of Jewish religious divorces, adoptions and conversions, (iii) certification of religious status; (iv) supervision of

shechita and kashrut.
General enquiries may be made from 9.00 a.m. to 5.00 p.m. (Monday to Thursday). Enquiries on kashrut should be made to the Kashrut Division, see below) Visitors may attend the Beth Din by appointment only. Messages left on the answerphone will be dealt with as soon as possible.
Kashrut Division. *Dir.* Rabbi J. Conway, B.A.; *Marketing Dir.* D. Steinhof, B.Sc; *Kashrut Admin.* N. Lauer. *Publ.:* The Really Jewish Food Guide, Snack 'n' Sweet Guide, Passover Supplement.

UNITED SYNAGOGUE
While the Act of Parliament under which it was created bears the date July 14, 1870, the United Synagogue had its origin much earlier in the history of London Jewry. Of the five Constituent Synagogues which joined to form the United Synagogue, the oldest–the Great Synagogue–had a history of more than 280 years; the Hambro dated from 1707 while the New Synagogue was founded in 1761. The Constituent Synagogues now number 42, and the Affiliated Synagogues 24, providing religious facilities for over 38,000 families (about 100,000 people). From the outset, the US has also taken a large share in the social and philanthropic work of the Community.

The **Youth and Community Service Committee** arranges Services for youths and children on Sabbaths and Festivals where required, and is directly concerned with the religious and cultural needs of Jewish youth, appointing Officers to administer such work in Clubs. The US together with the League of Jewish Women, is a sponsoring body of the Association of Jewish Friendship Clubs (see p.98).

The **Visitation Committee**, which is administered by the US, includes representatives not only of the US but of the Federation of Syns., the Union of Liberal and Progressive Synagogues, the Spanish and Portuguese Syn., the West London Syn., and the Western Syn. Its activities include: Visitation of Jewish inmates of hospitals prisons, and other public institutions, visitation and religious welfare of deprived, maladjusted and educationally subnormal children in the care of local Councils and Education Authorities, and children committed to Approved Schools and Remand Homes; aftercare of Jewish adult and young prisoners and assistance in the care of Borstal and probation cases (see p.101).

The work of the **Bequests and Trusts Committee** includes marriage portions, New Year, winter and Passover cash gifts, clothing, blankets, Commodity Cards and other necessities. In addition grants are made for the purpose of assisting persons not necessarily members of the US, to obtain a livelihood, or as temporary relief in cases of distress usually in consultation and in conjunction with Jewish Care. The Mutual Aid Fund, which is also under this Cttee., derives its income entirely from the voluntary contributions of seatholders.

The **Conjoint Passover Flour Committee**, which consists of reps. of the US, the Spanish and Portuguese Syn., the Federation of Syns. and the Regional Communities, is responsible for the distribution of Matzot to the needy and to the Jewish inmates of hospitals and other public institutions (see p.9).

The US bears the financial responsibility for the **Beth Din** (Court of the Chief Rabbi), whose duties include not only the determination of civil disputes, but also supervision of Kashrut, licensing of Shochetim and the granting of Jewish religious divorce (Get) (see p.7).

The US is the main contributor to the maintainance of the Chief Rabbinate of the United Hebrew Congregation (see p.7).

The US plays a large part in the work of the **Jewish Committee for H.M. Forces,** which provides facilities for Jewish members of H.M. Forces to maintain the practices of their faith (e.g. by the provision of religious services etc.), arranges for the appointment of Jewish ministers as Chaplains and Officiating Chaplains and for the provision of Jewish literature of a religious and devotional character (see p.?).

President Elkan Levy; *V. Presidents* Anthony Ansell; *Ts* Leslie Elstein, Stephen

Forman, Jeremy Jacobs; *Chairman, Bequests & Tr.* Anthony Cowen; *Chairman* Kashrus A. Kennard; *Chairman, Burial Cttee.* Elkan D. Levy; *Chairman, Visitation Cttee.* Mrs. J. Conway; *Chairman, BoM Beth Hamedrash Chairman, Aff. Syns.* Anthony Cowen; *Chairman, Min. Placements* Elkan Levy; *Jt. Chairmen, Conjoint Passover* Anthony Cowen, Stephen Forman; *Chief Exec.* J. M. Lew, B.Com., A.C.M.A. (Reg. Charity no. 242552.)
   Head Office: Adler House, 735 High Road, London N12 0US. ☎ 0181-343 8989. Fax: 0181-343 6262.
   Constituent, Affiliated & Assoc. Synagogues are listed on pp.76–79.
Burial Society, *Sexton* R. I. Ezekiel.

CONJOINT PASSOVER FLOUR COMMITTEE
Adler House, 735 High Road, N12 0US. ☎ 0181-343 8989.
Jt. Chairmen Anthony Cowen, Stephen Forman.

INITIATION SOCIETY
President Aaron Winegarten. *Medical Off.* Dr. M. Sifman, 47 The Ridgeway, NW11 8QP. ☎ 0181-455 2008. Fax 0181-731 6276; *Sec.* A. Minn, 15 Sunny Hill Ct., Sunningfields Cres. NW4 4RB. ☎/Fax: 0181-203 1352. (Est. 1745; Reg. Charity No. 207404) To train Mohalim and to supply Mohalim in cases where required. For a list of Mohalim practising in the British Isles and registered with the Society, apply to the Secretary.

JEWISH COMMITTEE FOR H.M. FORCES
25 Enford Street, W1H 2DD.
☎ 0171-724 7778 Fax: 0171-706 1710.
The Cttee. officially recognised by the Min. of Defence to appoint Jewish chaplains and to provide for the religious needs of Jewish members of H.M. Forces.
   Chairman George M. Gee, J.P.; T. Alfred Dunitz, J.P., C.C.; *Sen. Jewish Chaplain to H.M. Forces* Rev. Malcolm Weisman, M.A. (Oxon.); *Sec.* Miss Hilary Appell.
   Publ.: Menorah.

JEWISH MEMORIAL COUNCIL
25 Enford St., W1H 2DD.
☎ 0171-724 7778 Fax: 0171-706 1710.
(Est. 1919.) To commemorate the services rendered by Jews in the UK and British Empire in the war of 1914-18 by establishing an organisation which will carry on Jewish tradition as a permanent ennobling force in the lives of Jews in this country.
   Chairman E. Astaire; *General Manager,* J. Zaltzman. *President* Edmund L. de Rothschild, T.D.; *V. President* Chief Rabbi; *H. Sec.* T. M. Simon; *Hon. T.* A. Rosenzweig. *Sec.* Miss H.E. Appell.
   Public Schools Committee (which provides facilities for religious education for Jewish boarders in public schools). *Chairman* E. Astaire.
   Jewish Memorial Council Pensions Fund. A superannuation fund administered by the JMC, membership of which is open to all communal officials. *Chairman* A. Rosenzweig; *Admin.* J. Zaltzman.
   Scholarships. The following scholarships are admin. by the Council: Alfred Louis Cohen Fund: For students of the J.F.S. Comprehensive School.
   Higher Education Awards: For students of British nationality resident in the UK and studying at a UK univ. or equivalent academic institution.
   Sir Robert Waley Cohen Memorial Scholarship. To provide Jewish Ministers holding appointments in any part of the British Commonwealth with Travelling Scholarships to pursue Jewish studies.
   Provincial Hebrew Classes Committee. Promotes Jewish religious education by inspecting provincial classes and advising on methods and organisation.
   Chairman E. Astaire; *Educ. Adv.* D. Band.

JMC Bookshop. Admin. by the JMC to provide books and educational material to the Jewish community in the UK and overseas.
Small Communities Committee (Est. 1919). Admins. the funds for the Rev. Malcolm Weisman and his colleagues as visiting Mins. to the Small Communities and isolated families. The Cttee. organises regular conferences in the various regions.
Chairman Edgar Astaire.

NATIONAL COUNCIL OF SHECHITA BOARDS
P.O. Box 579, Adastra Suite, 401 Nether Street, N3 1YR
☎ 0181-349 9153. Fax: 0181-346 2209.
To centralise information on all matters relating to the performance and administration of shechita, and to act as liaison between the shechita boards and communities and the various Ministries and orgs. affecting shechita and the kosher meat and poultry industry.
   The Council registered a trademark with the Bd. of Trade in 1955 as a warranty of Kashrus and testifying that the holder of this trademark is a purveyor of kosher meat and/or poultry licensed as such by a Shechita Bd. affiliated to the Council and under the supervision of the Eccl. Auths. *President* N. C. Oster; *V. President* A. Schwalbe, R. Stern; *Ts.* S. Weingarten, I. Singer; *Exec.Dir.* M. T. Kester.

RABBINICAL COMMISSION FOR THE LICENSING OF SHOCHETIM
Est. under the Slaughter Houses Act 1974, Schedule 1, which provides for the shechita of animals and poultry by a shochet duly licensed for the purpose by the Rabbinical Com., and constitutes the Rabbinical Com. as follows: The Chief Rabbi, who shall be the permanent Chairman; one member appointed by the Spanish and Portuguese Syn. (London), who shall be a Vice-Chairman, three members appointed by the Beth Din (London); two members appointed by the Federation of Synagogues (London); one member appointed by the Union of Orthodox Hebrew Congregations (London); two members appointed by the *President* of the BoD to represent regional congregations.
   Chairman The Chief Rabbi.

SINGER'S PRAYER BOOK PUBLICATION COMMITTEE
Administered by the United Syn. (☎ 0181-343 8989). *Chairman* E. D. Levy. The purpose of Singer's Prayer Book, first published in 1890, is 'to place within the reach of the Community at large a complete daily prayer Book in Hebrew and English, equally suitable for use in syns. families, and schools.' 1st edn., 1890; 26 imp., 1891-1961; 2nd revd. edn., 6 imp., 1962-1988; 3rd revd. centenary edn., 1990; enlarged centenary edn. 1992.

SPANISH AND PORTUGUESE JEWS' CONGREGATION
The Community of Spanish and Portuguese Jews in London was founded by Marranos in the middle of the seventeenth century. The congregation 'Sahar Asamaim', worshipped in Creechurch Lane (where a tablet records the site) from 1657 to 1701, when the Bevis Marks Synagogue was built. It is the oldest extant syn. building in Britain except for the long-forgotten medieval syn. of Lincoln. The first branch syn. of the congregation in the West End was est. in Wigmore St. in 1853, and in 1861 removed to Bryanston Street, in 1896 the existing building in Lauderdale Road, Maida Vale was opened. In 1977 another branch of the S. & P. Jews' Cong. was opened in Wembley. The cong. is run by a Board of Elders as well as a Mahamad (five members) who act as Executive. An assessment (Finta) is levied on the Yehidim and congregational affairs are regulated by laws, termed Ascamot, the first code of which was drawn up in 1663.
   The congregation maintains the Medrash of Heshaim (founded in 1664). Hebrew religious instruction is given at the Communal Centre, Ashworth Road, W9 as well as in Redbridge and in Wembley.

RELIGIOUS ORGANISATIONS 11

A brotherhood Mikveh Israel (Lavadores), est. 1678, and a Burial Society, Hebrat Guemilut Hassadim (1665), attend to the last rites to the dead. A number of charitable and educational trusts exist for the benefit of Sephardim.
For the history of the Sephardi community in London see A. M. Hyamson: The Sephardim of England (reprinted 1991), L. D. Barnett: Bevis Marks Records Part I (1940), El Libro de los Acuerdos (1931); For geneaological records see Bevis Marks records [Part II and III (marriages), IV (circumcisions), V (births)]. Available from the Synagogue offices. Other publications include: Treasures of a London Temple (1952), edr. R. D. Barnett, Laws and Charities of the Spanish and Portuguese Congregation, by Neville J. Laski, The Mitsvot of the Spanish & Portuguese Jews' Congregation, by G. H. Whitehill.
(Reg. Charity no. 212517.)
President of Elders L. Gubbay; *V. President of Elders* C. Sacerdoti; *Chief Exec.*; *Sec., London Sephardi Trust.* Office: 2 Ashworth Road, W9 1JY. ☎ 0171-289 2573. Fax: 0171-289 2709.
Dayan P. Toledano, Ab Beth Din exercising his position as Ab Beth Din of the Congregation, Rabbi Dr. A. Levy, Communal Rabbi, exercising his position as Spiritual Head of the Congregation.
Synagogues and organisations are listed on pp.84–85.

FEDERATION OF SYNAGOGUES
65 Watford Way, NW4 3AQ.
☎ 0181-202 2263. Fax: 0181-203 0610.
The Federation of Synagogues, then embodying 16 small syns. in the eastern districts of London, was est. in 1887. It now comprises 14 Constituent syns. and 20 affiliated congregations situated in most parts of Greater London. The objects of the Federation include:
To provide the services of Orthodox rabbis, ministers and dayanim; the provision of a Burial Society; to assist syns. in the erection, reconstruction or redecoration of their Houses of Worship, to assist in the maintenance of Orthodox religious instruction in Talmud Torahs and Yeshivot; to obtain and maintain Kashrut; to support charitable and philanthropic works; to further the progress of Eretz Yisrael.
President A. J. Cohen, F.C.A.; *V. Presidents* W. Ungar & J. Winegarten; *Ts.* G. Halibard, A. Finlay; *Admin.* G. Kushner, A.C.M.A.

Associated Bodies
Emer. Rav Rashi: Dayan M. Fisher.
Beth Din of the Federation of Synagogues. Dayan Yisroel Yaakov Lichtenstein Rosh Beth Din, Dayan Berel Berkovits, LL.B., Dayan M. D. Elzas *Dayan Emer.* Dayan Z. J. Alony; *Clerk* Rabbi S.A. Zaidan.
London Kashrus Board. Kashrus Dir. Dayan M. D. Elzas; *Chairman* W. Ungar.
Federation Burial Society. ☎ 0181-202 3903. Fax 0181-203 0610. *Sexton* H. Brooks; *Admin.* M. L. Stuart; *Ts.* H. Dony, N. Bruckheimer.
Constituent and affiliated synagogues are listed on pp.79–80.

UNION OF ORTHODOX HEBREW CONGREGATIONS
140 Stamford Hill, N16 6QT.☎ 0181-802 6226. Fax 0181-809-7092. (Reg. Charity No. 249892).
The Union of Orthodox Hebrew Congregations was est. 1926 by the late Rabbi Dr. V. Schonfeld to protect traditional Judaism. The constituents consist of bodies affiliated to the Adath Yisroel Burial Society and others desirous of co-operating in the work of protecting Orthodoxy. Membership of the Union is stated to be more than 6,000.
Rabbinate Rabbi Henoch B. Padwa (Princ. Rab. Authority), Rabbi J. Dunner (Rabbi of the Union), Dayan A. D. Dunner; Dayan S. Friedman; Dayan D.

Grynhaus, Rabbi E. Halpern, Rabbi P. Roberts, Rabbi H. I. Feldman (for Kashrus Ctte.); *President* D. Frand; *Registrar* J. R. Conrad.

Associated Bodies
Kashrus Committee-Kedassia, address as above. ☎ 0181-800 6833. Fax 0181-809 7092. *Chairman* M. Hochhauser; *Admin.* I. Feldman.
Central Mikvaoth Board, address as above. ☎ 0181802 6226.
Adath Yisroel Burial Society, 40 Queen Elizabeth's Walk, N16 0HH. ☎ 0181-802 6262/3. Fax 0181-800 8764. *Sec.* A. Barnett. Cemeteries: Carterhatch Lane, Enfield. ☎ 0181-363 3384. Silver Street, Cheshunt Herts. ☎ 01707-874220.
Constituent and affiliated synagogues are listed on pp.81–82.

MASORTI
ASSEMBLY OF MASORTI SYNAGOGUES,
1097 Finchley Road, NW11 0PU. ☎ 0181-201 8772. Fax 0181-201 8917. Email: Masorti.uk@ort.org and www.ort.org/masorti
(Reg. Charity no. 801846). *President* F. Ashe Lincoln, QC; *Chairman* Alex Sklan; *Hon. Tr.* T. Lionel Halpern; *Dir.* Harry Freedman.
Constituent synagogues are listed on pp.82–83.

REFORM SYNAGOGUES OF GREAT BRITAIN
The Sternberg Centre for Judaism, 80 East End Road, N3 2SY.
☎ 0181-349 4731. Fax: 0181-343 0901.
Founded to co-ordinate a group of synagogues, the first of which - the West London Synagogue - was est. in 1840. Objects: to promote a living Judaism, to interpret the Torah in accordance with the spirit and needs of the present generation and through its positive, constructive, and progressive view of Jewish tradition, raise and maintain a high standard of Jewish religious life throughout the country.
Movement Chairman N. Sassienie; *T. S.* Licht; *Chairman of the Board* Della Carr; *Chief-Exec.* Rabbi T. Bayfield; *Education & Training: Chairman* J. Epstein, *Dir.* Rabbi Dr M. Shire; *Syn. partnership: Chairman* K. Price, *Dir.* D. Jacobs; *Youth & Students:* J. Boyd; *Admin.: Dir.* N. Landau; *Finance Dir.* M. Frankl; *Publ.:* Manna (quarterly), Reform Judaism (quarterly).

Constituent Synagogues: Metropolitan: Synagogues are listed on pp.85–86.
Regions: Cambridge Beth Shalom Syn.; Blackpool Ref. Jewish Cong.; Bournemouth Ref. Syn.; Bradford Syn.; Brighton & Hove New Syn.; Cardiff New Syn.; Glasgow New Syn.; Hull Reform Syn.; Maidenhead Ref. Syn.; Manchester Ref Syn.; Menorah Syn., Cheshire; Milton Keynes Ref. Syn.; Newcastle Ref Syn.; Sinai Syn., Leeds; Sha'arei Shalom N. Manchester Reform Cong.; South Hampshire Ref. Jewish Com.; Southend & Distr. Reform Syn.; Southport New Syn.; Thanet & Distr. Ref. Jewish Com.
Associated Communities: Beit Klal Yisrael (North Kensington Ref. Syn); Coventry Jewish Ref. Syn; Darlington Hebrew Cong.; Sheffield & Distr. Ref. Jewish Syn.; Swindon Jewish Com.; Beth Shalom (Munich).
Assembly of Rabbis: *Chairman* Rabbi D. Smith. ☎ 0181-958 9782; *H. Sec.* Rabbi A. Wright. ☎ 01923-856110.
Rabbinical Court: (Beit Din). ☎ 0181-349 2568. *Convenor* Rabbi Rodney Mariner.

RSY-Netzer (RSGB's Youth & Students Division); *Shaliach.* Yonathan Alter; *Northern Shaliach* Yishai Tarragano; *Mazkir* Ruth Mason. Student activities *Co-Ord.:* Nick Lambert (see p.49).
Reform Foundation Trust: *Chairman* Jeffery Rose.

WELFARE ORGANISATIONS 13

THE STERNBERG CENTRE FOR JUDAISM
80 East End Road, N3 2SY.
☎ 0181-346 2288. Fax: 0181-343-0901.
(Est. 1982 Reg. Charity No. 283083) A major national centre for the promotion of Jewish religious, educational, intellectual and cultural matters. The Centre includes a Holocaust Memorial Garden and a Biblical garden and a mikveh; it houses the Akiva School, Centre for Jewish Education; C. of Reform & Liberal Rabbis; Manor House Soc.; Jewish Museum, Finchley; Leo Baeck Coll.; Michael Goulston Educ. Foundation; Manor House Books; Plus U; Pro-Zion; Reform and Liberal Association of Mohalim; RSGB; and the Masorti New North London Synagogue.
Chairman of Trs. Sir Sigmund Sternberg KCSG., J.P.; *T.* H. Cohen; *Dir.* Rabbi Tony Bayfield, M.A. *Publ.:* Manna (quarterly).

UNION OF LIBERAL AND PROGRESSIVE SYNAGOGUES
(Jewish Religious Union) 21 Maple St., London W1P 6DS. ☎ 0171-580 1663. Fax 0171-436-4148. Email: montagu@ulps.demon.co.uk
Est. 1902 for the advancement of Liberal Judaism and to establish and organise Congregations, Groups and Religion Schools on Liberal Jewish principles.
Hon. Life President Rabbi John Rayner, C.B.E.; *Senior V. President* Rabbi Dr Sidney Brichto, M.A., D.D; *Chairman* Jeromé Freedman; *Dir.* Rabbi Dr Charles H. Middleburgh; *Admin. Dir.* Michael Burman.
Constituents: Barkingside Progressive Syn.; Birmingham Progressive Syn.; Brighton & Hove Progressive Syn.; Bristol & West Progressive Jewish Cong.; Chiltern Progressive Syn.; Crawley Jewish Com; Dublin Jewish Progressive Cong.; Ealing L. Syn.; East Anglia Progressive Jewish Com; Finchley Progressive Syn.; Harrow & Wembley Progressive Syn.; Hertsmere Progressive Syn.; Kent L. Jewish Community; Kingston L. Syn.; Leamington & Distr. Progressive Jewish Group; Leicester Progressive Jewish Cong.; The Liberal Jewish Syn., London; Lincoln Jewish Community; Liverpool Progressive Syn.; North London Progressive Syn.; Northwood & Pinner L. Syn.; Nottingham Progressive Syn.; Peterborough Liberal Jewish Com; South Bucks (Amersham) Liberal Jewish Com.; Southgate Progressive Syn.; South London L. Syn.; Thames Valley (Reading) Progressive Jewish Com.; West Central L. Syn. (Lond.); Woodford & Progressive L. Jewish Syn.
Rabbinic Conference: *Chair* Rabbi David J. Goldberg.
Associate Communities: Hereford Jewish Community; Oxford.
ULPS Youth Dept/ULPSNYC Netzer. *Dir.* Mark Bromley; *Admin.:* Karen Morris. For further information see under the respective headings.

ASSOCIATION OF REFORM AND LIBERAL MOHALIM
The Sternberg Centre for Judaism, 80 East End Road, London N3 2SY. ☎ 0181-349-4731; Fax. 0181-343-0901.
(Est. 1988.) A full list of practitioners may be obtained from constituent synagogues, from RSGB (0181-349 4731), ULPS (0171-5801663) or by writing to the Association at the Sternberg Centre.

COUNCIL OF REFORM AND LIBERAL RABBIS
The Sternberg Centre, Manor House, 80 East End Road, N3 2SY.
☎ 0181-349 4731.
Body est. to represent Progressive Rabbinate (RSGB & ULPS) in Britain. *Chairman* Rabbi W. Wolff.

WELFARE ORGANISATIONS

BRITISH ORT
The British branch of World ORT Union (Est. 1880)

126 Albert Street, London NW1 7NE.
☎ 0171-446 8520. Fax: 0171-446 8654.
(Reg. Charity No.: 225975).
(Est. 1920) Vocational Training and technical education for Jews throughout the world. *Patron* M. Naughton; *President* The Hon. David Sieff; *Chairman* M. Mishon; *Exec. Dir.* T. Zekaria. *Admin. Dir.* Mrs Peggy Ann King.

BRITISH TAY-SACHS FOUNDATION
Now under the administration of Jewish Care (see p.95). ☎ 0181-458 3282, ext. 317.

CENTRAL COUNCIL FOR JEWISH COMMUNITY SERVICES
17 Highfield Rd., NW11 9LS.
☎ 0181-458 1035. Fax: 0181-731 7462.
Est 1972 (Reg Charity No 269525.) to co-ordinate the work of Jewish communal organisations. Now has 57 member agencies throughout the UK.
Provides:- Atid Leadership Courses; Social Services Ombudsman; Arbitration & Mediation Service; and advice and support to small organisations.
Co-Ordinates Jewish Emergency Support Service (JESS) and **National Network of Jewish Housing Associations**
Publ. Directory of Jewish Social Services, 3rd ed. 1997.
President: The Lord Woolf, *Chairman:* Phillip Sober; *T. L.* Don; *Admin. Dir.* Daphne Band.
Ombudsman, PO Box 116, Pinner, Middx. HA5 3ND. ☎ 0181-458 9820.
National Network of Jewish Housing Associations. *Chairman* Robert Manning.

CHAI-LIFELINE
Norwood House, Harmony Way, off Victoria Road, London NW4 2BZ. ☎ Office: 0181-202-2211. Helpline: 0181-202-4567. Fax 0181-202-2111. (Reg. Charity no. 1000171). Provides emotional, spiritual and physical support to cancer patients, their families and friends. Telephone help-line, weekly support groups, educational lectures, resource library. Professional counselling available where required. WellWoman and WellMan Screening Clinics. Complementary Therapy Clinics offering aromatherapy, reflexology, healing, laughter therapy, relaxation classes with guided imagery, and a Homeopathic Clinic. For more information or appointments contact Ruth Baum.

FINNART HOUSE SCHOOL TRUST
707 High Road, London N12 0BT.
☎ 0181-445 1670. Fax: 0181-446 7370. Email: finnart@ort.org
(Reg. Charity No. 220917). A charitable trust, the object of which is to relieve children of the Jewish faith who are delinquent, deprived, sick, neglected and in need of care. *Chairman of Trustees* Dr Louis Marks; *Clerk* Peter Shaw.

GET (*Religious Divorce*) *Advisory Service*, 23 Ravenshurst Avenue, London NW4 4EE. ☎ 0181-203-6314. *Senior Negotiator:* Mr Leonard Finn, ACA. Has trained negotiators to help people who have problems in obtaining a Get.

JEWISH AIDS TRUST
Head Office: HIV Education Unit, Colindale Hospital, Colindale Avenue, London NW9 5HG. ☎ 0181-200 0369. Fax: 0181-905 9250. Helpline Mon-Thurs. 7.30 p.m. -10.00 p.m., Sun. 10 a.m.-1 p.m. Helpline ☎ 0181-206 1696.
(Est. 1988. Reg. Charity No. 327936). The Jewish AIDS Trust works across the entire Jewish community. Its aims are to raise awareness of HIV/AIDS; to provide educational programmes tailored to the needs of each community group; to provide counselling and a telephone helpline for those in need; and where appropriate to give financial support to people with an AIDS diagnosis.

WELFARE ORGANISATIONS 15

Patrons Professor Michael Adler, Mrs. Veronica Cohen, Lady Morris of Kenwood, The Hon. Miriam Rothschild; *Chairman of Tr.* Robin Gilbert; *Dir.* Mrs. Rosalind Collin.

JEWISH ASSOCIATION FOR THE MENTALLY ILL
(Reg. Charity No.: 1003345.)
707 High Rd., Finchley, London N12 0BT.
☎ 0181-343 1111. Fax: 0181-343 3355.
(Reg. Charity No. 1003345). JAMI provides guidance, support and advice for carers and sufferers. Principal objectives are: Recognition and support for the mentally ill; to encourage independence through education and training; to ensure the provision of efficient and effective Jewish social and welfare services. Day centre provides stimulating and interesting social activities. Promotes the establishment of residential care homes for the mentally ill.

JEWISH CHILD'S DAY
707 High Road, North Finchley, London N12 0BT
☎ 0181-446 8804. Fax: 0181-446 7370. Email: jcd@ort.org
(Est. 1947, registered charity no. 209266) Established under the joint auspices of the Central British Fund and of the Youth Aliyah Cttee. for Gt. Brit. Reconstituted 1951 on wide national basis. To assist necessitous children in the UK, Israel and overseas. *Life President* Mrs. J. Jacobs; *Chairman* Mrs. J. Moss; T. S. Moss, O.B.E.; H. *Sec.* S. Mehdi; *Exec. Dir.* Peter Shaw.

JEWISH LESBIAN AND GAY HELPLINE
BM Jewish Helpline, London WC1N 3XX
☎ 0171-706 3123.
Reg. Charity No. 1008035.
An information, support and confidential counselling service for Jewish lesbians, gay men, bisexuals, those unsure about their sexuality, and their family and friends.
It also provides a programme of outreach, educating individuals and organisations to be more aware of the needs and experiences of Jewish lesbians, gay men and bisexuals.
The Helpline is a nationwide service established in 1987. The phone line is open every Monday and Thursday 7.00 p.m. to 10.00 p.m. (except festivals and Bank Holidays).
Patrons Leo Abse; Rabbi A. M. Bayfield; Rabbi Lionel Blue; Prof. Sir Herman Bondi, K.C.B., F.R.S; Maria Charles; Dr. Wendy Greengross; Miriam Margolyes; Rabbi Julia Neuberger; Claire Rayner; *Co-ord.* Jack Gilbert; *Sec.* Sally Wexler.

JEWISH MARRIAGE COUNCIL
23 Ravenshurst Avenue, NW4 4EE.
☎ 0181-203 6311. Fax: 0181-203 8727.
Dir. Jeffery Blumenfeld, B.A. (Hons.); *Training Consultant:* Mrs. N. Berger B.A., M.S.W. The Council provides the following services: a counselling service for individual, marital and family problems; it assists anyone with a relationship problem whether they are single, married, divorced or separated (0181-203 6311); preventative counselling in the form of groups for engaged couples, newly-weds, adolescents as well as assertiveness and social skills courses; it provides a Get (religious divorce) Advisory Service (0181-203 6314) (see p. 14), Connect Marriage Bureau (0181-203 5207) and Miyad the Nationwide Jewish Crisis Helpline (0181-203 2611/01345 851 999).
JMC Manchester: Levi House, Bury Old Road, Manchester M8 6FX. ☎ 0161-795 1240. Appointments 0161-740 5764; 0345 585159.

JEWISH WOMEN'S AID (JWA)
BM JWAI, London WC1N 3XX.
☎ Admin: 0171-486 0860. Fax: 0171-486 0600; Helpline: 0800-591203.

(Est. 1992.) (Reg. Charity No. 1047045) A group of Jewish women from all sections of the community joined forces to support Jewish women who experience domestic abuse. JWA aims to break the silence surrounding domestic violence through education and awareness-raising programmes. JWA operates a freephone confidential helpline and its first refuge for Jewish women and their children is now open. Counselling and befriending services will be available.
Hon. President Judith Usiskin; *Chairperson* Tanya Novick; *H. Sec.* Stephanie Barnett; *H. T.* Jane Leaver.

THE MANOR HOUSE CENTRE FOR PSYCHOTHERAPY AND COUNSELLING
The Sternberg Centre, 80 East End Road, N3 2SY.
☎ 0181-371 0180. Fax: 0181-343 2558.
The Manor House Centre for Psychotherapy and Counselling provides counselling and psychotherapy skills for voluntary and professional workers in the community.
Course Dirs. & enquiries Judith Dell, Tina Simmonds.

MAZAL TOV: THE PROGRESSIVE JEWISH MARRIAGE BUREAU
c/o 21 Maple Street, London W1P 6DS.
☎ 01923 841527; 0171-580 1663. Email: montagu@ULPS.demon.co.uk
(Est. 1995) Non-profit making marriage bureau under aegis of the Union of Liberal and Progressive Synagogue.
Chairperson Management Team Rita Adler; *Admin* Ruth Green.

NATHAN AND ADOLPHE HAENDLER CHARITY
c/o World Jewish Relief, Drayton House, 30 Gordon Street, London WC1H 0AN.
☎ 0171-387 4747. Fax: 0171-383 4810. Email: wjr@ort.org
This charity is governed by a scheme which was approved by the Royal Courts of Justice in 1928, whereby the income of the Fund is applicable by the Trustees for the purpose of assisting poor Jews who, in consequence of religious persecution or other misfortune, have come or shall come to take refuge in England. Trustees now World Jewish Relief.

NATIONAL TAY-SACHS AND BIOCHEMICAL GENETICS CENTRE
Research Centre, Royal Manchester Children's Hospital, Pendlebury, Manchester, M27 4HA. ☎ 0161-794 4696 Ext. 2384.
(Reg. Charity No. 326403). Screening and counselling services for Tay-Sachs, Gauchers, Nieman-Pick etc. Community screening sessions in the North of England. Postal screening UK and Europe. Informative literature for students and families. Tay-Sachs Coordinator, any morning, or leave message on 24-hour answerphone. No fixed charge. Donations welcome. Medical enquiries to Dr. Sybil Simon (Research Centre).

OTTO SCHIFF HOUSING ASSOCIATION
The Bishop's Avenue, N2 0BG.
☎ 0181-209 0022. Fax: 0181-201 8089.
(Reg. Charity No.: 210396). (Est. 1934.) The Association is Britain's largest provider of care to Jewish refugees from Nazi persecution and accommodates over three hundred people in two Sheltered Housing Schemes, five Residential Care Homes and a Nursing Home. The Association also offers daycare and short-term respite care. During 1997, the Association launched OSHA Homecare Services, providing a comprehensive range of care and support services in clients' own homes. *Admission inquiries* Josephine Woolf. ☎ 0181-209 0022; *Homecare Services* Pam Kenward ☎ 0181-458 4088; *Council* Allan Blacher (*Chairman*), Frank Harding, Peter Held, Andrew Kaufman, Harry Kleeman, C.B.E., Rosemary Lewis and Ashley Mitchell; *Chief Exec.* Tony Shepherd; *General Mgr.* David

Lightburn; *Administrator* Esther Meyerson; *Financial Services Mgr.* David Lovell; *Campaign Mgr.* Edward Lord.

TAY-SACHS SCREENING CENTRE
SOUTH THAMES REGIONAL GENETICS CENTRE (EAST)
8th Floor, Guy's Tower, Guy's Hospital, St. Thomas Street, London SE1 9RT.
☎ 0171-955 4648. Fax 0171-955 2550.
Provides information, carrier testing and genetic counselling for Tay-Sachs disease. *Sec.* Mrs R. Demant.

WORLD JEWISH RELIEF
Drayton House, 30 Gordon Street, WC1H 0AN. ☎ 0171-387 3925. Fax: 0171-383 4810. Email: wjr@ort.org
(Est. 1933.) To advise and assist Jewish refugees in the UK who have fled from racial and religious persecution in any part of the world; to help Jews and Jewish communities in need outside the UK with their social, religious, cultural and development activities.
Presidents The Chief Rabbi, Communal Rabbi of Spanish & Portuguese Jews' Cong., Chairman, C. of Reform & Liberal Rabbis; K. D. Rubens; H. Kleeman, C.B.E; Sir Claus Moser, K.C.B., C.B.E., F.B.A.; Dame Simone Prendergast, D.B.E., D.L., J.P.; Lord Janner, Q.C.; D. Cope-Thompson; Lady Jakobovits; D. Lewis; Lord Nathan; Edmond de Rothschild; *Chairman* A. Mitchell; *Exec. Dirs.* Warren Alexander, Eli Benson.
Allocations (JTC Funds) Committee, est. 1953 to administer and make grants from funds received from the Jewish Trust Corporation for the benefit of former victims of Nazi oppression. *Chairman* K. D. Rubens; *Sec.*
Jewish Refugees Committee (est. 1933). ☎ 0171-387 4747. Case-working cttee. to assist and advise Jewish Refugees in the UK. *Chairman* Mrs. J. Cohen, J.P.; *Dir.* Ms L. Biasiolo.

REFUGEE ORGANISATIONS

45 AID SOCIETY HOLOCAUST SURVIVORS
46 Amery Road, Harrow, Middx HA1 3UQ.
☎ 0181-422 1512.
(Est. 1963) The Society consists mainly of survivors who came to England in 1945/6 and others who have immigrated subsequently. It maintains close links with members who have emigrated to Israel, USA, Canada and other countries. The Society is active in the community, helps members as well as others in need. It furthers Holocaust education and other charitable causes.
President Sir Martin Gilbert; *Chairman* Ben Helfgott; *V. Chairman* Harry Balsam; *Tr.* Krvlik Wilder; *Sec.* Mick Zwirek.

ACJR (Association of Children of Jewish Refugees)
c/o Ian Rosmarin, 47 Crown Reach, Grosvenor Road, London SW1V 3JY.
☎ 0171-931 9888/0171-976 6691. Fax: 0171-630 0893.
Cultural and social group for people whose parents suffered or fled from Nazi persecution in the 1930s and 1940s.
Chairman Ian Rosmarin; *Membership Sec.* Malcolm Wald.

AJR CHARITABLE TRUST (Association of Jewish Refugees in Great Britain)
1 Hampstead Gate, 1A Frognal, London NW3 6AL.
☎ 0171-431 6161. Fax: 0171-431 8454.
(Reg. Charity No. 211239). The Trust's aim is to assist Jewish refugees from Nazi oppression and their families, primarily from Central Europe, by providing a wide range of services. These include regular financial support for the needy, weekly advice

sessions on benefit and pension problems, the operation of a popular Day Centre, sheltered accommodation, financial aid for a number of residential homes for the aged, a meals-on-wheels service, a team of full-time social workers, volunteers, and a widely-read journal. *Director* Ernest David. *Publ.* A.J.R. Information (monthly).

ANNE FRANK EDUCATIONAL TRUST
Garden Floor, 43 Portland Place, London W1N 3AG. ☎ 0181-950 6476. Fax 0181-420 4520.
Touring exhibitions and resources on Anne Frank and the holocaust. *Contact* Gillian Walnes.

ASSOCIATION OF JEWISH EX-BERLINERS
33 Church Hill, London N21 1LN.
☎ 0181-882 1638.
(Est. 1990.) To exchange shared experiences of the most traumatic period of Jewish European history at social gatherings as well as record them in writings, individually and collectively.
Chairman P. H. Sinclair. ☎ 0181-882 1638; *T.* Manfred Alweiss, 22 Middleton Rd., London NW11 7NS. ☎ 0181-455 0115. *Publ.* 'So What's New?' (monthly).

CLUB 1943: ANGLO-GERMAN CULTURAL FORUM
51 Belsize Square, NW3 (Synagogue)
☎ 01442-54360.
The Society's aim and purpose was to preserve and develop their cultural standard attained in the country they had to leave. *Chairman* Hans Seelig, 27 Wood End Lane, Hemel Hempstead. ☎ 01442-54360; *Sec.* Julia Schwartz. ☎ 0181-209 0318. *Public Rel.* C. Krysler, 97 Hodford Road, NW11 8EH. ☎ 0181-455 8321.

COMMITTEE FOR THE WELFARE OF IRANIAN JEWS IN GT. BRITAIN
17 Arden Road, N3 3AB
☎ 0181-346 3121. Fax: 0181-343 7383.
(Est. 1981.) To act as a co-ordinating and referral agency for Iranian Jews requiring any form of assistance, and to act as a co-ordinating committee for those organisations or individuals who can provide for their needs, and to work closely with the BoD as to their welfare and interests. *President* Lord Clinton Davis, LL.B; *Chairman* S. Mehdi.

COUNCIL OF JEWS FROM GERMANY
1 Hampstead Gate, 1A Frognal, London NW3 6AL.
☎ 0171-431 6161. Fax: 0171-431 8454.
To protect the rights and interests of Jews who emigrated from Germany.
Founder Organisations: Association of Jewish Refugees in Great Britain, London; American Federation of Jews from Central Europe, Inc., New York; Irgun Oley Merkaz Europa, Tel Aviv.
Affiliated Organisations Almost all associations of former German Jews in their respective countries of resettlement. *Co-Chairmen* F. Estreicher (Tel Aviv), F. E. Falk (London); C. C. Silberman (New York); *H. Sec.* W. D. Rothenberg (London).

HOLOCAUST SURVIVORS' CENTRE
Corner of Parson Street/Church Road, London NW4 1QA.
☎ 0181-202 9844. Fax: 0181-202 2404.
To provide a centre for survivors of Nazi persecution.
Jointly founded by WJR and Jewish Care and administered by Jewish Care. Runs courses on public speaking for survivors, retirement workshops, art exhibitions and other courses of interest to survivors.
Co-ordinator Patricia Ward.

ORGANISATIONS CONCERNED WITH JEWS OF EASTERN EUROPE 19

POLISH JEWISH EX-SERVICEMEN'S ASSOCIATION
12 Antrim Grove, London NW3 4XR.
(Est. 1945.) To aid and protect Polish-Jewish ex-Servicemen in the UK, look after the interests of Polish-Jewish refugees, perpetuate the memory of Jewish martyrs of Nazi persecution. *Chairman* L. Kurzer; V. *Chairman* L. Feit; *H. Sec.* L. Kleiner. *H. T. J.* Tigner.

POLISH JEWISH REFUGEE FUND
143 Brondesbury Pk., NW2 5JL ☎ 0181-451 3425.
Chairman W. Schindler; *Sec.* Mrs. R. Gluckstein.

SOCIETY OF FRIENDS OF JEWISH REFUGEES
Reg. Charity No.: 227889.
Balfour House, 741 High Road, Finchley N12 0BQ.
☎ 0181-446 1477. Fax: 0181-446 1180.
Chairman G. Ognall; *H. Sec.* I. Connick; *Jt. H. Ts.* P. C. Leach, W. Sharron; *Fin. Sec.* E. H. Kraines.

ORGANISATIONS CONCERNED WITH THE JEWS OF EASTERN EUROPE

BRITISH COUNCIL FOR JEWS IN EASTERN EUROPE
Salisbury Hall, Park Road, Hull HU3 1TD.
☎ 01482 326848 (office), 01482 353981 (private). Fax 01482 568756.
(Est. 1990.) Support for Jewish revival in Eastern Europe. *Publ.* Working for a Cause.
(Belarus office: Apt. 19, 69a Pervomayskaya Str, Mogilev 212030. ☎ +7 1222 25 39 34 (Igor Ilyin)).

THE EAST EUROPEAN JEWISH HERITAGE PROJECT
Jarn, Old Boars Hill, Oxford, OX1 5JQ.
☎/Fax 01865 326578. Fax 01865 326922. E-mail: EEJHP@compuserve.com
(Reg. Charity No. 1061629.) The East European Jewish Heritage Project is a humanitarian, educational and research organization. It is dedicated to perpetuating East European Jewish Culture while improving the lives of Holocaust survivors. The EEJHP sends expeditions to East Europe to locate the last Shtetl Jews. Interviews conducted in Yiddish about pre-war life are tape-recorded and, along with a photographic record of architectural and other remains, are archived at the Taylorian Library of Oxford University. Courses in Yiddish and East European Jewish Studies are conducted in cooperation with East European Universities and other institutions. The East European Jewish Heritage Project also provides medical and other material and assistance to Holocaust survivors and their families. *Contact:* Frank Swartz.

EXODUS 2000
Sternberg Centre for Judaism, 80 East End Road, London N3 2SY.
☎ 0181-349 4731. Fax: 0181-343 0901.
Reform Synagogues of Great Britain Campaign for Progressive Judaism in Central and Eastern Europe. Exodus has a national exec. and grps. in many Reform Syns. Its major areas of work are: (i) supporting the growth of Progressive Judaism in the former Soviet Union (ii) twinning with new Eastern European Progressive Congregations; (iii) sending Rabbis and lay educators to teach. Exodus 2000 works closely with the World Union of Progressive Judaism in Jerusalem and Moscow, and the European Board in London. *Chairman* Rabbi David Soetendorp; *Admin* Linda Kann; *T.* Alan Langleben.

JEWISH RELIEF AND EDUCATION TRUST (JRET)
75 Abbotts Gardens, London N2.
☎ 0181883 7006.
(Est. 1991. Reg. Charity No.: 1007025.) The support of Jewish student and youth activities in the former Soviet Union.
Chairman Adam Rose.

NATIONAL COUNCIL FOR JEWS IN THE FORMER SOVIET UNION
Contact: Board of Deputies.
☎ 0171-543 5400.
(Est 1975.) Initiates and coordinates activities on behalf of Jews in the FSU including safeguarding and promoting their human, civic, religious and cultural rights. It acts as the umbrella org. for all bodies in Britain with similar objects. The Council is the voice of the community to Government and other bodies in the UK & internationally on FSU Jewish issues.
President E. Tabachnik Q.C.; *Acting Chairman* Jonathan Arkush.

WOMEN'S CAMPAIGN FOR SOVIET JEWRY (The 35's)
Pannell House, 779/781 Finchley Road, NW11 8DN.
☎ 0181-458 7148/9. Fax: 0181-458 9971.
An activist organisation which aims to help Jews in their efforts to leave the CIS and after they arrive in Israel. The campaign publicises the situation through a regular newsletter and through contacts with the media, political parties the Trade Unions and professional and religious associations. Support is given to Refuseniks and Poor Relatives in the CIS and to the new Olim in Israel with the organisation of the annual ONE TO ONE sponsored treks in Israel. *Co-Chairmen* Mrs. Rita Eker, Mrs. Margaret Rigal.

ZIONIST ORGANISATIONS

BRITISH ALIYA MOVEMENT
Balfour House, 741 High Road, Finchley, London N12 0BQ.
☎ 0181-446 2266. Fax: 0181-446 4419.
A support organisation providing practical information for future Olim and promoting Aliya. Local groups around Britain meet regularly with guest speakers and Shlichim in attendance on Israel-related topics. Fact finding tours to Israel organised for potential Olim. *BAM Org. for UK* Samantha Blakey.

BRITISH EMUNAH (formerly Child Resettlement Fund)
Norwood House, Harmony Way, off Victoria Rd., Hendon, NW4 2DR.
☎ 0181-203 6066. Fax: 0181-203 6668.
(Est. 1933. Reg. Charity No. 215398) A charity organisation with 37 groups throughout the country working to support our 26 projects in Israel for underprivileged children, children with learning difficulties, teenagers at risk, programme of social welfare, new immigrants and senior citizens. *H. L. President* The Lady Jakobovits; *H. President* Mrs. Elaine Sacks; *Founder President* Mrs. Gertie Landy; *Exec. President* Mrs. Guggy Grahame; *Exec. Vice Presidents* Mrs Vera Gorbacz, Mrs Della Worms.

BRITISH OLIM RELATIVES ASSOCIATION (BORA)
Balfour House, 741 High Road, Finchley, N12 0BQ
☎ 0181-343 9756/446 1477. Fax: 0181-446 0639.
(Est. 1984.) To maintain closer links between Brit. immigrants in Israel and their relatives in UK by providing services and concessions whenever possible, including reduced air fare, an emergency phone or Fax: link with Israel and monthly meetings. *President* Mrs. E. Imber-Lithman; *Chairman* J. Daniels.

ZIONIST ORGANISATIONS 21

BRITISH WIZO
(Federation of Women Zionists of Great Britain and Ireland)
105/107 Gloucester Place, London W1H 4BY.
☎ 0171-486 2691. Fax: 0171-486 7521.
(Est. 1918) WIZO (FWZ) is the British Branch of World WIZO and a constituent of the Zionist Fed. of Great Brit. & Ireland and is non-party. It has almost 200 affiliated societies with 14,000 members. *Co-Presidents* Mrs. J. Goldkorn, Mrs. G. Monty; *Chairman* Mrs. Ruth Sotnick; *H. Sec.* Mrs. B. Harding; *Co-Ts.* Mrs. S. Ronson, Mrs. M. Young.
Publs.: Vision Magazine (2 issues a year); Vision-Link (4 issues a year).

CHILDREN AND YOUTH ALIYAH COMMITTEE FOR GT. BRITAIN AND EIRE
Britannia House, 960 High Road, North Finchley, London N12 9YA.
☎ 0181-446 4321. Fax: 0181-343 7383.
Object: The rescue, absorption rehabilitation and educ. in Israel of immigrant, refugee and underprivileged Jewish children. Since 1933 more than 350,000 children have been helped in this way. More than 17,000 are in care at present. *Jt. Chairmen* Gerald Gaffin, Adrienne Sussman; *Vice Chairman* Alan Diamond; *H. T. M.* Josephs; *H. Sec.* Sheila Diamond; *H. Dir.* Mrs. N. Sacki; *Exec. Dir.* Sion Mehdi.
Publ.: Youth Aliyah Today. Committees in London and all parts of Gt. Britain support the work of Youth Aliyah in Israel.

GENERAL ZIONIST ORGANISATION OF GREAT BRITAIN
c/o Balfour House, 741 High Road, N12 0BQ.
President F. Ashe Lincoln, Q.C. *Chairman* A. Stanton; *T.* J. Chart; *H. Sec.* Mrs. Y. M. Stanton.

ISRAEL EMBASSY: 2 Palace Green, Kensington, W8 4QB. ☎ 0171-957 9500. Fax: 0171-957 9555. Email: isr-info@dircon.co.uk. Opening Hours: Mon.-Thur. 09.00-18.00 and Fri. 09.00-14.00. Defence Sec. 2A Palace Green, Kensington, W8 4QB; ☎ 0171-957 9548. Consular Sec. 15A Old Court Place, Kensington, W8 4QB. ☎ 0171-957 9516; *Ambassador* H. E. Dror Zeigerman-Eden; *Min. Plenipotentiary* Amiram Magid; *Min.-Cllr.* Y. D. Hadas-Handelsman; Ahuva Oren (Cultural Aff.); Ron Prosor (Press); Dov Lev (2nd Sec); Shalom Tourgeman (2nd Sec.); Gidon Siterman (Economic Aff.); Amos Wohl (Comm. Aff.); Yahalomah Shehory (Agricultural Aff.); Eliezer Hod, 1st Secretary (Information & Tourism); Menashe Bar-On (Consular Aff.); Shmuel Micha (Admin.); *Att.* Miss Iris Shoshani, Nissim Bracha, Moshe Aharonov; Brig. Gen. Itzhak Chen.
Travel Information: Internet site: http://www.israel-embassy.org.uk/london

JEWISH AGENCY FOR ISRAEL
London office: 741 High Road, Finchley, N12 0BQ.
☎ 0181-446 1144. Fax: 0181-446 8296.
The reconstituted Jewish Agency consisting of representatives of the World Zionist Organisation and of bodies raising funds on behalf of Israel, has assumed the following responsibilities: absorption of immigrants in Israel; social welfare services for immigrants; education in Israel: higher learning and research in Israel; youth care and training; agricultural settlement; immigrant housing. Project Renewal. *Chairman of the Exec.* Avraham Burg.

JEWISH NATIONAL FUND FOR ISRAEL
Head Office: 58-70 Edgware Way, Edgware, Middx HA8 8GQ.
☎ 0181-421 7600 (JNF); 0181-421 7601 (KKL Wills & Bequests); 0181-421 7602 (KKL Charity Accounts); 0181-421 7603 (Education). Fax: 0181-905 4299. Email: jnf@ort.org DX: 57159 Edgware.

President Gail Seal; *Jt. Vice-Presidents* Stanley Lovatt, Jeffrey Zinkin, F.C.A.; *Hon. Tr.* David Kibel, F.C.A.; *Chief Exec.* Simon Winters, M.IDM, M.IOD.
JNF Charitable Trust: *Chairman* Gail Seal; *Company Sec.* Harvey Bratt, LL.B.
KKL Executor & Trustee Co. Ltd.: *Chairman* Jeffrey Zinkin; *Company Sec.* Harvey Bratt, LL.B. Objects: Bequests, advisory and covenant services for charity.
Education Department: *Chairman* Helen Rosen; *Hd. of Dept.* Myrna Glass, B.Ed.(Hons), Cert. Ed. Supplies JNF/Israel educational resources to schools, nurseries, religion classes, youth movements and others. Arranges Bar/Bat Mitzvah ceremonies in Israel. Organises events in London and Provinces.
Young JNF: *Chairman:* Adam Caplin; *Co-ord.* Leesa Mather.
Bloomsbury Advertising Agency Ltd.: *Company Sec.* Harvey Bratt, LL.B.

LIKUD-HERUT MOVEMENT OF GREAT BRITAIN
143-145 Brondesbury Park, NW2 5JL.
☎ 0181-451 0003. Fax: 0181-459 8766.
(Est. 1970.) To promote the Zionist ideology as conceived by Ze'ev Jabotinsky. Member of Likud Haolami and affiliated to National Zionist Council of Gt. Britain and a member of the Board of Deputies. *Life President* E. Graus; *Life Vice-Presidents* M. Benjamin, J. Gellert; *Chairman* D. Bloom; *V. Chairmen* B. Gordon, LL.B., M. Kersh; *Hon. Tr.* M. A. Israel, F.C.A.; *H. Secs.* Miss F. Kutock & S. Mehdi. *Memb. Secs.* M. Kayne, M. Kahtan.
Affiliated Organisations: Young Likud Herut; (Brit Nashim Herut Women's League); Betar-Tagar, Brit Hashmonayim.

MAPAM/MERETZ FOR A PROGRESSIVE ISRAEL
Hashomer House, 37A Broadhurst Gardens, NW6 3BN. (Reg. Charity No. 269903).
☎ 0171-328 5451. Fax: 0171-624 6748.
An Anglo-Jewish organisation which identifies with Mapam's world outlook and strives to vitalise Anglo-Jewry in the spirit of Jewish humanism and democracy. It seeks to promote Socialist Zionism, the unity of the Jewish people, aliya, social justice in Israel; Jewish educ. and culture and peace as a vital element of Zionism, complete political, social and economic equality for all Israeli citizens, with religion left to the conscience of each individual. Affiliated to: World Union of Mapam; Z. Fed.; BoD; Monthly Newsletter. *Ch.* Pauline Levis; *Vice-Ch.* Michael Plight; *Sec.* Prof. Gertrude Falk.
Youth Org.: Hashomer Hatzair.
Student Org.: Kidmah.

MIZRACHI-HAPOEL HAMIZRACHI FEDERATION OF GREAT BRITAIN AND IRELAND
2b Golders Green Road, NW11 8LH.
☎ 0181-455 2243. Fax: 0181-455 2244.
(Est. 1918.) *President* A. L. Handler; *Co-Chairmen* Rabbi E. L. Jackson & M. Klausner; *V. Chairmen* A. Grant, D. Prins; *H. Ts.* N. A. Cohen, B.A, F.C.A., D. Cashdan, B.A. Berman; *H. Secs.* S. Sperber; I. Rubin; *H. V. Presidents* Dayan M. Fisher; Sir Sidney Hamburger, C.B.E.; Dayan P. Toledano; Rabbi E. Mirvis, Rabbi P. Greenberg; *V. Presidents* Dr. E. Jaffe, S. S. Levin, O.B.E., LL.B., K. Meyer, J. Reid.
Publ.: Jewish Review.
Constituent Orgs.: Emunah: Child Resettlement, Bachad; Bnei Akiva, Harel.
Affiliated Orgs.: National Zionist Council, Yavneh Olami.
Mifal Hatorah: Central Foundation for Yeshivot in Israel and Med. Aid Fund.
Education Committee: *Chairman* M.M. Wreschner, F.C.A.

Anglo-Jewry & Communal Affairs Committee: *Chairman* S. S. Levin, O.B.E.
Aliya Committee: *Chairman* I. Rubin.
Small Communities Committee: *Chairman* Rev. M. Weisman, M.A.(Oxon).
Midrasha Institute for Israel: *Chairman Exec. Cttee.* A. Handler; *Reg.* M. Shatzkes.

NATIONAL ZIONIST COUNCIL
2b Golders Green Road, NW11 8LH.
☎ 0181-455 2243/4. Fax: 0181-455 2244.
(Est. 1983.) Zionist rep. body for all Z. movements and individuals in Gt. Brit. & Ireland who subscribe to Zionist aims as defined in the Jerusalem programme. To work in particular in the fields of aliya, pub rel., information and economic activities and give maximum support to the J.I.A. It is affiliated with the Mizrachi Fed. Co-Chairman M. Klausner (Mizrachi); E. Graus (Herut); *V. Chairman* A. Stanton (Gen. Z. Org.); *Gen. Sec.* S. G. Kritz (Mizrachi).

POALE ZION—LABOUR ZIONIST MOVEMENT
(Affiliated to the British Labour Party.)
82 De Beauvoir Rd., N1 5AT.
Poale Zion, the Brit. section of the World Labour Z. Movement, is the sister party of the Israel Labour Party. It encourages aliya and demands effective internat. guarantees for the civil and political rights of Jews in the diaspora. It is affiliated to the BoD, the Z. Fed. and United Nations Assn. *President* Dr. S. Levenberg; *Chairman* Lawrie Nerva; *Regional V. Chairman* Allen Harris; *H. T. E.* Strauss; *H. Sec.* Henry Smith.

PRO-ZION: PROGRESSIVE RELIGIOUS ZIONISTS
The Sternberg Centre for Judaism, 80 East End Road, N3 2SY.
☎ 0181-349 4731.
(Est. 1978.) To work for full legal and rel. rights for Progressive Judaism in Israel, to affirm the centrality in Jewish life of the State of Israel. *Chairman* W. Heyman; *H. Sec.* C. Dalton; *H. Tr.* R. Stern.

UNITED JOINT ISRAEL APPEAL (UJIA)
(former Joint Israel Appeal and Jewish Continuity)
Balfour House, 741 High Road, Finchley N12 0BQ.
☎ 0181-446 1477. Fax: 0181-446 1180. Email: central@jia.org.
The majority of the work for which the UJIA is known is carried out by its associated charity, the Joint Jewish Charitable Trust (Charity Reg. No. 1060078), a company limited by guarantee. (Registered in England, No. 3295115). *Hon. Presidents* Chief Rabbi Dr Jonathan Sacks, Lord Sieff of Brimpton, O.B.E., M.A.; *President* Sir Trevor Chinn, C.V.O.; *Vice-Presidents* Stanley Cohen, Alan Fox, Ronald Preston, Stephen Rubin; *Chairman* Brian Kerner; *Vice-Chairman* Michael Sinclair; *T.* Howard Stanton, F.C.C.A.; *Chief Exec.* Jonathan Kestenbaum; *Finance Dir.* Eldred Kraines, C.A. (S.A.).

WORLD ZIONIST ORGANISATION
741 High Road, Finchley, N12 0BQ.
☎ 0181-446 1144. Fax: 0181-446 8296.
The WZO was established by the first Zionist Congress, which met in Basle on August 29, 1897. The aim of the Org., as defined in the programme adopted by the Basle Congress, was to secure for the Jewish people a home in Palestine guaranteed by public law. At the Congress a constitution providing for a self governing World Organisation, with the Zionist Congress as the supreme body, was adopted.
  In 1908 the Z.O. embarked upon the work of practical settlement and development in Palestine. When the Z.O. was recognised in 1922 as the Jewish Agency under the Palestine Mandate, it was already responsible for a wide field of devel-

opment and settlement activities and it commanded the support of important Jewish groups throughout the world.

The aims of Zionism, as enunciated in the 'New Jerusalem Programme' adopted by the 27th World Zionist Congress in June, 1968, are:
The unity of the Jewish People and the centrality of Israel in Jewish Life;
The ingathering of the Jewish people in its historic homeland, Eretz Israel, through Aliya from all countries;
The strengthening of the State of Israel which is based on the prophetic vision of justice and peace;
The preservation of the identity of the Jewish people through the fostering of Jewish and Hebrew education and of Jewish spiritual and cultural values;
The protection of Jewish rights everywhere.

The **Aliyah Department** has assisted more than 30,000 British Olim, and a team of Shlichim are available to offer advice, consultation and information for those considering Aliyah. ☎ 0181-446 4419.

The **Education Department** focuses on work within schools, as well as organising Ulpanim throughout Great Britain, catering for a wide range of skill levels and age groups. ☎ 0181-446 8109. Fax: 0181-446 8296.

The **Torah Department** concentrates on developing Torah education systems, as well as strengthening the commitment to Klal Yisrael the Community, the State of Israel and Zionism. Also available are a wide range of books and publications covering a broad spectrum of Jewish topics.

The **Youth & Hechalutz Department** specialises in educating Jewish Youth through informal means, and has very strong links with the Zionist Youth Movements operating n the UK. The Israel Desk section is responsible for the Israel Experience Programmes, enabling Jewish Youth from the UK to travel to Israel for both short and long term Israel Schemes, and the JPMP Pedagogic Centre has a wide selection of educational resources which are available for teachers, youth workers, etc. ☎ 0181-446 2277. Fax: 0181-343 9037.

ZIONIST FEDERATION OF GT. BRITAIN AND IRELAND
Balfour House, 741 High Road, N12 0BQ.
☎ 0181-343 9756. Fax: 0181-446 0639. Email: zion-fed@dircon.co.uk
(Est. 1899) The Zionist Federation is an umbrella organisation encompassing most of the Zionist organisations and individuals in the country and, as such, represents the Zionist Movement in the United Kingdom. Its function is to support, co-ordinate and facilitate the work of all its affiliates nationwide. The Zionist Federation aims to encourage the participation of Jews in Zionist activities including education, culture, Hebrew language and Israel information, underpinned by our belief that the main goal of Zionism is Aliyah.
Chairman Mr H. Schaverien; *V. Chairmen* Mr S. Pollock, Mr R. Stern; *H.T.* Mr I. Myers; *Hon. Sec.* Mrs E. Gilston; *Exec. Dir.* Mr D. Goldberg.
Committees: Constitution - *Chairman* Mr S. Shipton; Finance - *Chairman* Mr I. Myers; Fund Raising - *Chairman* Mr C. Rosen; Israel Conference - *Chairman* Mr S. Pollock; Israel Projects - *Chairman* Mrs E. Gilston; Moadon Ivri - *Chairman* Mr M. Novick; Recruitment - *Chairman* Mr R. Stern; Yom Ha'atzmaut - *Chairman* Mr D. Duke-Cohan. Other Committees: Youth Conference, Zionism 100.

OTHER ORGANISATIONS CONCERNED WITH ISRAEL

ACADEMIC STUDY GROUP ON ISRAEL AND THE MIDDLE EAST
25 Lyndale Avenue, NW2 2QB.
☎ 0171-435 6803. Fax: 0171-794 0291. Email: F01_ASG@msn.com
(Reg. Charity No. 801772) An academic org. which aims at forging and expanding contacts between academics in this country and their colleagues in Israel and develop among them an interest in their corresponding fields in Israel. Organises study

missions to Israel and lectures and meetings on campuses throughout Britain. *President* Sir Walten Bodmer, Hertford College, Oxon; *Chairman* Prof. J. Friend, Hull Univ.; *V. Chairman* Prof. Graham Zellick, QMW College, London; *Tr.* Aviva Petrie, London School of Hygiene; *Dir.* J. D. A. Levy.

AKIM
(Est. 1964. Reg. Charity No.: 241458) To assist with the rehabilitation of mentally handicapped children in Israel. *President* S. W. Samuelson C.B.E. *V. President* H. Steinhauer. *Chairman* D. Marlowe; *H. Ts.* L. Gamsa, W. Raychbart. Corresp. to: 45 Brampton Grove, NW4 4AH. ☎ 0181-202 0172. Fax: 0181-202 4747. Akim N.W.: D. Marlowe, 7 Faber Gardens, NW4. ☎ 0181-202 7481. Stanmore Akim: M. Marston, 35 Laburnum Ct., Dennis La., Stanmore, Middx. HA7 4JP. ☎ 0181-954 0543. Younger Akim: H. Turgel, 15 Longcroft Road, Canons Pk., Edgware, Middx. HA8 6RR. ☎ 0181-952 1586.

ANGLO-ISRAEL ARCHAEOLOGICAL SOCIETY
3 St. John's Wood Road, NW8 8RB.
☎ 0171-286 1176. Fax: 0171-289 5549.
(Reg. Charity No. 220367) Lectures on recent archaeological discoveries in Israel, publication of annual research bulletin and award of grants to students to participate in excavations in Israel.
Chairman Prof. H. G. M. Williamson, Oriental Instit., Pusey Lane, Oxford; *Admin.* Mrs. C. A. Murray.

ANGLO-ISRAEL ASSOCIATION
9 Bentinck Street, W1M 5RP.
☎ 0171-486 2300/935 9505. Fax: 0171-935 4690. E-mail: aia@dircon.co.uk
(Reg. Charity No. 313523) The Assn. exists to inform and educ. the Brit. public about Israel's achievements. It holds a unique position among orgs. in Brit. which support Israel. It was est. in 1949 by influential non-Jews who were convinced that others than Jews must support Israel and its membership consists of Jews and non-Jews in all walks of life. This joint support is its great strength. The Assn promotes Israel by org. lectures, meetings and study tours of Israel and Anglo-Israel colloquia, by publishing and commissioning literature about Israel, by awarding scholarships and making grants. Fdr. The late Sir Wyndham Deedes, C.M.G., D.S.O.; *H. President* The Israeli Ambassador; *President* The Lord Peter Shore; *Chairman of* C. The Hon. David Sieff; *Chairman, Exec. Cttee.* John L. Marshall; *H. T. G. R.* Pinto; *Dir.* David Sumberg.

THE BALFOUR DIAMOND JUBILEE TRUST
3rd Floor, 26 Enford Street, London W1H 2DD.
☎ 0171-258 0008. Fax. 0171-258 0344. Email: admin@bdjt.win-uk.net
(Est. 1977. Reg. Charity No. 276353) To consolidate and strengthen cultural relations between the UK and Israel. Provides the community with a diverse programme of topical activities throughout the year – in literature and the arts. Makes financial support available to individuals – both in the UK and Israel – whose work will make an enduring cultural contribution.
The Lord Goodman Fellowship Award, a joint venture with the British Council and the Foreign & Commonwealth Office, encourages the annual exchange of distinguished scholars between the UK and Israel by awarding scholarships for up to a full year of study or research in a field related to the Environment (see http://www.britcoun.org/israel/isrgoodmantm). *Exec. Sec.* Sasha Treuherz.

BANK LEUMI (UK) plc.
Head Office & Main Branch: 4/7 Woodstock Street, W1A 2AF.
☎ 0171-629 1205.

(One branch in London; Northern office in Manchester; subsidiary in Jersey, C.I., Bank Leumi: (Jersey) Ltd.) Inc. in 1959 as a subsidiary of Bank Leumi Le-Israel B.M., which was originally established in London in 1902 as the financial instrument of the Zionist Movement under the name of Jewish Colonial Tr. *Chairman* E. Raff; *Dep. Chairman* B. D. Schreier; *Dir. & Gen. Man.* U. Galili; *Dep. Gen. Mans.* G. Doubtfire, M. Shear.

BEN-GURION UNIVERSITY FOUNDATION
21-22 Grosvenor Street, W1X 9FE.
☎ 0171-499 2276. Fax: 0171-491 2649.
(Est. 1974. Reg. Charity No.: 276203). To promote Ben-Gurion University of the Negev in Beer-Sheva, Israel, as an international centre for academic excellence and advanced research in medicine, science and desert agriculture - by donations, books, equipment and subscriptions. *Presidents* Lord Weidenfeld of Chelsea; The Countess of Avon, Hyman Kreitman; *V. President* Suzanne Zlotowski; *Chairman* Harold Paisner; *V. Chairmen* Dr. Samuel S. Lawson, Miriam Hyams.

BRITAIN-ISRAEL PUBLIC AFFAIRS CENTRE
21/22 Great Sutton Street, EC1V 0DN.
☎ 0171-490 5373. Fax: 0171-490 4785. E-mail: Sutton@dircon.co.uk
(Est. 1976.) Bipac provides an information service on all aspects of Israel and Middle East politics. Maintains a photo-library, film catalogue, news and features service and information centre, and provides professional assistance in public relations to pro-Israel orgs. *Chairman* Sir Trevor Chinn; *Dir.* Helen Davis; *Admin.* Angela Silverman.

BRITISH & EUROPEAN MACHAL ASSOCIATION
6 Broadlands Close, London N6 4AF.
☎/Fax 0181-348 8695.
MACHAL (Mitnadvei Chutz L'Aretz). Volunteers from abroad in the 1948 Israel War of Independence. To collect stories and memorabilia appertaining to Machal's crucial contribution. To publicise Machal's endeavour and sacrifice. *Co-ordinator* Stanley Medicks.
On Israel's 50th anniversary, 1998, men, women, Jews and non-Jews, will gather from around the world and join their comrades in arms in Israel to celebrate this Golden Jubilee. As the late Yitzhak Rabin, who fought alongside Machal, said: 'You came to us when we needed you most, in those hard and uncertain days of the War of Independence.' Machalniks will gather at the Machal Memorial on the Burma Road on Yom Hazikoron to pray for their fallen comrades. A special stamp and medal will be issued in honour of Machal's crucial contribution.

BRITISH COMMITTEE OF BNEI BRAK HOSPITAL
273 Green Lanes, N4 2EX.
☎ 0181-800 2996
European Off. 21D Devonshire Place, W1. Est. 1979 as part of communal efforts in many countries to build an Orthodox hosp. with a special cardiac dept. in Bnei Brak. Maternity and other wards are open. *Chairman* Dr. L. Freedman; *V. Chairmen* Dayan M. Fisher, V. Lucas, F.S.V.A.; *H. T. B.* Freshwater; *Med. Dir.-Gen.* Dr. M. Rothschild.

BRITISH COMMITTEE OF KEREN YALDENU
(Est. 1955.) To protect Jewish children in Israel through the opening of special centres and institutions from missionary activities and influences alien to Judaism. *Chairman* Mrs. A. Finn, 4 Cheyne Walk, NW4 3W ☎ 0181-202 9689.

OTHER ORGANISATIONS CONCERNED WITH ISRAEL 27

COUNCIL OF SHAARE ZEDEK MEDICAL CENTRE
766 Finchley Road, NW11 7TH.
☎ 0181-201 8933. Fax: 0181-201 8935. http://www.szmc.org.il
(Hospital est. Jerusalem 1902.) (Reg. Charity No. 262870) Raising funds by way of donations and legacies to support the hospital's med. care, research and nursing educ. programmes. *President* Lord Mishcon DL; *Chairman* Mrs. M. Rothem; *H.T.* Alfred Frei, F.C.A.; *Exec. Dir.* Miss Angela Margolis, B.A.

BRITISH FRIENDS OF THE ART MUSEUMS OF ISRAEL
Accurist House, 44 Baker Street, P.O. Box 2283, London W1A 1NP.
☎ 0171-935 3954. Fax: 0171-224 0744.
(Est. 1948. Reg. Charity No. 313008) BFAMI raises funds to help maintain museums in Israel, acquire works of art and antiquities for them, sponsor exhibitions and youth-art educational programmes. *Patrons* H.E. The Ambassador of Israel, Avigdor Arikha, Sir Anthony Caro, CBE, the Duke of Devonshire, Walter Griessmann, Anish Kapoor; *Chairman* Edward Lee; *Exec. Dir.* Mrs Toni Zekaria.

BRITISH FRIENDS OF THE ASSAF HAROFEH MEDICAL CENTRE
707 High Road, N12 0BT.
☎ 0181-343 7068. Fax: 0181-446 7370. Email: jyf@ort.org
(Reg. Charity No. 281754). Provides assistance to the Assaf Harofeh Medical Centre, an 800 bed teaching hospital, affiliated with Tel Aviv University. The Assaf Hospital serves the whole spectrum of Israeli society - kibbutzim, moshavim, religious towns, secular cities, Jews, Arabs, a continuous flow of new immigrants and a major army base. It provides a full range of medical services encompassing every speciality in modern medicine. *President* David Elias, BEM, MWI, FINO; *Chairman* Helen French; *H.T.* Leon Simon MA, CA; *Hon. Sec.* Ann Silverman; *Dir.* Peter Shaw.

BRITISH FRIENDS OF HAIFA UNIVERSITY
26 Enford St., London W1H 2DD.
☎ 0171-724 3777.
(Reg. Charity No. 270733) To further the interests and development of Haifa Univ. by donations, books, equipment and subscriptions. The Brit. Frs. are represented at the Bd. of Govs. of Haifa Univ. *Chairman* Victor Conway, F.C.A.; Lord Jacobs (Chairman of Board of Govs).

BRITISH FRIENDS OF THE ISRAEL FREE LOAN ASSOCIATION
c/o Mrs. Audrey Druce, 30 Greyhound Hill, London NW4 4JP.
☎ 0181-203 7196. Fax: 0181-203 3394.
(Reg. Charity No.: 1009568). Provides interest free loans to Russian and Ethiopian immigrants in Israel and other needy Israelis, including small business loans, emergency housing, medical loans, and loans to families with handicapped children. Established in Jerusalem, 1990, and in 1992 in London.
Chairman Dr. Joshua Saper, 1 High Sheldon, Sheldon Avenue, London N6 4NJ; *Hon. T.* Mrs. A. Druce; *Patrons* Chief Rabbi Dr. Jonathan Sacks, Lady Jakobovits.

THE BRITISH FRIENDS OF THE ISRAEL PHILHARMONIC ORCHESTRA FOUNDATION
11 Radnor Mews, London W2 2SA.
☎ 0171-402 3167. Fax: 0171-706 3045.

BRITISH FRIENDS OF ISRAEL WAR DISABLED
23 Bentinck St., W1M 5RL
☎ 0171-935 5541.
(Est.1974. Reg. Charity No. 269269). To organise rehabilitation holidays in the UK

for groups of Israeli disabled soldiers injured whilst in service; staying in private homes on a community basis. Closely associated with Zahal Disabled Veterans Organisation in Israel. Finance raised in connection with the annual groups and for acquisition of specialised medical equipment. 7 local committees (London, Manchester, Birmingham, Bournemouth, Brighton etc.) *Chairman/Hon. Sol.* Brian B. Harris; *Sec./V.Chairman* Harold Newman; *Tr.* David Stetson; *Hon. Pres.* Mrs Ann Randall.

BRITISH FRIENDS OF RAMBAM MEDICAL CENTRE
34/36 Maddox Street, London W1R 9PD.
☎ 0171-495 8849. Fax: 0171-495 8859.
(Reg. Charity No. 028061) Voluntary organisation raising funds for the purchase of medical equipment for all hospital departments. Current projects include bone marrow transplant programme and pediatric renal units. *Director:* Anita Alexander-Passe.

BRITISH FRIENDS OF SARAH HERZOG MEMORIAL HOSPITAL (EZRATH NASHIM), JERUSALEM
15 Wildwood Road, London NW11 6UL.
☎ 0171-226 1732. Fax: 0171-226 3053.
(Reg. Charity No. 1024814) 300-bed teaching hospital affiliated with Hebrew Univ. Hadassah Med Sch, provides 210 geriatric beds and day hosp for health care and rehabilitation, plus 90 psychiatric beds. Community out-patient clinic has over 15,000 visits a year, gives comprehensive family and child counselling. In-depth research into Alzheimer's, Parkinson's diseases. Celebrated in 1995, 100 years service to Jerusalem area. *President* Lady Jakobovits; *V. President* Mrs Elaine Sacks, BA; *Chairman* Stuart I. Morganstein, BDS, FDSRCS.

BRITISH ISRAEL ARTS FOUNDATION
98 Belsize Lane, London NW3 5BB
☎ 0171-435 9878. Fax: 0171-435 9879.
(Est. 1985.) To promote all forms of bilateral culture between Britain and Israel. The Foundation organises concerts theatre, dance and literary events and exhibitions. Arts Liaison Group est. to coordinate Israeli culture activities in UK. *President* Lilian Hochhauser; *V. President* Norman Hyams; *Chairman* S. Soffair; *Dir.* Ruth Kohn-Corman.

BRITISH-ISRAEL CHAMBER OF COMMERCE
Accurist House, P.O. Box 2281, 44, Baker St., London W1A 1NN.
☎ 0171-486 2371. Fax: 0171-224 1783.
(Est. 1950.) To study and promote trade and econ. relations between the UK and Israel. *Chairman* Alan Fox; *V. Chairmen* R. Glatter, F.C.A., B. Morris; *Tr.* C. Lehmann, F.C.A.; *Exec. Dir.* Denise Arden, B.A.
 North-West Branch *Regional Dir.* Gideon Klaus, ☎ 0161-929 8916. Fax 0161-929 6277. **North-East Branch** *Regional Dir.* Sandra Levi, ☎ 0113-269 4891. Fax 0113-266 0604. **Midland Branch** *Sec.* Lynnette Jacobs. ☎ 0121-214 2547. Fax 0121-200 1991.
 Publ. British-Israel Review; *Edr.* Simon Mountford Communications, Cherry Tree House, Newton-upon-Ouse, York, YO6 2BN. ☎ 01347-848609. Fax: 01347-848301.

BRITISH ISRAEL FORUM
c/o 9 Farm Avenue, London, NW2 2EG.
☎ 0181-452 5236. Fax: 0181-452 7988.
(Est 1988. Reg. Charity No. 1042631) Non-political personal links with Israel and throughout Diaspora. Israel Forum 1983. North American Jewish Forum 1983.

OTHER ORGANISATIONS CONCERNED WITH ISRAEL 29

European Israel Forum 1983. In Britain 1988. *Chairman* Henry Grunwald; *Sec.* Marlena Schmool.

BRITISH-ISRAEL PARLIAMENTARY GROUP
House of Commons, SW1A 0AA. ☎ 0171-222 5853.
Hon. Sec. Stuart Bell, MP; *T.* Rev. Martin Smyth, MP.

BRITISH OVERSEAS TRADE GROUP FOR ISRAEL
P.O. Box 2283, Accurist House, 44 Baker St., London W1A 1NP.
☎ 0171-935 4351. Fax: 0171-268 2629. Email: melanie@botgi.easynet.co.uk
(Est. 1965.) To promote British exports to Israel. BOTGI is an 'Area Advisory Group' to the Brit. Overseas Trade Bd. (DTI) and organises British Trade delegations and exhibitions to Israel. *Chairman* A. Z. Stone; *Exec. Dir.* P. Style, OBE.

BRITISH TECHNION SOCIETY
62 Grosvenor Street, W1X 9DA.
☎ 0171-495 6824. Fax: 0171-355 1525.
(Est. 1951. Reg. Charity No. 206922) To further the development of the Israel Institute of Technology (the Technion) at Haifa. *H. President* Lord Mishcon Q.C, Hon. D.L.; *Chairman* Sidney Corob CBE; *V. Chairman* M. Heller; *Ts.* Lois Peltz, A.M. Sorkin; *Exec. Dir.* Bill Phillips. Social Cttees. in London & Regions.

CONSERVATIVE FRIENDS OF ISRAEL
45b Westbourne Terrace, W2 3UR.
☎ 0171-262 2493. Fax.: 0171-224 8941.
CFI is committed to the Conservative Party and to the welfare of the State of Israel and dedicated to establishing close links between GB and Israel. CFI distributes balanced and accurate information on events in the Middle East and through visits to Israel, gives MPs and candidates a greater understanding and insight into the Middle East. *President* Sir Robert Rhodes James DL; *Chairman* Rt. Hon. Sir Timothy Sainsbury; *Jt. V. Chairmen* Jeremy Galbraith, Mrs Betty Geller, John Taylor, CBE; *Tr.* David Meller; *Jt. V. Presidents* The Countess of Avon, MBE, JP, Lord Lane of Horsell, Sir Michael Latham D.L., Lord Sanderson of Bowden, Lord Sieff of Brimpton, Lord Thomas of Gwydir Q.C., Lord Thomas of Swynnerton; *Dir.* Stuart Polak.

FEDERATION OF JEWISH RELIEF ORGANISATIONS
143 Brondesbury Pk., NW2 5JL.
☎ 0181-451 3425. Fax: 0181-459 8059
(Reg. Charity No.: 250006.) *President* The Chief Rabbi; *Chairman* W. Schindler; *H. T.*; *Sec.* Mrs. R. Gluckstein.

FRIENDS OF ALYN
(Est. 1962. Reg. Charity No.: 232689) To assist the work of the Alyn Orthopaedic Hospital for physically handicapped children in Jerusalem, and provide free medical, surgical and educational aid for needy children. Mrs. Iris Landau, 1 Harford Walk, N2 0JB. ☎ 0181-883 3926.

FRIENDS OF BAR-ILAN UNIVERSITY
16 Wigmore St., W1H 9DE.
☎ 0171-436 9706. Fax: 0171-436 2483.
(Est. 1957. Reg. Charity No. 314139) To assist the development of the Bar-Ilan University at Ramat Gan. *Life President* Mrs Eileen Colman; *President*; *V. Presidents* Richard B. Mintz, A. Lawson, F.R.I.C.S.; *Jt. Chairmen* Hon. Mr. Justice Rix, Mr D. Brecher; *Dir.* Mrs. C. Torrance, M.A.

FRIENDS OF THE BIKUR CHOLIM HOSPITAL, JERUSALEM & BRITISH AID COMMITTEE
3A Princes Parade, Golders Green Road, NW11 9PS.
☎ 0181-458 8649.
Bikur Cholim, Jerusalem's oldest hosp. is now the largest med. centre in the heart of the city. Ladies Guild: *President* Lady Jakobovits; *V. President* Mrs. N. Freshwater; *Chairman* Mrs. R. Cohen; British Aid Committee: *Chairman* David Godfrey, M.A.; *V. Chairman* Morley Franks; *Jt. H. Trs.* B. S. E. Freshwater, P. Englard.

FRIENDS OF BOYS TOWN JERUSALEM
Heather House, Heather Gardens, NW11 9HS.
☎ 0181-731 9550. Fax: 0181-731 9599.
(Est. 1963. Reg. Charity No. 227895) To organise support for secondary education and technical training for 1,500 residential students at Boys Town Jerusalem (Kiryat Noar, Bayit Vegan). *Chairman* E. Tabachnik, Q.C.; *Tr.* J. Pinnick, F.C.A.; *Exec. Dir.* J. Gastwirth.

FRIENDS OF THE HEBREW UNIVERSITY OF JERUSALEM
3 St. John's Wood Road, NW8 8RB.
☎ 0171-286 1176. Fax: 0171-289 5549
(Est. 1926. Reg. Charity No. 209691) To promote the interests and development of the Hebrew University of Jerusalem through lectures, dinners, specialised events, student courses and donations.
President John Sacher C.B.E.; *Chairman* Michael Gee; *V. Chairman* Barry Townsley; *Exec Dir.* Stephen Goldman; *Dep. Dir.* Susan Coller.
The Brit. & Irish Friends are represented on the Hebrew Univ. Bd. of Govs.
Groups: Young Friends/Alumni; Womens' Groups; The Jewish & National University Library Group; British Friends of YISSUM (commercialisation of HU research); Jerusalem Botanical Gardens Group; Legal; Medical and 10 regional groups.

FRIENDS OF THE ISRAEL AGED
51 Woodlands, London NW11 9QS.
☎ 0181-455 1450.
To assist the work of the Women's Social Service (Re'uth) in maintaining sheltered housing, old age homes and the privately run Lichtenstaedter Hospital in Israel.
Est. in Israel 50 years ago. Committee in UK 1988. (Reg. Charity No. 278505).
President Arieh L. Handler; *Vice President* Anthony Rau; *H. Sec.* Carmel Gradenwitz; *H. T.* David Toledano.

FRIENDS OF THE ISRAEL CANCER ASSOCIATION
2 Serjeants' Inn, Fleet Street, London, EC4Y 1LT.
☎ 0171-583 5353. Fax: 0171-353 3683.
(Reg. Charity No. 260710).
The Charity is the UK fund raising arm of the Israel Cancer Association. The ICA, founded over 40 years ago, plays a prominent part in the fields of detection, research, treatment and education, supporting oncological institutes nationwide screening, patient care and information services. *President* Mrs. H. Gestetner, O.B.E.; *V. Presidents* Ruth Lady Wolfson, Mrs. V. Duffield, C.B.E., Stephan Wingate, Lady Alliance; *Hon. T.* Charles Corman; *Committee Chairman* Mrs V. Aaron.

FRIENDS OF ISRAEL EDUCATIONAL TRUST
25 Lyndale Avenue, NW2 2QB.
☎ 0171-435 6803. Fax. 0171-794 0291. Email: FO1_ASG@msn.com
(Reg. Charity No. 271983) To promote and advance the education of the public in

OTHER ORGANISATIONS CONCERNED WITH ISRAEL 31

the knowledge of the country of Israel and its citizens. F.O.I.E.T. undertakes an extensive UK education programme and sponsors a variety of young adult and professional scholarships in Israel. *Bd.:* Bronwen Lady Astor, Peter Levy (co-chair), Hon. Gerard Noel, Peter Oppenheimer, Rev. Dr. Isaac Levy, O.B.E., Harold Berwin, David Kaye, The Hon. Adrianne Marks (co-chair), Viscount Tonypandy, Carole Conrich; *Dir.* J. D. A. Levy.

FRIENDS OF THE JERUSALEM COLLEGE OF TECHNOLOGY
P.O. Box 9700, London NW6 1WF.
☎/Fax 0171-435 5501.
(Est. 1971. Reg. Charity No.: 263003). To promote the interests of the College and to support its charitable work. To endow and contribute towards campus projects and to further the work of development and research. *Chairman* R. Sherrington; T. H. Kramer.

FRIENDS OF JERUSALEM RUBIN ACADEMY OF MUSIC
11 Radnor Mews, W2 2SA.
☎ 0171-402 3167. Fax: 0171-706 3045.
To provide scholarships for talented children and to help in providing musical instruments, publications, etc. *Jt. Chairmen* Manja Leigh, Lilian Hochhauser.

FRIENDS OF MAGEN DAVID ADOM IN GREAT BRITAIN
Pearl House, 746 Finchley Road, NW11 7TH.
☎/Fax 0181-381 4849. Fax: 0181-381 4898.
(Reg. Charity No. 210770) To assist the work of Israel's voluntary emergency medical and national ambulance services which are responsible for supplying and maintaining first-aid posts and casualty stations, national blood services, medical wing of Israel Civil Defence, medical care of immigrants, missing persons bureaux, beach rescue stations , national responsibility for First-Aid training and all the other services usually supplied by a Red Cross Society.
Nat. Chairman Prof G. Westbury; *V. Chairman* Alan Michaelson; *H. T.* Alan N. Gainsford, F.C.A.; *Exec. Dir.* Moshe Portnoy.
Groups in many districts of London and the Regions.

FRIENDS OF THE MIDRASHIA
79 Princes Park Avenue, London NW11 0JS.
☎ 0171-515 9355. Fax: 0171-987 8719.
The British Commonwealth and Eire Cttee. was est. in 1952 to aid the Midrashia, the boys' boarding schools at Pardess Hana and Kfar Saba with over 1,000 pupils. (Reg. Charity No. 285047) *Founder* The late Dr. J. Braude; *Chairman* A. J. Braude.

FRIENDS OF PROGRESSIVE JUDAISM IN ISRAEL AND EUROPE
The Montagu Centre, 21 Maple Street, W1P 6DS.
☎ 0171-637 7442.
(Reg. Charity No. 241337) *Admin.* Neil Drapkin.

FRIENDS OF YAD SARAH
(Reg. Charity No. 294801). Yad Sarah, a volunteer operated home care organization, lends free, regular and hi-tech medical rehabilitative equipment and provides a spectrum of home care supportive services. Services available to tourists. Head offices, Jerusalem; 77 branches in Israel. *Trustee* D.S. Davis, c/o Cohen Arnold & Co., 13-17 New Burlington Place, London W1X 2JP. ☎ 0171-734 1362. Fax: 0171-434 1117.

HADASSAH MEDICAL RELIEF ASSOCIATION UK
26 Enford Street, London W1H 2DD.

☎ 0171-723 1144. Fax: 0171-723 1222.
(Est. 1986. Reg. Charity No. 1040848) Committed to fund-raising and promoting the work of the Hadassah medical organisation, Hebrew Univ. Med. Centre at Ein Kerem and the Hadassah Univ. Hosp. on Mt. Scopus in Jerusalem. *H.President* Lady Wolfson; *Chairman* Juliet Dalwood; *Hon. Sec.* Ruth David; *H.T.* Jonathan Prevezer; *Exec. Dir.* Norman Brodie.

HOLYLAND PHILATELIC SOCIETY
(form. British Association of Palestine Israel Philatelists)
(Est. 1952.) For the study and encouragement of all branches of the philately of Palestine and the State of Israel, and of other countries connected with the postal history of the territory form. known as Palestine. *H. Sec.* M. S. Davies, 3 St. Mary's Parsonage, Manchester, M3 2RD. ☎ 0161-832 3434. Fax: 0161-832 6650.

ISRAEL ACTION
Sternberg Centre for Judaism, Manor House, 80 East End Road, N3 2SY.
☎ 0181-349 4731. Fax: 0181-343 0901. Email: refsyn.org.uk
(Est. 1989.) Aims to create knowledge and love of Israel through theology, education and Israel action by raising Israel consciousness within the Reform Movement. *Co-Chairmen* Paul Langsford, Paul Usiskin; *Israel Desk* Pam Lewis.

ISRAEL DISCOUNT BANK LTD.
ISRAEL DISCOUNT BANK OF NEW YORK
(UK Representative Office) Suite 9, 22 Grosvenor Sq., W1X 0DY.
☎ 0171-499 1444. Fax. 0171-499 1414.
Israel Discount Bank Ltd. (est. 1935) is one of the three largest banks in Israel. The Bank offers, in Israel, a complete range of domestic and international banking services.
Israel Discount Bank of New York is the largest Israeli-owned bank operating overseas. It offers a full range of domestic and international banking services. *UK Rep.* Ilan Hadani.

ISRAEL GOVERNMENT TOURIST OFFICE
UK House, 180 Oxford Street, London W1N 0EL. ☎ 0171-299 1111. Fax. 0171-299 1112. (Est. 1954.) *Dir.* Eliezer Hod.
The office can provide a list of events making the Fiftieth Anniversary celebrations – Hatikvah 23, December 1997 – December 1998.

ISRAEL–JUDAICA STAMP CLUB
(formerly Judaica Philatelic Society)
☎ 0181-886 9331. Fax: 0181-886 5116.
A committee of the JNF and a ZF affiliate. Services collectors of the Jewish theme in philately; promotes KKL/JNF labels, Jewish education through philately, commemorative covers, and production of the Journal, the Judaica Collector, including an alphabetical listing of Jews and their achievements honoured on stamps world wide. Also illustrated lectures on this theme. *President* M. Persoff, M.A., F.R.S.A.; *Chairman* C. H. Rosen, F.B.C.O.; *Vice Chairman* A. Field; *Sec.* S. Kosky; T. E. Pollard; *Mem. Sec.* R. Slayer; *Jt. Eds*, The Israel–Judaica Collector, F. Knoller, E. Sugerman.

ISRAEL PHILATELIC AGENCY IN GREAT BRITAIN
P.O. Box 5, Watford, Herts. WD2 5SW. ☎ 01923-475555. Fax: 01923-475556.
Official Agents of the Philatelic Service, Israel Postal Authority, Tel Aviv-Yafo, Israel, for the distribution and promotion of postage stamps and related products of Israel (in the United Kingdom).
Agency Man. Mrs Pauline Cummins on behalf of Harry Allen (International Philatelic Agencies).

OTHER ORGANISATIONS CONCERNED WITH ISRAEL 33

JEWISH BLIND IN ISRAEL ASSOCIATION
c/o K. C. Keller F.C.A., Lynwood House, 373/375 Station Road, Harrow, Middx. HA1 2AW.
☎ 0181-863 2727. Fax 0181-863 2626.
(Reg. Charity No. 1006756) Provides financial support and equipment to the Jewish registered blind in Israel. *Adv:* Prof. Lutza Yanko & Prof. Eliezer D. Jaffe, Dr Ben-Zion Silverstone (Jerusalem), Joseph S. Conway, F.R.C.S. (London). *Chairman* Dr J. Saper.

LABOUR FRIENDS OF ISRAEL
BM LFI, London, WC1N 3XX.
☎ 0171-222 4323. Fax: 0171-222 4324.
To present the facts of the Middle East situation; To build bridges of understanding between the British and Israeli Labour Movements; To encourage study groups and visits to Israel, To welcome Israeli Labour representatives the UK. To forge strong links between the Jewish community and the British Labour Party.
Chairman Jane Kennedy, MP; *Dep. Chair* Mike Gapes, MP; *V. Chairs* Ivor Caplin, MP, Ivan Lewis, MP, Jim Murphy, MP, Stephen Twigg, MP; *Dir.* Nick Cosgrove.

LIBERAL DEMOCRAT FRIENDS OF ISRAEL
c/o 318 Whitchurch Lane, Canons Park, Edgware, Middlesex. ☎ 0181-952 8987. or 31 The Vale, London NW11 8SE. ☎ 0181-455 5140.
Open to all supporters of the Liberal Democrats in UK who recognise the right of Israel to a free, independent, permanent and prosperous existence as a member state of the United Nations. The Assoc. exists to foster good relations and understanding between Britain and state of Israel.
President Lord Jacobs; *V.Presidents* Alan Beith, MP, Alex Carlise, QC; *Chairman* Monroe Palmer, O.B.E.; *Sec.* David Lerner.

LIFELINE FOR THE OLD
6 Charlton Lodge, Temple Fortune Lane, NW11 7TY.
☎ 0181-455 9059.
(Reg. Charity No. 232084). to assist the work of Lifeline for the Old in Jerusalem, which aims to relieve poverty among the aged in Israel by providing training in occupational skills, and improve the welfare and quality of life of Jerusalem's elderly and disabled. *President* Mrs N. Winton; *Hon. Sec.* Miss J. Mitzman. *Leeds Branch: Chairman* Mrs A. Ziff.

MEDICAL AID COMMITTEE FOR ISRAEL
MAC-I: Reg. Charity No. 258697.
c/o 69 Hampstead Way, London NW11 7LG.
(Est. May 1969.) To provide med. and lab. equipment and offer techn. and prof. advice. To admin. Lewis Fellowships Fund (LFF) for post grad. study & exper. in Brit. hosp. & in the community. To assist and promote health and welfare projects in Israel. Applications from the Director Inter. Relations, Israel Min. of Health, 2 Ben Tabai Street, Jerusalem 93591. Dr. Lionel P. Balfour-Lynn, M.A., M.D., D.C.H.(Camb.).

NEW ISRAEL FUND
26 Enford St., W1H 2DD.
☎ 0171-724 2266. Fax: 0171-724 2299. Email: NIF@ort.org
(Est. 1992. Reg. Charity No. 1060081) The New Israel Fund awards grants to citizens' initiatives working to strengthen democracy and support social justice in these areas: civil and human rights, improving the status of women, Jewish–Arab co-existence, religious pluralism and tolerance, bridging social and economic gaps and environmental justice. Through SHATIL, its capacity-building centre for

social-change organisations, NIF also promotes action by coalitions of like-minded organisations. *Chief Exec.* Anna Josse.

OPERATION WHEELCHAIRS COMMITTEE
34/36 Maddox Street, London W1R 9PD.
☎ 0171-495 8849. Fax: 0171-495 8859.
(Est. 1970. Reg. Charity No. 263089) Voluntary organisation providing rehabilitation and general medical equipment and handmaster units to hospitals in Israel treating wounded soldiers. *Founder* Mrs. Lily Perry; *Chairman* Mrs. Anita Alexander-Passe.

POALE AGUDAT ISRAEL
Unites Orthodox religious workers to build up Eretz Yisrael in the spirit of the Torah.
World Central Off.: 64 Frishman Street, Tel Aviv. *President* Rabbi A. Werdiger.
European Office and Great Britain: P.A.I. Ho., 2A Alba Gardens, NW11 9NR.
☎/Fax 0181-458 5372. *Chairman* F. Wolkenfeld; *Corr.* D. Winter. *Publ.*: PAI Views.

STATE OF ISRAEL BONDS
Development Company for Israel (UK) Ltd.
34A North End Road, NW11 7PT.
☎ 0181-458 6559. Fax: 0181-455 6408.
(Est. 1981.) Promotes and sells State of Israel Bonds (Israel's gilt-edged securities). *Managing Dir.* Jack Gilenberg-Gilboa; *Sales Dir. UK* F. Knoller; *Comp. Sec.* G.B.S. Hausmann.

TEHILLA
Balfour House, 741 High Road, North Finchley, N12 0BQ.
☎ 0181-446 1477 Ext 2273. Fax: 0181-446 4419.
Tehilla is a non-political voluntary organisation dedicated to encouraging Aliyah and providing the support services needed by religious Jews coming to live in Israel.
U.K. Director:

TEL AVIV UNIVERSITY TRUST
1 Bentinck Street, W1M 5RN.
☎ 0171-487 5280. Fax: 0171-224 3908.
(Reg. Charity No. 314179) The principal aim of the Trust is to raise funds to promote the work of Tel Aviv University and to encourage support for academic projects, scholarships and campus development. The Trust also advises those who may wish to study at the University. *H. Presidents* Lord and Lady Wolfson, Sir Leslie and Dame Shirley Porter; *Chairman* John Porter.

TRADE UNION FRIENDS OF ISRAEL
BM LFI, London, WC1N 3XX.
☎ 0171-222 4323. Fax: 0171-222 4324.
To create and foster fraternal links between the Histadrut and the British Trade Union Movement; To educate and promote within the British Trade Union Movement the State of Israel and the Histadrut; To encourage study groups and delegations to visit Israel; to initiate dialogue between British Trade Union Movements and their Israeli counterparts.
Hon. Chairman Gavid Laird; *Dir.*; *Admin.* Suzanne Weiniger.

UK SOCIETY FOR THE PROTECTION OF NATURE IN ISRAEL
(Reg. Charity No. 327268)
25 Lyndale Avenue, London NW2 2QB.
☎ 0171-435 6803. Fax: 0171-794 0291. Email: FO1_ASG@msn.com

EDUCATIONAL AND CULTURAL ORGANISATIONS

(Est. 1986.) To generate interest in the beauty of Israel's natural landscapes; muster support for the conservation lobby in Israel. *Trs.* Godfrey Bradman, Edward Goldsmith, John D. A. Levy, Bob Lewin, Bill Oddie.

UNITED MIZRAHI BANK LTD.
Finsbury House, 23 Finsbury Circus, EC2M 7UB.
☎ 0171-360 3800. Fax. 0171-360 3810.
Br. of United Mizrahi Bank in Israel. *Gen. Man.* David Halperin.

WEIZMANN INSTITUTE FOUNDATION
Accurist House, 44 Baker St., P.O. Box 2282, London W1A 1NW.
☎ 0171-486 3954. Fax: 0171-268 2629. Email: 106042, ss@compuserve.com
(Est. 1956. Reg. Charity No. 232666) To stimulate financial, scientific and cultural support in the UK for the Weizmann Institute of Science in Rehovot. *Chairman of Exec. Cttee.* Hon. David Sieff; *Vice Chairman* Mrs V. Duffield, C.B.E.; *H. Sec.* J. O'Neill; *H.T.* Robert Glatter; *Exec. Dir.* Martha Schlesinger.

EDUCATIONAL AND CULTURAL ORGANISATIONS

Hebrew and Religion Classes are attached to most synagogues listed.
For University Centres and Institutions see p.43.

AGENCY FOR JEWISH EDUCATION
Education Resource Centre, 44a Albert Road, NW4 2SJ.
☎ 0181-203 6799. Fax: 0181-202 4668. E-mail: usbre@ibmpcug.co.uk
Training, resourcing and servicing full and part-time education community in Britain. Also organises Jewish Youth Study Group activities for teenagers through local and Israel based programmes.
Chief Exec. Simon Goulden; *Dir. Education.* Jeffrey Leader; *Chairman of Governors:* Jonathan Fine.

ASSOCIATION OF JEWISH TEACHERS
c/o Education Dept., Board of Deputies, Commonwealth House, 1-19 New Oxford St., London WC1A 1NF.
☎ 0171-543 5400. Fax 0171-543 0010.
(Est. 1986.) To promote, enhance and support the welfare and professional development of Jewish teachers in schools. *Chairman* Mrs Marilyn Nathan; *V. Chairman* Mrs D. Singer; *Publ.:* The Guide to Jewish Educational Resources.

ASSOCIATION OF ORTHODOX JEWISH PROFESSIONALS OF GREAT BRITAIN
53 Wentworth Road, NW11 0RT.
(Est. 1962.) To promote research in matters of common interest, and the general acceptance of Torah and Halacha as relevant and decisive in all aspects of modern life and thought. *President* Prof C. Domb; *Chairman* H. J. Adler.

BETH SHALOM HOLOCAUST MEMORIAL CENTRE
Laxton, Newark, Notts NG22 0PA.
☎ 01623-836627. Fax 01623-836647.
(Est. 1978 (as Beth Shalom Ltd.) Reg. Charity No. 509022). Holocaust education and commemoration. *Dir.* Stephen D. Smith, James M. Smith, Mrs Marina H. Smith.

CENTRE FOR JEWISH EDUCATION (CJE)
Sternberg Centre for Judaism, 80 East End Road, Finchley N3 2SY.
☎ 0181-343 4303. Fax: 0181-349 0694. Email: 106064.517@Compuserve.com
The Central Education Agency for the Progressive Movements offering teacher

training, community/family education, Hebrew programming, book service, offering a purchasing service for text books for schools, and three Resource Centres. Consultants are available to visit communities and offer programmes around the country. Established in 1987, amalgamating the RSGB Dept. of Education, ULPS Dept. of Education and Leo Baeck College Teacher Training Dept. *Dir.* Dr Michael J. Shire; *Admin.* Suzanne Ophir; *Chairman of Tr.* Rose Segal. **Branches:** Sternberg Centre Resource Centre, 80 East End Road, Finchley N3 2SY. ☎ 0181-343 4303. Fax: 0181-349 0694; Peggy Lang Resource Centre & Book Service, Montagu Centre, 21 Maple Street, W1P 6DS. ☎ 0171-580 0214. Fax: 0171-436 4184; Northern Resource & Learning Centre, Jackson's Row, Manchester M2 5WD. ☎ 0161-831 7092. Fax: 0161-839 4865.

CENTRE FOR THE STUDY OF JUDAISM AND JEWISH-CHRISTIAN RELATIONS
Central House, Selly Oak Colleges, Bristol Road, Birmingham B29 6LQ.
☎ 0121-472 4231. Fax: 0121-472 3206.
(Reg. Charity No. 328170) The centre offers lectures and programmes and courses in Jewish–Christian relations. The centre's projects roots are designed to satisfy the need for an understanding of Judaism and Jewish–Christian relations in the past and present. There is a special emphasis on theological colleges dioceses and other church bodies and also on schools and other educational bodies. *Chairman* Mrs E. Ferguson; *V. Chairman* Revd Eric Allen.

DAVAR, The Jewish Institute in Bristol
1/3 Percival Road, Clifton, Bristol, BS8 3LF.
☎/Fax: 0117-970 6594.
Email: davar@telecall.co.uk.URL:http://www.telecall.co.uk/~davar/davar.html
DAVAR was established in 1995 to provide a wide programme of cultural, educational and social activities for the Jewish community in Bristol and the South-West. A regular newsletter is available, free-of-charge, and Jewish groups in the area are encouraged to use the DAVAR mailing list to advertise their own events. *Chairman* David Prashker. *Admin.* Roz Wallace.

DVAR YERUSHALAYIM (London Jewish Academy)
24 Templars Avenue, NW11 0NS. Tel/Fax: 0181-455 8631.
(Est. 1978. Reg. Charity No. 284740) To provide full- and part-time courses in adult education to enable men and women of limited Jewish knowledge and background to further their understanding of Jewish thought and practice. *Princ.* Rabbi J. Freilich, Ph.C.

EVENING INSTITUTE OF ULPS
The Montagu Centre, 21 Maple Street, W1P 6DS.
☎ 0171-580 1663. Fax: 0171-436 4184. Email: montagu@ulps.demon.co.uk
The ULPS Evening Institute has been affirming the importance of continuing Jewish education for 35 years by providing people, whatever their age and background, with the opportunity to study Judaism and Hebrew at all levels. Courses are held on Mondays during the academic year and include the annual Rabbi Dr. David Goldstein Lecture. *Principal* Rabbi Stephen Howard.

FRIENDS OF YIDDISH
Contact Chaim Neslen, 232 Cranbrook Road, Ilford, Essex IG1 4UT. ☎ 0181-554 6112.
We meet every Saturday afternoon at Toynbee Hall, nr Aldgate East Tube Station, from 3 to 4.30pm. Our programme is (almost) entirely in Yiddish, and includes readings, live music and some discussion in a friendly and relaxed environment. Special events are advertised in the Jewish press.

HOLOCAUST EDUCATIONAL TRUST
BCM Box 7892, WC1N 3XX.
☎ 0171-222 6822/5853.
(Est. 1988.) To promote research into the Holocaust and the collection of archival materials and artifacts of the Holocaust period and the production of written and audio-visual materials. Also to promote teaching of the Holocaust in schools and assist individuals and orgs. involved in Holocaust educ. *Patrons* Prof. Elie Wiesel, The Lord Jakobovits, His Grace the Duke of Norfolk, The Rt. Rev. Lord Runcie; *President* Lord Sainsbury; *Chairman* Lord Janner, Q.C.; *Sec.* Sir Ivan Lawrence Q.C.; *Ts.* The Rt. Hon. Lord Merlyn Rees, David Sumberg; *Jt. Ts.* Martin Paisner; *Bd. of Man.* David Gryn, Kitty Hart, Ben Helfgott, Jonathan Kestenbaum, Paul Phillips and Martin Savitt; *Dir.* Jon Mendelsohn; *Assoc. Dir.* Janice Lopatkin; *Admin. Dir.* Danielle Rinberg.
British Video Archive for Holocaust Testimonies: *Admin:* Alberta Strage.

ISRAEL FOLK DANCE INSTITUTE
Balfour House, 741 High Road, London N12 0BQ.
Daytime tel/fax: 0181-446 6427. Evening tel/fax: 0181-445 6765.
(Reg Charity No. 279801) The Institute is an educational charity whose main work is in promoting Jewish and Israeli Cultural Heritage through the medium of song and dance. Recipient of the 13th Annual Award of the All-Party Parliamentary Committee for Soviet Jewry and the Chief Rabbi's Award for Excellence, 1995. The Institute has produced materials in both English and Russian, holds training seminars and runs classes for children, youth and adults. It is totally independent and has no political affiliation. *Chairman and Hon. Director:* Maurice Stone.

ISRAEL ZANGWILL FELLOWSHIP
(Est. 1954.) To perpetuate the memory of Israel Zangwill and to foster an appreciation and understanding of his works.
H. Sec. Harry S. Ward, 97 Shirehall Pk., NW4 2QU.

ISRAEL ZANGWILL MEMORIAL FUND
c/o Manor House Tr., Sternberg Centre For Judaism, 80 East End Road, N3 2SY.
☎ 0181-346-2288.
(Est. 1929.) To assist poor Jews engaged in literary, artistic, dramatic and scientific work.

JAT: THE JERUSALEM ACADEMY TRUST
Office: 1007 Finchley Road, NW11 7HB
☎ 0181-458 8563. Fax: 0171-431 3593
(Reg. Charity No. 262716) London Cttee: *Jt. Chairman* A. Maslo, B. Com., F.C.A., and M. A. Sprei, M.A. (Cantab), M. Sc. V. *Chairman* M. A. Toperoff. *Hon. G. S. Polikoff, LL.B. Hon. Sec.* C Cohen, B.A. *Patrons:* Chief Rabbi Dr Jonathan Sacks, Chief Rabbi Emeritus Lord I. Jakobovits, B.A., Ph.D., Rabbi J. Dinner, Dayan M. Fisher; Principal Rabbi B. Horovitz, M.A.; *President* Walter I. Hubert; *Vice Principal* Rabbi Aryeh Carmell, B. Sc.; *Exec. Dir.* Moshe Kahan.

JEWISH BOOK COUNCIL
28 Norfolk Road, NW8 6AU.
☎ 0171-722-7925.
(Est. 1947. Reg. Charity No. 293800) To stimulate and encourage the reading of books on Judaism and on every aspect of Jewish thought, life, history and literature; organizes annual Jewish Book Week, now Europe's largest Jewish bookfair, and associated events. *President* Mrs. M. R. Lehrer, M.A.(Oxon); *Chairman* Mrs. M. J. Cohen, M.Phil.; *H. Tr.* E. Grodzinski F.C.A.; *H. Sec.* R. Tager, Q.C. *Admin:* Mrs R. Goldstein.

JEWISH CHRONICLE
25 Furnival Street, London EC4A 1JT.
☏ 0171-415 1500. Fax: 0171-405 9040. Website: www.jchron.co.uk
(Est. 1841.) The world's oldest independent Jewish weekly newspaper.
Chairman Lionel Gordon; *Edr.* Mr. Ned Temko.

JEWISH COMMUNITY THEATRE
Reg. Charity No.: 1000187.
157 Denmark Hill, London SE5 8EH.
☏ 0171-737 4361.
To advance, develop and maintain public education and awareness of the history of British Jews by the presentation at theatres and other suitable venues of plays reflecting the cultural identity of Anglo-Jewry. Est. 1990. *Chairman* Ruth Franklin, 157 Denmark Hill, SE5 8EH; *Sec.* Freda Raingold, 1 Rosecroft Walk, Crawford Avenue, Wembley HA0 2JZ; *T.* Stephen Ross, 9 Orchard Avenue, N3 3NL.

JEWISH EDUCATION AID SOCIETY
(Est. 1896.) To investigate and advise on cases of highly talented students and in certain circumstances to provide interest-free loans to enable them to train for professions or the pursuit of art. Now under the administration of Anglo-Jewish Association (see p.3).

JEWISH EDUCATIONAL DEVELOPMENT TRUST
44 Albert Road, NW4 2SJ.
☏ 0181-203 6427. Fax 0181-203 6420.
(Est. 1971.) To promote Jewish educ., teacher training and the development of the day school network relating to all sections of the com. *President* The Chief Rabbi; *V. President* Sir Trevor Chinn, C.V.O.; *Chairman* Michael Phillips; *T.* Ronald Metzger.

JEWISH FILM FOUNDATION
c/o 46a Minster Road, London NW2 3RD.
The Jewish Film Foundation is an educational charity whose aim is to promote the exhibition, distribution, production and study of Jewish cinema, television and video programmes. It initiates and co-ordinates education and cultural activities involving film and video and advises those who make and use programmes on Jewish themes. Organises an annual Jewish Film Festival in London. *Bd. of Dir.* Michael Green, Dorothy Berwin, Jonathan Davis, Dominique Green, Jeremy Isaacs, Verity Lambert, Michael May, Louis Marks, Alan Yentob; *Prog. Dir.* Sam Maser.

JEWISH GENEALOGICAL SOCIETY OF GREAT BRITAIN
Membership: 2 Milton Close, London N2 0QH.
Genealogical enquiries: 14 St Helens Road, Alverstoke, Gosport, Hants, PO12 2RN.
(Est. 1992. Reg. Charity No. 1022738). To promote and encourage the study of Jewish geneaology on a secular basis. The Society organises lectures, seminars and family history workshops (including those at The London Museum of Jewish Life at the Sternberg Centre); publishes *Shemot*, a quarterly journal; promotes rsearch; and is building up a library. *V. Presidents* Dr Anthony Joseph, David Jacobs; *Chairman* George Anticoni; *Sec. and Membership* Anthony Winner; *T.* David Weingott; *Northern Groups* Janina Hochland; *Scottish Group* Harvey Kaplan; *South West Group* Alan Tobias; *South Coast Group* Geoffrey Keene.

JEWISH HISTORICAL SOCIETY OF ENGLAND
33 Seymour Place, W1H 5AP.
☏/Fax 0171-723 5852. E-mail: jhse@dircon.co.uk

(Est. 1893. Reg. Charity No. 217331) *President* Malcolm Brown; *H. T.* Alexander Rosenzweig; *H. Sec.* Cyril Drukker; *Admin.* Jeanette Cannon; Branches: **Birmingham:** *Chairman* Dr. Anthony Joseph, 25 Westbourne Road, Edgbaston, Birmingham B15 3TX; **Leeds:** *President* Judge Arthur Myerson QC, 20 Sandmoor Lane, LS17 7EA; **Liverpool:** *Chairman* Dr. Mervyn Goodman, 1 Hornby Lane, Liverpool L18 3HH; **Manchester:** *Chairmen* Dr. and Mrs. L. A. Kirk, 54 Waterpark Rd., Salford M7 4JL.

JEWISH MUSIC HERITAGE TRUST LTD.
PO Box 232, Harrow, Middx, HA1 2NN.
☎ 0181-909 2445. Fax: 0181-909 1030. Email: jewishmusic@jmht.org
(Reg. Charity No.: 328228) The Jewish Music Heritage Trust promotes study and performance of Jewish music to preserve this great heritage and teach it to successive generations.
Activities include:
Bnai Brith Jewish Music Festival: a biennial, month-long festival featuring concerts, recitals, workshops, masterclasses, lectures, Yiddish theatre and comedy; in major concert halls in London and around the country.
Commissioning of new Jewish Music.
Jewish Music Heritage Centre: supplies information and resources including recordings and sheet music, as well as related books, videos and other items to the media, educational establishments and general public.
Joe Loss Lectureship in Jewish Music at City University, London.
Jewish Music Heritage Recordings: Production of CDs and cassettes featuring music of special Jewish interest.
Gregori Schechter's Klezmer Festival Band: Founding and promotion of band for concerts and functions.
Klezmer Classes: Teaching sessions for youth and adults.
Trust and Festival Dir.: Mrs Geraldine Auerbach

KESHER – THE LEARNING CONNECTION
28 St Albans Lane, London NW11 7QE.
☎ 0181-455 2515. Fax: 0181-455 6656. Email: rsimon@kesher.org.uk
(Est. 1997. Reg Charity no. 1061689) Jewish Education and Outreach to singles and young couples. Reconnecting Jews of all backgrounds with their heritage. *Sec.* Mrs E. Cohen.

LEO BAECK COLLEGE
The Sternberg Centre for Judaism, 80 East End Road, N3 2SY.
☎ 0181-349 4525. Fax: 0181-343 2558. Email: Leo.Baeck.College@mailbox.ulcc.ac.uk
(Est. 1956. Reg. Charity no. 209777) Established for the study of Judaism and the training of rabbis and teachers. Under the joint auspices of the Reform Syns. of Gt. Britain and the Union of Liberal and Progressive Syns.
   President Prof. J. B. Segal; *V. Presidents* Rabbi Dr. A. H. Friedlander, Rabbi John Rayner; *Chairman* Willie Kessler; *Princ.* Rabbi Prof. J. Magonet; *Dean* Rabbi Dr. A. H. Friedlander; *Registrar* J. Olbrich.
   A five-year programme leads to Rabbinic Ordination; the College offers full-time and part-time B.A. (Hons.) in Jewish Studies, a one-year M.A., as well as Open Univ. M. Phil and D. Phil degrees.
   Chairman of Acad. B. Rabbi Prof. J. Magonet; *Lecturers* Rabbi L. Blue, Dr P. van Boxel, Rabbi C. Eimer, S. Gold, Rabbi Dr A. H. Friedlander, Mrs A. Kershen, R. Landau, H. Maccoby, Rabbi J. Neuberger, Rabbi J. Rayner, Dr E. Seidel, Rabbi S. Sheridan, Rabbi M. Solomon, Rabbi S. Shulman, Dr J. Weinberg, Rabbi C. Wiener, Rabbi A. Wright, Rabbi J. Wittenberg.

LEO BAECK INSTITUTE
4 Devonshire Street, W1N 2BH.
☎ 0171-580 3493.
Est. in 1955 (Reg. Charity No. 235163) for research and publications on history of Central European German-speaking Jewry. Organises conferences and seminars. *Chairman* Prof. Werner E. Mosse; *Dir.* Dr. A. Paucker. *Publ.:* Year Book (*Edr.* Prof. J. A. S. Grenville), symposia, monographs, etc.

LIMMUD
PO Box 13284, London N3 2WB.
☎/Fax: 0181-349 1154. E-mail: limmud@dial.pipex.com
(Reg. Charity No. 327111) Limmud is an innovative and thematic organisation. the main event Limmud organises is its annual 5-day residential Conference in December. In 1996, the Conference hosted close to 1,000 participants. In addition to the Conference, there are annual Leadership Development Days and Regional Days; a Family Conference is planned for August 1998. Limmud is in the process of developing a curriculum for the first-ever communal, thematic and systematic weekly learning course in the Anglo-Jewish community. The course will begin in January 1998. Limmud's sister organisation in the USA is CAJE, the Coalition for the Advancement of Jewish Education, whose annual conference in August Limmud also seeks to promote..
Chairperson Andrew Gilbert; *Conference Co-Chairs* Micah Gold, Jonny Persey, Marc Soloway; T. Graham Newman; *Development Chairs* Jack Gilbert, Naomi Cohen; *Fundraising Chair* Josh Levy; *Officer Worker* Zahavit Shalev.

LITTMAN LIBRARY OF JEWISH CIVILIZATION
PO Box 645, Oxford OX2 6AS. ☎/Fax: 01235-868104.
(Est. 1965. Reg. Charity No. 1000784) Established for the purpose of publishing scholarly works aimed at disseminating an understanding of the Jewish heritage and Jewish history and making Jewish religious thought and literary creativity accessible to the English-speaking world. *Dirs.* Mrs. C. C. Littman, R. J. Littman. *Contacts:* Connie Webber (Editorial); Ludo Craddock (Marketing & Admin.).

LONDON ACADEMY OF JEWISH STUDIES
2-4 Highfield Avenue, NW11 9ET.
☎ 0181-455 5938; 0181-458 1264.
Instit. for Rabbinics est. in 1975 to assist post-Yeshiva students to further their Jewish educ. and engage in advanced Talmudic res. Graduates are expected to take up rabbinical and teaching posts in the com. The Kolel also serves as a Torah-study centre for laymen. Its specialised library is open to the gen. public throughout the year incl. Shabbat and Yom Tov. *H. Princ.* Rabbi G. Hager.

MANOR HOUSE MEDIA
c/o Old School, High Street, Elstree, Herts WD6 3BY. ☎ 0181-386 9461. Fax: 0181-386 9462.
☎ 0181-343 4303. Fax: 0181-386 9462.
(Est. 1980.) MHM specialises in work for the Jewish Community using slides, audio and video media and cd-rom from its studio and two editing suites. Tenders for project design and production.
Contact J. M. Black.

MASORTI ACADEMY
1097 Finchley Rd., NW11 0PU.
☎ 0181-201 8772. Fax 0181-201 8917. Email: Masorti.uk@ort.org
Provides adult education in a number of different formats, offering seminars, evening classes, distance learning courses, residential study events and lectures, all

within the Masorti context of open-minded enquiry within a spirit of authentic traditional Judaism. *Dir.* Harry Freedman.

MICHAEL GOULSTON EDUCATIONAL FOUNDATION
Sternberg Centre for Judaism, Manor House, 80 East End Road, N3 2SY.
☎ 0181-343 4303. Fax: 0181-349 0694.
Est. 1972 in memory of Rabbi Michael Goulston to pub. Jewish educ. materials, including books, audio visuals and study programmes. *Dir.* Dr Michael J. Shire.

POLACK'S HOUSE, CLIFTON COLLEGE
1 Percival Road, Bristol BS8 3LF.
☎ 0117 9737634.
(Reg. Charity No. 1040218) Polack's House at Clifton College has provided boarding facilities and Jewish education since 1878,. Now reconstituted as the Polack's House Educational Trust it houses Jewish boys aged 13-18 within the House, and provides Jewish education and kosher meals for Jewish boys and girls aged 8-18, fully integrated into Clifton College. *Housemaster* Jo Greenbury; *Dir.* David Prashker.

PROJECT SEED EUROPE
Middlesex House, 29-45 High Street, Edgware, Middx, HA8 7UU.
☎ 0181-381 1555. Fax: 0181-381 1666.
London contacts: Mr Bobby Hill
(Est. 1980. Reg. Charity No. 281307) To provide Jewish adult educ. on a one-to-one teacher-student basis in communal study hall and regular weekend seminars for families and singles in January, May, August and December. *Dir.* Rabbi J. Grunfeld.
Weekly study sessions in Greater London: Men & Women in the following areas: Barnet, Edgware, Finchley/HGS, Kenton, Maida Vale, Mill Hill, Muswell Hill, Pinner, Ilford, Southgate, Stamford Hill/Tottenham. Men only: Belmont, Chigwell, Golders Green, Kingsbury, Wembley. Women only: Bushey, Hendon.
Weekly study sessions in the Regions: Men & Women in the following areas: Bury, Prestwich, Whitefield, Fallowfield, Glasgow, Leeds, Liverpool, Newcastle. Men only: Sunderland.

RSGB STUDENTS
The Sternberg Centre for Judaism, 80 East End Road, Finchley, London N3 2SY.
☎ 0181-349 4731 ext. 107; 346 2288. Fax: 0181-343 4972. Email: students.rsgb@ort.org
Provides rabbinic support, and political and cultural information for Progressive Jewish students on numerous campuses. Supports Jewish student groups and religious seminars. Cultivates Jewish–Arab student dialogue. Publishes NewsWatch, a religious and political news and information service via the Email. Contact the Student Co-ordinator for further details.

SCOPUS JEWISH EDUCATIONAL TRUST (formerly ZFET)
Balfour House, 741 High Road, N12 0BQ.
☎ 0181-343 9228. Fax: 0181-343 7309.
(Est. 1953. Reg. Charity No. 313154) To raise funds by way of endowment, legacy, bequest, gift or donation in order to provide a first class education in Jewish Studies and Hebrew throughout its national network of 14 day schools all of which have a Zionist ethos and emphasize the centrality of Israel in Jewish life. *Chairman* Peter Ohrenstein F.C.A; *H.T.* Philip Goodman, B.A., A.C.A.; *Hon. Sec.* Brenda Hyman; Schools: **London**: Harry & Abe Sherman Rosh Pinah School, Sebba Rosh Pinah Nursery, Mathilda Marks-Kennedy School, Ella & Ernst Frankel Kindergarten, Simon Marks School, Simon Marks Sherman Nursery, **Birmingham**: King David Primary School; **Glasgow**: Calderwood Lodge School; **Leeds**: Brodetsky Primary

and Nursery School; Deborah Taylor Playgroup; **Liverpool**: King David Kindergarten, King David Primary School, King David High School; **Manchester**: North Cheshire Primary School.

THE SEPHARDI CENTRE
2 Ashworth Road, Maida Vale, London W9 1JY.
☎/Fax 0171-266 3682.
(Reg. Charity No. 1039937.) The Sephardi Centre was opened in 1994. The Centre's aim is to promote Sephardi culture. Courses focus on Religion, History, Music, Art and Cuisine. Courses are open to all age groups and there is special programming for the Under 35's. A library and reading room specialising in Sephardi Literature is open to the public (see p.59).
Director: Rabbi Dr. Abraham Levy
For further information please contact: Michelle Shemtob, Assistant Director, The Sephardi Centre.

SOCIETY FOR JEWISH STUDY
(Est. 1946. Reg. Charity No. 283732) *Chairman* Michael Weitzman, B.Sc., Ph.D.; *Sec*. Rosemary Goldstein, 1A Church Mount, London N2 0RW. The Society's activities for the furtherance of learning and research include regular public lectures and support for the 'Journal of Jewish Studies'.

THE SPIRO INSTITUTE FOR STUDY OF JEWISH HISTORY & CULTURE
The Old House, c/o King's College, Kidderpore Avenue, NW3 7SZ.
☎ 0171-431 0345. Fax: 0171-431 0361. Email: spiro@booshie.demon.co.uk
(Est. 1978. Reg. Charity No. 1013594) To promote Jewish identity and self-awareness, the Institute engages in widespread teaching of Jewish history and culture including: literature, films, art, drama, Hebrew and Yiddish to adult classes; courses taught in secondary schools, and to others by correspondence; Holocaust education in schools and for LEAs including creation of teaching pack and accompanying video 'Lessons of the Holocaust' (with Holocaust Educational Trust and Rex Bloomstein); teacher training, preparation for GCSE and A-level in modern and biblical Hebrew; tutoring for BA Honours external degree in Jewish History at UCL; developing a Jewish film archive; public lectures and cultural events, international tours of Jewish interest. *Founding Dir*. Robin Spiro, MA, M.Phil, F.C.A.; *Dir. Cultural, Languages & Degrees* Nitza Spiro, M.Phil; *Dir. Schools, Univs, Seminars and Holocaust Studies* Trudy Gold, LLB; *Dir. Adult Educ*. Anthony Hammond, MA; *Dir. Admin*. Diana Midgen.

SPRINGBOARD EDUCATION TRUST
32 Foscote Road, London NW4 3SD.
☎ 0181-202 7147. Fax: 0181-905 4901.
(Est. 1979. Reg. Charity No. 277946). Whilst specialising in reminiscence and stimulation programmes for senior citizens, Springboard has extended its range of audio-visual and video productions to cover, at teenage and adult levels, Jewish and Zionist history, synagogue and home traditions, inter-faith projects.
Springboard also produces low-cost audio-visual/video programmes for other orgs. and provides seminars for teachers and welfare workers in the use of its programmes with substantial back-up materials.
Dirs. Aumie and Michael Shapiro.

YAKAR STUDY CENTRE
2 Egerton Gardens, NW4 4BA.
☎ 0181-202 5551/2. Fax: 0181-202 9653. Internet: http://www.yakar.demon.co.uk
(Est. 1978. Charity No. 277818) An independent Study Centre to promote Jewish

knowledge, tradition and culture, and to provide a place of learning and dialogue for people who are in search of a spiritual dimension. Educational courses, cultural events and seminars run weekly throughout the year. Also vibrant Synagogue Community. *Principal* Rabbi Dr Michael Rosen, Ph.D., Dip.Ed.; *M.* Rabbi Yehoshua Engleman; *Exec.* Rona Hart.

UNIVERSITY CENTRES AND ORGANISATIONS
(See also Organisations concerned with Jewish students on p.53, and Libraries on pp.54–59).

BRITISH ASSOCIATION FOR JEWISH STUDIES
(Est. 1975.) Membership is open to scholars concerned with the academic pursuit of Jewish studies in the British Isles. The Assoc. promotes and defends the scholarly study of Jewish culture in all its aspects and organizes an annual conference. *President* (1998): Prof. Raphael Loewe, Dept. of Hebrew & Jewish Studies University College London, WC1E 6BT. *Sec.* (1998) Dr Jonathan G. Campbell, Dept. of Theology & Religious Studies, University of Bristol, Bristol BS8 1TB. *T.* (1998) Dr Daniel Falk, Oriental Institute, Oxford, OX1 2LE.

CENTRE FOR JEWISH STUDIES (University of Leeds)
Leeds LS2 9JT. ☎ 0113-233 5197. Fax 0113-245 1977. Email: e.frojmovic@leeds.ac.uk
(Est. 1995) Teaching of Jewish Studies: taught MA in Modern Jewish Studies and supervision of research degrees. *Dir.* Dr Eva Frojmović.

CENTRE FOR JEWISH STUDIES (University of London)
School of Oriental and African Studies, Thornhaugh St., Russell Sq., WC1H 0XG.
☎ 0171-323-6089
Dir. Dr T. Parfitt.

CENTRE FOR GERMAN-JEWISH STUDIES
University of Sussex, Falmer, Brighton BN1 9QN. ☎ 01273-678495
Dir. Professor Edward Timms; *London Liaison Off.* Diana Franklin. ☎ 0181-455 4785. Fax: 0181-381 4721.

CENTRE FOR MODERN HEBREW STUDIES
Faculty of Oriental Studies, Sidgwick Ave., Cambridge CB3 9DA.
☎ 01223-335117. Fax 01223-335110.
A centre established within the University of Cambridge for the study and promotion of modern Hebrew language, literature and culture.
Hon. Dir. Dr R. Domb.

INSTITUTE OF JEWISH STUDIES
University College London, Gower Street, WC1E 6BT.
☎ 0171-380 7171. Fax: 0171-209 1026. Email: uclhvtm@uclh.ac.uk
Est. 1953 (Reg. Charity No. 213114.) by the late Prof. Alexander Altmann, located within the Dept. of Hebrew and Jewish Studies at Univ. College, London, while retaining its autonomous status. Funded by the private sector. Programme of activities dedicated to the academic study of all branches of Jewish history and civilisation, including series of public lectures, seminars, symposia, major internat. conferences, research projects and publs., especially of its conference proceedings. It brings together scholars, students, academic instits. from all sections inside and outside the Univ. of London and the scholarly scene in and outside the UK, worldwide. It equally reaches the community at large and brings scholars and the public together for regular exchange of ideas and interests. The Institute celebrated its 40th

anniversary in 1994 with a major international conference on "Aspects of Jewish Intellectual History". The theme of the 1997 conference was "The History and Culture of the Jews in the Low Countries". The 1998 conference will be on "Modern Hebrew Literature". List of publications and programme mailings available.
Patrons The Lord Mishcon, Sir Claus Moser, The Rt. Hon. The Lord Woolf; Bd. of Govs: *Chairman* Dr. Manfred Altman, Hon. Fel., Univ. College, London; *Hon. Ts.* David J. Lewis, BSc., F.R.I.C.S., Edward M.Lee, BSc (Econ), Philip L. Morgenstern, BA, Daniel Peltz, BA, Elliot E. Philipp, M.A., F.R.C.S., F.R.C.O.G., Nick Ritblat, MA; *Dir.* Prof. Mark J. Geller; *Hon. Sec.* J. Caplan, F.C.A.
The Trustees of the Institute of Jewish Studies, a non-profit making company limited by guarantee, registered in England No. 2598783.

JEWS' COLLEGE
Schaller House, Albert Road, Hendon NW4 2SJ.
☎ 0181-203 6427. Fax: 0181-203 6420.
(Est. 1855.) Educates the future teachers and leaders of the Jewish community through its BA, MA and PhD courses in Hebrew and Jewish Studies, and its rabbinical ordination and training programmes. It also houses one of the most extensive Judaica libraries in Europe which is visited regularly by scholars from around the world. The College hosts international conferences and evening lectures open to the public.
Governing Body: *President* The Chief Rabbi Dr Jonathan Sacks, MA (Cantab); *Deputy President* Rabbi Abraham Levy, BA, PhD; *Chairman* Alan Grant, BA, Clive Marks, FCA, ATII, Hon FLCM; *Ts.* Bernard Taub, Bernard Waiman, MA; *Hon. Sec.* Rabbi Edward Jackson BA.
Acting Principal Rabbi Sacha Stern, MA, D.Phil (Oxon); *Registrar* Clive Fierstone, MA; *Financial Officer* Esther Miller; *Admin.* Deborah Stanhill, BA; *Librarian* Esra Kahn.
Faculty Rabbi Elie Assis, MA; Fiona Blumfield, MA (Cantab), MA (Lon); John Fox, BSc, MSc, PhD, FRHistS; Rabbi Philip Ginsbury, MA; Harris Bor, PhD (Lon.); Dayan David C. Kaplin; Rabbi Reuven Livingstone, LLB, PgDipCPsych, PgDipLaw, MA, LLM; Rabbi Sholem Melinek, PhD; Rabbi Michael Newman, M.Phil; Rev Stephen Robins, ARCM; Rabbi Chaim S. Schmahl; Evelyn Stern, MA (Lon), MA (Cornell); Dr Michael Weitzman; Tamra Wright, MA, PhD.
Publ: Le'ela (twice yearly).

JOE LOSS LECTURESHIP IN JEWISH MUSIC
Music Dept., City Univ., Northampton Square, London EC1V 0HB.
☎ 0171-477 8283 (direct line); ☎ 0171-477 8576 (Music Dept. Fax.). Email: a.v.knapp@city.ac.uk
(Est. 1991.) Incorporates Jewish Music Resource Centre, and the Harry Rosencweig Collection of Jewish Music (see p.55). Sponsored by the Jewish Music Heritage Trust (see p.39). Research, lecturing, teaching, consultancy, and establishing City University as an international conference venue in this discipline. Studies cover the liturgical, semi-religious, folk, popular and art music of Ashkenazi, Sephardi and Oriental ethnic groups, in the context of Jewish culture, society, history, geography, language, psychology, religion and tradition (within wider Christian and Islamic environments). specialized resources comprise extensive collections of books and audio-visual materials kept in the Music Department and in the University Library.
Lect. Alexander Knapp.

UNIVERSITY CENTRES AND ORGANISATIONS 45

OXFORD CENTRE FOR HEBREW AND JEWISH STUDIES
Yarnton Manor, Yarnton, Oxford, OX5 1PY.
☎ 01865 377946. Fax 01865 375079. Email: ochjs@sable.oxford.ac.uk URL: http://associnst.ox.ac.uk/ochjs/shavuon
Additional Teaching Centre: 45 St Giles, Oxford OX1 3LP.
☎ 01865 511869/311961. Fax 01865 311791.
(Est. in 1972) The Centre is one of Europe's leading teaching and research institution in the area of Hebrew and Jewish studies. Its work includes Jewish history and literature, ancient, medieval and modern; Talmudic studies; Jewish/Islamic and Jewish/Christian relationships at all periods; Hebrew and Yiddish language; anthropology; sociology; law; and theology. It provides instruction in Jewish studies towards the Oxford University B.A., M.St., M.Phil, M.Litt and D.Phil degrees. The Centre's One-Year Graduate Programme in Jewish Studies which caters for a large and growing number of students from many countries leads to an Oxford University Diploma in Jewish Studies.

The Centre has its own faculty of 14 Fellows, the majority of whom are also Fellows of Oxford colleges and hold posts at the University. Some 20 visiting scholars come from all parts of the world each year.

Publications: Journal of Jewish Studies' (half-yearly); the Jewish Law Annual; Studies in Muslim-Jewish relations'; and numerous books and articles by Fellows past and present. The Programme of Activities, the Annual Report of the Centre and Merkaz (newsletter) are available on request. *President* Dr Bernard Wasserstein; *Chairman Bd. Gov.* Sir Richard Greenbury. (The Centre also houses the Leopold Muller Memorial Library, see p.58).

OXFORD INSTITUTE FOR YIDDISH STUDIES
Golden Cross Court, 4 Cornmarket, Oxford, OX1 3EX.
☎ 01865-798989. Fax: 01865-798987. Email: yiddishstudies@oxf-inst.demon.co.uk
(Est. 1994) The Institute is one of the world's leading centres for teaching, research and publishing in the field of Yiddish language, literature and culture. In 1996, a joint programme was initiated with the University of London to provide courses in Yiddish in the School of Oriental and African Studies.

The Institute incorporates the only Yiddish presses in Europe. Oksforder Yidish Press publishes the *Oxford Yiddish* series, scholarly works on Yiddish language and literature, and educational materials for universiyt-level study of Yiddish. Three Sisters Press publishes *Yiddish Pen*, the world's only literary monthly in Yiddish, and new books of Yiddish prose and poetry.

The Institute incorporates the Yonia Fain Collection of over one hundred paintings on East European and Holocaust motifs.

It has a full-time academic staff of three, and welcomes about a dozen visiting scholars each year. A descriptive brochure and a catalogue of publications are available on request. *Director of Projects* Marie Wright; *Academic Staff* Gennady Estraikh and Mikhail Krutikov.

QMW PROGRAMME FOR YIDDISH AND ASHKENAZIC STUDIES
Queen Mary & Westfield College, University of London, Kidderpore Avenue, London NW3 7ST.
☎ 0171-453 7141.
The Programme was primarily formed for the teaching of Yiddish language and literature towards the BA and MA degrees of London University. The Programme has expanded into the field of Ashkenazic Studies generally, including research into the history of Ashkenazic women. It hosts the weekly QMW Birnbaum Seminar, houses the Lisky Archive of East End Yiddish and has recently established its own publication series *(Editors* Dr. David Cesarani, Dr. Lewis Glinert, Dr. Devra Kay, Magdalena Pirozynska, Heather Valencia); *Dir. of Studies* Dr. Devra Kay.

SCHOOL OF ORIENTAL AND AFRICAN STUDIES (SOAS)
Dept. of the Languages and Cultures of the Near and Middle East, Thornhaugh St., Russel Sq., London WC1H OXG.
☎ 0171-637 2388. Fax 0171-436 3844. Internet: http://www.soas.ac.uk
SOAS is one of the world's greatest concentrations of expertise on Africa and Asia. The Near & Middle East Department offers a B.A. in Hebrew & Israeli Studies and degrees combining Hebrew with Law, Economics, Management, Arabic and with many other subjects – all affording a year's study at the Hebrew University of Jerusalem. The department also provides course-based M.A.s in Hebrew & Jewish Studies, Near Eastern Studies and a ground-breaking M.A. in Sephardi Studies, and research degrees in all these areas. A major new development is a Yiddish language and literature programme in partnership with the Oxford Institute for Yiddish Studies, designed for both degree students and external students. The one-year Diploma in Jewish Studies caters for postgraduates from around the world seeking an entrée into the field. These programmes have the benefit of one of the largest open-stack Jewish Studies libraries in Europe.
Also based at SOAS is the Centre for Jewish Studies, which hosts lecture series and symposia on a wide range of issues (see p.43).

STANLEY BURTON CENTRE FOR HOLOCAUST STUDIES
Dept. of History, University of Leicester, Leicester LE1 7RH.
☎ 0116-2522800 Fax: 0116-2523986
To promote the study of and research into the Holocaust. *Dir.* Steve G. Paulsson; *Hon. Assoc. Dir.* Aubrey Newman; *Hon. Res. Fellow* Dr. J. Scott.

UNIVERSITY COLLEGE LONDON
Department of Hebrew and Jewish Studies, Gower Street, WC1E 6BT.
☎ 0171-380 7171. Fax: 0171-209 1026.
The largest univ. dept. in the UK and Europe for obtaining honours degrees (B.A., M.A., M.Phil and PhD.) in Hebrew, medieval and modern Jewish history, Biblical Hebrew and Ancient Egyptian. The fields of teaching and research include: Ancient Near East, Hellenistic Jewish History; Jewish Mysticism; 18th and 19th century Hasidism; the ancient versions of the Hebrew Bible, application of statistics to linguistic problems; Modern Jewish History; History of Jewry in central and Eastern Europe, Jews in Islamic societies, Medieval Hebrew Literature; the History of the Jews in England; Medieval Jewry under Islam; Jewish Spirituality; Yiddish; History of Antisemitism; Holocaust Studies.
The dept. hosts regular visitors from the Hebrew Univ. and offers all students the opportunity to spend one year in Israel.
The dept. comprises eight full-time members of staff and six part-time, with over 80 undergraduate and 20 postgraduate students.
The dept. houses the Instit. of Jewish Studies (see p.43). *Head* John D. Klier.

ORGANISATIONS CONCERNED WITH JEWISH YOUTH

ASSOCIATION FOR JEWISH YOUTH
(Part of Norwood Ravenswood)
Norwood House, Harmony Way, London NW4 2BZ.
☎ 0181-203 3030. Fax: 0181-202 2030. E-mail: ajy@ort.org
Association for Jewish Youth Northern Office, 27 Bury Old Road, Prestwich, Manchester M25 0EY.
☎ 0161-740 6168. Fax 0161-740 6169. Email: north.ajy@ort.org
(Est. 1899. Now part of Norwood Ravenswood, see p.00).
AJY, working with Jewish youth workers, looks at the issues affecting young people today, which include eating disorders, drug abuse, Jewish identity and adolescent problems. AJY works in four main areas: an ongoing programme dealing with

issues affecting the lives of young Jewish people; developing new and existing youth provisions; providing the best professional training available; offering the highest quality of information advice and resources to those involved in Jewish youth work.
Publ. Jewish Youth Work (quarterly).
President The Rt. Hon. Lord Swaythling; *Hon. T.* M.R. Nathan; *Chairman and Hon. Sec.* Martin Bojam; *Head of AJY* Eric Finestone.

B'NAI B'RITH YOUTH ORGANISATION
1-2 Endsleigh Street, WC1H 0DS.
☎ 0171-387 3115. Fax: 0171-387 8014.
Part of the internat. B.B.Y.O. movement, it promotes a wide ranging programme in Jewish education, leadership training, welfare, arts and sports, in a totally youth led environment. (See p.67)

EDUCATION AND YOUTH COMMITTEE, BOARD OF DEPUTIES
(See p.1).

JEWISH GUIDE ADVISORY COUNCIL
J.G.A.C. furthers the Guide movement in the Jewish Com. *Nat. Chairman* Mrs D. Simonson, 61 Bute Road, Ilford, Essex IG6 1AG. ☎ 0181-554 9195; *T.* Mrs R. Davis, 19 Gibbs Green, Edgware, HA8 9RS.

JEWISH LADS' AND GIRLS' BRIGADE
H.Q.: Camperdown, 3 Beechcroft Road, South Woodford, E18 1LA.
☎ 0181-989 8990. Fax: 0181-518 8832.
(Est. 1895. Reg. Charity No. 286950) The JLGB is the longest-established Jewish youth movement in the UK. It serves about 4,000 young people, both through its *Uniformed groups and bands*, and also in Jewish schools, clubs, chedarim and in the smaller communities, through its *Outreach Kiruv Project*, for those not wishing to join a uniformed organisation. There are groups throughout the country, including at Ravenswood Village in Berkshire, and at the Delamere Forest School in Cheshire.
The wide range of activities include sports, crafts & hobbies, drama, camping, outdoor and adventure activities, public service (first aid, life saving, sign language etc), public speaking, discos and weekends away. It is the only Jewish Operating Authority for the *Duke of Edinburgh's Award*. The JLGB also offers its own *Challenge Award for Jewish Youth*, which includes sections on Jewish Heritage and Israel.
Members are encouraged to develop an awareness of the needs of others, through its voluntary service projects, and the JLGB has established partnerships with Ravenswood/Unity and Jewish Care to set up volunteer groups.
President: Edmund L. de Rothschild; *Commandant:* Dame Simone Prendergast, DBE, JP, DL; *Chairman:* E. C. Greenbury F.C.A.; *Chaplain-Emeritus:* Rev. Saul Amias MBE; *Chaplain:* Rev Stanley Cohen; *Brigade Sec.:* R. S. Weber.

JEWISH LEARNING EXCHANGE
Lincoln Gate, 152–154 Golders Green Road, London NW11 8HE. ☎ 0181-458 4588. Fax: 0181-458 4587. Email: 10626.1535@compuserv.com
A service of Ohr Somayach Institutions. Organises educational events for schools, universities, youth groups and yong adults and Jewish Learning programmes in Israel. *Dir.* Rabbi D. Kirsch, 29 The Drive, London NW11 9SX. ☎ 0181-458 4391. Fax: 0181-458 5694.

JEWISH NATIONAL FUND EDUCATION DEPT.
58-70 Edgware Way, Edgware, Middx HA8 8GQ.

☎ 0181-421 7603. Fax: 0181-905 4299.
Supplies JNF/Israel educ. material to schs., nurseries, rel. classes and youth movements. Arranges Bar/Bat Mitzvahs at the Western Wall, in Israel. Organises various activities in London and Provinces. *Head* Myrna Glass, B.Ed.(Hons.), Cert.Ed.

JEWISH PROGRAMME MATERIALS PROJECT (JPMP)
Balfour House, 741 High Road, N12 0BQ.
☎ 0181-446 8020. Fax: 0181-343 9037. Email: jpmp@jazouk.org
JPMP is a full-service resource centre for Jewish-Israel informal education and training - it is the educational arm of the Youth and Hechalutz Department. It promotes the centrality of Israel and enhances the Israel-Diaspora relationship, generates Jewish Identity and Jewish Literacy and fosters Jewish awareness and pride. JPMP provides consultants and trainers as well as technical and multi-media resources - including books, videos, tapes, exhibitions, educational programmes. JPMP seminars cover Jewish-Israel topics and various aspects of Jewish leadership development. It also draws upon a vast wealth of Israel-based educational resources as well as British-based Israeli Shlichim. It serves all of British Jewry but particularly the Zionist Youth movements, Jewish Youth Clubs and Jewish community professionals working in education. JPMP links up with Jewish resource centres in Manchester, Redbridge, Glasgow, Leeds and Liverpool. *Dir.* Roy Graham, LLB, MA.

JEWISH SCOUT ADVISORY COUNCIL
Furthers scouting in the Jewish com. *H. Sec.* P. Russell, 9 Graham Lodge, Graham Road, NW4 3DG. ☎ 0181-202 8613.

JEWISH YOUTH FUND
(Incorporating the Jewish Tercentenary Commemoration Fund)
(Est. 1937. Reg. Charity No. 251902.) To educate and advance religion among young members of the Jewish faith in the United Kingdom, and to help in the provision of leisure-time facilities for their social welfare; to assist and encourage the formation of clubs with the above objects. *Trs.* Lady Morris of Kenwood, Peter Levy, O.B.E., Jonathan Gestetner. *Chairman of Advisory Cttee.* Jonathan Gestetner; *Ts.* Peter Levy, O.B.E., Miss Wendy Pollecoff; *Sec.* Peter Shaw, 707 High Road, London N12 0BT. ☎ 0181-445 1670. Fax: 0181-446 7370. Email: jyf@ort.org.

JEWISH YOUTH ORCHESTRA OF GREAT BRITAIN
Rehearsals: Hillel House, 1-2 Endsleigh Street, WC1H 0DS. Email: jyo@ort.org
Reg. Charity No.: 294994. (Est. 1970) For young musicians (aged 13-20, Grade V and above) to give regular concerts in London and other cities. Occasional summer courses. Rehearsals Sunday mornings during term-time. *Co-founder and conductor* Sydney Fixman: *Chairman* S. Jessel (contact ☎ 0181-360 9403. Fax: 0181-364 0222); *Tr.* M. Chernick; *Hon. Sec.* J. Jessel.

JEWISH YOUTH STUDY GROUPS
(Agency for Jewish Education)
735 High Road, Finchley, London N12 0US.
☎ 0181-343 6289. Fax 0181-343 6298.
Holds weekly Sunday meetings for 13-18 age group on a variety of Jewish and secular topics in 13 areas around London and in the Regions as well as annual summer and winter schools, a post-GCSE Israel Tour and pre-university Year in Israel. This programme combines social events, intensive study and leadership training and discussion on a variety of Jewish issues. *Contact* Melanie Shutz.

ORGANISATIONS CONCERNED WITH JEWISH YOUTH 49

NOAM (NOAR MASORTI)
97 Leeside Crescent, London NW11 0JL.
☎ 0181-201 8773. Fax: 0181-458 4027. Email: noam@ort.org
(Est. 1985. Reg. Charity No. 801846).
NOAM is the Masorti Zionist youth movement. We run a wide variety of educational and social activities including clubs, weekends, summer camps and Israel tours for 8-16 year olds. NOAM also runs the MELTAM leadership course accredited by the University of Oxford delegacy of local examinations. Other activities include: Noam Israel Tour (post-GCSE); Amirim Europe Tour (pre-GCSE); Drachim – year-in-Israel including Machon, kibbutz, volunteer work and Jewish learning; summer camps in Britain and France; weekly clubs; weekends away; social action and charity projects; and contact with Masorti youth in Israel, Europe and America. *Mazkir* Ben Whine; *Camps Org.* Daniel Myers; *Shlicha* Lilach Tchleno; *Publ.* Hadashot Noam (termly newsletter); Norma ((bi-annual magazine).

R.S.Y.-NETZER/RSGB YOUTH DEPARTMENT
Manor House, 80 East End Road, N3 2SY.
☎ 0181-349 4731. Fax: 0181-343 4962. E-mail: rsy.rsgb@ort.org; students:rsgb@ort.org.
Northern Office Northern Resource & Learning Centre, Jacksons Row, Albert Sq., Manchester M2 5WD.
To educate young people towards a love of Reform Judaism and Reform Zionism and to offer them Jewish life options within an equal opportunity perspective.
RSY-Netzer is the autonomous reform Zionist youth movement of the Reform Movement and part of the worldwide Netzer youth movement. There are 26 anafim (branches) with weekly meetings around the country and a full calendar of residential activities, seminars and training courses for the four age groups - Garinim (10-12 yrs), Shtilim (13-16 yrs), Ilanot (16-18 yrs) and Bogrim (18+) Summer camps are run in England, Israel and Europe and a ten month leadership training programme (Shnat Netzer) in Israel,.
The Youth and Student Division offers youth work development and training to RSGB communities as well as developing innovative models of youth work practice and provides programmes, activities and support for Reform and Progressive Jewish students.

SIR MAX BONN MEMORIAL JEWISH YOUTH CENTRE
Leigh House, 63 Ethelbert Road, Cliftonville, Kent.
(Est. 1947.) To provide a holiday centre for young people and adolescents, conferences and discussion groups among clubs and institutions.
Contact Mrs. Doris Cohen, 2 Priory Court, Sparrows Herne, Bushey, Herts WD2 1EF. ☎ 0181-950 5141.

ULPS YOUTH DEPARTMENT/ULPSNYC - NETZER
The Montagu Centre, 21 Maple Street, W1P 6DS.
☎ 0171-631 0584. Fax: 0171-436 4184. Email: ulpsnyc.netzer.yd@ort.org
To informally educate young Jewish people towards a strong identity within a progressive Jewish and Zionist framework.
There are a network of youth clubs within the 28 ULPS synagogues which host weekly club sessions. The Youth Department in partnership with ULPSNYC Netzer offers residential activities, training in youth leadership and teaching. Summer camps are held in Britain and we offer tours to Israel, Europe and the USA. The Youth Dept. offers training, new models of youth work. Mind the Gap is the young adult group (21-35 age group) and offers social events and projects. We support and work with RSGB on student issues.
Dir. for Young People Mark Bromley; *Admin.* Katie Morris; *Mazkira* Katie Amber; *Schlichon* Amit Handelsman.

ORGANISATIONS CONCERNED WITH JEWISH YOUTH

UNION OF MACCABI ASSOCIATIONS IN GREAT BRITAIN AND IRELAND
Gildesgame House, 73A Compayne Gardens, NW6 3RS.
☎ 0171-328 0382. Fax: 0171-328 9118.
To promote the active participation in sports and education of young Jewish men and women, in order to enhance their Jewish identity, values and commitment to the community.
Chairman H. Minkoff; *Nat. Dir.* M. Herman; *H. Sec.* J. Barnett; *Hon. Sports Dir.* H. Moss; *Admin.* Mrs C. Green.
Affiliated clubs in the London area: Brady; Bushey; Catford; Chigwell & Hainault; E.D.R.S.; Ivri; Kadimah/Victoria, Kenton; Kinnor; Luton; Maccabi Assn. London; Southend-on-Sea.
Affiliated clubs in the provinces: Brighton and Hove; Cardiff; Dublin; Edinburgh; Glasgow; Liverpool; Leicester; Manchester; Newcastle; Sheffield.

The following groups are associated with the Zionist Movement.

BACHAD FELLOWSHIP
Friends of Bnei Akiva, Alexander Margulies Youth Centre, 2 Halleswelle Road, NW11 0DJ.
☎ 0181-458 9370. Fax: 0181-209 0107.
(Est. 1942. Reg. Charity No. 227509) To promote Jewish religious education and provide agricultural and vocational training for Jewish youth. Establishes and maintains Youth Centres in London, Leeds, Manchester, Glasgow and Dublin. *Hon. Presidents* Chief Rabbi Dr. Jonathan Sacks, The Rt. Hon. the Lord Jakobovits, Rabbi Cyril Harris, Chief Rabbi of South Africa; *V. President* Sir Sidney Hamburger, C.B.E., J.P.; *Chairman* Arieh L. Handler; *V. Chairmen* Herbert Kaufman, Jack Lass; *H. Ts.* Harry T. Klahr, Michael Wreschner; *H. Sec* Mrs. Susan Sperber. Bnei Akiva Scholarship Institute (BASI) arranges for senior members to spend one or two years in Israel working and studying to prepare for ultimate settlement in the country after returning here to act as youth leaders for a period.

BETAR-TAGAR
143-145 Brondesbury Park, NW2 5JL.
☎ 0181-451 0002. Fax: 0181-459 8766. E-mail: betar.tagar@ort.org
(Reg. Charity No. 290571.) Betar-Tagar Zionist students movement educates Jewish students and youth towards Zionism by stressing Aliya, the value of Jewish tradition and concern for Jewish people everywhere, self-defence and Jewish identity.

BNEI AKIVA
2 Halleswelle Road, NW11 0DJ.
☎ 0181-209 1319. Fax: 0181-209 0107. Email: bnei.akiva@ort.org
(Est. 1940.) Aims to educate young people, aged between 7 and 25 years, in ideals of Religious Zionism and Torah Ve-Avodah. More than 40 groups in UK meeting on Shabbat afternoons. Regular weekend and summer seminars are run throughout the year. Bnei Akiva runs a highly successful year scheme in Israel known as Hachshara which has two tracks – one yeshiva-based and the other kibbutz-based. Bnei Akiva is the largest religious Zionist youth organisation in the world.
Mazkir Jeremy Kaye; *Technical Dir.* Danny Newman; *Fieldworker* Sam Reisman; *Educ. Off.* Michael Laitner; *Northern Shaliach* Uri Berman; *Southern Shaliach* Dror Ben-Chaim; *Educ. Shaliach* Rabbi Benny Lau.
Publ.: Monthly education booklets, termly movement magazines, weekly Sidrah sheet. Supports Aliya to the State of Israel as the movement objective.
Regional centres: 72 Singleton Road, Salford M7 4LU. ☎ 0161-740 1621. Fax 0161-740 8018. Email: bnei.akiva.north@ort.org; Street Lane Gardens, Leeds 17. ☎ 01132-688 290.

ORGANISATIONS CONCERNED WITH JEWISH YOUTH 51

EZRA YOUTH MOVEMENT
British and European Off.: 2a Alba Gardens, London, NW11 9NR.
☎/Fax 0181-458 5372.
Associated with Poale Agudat Israel.
Orthodox Jewish movement based in London with a branch in Manchester and branches in Israel and other parts of the world.

FEDERATION OF ZIONIST YOUTH
25a Oakleigh Road North, London N20 9HE.
☎ 0181-445 6222. Fax 0181-445 6332. Email: fzy@ort.org.
FZY is an active and vibrant Zionist youth movement with societies throughout Britain. We are a pluralist movement, which means our members are drawn from all religious streams and are of all political colours. The movement aims to educate its members around Jewish and Zionist themes with the aim of fulfilling the four aims of FZY, namely: Aliya, Tarbut (promoting Jewish culture), Fund Raising and Defence of Jewish Rights.
FZY has weekly meetings all over the country organised around these aims which, when combined with weekend seminars for 14 to 18 year olds, our Winter Camp Shachar, our annual conference, our summer camp Kesher and our summer programmes in Israel, plus numerous other local and national events, create a dynamic and creative environment for Jewish Youth to express their heritage, culture and identity.
FZY Year Course is a prime example of our commitment to Israel. An exciting, stimulating and academic-year programme, with very strong leadership elements, Year Course allows FZYniks to explore and understand Israel and themselves, and encourages them to return as leaders in the community.
President Paul Lenga; *Hon. President* Abba Eban; *Mazkir* Adam Quint; *Oved Chinuch* Richard Pater; *Camps Org.* Sam Courts; *Org. Sec.* Louise Jacobs; *Northern Fieldworker* Judith Jackson; *Publ.* 'The Young Zionist' (quarterly) and 'The Bulletin' (monthly).

HABONIM–DROR
523 Finchley Road, NW3 7BD.
☎ 0171-435 9033/4. Fax: 0171-431 4503.
Habonim-Dror was created in 1979 when Habonim and Dror merged, and is part of the international Habonim-Dror movement.
It is a radical Zionist Youth Movement which educates Jewish Youth towards a realisation of their Jewish heritage, both traditional and historical. In particular, it educates at a later age towards chalutzic (pioneering) self-realisation in Israel, and the value of a more equal caring society.
Activities are run once or twice weekly covering drama, arts and crafts, educational games, and social events. There are Winter and Summer Camps for all ages, from 9 to 23, including adventure camps for 14-year-olds.
European Camp, including a Holocaust seminar, for 15-year-olds and Israel Camp for 16-year-olds.
A central feature of Habonim-Dror's programme is its well-established Year Course in Israel: Shnat Hachsharah. This involves living on Kibbutz, Youth Leadership training, tours of the country and a full educational programme about Judaism and Israel.
Habonim-Dror groups are to be found in most Jewish com. in Great Britain.
President Lady Morris of Kenwood; *Admin.* David Arram; *Nat. Sec.* James Rosenhead.
Youth Centres
London: North West & Central Office, 523 Finchley Road, London NW3 7BD (☎ 0171-435 9033. Fax: 0171-431 4503. E-mail: habonim@ort.org); Elstree & Borehamwood: c/o Central Office; Glasgow; Leeds: Fir Tree Lane, Leeds LS17 (☎ 01132 682055); Manchester: North, South Hale Barns, 11 Upper Park Road, Salford M7 0HY (☎ 0161-795 9447); Birmingham: 26 Somerset Road, Birmingham

B15 2QD (☎ Central Office); Oxford: Jewish Centre, Oxford (☎ Central Office); Bristol: c/o Central Office; Ilford: Sinclair House, Woodford Bridge Road, Ilford, Essex (☎ 0181-551 0017); all other coms.: inquire 523 Finchley Road, NW3 7BD; (☎ 0171-435 9033).
Publ.: Koleinu.

HANOAR HATZIONI
The Youth Centre, 31 Tetherdown, Muswell Hill, N10 1ND.
☎ 0181-8831022/3. Fax: 0181-365 2272.
A non-political Zionist youth movement catering for young people, 7–23 years, in groups in different parts of the country run with the help of central office. Holds national activities, annual summer and winter camps, outings, day hikes and educ. and leadership training seminars. Encourages local social activities. Promotes the Shnat Sherut Israel Year programme and 6-month gesher programme. Combines educ. objectives with a strong soc. network. *Mazkir* Spencer Gelding.

HASHOMER HATZAIR
Hashomer House, 37A Broadhurst Gardens, NW6 3BN.
☎ 0171-328 5451.
(Est. 1940.) The British constituent of a world movement to educate its members in Socialist Zionist ideals as a basis for life in Israel especially kibbutz. *Sec.* D. Sacks. *Shlicha* Sheva Friedman.
Youth Centre as above.

JOINT AUTHORITY FOR JEWISH/ZIONIST EDUCATION
Balfour House, 741 High Road, N12 0BQ.
☎ 0181-446 1144. Fax: 0181-446 8296.
The Joint Authority for Jewish Zionist Education was established in November 1990 to co-ordinate the educational activities provided by the Jewish Agency for Israel and the World Zionist Organisation. The Authority brings together the three World Zionist Organisation's education departments, i.e. the Departments of Jewish Education and Culture in the Diaspora, Torah and Youth & Hechalutz.
The Authority is the central policy-making body to which the various Education Departments are accountable.
The Authority sees its role as the provider of services responding to the needs of Diaspora communities and initially has identified the immediate areas of priority as:-
a) to develop 'Israel experience' programs.
b) to respond to personnel crisis in both formal and informal education.
c) to develop relevant educational materials and programmes.
Sponsors and administers a com.-wide educ. resource centre (J.P.M.P.).

KIBBUTZ REPRESENTATIVES
1A Accommodation Road, NW11 8ED.
☎ 0181-458 9235. Fax: 0181-455 7930. Email: enquiries@kibbutz.org.uk
(Reg. Charity No. 294564) Representing all the Kibbutz movements in Israel. The organisation arranges Working Visits on Kibbutz for persons aged 18-32. Kibbutz Ulpan for persons aged 18-28, including the 'Oren' enrichment programme; and a 2-month short Summer Ulpan, for persons aged 18-26. Religious Kibbutz options are available, and all applicants must be in good physical and mental health.

KIDMAH
c/o Hashomer House, 37a Broadhurst Gdns, London, NW6 3BN.
☎ 0171-328 5451.
Left-Zionist student organisation promoting Jewish-Arab recognisation, religious pluralism, anti-racism. Educational, social, political activities; provides lecturers to Jewish and non-Jewish groups. *Fieldworker* Daniel Marcus.

ORGANISATIONS CONCERNED WITH JEWISH STUDENTS

YOUNG MAPAM
Hashomer House, 37A Broadhurst Gardens, NW6 3BN.
☎ 0171-328 5451.
Anglo-Jewish youth and student group, ages 18-35, with a Socialist-Zionist outlook. Social, cultural, educ. and political programme stressing humanistic values of Judaism and progressive Zionist elements. Aliya of members encouraged. *Chairman* Marc Bernstein.

YOUNG JEWISH NATIONAL FUND FOR ISRAEL (YJNF)
58-70 Edgware Way, Edgware, Middx HA8 8GG.
☎ 0181-421 7693. Fax: 0181-905 4299. Email: jnf@ort.org.
(Est. 1958.) To support the work of the JNF in Israel in afforestation, land reclamation, environmental and ecological issues by fund-raising events organised through young committees (18-30) nationwide. Education and resources for students and youth movements groups. *Contact* Leesa Mather, B.A.(Hons.).

The following organisations are concerned with Jewish students

ASSOCIATION OF JEWISH SIXTH FORMERS
1-2 Endsleigh St., London WC1H 0DS.
☎ 0171-387 3384. Fax: 0171-387 3392. E-mail: aj6.hq@ort.org
(Est. 1977. Reg. Charity No. 1029445) Jewish youth organisation for fifth and sixth formers (membership 600, service outreach 1,200). Aims to educate and promote a positive Jewish identity. Five main objectives: preparation for the challenges of school and university campus life, outreach to unaffiliated youth, meaningful and lasting Jewish education, hadracha and leadership training, and shared responsibility (arevut). Services include campus visits, interview techniques, university and career information, regional weekly meetings, national weekends, shabbatons, social events (incl. Valentines ball and boat ball) and summer tours to Israel and Europe. *National Fieldworker* Simon Berman; *Dev. Worker* Joby Blume; *Sec./Admin* Anne Cutter.
Publ. AJ6 Guide to Jewish Student Life – info on Campus, University J-Socs, Hillel Houses, Chaplaincy; AJ6 Guide to Year Schemes in Israel; Sixth Sense (quarterly magazine); monthly mailings.

B'NAI B'RITH HILLEL FOUNDATION
Hillel House, 1-2 Endsleigh Street, WC1H 0DS.
☎ 0171-388 0801. Fax 0171-916 3973. Email: hillel@crt.org
(Reg. Charity No.: 313503.) Jewish Student Centre, devoted to social and educational activities among Jewish students at colleges and universities. Facilities include meeting rooms, common room, Kosher Restaurant. Closed Shabbat and Festivals, other than by arrangement.
President Fred S. Worms; *Chairman* Brenda Katten; *Dep. Chairman* Jeffrey Green; *Exec. Dir.* Gerry Lucas.
Residential and social facilities available at Hillel Houses in the following locations (contact person named for further details):
Birmingham: Frank Linden, ☎ 0121-4545042. **Bournemouth:** Marilyn Dexter ☎ 01202-304252, **Brighton:** Mrs. Annabelle Lee, ☎ 01273 880596. **Bristol:** Mrs. Sheila Tobias, ☎ 01454 412831. **Cardiff:** Mrs Paula Freed, ☎ 01222 758614. **Edinburgh:** Mrs Myrna Kaplan, ☎ 0131-399 8201. **Glasgow:** Dr. Simon Woldman, ☎ 0141-639 5869. **Hull:** Ian Dysch, ☎ 01482 54947. **Leeds:** Dr. Roger Pollard, ☎ 0113 332080. **Leicester:** Melissa Morrison, ☎ 01162 70-5771. **Liverpool:** Mrs. Carol Lewis, ☎ 0151-722 5021. **London:** (J. C. Gilbert House) Herman Greenbourne, ☎ 0181-998 7865, (Harold Godfrey House) Miss Evelyn Bacharach, ☎ 0171-722 01420. **Manchester:** Dr. Sydney Baigel, ☎ 0161-740 2521.

Newcastle: Geoffrey Lurie, ☎ 0191-285 7928. **Nottingham:** Mrs. Sandra Flitterman, ☎ 01152 937 5403. **Reading:** Richard Sassoon, ☎ 01734 613367. **Sheffield:** Mrs. Elaine Jacob, ☎ 01142 308688. **Southampton:** Irene Weintroub, ☎ 01202 527527.

UNION OF JEWISH STUDENTS
of the United Kingdom and Ireland
(formerly: Inter-University Jewish Federation of Gt. Britain and Ireland).
Hillel House, 1/2 Endsleigh Street, WC1H 0DS.
☎ 0171-387 4644/380 0111. Fax 0171-383 0390. Email: ujs@brijnet.org
Co-ordinates the activities of the Jewish and Israel societies in the universities and colleges of the UK and Ireland. It stimulates an interest among Jewish students in Judaism, Zionism, Jewish history and education, and in Jewish thought. It encourages members to play their part in the religious and social life of the community. (Est. 1919.) *Chair* Danny Newman; *Admin.* Shirley Goldwater.

Jewish student societies are attached to many universities and colleges. See under separate towns.

London Region, Hillel House, 1/2 Endsleigh Street, WC1H 0DS. ☎ 0171-388 4919. There is a full cultural and social programme at the Centre in Hillel House and at Jewish Socs. in the region.

UNIVERSITY JEWISH CHAPLAINCY BOARD
Office of the Chief Rabbi.
(Est. 1968.) Its object is to appoint full-time chaplains to Jewish students at univ. *President* The Chief Rabbi; *Chairman* Hilton Lorie; *V. Chairman* Anthony Cowen; *Tr.* Michael Weinstein; *Sec.*

WINGATE YOUTH TRUST
(Est. 1975. Reg. Charity No. 269678) To provide facilities for youth, for recreation and leisure. *Chairman* F. Davis; T. M. Rebak, 58 Southwood Park, Southwood Lawn Road, N6 5SQ. ☎ 0181-340 1287; *Sec.* Malcolm Davis.

LIBRARIES, MUSEUMS AND EXHIBITIONS

AJEX Military Museum, AJEX House, East Bank, Stamford Hill, London N16 5RT. ☎ 0181-800 2844. Fax: 0181-880 1117.
A display of books, photographs and memorabilia from the reign of George III to the present. *Archivist:* H. Morris.

Anglo-Jewish Archives. An independent Registered Charity under the auspices of the Jewish Historical Society of England. The genealogical collections have been deposited at the Society of Genealogists and the main archive collection has been deposited with the Hartley Library, University of Southampton (see p.55). *H. Sec.* Cyril Drukker, (JHSE), 33 Seymour Place, London W1H 5AP. ☎/Fax: 0171-723 5852.

Ben Uri Art Society and Gallery, 126 Albert Street, London NW1 7NE. ☎ 0171-482 1234. Fax 0171-482 1414. Email: benuri@ort.org. (Reg. Charity No. 280389) Open Mon.-Thurs., 10-5, Sun. 2-5 during exhibitions. Closed Jewish Holy-days, Bank holidays and August. The aim of the Society, which is a registered charity founded in 1915, is to promote Jewish Art as part of the Jewish cultural heritage. The Gallery provides a showcase for exhibitions of contemporary art as well as for the Society's own permanent collection of over 700 works by Jewish artists. A full programme of activities is provided for members of the Society including lectures, visits to other galleries and the popular annual picture fair. *Chairman* Leslie Michaels; *V. Chairmen* Mrs Lois Peltz, Lewis Goodman, O.B.E.;

Hon. Sec. David Kut; *Jt. Hon. Trs.* David Shaw, Raymond Bernstein; *Chairman of Art Cttee.* David Glasser; *Dir.* Mrs Jo Velleman.

Beth Hammidrash, The library of the London Beth Din. Facilities available to bona fide scholars on application to the Registrar.

Bodleian Library, Broad Street, Oxford OX1 3BG. ☎ 01865 277000. *Bodley's Librarian:* Mr R. Carr. The Hebrew and Yiddish collections comprise 3000 manuscript volumes and 60,000 printed books, including many incunabula, fragments from the Cairo Genizah and the Oppenheimer library, the finest collection of Hebrew books and manuscripts ever assembled. Intending readers should always contact the Admissions Office in advance. Open to holders of a reader's ticket Mon. to Fri. 9-7, Sat. 9-1. *Hebrew Specialist Libr.* R. C. Judd, M.A., M.Phil.

The British Library, Oriental and India Office Collections, 197 Blackfriars Road, London SE1 8NG. ☎ 0171-412 7657/7646. The Hebrew collection comprises more than 3,000 manuscript volumes and 10,000 fragments (incl. Haham Moses Gaster's collection and many fragments from the Cairo Genizah); Hebrew printed books, about 70,000 titles, incl. 100 incunabula, rabbinic and modern Hebrew literature; Yiddish, Ladino, Judeo-Arabic and Judeo-Persian books; some 1,000 Hebrew periodicals and newspapers. Oriental Reading Room open to holders of readers' passes: Mon. to Fri. 9.30-5.45; Sat., 9.30-12.45.
The Reading Room is due to close in April 1998 for at least four months, after which it will re-open at 96 Euston Road, London NW1 2DB. Please contact the Library for further information.

Brotherton Library, University of Leeds, Leeds LS2 9JT. ☎ 01132 335501. Fax: 01132 335561. *Librarian* Lynne Brindley. Holdings include substantial materials for Hebrew and Jewish studies and the Travers Herford Collection on Judaism and Talmudic studies. The primary Judaica collection is the Roth Collection comprising the manuscripts and printed books from the library of Cecil Roth, including 350 mss., 900 printed books (pre-1850) 6,000 modern books and other archival material. Available to bona fide scholars who should write to the Librarian in the first instance enclosing an appropriate recommendation. *Asst. Libr. (Semitic)* M. C. Davis. *Publ.* Selig Brodetsky lecture series.

Cambridge University Library, West Rd, Cambridge CB3 9DR. ☎ 01223 333000. Fax: 01223 333160. Email: library@ula.cam.ac.uk. *Dir.* Mr P.K. Fox. The Hebraica and Judaica collections comprise c. 140,000 Cairo Genizah fragments (being catalogued in the Genizah Series, CUP); 1,000 complete Hebrew codices (see S.C. Reif, Hebrew Manuscripts at Cambridge University Library, CUP 1997); approximately 40,000 printed books. Available to members of the University and bona fide scholars by application in person to the Admissions Officer. Reading rooms open 9.30-6.45; Admissions Office: 9.30-12.30, 2.00-4.15. *Dir. Genizah Res. Unit and Oriental Div.* Dr. S. C. Reif; *Hebraica Libr.* Mrs. J. Butterworth.

Harry Rosencweig Collection of Jewish Music.
University Library, City University, Northampton Square, EC1V 0HB.
☎ 0171-477 8193. Fax 0171-477 8194. Email: library@city.ac.uk.
Printed sheet music includes 17th–20th century European, American and Israeli liturgical and art music, and various anthologies of folk music. Text books on Jewish music and dance. A few LPs. Many rare items. *Libr.* John McGuirk.

The Hartley Library, University of Southampton, Highfield, Southampton SO17 1BJ. Holdings of the Special Collections Division include (i) the **Parkes Library**, founded

56 LIBRARIES, MUSEUMS AND EXHIBITIONS

by the late Revd. Dr. James Parkes in 1935 to promote the study of relations between the Jewish and the non-Jewish worlds, now containing 14,000 books and periodicals; (ii) extensive collections of manuscripts relating to Anglo-Jewry (containing many of the collections of **Anglo-Jewish Archives**) and encompassing the papers of the Council of Christians and Jews, the Anglo-Jewish Association, the papers of Rabbi Solomon Schonfeld and the Chief Rabbi's Religious Emergency Fund, archives of the Union of Jewish Women, private papers of Chief Rabbi Hertz, early records of the Board of Shechita, archives of the Federation of Jewish Relief Organisations, and the papers of the Jewish Board of Guardians and of the Jewish Blind Society. A catalogue of the archives was published by the library in 1992. Open Mon., Tue., Thur. and Fri., 0900-1700; Wed. 1000-1700; by appointment. ☎ 01703 593335 (Parkes); 01703 592721 (MSS); Fax: 01703 593007. E-mail: library@soton.ac.uk (for Parkes); archives@soton.ac.uk (for MSS). *Archivist* Dr. C. M. Woolgar.

The Hillel Brodetsky Library, Formerly at Hillel House, now transferred to the new Sephardi Centre at Lauderdale Road Syn. (see p.59).

Institute of Contemporary History and Wiener Library, Ltd., 4 Devonshire Street, W1N 2BH. Reg. Charity No. 313015. ☎ 0171-636 7247. Fax: 0171-436 6428. Email: lib@wl.u-net.com
Founded by Dr. A. Wiener in Amsterdam, 1933, and since 1939 in London. Research Library and Institute on contemporary European and Jewish history, especially the rise and fall of the Third Reich; survival and revival of Nazi and fascist movements; antisemitism; racialism; the Middle East; post-war Germany. Holds Britain's largest collection of documents, testimonies, books and videos on the Holocaust. Active educ. programme of lectures, seminars and conferences. *Chairman of Exec. Cttee.* Ernst Fraenkel; *Dir.* Prof. David Cesarani; *Libr.* Rosemarie Nief.

Institute for Jewish Policy Research Library, 79 Wimpole Street, London W1M 7DD. ☎ 0171-935 8266. Fax: 0171-935 3252. E-mail: JPR@ort.org.
The Edgar M. Bronfman library is open to JPR members and postgraduate researchers by appointment. Books and press cuttings collections include material on past and present Jewish issues: antisemitism, the Holocaust, Jewish Christian relations, world Jewry, Israel and inter-faith relations. *Libr.* Patricia Schotten, B.A.

Jewish Community Exhibition Centre, c/o David Turner, 1 Village Close, Belsize Lane, London NW3. ☎ 0171-794 1542. (Est. 1985.) To provide exhibition material on subjects of Jewish interest. The central exhibition under the responsibility of the Education Dept. of the BoD is 'The Jewish Way of Life' which has travelled to many venues in the UK. Other exhibitions include 'The Anschluss', 'Sir Moses Montefiore', 'Shalosh Regalim', the three Foot Festivals and 'The Anglo Jewish Experience 1066-1990', the history of the Jews in England.
Co-Chairmen David Turner and Mrs. Ruth Winston Fox, MBE, J.P.

The Jewish Museum - London's Museum of Jewish Life
Website: http://www.ort.org/jewmusm/
(Est. 1932. Reg. Charity No. 10098819.) In 1995, The Jewish Museum re-opened in new premises and amalgamated on a two-site basis with the former London Museum of Jewish Life. The combined Museum now has locations in Finchley and Camden Town. It seeks to recover, preserve and exhibit material locating to the roots and heritage of Jewish people in Britain and to illustrate and explain Jewish religious practice and objects of rarity and beauty. Publ. include: Research Papers, Map of the Jewish East End, *Living up West - Jewish Life in London's West End, The Jews of Aden, What about the Children - 200 years of Norwood Child Care, The Portuguese Jewish Community in London (1656-1830)*; Immigrant Furniture

LIBRARIES, MUSEUMS AND EXHIBITIONS 57

Workers in London, 1881-1939.
Dir. Rickie Burman, M.A., M.Phil.; *Chairman:* Kenneth Rubens, FRSA; *Dep. Chairman:* Robert Craig, LLM; *Friends Admin.:* Sidney Berg.

The Jewish Museum - Camden Town
Outstanding collections of objects and antiquities of artistic merit, illustrating Jewish life, history and religion. History and Ceremonial Art Galleries and a Temporary Exhibitions Gallery with changing exhibitions (educational programmes available). Open: Sun-Thurs, 10 am-4 pm. Closed Jewish Festivals and Public Holidays. Address: Raymond Burton House, 129-131 Albert Street, NW1 7NB. ☎ 0171-284 1997. Fax: 0171-267 9008.

The Jewish Museum - Finchley
Displays relating to Jewish social history, and an active programme of Holocaust education. Travelling exhibitions, Educational Programmes and Walking Tours of Jewish London. 80 East End Road, N3 2SY. For details of opening hours, please telephone: ☎ 0181-349 1143. Fax: 0181-343 2162.

Jewish Studies Library (Incorporating the Library of the Jewish Historical Society of England), University College London, Gower Street, WC1E 6BT. ☎ 0171-387 7050 (ext. 2598). Fax: 0171-380 7373. E-mail: library@ucl.ac.uk.
All collections are housed together in the Arnold Mishcon Reading Room. These are the Mocatta Library, the Brodie Library, the Altmann Library, the Abramsky Library, the William Margulies Yiddish Library and the Gaster Papers, in addition to books and periodicals acquired for the support of teaching and research by the College's Department of Hebrew and Jewish Studies. The Jewish Studies Library, as well as serving the academic community of UCL and affiliated institutions, is open for reference purposes to the general public engaged in research. The Arnold Mishcon Reading Room is part of the Main Library. Please contact the library to obtain current opening hours and admissions procedure. Geneaological enquiries are referred to a professional geneaologist unless specifically related to collections in the Library. *Libr.* F. J. Friend, B.A.

Jews' College Library, Schaller House, Albert Road, London NW4 2SJ. ☎ 0181-203 6427. Fax: 0181-203 6420.
(Est. 1855. Reg. Charity No. 310023) Open (during terms) Mon.-Thurs. 9 a.m.-6 p.m.; Fri. and eve of festivals, 9 a.m.-1 p.m.; Sun., 9.30 a.m.-12.30 p.m. (summer and term breaks). Mon.-Thurs. 9 a.m.-5 p.m., Fri. 9 a.m.-1 p.m. Closed Jewish holidays and fast days. One of the most extensive Judaica libraries in Europe, the library contains 80,000 volumes, 20,000 pamphlets and 700 manuscripts. *Hd. Libr.* Esra Kahn.

John Rylands University Library of Manchester, Oxford Road, Manchester M13 9PP. The Special Collections Repository, 150 Deansgate, Manchester M3 3EH. ☎ 0161-834 5343. Fax: 0161-834 5574. The library collection of Hebraica and Judaica comprises over 10,500 fragments from the Cairo Genizah; manuscripts and codices from the Crawford and Gaster collections; Samaritan manuscripts from the Gaster collection; 6,600 items of printed Hebraica and Talmudic literature in the Marmorstein collection; 1,000 volumes of the Haskalah collection; the Moses Gaster collection; and some 5,000 volumes in the Near Eastern collection in the main library dealing with Hebrew language and literature. Although primarily serving the staff and students of the University, other readers may obtain reference only access to the library on application (letter of introduction and evidence of identity required). A fee is charged to external readers requiring regular access to the main library. *Head of Special Collections* Dr. P. McNiven.

LIBRARIES, MUSEUMS AND EXHIBITIONS

Keren Hatorah Library, 97 Stamford Hill, London N16 5DN. ☎ 0181-800 6688. A comprehensive collection of Torah literature for the whole family, including a children's section. Operates as a lending library with opening hours Sun., Tues., and Thurs. mornings, 10.30-12.30. *Libr.* Mrs. Grossnass.

Keren Hatorah Tape Library, 97 Stamford Hill, London N16. ☎ 0181802 6388. Over ten thousand cassette recordings of Shiurim, lectures and conventions. The collection includes the complete Talmud in either English or Yiddish. Other subjects: Jewish History, Holocaust, the Festivals, Nach, Siddur, Hashkafa and Halacha. Open Sun 10.30-1.00, Mon to Thurs 11.00-4.00. *Libr.* A. Lauer.

Leo Baeck College Library The Sternberg Centre for Judaism, 80 East End Road, N3 2SY. ☎ 0181-349 4525 (ext. 400). Est. 1956 to provide a library for Jewish Studies and research. Holdings: 35,000 vols.; 60 current periodicals; 3,000 pamphlets; 1,500 sound records (shiurim and public lectures); 160 rabbinic theses. Range: Bible, rabbinic literature, codes, liturgy, education, language, literature, arts, history, holocaust, Israel and Zionism. Library loan facilities. *Libr.* Dr. P.W. van Boxel.

Leopold Muller Memorial Library, Oxford Centre for Hebrew & Jewish Studies, Yarnton Manor, Yarnton, Oxford OX5 1PY. ☎ 01865-377946. Fax: 01865-375079. (Reg. Charity No. 309720). The Oxford Centre houses the Leopold Muller Memorial Library whose main constituents are the Kressel and Elkoshi collections comprising a total of some 35,000 volumes in Hebrew and over 7,000 volumes in western languages. The collections cover the full range of Hebrew and Jewish studies, with special focus on Hebrew literature of the 19th and 20th centuries, Haskalah, modern biographical and historical archive of some 500 box files of Hebrew newspaper and periodical cuttings on 12,000 Jewish pesonalities and on the early Yishuv in Palestine, as well as representative samples of the Hebrew and Yiddish press. *Libr.* Brad Sabin Hill.

London Museum of Jewish Life
See: The Jewish Museum (above p.56).

Lubavitch Lending Library, 107-115 Stamford Hill, N16 5RP. ☎ 0181-800 5823. Est. 1972 to help the Jewish public study traditional Jewish culture and aid scholarship. The library contains 12,000 volumes in Hebrew, English & Yiddish. Services include a reference libr., a children's libr. and postal lending. Lectures and displays org. anywhere. Open Sun., 10 a.m.-12.30 p.m., 4 p.m.-8 p.m.; Mon.-Fri., 10 a.m.-4 p.m. Some weekday evgs. Other times available by appointment. *Libr.* Z. Rabin, A.L.A.

National Life Story Collection at the British Library National Sound Archive, Exhibition Road, South Kensington, London SW7 2AS. ☎ 0171-412 7404. Fax: 0171-412 7441. Est. 1987 to create Britain's first national archive of oral history and provide a central focus for life oral story interviewing. The **Living Memory of the Jewish Community** is an extensive and growing collection of the stories of Jewish men and women. The initial focus is on those fleeing from Nazi persecution and includes testimonies from survivors from many parts of Europe, now extending to second generation interviews.

Porton Collection, Central Library, Municipal Buildings, Leeds LS1 3AB. ☎ 0113 2478282. About 6000 items on all aspects of Jewish life in English, Hebrew and Yiddish. For reference use only.

School of Oriental and African Studies (Univ. of London), Thornhaugh Street, Russell Square, London WC1H 0XG. ☎ 0171-323 6098. Fax: 0171-636 2834.

Email: ps4@soas.ac.uk.
Ancient Near East, Semitics & Judaica Section of SOAS Library. *Section Head* P. S. Salinger. The Semitics and Judaica collections comprise about 15,000 Hebrew items covering the fields of modern Hebrew language and literature (one of the finest collections in Europe), biblical and intertestamental studies, Judaism, the Jewish people, and the land of Israel. There are also a considerable number of books in Western languages covering the above mentioned fields. In addition, largely owing to the acquisition of the Stencl and Leftwich collections in 1983 and some books from the Whitechapel collection in 1984, there are about 3000 books on Yiddish language and literature. Periodicals, of which the Library holds about 200 Hebrew titles are shelved separately. For details of services, please refer to the Library Guide.

Spanish & Portuguese Jews' Congregation, 2 Ashworth Road, W9 1JY. ☎ 0171-289 2573. Fax: 0171-289 2709. **Archives**: The archives of the Spanish & Portuguese Jews' Congregation, London, and its institutions, which date from the mid-17th century, include Minute and Account Books, Registers of Births, Circumcisions, Marriages and Burials. Some of the Registers have been published and copies may be purchased from the Congregation's offices. The archives are not open to the public. Queries and requests by bona fide researchers should be submitted in writing to the Hon. Archivist. Advice and help will be given to general enquirers wherever possible. A search fee may be charged. *Hon. Archivist*: Miriam Rodrigues-Pereira. **Shasha Library** (Est 1936.) Designed to contain books on Jewish history, religion, literature and kindred interest from the Sephardi standpoint. The Library is intended for the use of members of the congregation. It contains over 1,200 books. These collections have been bought into the new Sephardi Centre opened at the end of 1994 (see p.42). *Libr.* Jack Epstein.

PROFESSIONAL ORGANISATIONS

AGUDAS HARABBONIM (ASSOCIATION OF RABBIS OF GREAT BRITAIN) (in association with the Agudas Israel World Rabbinical Council) 273 Green Lanes, N4 2EX. ☎ 0181-802 1544. (Est 1929.) *Chairman Princ.* Rabbi H. Padwa, Av Beth Din, U.O.H.C.; *H. Dir.* Rabbi Ben Zion Blau; *H. Gen. Sec.* vacant.

AGUDATH HASHOCHTIM V'HASHOMRIM OF GREAT BRITAIN
Cattle Section: *H. Sec.* S. B. Spitzer, 33 Elm Park Avenue, N15 6AR.
Poultry Section: *H. Sec.* S. Leaman, 25 Rostrevor Road, N.15.

ASSOCIATION OF JEWISH COMMUNAL PROFESSIONALS
PO Box 73, Bushey, WD2 8XD. ☎/Fax: 0181-386 1857. The aims of the Association are to enhance the standing of the communal professional, represent their needs and interests, improve professional practice, provide a forum for professionals to discuss common issues and give mutual support, and to be a resource of relevant information. The Association publishes a Code of Practice which gives guidelines to Jewish communal organisations. *Chair* David Goldberg; *V. Chair* Alan Curtis, Angela Margolis; *H. Sec.* Rhoda Goodman; *H.T.* Maurice Ross.

ASSOCIATION OF MINISTERS (CHAZANIM) OF GREAT BRITAIN
Chairman Rev. S. I. Brickman, 9 Marlborough Mansions, Cannon Hill, London NW6 1JP. ☎ 0171-431 0575. *V. Chairman* Rev. A. Levin. ☎ 0181-554 0499. *Sec.* Rabbi D.A. Katanka. ☎ 0181-905-5473.

GUILD OF JEWISH JOURNALISTS
Affiliated to the World Federation of Jewish Journalists. L. *President* D. Pela; *V. Presidents* G. M. Smith; G. Tessler; *Chairman* J. Finklestone; *H.T.* Freda Riseman, 2 Holmdale Gardens, Hendon NW4 2LX. ☎ 0181-203 2540.

JEWISH NURSES & MIDWIVES ASSOCIATION
104 Gilling Court, Belsize Grove, London NW3 4XD.
☎ 071-722 5919. Fax 0171-493 4895.
(Est. 1993) A social, educational and support group for all Jewish nurses, midwives and members of allied professions. Students welcome. *Chair* Sara Barnett (address above); *T.* Evelyne Moss, 41 Burnham Court, NW4. No regional offices at present but membership extends to Wales, Manchester, Nottingham and Leeds.

PROVINCIAL JEWISH MINISTERS' FUND
To assist small provincial congregations in providing a sufficient income for Ministers qualified to teach and preach in the English language. (Est 1884.) *H. Sec.* Rev. Dr. I. Levy, O.B.E., T.D.

RABBINIC CONFERENCE OF THE UNION OF LIBERAL & PROGRESSIVE SYNAGOGUES
The Montagu Centre, 21 Maple Street, W1P 6DS.
☎ 0171-5880 1663. Fax: 0171-436 4184. Email: montagu@ulps.demon.co.uk
Rabbinic Chairperson: Rabbi David J. Goldberg.

RABBINICAL COUNCIL OF EAST LONDON AND WEST ESSEX
8 The Lindens, Prospect Hill, Waltham Forest, E17 3EJ.
☎ 0181-5201759.
(Est 1981.) To co-ordinate and enhance Jewish com. and educ. facilities within the East London and West Essex area. Patron The Chief Rabbi; *Chairman* Rabbi E. Salasnik; *V. Chairman* Rev. S. Black; *Sec.* Rev. S. Kreiman.

RABBINICAL COUNCIL OF THE PROVINCES
151 Shadwell Lane, Leeds LS17 8DW.
☎ 0113-2370852. Fax: 0113-2370851.
President The Chief Rabbi Dr. Jonathan Sacks; *Chairman* Rabbi Y. Rubin; *V. Chairman* Rabbi J. Guttentag; *H. Tr.* Rabbi M. Ginsbury; *Sec.* Rabbi I. Goodhardt.

RABBINICAL COUNCIL OF THE UNITED SYNAGOGUE
Chairman Rabbi Y. Fine, 274 Chase Side, London N14 4PR. *Hon. Sec.* Rabbi Emanuel Levy, BA (Hons.), 11 Morton Cresc., London N14 7AH. ☎ 0181-882-2943; *V. Chairmen* Rabbi Dr. J. M. Cohen, BA, MPhil., Rabbi Z. M. Salasnik, BA (Hons.), FJC; *H. T.* Rabbi E. Mirvis, B.A.

SOUTH LONDON COMMUNAL COUNCIL
c/o 40 York Road, Cheam, Surrey, SM2 6HH.
☎ 0181-643 3228.
A grouping of Orthodox Synagogues in South London, meeting regularly to discuss matters of common concern in the fields of social, educational and other communal endeavours, also as a means of arranging joint activities where appropriate. *Correspondent* Michael Harris, 40 York Road, Cheam, Surrey, SM2 6HH. Communities involved include: Catford & Bromley, Croydon, Kingston & Surbiton, Richmond, South London, Staines, Sutton and Chabad House (Wimbledon).

UNITED SYNAGOGUE SECRETARIES' ASSOCIATION
☎ 0181-958 750. Fax: 0181-905 4449.
Chairman L. J. Ford, Edgware United Syn., Parnell Close, Edgware, Middlesex HA8 8YE.

MISCELLANEOUS ORGANISATIONS

ADVISORY COMMITTEE FOR THE ADMISSION OF JEWISH ECCLESIASTICAL OFFICERS
5 Mapesbury Road, NW2 4HZ. ☎ 0181-451 0233. Fax: 0181-830 2203. Est. 1932 to advise the Home Office in connection with applications for the admission of eccl. officers, including rabbis, ministers, readers, Talmudical students, etc. The Cttee. comprises nominees from the major synagogal and religious orgs. in the UK. Its work is conducted from the Jews' Temporary Shelter Offices. *H. Sec.* C. Lauder.

ALL-PARTY PARLIAMENTARY WAR CRIMES GROUP
House of Commons, London SW1A 0AA.
☎ 0171-222 6822
(Est. 1986.) To monitor the implementation of the War Crimes Act 1991, which enables the prosecution of alleged Nazi war criminals living in the UK. *Chairman* Rt. Hon. Lord Merlyn-Rees, P.C.; *V. Chairmen* Rt. Hon. Lord Archer of Sandwell, Q.C.; *Hon. Sec.* Lord Greville Janner, Q.C.; *Hon. Ts.* Rt. Hon., The Lord Mason.

ASSOCIATION OF JEWISH EX-SERVICEMEN AND WOMEN (AJEX)
Ajex House, East Bank, Stamford Hill, N16 5RT.
☎ 0181-800 2844. Fax: 0181-880 1117.
(Est. 1923.) *Nat. Chairman* Gerald Bean; *Gen. Sec.* J. Weisser; *Hon. Secs.* Gabriel Kaufman, David van Loen; *H. Chaplain* Rev. Dr. I. Levy, O.B.E., T.D. A list of London and Regional Branches can be obtained from the Secretary. For the Military Museum contact H. Morris, *Archivist*.

ASSOCIATION OF JEWISH GOLF CLUBS & SOCIETIES
Officers: *President* Gerald N. Tankel, Flat 9 Darnhills, Watford Road, Radlett, Herts, WD7 8LQ; *V. President* Ralph Curtis; *Sec.* Martin S. Caller, 2 Sergeants Lane, Whitefield, Manchester, M45 7TS; *Tournament Sec.* Mervyn Berg; *Assist Tournament Sec.* Stanley Fingret.

ASSOCIATION OF JEWISH HUMANISTS
12 Woodland Court, Woodlands, NW11 9QQ.
☎ 0181-455 2393.
(Est. 1983). Humanistic Jews believe each Jew has the right to create a meaningful Jewish lifestyle free from supernatural authority and imposed tradition.
Humanistic Jews believe the goal of life is personal dignity and self-esteem. Humanist Jews believe the secular roots of Jewish life are as important as the religious ones, and the survival of the Jewish people needs a reconciliation between science, personal autonomy and Jewish loyalty.
The Association of Jewish Humanists is a constituent member of the International Institute for Secular Humanistic Judaism (Jerusalem). An Associate of the Society for Humanistic Judaism, Farmington Hills, MI, U.S.A. An Affiliate of the British Humanist Association, London WC1R 4RH.
Hon. Jt. Chairmen M. Miller, 12 Woodland Court, Woodlands, NW11 9QQ, D. Wilkes, 7 Ashley Close, Hendon, N.W.4.; *Hon. Sec.* M. Miller, 12 Woodland Court, Woodlands, NW11 9QQ; *Hon. Tr.* J. Hulman, 60 Morley Crescent East, Stanmore, Middlesex.

CAMPAIGN FOR THE PROTECTION OF SHECHITA
66 Townshend Court, Townshend Road, Regents Park, London NW8 6LE.
☎ 0171-722 8523.
(Est. 1985.) To protect the freedom of Jews to perform Shechita; to make representations to Government on proposed legislation or other measures which may affect the proper performance of Shechita. Neville Kesselman, *Nat. Co-ord.* and

Hon. Solicitors; Prof. Geoffrey Alderman, M.A., D. Phil. (Oxon), F.R. Hist S.; *Political Adv.*; Chanoch Kesselman, London. Reg. *Coord.;* Rabbi Benjamin Vorst and Rabbi Dr. David Miller, M.A., M.Sc., D. Phil. (Oxon), *Rabbinical Adv.*

CELEBRITIES GUILD OF GREAT BRITAIN
Knight House, 29-31 East Barnet Road, New Barnet, Herts EN4 8RN.
☎ 0181-449 1234, 0181-449 1515, weekdays 10.00-4.00.
(Est. 1977. Reg. Charity No. 282298.) A social and fund-raising Guild of prominent people in British Jewry who organise events to raise funds to provide equipment for disabled and handicapped people. *H. Exec. Guilder* Mrs. Ella Glazer; *H. Life President*: Stanley Black, O.B.E.; *Master Guilder* Ronnie Wolfe; *Ass. Master Guilder* Leonard Fenton.

CONNECT – THE JEWISH MARRIAGE BUREAU
23 Ravenshurst Avenue, NW4 4EE.
☎ 0181-203 5207.
See Jewish Marriage Council, p.15.

CZECH MEMORIAL SCROLLS CENTRE (MEMORIAL SCROLLS TRUST)
Kent House, Rutland Gardens, London SW7 1BX.
☎ 0171-584 3741.
(Reg. Charity No.: 278900.) This permanent exhibition tells the unique story of the rescue from Prague, in 1964, of 1,564 Torah Scrolls and of their restoration and distribution on permanent loan to communities throughout the world. The exhibits include some of the scrolls, a remarkable display of Torah binders, some dating from the 18th century, and other moving reminders of the vanished communities of Bohemia and Moravia. The centre is open on Tuesdays & Thursdays from 10am to 4pm. *Jt. Chairmen* Mrs R. Shaffer, Miss C. Stuart.

HIGH SEAS SAILING CLUB
6a Langford Place, London NW8 0LL.
☎ 0171-624 0201.
(Est. 1989.) The UK's only sailing club for people with a 'Jewish affinity or friendship'. Dinghy and motorboat sections also. Membership of 180 from throughout UK and overseas. The club holds coastal sailing meets throughout the summer months. During the winter there is an active programme of lectures, sail training and social activities in the NW London area. Crewing Register maintained. Monthly newsletters. *Publ.* Wavelength (annual). *Club Commodore* Gillian Woodbridge; *V. Commodore* Brian Baumal; *Rear Commodore* Michael Doctors; *Tr.* Laurence Factor; *Sec.* Uta Gosling.

INSTITUTE OF COMMUNITY RELATIONS
101 Dunsmure Road, London N16 5HT.
☎ 0181-800 8612.
(Est. 1975) Objects: To promote racial equality and good community relations in particular between Orthodox Jews and other ethnic groups. It seeks to promote marriage and the family, human rights and moral values, and to foster Franco-British friendship. Activities: Running a number of projects including campaigns for racial equality in education and television, a campaign for single sex health services, a campaign to support marriage and the family, an information project and a project to relieve poverty. *Dir.* Rabbi Henri Brand, *Hon. Tr.* Rabbi C. Pinter; *Hon. Sec.* I. Kraus.

MISCELLANEOUS ORGANISATIONS 63

JEWISH ASSOCIATION FOR BUSINESS ETHICS
P.O. Box 3840, The Hyde, Colindale, NW9 6LG
☎ 0181-200 8007 Fax 0181-200 8061. Email: jabe@brijnet.org
(Reg. Charity No. 1038453) To encourage the highest standards of integrity in business and professional conduct by promoting the Jewish ethical approach to business.
Chairman: Stephen Rubin; *Exec. Dir.* Lorraine Spector.

JEWISH ASSOCIATION OF SPIRITUAL HEALERS
24 Greenacres, Hendon Lane, Finchley N3 3SF.
☎ 0181-349 1544.
(Est. 1966. Reg. Charity No. 275081) Aims: (1) To attempt to relieve sickness and suffering; (2) To demonstrate that Spiritual Healing is in keeping with the teachings of Judaism.
Chairman Steve Sharpe, 22 Boldmere Road, Pinner HA5 1PS; *Sec.* Audrey Cane, 24 Greenacres, Hendon Lane, Finchley N3 3SF; *Healing Centre* Ruth Green, West London Synagogue, 33 Seymour Place, London W1.

THE JEWISH COUNCIL FOR RACIAL EQUALITY
33 Seymour Place, W1H 6AT.
☎ 0181-455 0896. Fax: 0181-458 4700.
(Est. 1976. Reg. Charity No. 281236.) To improve race relations in Britain, encourage awareness in the Jewish community of responsibilities of a multi-racial society and join other organisations to combat racism; *Chairman* R. Stone; *V. Chairman* Mrs June Jacobs; *H.T.* Dr Len MacDonald; *Dir.* Dr Edie Friedman.
Projects: Developing Jewish anti-racist educational materials for schools, cheders and youth clubs; training for teachers and youth leaders on the use of anti-racist materials; the setting-up of a resource centre for youth leaders, teachers and community workers; additional campaigning on refugee and immigration issues, practical involvement with refugees and divided families; seminars with other Jewish organisations; extending cooperation with other minority groups to combat racism; establishing a campaigning role, working in solidarity with other minority organisations.

JEWISH FEMINIST GROUP
Box 39, Sisterwrite, 190 Upper Street, N1.
(Est. 1979.) To raise consciousness among Jewish women about their position in society, both as Jews and as women, and strive to improve both and combat antisemitism
Publ.: Quarterly newsletter.

JEWISH FRIENDLY SOCIETIES
Grand Order of Israel and Shield of David. *Grand Sec.* R. Salasnik
11, The Lindens, Prospect Hill, Waltham Forest, E17 3EJ.
☎ 0181-520 3531. Email: goisd@brijnet.org.
(Est. 1896.) The membership is contained in five Lodges in Metropolitan area amd one in Birmingham.

THE MAIMONIDES FOUNDATION
BCM Box 6764, London WC1N 3XX.
☎ 0171-222 1992. Fax 0171-233 0161.
(Est. 1995. Reg. Charity No. 1044028) To foster understanding and promote and facilitate dialogue, interaction and co-operation between Jews and peoples of different faiths – especially between Jews and Muslims – and to build alliances between them based on mutual respect and trust. To strengthen the cultural, spiritual and intellectual ties between Jews and Muslims as the basis of a peaceful and meaningful co-existence. *President* Lord Janner, QC; *Chairman* Dr David Khalili; *T.* Dr Richard Stone; *Exec. Cttee* Sydney S. Assor, Michael Bradfield, Denise

Cotton, Naomi Gryn, Alan Lee, David Meller, Freddy Salem, Robert Yentob; *Exec. Dir.* Douglas Krikler; *Admin.* Ilanit Chalif.

MONTAGU JEWISH COMMUNITY TRUST
North London Jewish Centre, Henriques House, 120 Oakleigh Road North, N20 9EZ.
☎ 0181-423 5840.
(Est. 1893 as West Central Club and Settlement.) A Trust concerned with the allocation of grants for community activities principally in the field of training and education. *President* B. de C. S. Montagu.

OPERATION JUDAISM
95 Willows Road, Birmingham B12 9QF.
☎ 0121-440 6673 (24 hrs ansaphone) Fax 0121-446-4199.
(Est. 1986.) Operation Judaism is the communities' defence against missionary attack. It operates nationally an information and counselling service. Man. Cttee. consists of representatives from: Office of the C. Rabbi, Board of Deputies & Lubavitch Foundation.

ROYAL BRITISH LEGION (MONASH BRANCH)
26 The Vale, NW11 8SH.
☎ 0181-458 3609. Fax 0181-455 2793.
(Est. 1936.) *Chairman* W.M. Fisher, F.C.A.; *H. Sec.* H. Goldsmith.

SHATNEZ CENTRE TRUST
22 Bell Lane, Hendon, NW4 2AD
☎ 0181-202 4005
(Est. 1990. Reg. Charity No. 1013840.) To provide Shatnez checking at the Shatnez Centre and promote Shatnez observance in the community. *Ts.* A. E. Bude, David Rabson.

TZEDEK
(Jewish Action for a Just World)
Steven Derby, Development Officer, 61 Pine Road, London NW2 6SB.
☎ 0181-452 5146. Email: tzedekuk@aol.com
(Est. 1990. Reg. Charity No. 1016767.) To provide direct support to the developing world working towards the relief and elimination of poverty regardless of race or religion; to educate people, particularly in the Jewish community as to the causes and effects of poverty and the Jewish obligation to respond.
Programmes: support for development projects through a grant making programme targeted at self-help, sustainable developments in Africa, Asia and South America; providing educational workshops on the themes of aid, development and Jewish values to schools, youth clubs and adult groups; Zimbabwe Volunteer Programme – in which Jewish volunteers have the opportunity to work for six weeks during the summer at development projects in Zimbabwe; fundraising activities.

UNITED KINGDOM JEWISH AID AND INTERNATIONAL DEVELOPMENT
33 Seymour Place, W1H 6AT.
☎ 0171-723 3442. Fax 0171-723 3445. Email ukjaid@ort.org
(Est. 1989.) UKJAID is a Jewish humanitarian organisation which responds to international disasters and promotes sustainable development, aimed at reducing deprivation and suffering, irrespective of ethnicity, gender or religion. Current projects include an orphanage in Rwanda, training community workers in trauma relief in the former Yugoslavia and a community care project for the elderly in Sarajevo. *Patrons* The Chief Rabbi, Communal Rabbi of the Spanish & Portuguese Jews' Cong., Chairman of the Council of Reform and Liberal Rabbis, President of

the Masorti Rabbinic Liaison Committee, President of the Board of Deputies of British Jews, The Lord Mishcon Q.C. Hon. D.L., Lord Janner Q.C..; *President* Kenneth D. Rubens; *Chairman* Ansel Harris; *H. Projects Dir.* Dr T. Scarlett Epstein; *Act. Dir.* Danielle Gold.

INTERNATIONAL ORGANISATIONS

JEWISH ORGANISATIONS HAVING CONSULTATIVE STATUS WITH THE ECONOMIC AND SOCIAL COUNCIL OF THE UNITED NATIONS

Agudas Israel World Org.; Coordinating Bd. of Jewish Orgs. (comprising the British BoD, the South African BoD, and the B'nai B'rith); Consultative Council of Jewish Orgs. (comprising the Anglo-Jewish Assn., the Alliance Israélite Universelle, and the Canadian Friends of the Alliance); W.J.C. Internat. Council on Jewish Social and Welfare Services (comprising American Joint Distribution Committee, World Jewish Relief, Jewish Colonization Assn., European Council of Jewish Community Services, United Hias Service, World ORT Union); Internat. Council of Jewish Women.

AGUDAS ISRAEL WORLD ORGANISATIONS

The organisation was founded in Kattowitz in 1912. Its programme was defined as being 'the solution–in the spirit of the Torah–of problems which periodically confront the Jewish people in Eretz Yisroel and the Diaspora'. This object was to be fulfilled 'by coordination of Orthodox Jewish effort throughout the world ... by the representation and protection of the interests of Torah-true Jewish communities. The programme was formulated by our ancestors for the unconditional acceptance by all Jewish generations of the Biblical injunction 'And ye shall be unto Me a kingdom of priests and a holy nation.' The organisation seeks to implement this injunction by its endeavours. It opposes assimilation and different interpretations of Jewish nationhood.' Consult. status with United Nations, New York and Geneva, and Unesco in Paris.

Agudas Israel of Gt. Britain. *Presidium:* Rabbi J. H. Dunner, Rabbi Y. H. Rosenbaum, 95-99 Stamford Hill, N16 5DN. ☎ 0181-800 6688. Fax 0181-800-5000.
Publ.: Jewish Tribune (weekly).

Zeire Agudas Israel, (Reg. Charity No. 253513.), 95 Stamford Hill, N16; 35a Northumberland Street, Salford, 7. *Chairman* J. Schleider. *Sec. Gen.*

Agudas Israel Community Services, (Reg. Charity No. 287367), 97 Stamford Hill, N16 5DN. ☎ 0181-800 6688 & 802 6627. Est. 1980 to help find suitable employment for observant Jews, including immigrants and Yiddish speakers and other social services.

Beth Jacob Council of Great Britain, 97 Stamford Hill, N16 5DN. The following institutions are under the auspices of the Council: Teachers' Training Seminar, 69 Allerton Road, N16. *Princ.* Rabbi J. H. Dunner. *Menahel:* Rabbi B. Dunner, Beth Jacob Classes and Groups, 65 Amhurst Pk., N16 5ND. Gateshead Training Colleges for Teachers. (See p. 103.)

Jewish Rescue and Relief Cttee., (Reg. Charity No. X99706ES), 215 Golders Green Rd., NW11 9BY. ☎ 0181-458 1710. *Chairman* A. Strom.

Keren Hatorah Cttee., (Reg. Charity No. 281384). (For the relief of religious, educational and social institutions, a division of Agudas Yisroel in Great Britain.), 97 Stamford Hill, N16 5DN. ☎ 0181-800 6688. *Exec. Dir.* Rabbi C. Y. Davis.

Russian Immigrant Aid Fund, for the material and spiritual rehabilitation of Russian immigrants in Israel. 97 Stamford Hill, N16 5DN. ☎ 0181-800 6688. *Chairman* I. M. Cymerman.

Society of Friends of the Torah, (Reg. Charity No. 238230), 97 Stamford Hill, N16 5DN, and, 215 Golders Green Rd., NW11 9BY. ☎ 0181-800 6687, 0181-458 9988. *Dir.* J. Davis.

ALLIANCE ISRAELITE UNIVERSELLE
45 rue la Bruyère, F 75425 Paris Cedex 09.
☎ (1)42803500. Fax (1) 48 74 51 33. E:mail aiu@imaginet.fr
(Est. 1860.) This educative and cultural-oriented organisation essentially works through a network of schools which affects today more than 20,000 pupils and its century-old defence of human rights before governmental and international institutions all over the world. Has two quarterly pubs: Les Cahiers de L'Alliance Israélite Universelle and Les Nouveaux Cahiers; and a centre for pedagogical pubs: Créer-Didactique. Its library with more than 120,000 books in the field of Hebraica-Judaica and its College des Etudes juives make it one of the most important Jewish centres in Europe. Today the Alliance operates in Belgium, Canada, France, Iran, Israel, Morocco, Spain. *President* Prof. A. Steg; *Dir.* Jean-Jacques Wahl.

ASIA PACIFIC JEWISH ASSOCIATION
G.P.O. Box 5402 CC, Melbourne, Victoria, Australia 3001.
☎ (03) 9828 8570. Fax (03) 9828 8584. E:mail aija@ozemail.com.au
The Assn. is the regional rep. org. for the Jewish coms. in Australia, Fiji, Hawaii, Hong Kong, India, Japan, Korea, New Caledonia, New Zealand, Papua New Guinea, Philippines, Singapore, Sri Lanka, Tahiti, Taiwan and Thailand. *Contact* Charla Smith.

B'NAI B'RITH
B'nai B'rith is over 150 years old and is open to all Jews whatever their religious background and affiliation. We operate in 54 countries, with headquarters in Washington DC and consultative status at the United Nations in New York, providing a high political profile for B'nai B'rith in the U.S.A.

In the United Kingdom B'nai B'rith has a major series of service, cultural and social activities. B'nai B'rith works with youth through Hillel and BBYO, and with the elderly through the B'nai B'rith Housing Society. B'nai B'rith donates scholarships to Quiryat Gat in Israel. It supports the Jewish Community Information intiative (JCI, see p.000) which is now in a position to provide a resource of all Jewish communal activities across Britain.

With the backing of the UK Government it has been introducing Western "free market" concepts to emerging East European democracies through the B'nai B'rith consultancy and training scheme. The B'nai B'rith Music Festival has created new interest in Jewish music and the arts. Newer projects include the computerised database of all the resources of Jewish Continuity. Its latest project, the B'nai B'rith Family Services group, will maintain the integrity of the Jewish family unit through seminars and projects. First steps in creating a European Jewish union of B'nai B'rith have been taken with the signing of a Declaration of Intent for a form of joint organisation with B'nai B'rith on the continent of Europe. B'nai B'rith local groups enjoy their own cultural, social and service programmes in addition to the above.

International HQ., 1640 Rhode Island Avenue, N.W., Washington D.C., U.S.A. ☎ (202) 857 6600. Fax (202) 857 1099. *President* Tommy Baer; *Exec. V. President* Dr Sidney Clearfield.

District 15 of Gt. Britain and Ireland, B'nai B'rith, Hillel House, 1/2 Endsleigh Street, WC1H 0DS. ☎ 0171-387 5278 and 5954. Fax 0171-387 8014. *Nat. President* Alan Cohen; *V. Presidents* S. G. Saideman, Valerie Belle; *Nat. T. G.* Weinberg; *Nat. Sec.* Norman King; *Exec. Dir.* Mark Marcus, B.A. (Com.).

Lodges
Abraham Lewin (Enfield) Unity: Ben Gurion (Southgate) Unity; Birmingham Joint;

Bournemouth Unity; Cheshire Unity; Ealing (Selig Brodetsky) Joint; Edgware Women; Finchley Joint; First Lodge of England; First Women; First Unity; Ilford (Golda Meir) Unity; Jerusalem (Wembley and District); Kentgate Joint; Leeds Unity: Leo Baeck Men's; Leo Baeck Women's; Manchester; North Manchester Unity; Nottingham Joint; Pegasus Unity; Raoul Wallenberg Unity; Shlomo Argov Unity; Southend and District Unity; Surrey Joint; Thames; Thanet Montefiore Unity; West Riding Shalom; Wolverhampton Men; Yad B'Yad Unity; Yitzchak Rabin.

BRITISH ASSOCIATION OF ETHIOPIAN JEWRY
(formerly Falasha Welfare Association)
World Jewish Relief, Drayton House, 30 Gordon Street, WC1H 0AN.
☎ 0171-387 3925.
Est. 1967 and now merged with WJR. All aid for Ethiopian Jewry is now directed towards their resettlement in Israel.

COMMONWEALTH JEWISH COUNCIL
BCM Box 6871, London WC1N 3XX.
☎ 0171-222 2120. Fax 0171-222 1781.
(Est. 1982.) To provide links between Commonwealth Jewish coms.; to provide a central rep. voice for Commonwealth Jewish coms. and to help preserve their religious and cultural heritage; to seek ways to strengthen Commonwealth Jewish coms. in accordance with their individual needs and wishes and provide mutual help and cooperation. *President* Lord Janner, Q.C.; *Chairman* Jeff Durkin; *V. Chairman* Paul Secher; *Sec.* J. Galaun, F.C.A.; *H. T. H.B.* Lipsith; *Dir.* Maureen Gold.
There are 36 member coms. including those in Antigua, Australia, Bahamas, Barbados, Belize, Bermuda, Botswana, Canada, Cayman Is., Cyprus, Fiji, Gibraltar, Guernsey, Hong Kong, India, Isle of Man, Jamaica, Jersey, Kenya, Mauritius, Namibia, New Zealand, Nigeria, Singapore, Sri Lanka, Trinidad & Tobago, Turks & Caicos Is., United Kingdom, Zambia and Zimbabwe.

Commonwealth Jewish Trust. (Reg. Charity No. 287564). *Trs.* Lord Janner, Edward Bronfman, Harvey Lipsith, Dorothy Reitman, Jack Galaun, Sir Jack Zunz.
The Trust undertakes charitable projects in Jewish coms. throughout the Commonwealth, with special emphasis on smaller coms.

CONFERENCE OF EUROPEAN RABBIS
735 High Road, N12 0US.
☎ 0181-343 8989.
President Emer. Chief Rabbi Lord Jakobovits; *V. President* Grand Rabbin, J. Sitruk, Chief Rabbi of France; *Dir.* Rabbi A. M. Rose, P.O.B. 5324, Jerusalem, Israel.
Est. 1957, to provide a medium for co-operation on matters of common concern to rabbis of European communities.

CONFERENCE ON JEWISH MATERIAL CLAIMS AGAINST GERMANY, Inc.
15 East 26th Street, New York, N.Y. 10010.
☎ 212-696 4944. Fax 212-679 2126.
President Rabbi I. Miller. *Sec.* S. Kagan; *Tr.* A. Lewinsky. (Est 1951.) Has admin. funds received from the Federal German Republic for relief, rehabilitation and resettlement of victims of Nazi persecution residing outside Israel. Residual funds are now used for com. leaders of destroyed Jewish coms. or their widows, and for needy non-Jews who saved Jewish life at the risk of their own. Now also admin. Hardship Fund intended primarily for Jewish victims of Nazi persecution who left Eastern Europe after 1965. Since January, 1993 also administers Article 2 Fund for

the benefit of severely persecuted Nazi victims. The FDr President was the late Dr Nahum Goldmann.

CONSULTATIVE COUNCIL OF JEWISH ORGANISATIONS
420 Lexington Avenue, New York City, N.Y. 10170.
☎ (212) 808-5437. Fax (212) 983-0094.
Est. 1946 for the purpose of cooperating with the U.N. and other intergovernmental orgs. and agencies in the advancement of human rights and the safeguarding of Jewish interests. Constituent Orgs.: Alliance Israelite Universelle, AJA, Canadian Frs. A.I.U. *Chairmen* Prof. Ady Steg, Clemens Nathan, Joseph Nuss; *Sec. Gen.* Warren Green.

EUROPEAN ASSOCIATION FOR JEWISH STUDIES
Secretariat: Oxford Centre for Hebrew and Jewish Studies, Yarnton Manor, Yarnton, Oxon OX5 1PY. ☎ 01865 377946.
Publ. Newsletter.

EUROPEAN COUNCIL OF JEWISH COMMUNITIES
74 Gloucester Place, London W1H 3HN.
☎ 0171-224-3445. Fax 0171-224-3446. Email: ecjc@ort.org. Home page: JEWL-Jewish Euro Web Link: http://www.ort.org/ecjc/
Est. 1968 as the European Council of Jewish Community Services. The mission of the ECJC is to provide a forum for inter-European planning and co-operation in the areas of social welfare, formal and informal Jewish education, leadership training and culture. Projects and activities include: MA'AYAN – The European Conference on Jewish Education; CARELINK – The European Jewish Welfare Fund; The European Centre for Jewish Leadership–LE'ATID EUROPE; Social Commission; European Commission Liaison Group.
A wide range of activities are organised in the framework of four ECJC regional co-operation projects: Central European Co-operation Region; Mediterranean Co-operation Region; Nordic Co-operation Region; Southeastern European Co-operation Region.
Publ.: FAX-LINK The European Bulletin Board, Current Trends in European Jewry.
Fifty member organisations in 35 European countries. *President* David J. Lewis; *Chair* Ruth Zilkha; *Exec. Dir.* Michael May.

EUROPEAN JEWISH FORUM
c/o 31 Ridge Hill, London NW11 8PR.
☎ 0181-202 2699. Fax 0181-202 1276.
(Est. 1989) Development of individual personal links between European Jewish community and Israel. *Chairman* Dr Shimon Samuels (France); *Vice Chairman* Miklos Hernadi (Hungary); *Sec.* Thelma Epstein (G.B.).

EUROPEAN JEWISH PUBLICATION SOCIETY
c/o 1st Floor, Pegasus House, 37/43 Sackville St., London W1X 2DL.
☎ 0171-333 8111. Fax 0171-333 0660.
(Est. 1994. Reg. Charity No. 3002158) A registered charity which makes grants to assist in the publication and distribution of books relating to Jewish literature, history, religion, philosophy, politics and culture. *President* Sir Isaiah Berlin; *Chairman* Frederick Worms; *Hon. Sec.* Dr Sidney Brichto; *Editorial Coord.* Colin Shindler, 80 Stanhope Ave., N3 3NA. ☎ 0181-349 1264

EUROPEAN UNION OF JEWISH STUDENTS
89 Chaussée de Vleurgat, B-1050, Brussels, Belgium.
☎ 010-32-2-647 72 79. Fax 010-32-2-6482431. Email: 106211.2511@compuserve.com. Website: http://www-students.unisg.ch/eujs/

Est. 1978 for co-ordination purposes between nat. unions in 32 countries. It represents more than 170,000 European Jewish students in international Jewish and non-Jewish forums dealing with cultural and political matters and opposes all forms of racism and fascism. The E.U.J.S. is also a 'service org.' for students. It helps with courses abroad, supplies material on different subjects for univ. students and organises visits and seminars. *H. Presidents* Mrs Simone Veil, Maram Stern; *H. Mems.* Hon. Greville Janner, Q.C., M.P. (Brit.), David Susskind (Belgium), Suzy Jurysta (B.), Laslov Kadelburg (Yu.); *President* Ariane Platt.

Member unions in: Austria, Belgium, Belorus, Britain, Bulgaria, Czech, Croatia, Denmark, Estonia, Finland, France, Germany, Gibraltar, Greece, Holland, Hungary, Ireland, Italy, Latvia, Lithuania, Luxembourg, Norway, Poland, Portugal, Russia, Serbia, Slovakia, Spain, Sweden, Switzerland, Turkey, Ukraine.

FRIENDSHIP WITH ISRAEL (European Parliament)
51 Tavistock Court, Tavistock Square, WC1H 9HG.
☎ 0171-387 4925.
(Est. 1979.) All-Party Group in European Parl. with more than 120 MEPs. Aims at promoting friendship and co-operation between the European Com. and Israel. Provides up-to-date inf. on Israeli matters and a balanced view of Middle East events. Holds regular meetings in Strasbourg at Palais de l'Europe when the Euro-Parl. sits. Recognised as an official 'Inter-Parl. Group'. H. Patron Mrs. Simone Veil MEP, past President, Euro-Parl.; *Chairman* Tom Normanton, MEP (UK); *V. Chairmen* Erik Blumenfeld, MEP, Hans-Joachim Seeler, MEP (West Germany), Hans Nord, MEP (Holland), John Tomlinson, MEP (UK); *H. Sec.* John Marshall, MEP (UK); *Dir.* Mrs. Sylvia Sheff, J.P., B.A.

HEBREWARE® USER GROUP
46 Norfolk Avenue, N15 6JX.
☎ 0181-802 6143. Fax 0181-802 1130
HEBREWARE® is the leading User Group for Hebrew computer software users in Europe.
Contact: Mr Menasche Scharf. Branches: USA, Belgium, Israel.

HEIMLER INTERNATIONAL
(Formerly The Heimler Foundation)
Peter Hudson, 47 Rosebery Road, SW2 4DQ
☎ 0181-674 6999.
(Est. 1972.) Heimler International was set up to facilitate the work and ideas of Prof. Eugene Heimler. Its aims are: 1. to provide counselling and therapy for individuals and groups, using the Heimler approach; 2. to provide basic and advanced training in the Heimler Method; 3. to recognise advanced practitioners and lecturers in the Heimler Method; 4. to sanction and collect bona fide research, act as a focal point, publish books/tapes describing the Heimler Method.

There are Branches in several different countries in Europe, Canada, USA.

HIAS
333 7th Avenue, New York, N.Y. 1000, U.S.A.
European H.Q.: 75 rue de Lyon 1211, Geneva 13, Switzerland.
Est. August, 1954, through merger of the Hebrew Sheltering and Immigrant Aid Society (HIAS), United Service for New Americans (USNA) and the migration service of the American Joint Distribution Committee (AJDC).

HIAS, the Hebrew Immigrant Aid Society, has been the internat. migration agency of the organised Amer. Jewish com. since its founding in 1880. It assists Jewish migrants and refugees to countries of freedom and security, arranges reception on arrival, helps newcomers become integrated in their new coms. Works with Govt. agencies and other orgs. to promote increased immigration opportunities. *President* Ben Zion Leuchter.

INSTITUTE FOR JEWISH POLICY RESEARCH
79 Wimpole Street, W1M 7DD.
☎ 0171-935 8266. Fax 0171-935 3252. Email: jpr@ort.org. Website: http://www.ort.org/communit/jpr.
President Lord Rothschild; *V. President* William Frankel CBE; *Chairman* Peter L. Levy OBE; *Dep. Chairman* Lord Haskel; *Tr.* Milton Z. Levine; *Int. Adv. Bd.*, Lord Weidenfeld; *Res. Bd.* Peter M. Oppenheimer; *Exec. Director* Antony Lerman; *Res. Dir.* Prof. Barry Kosmin; *Assist. Dir.* Lena Stanley-Clamp and Jacqueline Sallon.

JPR is an independent think-tank which informs and influences policy, opinion and decision-making on issues affecting Jewish life worldwide by conducting and commissioning research, developing and disseminating policy proposals and promoting public debate. JPR's public activities include lectures, symposia, policy seminars and conferences.

Publications: Antisemitism World Report (annual survey); East European Jewish Affairs (twice a year); Patterns of Prejudice (quarterly); JPR Policy Papers, Research Findings.

INTERNATIONAL ASSOCIATION OF JEWISH LAWYERS & JURISTS
4 Brick Court, Temple, London EC4Y 9AD
☎ 0171-583 8455. Fax 0171-353 1699.
(Est. 1990) The objectives of the Association are: to contribute, alone or in co-operation with other international or national organisations, towards the establishment of an international legal order based on the Rule of Law in relations between all nations and states; to promote human rights and the principles of equality of men and the right of all states and peoples to live in peace; to act against racism and antisemitism, whether openly expressed or covertly exercised, *inter alia*, where necessary, by legal proceedings; to promote the study of legal problems affecting the world's Jewish communities in the context of national and international law; to promote, in consultation with the legal profession within the State of Israel and its agencies, the study of legal problems of particular concern to the State of Israel; to promote the study of Jewish law in comparison with other laws and facilitate the exchange of any information resulting from research thereto among member groups; to collect and disseminate information concerning the *de facto* and *de jure* status of the Jewish communities and other minority ethnic and religious groups throughout the world and where the occasion arises, to give help and support pursuant to human rights treaties; to promote and support co-operation and communication between the Association's member groups; to concern itself with any other matter of legal interest considered of relevance by any of the member groups.
President Lord Woolf; *V. Presidents* Mr F. Ashe Lincoln, His Honour Israel Finestein QC, Jonathan Goldberg QC; *Chairman* Her Honour Myrella Cohen QC; *V. Chairman* Mr Jonathan Lewis; *Sec.* Mrs Patricia May; *T.* Miss Jane Mirwitch.

INTERNATIONAL COUNCIL OF CHRISTIANS AND JEWS
Martin Buber Haus, Werlestrasse 2, Postfach 1129, D-64629, Heppenheim, Germany.
☎ (0 62 52) 5041. Fax (0 62 52) 68331.
President Prof. Dr Martin Stohr; *Gen. Sec.* Rev. Dr Jacobus Schoneveld; *Chairman Exec. Cttee.* Sir Sigmund Sternberg, O.St.J., K.C.S.G., J.P.
Est. 1974 to strengthen Jewish-Christian understanding on an international basis and to co-ordinate and initiate programmes and activities for this purpose.

INTERNATIONAL COUNCIL OF JEWISH WOMEN
1110 Finch Avenue West, Suite 518, Downsview, Ontario, Canada M3J 2T2.
(Est. 1912.) The Council promotes through its 42 autonomous National affiliates in 40 countries throughout all continents, friendly relations among Jewish women all over the world. It seeks to promote co-operation among Jewish women and

advance their status in Jewish and secular law; guides in developing Jewish education, social welfare and volunteer training programmes. It has consultative status with the Council of Europe, the U.N. Economic and Social Council (Ecosoc), the Unicef and Unesco. The British affiliate is The League of Jewish Women (see p.4). *V. President* Mrs Addrianne Sherman.

INTERNATIONAL COUNCIL ON JEWISH SOCIAL AND WELFARE SERVICES
Drayton House, 30 Gordon Street, London WC1H 0AN. ☎ 0171-387 3925. Fax 0171-383 4810.
Est. 1961. Member Organisations: Amer. Jt. Distribution Cttee.; CBF-WJR.; European Council of Jewish Com. Services; Hias; World ORT Union. *Exec. Sec.* C. R. Mariner.

INTERNATIONAL JEWISH GENEALOGICAL RESOURCES [IJGR(UK)]
25 Westbourne Road, Edgbaston, Birmingham B15 3TX.
☎ 0121-454 0408. Fax 0121-454 9758.
(Est. 1988). Provides guidance on Jewish geneaology; has a library including material on Anglo-Jewry/Anglo-Australasian Jewry; microfilm of Jewish Chronicle, etc. Research undertaken.
Org. Dr Anthony P. Joseph and Mrs Judith Joseph.

INTERNATIONAL JEWISH VEGETARIAN SOCIETY
Bet Teva, 853/855 Finchley Road, NW11 8LX.
☎ 0181-455 0692. Fax 0181-455 0692
(Est. 1965. Reg. Charity No. 258581.) Affiliated to the International Vegetarian Union. Branches: N. and S. America, S. Africa, Israel, Australia. *Chairman* A. Jackson; *H. Sec.* S. Labelda.

JCA CHARITABLE FOUNDATION
Victoria Palace Theatre, Victoria St., SW1E 5EA..
☎ 0171-828 0600. Fax 0171-828 6882.
(Reg. Charity No. 207031) Charitable company est. in 1891 by Baron Maurice de Hirsch to assist poor and needy Jews. The JCA was instrumental in promoting the emigration from Russia of thousands of Jews who were settled in farm 'colonies' in North and South America, Palestine/Israel and elsewhere.
Today JCA's main efforts are in Israel in rural areas where it supports schs., instits. of higher learning, agricultural research and helps to promote the subsistence of needy Jews. *President* Sir Stephen Waley-Cohen, Bt.; *Manager* Y. Lothan.

JEWISH RECONSTRUCTIONIST FEDERATION (JRF, formerly FRCH)
1299 Church Road, Wyncote, PA 19095.
☎ (215) 887-1988. Fax (215) 887-5348.
(Est. 1955) JRF is the congrgational arm of the Reconstructionist movement, representing over eighty affiliates in North America. Dedicated to the concept of Judaism as an evolving religious civilisation, JRF provides outreach, consulting, programmatic and educational support to its congregations and havurot. JRF is the publisher of a variety of books, magazines and the *Kol Haneshamah* prayerbook series.

JEWS OF ZAMBIA PROJECT
34 John Street, London WC1N 2EU, and Dr Michael Bush, PO Box 30020, Lusaka, Zambia.
☎ 0171-831 0551. Fax 0171-405 3280.
(Est. 1989.) To record the history of the Jews in Zambia.
Committee Edwin Wulfsohn, Michael Galaun, Malcolm J. Gee, F.C.A.; *Jt. Authors* Frank Shapiro, M.A. and Hugh Macmillan.

JORDAN IS PALESTINE COMMITTEE (UK)
Citi Box 157, 2 Old Brompton Road, London SW7 3DQ.
☎ 0171-584 1844.
The aims and objectives of the Jordan is Palestine Committee are: To show that the Palestine Arabs are not a homeless people; To show that Israel is only one-fifth of Mandated Palestine; To show that Jordan, in other words, is Arab Palestine; To show that the real problem is the continuing rejection, by most Arab states, of Israel – in any part of former Palestine; To help advance the peace process by making these facts widely known.
JIP has no party political affiliation, and is an independent International Organisation.
President The Earl of Balfour; *Nat. Dir.* Mrs. Mia Silver; *Tr.* Uri Rabin.

MACCABI WORLD UNION
Kfar Maccabiah, Ramat Gan 52105, Israel.
The Union (est. 1921) is a coordinating body for the promotion and advancement of sports, educational and cultural activities among Jewish communities worldwide. *President* R. Bakalarz; *Chairman* Uzi Netanel; *Chairman, European Maccabi Confederation* Michel Grun. *Exec. Dir.* E. Tiberger. See Maccabi Assns., p.?.

MEMORIAL FOUNDATION FOR JEWISH CULTURE
15 East 26th Street, New York N.Y. 10010.
☎ 212 679-4074.
(Est. 1964.) Supports Jewish cultural and educational programmes all over the world in co-operation with educational research and scholarly orgs., and conducts annual scholarship and fellowship programmes in Jewish fields.
President J. Spitzer; *Chairman of Exec. Cttee.* Rabbi A. Schindler; *Sec.* J. Jacobs; *Exec. V. President* Dr J. Hochbaum.

SHAPE INTERNATIONAL JEWISH COMMUNITY
c/o SHAPE Chaplains' Office, B-7010 SHAPE, Belgium.
☎/Fax (32) 6572 8769.
(Est. 1967). To meet the spiritual, social and educational needs of Jewish military and civilian personnel and their families serving at or temporarily assigned to SHAPE, Mons, Belgium. *Lay Leader* Wing Commander Stephen Griffiths, MBE, RAF.

SIMON WIESENTHAL CENTRE, EUROPEAN OFFICE
64 Avenue Marceau, 75008 Paris, France.
☎ (331) 4723-7637. Fax (331) 4720-8401.
London office: Simon Wiesenthal Centre UK, 27 Old Gloucester Street, WC1N 3XX.
☎ 0171-419 5014. Fax 0171-831 9489. Email: csweurope@compuserve.com.
(Est. Los Angeles, 1979). To study the contemporary Jewish and general social condition in Europe by drawing lessons from the Holocaust experience.
To monitor, combat and educate against Anti-Semitism, Racism and Prejudice.
Int. Dir. Rabbi Marvin Hier; *Chairman, Board of Trustees* Samuel Belzberg; *Dir. for Int. Affairs* Dr Shimon Samuels. 400,000 members. Head-quarters: Los Angeles Offices in: New York, Chicago, Washington D.C., Miami, Toronto, Jerusalem, Paris, Buenos Aires.

WORLD COUNCIL OF CONSERVATIVE/MASORTI SYNAGOGUES
155 Fifth Avenue, New York, N.Y. 10010.
☎ 212-533 7800 (Ext 2014); Fax 212-353 9439.
2 Agron St., PO Box 7456, Jerusalem 91073.
☎ 02-256 386.

(Est. 1957.) To foster the growth of Conservative Judaism in more than 30 countries in which it operates and to coordinate the activities of its autonomous orgs. and regions. Its constituents include the Utd. Syn. of Conservative Judaism, Rabbinical Assembly, Women's League for Conservative Judaism, Nat. Fed. of Jewish Men's Clubs, Jewish Educators Assembly, Israeli Masorti Movement, British Masorti Assembly of Synagogues, Utd. Syn. of India, and the Seminario Rabinico Latinamericano, Buenos Aires. *President* Rabbi Marc N. Liebhaber; *Co-President* Rabbi Benjamin Z. Kreitman; *Chairman of Exec. Cttee.* Rabbi Alan Silverstein; *Chairman of Bd.* Rabbi Jack Topal.

WORLD JEWISH CONGRESS
(a) To co-ordinate the efforts of its affliated orgs., in respect of the political, economic, social, religious and cultural problems of the Jewish people; (b) to secure the rights, status and interests of Jews and Jewish communities and to defend them wherever they are denied, violated or imperiled; (c) to encourage and assist the creative development of Jewish social, religious and cultural life throughout the world; (d) to represent and act on behalf of its affiliated orgs. before governmental, intergovernmental and other international authorities in respect of matters which concern the Jewish people as a whole. *FDr President* Late Dr N. Goldmann; *Emer, President* P. M. Klutznick; *President* Edgar M. Bronfman; *Sec. Gen.* Israel Singer; *Chairman, Gov. Bd.* Mendel Kaplan; *Co-Chairman Gov. Bd.* Isi J. Leibler, A.O., C.B.E.; *Chairmen of Regions:* North America, Prof Irwin Cotler, Mrs Evelyn Sommer; Latin America, Dr David Goldberg, Dr Benno Milnitzky; Europe, Jean Kahn, Judge Israel Finestein, Q.C.; Israel, Matityahu Droblas, Yehiel Leket; Russia, Dr Michael Chlenov, Roman Spektor.
Principal Offices: New York, 501 Madison Avenue, 17th Fl., NY 10022. ☎ 755 5770; Geneva, 1 rue de Varembe. ☎ 734-13-25; Paris, 78 Av. des Champs Elysées. ☎ 4359 9463, Fax 4225 4528; Buenos Aires, Casilla 20, Suc. 53. ☎ 962-5028; Jerusalem, P.O.B. 4293, Jerusalem 91042, Rehov Jabotinsky 21. ☎ 635 261/4.
Publ.: Report W.J.C. (monthly), Boletin de Información O.J.I. (Spanish) (fortnightly), Gesher (Hebrew) (quarterly), Batfutzot (Hebrew).

WORLD ORT UNION
1 Rue de Varembé, Geneva, Switzerland.
☎ (022) 73414 34. Fax (022) 734 1096.
(Est. 1880.) Organisation for educational Resources and Technological training. Over three and a half million students have been trained since 1880, and currently 260,000 students are being trained in 60 countries in different parts of the world.
Operational Headquarters in U.K.: World ORT Trust, 126 Albert St., London NW1 7NF. ☎ 0171-446 8500.

WORLD UNION FOR PROGRESSIVE JUDAISM
13 King David Street, 94101 Jerusalem. ☎ 972 26203 447. Fax 262 203 446
(Est. 1926.) To foster the international growth and practice of Progressive Judaism, and to coordinate the activities of its autonomous constituent organisations. Affiliates are located in 25 countries. *President* Austin Beutel; *Exec. Dir.* Rabbi R. Hirsch; *Dir. N.A. Operations* Clifford Kielwin.
European Office: *Hon. Sec.* Oliver Kurer, The Montagu Centre, 21 Maple Street, London, WIP 6DS. ☎ 0171-637 7442; Fax 0171-436 4184. Email: es_wupj@compuserve.com.

WORLD UNION OF JEWISH STUDENTS
P.O. Box 7914, Jerusalem 91077, Israel.
☎ 02 610133. Fax 02 610741.
Est. 1924 to fight antisemitism and to act as an umbrella organization for national Jewish students' bodies; organizes educational programmes, leadership training

seminars, and Project Areivim, a service programme for Diaspora coms.; divided into six regions; Congress every three years; members: 51 national unions representing over 700,000 students; NGO member of UNESCO; Youth affiliate of the World Jewish Congress; member organization of the World Zionist Organization. *First President* Prof. Albert Einstein; *Chairman* David Gold; *Exec. Dir.* Eiran Gazit. *Publs.* Heritage & history, WUJS Reports, WUJS Leads, the Jewish student activist handbook.

LONDON (219,000)

SYNAGOGUES

(D) where shown indicates regular daily services are held.

Ashkenazi

United Synagogue

Constituent and Affiliated Synagogues of the United Synagogue, Adler House, 735 High Road, N12 0US. *Chief Exec.* J. M. Lew, B.Comm., A.C.M.A. ☎ 0181-343 8989. Fax 0181-343 6262.

CONSTITUENT SYNAGOGUES
Belmont Synagogue, 101 Vernon Dr, Stanmore, Middx. HA7 2BW. *M.* Rabbi D. Roselaar; *Admin.* Mrs C. Fletcher. ☎ 0181-426 0104 Fax 0181-427 2046. (D)
Borehamwood & Elstree Synagogue, Croxdale Road, Borehamwood, Herts. WD6 4QF. ☎ 0181-386 5227. Fax 0181-386 3303. (Est. 1955.) *M.* Rabbi A. Plancey; *Admin.* B. Winterman. (D)
Bushey & District Synagogue, 177/189 Sparrows Herne, Bushey, Herts. WD2 1AJ. ☎ 0181-950 7340. Fax 0181-421 8267, *M.* Rabbi Z. M. Salasnik, B.A., F.J.C.; *Admin.* Mrs M. Chambers. (D)
Central Synagogue, (Great Portland St.), 36-40 Hallam St., W1N 6NN. ☎ 0171-580 1355. Fax 0171-636 3831. (Consecrated 1870, destroyed by enemy action May, 1941, rebuilt 1958.) Admin.'s Office 36 Hallam Street, W1N 6NN; *M.* Rabbi B. Marcus; *R.* J. Morgraff; *Admin.* Mrs C. Jowell.
Chigwell and Hainault Synagogue, Limes Ave., Chigwell, Essex IG7 5NT. ☎ 0181-500 2451. *M.*; *Admin.* W. Land. (D)
Clayhall Synagogue, Sinclair Hse., Woodford Bridge Rd., Ilford, Essex IG4 5LN. ☎ 0181-551 6533. Fax 0181-551 9803. *M.* Rabbi A.M. Sufrin; *Admin.* Mrs L. Brandon.
Cockfosters & N. Southgate Synagogue, Old Farm Av., Southgate, N14 5QR. ☎ 0181-886 8225. (Est. 1948. Consecrated Dec., 1954). *M.* Rabbi Y. Fine, B.A.; *R.* Rev. D. Speier; *Admin.* Mrs R. Graye.
Cricklewood Synagogue, 131 Walm Lane, NW2 3AU. ☎ 0181-452 1739. (Consecrated 1931.) *M.* Rev. G. Glausiusz; *Admin.* K. N. Gamse. (D)
Dollis Hill Synagogue, Parkside, Dollis Hill Lane, NW2 6RJ. ☎ 0181-452 7172. *R.*; *Admin.* Warren Land.
Ealing Synagogue, 15 Grange Road, Ealing, W5 5QN. ☎ 0181-579 4894. *M.* Rabbi Dr J. G. Jacobs, M.A.; *Admin.* Mrs S. Hayman.
Edgware Synagogue, Parnell Close, Edgware Way, Edgware, Middx. HA8 8YE. ☎ 0181-958 7508. Fax 0181-905 4449. *M.* Rabbi B. Rabinowitz, B.A., M.Phil.; *R.* Rev. S. L. Robins, A.R.C.M.; *Admin.* L. Ford. (D)
Finchley Synagogue, Kinloss Gdns., N3 3DU. ☎ 0181-346 8551. Fax 0181-343 1180. (Consecrated 1935.) *M.* Rabbi E. Mirvis; *Admin.* Mrs B. Fireman. (D)
Finsbury Park Synagogue, 220 Green Lanes, N4 2NT. ☎ 0181-800 3526. Fax 0181-383 4934. *M.* Rabbi A. Cohn; *R.* Rev. E. Krausher; *Admin.* H. Mather.
Golders Green Synagogue, 41 Dunstan Road, NW11 8AE. ☎ 0181-455 2460. (Consecrated 1922.) *M.* Rev. S. Djanogly; *R.* Rabbi D. Katanka, M.A.; *Admin.* Mrs S. Alexander. (D)
Hackney & East London Synagogue, Brenthouse Road, Mare Street, E9 6QG. ☎ 0181-985 4600. Fax 0181-986 9507. (Consecrated 1897; enlarged and reconsecrated 1936, amalgamated 1993.) *M.* Rev. A. Greenbat; *Admin.* Mrs B. Heumann.
Hammersmith and West Kensington Synagogue, 71 Brook Green, Hammersmith,

W6 7BE. ☎ 0171-602 1405. (Consecrated 1890.) *M.* ; *Admin.* S. Williams.
Hampstead Garden Suburb Synagogue, Norrice Lea, N2 0RE. ☎ 0181-455 8126. Fax 0181-201 9247. (Consecrated 1934). *M.* Rabbi E.L. Jackson, B.A.; *R.* Chazan A. Freilich; *Admin.* Mrs M. S. Wolff. (D)
Hampstead Synagogue, Dennington Park Road, West Hampstead, NW6 1AX. ☎ 0171-435 1518. Fax 0171-431 8369. (Consecrated 1892. Reg. Charity No. 242552) *M.* Rabbi M.J. Harris; *R.* S. Brickman; *Admin.* I. Nadel. (D)
Hendon Synagogue, 18 Raleigh Close, Wykeham Road, NW4 2TA. ☎ 0181-202 6924. Fax 0181-202 1720 (Consecrated 1935.) *M.* ; *Emer. M.* Rev. L. Hardman, M.A.; *R.* Rev. S. Neuman; *Exec. Sec.* J. Benson. (D)
Highgate Synagogue (Est. 1929.) Grimshaw Close, 57 North Road, Highgate, N6 4BJ. ☎ 0181-340 7655. *M.* Rabbi I.H. Sufrin, ☎ 0181-341 1714; *Admin.* Mrs J. Rubin.
Ilford Synagogue, 22 Beehive Lane, Ilford, Essex IG1 3RT. ☎ 0181-554 5969. (Est. 1936.) *M.* ; *R.* Rev. A. Levin; *Admin.* Ms. H.R. Michaels. (D)
Kenton Synagogue, Shaftesbury Avenue, Kenton, Middx., HA3 0RD. ☎ 0181-907 5959. Fax 0181-909 2677. *R.* Rabbi S. Zneimer, M.A.; *Admin.* Mrs A Primhak; *Youth Dir.* Rabbi S. Miller, ☎ 0181-907 3643.
Kingsbury Synagogue, Kingsbury Green, NW9 8XR. ☎ 0181-204 8089. *M.* Rabbi M. Hool; *R.* Rev. M. Rothstein; *Admin.* Mrs N. Hill. (D)
Mill Hill Synagogue, Brockenhurst Gdns., NW7 2JY. ☎ 0181-959 1137. Fax 0181-959 6484. *M.* Rabbi Y.Y. Schochet; *Admin.* Mrs M. Vogel. *Sec.* Mrs R. Polus. (D)
Muswell Hill Synagogue, 31 Tetherdown, N10 1ND. ☎ 0181-883 5925. (Est. 1908.) *M.* Rabbi Dr J. Shindler; *Admin.* A. Hankin.
New Synagogue, Victoria Community Centre, Egerton Rd., Stamford Hill, N16 6UB. (Est. in Leadenhall St., 1761.) ☎ 0181-800 6003. *Admin.* Mr. A. Levenson. (D)
New West End Synagogue, St. Petersburgh Place, Bayswater Road, W2 4JT. ☎ 0171-229 2631. Fax 0171-229 2355. (Consec. 1879.) *M.* ; *Admin.* Mrs S. Hayman.
Newbury Park Synagogue, 23 Wessex Close, off Suffolk Road, Newbury Pk., Ilford, Essex, IG3 8JU. ☎ /Fax 0181-597 0958. *M.* Rev. S. Myers, BA; *Admin.* Mrs E.M. Benjamin. (D)
Northwood Synagogue, 21-23 Murray Road, Middx. HA6 2YP. ☎ 01923 820004. Fax 01923-820020. *M.* Rabbi N.Y. Brawer; *Admin.* Mrs E. Granger.
Palmers Green and Southgate Synagogue, Brownlow Road, N11 2BN. ☎ 0181-881 0037. *M.* Rabbi E. Levy B.A.; *R.* B. Segal; *Emer. M.* Rabbi J. Shaw, B.A.; *Admin.* M. Lewis. (D)
Pinner Synagogue, 1 Cecil Park, Pinner, Middx. HA5 5HJ. ☎ 0181-868 7204. Fax: 0181-868 7011. *M.* Rabbi J. Grunewald, B.A.; *Admin.* Mrs C. Lipman; *Youth Leader* Andy Sollofe. ☎ 0181-868 7938. (D)
Radlett Synagogue, P.O. Box 28, Radlett, Herts. WD7 7PN. ☎ 01923-856878. Fax 01923-856698. *M.*
Richmond Synagogue, Lichfield Gardens, Richmond-on-Thames, Surrey, TW9 1AP. ☎ 0181-940 3526. (Est. 1916.) *M.* Rabbi M. Junik; *Admin.* J. Bobrofsky.
St. John's Wood Synagogue, 37/41 Grove End Road, St. John's Wood, NW8 9NG. ☎ 0171-286 3838. Fax 0171-266 2123 (Est. in Abbey Road 1882; present building consecrated 1964.) *M.* Dayan I. Binstock, B.Sc.; *R.* Rev. M. Haschel; *Admin.* Mrs Loraine Young. (D)
South Hampstead Synagogue, 20/22 Eton Villas, Eton Road, NW3 4SP. ☎ 0171-722 1807. Fax 0171-586 3459. *M.* Rabbi S. Levin; *Admin.* Mrs M Spector.
South London Synagogue, 45 Leigham Ct. Road, SW16 2NF. ☎ 0181-677 0234. Fax 0181-677 5107. *M.* Rabbi P. N. Ginsbury, M.A.; *Admin.* D. Saul.
South Tottenham Synagogue, 111 Crowland Road, N15 6UL. (Call Box; Sun 10.15-11.30am; Wed. 7.00-7.45pm): ☎ 0181-880 2731. (Est. 1938.) *M.*; *R.* Rev. D. Acoca; *Admin.* R. Danan (D)

Stanmore and Canons Park Synagogue, London Road, Stanmore Middx., HA7 4NS. ☎ 0181-954 2210. Fax 0181-954 4369. *M.* Rabbi Dr J. M. Cohen, B.A., M.Phil., A.J.C., Ph.D;. *R.* H. Black; *Admin.* Mrs B. S. Dresner. (D)
Watford Synagogue, 16 Nascot Road, Watford, Herts., WD1 3RE. ☎ 01923-222755 (Est. 1946.) *M.* ; *Admin.* Mrs C. Silverman.
Wembley Synagogue, Forty Avenue, Wembley Park, Middx., HA9 8JW. ☎ 0181-904 6565. Fax 0181-908 2740. *M.* Rabbi M. van den Bergh; *R.* Rev. A. Wolfson, B.Ed., M.A.; *Admin.* Mrs R. Garfield. (D)
West Ham and Upton Park Synagogue, 95 Earlham Grove, Forest Gate, E7 9AN. ☎ 0181-522 1917. *M.* Rabbi R. Broder; *Admin.* Mrs E. Benjamin.
Willesden and Brondesbury Synagogue, 143 Brondesbury Park NW2 5JL. ☎ 0181-459 1083. (Est. 1934.) *R.* Rev. Y. Landenberg; *Admin.* Mrs J. Questle. (D)
Woodside Park Synagogue, Woodside Park Road, N12 8RZ. ☎/Fax 0181-445 4236. *M.* Rabbi H. Rader; *R.* Rev. M. L. Plaskow A.L.C.M.; *Chairman*: Dr M. Cohen; *Admin.* Mrs D. Bruce. (D)

ASSOCIATE SYNAGOGUE
Western Marble Arch, 32 Great Cumberland Place, London, W1H 7DJ. ☎ 0171-723 9333. Fax 0171-224 8065. *M.* Rabbi S. Harris; *Admin.* Malcolm E. Howard.

AFFILIATED SYNAGOGUES
These are syns., belonging to U.S. by means of a scheme for small and newly est. congregations.
Barking and Becontree (Affiliated) Synagogue, 200 Becontree Avenue, Dagenham, Essex RM8 2TR. ☎ 0181-590 2737. R. D. Hackner. *Chairman* H. Dent; *Hon. Sec.* Mrs B. Berman.
Barnet and District Affiliated Synagogue, Eversleigh Road, New Barnet Herts. EN5 1NE. ☎ 0181-449 0145. *M.*; *H. Admin.* Mrs H. Spillman, ☎ 0181-441 2783.
Catford & Bromley Affiliated Synagogue (est. 1937). 6 Crantock Road, SE6 2QS. ☎ 0181-698 9496. *M.* Rev J. Kleiman. Enq. P.O. Box 4724, London SE6 2YA. *Admin.* Mrs E. Govendir. ☎ 01322-527239.
Chelsea Affiliated Synagogue, Smith Terrace, Smith Street, Chelsea, SW3 4DL. (Reg. Charity No. 242552) ☎ 0171-351 6046. *M.* Rabbi M. Atkins, ☎ 0171-351 6292; *Admin.* Diana Davis. ☎ 0181-747-3931.
Elm Park Affiliated Synagogue, Woburn Avenue, Elm Park, Hornchurch Essex, RM12 4NQ. *M.* Rabbi. Saul Wiseman; *Admin.* Mrs S. Gaynor. ☎ 01708 449305.
Enfield & Winchmore Hill Synagogue, 53 Wellington Road, Bush Hill Park, Middx. EN1 2PG ☎ 0181-363 2697. (Est. 1950.) *M.* Rabbi. C. Silverman; *Hon. Sec.* B. Bowman, 204 St Edmunds Road, N9 7PJ, ☎ 0181-292 0229.
Harold Hill and District Affiliated Synagogue, Trowbridge Road, Harold Hill, Essex RM3 0YW. (Est. 1953.) *H. Sec.* Miss D. Meid, 4 Portmadoc House, Broseley Road, Harold Hill, Essex RM3 9BT. ☎ 01708-348904.
Hemel Hempstead and District Affiliated Synagogue, c/o 1 Devreaux Drive, Watford WD1 3DD. *Admin.* H. Nathan. ☎ 01923 232007.
High Wycombe Affiliated Synagogue. *Hon. Sec.* Mrs R. Weiss, 33 Hampden Road, High Wycombe, Bucks. HP13 6SZ. ☎ 01494 529821.
Highams Park and Chingford Affiliated Synagogue, Marlborough Road, Highams Pk., E4 9AZ. *M.* Rev. M. Lester; *Admin.* Mrs S.R. Benjamin, 77 Royston Avenue, Chingford E4 9DE. ☎ 0181-527 4750.
Hounslow, Heathrow and District Affiliated Synagogue, 100 Staines Road, Hounslow, Middx. (Est. 1944.) ☎ 0181-572 2100. *H. Admin.* L. Gilbert, 9 Park Ave., Hounslow, Middx. TW3 2NA. ☎ 0181-894 4020.
Kingston, Surbiton and District Affiliated Synagogue, 33-35 Uxbridge Road, Kingston on Thames, Surrey KT1 2LL. (Est. 1947) ☎ 0181-546 9370. Email: rabbicoten@panther.netmania.co.uk. *M.* Rabbi S. Coten. ☎/Fax 0181-399 8689.

H. Admin. S. Nakar, 85 Alexandra Dr, Surbiton KT5 9AE. ☎ 0181-399 7403.
Peterborough Affiliated Synagogue, 142 Cobden Avenue, Peterborough PEI 2NU. *Admin.* C. Conn. ☎ 01733 571282.
Potters Bar and District Affiliated Synagogue. Meadowcroft, Great North Road, Bell Bar (Nr. Potters Bar), Hatfield, Herts. AL9 6DB. *M.* Rev D. Levy. ☎ 01707 656202; *Sec.* J. Bellman.
Romford and District Affiliated Synagogue, (Reg. Charity No. 242552) 25 Eastern Road, Romford, Essex. (Est. 1929.) *Admin.* J. Rose. ☎ 01708-748199.
Ruislip and District Affiliated Synagogue, Shenley Avenue, Ruislip Manor, Middx., HA4 6BP. ☎ 01895 622059. (Est. 1946.) *M.* Rev D. Wolfson; *Sec.* Mrs M. Petrook.
St. Albans Affiliated Synagogue. Oswald Road, St. Albans, Herts. ☎ 01727 854872. *Admin.* H. Turner. ☎ 01727 825295.
Staines and District Affiliated Synagogue, Westbrook Road, South Street, Staines, Middx. TW18 4PR. *M.* ; *Hon. Sec.* Mrs P. D. Fellman. ☎ 01784 254604.
Sutton & District Synagogue, 14 Cedar Road, Sutton, Surrey, SM2 5DA. ☎ 0181-642 5419. Rev. Dr Z.H. Amit. ☎ 0181-642 8029; *Admin.* Mrs T. Raphael, 43 Avenue Rd., Belmont, Sutton SM2 6JE. ☎ 0181-642 9285.
Wanstead and Woodford Affiliated Synagogue, 20 Churchfields, South Woodford E18 2QZ. ☎ 0181-504 1990. *M.* Rabbi A. Lewis; *Admin.* Mrs S. Braude. (D)
Welwyn Garden City Affiliated Synagogue, Barn Close, Handside Lane, Welwyn Garden City, Herts. AL8 6ST. ☎ 01582-762829. *Hon. Admin.* Mr. S. Hirschfield.

BURIAL SOCIETY
Office: *Sexton* R. I. Ezekiel, Finchley Synagogue, P.O. Box 9537, Kinloss Gardens, N3 3DU. ☎ 0181-343 3456. Fax 0181-346 3402 (Bushey & Willesden).
Ilford office, Schaller House, Ilford Synagogue, 22, Beehive Lane, Ilford, Essex IG1 3RT. ☎ 0181-518 2868 (Waltham Abbey, East Ham, West Ham, and Plashet). *Admin* Mrs M.J. Wohlman.

CEMETERIES
Willesden, Beaconsfield Road, NW10. Opened 1873. ☎ 0181-459 0394. Fax 0181-451 0478; East ham, Marlow Road, High St. South, E6. Opened 1919. ☎ 0181-472 0554. Fax 0181-471 2822; Bushey, Little Bushey Lane, Bushey, Herts. Opened 1947. ☎ 0181-950 6299. Fax 0181-420 4973; Waltham Abbey, Skillet Hill (Honey Lane), Waltham Abbey, Essex. Opened 1960. ☎ 01992 714492. Fax 01992-650 735. Plashet, High Street, North, E12. Opened 1896. ☎ 0181-472 0554. West Ham, Buckingham Road, Forest Lane, E15. Opened 1857. ☎ 0181-555 2193. Alderney Road, E1. Opened for Great Syn. in 1696 (disused). ☎ 0171-790 1445. Brady street, E1. Opened for the New Syn, in 1761; subsequently used also by Great Syn. (disused), Hackney, Lauriston Road, E9. Opened for Hambro' Syn. in 1788 (disused). ☎ 0181-985 1527.

Federation of Synagogues

Constituent and Affiliated Synagogues of the Federation of Synagogues, 65 Watford Way, NW4 3AQ. ☎ 0181-202 2263 Fax 0181-203 0610.

CONSTITUENT SYNAGOGUES
Clapton Federation Synagogue (Sha'are Shomayim), 47 Lea Bridge Road, E5 9QB. ☎ 081-806 4369.(Est. 1919.) *M.* Rev. H. Daviest; *Sec.* R. Jacobs. ☎ 0181-530 5816.
Croydon & District Synagogue, The Almonds, Shirley Oaks, CRO 8YX. *M.* Rabbi H. Vogel; *H. Sec.* Mrs S. Hanover. ☎ 0181-662 0011.
East London Central Synagogue, 30/40 Nelson Street, E1 2DE. ☎ 0171-790 9809. *Sec.* L. Gayer. ☎ 0181-554 5267.

Finchley Central Synagogue, Redbourne Avenue, N3 2BS. ☎ 0181-346 1892. *Rab.* Rabbi Z. H. Telsner; *Sec.* M. Moller.
Ilford Federation Synagogue, 16 Coventry Road, Ilford, Essex IG1 4QR. ☎ 0181-554 5289. (Est. 1927.) *M.* Rabbi R. Livingstone; *R.* Rev. E. Sufrin; *Sec.* Mrs P. Hackner. ☎ 0181-554 5289. (D)
Ohel Jacob Beth Hamedrash: (1st Floor) 478 Cranbrook Road, Ilford, Essex IG2 2LE. *H. Sec.* Mrs R. Pressman. ☎ 0181-550 4596.
Shomrei Hadath Synagogue, 64 Burrard Road, NW6 1DD. *Sec.* Mrs J. Segal. ☎ 0171-431 0017.
Sinai Synagogue, 54 Woodstock Avenue, NW11 9RJ. (Est. 1935.) *Rab.* Rabbi B. Knopfler; *Sec.* I. Leskin. ☎ 0181-455 6876. (D)
Woolwich & District Synagogue, Anglesea Road, Woolwich, SE18 6EG. ☎ 0181-854 6680. *M.* Rev. M. Gingold; *Sec.* B. Greenberg. ☎ 0181-658 0448.
Yavneh Synagogue, 25 Ainsworth Road, E9 9JE (Est. 1904.) *Sec.* R. I. Jacobs. ☎ 0181-530 5816.
Yeshurun Synagogue, Fernhurst Gdns., Stonegrove, Edgware, Middx. HA8 7PH. ☎ 0181-952 5167. (Est. 1946.) *Rab.* Dayan G. Lopian; *Sec.* D. Cohen. ☎ 0181-952 3844 (eves).

AFFILIATED SYNAGOGUES
Congregation of Jacob, 351/355 Commercial Road, E1. (Est. 1904.) *Sec.* P. Da Costa. ☎ 0958 486792.
Fieldgate Street Great Synagogue, 41 Fieldgate Street, E1. ☎ 0171-247 2644. *M.; Sec.* Mrs D. Jacobson. (D)
Finchley Road Synagogue, 4 Helenslea Avenue, NW11. (Est. 1941.) *Rab.* Rabbi S. Rubin. ☎ 0181-455 4305.
Greenford & District Synagogue, 39-45 Oldfield Lane South, Greenford, Middx. UB6 9LB. *H. Sec.* R. A. Hyams. ☎ 0181-421 6366.
Leytonstone & Wanstead Synagogue, 2 Fillebrook Road, E11. (Est. 1932.) *Sec.* S. Pizer. ☎ 0181-924 7505.
Loughton, Chigwell & District Synagogue, Borders La., Loughton, Essex IG10 3HT. *M.* Rev. J. D. Lorraine. ☎ 0181-508 0270. *Sec.* A. Fell. ☎ 0181-504 2248.
Machzike Hadath Synagogue, Highfield Road, NW11 9LU. ☎ 0181-455 9816 (Reg. Charity No. 289999). *H. Sec.* R. Shaw. ☎ 0181-204 1887.
New Wimbledon & Putney District Synagogue, The Clubroom, Toland Sq., Eastwood Estate, Roehampton Lane, SW15. *H. Sec.* J. Leigh, 5 Greenfield House, Inner Park Road, SW19. ☎ 0181-788 0176.
Notting Hill Synagogue, 206/8 Kensington Park Road, W11 1NR. (Est. 1900.) *Warden* P. Fogelman, ☎ 0181-969 8416; *Sec.* H. Lamb, ☎ 0181-952 4354.
Springfield Synagogue, 202 Upper Clapton Road, E5 9DH. ☎ 0181-806 2377. (Est. 1929.) *Rab.* Dayan I. Gukovitski; *Sec.* L. Blackman, 45 Midhurst Avenue, Westcliff on Sea, Essex SS0 0NP. ☎ 01702 340 762.
Stamford Hill Beth Hamedrash, 50 Clapton Common, E5 9AL. *M.; Sec.* M. Chontow. ☎ 0181-800 5465.
Tottenham Hebrew Congregation, 366A High Road, N17 9HT. (Est. 1904.) *M.* Rev. M. Davis; *Sec.* Dr S. S. Cohen. ☎ 0181-368 4158.
West Hackney Synagogue & Montague Rd Beth Hamedrash, 233A Amhurst Road, E8 2BS (Est. 1903.) *Chairman* I. Leigh. ☎ 0181-550 9543. *Sec.* Mrs R. Glaser. ☎ 0171-254 8078.

BURIAL SOCIETY
Office: 65 Watford Way, Hendon NW4 3AQ. ☎ 0181-202 3903; Fax 0181-203 0610. *Sexton* Mr. H. Brooks; *Admin.* M. L. Stuart; *Tr.* H. Dony, N. Bruckheimer.

LONDON 81

CEMETERIES
Montague Rd., Angel Road, Lower Edmonton, N.18. ☎ 0181-807 2268.
Upminster Road North, Rainham, Essex. Supt. E. Brown. ☎ 017085-52825.

Union of Orthodox Hebrew Congregations
140 Stamford Hill, N16 6QT.
☎ 0181-802 6226 Fax 0181-809 7092.

CONSTITUENTS
Adath Yisroel (Parent) Synagogue, 40 Queen Elizabeth's Walk, N16 0HH. *Rab.* Rabbi J. Dunner; *Sec.* A. Barnett. ☎ 0181-802 6262/3. (D)
Adath Yisroel Tottenham Beth Hamedrash, 55/57 Ravensdale Road, N16. *Rab.* Dayan A. D. Dunner. ☎ 0181-800 3978. (D)
Ahavat Israel Synagogue, D'Chasidey Viznitz, 89 Stamford Hill, N16. ☎ 0181-800 9359. *Rab.* Rabbi F. Schneebalg. (D)
Beit Knesset Chida, Egerton Road, N16.
Beth Abraham Synagogue, 46 The Ridgeway, NW11. *Rab.* Rabbi C. Schmahl.
Beth Chodosh Synagogue, 51 Queen Elizabeth's Walk, N16. ☎ 0181-800 6754.
Beth Hamedrash Beis Nadvorna, 45 Darenth Road, N16 6ES. ☎ 0181-806 3903. *Rab.* Rabbi M. Leifer. (D)
Beth Hamedrash Cheishev Sofer d' Pressburg, 103 Clapton Common, E5. *Rab.* S. Ludmir. (D)
Beth Hamedrash Chelkas Yehoshua (Biala), 110 Castlewood Road, London N15. *Rab.* Rabbi L Rabbinowitz.
Beth Hamedrash D'Chasidey Belz, 99 Bethune Road, N16. ☎ 0181-802 8233. (D)
Beth Hamedrash D'Chasidey Belz, 96 Clapton Common, E5. *Rab.* Dayan J. D. Babad. (D)
Beth Hamedrash D'Chasidey Gur, 2 Lampard Grove, N16. ☎ 0181-806 4333, and 98 Bridge Lane, NW11. ☎ 0181-458 6243. (D)
Beth Hamedrash D'Chasidey Ryzin, 33 Paget Road, N16. ☎ 0181-800 7979. (D)
Beth Hamedrash D'Chasidey Sanz Klausenburg, 42 Craven Walk, N16. (D)
Beth Hamedrash D'Chassidey Square, 22 Dunsmure Road, N16. ☎ 0181-800 8448.
Beth Hamedrash Divrei Chaim, 71 Bridge La., NW11. ☎ 0181-458 1161. *Rab.* Rabbi Chaim A. Z. Halpern. (D)
Beth Hamedrash Hendon, 3 The Approach, NW4 2HU. *Rab.* Rabbi D. Halpern (D)
Beth Hamedrash Imrey Chaim D'Chasidey Vishnitz-Monsey, 121 Clapton Common, E5. ☎ 0181-800 3741. *Rab.* Rabbi D. Hager (D)
Beth Hamedrash Kehillas Yacov, 35 Highfield Av., NW11 ☎ 0181-455 3066. (D)
Beth Hamedrash Ohel Moshe, 202B Upper Clapton Road, E5. (D)
Beth Hamedrash Ohel Naphtoli (Bobov), 87 Egerton Road, N16. ☎ 0181-802 3979. *Rab.* Dayan B. Blum (D)
Beth Hamedrash of the Agudah Youth Movement, 69 Lordship Road, N.16. Also 95 Stamford Hill, N16. ☎ 0181-800 8873. *Rab.* Rabbi M. J. Kamionka. (D)
Beth Hamedrash Or Yisroel (Sadigur), 269 Golders Green Road, NW11. *Rab.* Y.M. Friedman. (D)
Beth Hamedrash Spinke, 36 Bergholt Cres., N16 5SE. ☎ 0181-809 6903. *Rab.* Rabbi M. Kahana.
Beth Hamedrash Torah Etz Chayim, 69 Lordship Road, N16. ☎ 0181-800 7726. *Rab.* Rabbi Z. Feldman. (D)
Beth Hamedrash Torah Chaim Liege, 145 Up. Clapton Road, E5. *Rab.* Rabbi Y. Meisels. (D)
Beth Hamedrash Toras Chaim, 37 Craven Walk, N16 6BS. ☎ 0181-800 3868. *Rab.* Rabbi J. Meisels. (D)
Beth Hamedrash Vayoel Moshe, 14 Heathland Road, N16.

Beth Hamedrash Yetiv Lev, D'Satmar, 86 Cazenove Road, N16. ☎ 0181-800 2633. (D) Also 26 Clapton Common, E5. ☎ 0181-806 7439. *Rab.* Rabbi C. Wosner. (D)
Beth Israel (Trisker) Synagogue, 146 Osbaldeston Road, N16. ☎ 0181-806 3551. (D)
Beth Shmuel Synagogue, 171 Golders Green Road, NW11. ☎ 0181-458 7511. *Rab.* Rabbi E. Halpern. (D)
Beth Sholom Synagogue, 27 St. Kilda's Road, N16. ☎ 0181-809 6224. *Rab.* Rabbi M. Deutsch. (D)
Beth Talmud Centre, 78 Cazenove Road, N16.
Beth Yisochor Dov Beth Hamedrash, 2-4 Highfield Avenue, NW11. *Rab.* Rabbi G. Hager. (D)
Birkath Yehuda (Halaser) Beth Hamedrash, 47 Moundfield Road, N16 6DT. *Rab.* Rabbi M. Lebovits. ☎ 0181-806 6448. (D)
Bridge Lane Beth Hamedrash, 44 Bridge Lane, NW11 0EG. *Rab.* Rabbi S. Winegarten. (D)
Etz Chaim Yeshiva, 83/85 Bridge Lane, NW11. *Rab.* Z. Rabi. (D)
Finchley Road Synagogue, 4 Helenslea Avenue, NW11. ☎ 0181-455 4305 *Rab.* Rabbi S. Rubin. (D)
Garden Suburb Beth Hamedrash, 5 The Bishop's Avenue, N2. ☎ 0181-458 3765. *Rab.* Rabbi C. Wilschanski. (D)
Heichal Hatorah, 27 St. Kildas Road, N16. ☎ 0181-809 4331. R. L. Rakow.
Hendon Adath Yisroel Synagogue, 11 Brent Street, NW4 2EU. ☎ 0181-202 9183. *Rab.* Rabbi P. Roberts; *Sec.* N. Hammond. (D)
Kehal Chasidim D'Munkatch Synagogue, 85 Cazenove Road, N16.
Kingsley Way Beth Hamedrash (Lubavitch), 3-5 Kingsley Way, London N2. ☎ 0181-458 2312. *Rab.* Rabbi Y. Hertz.
Knightland Road Synagogue of the Law of Truth Talmudical College, 50 Knightland Road, E5 9HS. Corr: 27 Warwick Grove, E5 9HX. ☎ 0181-806 2963. *Rab.* Rabbi S.A. Halpern.
Lubavitch Synagogue, 107-115 Stamford Hill, N16. ☎ 0181-800 0022. *Rab.* Rabbi N. Sudak. (D)
Machzikei Hadass Edgware Beth Hamedrash, 269 Hale Lane, Edgwarev HA8. R. Rabbi E. Schneelbag. ☎ 0181-958 1030. (D)
Mesifta Synagogue, 82-84 Cazenove Road, N16. (D)
North Hendon Adath Yisroel Synagogue, Holders Hill Road, NW4 1NA. *Rab.* Rabbi D. Cooper; *Sec.* A. H. Ehreich. ☎ 0181-203 0797; corr.: 31 Holders Hill Crescent, NW4 1NE. (D)
Ohel Israel (Skoler) Synagogue, 11 Brent Street, NW4. (D)
Shaare Zion, 10 Woodberry Down, N4.
Stanislowa Beth Hamedrash, 93 Lordship Park, N16. ☎ 0181-800 2040. *Rab.* Rabbi M. Aschkenasi. (D)
Yeshiva Horomoh Beth Hamedrash, 100 Fairholt Road, N16 5HH. ☎ 0181-809 3904; 0181-800 4522 (students). *Rab.* Rabbi E. Schlesinger. ☎ 0181-800 2194. (D)
Yeshuath Chaim Synagogue, 45 Heathland Road, N16. ☎ 0181-800 2332. *Rab.* Rabbi S. Pinten; *H. Sec.* I. Kohn. (D)
Yesodey Hatorah Synagogue, 2/4 Amhurst Pk., N16.
Zichron Shlomo Beth Hamedrash, 9 Elm Park Av., N15. ☎ 0181-809 7850. R. Rabbi S. Meisels.

The Assembly of Masorti Synagogues

1097 Finchley Road, NW11 0PU..
☎ 0181-201 8772, Fax 0181-201 8917. Email: Masorti.uk@ort.org. Website: http://www.ort.org/masorti
(Est. 1985. Reg. Charity No. 801846). *Dir.* H. Freedman, *Chairman:* A. Sklan.

New London Synagogue, 33 Abbey Road, NW8 0AT. ☎ 0171-328 1026.

LONDON 83

(Est. 1964) *M.* Rabbi Louis Jacobs, C.B.E.; *Chairman* Eleanor Lind Q.C.; *Off.* D. Lewis.
New North London Synagogue, The Manor House, 80 East End Road, N3 2SY. ☎ 0181-346 8560. (Est. 1974.) An independent traditional com. following the philosophy of Rabbi Dr L. Jacobs. *M.* Rabbi J. Wittenberg;. *Chairman* P. Shrank; *Tr.* G. Kirsh; *Sec.* P. Tobin; *Off.* Mrs Barbara Anders.
Edgware Masorti Synagogue. Synagogue Office/Post/Weekly entrance: Pearl Community Centre, Stream Lane, Edgware, Middx. HA8 7YA. Shabbat entrance: Bakery Path (off Station Road), Edgware, Middx. HA8 7YE. ☎/Fax 0181-905 4096. *M.* Rabbi Chaim Weiner, ☎ 0181-931 1673; *Co-Chairpersons* Mrs C. Sklan, H. Segal; *T.* D. Davis.
Hendon Masorti Minyan. *Contact* H. Defries ☎ 0181-202 9058.
New Essex Masorti Congregation, Services: Prince Regent Hotel, Woodford Bridge, Essex. Enqs. ☎ 0181-554 0158/0181 504 0010. *Chairman* A.M. Pearl; *Jt.V. Chairmen* Mrs B. Cohen, Mrs R. Bravo; *Tr.* M. Foulds; *Sec.* Mrs M. Berger
New Whetstone Synagogue, Enquiries: 0181-368 3936. *Chairman* E. Slater.
St. Albans Masorti Synagogue, *Chairman* S. Gess; *Tr.* N. Grant; *Sec.* N. Freedman. ☎ 017278 48778.

Independent Congregations

Belsize Square Synagogue, 51 Belsize Square, London NW3 4HX. ☎ 0171-794 3949. Fax 0171-431 4559. (Est. 1939. Reg. Charity No. 233742.) An Independent Synagogue combining traditional forms of worship with progressive ideals. *M.* Rabbi Rodney J. Mariner; *Cantor* Rev. Lawrence Fine; *Sec.* Ms. J. Berman; *Chairman* Harry L. Davies; *H. T.* Max Kochmann; *H. Sec.* Thomas Tausz. Totteridge Branch twice monthly at Badgers Croft.
Commercial Road Talmud Torah Synagogue (formerly 9-11 Christian Street, E1.) 153 Stamford Hill, London N16 5LG. ☎ 0181-800 1618. (est. 1898) *Sec.* A. Becker. Burial Society. Cemeteries: Carterhatch Lane, Enfield. ☎ 0181-363 3384. Silver Street, Cheshunt, Herts. ☎ 01707 874220.
Edgware Adath Yisroel Synagogue, 261 Hale Lane, Edgware HA8 8NX. ☎ : 0181-958 9003. Fax 0181-958 8121. Email: Rabbi@eayc.demon.co.uk. *Rab.* Rabbi Zvi Lieberman. (Affiliated to Adath Yisroel Burial Soc. p.00) (D)
Golders Green Beth Hamedrash Congregation, The Riding, Golders Green Road, NW11 8HL. ☎ 0181-455 2974. (Est. 1934.) *Rab.* Rabbi H. I. Feldman; *R.* Rev. N. Gluck.
Ner Yisrael, The Crest (off Brent St.), Hendon, NW4. ☎ 0181-202 6687. Fax 0181-203 5158. *M.* Rabbi A.A. Kimche. ☎ 0181-455 7347.
Porat Yosef (est. 1988.) Moroccan Hebrew Congregation. 9 Burroughs Gardens, Hendon, NW4 4AU. ☎ 0181-203 7809. *President* Jacques Onona; *R.* Rabbi Leon Benarroch; *Sec.* B. Benarroch.
Sandy's Row Synagogue, (est. 1854), Sandy's Row, Middlesex Street, E1 7HW. *M.* Rev. Y. Moses; *Sec.* E. Wilder. ☎ 0171-253 8311; 0171-377 5854. (D)
Synagogue Française de Londres (La), 101 Dunsmure Road, N16 5HT. Le Grand Rabbin Henri Brand, 54 Bethune Road, N16 5BD. ☎ 0181-800 8612. *Hon. Tr.* Rabbi C. Pinter; *Hon. Sec.* I. Kraus.
Walford Road Synagogue, 99 Walford Road, Stoke Newington, N.16. *M.* Rabbi H. Gluck; *Sec.* Mrs S. Raymond. ☎ 0171-249 5604.
Waltham Forest Hebrew Congregation, 140 Boundary Road, E17 8LA. (Est. 1902.) ☎ *Off.*: 0181-509 0775. Fax 0181-518 8200. *M.* Rev. L. Mockton. *President* W. Jacobs; *Admin.* A. Wolpert. (D)
West End Great Synagogue, 32 Great Cumberland Place, W1H 7DJ. ☎ 0171-724 8121. Fax 0171-723 4413. (Est. 1880.) *M.*; *Sec.* S. B. Levy.
Chesed V'Ameth. Cemeteries: Rowan Road, Greyhound Lane, SW16. ☎ 0181-764 1566; Cheshunt Cemetery (Western), Bullscross Ride, Cheshunt, Herts.

☎ 01992 717820.
Affiliated Synagogues: retaining burial rights: *Commercial Road Great Syn., Teesdale Street Syn., *Great Garden Street Syn., *Cong. of Jacob, *Ezras Chaim Syn., *Nelson Street Sephardish Syn., Sandy's Row Syn., *Fieldgate St. Syn.
The synagogues marked * still have a section of members affiliated for burial rights under the Federation of Synagogues.

Western Marble Arch Synagogue, successor to the Western Synagogue (est. 1761) and the Marble Arch Synagogue, 32 Great Cumberland Place, W1H 7DJ. ☎ 0171-723 9333. Fax 0171-224 8065. *M.* Rabbi S. Harris; *Community Admin*, Malcolm E. Howard; Affiliated for burial rights with Western Charitable Foundation in the following Cemeteries: Edmonton, Montague Road, N18, Bullscross Ride, Cheshunt, Herts; *Supt.* M. Clements, Bullscross Ride, Cheshunt, Herts. ☎ 01992 717820.
Affiliated Orgs.: Western Charitable Foundation. *Chairman* S. Jacque, J.P.; *Tr.* W. Ward.
Westminster Synagogue (Est. 1957), Rutland Gdns., Knightsbridge, SW7 1BX. ☎ 0171-584 3953. Fax 0171-581 8012. *M. Emer.* Rabbi A. H. Friedlander, Ph.D., Rabbi T. Salomon; *President* H. I. Connick; *Chairman* E. D. Glover; *Jt. H. Secs.* Mrs D. Barnard, Mrs B. Naggar; *Sec.* Mrs M. R. Henriques.

Sephardi

Spanish and Portuguese Jews' Congregations (Reg. Charity No. 212517) 2, Ashworth Rd, Maida Vale, W9 1JY. ☎ 0171-289 2573. Fax 0171-289 2709.

SYNAGOGUES
Bevis Marks (1701), EC3A 5DQ. ☎ 0171-626 1274. Fax 0171-283 8825. Rabbi Dr A. Levy B.A. *M.* Rev. H. Benarroch, B.A.
Lauderdale Road Syn. (1896), Maida Vale, W9 1JY.☎ 0171-289 2573. *Rabbi & M.* Rabbi Dr A. Levy, B.A.
Wembley Synagogue, 46 Forty Ave., Wembley, Middx HA9 8LQ. ☎ 0181-904 9912. *Rabbi & M.* Dayan Dr P. Toledano, B.A.
Sir Moses Montefiore Synagogue, Honeysuckle Road, Ramsgate, Kent.

OTHER INSTITUTIONS
Burial Society, 2 Ashworth Road, W9 1JY. ☎ 0171-289 2573.
Welfare Board, 2 Ashworth Road, W9 1JY. ☎ 0171-289 2573. (Est. 1837.) *H. Sec.* J. Politi.
Sephardi Kashrut Authority, 2 Ashworth Road, W9 1JY. ☎ 0171-289 2573. *Chairman* E. H. Silas; *Dir.* Rabbi I. Abraham.
Communal Centre, Montefiore Hall, 2 Ashworth Road, W9 1JY. ☎ 0171-289 2573.
Beth Hamedrash Heshaim, (Instituted 1664.) *T.* Prof. R.J. Loewe. Ad: 2 Ashworth Road, W9 1JY. ☎ 0171-289 2573.
Montefiore Endowment at Ramsgate (incorporating the **Judith Lady Montefiore College Trust**), 2 Ashworth Road, W9 1JY. (☎ 0171-289 2573.) Est. by Sir Moses Montefiore 1866; New scheme est. by the Charity Commission in 1989 'for the maintenance of the Synagogue, the Mausoleum and the Jewish Cemetery in Ramsgate', also 'for the promotion of the advanced study of the Holy Law as revealed on Sinai and expounded by the revered sages of the Mishna and Talmud' by making grants to charitable institutions for the training of Orthodox Jewish Teachers, Ministers and Rabbis and by awarding scholarships to such trainees.
The Mausoleum with the remains of Sir Moses and Lady Montefiore is situated next to the Synagogue in Ramsgate (see above). Sir Moses's seats in Bevis Marks

and Ramsgate Syns. are still preserved.
Edinburgh House (Beth Holim), 36/44 Forty Avenue, Wembley. (Est. 1747.) Home for the Aged. *Hd. of Home* C. Gilmour. ☎ 0181-908 4151.

CEMETERIES
253 Mile End Rd., E1. (Disused.) Opened in 1657, the oldest Jewish burial ground in the United Kingdom. 329 Mile End Road, E1. (Opened 1725. Disused.) Hoop Lane, Golders Green, NW11. *Keeper* B. H. Calo. ☎ 0181-455 2569. Edgwarebury Lane, Edgware. ☎ 0181-958 3388. *Keeper* B. H. Calo. Dytchleys, Coxtie Green, Brentwood. (Disused.)

Other Sephardi Synagogues
Aden Jews' Congregation, 117 Clapton Common, E5. *H. Sec.* M. A. Solomon. ☎ 0181-806 1320.
David Ishag Synagogue, Neveh Shalom Community, 352-4 Preston Road, Harrow, Middx., HA3 0QJ. *H. Sec.* F. Lichaa; *T.* J. M. Sitton. ☎ 0181-904 3009.
Eastern Jewry Community (Est. 1955.) Newbury Park Station, Newbury Park. *M.* Rabbi C. Tangy; *H. Sec.* D. Elias. ☎ 0181-809 4387.
Ilford Congregation (Ohel David), Newbury Park Station, Ilford. *H. Sec.* D. Elias, 7 Kyverdale Road, N16. ☎ 0181-809 4387. Fax 0181-809 4441; 0181-458 1468.
Jacob Benjamin Elias Synagogue, 140 Stamford Hill, N16. *M.* Rabbi C. Tangy; *H. Sec.* D. Elias. ☎ 0181-809 4387. Fax 0181-809 4441; 0181-458 1468.
Ohel David Eastern Synagogue, Lincoln Institute, Broadwalk Lane, Golders Green Road, NW11. (Reg. Charity No. 243901) *M.* Rabbi Abraham Gubbay; ☎ 0181-455 8125. *H. Sec.* M. Lanyado. ☎ 0181-455 9581.
Persian Hebrew Congregation, 5a East Bank, Stamford Hill, N16. ☎ 0181-800 9261. Corr. *H. Sec.* 17 Arden Road, London N3 3AB. ☎ 0181-446 4321. Fax 0181-343 7383.
Spanish & Portuguese Synagogue, Holland Park, (Est. 1928 under Deed of Association with Spanish and Portuguese Jews' Congregation), 8 St. James's Gdns. W11 4RB. ☎ 0171-603 7961/3232. Fax 0171-603 9471. *Sec.* Mrs Z. Fineburgh.
Manchester, Sha'are Sedek: Sha'are Tefillah: Withington (p.117.)

OTHER INSTITUTIONS
Friends of Sephardi and other Jewish Refugees, New House, 67-68 Hatton Gdn., EC1N 8JY. ☎ 0171-242 4556. Fax 0171-242 2418. *Chairman* ; *Hon. Sec.* Sidney L. Shipton, LL.B., M.B.A., F.R.S.A., F.INST.M.

Reform

(Constituents of the Reform Synagogues of Great Britain), The Sternberg Centre for Judaism, 80 East End Road, N3 2SY. *Chief Executive* Rabbi Tony Bayfield. ☎ 0181-349 4731. Fax 0181-343 0901.
West London Synagogue of British Jews, 34 Upper Berkeley Street, W1. Office, 33 Seymour Place, W1H 6AT. ☎ 0171-723 4404. Fax 0171-224 8258 (ca. 2,500 families.)
The congregation was organised April 15, 1840, to establish a synagogue "where a revised service may be performed at hours more suited to our habits and in a manner more calculated to inspire feelings of devotion, where religious instruction may be afforded by competent persons, and where, to effect these purposes, Jews generally may form a united congregation under the denomination of British Jews."
M. Rabbi Mrs Jacqueline Tabick; *President* G. D. Leuw; *Chairman* J. Samson; *Exec. Dir.* M. Ross.
Funerals: ☎ 0171-723 4404. Fax 0171-224 8258.
Cemeteries: Golders Green, Hoop Lane, NW11; Edgwarebury, Edgwarebury Lane,

Middx. *Supt.* B. H. Calo. ☎ 0181-958 3388.
Beit Klal Yisrael (North Kensington Reform Syn.) (Reg. Charity No.1034282), P.O. Box 1828, W10 5RT. Services in Notting Hill Gate. *M.* Rabbi Sheila Shulman. *Chairman* S. Ambalu. ☎/Fax 0181-969 5080.
Bromley Reform Synagogue (Est. 1964. Reg. Charity No. 1059190). 28 Highland Road, Bromley, Kent BR1 4AD. ☎/Fax 0181-460 5460. *M.* Rabbi Sylvia Rothschild; *H. Sec.* Ms B. Kurtz.
Edgware and District Reform Synagogue, (Reg. Charity No. 1038116). 118 Stonegrove, Edgware HA8 8AB. (Est. 1934.) ☎ 0181-958 9782. Fax 0181-905 4710. *M.* Rabbi A.D. Smith, M.A.; *Assoc. M.* Rabbi M. Michaels, Rabbi Dr M. Leigh, M.A., (Emer); *Admin.* Mrs J. Altman.
Finchley Reform Synagogue, Fallow Court Avenue, Finchley, N12 0BE. ☎ 0181-446 3244. Fax 0181-446 5980. *M.* Rabbi J. Newman; *Admin.* Jo-Anne Parker.
Hampstead Reform Jewish Community, 37a, Broadhurst Gdns., NW6. *Warden* M. Teper. ☎ 0171-794 8488. *Sec.* S. Gold.
Harlow Jewish Community, Harberts Road, Hare Street, Harlow, Essex CM19 4DT. ☎ 01992-573448. *Sec.* Mrs C. Petar.
Hendon Reform Synagogue, Danescroft Avenue, NW4 2NA (Est. 1949.) ☎ 0181-203 4168. Fax 0181-203 9385. *M.* Rabbi S. Katz; *Sec.* Mrs M. Djora. Cemetery: New Southgate Cemetery, Brunswick Park Road, N.11. ☎ 0181-203 4168.
Kol Chai-Hatch End Jewish Community. (Reg. Charity No. 299063). *M.* Rabbi S. Pereira; *Sec.* Peter Lewy, 21 New Rd., Croxley Green, Rickmansworth, Herts. WD3 3EJ. ☎ 01923-771856.
Middlesex New Synagogue, 39 Bessborough Road, Harrow, HA1 3BS. ☎/Fax 0181-864 0133/4. (Est. 1959.) *M.* Rabbi S.J. Franses; *Sec.* Mrs A. Simon.
North West Surrey Synagogue, Horvath Close, Rosslyn Pk., Oatlands Dr, Weybridge, Surrey KT13 9QZ. ☎/Fax 01932 855400. *M.* Rabbi F. Morgan; *H. Sec.* B. Press.
North Western Reform Synagogue, Alyth Gdns., Finchley Road, NW11 7EN. ☎ 0181-455 6763/4. Fax 0181-458 2469 (Est 1933 Reg. Charity No. 247081.) *M.* Rabbi C. Emanuel. (D)
Jewish Joint Burial Society. (Est. 1968.) *H. Sec.* P. S. Michaelis; *Sexton* E. S. Mansell. ☎ 0181-455 8579.
Radlett & Bushey Reform Synagogue, 118 Watling Street, Radlett, Herts WD7 7AA. ☎ 01923 85 6110. *M.* Rabbi Alexandra Wright. *H. Sec.* K. Young.
South West Essex and Settlement Reform Synagogue, Oaks Lane, Newbury Park, Ilford IG2 7PL. ☎ 0181-599 0936. (Est.1956.) *M.* Rabbi L. Rigàl, Rabbi H. Goldstein; *Office:* Angela Jacobs.
Southgate and District Reform Synagogue (Reg. Charity No. 145 765), 45 High Street, N14 6LD. ☎ 0181-882 6828 Fax 0181-882 7539. *M.* Rabbi C. Eimer; *Chairman* Michael Wohl.
Sukkat Shalom (formerly Buckhurst Hill Reform) (Reg. Charity No. 283615). Hermon Hill, London E11. ☎ 0181-530 3345. *M.*; *Chairman* R. Brody.
Wimbledon and District Synagogue, 44-46 Worple Road, SW19 4EJ. ☎ 0181-946 4836 Fax 0181-944 7790. (Est. 1949. Reg. Charity No. 1040712) *M.* Rabbi W. Wolff; *Admin.* Mrs F. Solomon.

Liberal and Progressive

(Constituents of the Union of Liberal and Progressive Synagogues, The Montagu Centre, 21 Maple St., W1P 6DS.) *Senior V. President* Rabbi Dr Sidney Brichto, M.A., D.D.; *Dir.* Rabbi Dr Charles H. Middleburgh; *Admin. Dir.* Michael Burman. ☎ 0171-580 1663; Fax 0171-436 4184. Email: montagu@ulps.demon.co.uk
Barkingside Progressive Synagogue (Reg. Charity No. 283547), 129 Perrymans Farm Road, Barkingside, Ilford, Essex IG2 7LX. *Sec.* B. Lautman. ☎ 0181-554

9682; *M.* Rabbi D. Hulbert.
Chiltern Progressive Synagogue, c/o The ULPS, The Montagu Centre, 21 Maple St., W1P 6DS. ☎ 01582-873414.
Ealing Liberal Synagogue, Lynton Av., Drayton Green, Ealing, W13 0ED. ☎/Fax: 0181-997 0528. (Est. 1944. Reg. Charity No. 1037099) *M.* Rabbi Melinda Carr, M.A.; *Admin.* A. Aarons.
Finchley Progressive Synagogue, 54a Hutton Gro. N12 8Dr (Est. 1953.) ☎ 0181-446 4063. Fax 0181-446 4063. *M.* Rabbi Dr F. Hellner; *Admin.* Mrs R. Lester.
Harrow & Wembley Progressive Synagogue, 326 Preston Road, Harrow, HA3 0QH. (Reg. Charity No. 251172) ☎ 0181-904 8581. Fax 0181-904 6540. Email: info@hwps.win-uk.net. Internet: www.ibmpcug.co.uk./~hwps/ (Est. 1947.) *M.* Rabbi Frank Dabba Smith; *Admin.* Mrs S. Rose.
Hertsmere Progressive Synagogue, High Street, Elstree, Herts. WD6 3BY. ☎ 0181-953 8889. *M.* Rabbi J. Black; *H. Sec.* Valerie Dickson. ☎ 0181-950 3268.
Kingston Liberal Synagogue, Rushett Road, Long Ditton, Surrey, KT7 0UX., Reg. Charity No. 270792. ☎ 0181-398 7400. *M.* Rabbi Danny Rich. ☎/Fax 0181-398 4252; *Chair* P. Levene, ☎ 0181-399 7887.
The Liberal Jewish Synagogue, (Reg. Charity No. 235668), 28 St. John's Wood Road, London, NW8 7HA. ☎ 0171-286 5181. Fax 0171-266 3591. Est. 1910 by the Jewish Religious Union, now known as the ULPS, the LJS, as it is known, was the first Liberal synagogue in the UK. Syn. rebuilt 1991. Membership. c.1,800 adults. *Chairman* Rita Adler. *Ms.* Rabbi Emeritus Dr J.D. Rayner, C.B.E.; *Senior Rabbi* Rabbi D.J. Goldberg; *Assoc.* Rabbi Helen Freeman; *Org. Sec.* D. Rigal.
North London Progressive Synagogue, (Est. 1921) 100 Amhurst Pk., N16 5AR. ☎ 0181-800 8931. Fax 0181-800 0416. *M.* Rabbi Marcia Plumb M.A.; *Emeritus M.* Rabbi B. Hooker; *Chair* Mrs J. Fox; *Hon. Sec.* David Selo; *Admin.* David Sylvester.
Northwood and Pinner Liberal Synagogue, Oaklands Gate, Green La., Northwood HA6 3AA. (Est. 1964. Reg. Charity No. 243618) *M.* Rabbi A. Goldstein, B.Sc.; *H. Sec.* Mrs J. Bullock. ☎ 01923 822592. Fax 01923-824454.
South London Liberal Synagogue, (Reg. Charity No. 236771), P.O.Box 14475, Streatham, SW16 1ZW. (Est. 1929.) ☎ 0181-769 4787. *M.* Rabbi N.S. Kraft; *Sec.* Mrs R. Edwards.
Southgate Progressive Synagogue, 75 Chase Road, N14 4QY. (Reg. Charity No. 239096). ☎ 0181-886 0977. Fax. 0181-882 5394. (Est. 1943.) *M.* Rabbi S. Howard; *Sec.* Mrs P. A. Freedman.
West Central Liberal Synagogue, The Montagu Centre, 21, Maple St., W1P 6DS. ☎ 0171-636 7627. Fax 0171-436 4184. (Cong. est. 1928; present syn. opened 1954.) *M.* Rabbi M.L. Solomon B.A., *Cantor* Rev. A. Harman ALCM; *Chairman*: Dr L. Hepner; *H. Sec.* H. Berman.
Woodford Progressive Synagogue, Marlborough Road, South Woodford, E18. (Est. 1960.) *M.* Rabbi M. Goldsmith; *Sec.* Mrs E. Cross. ☎ 0181-989 7619.

CEMETERIES
Funeral-Dir. Martin Board and Son. ☎ 0181-455 2797. Fax 0181-343 9463.
Edgwarebury Lane, Edgware, Middx. ☎ 0181-958 3388. *Supt.* Mr B. Calo.
Liberal Jewish Cemetery, Pound Lane, Willesden, NW10. *Supt.* Frank Quinn. ☎ 0181-459 1635. *Funeral Dir.* Bernard Foreman, ☎ 0181-459 5848.

Religious Organisations

Association of United Synagogue Women. (Est. 1968.) To promote the observance of traditional Judaism and encourage women's participation in Synagogue and communal affairs. *President* Mrs E. Sacks; *Chairman* Mrs S. Cohen; *Jt. H. Secs.* Mrs S. Webber, Dr S. Levene; *Admin.* Off. Mrs J. Wayne, c/o United Synagogue,

Adler House, 735 High Rd., N12 0US. ☎ 0181-343 6226. Fax 0181-343 6262. *Chair* Mrs R. Ross; *Jt. Hon. Secs.* Mrs R. Burns, Mrs S. Mann.
London Board for Shechita, (Reg. Charity No. 233467). P.O. Box 579, Adastra Suite, 401 Nether Street, N3 1YR. ☎ 0181-349 9160. Fax 0181-346 2209 (Est. 1804.) To administer the affairs of Shechita in London. *President* Dr M. Segal; V. *Presidents* M.A. Cohen, P. Sheldon; *H. T.* A. Kennard; *Sec.* M. T. Kester. ☎ 0181-349 9160/9153. Fax 0181-346 2209.

Ritual Baths (Mikvaot)

Central Mikvaot Board, 140 Stamford Hill, N16 6QT. ☎ 0181-802 6226/7.
Edgware & District Communal Mikvah, Edgware United Synagogue, Edgware Way, Edgware, Middlesex. (Reg. Charity No. 281586). ☎ 0181-958 3233. Fax 0181-951 5208. Email: estrin4488@aol.com.Gen. enquiries: Mrs Mandy Estrin ☎ 0181-958 4488 (eve), 0181-952 5292 (day).
Ilford Mikvah, 463 Cranbrook Road, Ilford. ☎ 0181-554 5450.
Kingsbury Mikvah, see below. United Synagogue Mikvah.
Lordship Park Mikvah, 55 Lordship Park, N16 (entrance in Queen Elizabeth's Walk). ☎ 0181-800 9621 (day) 0181-800 5801 (evening).
North London Mikvah, adjoining 40 Queen Elizabeth's Walk, N16 (entrance, Grazebrook Road). ☎ 0181-802 2554. Fax 0181-800 8764. *H. Sec.* A. Barnett.
Northwest London Communal Mikvah, 10a Shirehall Lane, Hendon, NW4. ☎ 0181-202 1427 (day), 0181-202 8517/5706 (evening).
Mikveh of the Reform Synagogues of Great Britain, Sternberg Centre, 80 East End Rd., N3 2SY. Appointments ☎ 0181-349 4731.
Satmar Mikvah, 62 Filey Avenue, N16. ☎ 0181-806 3961.
South London Mikvah, 42 St. George's Rd., Wimbledon SW19 4ED. (Reg. Charity No. 1009208) ☎ 0181-944 7149. Fax 0181-944 7563. *Hon. Sec.* L. Cohen. *Contact:* Mrs S. Dubov.
Stamford Hill Mikvah, 26 Lampard Grove, N16 (entrance in Margaret Road). ☎ 0181-806 3880.
United Synagogue Mikvah, Kingsbury United Synagogue, Kingsbury Green, NW9 8XR. ☎ 0181-204 6390. (See also Friends Group, p.00.)

Sabbath Observance Employment Bureau. (Est. 1909. Reg. Charity No. 209451) Commonwealth House, 1-19 New Oxford St., WC1A 1NF. ☎ 0171-831 6899. To obtain employment for those desirous of observing the Sabbath and Holydays. *Man.* Mrs E. Statham; *Chairman* E. F. Kestenbaum.

Memorials

Holocaust Memorial and Garden, Hyde Park, near Hyde Park Corner. Opened in July 1983, on a site given to the Board of Deputies by the British Government.
Holocaust Memorial, Waltham Abbey Cemetery, Skillet Hill, Honey La., Waltham Abbey, Essex. Consecrated 1985 under U.S. auspices.
Holocaust Memorial, Sternberg Centre, 80 East End Road, Finchley N3.
Memorial in Willesden Jewish Cemetery, Beaconsfield Road, NW10, to Jewish Servicemen and Women in the British Armed Forces who died in the two World Wars and have no known graves. Annual service organised by Ajex.
Prisoners' Memorial, Gladstone Park, Dollis Hill Lane, NW2, to those who died in prisoner-of-war camps and concentration camps during the Second World War. Annual service jointly org. by Ajex and the Royal Brit. Legion.
Royal Fusiliers, City of London Regiment Memorial, High Holborn, by City boundary. The names of the 38th, 39th and 40th Battalions are inscribed on the monument, together with all other battalions, which served in the First World War. Ajex is represented at the annual service.

Cemeteries

US = United Synagogue. F = Federation of Synagogues. UO = Union of Orthodox Hebrew Congregations. SP = Spanish and Portuguese Synagogue. W = Western Marble Arch Synagogue. WG = West End Great Synagogue. R = Reform. L = Liberal.
Alderney Road Cemetery (disused) E1. ☎ 0181-790 1445. (US).
Brady Street Cemetery, E1. (US).
Bullscross Ride Cemetery, Cheshunt, Herts. ☎ 01992 717820 (W and WG)
Bushey Cemetery, Little Bushey Lane, Bushey, Herts. ☎ 0181-950 6299. (US).
East Ham Cemetery, Marlow Road, High St. South, E6. (US).
Edgwarebury Cemetery, Edgwarebury Lane, Edgware, Middx. ☎ 0181-958 3388. (SP and R).
Edgwarebury Cemetery, Edgwarebury Lane, Edgware, Middx. ☎ 0181-580 1663. (L).
Edmonton Federation Cemetery, Montagu Road, Angel Road, Lower Edmonton, N18. ☎ 0181-807 2268. (F).
Enfield Cemetery, Carterhatch Lane, Enfield, Middx. ☎ 0181-363 3384. (UO).
Hackney Cemetery, (disused) Lauriston Road, E9. ☎ 0181-985 1527. (US).
Hoop Lane Cemetery, Golders Green, NW11. ☎ 0181-455 2569. (SP and R).
Kingsbury Road Cemetery, Balls Pond Road, N1. (R).
Liberal Jewish Cemetery, Pound Lane and Harlesden Road, NW10. (L).
Mile End Road (disused), E1. (SP).
Plashet Cemetery, High St. North E12. ☎ 0181-472 0554. (US).
Queen's Elm Parade Cemetery, (disused), Fulham Road, SW3. (W).
Rainham Cemetery, Upminster Road North, Rainham, Essex. ☎ 017085-52825. (F).
Rowan Road Cemetery, Greyhound Lane, SW16. ☎ 0181-764 1566. (WG).
Silver Street Cemetery, Cheshunt, Herts. ☎ 0181-802 6262. (UO).
Waltham Abbey Cemetery, Skillet Hill (Honey Lane), Waltham Abbey, Essex. ☎ 0992 714492. (US).
West Ham Cemetery, Buckingham Road, Forest Lane, E15. ☎ 0181-534 3006. (US).
Western Synagogue Cemetery, Montagu Road, N18. ☎ 0181-971 7820. (W).
Willesden Cemetery, Beaconsfield Road, NW10. ☎ 0181-459 0394. (US).

EDUCATIONAL ORGANISATIONS
Withdrawal on Friday Afternoons:
When the Sabbath begins at 5 p.m. or earlier, parents of Jewish children attending either State or State-aided schools can request that their children be withdrawn at such time as to reach their homes before the commencement of the Sabbath. Such requests should be submitted to the Head Teacher in writing. Hebrew and Religion Classes are attached to nearly all the syns. listed.
Agency for Jewish Education. (See p.35).
Schools' J-Link, 44a Albert Road, Hendon, London NW4 2SJ. ☎ 0181-202 2236. Fax 0181-202 4668. Email: j-link@dircon.co.uk (Est. 1993. Reg. Charity No. 1062551) Schools' J-Link is an outreach programme to Jewish children in non-Jewish secondary schools aimed at raising their level of Jewish knowledge, commitment and involvement. Within the school system, it addresses Jewish pupils in Jewish Assemblies and/or Society meetings, as well as at main school assembly, the classroom and at 6th form discussion sessions. It provides a broad spectrum of Jewish input by coopting rabbis, youth workers, knowledgeable lay men and women, representatives of various Jewish organisations and visiting speakers from abroad. It also runs training programmes for non-Jewish teachers who are teaching Judaism. Schools' J-Link currently visits over 60 schools in the London area and meets upwards of 4,000 young Jews in the course of the school year.*Dir* Rabbi Arye Forta, BA; *Programme Coord.* Mrs Susan Bolsom.
Akiva School, Levy House, The Steinberg Centre, 80 East End Road, N3 2SY. ☎

0181-349 4980. (Est. 1981.) Primary educ. for pupils, aged 4-11 years, under Reform & Liberal Synagogue auspices. *Head Teacher* Mrs L. Bayfield, B.A. (Hns), p.00; *Admin.* Mrs R. Black.

Avigdor Primary School, 63-67 Lordship Road, N.16. Voluntary-aided school for boys and girls, 3-11. *H.M.* Mrs R. Springer; *Sec.* Mrs Y. Ricketts. ☎ 0181-800 8339.

Binoh: The Jewish Special Educational Needs Service, Norwood House, Harmony Way, off Victoria Road, London NW4 2BA. ☎ 0181-203 3030/954-4555. Fax 0181-202 3030. (Reg. Charity No. 291978). Web Site: WWW.Shema Yisrael.co.il Email: Norwood@ort.org. Part of Norwood Ravenswood (see p.00), Binoh is a multi-disciplinary Special Education Service for Jewish children. A range of services is provided for children with special educational needs from birth to the end of their school years. Learning difficulties can include dyslexia, developmental problems or behavioural difficulties – anything that is holding back a child's progress. Our educational psychologists, therapists, support teachers and other staff, aim to help children with special needs to remain within the ordinary school system and to access the best opportunities for developing their potential. *Dir. of Education* Ruth Deutsch.

Training courses and workshops for parents and teachers, Parent Advisory Service and multi-disciplinary services including teaching and therapeutic services. Local teams in Hackney and Redbridge. Part-time Special Needs Unit for children with learning difficulties located at Norwood House. Binoh is part of Norwood Ravenswood.

Gan Aviv Kindergarten, Bushey & District Synagogue, 177–189, Sparrows Herne, Bushey, Herts., WD2 1AJ. ☎ 0181-386 1616. Fax 0181-421 8267. (For children 3-5). *H. Princ.* Rabbi Z. M. Salasnik B.A.; *H. M.* Mrs E. Levine, Cert. Ed.

Hasmonean High School:
Boys, 11/18, Holders Hill Road, NW4 1 NA. ☎ 0181-203 1411. Fax 0181-202 4526.
Girls, 2/4, Page Street, NW7 2EU. ☎ 0181-203 4294. Fax 0181-202 4527.
Recognised by Dept. of Education. Grant maintained London Borough of Barnet. *H. T. D.* Coleman Ph.D., M.A., B.Sc.; *Dep. Heads* D. Gilman, B.Ed.; Rabbi A. Cohen B.A.; Rabbi C. Baddiel, B.A.; *Admin* J. Cutzon.

Hasmonean Primary School, 8-10 Shirehall Lane, NW4 2PD. ☎ 0181-202 7704. Fax 0181-202 1605. (Boys and Girls 2-11.) *Hd.* Mrs J. Rodin; Cert Ed. Premier Degré (Paris). Rabbi M. Beaton, Rav of the School.

Ilford Jewish Primary School, Carlton Dr, Ilford, Essex IG6 1LZ. ☎ 0181-551 4294. Fax 0181-551 4295. *H. M.* Rev. A. Shaw, M.A. Cert.Ed.

Immanuel College, (The Charles Kalms, Henry Ronson Immanuel College) 87/91 Elstree Road, Bushey, Herts., WD2 3RH. ☎ 0181-950 0604. Fax: 0181-950 8687. Email: immcoll@rmplc.co.uk (Reg Charity No. 803179) Independent mixed selective school. *H.* Mrs Myrna Jacobs, BA; *Dep. H.* Rabbi D. Radomsky, BA(Hons), MA.; *Sec. Dep. H.* Richard Felsenstein BA(Hons), Cert Ed.

Independent Jewish Day School, 46 Green Lane, NW4 2AH. ☎ 0181-203 2299. Orthodox Primary Sch. & Kindergarten (est. 1979). *Chairman* S. Benaim. *Princ.* A. A. Kimche, B.A.; *H. T.* Mrs H. Cohen, B.A.

Jewish Resource Centre (JRC at CREDE), Centre for Religious Education and Development, Roehampton Institute London, Digby Stuart College, Roehampton Lane, SW15 5PH. ☎/Fax 0181-392 3349. JRC at CREDE was set up in 1996 – with the support of the Jewish Community Allocations Board – to serve as a resource for all sections of the Jewish community in South London, as well as for the non-Jewish teaching community. The Centre houses a large stock of books and religious articles for purchase, loan and consultation, and provides a base for educational and cultural activities. Staff are available to visit synagogues, religion schools/chadarim and teachers' centres in the area to run book

sales and other events. JRC at CREDE is open on Wednesday afternoons during term-time from 2.00 to 5.00 p.m., and at other times by appointment. *Co-ord.* Anne Clark, B.A. (Hons.), M.A., Dip. Couns.
Jewish Secondary Schools Movement, Holders Hill Road, NW4. ☎ 0181-203 1411. Fax 0181-202 4526. (Est. 1929.) *Principal.* J.F.S., 175 Camden Road, NW1 9HD. ☎ 0171-485 9416. Fax 0171-284 3948. (Est. 1958.) *H. T.* Miss R. Robins, B.A., TTHD; *Clerk to Govs.* Mr. N.C.G. Cann, MIM, MInst AM. Goldbloom (Hebrew Studies) Dept.
Kerem House, 18 Kingsley Way, N2 0ER. ☎ 0181-455 7524. (Boys and Girls 3-5.) *H. Princ.* Rabbi E. Jackson, B.A.; *H. T.* Mrs D. Rose, Cert. Ed.
Kerem School, Norrice Lea, N2 0RE. ☎ 0181-455 0909. (Boys and Girls 4-11.) *H. Princ.* Rabbi E. Jackson, B.A.; *H. T.* Mrs R. Goulden, M. Ed.
King Solomon High School, Forest Road, Barkingside, Ilford Essex IG6 3HB. ☎ 0181-501 2083. Fax 0181-559 9445. *H.M.* A. Falk; *Chairman of Govs.* A. Sugar; *H. Corr.* D. Lerner; *Denominational Body:* United Synagogue; *Auth.* London Borough of Redbridge.
Kisharon, (Reg. Charity No.: 271519). 1011 Finchley Road, NW11 7HB. ☎ 0181-455 7483. Fax 0181-731 7005. (Est. 1976). *Chairman* S. Greenman; *H. T.* Mrs Ch. Lehman.
Day School: (Mild-Moderate Learning Difficulties, age 3-16). In addition to the subject requirements of the National Curriculum each child has an Individual Educational Programme which focuses on their specific needs. The staff team include a Music Teacher, Music Therapist, Speech therapist, Consultant Physiotherapist and Occupational Therapist.
Senior Centre 1: Josselson Building, 37 Moss Hall Grove, N12 8PE, 0181-343 9412. Centre 1 offers an independence based programme for young adults with severe learning difficulties aged 16-30. The centre has an on-site established workshop, and Autistic students.
Senior Centre 2: Highfield House, 261 Hale Lane, Edgware HA8 8NX, 0181-905 4583. Centre 2 offers further education and vocational opportunities to young adults with mild to moderate learning difficulties. Basic education and religious studies forms a basis for the programme with craft sessions and bookbinding underpinning the students vocational development. All the students have work experience opportunities in the wider community and attend courses at Barnet College.
Early Childhood Development Centre: Opening January 1998.
Residential Provision: Hannah Schwalbe Home, 48 Leeside Crescent NW11 0LA, offers residential provision for eight young adults with moderate learning difficulties.
Law of Truth Talmudical College, (Reg. Charity No.: T31648Z/1). 50 Knightland Road, E5 9HS. *Corr.* 27 Warwick Grove, E5 9HX. ☎ 0181-806 2963. Fax 0181-806 9318. Students: 0181-806 6642. (Est. by Rabbi M. Szneider in Memel, 1911, Frankfurt 1918, London 1938.) *Princ.* Rabbi S. A. Halpern.
Lubavitch Foundation, 107-115 Stamford Hill, N16 5RP. ☎ 0181-800 0022. fax 0181-809 7324. (Est. 1959.) To further Jewish religious education, identity and commitment. Separate depts. for adult education, summer and day camps, youth clubs and training, univ. counsellors, publications, welfare, and orgs. concerned with Israel. *Princ.* Rabbi N. Sudak; *Dir. of Educ.* Rev. A. D. Sufrin; *Dir.* Rabbi S. F. Vogel. Lubavitch House School–Boys' Senior, 133 Clapton Common, E5. ☎ 0181-809 7476. Girls' Senior, 107 Stamford Hill, N16. ☎ 0181-800 0022. *H. M.* Rabbi S. Lew. Boys' Primary, 135 Clapton Common E5. ☎ 0181-800 1044. *H. M.* Rabbi Y.D. Chaiton. Girls' Primary, 113-115 Stamford Hill, N16 5RP. ☎ 0181-800 0022. Fax 0181-809 7324. Kindergarten, 107 Stamford Hill, N16. ☎ 0181-800 0022. *H. T.* Mrs F. Sudak. *Librarian* Zvi Rabin, ALA. ☎ 0181-800 5823. Women's Centre, 19 Northfield Rd, N16 5RL. ☎ 0181-809 6508. *Admin.* Mrs R. Bernstein. *Publ.* Lubavitch Direct.

Menorah Foundation School, Abbotts Road, NW9. ☎ 0181-906 9992. Fax 0181-906 9993. *H. T.* Anne Albert Cert.Ed., Dip.Ed.; *Principal* Rabbi H.I. Feldman; *Chairman* Jeremy Kon.
Menorah Grammar School for Boys, (Private), Beverley Gdns., NW11 9DG. ☎ 0181-458 8354. Fax 0181-458 1096. *H. M.* Rabbi A. M. Goldblatt.
Menorah Primary School, Woodstock Avenue, NW11. ☎ 0181-458 1276. Vol. Aided (Lond. Borough of Barnet) for Boys & Girls 5-11. (Est. 1944.) *Princ.* Rabbi H.I. Feldman; *Hd.* Mrs S. Kestenbaum.
Michael Sobell Sinai School, Shakespeare Dr, Kenton, Harrow, Middx HA3 9UD. ☎ 0181-204 1550. (Est. 1981.) Vol. aided primary sch. for boys & girls, aged 3-11. *Chairman Govs.* Mrs C. Hart; *H. T.* Mrs V. Orloff; *H. Corr.* D. Lerner; *Denominational body* Bd. of Rel. Educ.; *Auth.* Lond. Borough of Brent.
MST (formerly Massoret), 240-242 Hendon Way, NW4 3NL. ☎ 0181-202 2212. ☎/Fax 0181 203 2212. Orthodox women's college providing tertiary education and professional training. Operates within four faculties – Education (Teacher Training); Health and Community Care; Art, Design and Technology; I.T. (Computing) and Business Studies. Full-time and part-time courses combined with essential Torah and Hebrew studies. *Dean* Mrs J. Nemeth; *Exec. Dir.* Mrs O. Joseph.
Naima Jewish Preparatory School, 21 Andover Place, NW6 5ED. ☎ 0171-328 2802. Small caring school for children aged 3-11 years offering a broad secular curriculum together with rich programme of Orthodox Jewish studies. Catering for all children of all abilities through flexible learning programme. *H. Princ.* Rabbi Dr A. Levy; *Hd. T.* Mrs K. Peters.
North-West London Jewish Day School, 180 Willesden Lane, NW6 7PP. ☎ 0181-459 3378/3797. Fax 0181-451 7298. Grant maintained Orthodox Primary sch. and nursery for boys and girls, 3-11 (Est. 1945). *Act. Principal* Dayan J. Binstock; *H. M. D.* Collins, B.Sc., Dip. Ed. Admin., A.C.P.
Pardes House Primary School, Hendon Lane, N3 1SA. ☎ 0181-343 3568. *H. Princ.* Rabbi E. Halpern. *Head M.* Rabbi D. M. Kornhauser. Kindergarten: Golders Grn. Syn., Dunston Rd., NW11. *Matron* Mrs Y. Wilhelm.
Pardes House Grammar School, Hendon Lane, N3 1SA. ☎ 0181-343 3568. *H. Princ.* Rabbi E. Halpern; *Head M.* Rabbi D. Dunner.
Scopus Jewish Educational Trust Schools:
(see p.41)
Harry & Abe Sherman Rosh Pinah Jewish Primary School Glengall Road, Edgware, HA8 8TE. ☎ 0181-958 8599. (Est. 1956.) *H. Princ.* Rev. S. Amias, M.B.E.; *H. T.* M. Leviton, B.Ed.
Sebba Rosh Pinah Nursery School and Play Group, Mowbray Road, Edgware, Middx., HA8 8JL. ☎ 0181-958 1597. For children aged 2½-5. *H. T.* Mrs B. Mailer, Dip. Ed. (SA).
Mathilda Marks-Kennedy School, 68 Hale Lane, NW7 3RT. ☎ 0181-959 6089. (Est. 1959.) For children between 2½-11, emphasising traditional Jewish education within a Zionist framework. *H. Princ.* Rev. R. Turner; *H. T.* Mrs Jean Shindler, B.Ed., Dip. Ed.
Simon Marks Jewish Primary School & Nursery, 75 Cazenove Road (cnr. Kyverdale Road) N16 6PD. ☎ 0181-806 6048. Fax 0181-442 4722. *H.T.* Miss D. Kavanagh, Cert. Ed., Dip. Ed.
Sharon Kindergarten, Finchley Synagogue, Kinloss Gdns., N3 3DU. ☎ 0181-346 2039. (For children 2½-5.) – *H. T.* Mrs E. Elek.
Torah Centre Trust, 84 Leadale Road, N15 6BH. ☎ 0181-802 3586. (Est. 1975.) To provide full or part-time facilities for children, in particular those from 'uncommitted' families, to enable them to further their secular and Hebrew educ. *Chairman* Rabbi J. Dunner; *Educ. Dir.* Rabbi M. Bernstein, B.Ed.
Wolfson Hillel Primary School, Chase Road, Southgate, N14 4LG. ☎ 0181-882 6487. Fax 0181-882 7965. (Est. 1992). Vol. aided primary school for boys &

girls aged 3-11. *Chairman Govs.* P. Musgrave; *H. T.* Mrs S. Margolis. (United Synagogue Board of Religious Educ.; *Auth.* London Borough of Enfield.)
Yeshiva Gedola, 3/5 Kingsley Way, N2. ☎ 0181-455 3262. *Rosh Yeshiva* Rabbi I. M. Hertz.
Yeshivah Ohel Moshe Etz Chaim, 85 Bridge Lane, NW11.(Reg. Charity No. 312232) ☎ 0181-458 5149. *Princ.* Rabbi Z. Rabi.
Yesodey Hatorah Schools, 2 and 4 Amhurst Park, N16 5AE. ☎ 0181-800 8612. (Est. 1943.) *Princ.* Rabbi A. Pinter; *V. President* Rabbi C. Pinter.
Yesodey Hatorah Nursery, 2 Amhurst Pk., N16 5AE. ☎ 0181-800 9221. *Hd.* Mrs R. Greenberg.
Yesodey Hatorah Kindergarten, 2 Amhurst Pk., N16 5AE. ☎ 0181-800 8612. *Matron* Mrs B. Gottlieb.
Yesodey Hatorah Primary School (Boys), 2 Amhurst Pk., N16 5AE. ☎ 0181-800 8612. *Princ* Rabbi A. Pinter; *Menahel* Rabbi D. Mapper.
Yesodey Hatorah Senior School (Boys), 4 Amhurst Pk., N16 5AE. ☎ 0181-800 8612. *Princ.* Rabbi A. Pinter; *Menahel* Rabbi D. Mapper.
Yesodey Hatorah Primary School (Girls), 153 Stamford Hill, N16 5LG. ☎ 0181-800 8612. *Princ.* Rabbi A. Pinter; *H. M.* Mrs D. Luria; *Dep. H. M.* Mrs C. Berger.
Yesodey Hatorah Senior School (Girls) 153 Stamford Hill, N16 5LG. ☎ 0181-800 8612. *Princ.* Rabbi A. Pinter; *H. M.* Mrs R. Pinter

WELFARE ORGANISATIONS

Abbeyfield (Camden) Society, 178 Walm Lane, London NW2 3AX. ☎ 0181-452 7375. The Abbeyfield Camden Society run two small residential homes for the able-bodied elderly, with facilities for short-stay visitors. Each resident has his/her own room for which they are responsible, and lunch and supper are provided by the resident housekeeper in the communal dining-room. We aim to preserve independence within a secure and friendly community. *Chairman* Mrs B. Richenberg, 16 Greenacre Walk, Cannon Hill, N14 7DB. *Hon. Sec.* Mrs J. Kessler, 20 Seaforth Gdns., N21 3BS. Branches: Peggy Lang House, 178 Walm Lane, NW2 3AX. Lily Montagu House, 36-38 Orchard Dr, Stanmore, Middx. HA8 7SD.
Agudas Israel Housing Association Ltd., 206 Lordship Rd., N16 5ES. ☎ 0181-802 3819. Fax 0181-809 6206 (Reg. Charity No. 23535).
Schonfeld Square Development, Fradel Lodge Sheltered Accommodation and Beis Pinchos Residential Home (Reg. Charity No. 1049179). ☎ 0181-802 7477. *Chief Exec.* Mrs Ita Symons, MBE.
Ajex Housing Association Ltd. ☎ 0181-802 3348 Warden. Fax 0181-880 1117. Provides flatlets for elderly and disabled ex-servicemen and women and/or their dependants. *Chairman* H. Newman; *H. Sec.* L. Primack; *Admin.* Ajex House, East Bank, N16 5RT.
Arbib Lucas Trust, (Reg. Charity No. 208666). Provides financial assistance to women in reduced circumstances and helps with vocational training for them. *H. Sec.* Mrs Anita Kafton, 16 Sunny Hill, NW4 4LL.
Bnai Brith (JBG) Housing Association, Harmony Close, Princes Park Ave. NW11 0JJ. ☎ 0181-381 4901. Fax 0181-458 1772. *Chairman* E. Shapiro; *T. L.* Sterling; *Chief Exec.* S. Clarke. The Association provides sheltered housing in London, Margate and Hemel Hempstead, together with a range of accommodation for people with special needs. Special Need accommodation is managed by Norwood Ravenswood and Jewish Care. Hostel accommodation for young people is located in Golders Green.
Drugsline Chabad (Reg. Charity No. 227638), 372 Cranbrook Road, Gants Hill, Ilford, Essex IG2 6HW. Crisis Helpline: Freephone 0800 731 0713 or 0181-518 6470. Office: 0181-554 3220. Fax: 0181 518 2126. Drop in service for those people with drug-related problems, their families and friends. Drug and alcohol

education services offered to schools, youth clubs and other organisations. *Dir.* Rabbi Aryeh Sufrin; *Project Worker* Debbie Epstein.

Finchley Kosher Lunch Service, (Meals-on-Wheels for the housebound and disabled), Covers Edgware, Finchley, Golders Green, Hampstead Garden Suburb, Hendon, Mill Hill. *H. T.* Mrs Ruth Freed, ☎ 0181-202 8129. Admin. by the League of Jewish Women. (See p.?.)

Food for the Jewish Poor, To provide (a) food throughout the year; (b) grocery during Passover; (c) special relief for approved emergency cases. (See Jewish Care).

Friends of the Kingsbury Mikveh – Educational and Support Group, Kingsbury United Synagogue, Kingsbury Green, NW9 8XR. ☎ 0181-204 6390. *Hon.T.* Janet Rabson, 16 Broadfields Ave., Edgware, HA8 8PG. ☎ 0181-958 9035.

Friends of the Sick (Chevrat Bikkur Cholim), (Reg. Charity No. 91468A), 463a Finchley Road, NW3 6HN. ☎ 0171-435 0836. (Est. 1947.) To nurse sick and aged needy persons in their own homes. *President* Peter Gillis; *H. T. M.* Wechsler; *Gen. Sec.* Mrs E. Weitzman.

Hagadolim Charitable Organisation, (Est. 1950.) To provide financial assistance to Homes and charities in England and Israel, and to visit and provide comforts in private homes in the Home Counties. *Chairman* L. Dunitz; *Jt. Ts.* B. Wallach, Mrs R. J. Dunitz; *Sec.* Mrs S. Levy, 4 Edgwarebury Ct., Edgwarebury La., Edgware, Middx. HA8 8LP. ☎ 0181-958 8558.

Haven Foundation (Regd. Charity No. 264029), Alfred House, 1 Holly Park, Crouch Hill, N4 4BN. ☎ 0171-272 1345 (Admin. by Ravenswood Foundation). Est. 1971. To provide permanent residential care and development training for Jewish mildly mentally handicapped adults in its hostel, group homes and soc. development unit. *L. President* Eve Alfred; *Chairman* N. Freeder; *Jt. V. Chairman* R. Rosenberg, A.C.A.

Hospital Kosher Meals Service, (Reg. Charity No.: 1025601), Lanmor House, 370/386 High Road, Wembley, Middx. HA9 6AX. ☎ 0181-795 2058. Fax 0181-900 2462. Provides supervised kosher meals to patients in hospitals throughout Greater London. *Chairman* M.G. Freedman, M.Sc., F.C.A.; *V. Chairman* H. Glyn, B.Sc., FRICS; *H. T. M.* Blum, F.C.A.

JBG Housing Society Ltd., 17 Highfield Road, NW11 9LS. ☎ 0181-381 4901. Fax 0181-731 7462. (Est. 1965). Sheltered housing for elderly and young people with disabilities. Group homes and hostels for people with mental illness, people with learning difficulties and young people leaving care. Registered care home for people with physical disabilities. *Chairman* E. Shapiro; *Dir.* S. Clarke; *Housing Man.* E. Kurrant.

Jewish Aged Needy Pension Society (Est. 1829.) Provides pensions for members of the Jewish community aged 60 or over, who have known better times and who, in their old age, find themselves in reduced circumstances. Also supplements income provided from statutory sources. Services to the middle-class of society who find themselves in greater financial need and who do not seem to fall within the purview of any other charitable organisations. *President* I. Lewisohnv; *Ts.* R. W. Gollance, M. E. G. Prince; *H. Sec.* Mrs G. B. Rigal; *Sec./Admin.* Mrs Sheila A. Taylor, 34 Dalkeith Grove, Stanmore, Middx. ☎ 0181-958 5390.

Jewish Bereavement Counselling Service, (Est. 1980), P.O. Box 6748, London N3 3BX. ☎ 0181-343 6226, 0181-349 0839 (24 hour answerphone). Offers bereavement counselling and support to members of the Jewish community who have been bereaved. Covers North, NW and SW London. *Chairman* Joy Conway, *Co-ord.* June Epstein, *Consults.* Roni Goldberg, Jacqueline Toff.

Jewish Blind & Disabled (JBD), the working name of the Jewish Blind & Physically Handicapped Society, a company limited by guarantee. Reg. Charity No. 259480. Head Office: 118 Seymour Place, London W1H 5DJ. Care & Campaign Office: 164 East End Road, London N2 0RR. ☎ 0181-883 1000. Fax 0181-444 6729. Email: info@jblind.cix.co.uk. Jewish Blind & Disabled (JBD) provides caring sheltered housing with communal and welfare services for visu-

ally and physically disabled people, to improve the quality of life, maximise freedom of choice, respect dignity at all times and help achieve independent living.
JBD is an independent charity providing independent living. Founded in 1969 by the late Cecil Rosen, who recognised the need for purpose-built, sheltered housing for blind, partially sighted and disabled people of all ages, within the community. JBD currently has five modern sheltered projects providing 193 purpose-built apartments able to accommodate up to 300 residents. Resident House Managers are on site twenty-four hours a day. Jewish Blind & Disabled is the UK's largest Jewish sheltered housing provider for blind and disabled people.
Chairman John Joseph; *Hon. Chief Exec.* Malcolm J. Ozin; *Housing & Care Dir.* David A. Brodtman; *Campaign Dir.* Jason J. Ozin; *Trust Dir.* Marilyn Leveson.
JBD Projects: *Sheltered housing schemes:* Fairacres, 164 East End Road, Finchley, N2; Cherry Tree Court, Roe Green, Kingsbury, NW9; Cecil Rosen Court, 331 East Lane, North Wembley, Middx; Milne Court, 14 Churchfields, South Woodford, E18; New Project: 34 Sylvan Road, Wanstead, E11.
Day Centres: Monday Club, Fairacres, Finchley, N2; Monday Club, Milne Court, South Woodford, E18; Milne Court Clubbers, Milne Court, SouthWoodford, E18; Wednesday Club, Cecil Rosen Court, Wembley, & Cherry Tree Court, Kingsbury.
Hostel: Aldun House, Pulham Avenue, Finchley, N2 (hostel for homeless youths, managed by Norwood/Ravenswood).

Jewish Blind Society (incorporating Jewish Assn. for the Physically Handicapped). See below: Jewish Care.

Jewish Care, a company limited by guarantee. Reg. in England No.: 2447900, Stuart Young House, 221 Golders Green Road, London NW11 9DQ. ☎ 0181-458-3282, Fax. 0181-455-7185. Formed on 1st January 1990 by the merger of the Jewish Blind Society (est. 1819) and the Jewish Welfare Board (est. 1859 Reg. Charity No. 802559). Since then the following organisations have also merged their activities with Jewish Care: The Jewish Home & Hospital at Tottenham; Food for the Jewish Poor (Soup Kitchen); Jewish Assn. for the Physically Handicapped; Brit. Tay-Sachs Foundation; Waverley Manor (Friends of the London Jewish Hospital).; Brighton and Hove Jewish Home: Stepney Jewish (B'nai B'rith) Clubs and Settlement; Redbridge Jewish Youth and Community Centre.

Services are provided for over five thousand elderly, mentally ill, visually impaired and physically disabled people and their families every single day. Resources include residential and nursing homes, hostels, day centres, sheltered housing, domiciliary care and social work teams in London and South East England.

Jewish Care is Anglo-Jewry's largest social services organisation catering for the needs of the community living in London and south-east England.. The organisation provides a wide and comprehensive range of services employs over 1,000 people and works in partnership with nearly 2,500 volunteers. Jewish Care relies on funds from generous donations from members of the community, central and local government, and from The European Union which help Jewish Care in its mission to provide the highest quality of service and ensure that people who are not in a position to pay can still receive our help. Jewish Care has a current budget of £30 million. The Guide to Jewish Care is available on request.
President The Rt. Hon. Lord Young of Graffham; *Chairman* Michael Levy; *Chief Exec.* Melvyn I. Carlowe; *Assoc. Chief Exec.* Jeff Shear; *Dir. Special Projects* Anthony Krais. *Dir. Quality Assurance* Alex Sklan. *Finance Dir.* Henry Solomon.
Publ. Guide to Jewish Care.
Establishments administered by Jewish Care:
Residential Homes -
Braemar Royal, Bournemouth; Carlton Dene (holiday home), Bournemouth; Charles Clore, N10; Brighton & Hove Jewish Home; Ella & Ridley Jacobs, NW4; Kay Court, NW3; Morton House, Hemel Hempstead; Raymond House,

Southend-on-Sea; Rela Goldhill Lodge (specialist for younger people with a physical disablity), NW11; Rokefield, Dorking; Rubens, N3; Sarah Tankel, N5; Home & Hospital at Tottenham, N15; Vi & John Rubens, Redbridge; Waverley Manor, NW4; Wolfson House, N4.
Day Centres -
Michael Sobell Community Centre, NW11; Stamford Hill Community Centre, N16; Redbridge Jewish Day Centre (in conjunction with Redbridge Jewish Youth & Com. Centre); Stepney Jewish Day Centre (in conjunction with B'nai B'rith), E1; Southend & Westcliff Jewish Day Centre.
Special Day Care Units -
Sam Beckman Special Day Care Centre, NW4; Stanmore & Edgware Special Day Care Centre; Stepney Special Day Care Unit, E1; Wolfson House Special Day Care Centre, N4.
Specialist units: Employment Resource Centre, N3; Holocaust Survivors Centre, NW4, Carers' Centre, NW11.
Flatlet Schemes (sheltered housing) -
Shine House (in conjunction with JBG Housing Ltd), N3; Maitland House (in conjunction with JBG Housing Ltd), Hemel Hempstead; Rosetta House (in conjunction with JBG Housing Ltd), Hemel Hempstead; Rabbi Pinchas Shebson Lodge, Southend-on-Sea; Sir John & Lady Cohen Court (Joel Emanual Almshouse Trust), N.16; Posnansky Court (in conjuction with JBG Housing Ltd), N4.
Mental Health Provision -
Mitkadem, Redbridge; Shalvata Centre, NW4; 7A Mapesbury Road (therapeutic hostel), NW2; Ealon House, 7B Mapesbury Road (support hostel), NW2; 6 sheltered homes.
Social Work Teams -
Edgware Jewish Family Service, ☎ 0181-951 0166; Hackney Jewish Family Services, ☎ 0181-880 2244; North West Area Office, ☎ 0181-458 3282; Redbridge Jewish Family Services, ☎ 0181-554 8299; South London Jewish Family Service, ☎ 0181-458 3282.

Jewish Children's Holidays Fund (Formerly The Jewish Branch of the Children's Country Holidays Fund). (Reg. Charity No.: 295361). (Est. 1888.) *President* Mrs Maud Whiteley; *Chairman* Sydney Harvey; *Sec.* Mrs F. Warshawsky, 60 Oundle Ave., Bushey, Herts WD2 3QQ. ☎ 0181-950 3383.

Jewish Crisis Help Line, Miyad. ☎ 0181-203 6211. Confidential listening service for those experiencing stress in their lives. Sponsored by the Jewish Marriage Council.

Jewish Deaf Association, 26 Aylmer Parade, Aylmer Rd., N2 0PE. ☎ 0181-347 7366. Fax 0181-347 7558; 21a Accommodation Rd., NW11 8EP. ☎ 0181-455 1557. (Reg. Charity No. 209892). Provides a welfare and social environment for the profoundly deaf and hearing-impaired. Maintains a Day Centre for deaf people. Runs two Advisory and Resource Centres exhibiting aids to daily living for deaf and hard of hearing people of all ages. *President* G. M. Gee, J.P.; *Chairman* Mrs E. Gee; *Exec. Dir.* Mrs P. Goldring; *H. Chaplain* Rev. M. Plaskow.

Jewish Society for the Mentally Handicapped, Now merged with Ravenswood Foundation (See below).

Jewish Welfare Board (incorporating the Jewish Bread, Meat and Coal Society, est. 1779), See: Jewish Care, above.

Jews' Temporary Shelter (Reg. Charity No. 212071), 5 Mapesbury Road, NW2 4HZ. ☎ 0181-451 0233. Fax 0181-830 2203. (Est. 1885. Reg. Charity No. 212071) *Jt. H.* T. H. Arnold, F.C.A., H. Kleeman, C.B.E.; *Jt. H. Secs.* Mrs A. Elman, D. Feldman; *House Cttee Sec.* C.L. Lander.

Lewis Hammerson Memorial Home, Hammerson House, The Bishop's Avenue, N2 OBE. ☎ 0181-458 4523. Fax 0181-458 2537. (Est. 1962 Reg. Charity No. 286002) *President* Mrs S. Hammerson, O.B.E.; *Chairman* Philip Balcombe. Applications for admission: 0181-458 4523.

MIYAD: Jewish Telephone Crisis Line, ☎ 0181-203 6211, 0345 581999. Sponsored by the Jewish Marriage Council. Confidential telephone line offered to the Jewish community for people needing heip in crisis situations.
Necessitous Ladies' Fund, Incorporating Delissa Joseph Memorial Fund (both funds founded by Union of Jewish Women). For the relief of Jewish women who are in need, hardship or distress (Reg. Charity No. 266921 A3L1). *Chairman* Mrs Freda Davis; *H. Sec.* Mrs D. Curzon, 14 Blessington Close, SE13 5ED.
Nightingale House (Home for Aged Jews), 105 Nightingale Lane, SW12 8NB. ☎ 0181-673 3495. Fax 0181-675 2258 (Reg. Charity No. 207316) (Est. 1840.) Patrons Lord Rayne, Mrs V. Duffield, C.B.E.; *Chairman* G. Lipton; *Jt Ts.* M. Lawson; L. Green, FCA; K. Goodman, FCA; *Exec. Dir.* Leon Smith. Aid Societies: N.W. London; S.W. London; The Nightingales; Zamir; Nightingale Ladies' Cttee. Bazaar; The Kentongales . Also manages Rayne House sheltered housing flats.
Norwood Ravenswood, Broadway House, 80/82, The Broadway, Stanmore, HA7 4HB. ☎ 0181-954 4555. Fax 0181-420 6800. Email: Norwood@ort.org. Locally based social service teams are in Hackney (0181-880 2244), North West London (0181-203-3030), Edgware (0181-951-0166), Redbridge (0181-550 6114). Norwood Ravenswood is now the largest Jewish child and family services charity in Europe, working with over 6,000 children, young people, adults, people with learning disabilities and their families every year. We will provide a 'one stop' family service where children can if necessary continue to receive ongoing help throughout their lives. Included are: **Community services** offering a comprehensive range of counselling and support services to children and their families, dealing with problems of child abuse, financial hardshp and family breakdown. Extensive community services are also provided to people with learning disabilities and their families, including **Unity** and **Links** providing recreation schemes for children and adults. The Deli and Horticultural Project provide vocational training.
Presidential services include an adolescent unit, semi-independent bedsits, a respite care house, a network of community homes and Ravenswood Village. Day services include the **Kennedy Leigh Centre** and **Family Centre** in Hendon and many day opportunity schemes for young people and adults.
Binoh is our special educational needs service (see p.89), and the Association for Jewish Youth provides training and development services for youth organisations. **Koleinu** is an activity-based service for young Jewish deaf people. **Buckets and Spades Lodge** is Norwood Ravenswood's respite care house.
Patron HM The Queen; *President* Sir Trevor Chinn; *Chairman* Ronald Gottleib; *Exec. Dirs.* Sam Brier, MA, Norma Brier, MSc.
Raphael Centre, (a Jewish Counselling Service). (Reg. Charity No.: 278522). c/o Shalvata, Parson St., Hendon, NW1 4EB. Intake Counsellor. ☎ 0181-203 9881. Aims: To provide short- or long-term counselling by professional counsellors and psychotherapists for Jewish people with emotional or psychological problems, such as depression, stress, anxiety, loss or bereavement, relationship or family problems. Counselling supports, and helps with personal growth and the development, of personal resources. Fees are charged on a sliding scale within every clients reach. *Contact:* Hazel Stein.
Rishon Multiple Sclerosis Aid Group, 1 Mersham Dr, Kingsbury NW9 9PP. ☎ 0181-204 8622. (Est. 1966. Reg. Charity No. 252359) Affiliated to the Multiple Sclerosis Society of Great Britain. Provides social and cultural activities, help and welfare, for Multiple Sclerosis sufferers and raises funds for this and the encouragement of research into the causes and cure of the disease. *H. Sec.* B. Gold.
Stamford Hill Community Centre, 91-93 Stamford Hill, N16 5TP. ☎ 0181-800 5672. Fax 0181-800 1678 (Reg. Charity No. 802559). Administered by Jewish Care. Community Centre for the elderly and visually handicapped and others with special needs. *Director:* Mrs B. Hart.
Sunridge Housing Association Ltd., 76 The Ridgeway, NW11; *Chairman* David

Stern; *H. Sec.* Robin Michaelson.
Westlon and Westmount, 850 Finchley Road, NW111 6BB. ☎ 0181-201 8484. Fax 0181-731 8847.
Westlon Housing Association. *H. L. President* His Hon. Alan King-Hamilton, Q.C.; *President* H. Steel; *Chairman* Jennifer Ellis; *Admin.* J.W. Silverman. **Annette White Lodge,** 287/289 High Road, N2 8HB. **Deborah Rayne House,** 33b Sunningfields Road, NW4 4QX. **The Woodville,** Woodville Road, W5 2SE. Applications to 0181-201 9494.
Westmount Charitable Trust (Est. 1978) and **Westmount Housing Association.** *Chairman* Mrs E. Corob; *T.* S. Corob; *Sec.* Mrs S. Berg; *Admin.* J.W. Silverman. Accommodation and amenities for the elderly. **Westmount,** 126 Fortune Green Road, NW6 1DN. Residence for 40 elderly persons. Applications to 0181-201 8484.
Yad Voezer, 80 Queen Elizabeth's Walk, N16 5UQ. ☎/Fax 0181-809 4303. (Est. 1975). (Reg. Charity No. 277771). Care for Jewish children and adults with learning disabilities. Services include residential/respite care, Sunday and Holiday Clubs, day care, employment schemes, advice, counselling and family support. Services are managed and run within the N16 area. *Chairman* Rabbi E. Landau; *Ts.* R. Spitzer, S. Singer; *President* Lady A. Jakobovits; *Exec. Dir.* Zelda Landau.

Clubs and Cultural Societies

See also under Synagogues (pp.76–87); Organisations concerned with Jewish Youth (pp.46–54).
London Diary of Jewish Events, 12 Holne Chase, N2 0QN. ☎ 0181-458 2466. Fax 0181-458 5457 (Est. 1995) Monthly publication listing events organised by Jewish institutions for the Jewish community in London. *Ed.* Jazmin Naghar.

Alyth Choral Society, North Western Reform Synagogue, Alyth Gdns., NW11 7EN. ☎ 0181-455 6763 (Est. 1983.) *Ldr* Vivienne Bellos; *Chairman* F. Abrahams; *Sec.* Ms. C. Holmes.
Association of Jewish Friendship Clubs, 26 Enford St., W1H 2DD. ☎ 0171-724 8100. Fax 0171-706 1710 (Head Office). An umbrella organisation for men and women in the 50 plus age group, providing companionship throughout 70 clubs in London and the Provinces. A network of social clubs joining together for activities on a National basis, e.g. group holidays and central London based functions. *Jt Hon. Life Presidents* Lady Jakobovits and Rabbanit Elaine Sacks; *National Chairman* Mrs Stella Harris; *Hon. Chaplain* Rev. Dr Norman Gale.
Bernhard Baron St. George's Jewish Settlement (Reg. Charity No. 207191), 120 Oakleigh Road North, N20 9EZ. ☎ 0181-446 3101/2. Founded in 1914 by the late Sir Basil Henriques. Aims to meet the spiritual, cultural and recreational needs of Jewish people in the area. *Dir.* J. Wosner.
Besht Tellers, Maccabi House, 73 Compayne Gardens, NW6 3RS. ☎ 0171-624 4343. Email: 100645.3632@compuserve.com. Professional Jewish Theatre company producing national and international public performances of original Jewish Theatre. Touring community performances and educational workshops available for booking. *Dirs.* Robbie Gringras, Rebecca Wolman; *Admin.* Olivia Jacobs.
Brady-Maccabi, Youth and Community Centre, 4 Manor Pk. Cresc., Edgware, Middx. HA8 7NL. ☎ 0181-952 2948. Fax 0181-952 2393. (Est. 1979.) Open Sun. to Thurs. Snr. Citizens clubs meet Tues. and Thurs. aft. *President* John Cutner J.P., F.C.A.; *Chairman* Stuart Ansher; *Dir.* Miss S. Muscovitch.
Chabad Lubavitch Centre (Reg. Charity No. 227638), 372 Cranbrook Rd., Ilford, Essex IG2 6HW. ☎ 0181-554 1624. Fax 0181-518 2126. (Est. 1986). *Dir.* Rabbi A.M. Sufrin; *Programme Co-ord.* Rabbi M. Muller.
Friends of Jewish Youth, formerly Old Boys' Association. Martin Shaw, c/o A. J. Y.,

128 East Lane, Wembley, Middx. ☎ 0181-908 4747. Fax 0181-904 4323.
The Half-Empty Bookcase, for Progressive Jewish Women's Studies, 80 East End Rd., N3 2SY. ☎ 0181-447 8444. *Co-ord.* Dee Eimer.
Institute for Jewish Music Studies and Performance, 33 Seymour Pl. W1H 6AT. ☎ 0171-723 4404. (Est. 1982). To further the study and knowledge of Jewish music, both liturgical and secular, at the highest academic and performing level. *Dir.* S. Fixman.
Jewish Appreciation Group Tours, 32 Anworth Close, Woodford Green, Essex IG8 0DR ☎ 0181-504 9159. (Est. 1960.) Full history tours of the Jewish East End and the Jews in England from 1066. Historic walks and tours throughout the year. *Tours Org.* Adam Joseph.
Jewish Association of Cultural Societies (J.A.C.S.), Edgware Synagogue, Edgware Way, Edgware Middx. HA8 9YE. ☎ 0181-954 1353. (Est. 1978.) Thirty clubs have been opened throughout the Greater London com., with two in Surrey, one in Bournemouth, one in Brighton, one in Westcliff-on-Sea and one in Cardiff, providing weekly meetings for the 50+, embracing cultural and social programmes. *H. President* Rev. Saul Amias, M.B.E.; *Nat. Chairman* Mrs Annette Pearlman; *V. Chairman* Leslie Curtis; *H. Sec.* Mrs June Leader.
Jewish Research Group, c/o 43 Churchill Ct., Ainsley Close, Edmonton, N9 9XJ. ☎ 0181-886 6234. The Jewish Research Group is an autonomous part of the Edmonton Hundred Historical Society and was established in 1978 when the Committee of the 1st Jewish Way of Life Exhibition, held to mark the 50th Anniversary of the Palmers Green and Southgate Synagogue, decided not to disband. The main aim of the J.R.G. is to research the Jewish history in the 'Edmonton Hundred' which corresponds approximately to the boundaries of the London Boroughs of Enfield and Haringey and publish its findings.
   Membership is now 90. Monthly meetings are held at which prominent speakers are invited to address the Group on Jewish historical subjects. Four publications have been printed under the title of 'Heritage'. *President* Mrs Marjorie Glick, BA; *Chairman* Robert Landau, B.Sc; *V. Chairman* Anita Shapiro; *H. Sec.* Jeffrey Baum; *H. T.* Harold Temerlies.
Kadimah/Victoria Youth Club (Reg. Charity No.: 299323), 127/129 Clapton Common, E5 9AB. ☎ 0181-809 3618. Catering for the traditional and non-traditional, Ashkenazi and Sephardi communities. Membership for 5-14 yrs. *Senior Youth Worker* Rob Berg; *Chairman* Yoel Salem.
London Jewish Male Choir. *H. Sec.* Bernard Jackson, 62 Rotherwick Rd., NW11 7DB. ☎ 0181-458 6803. Fax 0181-731-8722. (Inland Revenue Number: X 91533). Rehearsals Thurs. evgs., Hendon Synagogue.
London Jewish Music Centre, PO Box 2268, NW4 3UW. ☎ & Fax 0181-203 8046. Founded in 1991 by The Jewish Music Festival Trust. The Jewish Music Centre is an information and resource centre on all aspects of Jewish music. Cassettes, Songbooks, CD's and Videos available for purchase. *Dirs.* Rachel Wetstein and Daniel Tunkel.
Lubavitch of South London (Reg. Charity No. 227638), 42 St. George's Road, Wimbledon, SW19 4ED. ☎ 0181-944 1581. Fax 0181-944 7563. (Est. 1988) Adult Jewish educ., library, food and bookshop, mailings, assemblies, tuition, Mitzva campaigns, youth activities. *Dir.* Rabbi Nissan Dubov.
The Maccabaeans. (Est. 1891.) Consisting primarily of those engaged in professional pursuits, its aims being to provide 'social intercourse and co-operation among its members with a view to the promotion of the interests of Jews, including the support of any professional or learned bodies and charities.' *President* Rt. Hon. Sir John Balcombe; *H. T.* D. D. Rosenfelder; *H. Sec.* L. Slowe, 4 Corringway, NW11 7ED.
Manor House Society, Sternberg Centre for Judaism, Manor House, 80 East End Road, N3 2SY. ☎ 0181-346 2288. Fax 0181-343 0901. Jewish cultural soc. pro-

viding art exhibitions, concerts and many other activities. *Chairman* L. Hepner; *Admin.* Mrs P. Lewis. Quarterly journal: 'Manna'.

Oxford & St. George's North London Jewish Centre (Reg. Charity No. 207191), 120 Oakleigh Road North, N20 9EZ. ☎ 0181-446 3101/2. Communal provision, youth clubs and Henriques House Jewish Day Centre (for the elderly). *Dir.* J. Wosner.

Redbridge Jewish Community Resource Centre (JPMP), Sinclair House, Woodford Bridge Road, Ilford, Essex, IG5 4LN. ☎ 0181-551 0017. Fax 0181-551 9027. The Resource Centre is a creative dynamic centre for informal Jewish and Zionist education. The Centre has operated in the community for ten years as a resource for educators who require support and advice in this field. The Resource Centre is a focus for leadership training in the community. The Redbridge Jewish Community Resource Centre is a Sinclair House project in association with JPMP (see p.?).

Redbridge Jewish Youth and Community Centre (Reg. Charity No.: 3013185), Sinclair House, Woodford Bridge Road, Ilford, Essex, IG4 5LN. ☎ 0181-551 0017. Fax 0181-551 9027. *Jt. Presidents* E. S. Birk, F. Cass; *Dir.* Neil Taylor. Sinclair House, home of the Redbridge Jewish Youth and Community Centre, meets the social, educational and welfare needs of all sections of the Redbridge and District Jewish Community. More than 3,500 people make use of the centre's facilities each week. The Redbridge Jewish Day Centre provides a high level of essential care for over 450 elderly and disabled people. There are programmes and services for young people, including those with special needs, and social, educational, welfare and active sports programmes for young and adults alike. The Centre is also the base for the Community Shlicha, Clayhall Synagogue, Redbridge Jewish Community Resource Centre (JPMP), Habonim Dror, Essex Teenage Centre, Sephardi Hebrew Classes, the Redbridge Jewish Youth Council and many communal events and activities.

The Redbridge Jewish Youth and Community Centre and Jewish Care are to merge subject to the approval of the Charity Commissioners.

Spec Jewish Youth and Community Centre, (Reg. Charity No. 302921), 87 Brookside South, East Barnet, Herts EN4 8LL. ☎ 0181-368 5117. Est. 1962 to enable Jewish young people to meet in a secure environment and offer opportunities for personal growth. Activities include youth clubs for 5½-16 age grps. *Chairman* N. Kingsley; *Tr.* C. Niren; *H. Sec.* Jeffrey Leifer; *Sec.* Linda Rich; *Dir.* Elizabeth Gordon.

Stepney Jewish Community Centre, 2-8 Beaumont Grove, E1 4NQ. ☎ 0171-790 6441. Fax 0171-265 8342. (Reg. Charity No. 802559) **Administered by Jewish Care**. Community Centre for the Elderly; Special Care Centre for Physically and Mentally Frail; Kosher Meals on Wheels; and Friendship Clubs. *Dir.* Barry Marcus.

Western Charitable Foundation, 32 Gt. Cumberland Place, W1H 7DJ. ☎ 0171-723 7246. *Chairman* Sidney Jaque, J.P.; *V. Chairman* Harold Pasha; *Tr.* W Ward.

Zemel Choir, (Reg. Charity No. 252572/ACL), Britain's leading mixed Jewish Choir performing a varied repertoire, with an emphasis on Hebrew, Yiddish, Israeli and liturgical music, and contemporary compositions of Jewish interest. Overseas tours, prestige concerts in London and provinces, recordings, social events. Zemel welcomes enthusiastic and committed singers who read music fairly fluently. Rehearsals most Mondays 8-10.30 p.m. North West London. *Musical Dir.* Robert Max. *Contact:* Concert Manager Peter Pollak, 5 Gable Lodge, 17-19 Torrington Park, N12 9TB. ☎ 0181-343 9819 (eves.). Fax 0181-933 6375.

Miscellaneous Organisations

All Aboard Charity Shops (0171-543 5404) are dedicated to raising funds for UK based Jewish charities only. All Aboard welcome donations of clothes and new

volunteers to assist in the shops and with management. Our stores are at: 1&2 Boot Parade, 88 High Street, Edgware; 125 Golders Green Road NW11; 107 Cranbrook Road, Ilford, Essex; 2a Regent Parade, Amhurst Park, Stamford Hill, N16; 616 Finchley Road, NW11; 98 Brent Street, Hendon, NW4; 124 High Road, East Finchley, N2; 14 Cricklewood Broadway, NW2; 59 Camden High Street, NW1; 1111 Finchley Road, NW11; 132 Ballards Lane, N3; 83 Streatham High Road, SW16; also Unit 10, the Longfield Centre, Prestwich, Manchester M25.
Central Enquiry Desk. See page 1.

LONDON JEWISH MEDICAL SOCIETY
The Medical Society of London, 11 Chandos Street, W1M 0EB. ☎ 0181-959 5674.
(Est. 1928.) A learned society for doctors, senior medical students and members of allied professions. 1996-97: *President* Dr A. Hirsh; *V. Presidents* Mr S. Stanton, Dr D. Golding, Dr B. Fehler; *Hon. Sec.* Dr J. Schwartz, *Hon. T.* Dr A. Rinsler.

LONDON SOCIETY OF JEWS AND CHRISTIANS
28 St John's Wood Road, NW8 7HA.
☎ 0171-286 5181. Fax 0171-266 3591.
(Est. 1924.) To give an opportunity to Jews and Christians to confer together on the basis of their common ideals and with mutual respect for differences of religion. *President* The Rev. Professor Geoffrey Parrinder; *Jt. Chairman* Rabbi David J. Goldberg, Dr Anthony Harvey; *Org. Sec.* Ron Pluck;. *T.* Alan Rainer.

VISITATION COMMITTEE
A list of hospitals and other public institutions numbering more than 50, to which Jewish Visiting Ministers are attached under the auspices of the Visitation Cttee., may be consulted on application to Josephine Wayne, 735 High Rd., N12 0US. ☎ 0181-343 6226. Fax 0181-343 6262. *Chairman* Mrs Joy Conway.
Bereavement Counselling Service (see p.94).
Hospital Visitors Branch. *Chairman* Mrs Joy Conway.

THE REGIONS

Figures in brackets after place names indicate estimated Jewish population (see pp.191–196).

There are Zionist societies in almost every Jewish regional centre, and Women's Zionist societies in most of them.
Details of current burial arrangements have been listed where forthcoming.

Disused cemeteries are maintained by the Board of Deputies of British Jews at a number of towns in the British Isles. **Bath:** Bradford Road, cnr of Greendown Place, abt. 2 miles from town centre. Keys held by City of Bath Probation Office. **Canterbury:** Entrance at end of passageway between 26 and 28 Whitstable Road **Douglas:** Jewish enclosure in municipal cemetery. **Falmouth:** On main Penryn Road, Ponsharden. Keys from Vospers Garage (adjacent) ☎ 01326-372011. **Ipswich:** In Salthouse La. (unmarked passageway) off Salthouse St. Access only on workdays. **King's Lynn:** In Millfleet (pedestrian precinct). Keys from Mr. Colin Drew, West Norfolk District Council, Hardwick Narrows Estate, King's Lynn. **Penzance:** Historic walled Georgian Cemetery; approx. 50 headstones. Passage between 19 and 20 Leskinnick Ter., right at end of arch, cemetery on left. (Access road unsuitable for cars). Key from Keith Pearce, ☎ 01736-368778. **Sheerness:** Jewish enclosure in municipal cemetery. Another site is behind estate agents at cnr. Hope St./High St. Key from Mr. G. Lancaster, 15 Grange Way, Rochester. **Yarmouth:** On Blackfriars Road, Alma Road, on perimeter of old city walls. Key from Dept. of Technical Services, Gt. Yarmouth town hall.

(See also Listed Synagogues and Other Jewish Monuments in the UK, pp.204–205.)

Mikvaoth are maintained in the following centres: Birmingham, Bournemouth, Brighton, Gateshead, Leeds, Leicester, Liverpool, Manchester, Newcastle, Southend, Southport, Sunderland, Cardiff and Glasgow.

AMERSHAM (50)
South Bucks. Jewish Community (ULPS).
Services: Every Fri. at 8.00 p.m. and one Sat. per month at The Friends Meeting House, Whielden St., Amersham. Religion School at Dr Challoner's Grammar School. Enq.: David Sacker. ☎ 01494 431885. Gill Noach ☎ 01923-771451.
Cemetery: See Edgwarebury Cemetery (p.89).

BASILDON (Essex) (12)
Services are held in members' homes. *Chairman* M. M. Kochmann, 3 Furlongs, Basildon, Essex SS16 4BW. ☎ 01268 524947. Fax 01268-271358.
Burials arranged through Southend & Westcliff Hebrew Congregation at their cemetery in Southend.

BATH
The last synagogue closed in 1910. Services are currently being revived under the auspices of the Bristol and West Progressive Jewish Congregation (see p.106) at The Friends' Meeting House, York St.

BEDFORD (ca. 35)
In medieval times Bedford was one of the centres of English Jewry. A number of congregations existed at various times from 1803 onwards. The present com. originated during the 1939-45 war.
Hebrew Congregation. *Sec.* R. Berman. ☎ 01234 364723.

BIRMINGHAM (3,000)
This Jewish community is one of the oldest in the provinces, dating from 1730, if not earlier. Birmingham manufacturing attracted early Jewish settlers. In the Anglo-Jewish economy Birmingham's position was similar to a port, a centre from which Jewish pedlars covered the surrounding country week by week, returning to their homes for the Sabbath. The first synagogue of which there is any record was in The Froggery in 1780. But there was a Jewish cemetery in the same neighbourhood in 1730, and Moses Aaron is said to have been born in Birmingham in 1718.
Representative Council of Birmingham and Midland Jewry. (Est. 1937.) *President* R. Diamond, 35 Huntstanton Ave., B17 8SX. ☎ 0121-554 2234; *Chairman* Sir B. Zissman; *H. Sec.* L. Jacobs, 37 Wellington Road, Birmingham 15. ☎ 0121-236 1801. Fax 0121-236 9906.
Board of Shechita, c/o Hebrew Cong., Singers Hill B1 1HL; *Sec.* B. Gingold.

SYNAGOGUES
Hebrew Congregation, Singers Hill, Blucher Street B1 1QL. ☎ 0121-643 0884. The present syn. was consecrated on September 24, 1856. *M.* Rabbi L. L. Tann; *Admin.* B. Gingold.
Central Synagogue, 133 Pershore Road, B5 7PA. ☎/Fax 0121-440 4044. *M. R.*; *Sec.* S.Cohen.
Progressive Synagogue (ULPS), 4 Sheepcote Street, B16 8AA. ☎ 0121-643 5640 (9.30 a.m.-1.00 p.m. w/d). *H. Sec.* Mr. B. Grant; *M.* Rabbi Dr Margaret Jacobi.

OTHER INSTITUTIONS
Birmingham Jewish Youth Trust, Youth Centre, 19 Sandhurst Road, Birmingham 13. ☎ 0121-442 4459. *Youth Worker* C. Jennings.
Birmingham Union of Jewish Students. C/o Hillel House, 26 Somerset Road, Edgbaston, B15 2QD. ☎ 0121-454 5684.
Hillel House, 26 Somerset Road Edgbaston, B15 2QD. ☎ 0121-454 5684. Applications for admission to F. M. Linden, 7 Westbourne Gardens, B15. ☎ 0121-454 5042 or Mrs R. Jacobs ☎ 0121-440 4142/643-2688.
B'nai Brith Joint Lodge. *Jt. Secs.* F. & H. Linden, 7 Westbourne Gardens, Edgbaston, B15 3TJ. ☎ 0121-454 5042.
Home for Aged, Andrew Cohen House, Riverbrook Drive, Stirchley, B30 2SH. ☎ 0121-458 5000.
Jewish Graduates Association. *Sec.* Mrs C. Jacobs, 54 Sir Richards Dr, B17 8SS. ☎ 0121-429 4375.
Jewish Welfare Board, 1 Rake Way, Tennant Street, B15 1EG. ☎ 0121-643 2835. Fax 0121-643 5291. *President* M. Abrams.
King David School, 244 Alcester Road, B13 8EY. ☎ 0121-499 3364. *H.T.* Mrs E. Lesser.
Lubavitch Centre & Bookshop, 95 Willows Road, B12 9QF. ☎ 0121-440 6673. *M.* Rabbi S. Arkush.
Mikva at Central Synagogue, For appointments ☎ 0121-440 5853.
Israel Information Centre, Bookshop and Reference Library, Hebrew Cong., Singers Hill, B1 1HL. *Dir.* Mrs R. Jacobs ☎ 0121-643 2688.
Jewish Education Board, Central Syn., 133 Pershore Road, B5 7PA. ☎ 0121-440 4044.

CEMETERIES
Brandwood End Cemetery, Kings Heath 14. Enqs. to Hebrew Congregation (☎ 0121-643 0884).
Witton Cemetery, The Ridgeway, College Road, Erdington 23. ☎ 0121-356 4615.

BLACKPOOL (1,500)
United Hebrew Congregation, Leamington Road (Consecrated 1916.) Services

were first held in the 1890s in a private house. Later a syn. was built in Springfield Road. *M. Rev.* D. Braunold. ☎ 01253 392382; *President* F. H. Freeman. ☎ 01253 393767.
Reform Synagogue, 40 Raikes Parade, FY1 4EX. (A constituent of R.S.G.B.). ☎ 01253 23687. *H. T.* Mrs E. R. Ballan, 177 Hornby Road, Blackpool, FY2 4JA. ☎ 01253 25839.
Blackpool Council of Christians and Jews. Rev D. Braunold, 31 Marlborough Road, Blackpool North. ☎ 01253 392382. *H. Sec.* Mrs G. Kay.
Blackpool and Fylde Ajex. *H. Sec.* F. Tomlinson. ☎ 01253 728659.
Blackpool and Fylde Jewish Welfare Society. *President*: Mrs G. Kay; *H. T.* D. Lewis ☎ 01253 295608.
Fylde League of Jewish Women. *H. Sec.* Mrs J. Weinbren, 50 Riverside Drive, Hambleton, Lancs. FY6 9EB. ☎ 01253 701012.

BOGNOR REGIS (40)
Hebrew Congregation. *H. Sec.* J. S. Jacobs, Elm Lodge, Sylvan Way. ☎ 01243-823006.

BOURNEMOUTH (3,000)
The Bournemouth Hebrew Cong. was est. in 1905 and met in the Assembly Rooms, where the Bournemouth Pavilion now stands. A syn., built in Wootton Gdns. in 1911, was rebuilt in 1961 to seat some 950 congregants. The Menorah suite was added in 1974, and a mikva in 1976.
Bournemouth Reform Synagogue was started by a small band of enthusiasts in 1947. Ten years later the congregation was large enough to build the present synagogue building at 53 Christchurch Road. It was extended in 1980 and now has a membership of over 700 persons, with a voluntary mixed choir, active Cheder, many social activities and is host to the Jewish Day Centre every Monday.
Bournemouth is the religious and social centre for the fast growing community in Dorset, West Hampshire and Wiltshire.
Bournemouth District Jewish Representative Council. (incorp. Southampton). *Chairman* Mrs H. Greene, P.O. Box 2287, BH3 7ZD. ☎ 01202-762101; *H. Sec.* Mrs M. Perry.
Wessex Jewish News (community news letter), P.O. Box 2287, BH3 7ZD.
Hebrew Congregation, Wootton Gdns. BH1 1PW. ☎ 01202 557433. *President* S. White; *M.* Rabbi G. Shisler.
Mikva, Gertrude Preston Hall, Wootton Gdns. ☎ 01202 557433.
Yavneh Kindergarten, Gertrude Preston Hall, Wootton Gdns. BH1 3PW. ☎ 01202 295414. *Princ.* Mrs E. Devine.
Reform Syngagogue, 53 Christchurch Road, P.O. Box 8, BH1 3PN. (Est. 1947.) (A Constituent of the R.S.G.B.) ☎ 01202-557736. *M.* Rabbi D. Soetendorp; *Chairman* Mrs C. Bradley; *H. Sec.* Mrs J. Gee.
Day Centre, *Co-ordinator* Mrs R. Lesser, 40A East Avenue, BH3 7DA. ☎ 01202 766039.
Bournemouth University Jewish Society, Wallisdown Road, Poole. ☎ 01202 524111.
Friendship Club (over 60s). *H. Sec.* S. Mazin. ☎ 01202 551255.
Home for Aged: Hannah Levy House, 15 Poole Road, Bournemouth. ☎ 01202 765361.
Jewish Care, Braemar Royal, Grand Avenue, Southbourne, Bournemouth. ☎ 01202 423246.
Lubavitch Centre, Chabad House, 8 Gordon Road, Boscombe, Bournemouth. ☎ 01202 396615.
Cemeteries: Kinson Cemetery (used by both Hebrew Cong. and Reform Syn.); Boscombe Cemetery (used by old established mems. Hebrew Cong.).

BRADFORD (170)

Jews of German birth, who began settling in Bradford in the first half of the nineteenth century, were in a large measure responsible for the development of its wool yarns and fabrics exports to all parts of the world. Jewish services, first held in the 1830s in private houses, were held in 1873, on Reform lines, in a public hall. About the same period saw the beginnings of the Orthodox community.
Hebrew Congregation. (Orthodox). Springhurst Road, Shipley, West Yorks. BD18 3DN. (Cong. est. 1886, Syn. erected 1970.) *President* A. A. Waxman; *H. Sec.* Mrs M. D. Freund, 'High Winds', 513 Harrogate Rd., Leeds, LS17 7DU.
Synagogue, Bowland Street, Bradford, BD1 3BW. ☎ 01274 584431. (Est. 1880). (A constituent of R.S.G.B.). *Chairman* K. Fabian, 26 Thorndale Rise, Poplars Farm, King's Rd., BD2 1NU; *H. Sec.* Mr. T. Dyson, 8 Northlea Ave., Thackley, Bradford, BD10 8LX. ☎ 01274 615023.
Jewish Benevolent Society. *President* Michael Levi; *Hon. Tr.* L. Solity; *Hon. Sec.*
Cemetery: (Both Orthodox and Reform). Scholemoor, Necropolis Road, Cemetery Road, Bradford.

BRIGHTON & HOVE (8,000)

There were Jews resident in Brighton in the second half of the eighteenth century, and by the beginning of the nineteenth century there was an organised community. (The earliest syn. was founded in Jew Street in 1792.)
Brighton and Hove Jewish Representative Council. Meetings at Ralli Hall, Denmark Villas, Hove. P.O. Box 2001, Hove, BN3 4HY. ☎ 01273 270649/ 550445.
Joint Kashrut Board. ☎ 01273 506574.
Sussex Jewish News, P.O. Box 1623, BN1 5NX. ☎ 01273 504455.
Brighton & Hove Hebrew Congregation, (Reg. Charity No. 233221).
Synagogues:
66 Middle Street, BN1 1AL. *M.* Rabbi P. Efune; *Hon. Sexton* B. Goldberg. ☎ 01273 601088.
31 New Church Road, Hove BN3 4AD; *Admin.* Mrs S. Bourne. ☎ 01273 888855. Fax 01273 888810
Mikva, Prince Regent Swimming Complex. ☎ 01273 685692.
Hove Hebrew Congregation, 79 Holland Road, Hove. *M.* Rabbi V. Silverman. ☎ 01273 732035.
Brighton & Hove New Synagogue (Reform, Est. 1955, Constituent of RSGB), Palmeira Avenue, Hove, BN3 3GE. ☎ 01273 735343.
J.A.C.S. meet every Wednesday at 2pm at the Ajex Hall of the New Synagogue. ☎ 01273 774037.
Brighton & Hove Progressive Synagogue (ULPS), (Est. 1935). 6 Lansdowne Road, Hove, BN3 1FF. ☎ 01273 737223. *M.*
Brighton and Hove Jewish Housing Association. ☎ 01273 207328.
Brighton & Hove Jewish Centre, (Reg. Charity No. 269474) (Incorporating Brighton and Hove Maccabi, B.B.Y.O.; Ralli Hall Amateur Theatrical Society; New Ralli Bridge Club and Jewish Community Art Society), Ralli Hall, 81 Denmark Villas, Hove BN3 3TH. ☎ 01273 202254. *Admin.* Norina Duke; *Chairman* Roger Abrahams. Meeting centre for various senior citizens clubs and youth clubs. Facilities include snooker room, work-out gym, library/reading room, cafeteria, etc. Kosher lunch available on Thursdays.
Ajex. Contact Philip Sions. ☎ 01273 772172.
Ben Gurion University Foundation. *Contact* Godfrey Gould. ☎ 01273 419412.
B&H Arts Society. *Contact* Audrey Davis, 396 Whittingham Gdns, BN1 6PU.
JIA Ladies Committee. Mrs S. Carlton. ☎ 01273 5522821.
Jewish Welfare Board. ☎ 01273 722523. Est. 1846. *H. T.* G.E. Burkeman.
Lubavitch Foundation. ☎ 01273 321919.
Magen David Adom. Mrs E. Hagard, 53a New Church Rd., Hove.

Torah Academy. Rabbi P. Efune, 31 New Church Road ☎ 01273 328675.
Brighton and Hove Jewish Home, 20 Burlington Street, BN2 1AU. ☎ 01273 688226.
Hillel House, 18 Harrington Road, Brighton BN1 6RE. *Admin.* Mrs A. Lee. ☎ 01273 503450.
Sussex Jewish Continuity. *Contact* Simon Seligman. ☎ 01273 557755.
Sussex ORT. *Contact* Estelle Josephs. ☎ 01903 232932.
Sussex Jewish Golfing Society. *Contact* Ivor Richards. ☎ 01273 720366.
Sussex Tikvah (Home for Jewish adults with severe learning difficulties) ☎ 01273 564021. *Chairman* Peter Senker; *Head of House* Mrs C. Nicholls; *Bursar* Mrs M. Bomzer. ☎ 01273 506665.
Youth Aliyah. *Contact* Mrs E. Posner. ☎ 01273 776671.
Centre for German–Jewish Studies at Sussex University, see p.43.
Cemetery: ☎ 01273 606961.

BRISTOL (375)
Bristol was one of the principal Jewish centres of medieval England. Even after the Expulsion from England in 1290 there were occasional Jewish residents or visitors. A community of Marranos lived here during the Tudor period. There had been a Jewish community in the City before 1754 and the original Synagogue opened in 1786. The present building dates from 1871 and was renovated in 1981-83. Polack's House (Clifton College) was founded in 1878. The Progressive Synagogue was founded in 1961 and their present building was consecrated in 1971.

Bristol Jewish Liaison Committee, *Chairman* Bernard Barnett, 14 Tennyson Rd., Horfield BS7 8SB. ☎ 0117-942 4837. *Sec.* Mrs V. Freedman, ☎ 0117-958 6646. Email: bjlc@fishpond.demon.co.uk.
Synagogues: Bristol Hebrew Congregation, 9 Park Row BS1 5LP, Rabbi Hillel Simon. ☎ 0117-925 5160. Enq. to Mrs L. Tanklovitch, ☎ 0117-970 6938. Services: Sat. 9.45am, Fri. Summer 8.30pm, Winter 7.30 pm; Bristol & West Progressive Jewish Cong (ULPS). (Reg. Charity No. 73879), 43-45 Bannerman Road, Easton BS5 0RR. M. Rabbi Hadassah Davis. ☎ 0118-954 3768. Enq. to Mrs. I. Wagen. ☎ 0117 973 8633. Services: Sat. 11.00am Fri. 8.00pm Email: bwpjc@fishpond.demon.co.uk.
Bristol University Jewish & Israel Soc., c/o Hillel House.
Hillel House, 45 Oakfield Road, Clifton, BS8 2BA. ☎ 0117-946 6589. Accommodation enquiries: Mrs S. Tobias, ☎ 01454 412831.
Davar, The Jewish Institute in Bristol, cultural and educational organisation aims to encourage Jewish identity with the widest possible spectrum. ☎ 0117 970 6594. *Admin.* Roz Wallace.
Polack's House, Clifton College, Housemaster, Mr Jo Greenbury. ☎ 0117-973 7634.
Cemetery: Oakdene Avenue, Fishponds, Bristol BS5 6QQ.

CAMBRIDGE (Resident Jewish pop. 500, Students 500 approx.)
Cambridge Traditional Jewish Congregation (Reg. Charity No. 282849). *President* Sharon Blaukopf, 28, Harvey Goodwin Avenue, CB3 4 3EU. ☎ 01223-352145. During university terms there are services three times a day. During vacations there are regular services on Friday night, Shabbat morning, Sunday morning, Tuesday evening and other times by arrangement. Shiurim are held throughout the year, including a women's learning group; Cheder Kosher food can be obtained. ☎ 01223 352145.
The Cambridge University Jewish Society was formed in 1937. It organises services every day during term-time. Kosher meals are served at lunchtime during the week and Shabbat and on Friday nights. There is a resident full-time Student Chaplain. ☎ 01223 354783. *Chaplain* Rabbi S. Robinson ☎ 01223 358356.

Traditional Synagogue, Thompson's Lane, CB5 8AQ. Present cong. founded 1888, but there was an organised com. from 1774. Present syn. opened 1937.
Beth Shalom Reform Synagogue. (A Constituent of R.S.G.B.) *Chairman* L. Coppersmith, 3 Cranmer Road, Cambridge CB3 9BL. ☎ 01223 365614.
Cambridge Jewish Residents' Association. ☎ 01223-352963.

CANTERBURY & DISTRICT (160)
Jewish Community, includes members in Folkestone and Whitstable areas. Regular monthly programme. *Chairman* John Lipitch; *H. Sec.* G. Rickayzen; Contact J. Morris, 26 Meadow Road, Sturry, Canterbury CT2 0JF. ☎ 01227 711455. There are a number of Jewish students at Kent University.

CHATHAM (ca. 50)
There was an organised Jewish community in Chatham from the first half of the eighteenth century. The present syn., erected in 1869 in memory of Captain Lazarus Simon Magnus, by his father, Simon Magnus, is on the site of its predecessor, erected about 1740. A Centenary Hall and Mid-Kent Jewish Youth Centre was consecrated in 1972. The old cemetery, dating back to about 1790, is behind the syn.
Chatham Memorial Synagogue, 366 High Street, Rochester. Inquiries: Dr C. Harris, Sutton Place, Sutton Road Maidstone, Kent ME15 9DU. ☎ 01622 753040.

CHELMSFORD (145)
Jewish Community. (Reg. Charity No. 281498). 11 Haig Court, CM2 0BH. ☎ 01245 266150. The community, est. in 1974, holds regular services, religion classes and social activities. It has burial arrangements through the Joint Jewish Burial Society.

CHELTENHAM (70)
The congregation was est. in 1824 and the present syn. in St. James's Sq. opened in 1839. After two generations, the cong. dwindled and the syn. closed in 1903. Refugees from Central Europe and evacuated children and others from Jewish centres in England, however, formed a new community and a cong. was re-formed in 1939 and the old syn. reopened. The cemetery, dating from 1824, is in Elm St.
Hebrew Congregation, St. James's Sq. *H. Sec.* H. Bazar, Kynance, 22 Sydenham Road, Cheltenham, GL52 6EA. ☎ 01242 525032.

CHESTER (35)
Hebrew Congregation, Helen & Gordon Viner, 5 Nield Ct., Upton Chester, CH2 1DN. ☎ 01244 383745. Ian & Lesley Daniels, Riverslea, 61 Dee Banks, Chester. ☎ 01244 313033. Monthly Fri. evg. services.

COLCHESTER (100)
Colchester and District Jewish Community (Reg. Charity No. 237240), Synagogue, Fennings Chase, Priory St,. CO1 2QG. Services held on Friday evenings and on all Festivals. The Community has many families with young children and there is a Cheder every Sunday morning. The community has close links with the University of Essex at Colchester which is a popular choice for Israeli students wishing to study for a law degree. For information about services, Cheder and social events please contact the Hon. Secretary, Mrs N. B. Stevenson, ☎ 01206 545992.

COVENTRY (140)
There were Jews settled in Coventry in 1775, if not earlier, and by the beginning of the nineteenth century there was a relatively large community.
Synagogue, Barras Lane. (Consec. 1870) ☎ (01203) 220168. *H. Sec.* L. R. Benjamin,

25 Hathaway Drive, Warwick CV34 5RD. ☎ 01926 499272. Email: laurence.benjamin@warwick.source.co.uk
Reform Community, *Chairman* Dr M. Been, 24 Nightingale Lane, Canley Gardens, CV6 6AY. ☎ 01203-672027.

CRAWLEY (ca. 50)
Progressive Jewish Community (ULPS). (Est. 1959.) *H. Sec.* Mrs L. Bloom, 44 Brighton Road, Crawley, West Sussex RH10 6AT. ☎ 01293 534294.

DARLINGTON (40)
Hebrew Congregation (RSGB), Bloomfield Road (Est 1904.) *Sec.* J. Starr, 2 Desmond Rd., Middleton St. George, DL2 1AN. ☎ 01325 333736; *President* M. Finn, 17 Thornbury Rise, DL3 9NE. ☎ 01325 252234.
Cemetery: Contained in a consecrated section of: The West Cemetery, Carmel Road, Darlington.

EAST GRINSTEAD AND DISTRICT (35)
Jewish Community (Reg. Charity No. 288189). (Est. 1978). *Hon.* M. Rev. M. Weisman, M.A.; Correspondence and Warden E. Godfrey, 7 Jefferies Way, Crowborough, Sussex TN6 2UH. ☎ 01892 653949. *Hon. Sec.* Mrs C. Harris, 5 Sandown Grove, Tunbridge Wells, Kent TN2 4RW. ☎ 01892 823332. Fax 01892 822311

EASTBOURNE (63)
Hebrew Congregation, 22 Susans Road, BN21 3HA. *M. Rev.* C. H. Zack; *H. Sec.* Mrs M. J. Mindell. ☎ 01435 866928. Fax 01435-865783.
Cemetery: Eastbourne Borough Cemetery has a part set aside for the comm. in conjunction with the Brighton Chevra Kedusha.

EXETER (150)
Before the expulsion, Exeter was an important Jewish centre.
The syn. off Mary Arches St. was built in 1763, and the cemetery in Magdalen Road dates from 1757, but Jews are known to have lived in Exeter 30 years earlier and the com. is said to have been founded as early as 1728. The community greatly decreased during the 19th century, but has revived in recent years. Ring for dates of monthly Shabbat services. High Holy-days and Festivals 10am. Synagogue ☎ 01392 51529.
Hebrew Congregation. Synagogue, Synagogue Place, Mary Arches St., EX4 3BA. ☎ 01392 251529. *President* Sonia Fodor. ☎ 01392 254360.

GATESHEAD (1,400)
Synagogue, 180 Bewick Road, 8. ☎ 0191 4770111, (Mikva. ☎ 0191-477 3552). *Rab.* Rabbi B. Rakow, 138 Whitehall Road, 8. ☎ 0191-477 3012; Senior Warden M. Guttentag, 205 Dryden Road, Lowfell NE9 5DA. ☎ 0191-477 3871.
Kolel Synagogue, 22 Claremont Place, Gateshead NE8 1TL. (Constituent of the Union of Orthodox Hebrew Congregations.) *Sec.* S. Ehrentreu. ☎ 0191-477 2189.
Beis Hatalmud, 1 Ashgrove Tce. Gateshead 8. *Princ.* Rabbi S Steinhouse. ☎ 0191-478 4352.
Beth Midrash Lemoroth, 50 Bewick Road 8. (Teachers Training College for Girls.) ☎ 0191-477 2620. *Princ.* Rabbi M. Miller. *H. T.* M. Pearlman.
Institute for Higher Rabbinical Studies (Kolel Harabbonim), 22 Claremont Place, Gateshead NE8 ITL. ☎ 0191-477 2189. *Sec.* S. Ehrentreu.
Project SEED, 160 Whitehall Rd., NE8 1TP. ☎ 0181-478 5434.
Sunderland Talmudical College and Yeshiva, Prince Consort Road, Gateshead-on-Tyne NE3 4DS. ☎ 0191-490 0195 (Off.); 0191-490 0193 (Students). *Princ.* Rabbi S. Zahn. ☎ 0191-565 0224.

GRIMSBY 109

Yeshiva, 88 Windermere Street, 8. ☎ 0191-478 5210 and 477 2616. Students, 179 Bewick Road ☎ 0191-477 1646. *Sec.* S. Esofsky
Yeshive Lezeirim, Cambridge Tce., Gateshead 8. *Princ.* Rabbi E. Jaffe. ☎ 0191-477 0744.
Gateshead Girls High School, 6 Gladstone Tce., NE8. ☎ 0191-477 3471. *Princ.* Rabbi D. Bowden; *H. Sec.* Mrs C. Rabinowitz.
Jewish Boarding School (Boys, aged 10-16), 36-38 Gladstone Terr. (Union of Orthodox Hebrew Congregations.) *Princ.* Rabbi R. Kohn; *Sec.* J. Salomon. ☎ 0191-477 1431 & 477 2066 (Students).
Jewish Primary School, 18 Gladstone Terr., 8. ☎ 0191-477 2154. *Princ.* Rabbi S. Wagschal; *H. Sec.* Mrs C. Rabinowitz.
Ohel Rivka Kindergarten, Alexandra Road, NE8. ☎ 0191-478 3723; *H. Sec.* Mrs Esofsky, 13 Grasmere St. ☎ 0191-477 4102.

GRIMSBY (45)
Sir Moses Montefiore Synagogue, Holme Hill, Heneage Road, Grimsby DN32 9DZ. *President* L. Solomon; *T.* H. Kalson; *H. Sec.* B. Greenberg, 21 Abbey Park Road, Grimsby DN32 0HJ. ☎ 01472 351404.
Cemetery: (Chevra Kadisha) First Avenue, Nunsthorpe, Grimsby. *Sec.* B. Greenberg; *T.* H. Kalson, 12A Welholme Avenue, Grimsby DN32 0HP.

GUILDFORD (100)
Synagogue (1979), York Road, GU1 4Dr The community itself has grown up since the Second World War. Regular services; Cheder and social activities. *Chairman* Dr S. Cornbleet. ☎ 01483 575787; *Sec.* Mrs B. Gould. ☎ 01483 576470.
University of Surrey Jewish Society, c/o Professor R. Spier. ☎ 01483 259265.
Cemetery: Consecrated section of municipal cemetery.

HARLOW (190)
Jewish Community, Harberts Road, Hare St, CM19 4DT. ☎ 01992 573448. (A Constituent of R.S.G.B.) *President* E. Clayman; *Chairman* I. Jackson, 34 Greenhills, Harlow, Essex CM20 3SX. ☎ 01279-416138. *Sec.* Mrs C. Petar.

HARROGATE (150)
Hebrew Congregation, St. Mary's Walk, HG2 0LW. (Est. 1918.) *President* Sandy Royston. ☎ 01423 561188; *Sec.* P.E. Morris. ☎ 01423 871713. *Corr.* L. Fox, 20 Park Parade, HG1 5AF. ☎ 01423 523439.
Zionist Group. *Chairman* Anita Rouston. ☎ 01423 561188.

HASTINGS (33)
Hastings and District Jewish Society (Reg. Charity No. 273806) Regular meetings of the Society including a short service are held on the first Friday of the month in Bexhill, at 7 p.m. *H. Sec.* Mrs I. J. Eton, 6 Gilbert Road, St. Leonards-on-Sea, E. Sussex, TN38 0RH. ☎ 01424 436551.

HEMEL HEMPSTEAD (270)
Hebrew Congregation (affiliated to U.S.) Est. 1956. Synagogue, Lady Sarah Cohen Community Centre, Midland Road, Hemel Hempstead, Herts. HD1 1RP. *H. Sec.* H. Nathan. ☎ 01923 32007.

HEREFORD
Hereford Jewish Community (Associate Community of ULPS). Enquiries to Josephine Woolfson. ☎ 01432 271678.

HIGH WYCOMBE (35)
Hebrew Congregation (affiliated to the U.S.). *H. Sec.* Mrs R. Weiss, 33 Hampden

Road, High Wycombe, Bucks. HP13 6SZ. ☎ 01494 529821.

HOVE (see Brighton & Hove)

HULL (1,120)
In Hull, as in other English ports, a Jewish community was formed earlier than in the neighbouring inland towns. The exact date is unknown, but as a Catholic chapel, damaged in the riots of 1780, was acquired as a syn., the formal constitution of a community was probably about that date. In 1810 a cemetery had been in existence some years. Hull was then the principal port of entry from Northern Europe and most of the Jewish immigrants came through it. In 1851 the Jewish community numbered about 200. Both the old syn. in Osborne St. and the Central Syn., in Cogan St. were destroyed in air raids during the Second World War.
Jewish Representative Council. *President* Mrs Doreen Rose. ☎ 01482 655367; *H. Sec.* Mrs A. Segelman, 251 Beverley Road, Kirkella, Hull HU10 7AG. ☎ 01482 650288.

SYNAGOGUES
Hull Hebrew Congregation, 30 Pryme Street, Anlaby HU10 6SH. *Hon. Sec.*: Mr. E. Pearlman, 277 Beverley Road, Kirkella HU10 7AQ. ☎ 01482 653398.
Reform Synagogue. (A Constituent of R.S.G.B.) Great Gutter Lane, Willerby HU10 7JT. *H. Sec.* L. Sugarman, 36 Kerry Pit Way, Anlaby HU10 7NB. ☎ 01482 656469.

OTHER INSTITUTIONS
Board of Guardians. (Est. 1880.) *H. Sec.* V. Appleson, 1 Tranby Ride, Anlaby, HU10 7ED. ☎ 01482 653018.
Hillel House, 18 Auckland Avenue. ☎ 01482 48196. Enquiries to: *H. Sec.* I. Dysch, 1000 Anlaby High Road, HU4 6AT. ☎ 01482 54947.
Hull Synagogue Museum, Linnaeus St., HU3 2PD. (Est. 1994). *Exec. Dir.* 771 Anlaby Rd., HU4 6DJ. ☎ 01482 53981/26848 (office). Fax 568756.
Parkfield Centre, Parkfield Drive. *H. Sec.* A. Rowland, 24 Wolfreton Garth, Kirkella, HU10 7AB. ☎ 01482 655886.
Talmud Torah, 30 Pryne St., Anlaby, HU10 6SH. *H. Sec.* J. Levine, 11 Oaklands Dr, Willerby HU10 6BJ. ☎ 01482-657188.
University Jewish Students' Society, c/o Hillel House, 18 Auckland Ave. ☎ 01482 48196.
Board of Shechita, *H. Sec.* E. Pearlman, 277 Beverely Rd., Kirkella HU10 7AQ.

LEAMINGTON & DISTRICT (132)
Progressive Jewish Group. (A branch of the Progressive Synagogue Birmingham, ULPS). Inq.: 12 Church La., Lillington, Leamington Spa CV32 7RG. ☎ 01926 421300.

LEEDS (8,250)
Leeds has the third largest Jewish community in Britain. Jews have lived in Leeds at least from the middle of the eighteenth century, but it was only in 1840 that a Jewish cemetery was acquired. The first so-called synagogue was a converted room in Bridge Street, where services were held up to 1846. Thereafter the place of worship was transferred to the Back Rockingham Street Synagogue, which was replaced by the Belgrave Street Synagogue built in 1860. Another syn. was built in 1877, but this closed in 1983.
The Leeds Jewish community is mainly the product of the persecution of Russian Jewry in the latter half of the nineteenth century. The bulk of immigration settled in Leeds between 1881 and 1905, enhancing the growth of the clothing industry which developed from the woollen and worsted manufacturing in the West Riding

of Yorkshire. This industry was made world famous by John Barran, a non-Jew, and his Jewish associate Herman Friend, who was responsible for introducing division of labour into the clothing industry. While the sweating system existed in Leeds, both wages and working conditions were better than in London or Manchester. Trade unionism was successful and the first recorded strike by Jewish industrial workers took place spontaneously in Leeds in 1885.

During the early decades of this century the old Leylands ghetto, where most of the immigrants lived, began to break up. The main move of the Jewish people was to northern districts of Leeds, first to Chapeltown, which flourished in the 1940s, and then to the Moortown and Alwoodley suburbs.

The Leeds Rep. C. republished in 1985 the late Louis Saipe's 'A History of the Jews of Leeds'.

Today this well-organised strong community of approx. 8,500 provides for Leeds Jews with over 100 organisations which are affiliated to the Leeds Jewish Representative Council, the official spokesman of the Leeds Jewish community.

Among the organisations are seven orthodox and one reform synagogue, a voluntary Chevra Kadisha, Jewish nursery and day schools, Talmud Torah and adult education. Welfare organisations include the Jewish Welfare Board, The Home for Aged Jews, League of Jewish Women, Kosher meals for hospitals, Day and Leisure Centres.

A Hillel House and Chaplaincy with Campus Chaplain are provided for students. There are also numerous Zionist organisations, Speakers' Panels and A.J.E.X.

GENERAL ORGANISATIONS
Jewish Representative Council, Shadwell La. Synagogue, 151 Shadwell La., LS17 8DW. ☎ 0113 2697520. Fax 0113 2370851. Nearly every syn., charitable org., social and cultural instit. and Zionist Soc. is affiliated to this council and on its exec. cttee. serve ex-officio all local Jewish magistrates, public reps. and BoD members. *President* Tim Friedman, B.Com., F.C.A., S.T.E.P.; *V. Presidents* Dr K.D. Shenderey, M.B., B.S., Hillary Miller, JP, M.R. Pharm. S.; *T.* Ian Goldman, LL.B., F.Inst.D.; *Sec.* Sue Baker, JP; *Exec. Off.* Barry Abis, JP.
A.J.E.X. *Chairman* Stanley Graham; *H. Sec.* Leonard Cohen, 76 The Avenue, LS17 7NZ.
Beth Din, Etz Chaim Synagogue, 411 Harrogate Rd., LS17 7BY. ☎ 0113 2696902. Fax 0113 370893. *M.* Dayan Y. Refson; Rev. A. Gilbert, B.A.
Community Shaliach, 411 Harrogate Rd., LS17 7TT. ☎ 0113 2680899. Fax 0113 2668419.
J.I.A. Office, Balfour House, 399 Street La., LS17 6HQ. ☎ 0113 2693136. Fax 0113 2693961.
J.N.F. and Zionist Council, 411 Harrogate Rd., LS17 7BY. ☎ 0113 2693134. Fax 0113 2668419. *District org.* S. Cohen.
Kashrut Authority. *Admin. Sec.* Barry Abis, J.P., 151 Shadwell Lane, LS17 8DW. ☎ 0113 2697520. Fax 0113 2370851.
Leeds Emunah Council. *Co-ordinator* Hazel Broch, 4 Sandmoor Ct., Harrogate Rd., LS17 7JY. ☎ 0113 2662117.
Mikvah. 411 Harrogate Road, LS17 7BY. ☎ 0113 2681461 (Answer machine).
Women's Zionist Council (Wizo), 411 Harrogate Rd., LS17 7BY. ☎ 0113 2684773. *Chairman* Mrs L. Jacoby.
Yorkshire Israel Office. 411 Harrogate Rd., LS17 7TT. ☎ 0113 2680899. Fax 0113 2688419.

SYNAGOGUES
Beth Hamedrash Hagadol Synagogue, 399 Street Lane Gdns., LS17 6HQ. (Est. 1874.). *M.* Rabbi Y. Shemaria; *R. D.* Apfel; *Exec. Off.* Mrs M. Wilson. ☎ 0113 2692181.
Chassidishe Synagogue, (Est. 1897.) c/o Donisthorpe Hall, Shadwell Lane, LS17 6AW. All enq. to M. Kent, Flat 8, Sandhill Lawns, Sandhill Lane, LS17 6TT.

Etz Chaim Synagogue, 411 Harrogate Road, LS17 7BY. *Rab.* Rabbi Y. Angyalfi; *M. Rev.* G. Harris; *R. Rev.* A. Gilbert; *Sec.* 584 Harrogate Road, Sandhill Pde., LS17 7DP ☎ 0113 2662214. Fax 0113 2371183.
Masorti, *Contact* A. Selman ☎ 01132 612700.
Queenshill Synagogue, 26 Queenshill Avenue, LS17 6AX.
Shomrei Hadass Congregation, 368 Harrogate Road, LS17 6QB. ☎ 0113 2681461. *M.* Dayan Y. Refson.
Sinai Synagogue, Roman Avenue, Street Lane, LS8 2AN. ☎ 0113 2665256. (A Constituent of R.S.G.B.) (Est. 1944). *M.* Rabbi I. Morris; *H. Sec.* Mrs P. Mason. Mon-Fri 9.30am-2pm.
United Hebrew Congregation (Reg. Charity No. 515316) 151 Shadwell La., LS17 8DW. ☎ 0113-269 6141. Fax 0113-237 0851. *M.* Rabbi I. Goodhart. ☎ 0113-237 0852; *R. Rev.* H. Miller; *Admin.* Mrs A. Silver.

Cemeteries: For information refer to the Representative Council as above.

CULTURAL AND EDUCATIONAL ORGANISATIONS
B'nai B'rith Lodge of Leeds. *President* Mrs Shirley Casden. ☎ 0113 226447.
Jewish Education Board (Talmud Torah), 2 Sandhill La., LS17 6AQ. (Est. 1879.) Houses the Talmud Torah classes. Administers Jewish Assemblies for pupils attending State schools. ☎ 0113 2683390/2680836.
Jewish Education Bureau, 8 Westcombe Avenue, LS8. ☎ 0113 663613. Provides information and materials on all aspects of Judaism to non-Jewish educationalists and clergy. *Dir.* Rabbi D. S. Charing.
Scopus Jewish Educational Trust:
Brodetsky Jewish Primary School & Nursery, George Lyttleton Centre, Wentworth Avenue, LS17 7TN. *H. M.* Mrs L. Hastings. ☎ 0113 2692218.
Deborah Taylor Playgroup, George Lyttleton Centre, Primley Park Road, LS17 7HR. *H. M.* Mrs J. Fineberg. ☎ 0113 2692831.
Jewish Day Schools' Administrative Office, George Lyttleton Centre, Wentworth Avenue, LS17 7TN. *Admin.* Mrs Z. Fiddler. ☎ 0113 2693176.
Jewish Historical Society (Branch). *H. Sec.* Rita Biehal, 16 The Poplars, Bramhope, LS16 9DL. ☎ 0113 2677262.
Jewish Social Centre, Street Lane Gdns., 393 Street La., LS17 6HQ. ☎ 0113 2693381. *Manager* R.A. Ross.
Jewish Students' Association, Hillel House, 2 Springfield Mount, LS2 9NE. ☎ 0113 2433211. (Est. 1912.) *Sec.,* c/o Leeds University Union, LS2.
Judean Youth Service, *Admin. Office,* 151 Shadwell Lane, LS17 8DW. ☎ 0113 2697520. Fax 0113 2370851; *Youth Worker* Louise Williams, 411 Harrogate Rd., LS17 7TT. ☎/Fax 0113 2370751.
Leeds Council of Christians and Jews (Reg. Charity No. 238005), *Chairman* A.M. Conway, ☎ 0113 2680444; *H. Sec.* L. Collins ☎ 0113 2687556, Mrs S. Crowther ☎ 0113 2561407.
Leeds Jewish Dental Society. Correspondence to Minutes *Sec.* Paul H. Leslie, 16 High Ash Ave., LS17 8RG. ☎ 0113-2694510.
Leeds Jewish Medical Society. *H. Sec.* A. L. Green, 47 High Ash Avenue, LS17 8RS. ☎ 0113 2695285.
Leeds University Library, Judaica collections (see p.56).
Limelight Drama Group. *Chairman* Lawrence Gorsden.
Makor—Jewish Resource Centre and Israel Information Centre (JPMP), 411 Harrogate Rd., LS17 7TT. ☎ 0113 2680899. *Sec.* Anita Buxbaum.
Menorah School, 2 Sandhill Lane, Leeds 17.
Porton Collection, Central Library, LS1 3AB (see p.58). ☎ 0113 2462016
Reform Hebrew Classes, Sinai Synagogue, 22 Roman Avenue, LS8 2AN. ☎ 0113 2665256.
S.E.E.D. Project. Contact: Rabbi Y. Angyalfi, ☎ 0113 2663311.

WELFARE ORGANISATIONS
Chaplaincy Board–Yorkshire & Humberside, 17 Queens Road, LS6 1NY. ☎ 0113 2789597.
Chevra Kadisha. Leeds Jt. Chairmen Jackie Nathan and Melvyn Sumroy; Org. I. Baum. ☎ 0113 2955748. Correspondence: Mrs L. Baker, 8 Lakeland Crescent, LS17 7PR.
Jewish Day Centre, 26 Queenshill Avenue, Leeds 17. ☎ 0113 2692018. Org. Jackie King.
Jewish Welfare Board, 311 Stonegate Road, LS17 6AZ. ☎ 0113 2684211. Fax 0113 2664754. President R. Manning; Chief Exec. Ms. S. Saunders.
Miyad Helpline. ☎ 0345-581999.
Residential Nursing Home for the Jewish Elderly, Donisthorpe Hall, Shadwell Lane, LS17 6AW. (Est. 1923.) ☎ 0113 2684248. Admin. S. Stone.
Hospital meals and visitation. Non-residents of Leeds who may be admitted to one of the city's hospitals should contact the Exec. Officer, Leeds Jewish Representative Council, ☎ 0113 2697520.

LEICESTER (670)

There have been Jewish communities in Leicester since the Middle Ages, but the first record of a Jews' Synagogue appears in the 1861 Leicester Directory and the first marriages were consecrated in 1875. The present syn. dates from 1897.
Synagogue, Highfield St. M. Rabbi A.S. Hill, B.A.; ☎ 0116 2706622. H. Sec. G. J. Louis, 4 Lyndhurst Ct., London Road, LE2 2AP. ☎ 0116 2700997.
Mikva, Synagogue building, Highfield St.
Communal Centre, Highfield St. ☎ 0116 2540477.
Shalom Club for Sr. Citizens. ☎ 0116 2540477.
Jewish Library, Communal Centre, Highfield St.
Ladies' Guild. Chairman Mrs H. Reggel, 22 Sackville Gardens, ☎ 0116 270 9687.
Jewish Students' Society, c/o The Union, Leicester University.
Maccabi Association, Communal Centre, Highfield St. ☎ 0116 2540477.
Leicester Progressive Jewish Synagogue (ULPS). (Est. 1950) 24 Avenue Rd., H. Sec. M. Gibby, ☎ 01162 711129. Services alternate Fri. evgs. and Saturday twice monthly. Religion Sch., Sundays.
Cemeteries: Leicester Hebrew Cong. uses a section of the Gilroes Cemetery, Groby Road. The Progressive congregation uses a section of the Loughborough Municipal C.

LINCOLN

Lincolnshire Jewish Community (Associate Community of ULPS). Enquiries to Don Gould, 2 Barleyfield Close, Heighington, Lincoln. ☎ 01522 793994; Dr Karen Genard ☎ 01469 588951.

LIVERPOOL (3,000)

Liverpool, for centuries an important port, first for Ireland, later also for America, had a natural attraction for Jews looking for a place in which to start their new lives. There is evidence of an organised community before 1750. It appears to have had a burial ground attached. Little is known of this early community. It declined but about 1770 was reinforced by a new wave of settlers chiefly from Europe, who worshipped in a house in Frederick Street, near the river front, with a Mikva and a cemetery. In 1807 a synagogue of some size was built in Seel Street, the parent of the present syn. in Princes Road, one of the handsomest in the country. At this time Liverpool was already one of the four leading regional coms. The site for the Seel St. Synagogue was a gift of the Liverpool Corporation.
Merseyside Jewish Representative Council. President Mrs S. Lander; H. Sec. Mrs A. Irving, Shifrin House, 433 Smithdown Road, Liverpool L15 3JL. ☎ 0151-733 2292. Fax 0151-734 0212. Communal Archivist J.Wolfman, MA.

Liverpool Kashrut Commission, c/o 433 Smithdown Road, Liverpool L15 3JL. ☎ 0151-733 2292. Fax 0151-734 0212. *Rab.* Rabbi L. Cofnas.
Mikva. Childwall Synagogue. *Chairman* Rabbi L. Cofnas. ☎ 0151-722 2079.

SYNAGOGUES
Old Hebrew Congregation, Princes Road, Liverpool L8. ☎ 0151-709 3431 (Congregation founded c. 1740; Synagogue consecrated 1874.) *M.* Rev. S. Cohen; *Sec.* Mrs D. Spratt.
Allerton Hebrew Congregation, Mather Avenue, Liverpool L18. ☎ 0151-427 6848. *Emer. Rabbi* M. Malits, M.A.; *M.* Rabbi M. Barron. *Admin.* P. Fisher.
Childwall Synagogue, Dunbabin Road, Liverpool L15. ☎ 0151-722 2079. (Est. 1935; consecrated 1938.) Rabbi L. Cofnas; *Admin.* Mrs A. Reuben.
Greenbank Drive Synagogue. (Incorporating Hope Pl. and Sefton Park Hebrew Congregations.) (Est. 1836. Syn. consecrated 1937.) ☎ 0151-733 1417. *Sec. & Reg. Cantor* Rev. H. M. Chait.
Ullet Road Synagogue, 101 Ullet Road, Liverpool L17. *H. Sec.* A. Segal.
Progressive Synagogue (ULPS), 28 Church Road North, Liverpool, L15 6TF. ☎ 0151-733 5871. (Est. 1929. Affiliated to U.L.P.S.). *M.* Rabbi N. Zalud; *H. Sec.* Jeanne Doft. ☎ 0151-733 5871.
Cemeteries: Liverpool Jewish Cemeteries: Springwood; Lowerhouse Lane; Broad Green; Long Lane.

CULTURAL AND EDUCATIONAL ORGANISATIONS
Adult Jewish Education Committee. Mr. E. Rosen. ☎ 0151-475 5671.
Community Centre, (Harold House), Dunbabin Road, L15 6XL. ☎ 0151-475 5825.
Crosby Jewish Literary Society. *H. Secs.* Mrs C. Hoddes, Mrs Y. Mendick. ☎ 0151 924 1795.
Hillel House, 12 Greenbank Dr, L17 1AW. ☎ 0151-735 0793. Applications to: Mrs C. Lewis. ☎ 0151-733-2292/722-5021; *Chaplain* Rabbi Y.Y. Rubinstein. ☎ 0161-721 4066.
Jewish Bookshop, *Chairman* M. Turner. Open at Youth and Community Centre, Sundays 11-1.
Jewish Historical Society, (Branch). *Chairman* Dr M. Goodman, 1 Hornby Lane, L18 3HH.
Jewish Youth Centre, Dunbabin Road, L15 6XL. ☎ 0151-475 5671.
King David Foundation, 433 Smithdown Road, Liverpool L15 3JL. ☎ 0151-733 2292. Fax 0151-734 0212. *President* J. Max; *Clerk* Mrs N. Sneeden.
King David High School, Childwall Road, L15 6UZ. ☎ 0151-722 7496. Clerk to Govs. 433 Smithdown Road, L15 3JL. ☎ 0151-733 2292. Fax 0151-734 0212. *H. T.* J. Smartt, B.Ed., Cert Ed.
King David Kindergarten, Community Centre, Dunbabin Road, L15 6XL. *Teachers-in-charge.* ☎ 0151-475 5661.
King David Primary School, Beauclair Drive, L15 6XH. ☎ 0151-722 3372. Clerk to Govs. 433 Smithdown Road, L15 3JL. ☎ 0151-733 2292. Fax 0151-734 0212; *H. T.* Mrs E. Spencer, Cert.Ed.
Liverpool Jewish Resource Centre, Harold House, Dunbabin Road L15 6XL. ☎ 0151-722 3514. Fax 0151-475 2212. Sundays 11-1, Mon.-Thurs. 1-5pm. *Admin.* Mrs H. Cohen.
Liverpool Yeshivah, Childwall Synagogue, Dunbabin Road, L15. *Rosh Yeshiva* Rabbi M. L. Cofnas.
Merseyside Amalgamated Talmud Torah, King David Primary School. *Chairman* Mrs J. Bennett.
Midrasha for Girls, c/o Childwall Synagogue, Dunbabin Road, Liverpool L15.
University Jewish Students' Society, c/o Students' Union, Bedford Street, 7.

WELFARE ORGANISATIONS
Jewish Welfare Council. (Est. 1875.) *Chief Exec.* Ms M. Fetcher, 433 Smithdown Road, Liverpool L15 3JL. ☎ 0151-733 2292. Fax 0151-734 0212.

Jewish Women's Aid Society. *H. Sec.* Mrs S. Gore, 433 Smithdown Road, L15 3JL.
Stapely Residential Home for Aged Jews, North Mossley Hill Road, Liverpool, 18.
Admin. ☎ 0151-724 3260 (Adm.), 0151-724 4548 (Hosp. wing).

LUTON & DUNSTABLE & DISTRICT (550)
Luton Hebrew Congregation Synagogue, Postal address: P.O. Box No. 215, LU1 1HW. ☎ 01582 725032. R. Rabbi Y. Y. Schewi; *President* C. Davis; *V. President* I.S. Rapstone; *H. Sec.* H. Podgorney. Office hrs., Sun. 9.45 am-12.15 pm.
Ladies' Guild. *Chairman* P. Freeman.
Judean Youth Club. *Chairman* Mrs L. Seltzer, c/o Synagogue.
Chiltern Progressive Synagogue (ULPS), c/o David Corfan, 39 Broadacres, Bushmead LU2 7FY. ☎ 01234-218387.

MAIDENHEAD (1,240)
Synagogue, 9 Boyn Hill Avenue, SL6 4ET. ☎ 01628 73012. (A Constituent of R.S.G.B.). *M.* Rabbi Dr J. A. Romain. ☎ 01628 71058.
Cemetery: Braywick Cemetery, Maidenhead.

MAIDSTONE
Kent Liberal Jewish Community. Enquiries to John Lloyd. ☎ 01843 85150, or Judy Taylor. ☎ 01233 502738.

MANCHESTER (27,000)
The Manchester community of about 27,000 Jews is the second largest in the U.K. In 1865 there were less than 5,000. The rapid and great increase came between 1883 and 1905, a consequence of the intensified persecution of the Jews in Russia.

Newcomers to England in the eighteenth century were encouraged by their co-religionists in London to go farther afield. This they did, generally financed by their longer-settled fellow-Jews in London, as pedlars along the countryside. As these newcomers prospered they settled in the ports, on their part sending out a wave of later arrivals similarly supplied with small stocks to peddle them in the inland towns and villages. This new wave also ultimately settled down, but for the most part in the interior of the country. Thus was laid the foundation of the Jewish community of Manchester.

Later, a very different class of settler came – merchants and men of substance from Central Europe, some of them political refugees seeking a freer life, others, for instance the first English Rothschild, in the normal course of commercial development. A later influx, a small one, was from North Africa and the Levant, lands closely connected with the cotton business of which Manchester was then the centre. The great immigration came, however, in the last two decades of the nineteenth century, consisting of refugees from Eastern Europe.

Although a few Jews were known to have lived in Manchester in preceding years, a community was not organised until 1780 or a cemetery acquired until 1794. The present Great Synagogue (now amalgamated with the New) claims to be the direct descendant of this earlier community. The leaders of Manchester Jewry in those early days came from the neighbouring Liverpool Jewish community.

GENERAL ORGANISATIONS
Jewish Representative Council of Greater Manchester and Region. The rep. body of the Manchester, Salford and Distr. Jewish com., constituted of reps. from all syns., MPs and MEPs, and other orgs., the local members of the BoD, Magistrates and town councillors. Offices Jewish Cultural Centre, Bury Old Road, Manchester, M8 6FY. ☎ 0161-720 8721. *President* Isidore Fromson; *H. Secs.* Mrs M.R. Landsman, JP, D. Arnold.
Council of Synagogues (Orthodox). *Chairman* S. Goldblatt; *Sec.* M. Green, c/o Central-North Manch. Syn., Leicester Road, Salford M7 4GP. ☎ 0161-740 4830.

Beth Din, 435 Cheetham Hill Road, M8 7PF. ☎ 0161-740 9711. Fax 0161-721 4249. Dayan G. Krausz (Rosh Beth Din); Dayan O.Y. Westheim. *Registrar* Y. Brodie, B.A. (Hons.)
Kashrus Authority, 435 Cheetham Hill Road, M8 0PF. ☎ 0161-740 9711. Fax 0161-721 4249. *President* A. Schwalbe; *Admin.* Y. Brodie.
Community Mikva (under Beth Din authority), Broom Holme, Tetlow La., Salford, M7 0BU. ☎ 0161-792 3970.
Manchester Trades Advisory Council, Jewish Cultural Centre, Bury Old Road, Manchester M8 6FY. ☎/Fax 0161-720 8721. *Chairman* Sir S. C. Hamburger, C.B.E., J.P., D.L.
(Naomi Greenberg) South Manchester Mikva (under Beth Din Authority), Shay Lane, Hale Barns, Altrincham, Cheshire. ☎ 0161-904 8296.
Torah Corps. *President* Rabbi R. Margulies, 24 Hilton Cres., Prestwich M25 8NQ. ☎ 0161-773 1045.
Whitefield Mikveh, Telephone for appointments 0161-796 1054.
Zionist Central Council of Greater Manchester, Joseph Mamlock House, 142 Bury Old Road, M8 4HD. ☎ 0161-740 1825/8835. *President* J. S. Wolfe. Jewish Agency Aliyah Dept. ☎ 0161-740 2864. WIZO *Chairmen* Beryl Steinberg, Elaine Hamburger. ☎ 0161-740 3367.

SYNAGOGUES
Adass Yeshurun Synagogue, Cheltenham Cres., Salford, M7 0FE. ☎ 0161-740 4548. *M.* Dayan G. Krausz; *H. Sec.* M.R. Goldman. ☎/Fax 0161-740 3935.
Adath Israel Synagogue, Up. Park Road, Salford M7 0HL. (Form. Kahal Chassidim Syn., present building opened in 1957). Inq.: 105 Leicester Road, Salford 7. *Sec.* Rev. S. Simon. ☎ 0161-740 3905.
Bury Hebrew Congregation. Sunnybank Road, Bury, BL9 8HE. ☎ 0161-796 5062. *M.* Rabbi B. Singer; *Admin.* Mrs M. Wilson.
Central-North Manchester Synagogue (merged 1978), Leicester Road, Salford M7 4GP. *M.* Rabbi J. Rubinstein. ☎ 0161-740 7762; *Sec.* M. Green. ☎ 0161-740 4830. (Central Syn. est. 1871; N. Manch. Syn. est. 1899).
Cheetham Hebrew Congregation, 453 Cheetham Hill Road, M8 9PA. ☎ 0161-740 7788. *President* B. M. Stone. *M.* Rabbi Y. Abenson.
Cheshire Reform Congregation, (Reg. Charity No. 234762), Menorah Synagogue, 198 Altrincham Road, M22 4RZ. ☎ 0161-428 7746. (Est. 1964.) (A Constituent of R.S.G.B.). *M.* Rabbi M. Hilton; *H. Sec.* R. Farshi. Disabled access. Nursery school.
Damesek Eliezer Synagogue, 74 Kings Road, Prestwich. *M.* Rabbi S. Goldberg. ☎ 0161-740 2486.
Great and New (Stenecourt) Synagogue, (Est. 1806). Singleton Road, Holden Road, Salford, M7 4LN. *M.* Rev. G. Brodie, 43 Stanley Road, Salford M7 0FR. ☎ 0161-740 2506; *Sec.* E. Levene. ☎ 0161-792 8399.
Hale and District Hebrew Congregation, Shay Lane, Hale Barns, Cheshire WA15 8PA. ☎ 0161-980 8846. (Est. 1976.) *M.* Rabbi J. Portnoy; *H. Sec.* F. Greibach.
Heaton Park Hebrew Congregation, Ashdown, Middleton Road M8 6JX. *M.* Rev. L. Olsberg, ☎ 0161-740 2767; *Sec.* K.D. Radivan. ☎ 0161-740 4766.
Higher Crumpsall and Higher Broughton Hebrew Congregation, Bury Old Road, Salford, M7 4PX. ☎ 0161-740 1210. *M.* Rabbi A. Saunders. *Sec.* Mrs E. Somers. ☎ 0161-740 8155.
Higher Prestwich Hebrew Congregation, Highbury House, 445 Bury Old Road, Higher Prestwich M25 1QP. ☎ 0161-773 4800. *M.* Rabbi A. Z. Herman.
Hillock Hebrew Congregation, Ribble Drive, Whitefield, M45. *H. Sec.* R. Walker, 13 Mersey Close, Whitefield, M25 6NJ. ☎ 0161-766 1162
Holy Law and South Broughton Congregation, Bury Old Road, Prestwich M25 0EX. ☎ 0161-740 1634. Fax 0161-720 6623. (Est. 1865, present building opened 1935, merged with South Broughton Syn., 1978). *M.* Rabbi Y. Chazan.

☎ 0161-792 6349 (Study 0161-721 4705); *Admin.* Mrs P. Mann. (D)
Hulme Hebrew Congregation, Hillel House, Greenheys La., Manchester M15 6LR.
Kahal Chassidim Synagogue (Lubavitch), 62 Singleton Road, Salford M7 0LU. ☎ 0161-740 3632. *M.* Rabbi A. Jaffe; *Sec.* S. Topperman. ☎ 0161-740 4468.
Lubavitch Foundation (Reg. Charity No. X98704), 62 Singleton Road, Salford M7 4LU. ☎/Fax 0161-720 9514. *M.* Rabbi L. Wineberg.
Machzikei Hadass Communities, 17 Northumberland Street, Salford M7 0FE. ☎ 0161-792 1313. *Rav.* Rav. M. Schneebalg. ☎ 0161-792 3063. *Sec.* A. Vogel. ☎ 0161-792 1313.
Constituent Syn.: Machzikei Hadass. **Mikva:** Sedgley Park Road, Prestwich. ☎ 0161-773 1537/0161-721 4341.
Machzikei Hadass Synagogue, Legh Street, Northumberland Street, Salford M7 0FE. ☎ 0161-792 1313. *Rav.* Rav. M. Schneebalg.
Manchester Reform Synagogue, Jackson's Row, M2 5NH. ☎ 0161-834 0415. (Est. 1856). (A Constituent of R.S.G.B.). The former syn. in Park Pl. was destroyed by enemy action in 1941; present premises occupied since 1953. *M.* Rabbi R. Silverman; *Sec.* N. Franks. ☎ 0161-834 0415. Fax 0161-834 0415.
North Salford Synagogue, 2 Vine St., Kersal, Salford M7 0NX. *M.* Rabbi L. W. Rabinowitz. ☎ 0161-740 7958.
Ohel Torah Congregation, 132 Leicester Road, Salford M7 0ES. (Constituent of the Union of Orthodox Hebrew Congregations.) *M.* Rabbi M. Ellinson; *Sec.* S. Spielman. ☎ 0161-792 2413.
Prestwich Beth Hamedrash, 74 Kings Road, Prestwich M25 8HU. *M.* Rabbi S. Goldberg. ☎ 0161-740 2486.
Prestwich Hebrew Congregation, Bury New Road, Prestwich M25 9WN. ☎ 0161-773 1978. *M.* Rabbi M. Ginsbury; *Sec.* A. Frankel.
Sale and District Hebrew Congregation, Hesketh Road, Sale, M33 5AA. ☎ 0161-973 3013. *Sec.* Mrs I. Gould, 32 Kenilworth Rd., M33 5FB.
Sedgley Park Synagogue (Shomrei Hadass), Parkview Road, Prestwich M25 5FA. *H. Sec.* G. R. Marks. ☎ 0161-773 6092.
Sephardi Communal Torah Centre, 2 Upper Park Road, Salford M7 0HF. *Dir.* Rabbi Y. Levy. ☎ 0161-740 2050/0321.
Sha'are Sedek Synagogue, Old Lansdowne Road, West Didsbury M20 8NZ. (Opened 1924.) ☎ 0161-445 5731. *M.* Rabbi S. Ellituv; *Sec.* Mrs J. Stewart
Sha'arei Shalom, North Manchester Reform Congregation, (Reg. Charity No. 506117), Elms Street, Whitefield, M45 8GQ. (Est. 1977). (A Constituent of R.S.G.B.). *M.* Rabbi W. Elf; *Hon. Sec.* Mrs S. Cohen. ☎ 0161-796 6736.
South Manchester Synagogue, (Reg. Charity No. 231976), Wilbraham Road, M14 6JS. (Est. 1872.) ☎ 0161-224 1366. Steel Memorial Hall. ☎ 0161-224 3744. *M.* Rabbi Y. Rubin; *Admin.* S. L. Rydz, M.A.
Spanish & Portuguese Synagogue, (Est. 1873), 18 Moor La., Salford M7 0WX. ☎ 0161-792 7406. Fax 0161-225 8033. *Hon. Sec.* J. Jacobs.
Talmud Torah Chinuch N'orim Synagogue, 11 Wellington Street, East, Salford M7 9AU. ☎ 0161-792 4522. (Constituent of the Union of Orthodox Hebrew Congregations.) *Ms.* Rev. N. Friedman, Rev. P. Koppenheim; *H. Sec.* S. Kornbluh.
United Synagogue, Meade Hill Road, M8 6LS. ☎ 0161-740 9586. *President* Sidney Huller; *Sec.* Reuben Wilner. ☎ 0161-740 9586.
Whitefield Hebrew Congregation, Park Lane, M45 7PB. ☎ 0161-766 3732. Fax: 0161-767 9453. (Est. 1959). *M.* Rabbi J. Guttentag, (B.A. Hons.); *Admin.* Mrs P.M. Deach.
Withington Congregation of Spanish and Portuguese Jews, (Reg. Charity No. 235960), 8 Queenston Road, West Didsbury M20 8WZ. ☎ 0161-445 1943. Fax 0161-434 8094. *M.* ☎ 0161-445 6300.
Yeshurun Hebrew Congregation, Coniston Road, Gatley, Cheshire SK8 4AP. ☎ 0161-428 8242 Fax 0161-491 5265. *M.* Rev. Dr A. Unterman; *Admin.* Mrs N.

Shepherd.
Zerei Agudas Israel Synagogue, 35 Northumberland Street, Salford M7 0DQ. *M. Dayan O. Westheim.*

CULTURAL ORGANISATIONS
Institute of Contemporary Jewish Studies, ICJS Conference Facility, Abramovitch Wing, Machon Levi Yitschok, Bury Old Road, Manchester. *Youth & Outreach Dir.* Rabbi Peretz Chein. *Contact* ☎ 0161-795 4000. *Admin.* ☎ 0161-720 9908. Fax 0161-720 9998.
Israel Information Centre, 142 Bury Old Road, M8 6HD. ☎ 0161-721 4344. Fax 0161-740 7407. Email: iicmcr@dircon.co.uk. Information and presentation of Israel's culture. *Dir.* Doreen Gerson. (Est. 1984.)
Jewish Graduates' Association, *Chairman* E. Leigh, Flat 17, Moorfield, Moor La., Salford M7. ☎ 0161-792 4409.
Jewish Historical Society of England (Branch), *Chairmen* Dr & Mrs L. A. Kirk. 54 Waterpark Rd., Salford M7 4JL.
Jewish Library, Central Library. ☎ 0161-236 9422. Stock now absorbed into main Social Sciences Library collection.
Jewish Museum, 190 Cheetham Hill Road, M8 8LW. ☎ 0161-834 9879 and 0161-832 7353. Fax 0161-832 7353. Mon.-Thurs., 10.30 a.m. to 4 p.m. Sun., 10.30 a.m. to 5 p.m. (Reg. Charity No. 508278). Admission charge. Exhibitions, Heritage trails, Demonstration and Talks. Calendar of events available on request. Educational visits for schools and adult groups must be booked in advance with the Administrator. Contact Don Rainger.
Jewish Male Voice Choir. *Cond.* A. Isaacs. ☎ 0161-740 1210.

EDUCATIONAL ORGANISATIONS
Academy for Rabbinical Research (Kolel), (Reg. Charity No. 526665), 134 Leicester Road, Salford M7 4GB. ☎ 0161-740 1960. *Princ.* Rabbi W. Kaufman; *Sec.* Rev. J. Freedman.
Association For Jewish Youth Northern Office, 27 Bury Old Road, Prestwich, M25 0EY. ☎ 0181-203 3030, 0161-740 6168. Fax 0161-740 6169. Email: north.ajy@ort.org.
Bnos Yisroel School, Leicester Road, Salford, M7 0AH. ☎ 0161-792 3896.
Bury & Whitefield Jewish Primary School, Parr La., Bury, Lancs. BL9 8JT. ☎ 0161-766 2888. Fax 0161-766 5426. *H. T.* Mrs N. Massel; *Chairman of Govs.* Rabbi A.J. Jaffe. Nursery School, Parr La., Bury, Lancs. ☎ 0161-767 9390. (Children 2 yrs. plus).
Delamere Forest School, Norley, Nr. Frodsham, Cheshire WA6 6NP. (Reg Charity No. 525913). For Jewish children with special needs: Office: 9 Leicester Avenue, Salford M7 4HA. ☎ 0161-740 5676. *Co. Chairmen* R. J. Wax, D. Clayton; *H.T.* Mrs J. Vegoda.
Hillel House, Greenheys La., M15 6LR. ☎ 0161-226 10161.
Hubert Jewish High School for Girls, 10 Radford Street, Salford, M7 4NT. ☎ 0161-792 2118. Fax 0161-792 1733. *Princ.* Rabbi Y. Goldblat, MA (Oxon), PGCE.
Jerusalem Academy Study Groups. *Chairman* Rev. G. Brodie, 43 Stanley Road, Salford M7 4FR. ☎ 0161-740 2506.
Jewish Senior Boys School - Kesser Torah, Hubert House, 4 New Hall Road, Salford M7 4EL. ☎ 0161-708 9175.
Jewish Education Bureau Resources Centre, Sacred Trinity Centre, Chapel Street, Salford M3 7AJ. ☎ 0161-832 3709. *Dir.* Rabbi D. S. Charing; *Org. Sec.* Mrs G. Abrahams.
Jewish Programme Materials Project (JPMP), 34 Ashley Road, Altrincham, Cheshire WA14 2DW. ☎ 0161-929 5008. Fax 0161-928 6630. Email: s.manchester.jyt@ort.org.

King David Schools. (Est. 1838. Reg. Charity No. 526631)
King David High School, Eaton Road, M8 5DY. ☏ 0161-740 7248. Fax 0161-740 0790. *H. of Upper Campus* E.S. Wilson, J.P., B.A., BEd., F.R.S.A.; *Act. H.T.* B.N. Levy, B.Ed.; *H. of Sixth Form* Mrs J. Bentley, B. Comm, STCSE; *H. of Yavneh* Rabbi J. Kennard, M.A. (Oxon).
King David Junior School, Wilton Polygon, M8 5DJ. ☏ 0161-740 3343. *H.T.* E.S. Wilson, J.P., B.A., B.Ed., F.R.S.A.
King David Infant School, Wilton Polygon, M8 6DR. ☏ 0161-740 4110. *H.T.* Mrs J. Rich, B.A.
King David Nursery & Crèche, Eaton Road, M8 5DY. ☏ 0161-740 3481. *Nursery Man.* Mrs S. Isaacs; *Crèche Man.* Mrs L. Marks.
Governors' Admin. Michael D. Epstein. ☏ 0161-740 3181. Fax 0161-740 3182.
Lubavitch Yeshiva, Lubavitch House, 62 Singleton Road, Salford M7 0LU. ☏ 0161-740 7649. *Dean* Rabbi A. Cohen. *Admin.* S. Weiss, ☏ 01161-740 4243.
Manchester Central Board for Hebrew Education and Talmud Torah (Reg. Charity No. 526164), Emanuel Raffles House, 57 Leicester Road, Salford M7 4DA. ☏/Fax 0161-708 9200. *Chairman* S. Pine; *Admin.* Mrs Y. E. Klein & Mrs M. Gaus. Study Centres: Prestwich Talmud Torah Prestwich Synagogue;. *H. T.* Mrs Joan Yodaiken, B.A. (Hons). North Manchester Jewish Teenage Centre at the Bury & Whitefield Jewish Primary School. *H. T. S.* Lader. Shaarei Deoh Special Needs Cheder. *H. T.* Mrs M. Gold.
Manchester Jewish Grammar School, (Reg. Charity No. 526607), Beechwood, Charlton Avenue, Prestwich M25 0PH ☏ 0161-773 1789. *Princ.* Rabbi L. W. Rabinowitz; *H. M. P.* Pink, B.Sc.(Econ), Dip.Ed.
Mechinah Leyshiva, 13 Up. Park Road, Salford M7 0HY. ☏ 0161-795 9275.
Moriah Institute for Further Education, Y. Y. Rubinstein, 97 Singleton Road, Salford M7.
North Cheshire Jewish Primary School, St. Anns Road North, Heald Green, Cheadle, Cheshire SK8 4RZ. ☏ 0161-282 4500. Fax 0161-282 4501. (Scopus Jewish Educational Trust). *H. M.* Mrs J. Brown, M.Sc., Cert. Ed.
North Manchester Jewish Teenage Centre (Reg. Charity No. 1009785), at the Bnei Akiva Bayit, 72 Singleton Road, Salford M7 4LU. Open Sunday morning only. Under the auspices of the Manchester Centre Hebrew Board, 57 Leicester Road, Salford M7 4DA. ☏/Fax 0161-708 9200. *Corres.* D. Black.
Project SEED, (Reg. Charity No. 281307), 47 Stanley Rd., Salford M7 4FR. ☏ 0161-740 0906. Rabbi A. Hassan.
Reshet Torah Education Network, Rabbi S.M. Kupetz, 4 Hanover Gdns., Salford M7 4FQ. ☏ 0161-740 5735.
South Manchester Jewish Youth Trust, (Reg. Charity No. 1040648), c/o North Cheshire Jewish Primary School, St Anne's Road North, Heald Green, Cheshire SK8 4RZ. ☏ 0161-428 3623. Fax 0161-491 0140. Email: s.manchester.jyt@ort.org. *Community Youth Worker* Andy Sollofe; *Chair* David Zucker. Working with young people in the South Manchester community.
Talmud Torah Chinuch N'orim, 11 Wellington Street, East, Salford M7 9AU. ☏ 0161-792 4522. *Chairman, Bd. of Govs.* B. Waldman.
Whitefield Community Kollel, c/o Whitefield Hebrew Congregation, Park Lane, Whitefield, M45 7PB. *Hon. Admin. P.* Struel. ☏ 0161-766 2150.
Academy of Higher Jewish Learning & Rabbinical Training College. *One to One Learning. Contact* Rabbi Malcolm Herman. ☏ 0161-766 6518/8138.
The Kollel also runs two informal educational programmes.
J.A.M. (Judaism and Me) Post-Barmitzvah groups through to students with an associated girls group.
C.A.F.E. (Community & Family Education) Lectures and discussions for adults in local homes.
Missing Link Adult Education lecture series, particularly refresher courses in Judaism and a Shabbas morning Explanatory Service. *Contact* Rabbi Malcolm

Herman.
Whitefield Jewish Youth Centre. *Co-ord.* Mrs B. Howard. ☎ 0161-796 8564.
Yeshiva (Talmudical College), Saul Rosenberg House, Seymour Road, Higher Crumpsall, M8 5BQ. (Est. 1911). ☎ 0161-740 0214. *Princ.* Rabbi M. Z. Ehrentreu; *Sec.* Rev. G. Brodie.
Yesoiday HaTorah School, Sedgley Park Rd., off Bury New Rd., Prestwich M25 0JW. ☎ 0161-798 9725. Fax 0161-773 3914. *Princ.* Rabbi Y. Yodaiken; *Clerk* Mrs V. Fagleman.
Yocheved Segal Kindergarten, Sedgley Pk. Road, Prestwich M25 0JW. ☎ 0161-773 8413.

WELFARE ORGANISATIONS
Manchester Jewish Federation, (Reg. Charity No. 220165). 12 Holland Road, M8 4NP. ☎ 0161-795 0024. *Chief Exec.* K. Phillips. (Incorporating Jewish Social Services and Manchester Jews' Benevolent Society.).
Aguda Community Services, 35 Northumberland Street, Salford M7 4DQ. ☎ 0161-792 6265. Seeks to provide employment for Jewish people wishing to observe the Sabbath and Holy-days. *Sec.* Mrs O. Weissler.
Brookvale, Caring for People with Special Needs, (Reg. Charity No. 526086), Simister Lane, Prestwich, M25 2SF. ☎ 0161-653 1767. Fax 0161-655 3635. *Exec. Dir.* Mrs L. Richmond; *Fin. Dir.* M. Walters.
Heathlands Village (Reg. Charity No. 221890), Heathlands Dr., Prestwich, M25 9SB. ☎ 0161-772 4800. Fax 0161-772 4934. *L. President* Sir S.C. Hamburger, C.B.E., JP, D.L., LL.D., MA; *President* Mrs J. Cainer. Accommodates 148 residents in self-contained flats and 161 patients in nursing areas.
Jewish Marriage Council, Manchester Branch, Levi House, Bury Old Road, M8 6FX. ☎ 0161-795 1240. Appointments: 0161-740 5746. Offers: Confidential family and marriage counselling, assisting couples and individuals with relationship problems whether they are single, married, widowed, divorced or separated. Cookery Demonstration Group. Discussion & talks on subjects relating to family life and interpersonal relationships.
Jewish Soup Kitchen (Meals-on-Wheels Service), (Reg. Charity No. 226424), Rita Glickman House, Ravensway, Prestwich M25 0EX. ☎ 0161-795 4930. *H. Sec.* Mrs D. Phillips, B.E.M. ☎ 0161-740 1287.
Manchester Jewish Community Care (formerly Manchester Jewish Blind Society), (Reg. Charity No. 257238), Nicky Alliance Day Centre, 85 Middleton Road M8 4JY. ☎ 0161-740 0111. Fax 0161-721 4273. Day Centre and social work services for visually and physically handicapped and isolated elderly. *Chief Exec.* M. Galley; *Chairman* Mrs L. Simons.
Manchester Jewish Visitation Board. (Est. 1903). *Convenor* Y. Brodie; *Chairman* Rev. L. Olsberg. ☎ 0161-740 9711.
Manchester Jews' Benevolent Society, (Reg. Charity No. 224318). Levi House, Bury Old Road, Manchester 8. ☎ 0161-740 4089. *President* H. Weisberg. *H. Sec.* P. Weisberg. (Now merged with Manchester Jewish Federation.)
Morris Feinmann Home (Residential/Nursing Home for the Discerning), 178 Palatine Road, Didsbury, M20 2YW. ☎ 0161-445 3533.
Outreach Community & Residential Services (Reg. Charity No. 509119), 24A Bury New Road, M25 0LD. ☎ 0161-798 0180. Fax 0161-798 5596. Email: gk97@dial.pipex.com. *Dir.* P. Elton. *Chief Exec.* Mrs S. Bitaye; *Dir. of Care* P. Williamson.

MARGATE (200)
Synagogue, Godwin Road, Cliftonville. (Est. 1904; new syn. consecrated 1929.) *President* D. Coberman. ☎ 01843 228550. *H. Sec.* D. Kaye. ☎ 01843 223219.
  Outings catered for: contact *H. Sec.*
Thanet and District Reform Synagogue, 293A Margate Road, Ramsgate, Kent

CT12 6TE. ☎ 01843 851164. *Enquiries to:* David Mirsky (*President*) ☎ 01843 603241.
Cemetery: For Margate Hebrew Congregation & Thanet Reform at Manston Road, Margate.

MIDDLESBROUGH (65)
(Incorporating Stockton and Hartlepool.)
Synagogue, Park Road South. (Est. 1873.) *H. Sec.* L. Simons. ☎ 01642 819034 (for details of services). J. Bloom. ☎ 01642 781363.
Cemetery: Ayresome Green Lane, Middlesbrough.

MILTON KEYNES & DISTRICT (182)
Reform Synagogue (Est. 1978). (Affiliated to R.S.G.B) Inq: Stanley Cohen, 74 Corn Hill, Two Mile Ash, MK8 8JR. ☎ 01908 569661.

NEWARK
Beth Shalom Holocaust Memorial Centre, Laxton, Newark NG22 0PA. ☎ 01623 836627. Fax 01623 836647. *Dirs.* S.D. Smith, J.M. Smith, Mrs M.H. Smith.

NEWCASTLE UPON TYNE (1,110)
The community was est. in the 1820s, when services were held and a Shochet employed. A cemetery was acquired in 1831. Jews, however, had been resident in Newcastle since before 1775. In the Middle Ages Jews are known to have been est. in Newcastle in 1176. The population figure quoted is that of the community's recent census.
Representative Council of North-East Jewry. *President* Mrs Susan Olsburgh; *V. Presidents* V. Gallant, G. Lurie; *Hon. Sec.* M.A. Levinson, 39 Kenton Road, NE3 4NH. ☎ 0191-284 4647.
North East Jewish Recorder (communal journal published by the Representative Council), c/o 28 Montagu Court, Gosforth NE3 4JL. *Edr* Mrs E. Franks.
United Hebrew Congregation (Est. 1973.). The Synagogue, Graham Park Road, Gosforth NE3 4BH. ☎ 0191-284 0959. *President* D. Simon; *M.* Rabbi Y. Black; *Sec.* Mrs P. Ashton. Mikva on premises. Burial Cttee: *Chairman* N. Sterrie. ☎ 0191-285 5501.
Reform Synagogue, The Croft, off Kenton Road, Gosforth, NE3 4RF. ☎ 0191-284 8621. (Est. 1965.) (A Constituent of R.S.G.B.). *Chairman* A. Gilbert; *M.* Rabbi F. Berry. Burial Cttee. Contact ☎ 0191-284 8621.

OTHER ORGANISATIONS
AJEX, *Chairman* C. Topaz. ☎ 01661 824819.
Awakenings (Singles and Young Couples). Contact Susan and Russel Eisen. ☎ 0191 276 7031.
Education and Youth Cttee. c/o United Hebrew Cong. *Chairman* H. Ross.
Jewish Care North East. *Chairman* V. Gallant. ☎ 0191-285 7533.
Jewish Students' Society and Hillel House, 29-31 Hawthorn Road, Gosforth, NE3 4DE. ☎ 0191-284 1407.
Jewish Welfare Society, Lionel Jacobson House, Graham Park Road, Gosforth NE3 4BH. *Sec.* Mrs P. Ashton. ☎ 0191-284 0959.
Joint Israel Appeal. *H. Sec.* J. Mark. ☎ 0191-284 1903.
Newcastle Jewish Housing Association Ltd., *Chairman* J. Fox, c/o Lionel Jacobson House, Graham Park Road, Gosforth NE3 4BH.
Newcastle Jewish Players, *Co-Chairmen* Louise Kaiter ☎ 0191-284 6619; Deanna Van der Velde ☎ 0191-285 1253.
North East Jewish Community Services. *Chairman* V. Gallant, ☎ 0191-285 7533; *Community Dev. Off.* Bernard Shaffer, Lionel Jacobson House, ☎ 0191-284 1968.

North East Jewish Golfing Society. Contact Anthony Josephs. ☏ 0191 285 7173.
The Swingers (Ladies' Section of Golfing Society). Contact Faga Speker. ☏ 0191 285 3101.
Philip Cussins House (Residential Care for Jewish Aged in the North East), 33/35 Linden Road, NE3 4EY. ☏ 0191 213 5353. Fax 0191 213 5354. Residents 0191 213 5355.
Kashrus Cttee., c/o United Hebrew Cong. *Chairman* M. Spodick.
WIZO:
  Sharon Group, *Chairmen* Pam Peterson, ☏ 0191-286 2892; Audrey Veeder, ☏ 0191-285 8013.
  Rosa Wollstein Group, *Chairman* Lady Beecham, ☏ 0191-285 1888.
Zelda's (Kosher meats and delicatessen), Unit 7, Kenton Park Shopping Centre, NE3 4RU. ☏ 0191-213 0013.
Cemeteries: Hazelrigg and Heaton, Newcastle upon Tyne; North Shields (Reform).

NORTHAMPTON (185)

The community marked its centenary in 1988. Services, 8 p.m., Fri. evgs., Yom Tovim and occasional morning services.
Hebrew Congregation, Overstone Road, Northampton, NN1 3JW. ☏ 01604 33345. *M.*; *Sec.* A. Moss, ☏ 01604-33345.
Cemetery: Towcester Road.

NORWICH (170)

The present community was founded in 1813, Jews having been resident in Norwich during the Middle Ages, and connected with the woollen and worsted trade, for which the city was at that time famous. A resettlement of Jews is believed to have been completed by the middle of the eighteenth century. A synagogue was built in 1848 and destroyed in an air raid in 1942. A temporary synagogue opened in 1948 and the present building was consecrated by the Chief Rabbi in 1969. The congregation serves a large area, having members in Ipswich, Gt. Yarmouth, Lowestoft and Cromer.
Norwich Hebrew Congregation Synagogue, 3a Earlham Road, NR2 3RA. ☏ 0163 623948. *M.* Rev. M. Daniels; *President* Mrs E. Imber-Lithman; *H. Sec.* J. Griffiths, 23 Varvel Avenue, Sprowston, NR7 8PH. ☏ 01603 417 810.
Progressive Jewish Community of East Anglia (Norwich). A new community based in Norwich. Affiliated to the ULPS. Regular services at The Octagon, Colegate, Norwich. *Chairman* Dr P. Lawrence. *M.*; Enquiries to: *H. Sec.* Alison Knight, ☏ 01603 259271.
Jewish Ladies' Society, 3a Earlham Road. *President* Mrs P. Simons; *H. Sec.* Mrs F. Cadywond.
Chevra Kadisha, 3a Earlham Road, Norwich. *President* B. C. Leveton.
Norfolk and Norwich Branch of the Council of Christians and Jews, Dale Lodge, Sandy Lane, East Dereham, NR19 2EA. ☏ 01362 694131. (Est. 1991). *H. Sec.* Mrs M. Agombar, 3 Purtingay Close, Eaton NR4 6HU. ☏ 01603 461406.
Norwich Israel Social Society (NISS), *Chairman* P. Stein; 2 Leeds Way, Horning, NR12 8LU. ☏ 01692 630086.

NOTTINGHAM (1,050)

A small community has lived in Nottingham since the early 19th century, and in 1890, with a com. increased by immigrants to some 100 families, the Hebrew Congregation built its first synagogue in Chaucer St. During the Second World War, there was a sharp growth in the community, and the congregation acquired its present synagogue in 1954. With the closure of the Derby syn. in 1986, many of its members joined the Nottingham Hebrew Cong. The Progressive Jewish Cong. was est. in 1959.
Hebrew Congregation, Shakespeare Villas, NG1 4FQ. ☏ 0115 472004. *President* Paul Levin.

Progressive Jewish Congregation (ULPS), Lloyd Street, NG5 4BP. ☎ 0115 9624761. *Chairman* B. Peters. ☎ 0115 913 2619. *H. Sec.* Mrs L. Chapman. ☎ 0115 9281613.
Nottingham Representative Council, 42 Weardale Rd., Sherwood NG5 1DD. ☎ 0115 413553. *President* D. Lipman. ☎ 01159 212018. *Chairman* M. Spungin, O.B.E.; *Sec.* Mrs A. Lewis. ☎ 0115 6016121.
Federation of Women Zionists. *H. Sec.* Mrs S. Flitterman, 11 Priory Road, West Bridgford, NG2 SHU.
Jewish Welfare Board. *Chairman* Dr M. Caplan. ☎ 0115 260245. *Hon. Sec.* P. Seymour, 115 Selby Rd., West Bridgford, NG2 7BB. ☎ 0115 452895.
Miriam Kaplowitch House, Jewish rest home, 470 Mansfield Road, NG5 2Dr ☎ 0115 624274 (Residents) & 0115 9622038 (Matron & Admin.) (Est. 1986).
University of Nottingham Jewish and Israel Society, c/o The University of Nottingham, NG7 2RD.
Women's Benevolent Society. *Chairman* Mrs E. Litman, J.P. ☎ 0115 9231102.

OXFORD (Resident Jewish pop. 700 approx.)
An important centre in the medieval period. The modern community was est. in 1842. In 1974 the Oxford Synagogue and Jewish Centre was built on the site of the earlier synagogue. It serves the resident community and a fluctuating number of university students, and is available for all forms of Jewish worship.
Jewish Congregation, The Synagogue, 21 Richmond Road, OX1 2JL. ☎ 01865 53042. *President* Penny Faust, 22 Feilden Grove, Headington, OX3 0DU. ☎ 01865 68140.
Oxford University L'Chaim Society, Albion House, Albion Place, Little Gate, OX1 1QZ. ☎ 01865 794462.
University Jewish Society. (Est. 1903). *Senior Member* Mike Woodin, Balliol College, ☎ 01865 248073; *Sec.* T. J. Montagu, 171 Iffley Road, OX4 1EL. ☎ 01865 726037; *Chaplain* Rev. M. Weisman, M.A. (Oxon.). ☎ 0181-451 3484.
Progressive Services. Inq.: Katherine Shock. ☎/Fax 01865 515584.

PETERBOROUGH (105)
Hebrew Congregation, 142 Cobden Avenue, PE1 2NU. ☎ 01733 571282. (Congregation est. 1940. Syn. opened 1954. Affiliated to the U.S.) *Admin.* C. Conn. ☎ 01733 571282. Services Kabbalat Shabbat 8pm. Liberal Jewish Community. *Admin.* N. Gordon ☎ 01733 22813; Juliet Vart ☎ 01733 53269. Services first and third Shabbat at 10.30am.
Liberal Jewish Community (ULPS). Enquiries to Elisabeth Walker. ☎ 01733 266188.

PLYMOUTH (100)
The Plymouth cong. was founded in 1745, when a cemetery was opened. Jews lived in the city even earlier. The syn., built in 1762, is the oldest Ashkenazi house of worship still standing in the English-speaking world. Its 225th anniversary in 1987 was marked by a service attended by representatives of the United Synagogue, the Board of Deputies and the Civic Authorities. In the early 19th century, Plymouth was one of the four most important provincial centres of Anglo-Jewry.
Hebrew Congregation (Reg. Charity 220010), Catherine Street, PL1 2AD. ☎ 01752 664995. (Est. 1761.) *H. Sec.* Dr P. Lee. ☎ 01822 612281.

PORTSMOUTH (385)
The com. was est. in 1746 and opened a syn. in Oyster Row, later to move to a building in White's Row, off Queen St. which was occupied for over 150 years. The present syn. was built in 1936. The cemetery was acquired in 1749 and is the oldest in the Regions still in use. It is situated in Fawcett Road, which has been known for more than 200 years as Jews' Lane. By 1815 Portsmouth was one of the four main Jewish centres outside London, the others being Plymouth, Liverpool and

Birmingham. Portsmouth's prosperity declined after the Napoleonic Wars.
See also under Winchester.
Synagogue, The Thicket, Southsea PO5 2AA. ☎ 01705 821494. *M.* Rev. H.
Caplan; *Hon. Sec.* Mrs Y.E. Davis.
Board of Guardians, The Thicket (Est. 1804)
Chevra Kadisha, The Thicket.
Jewish Ladies' Benevolent Society, (Est. 1770.) The Thicket.
Cemeteries: Fawcett Road, Kingston, New Road; Catherington.

POTTERS BAR (205)
Synagogue, (affiliated to the United Synagogue). *M.* Rev. D. Levy. Correspondence to: P.O. Box 119, Potters Bar, Herts.

PRESTON (25)
Synagogue, est. 1882, now closed. *H. Sec.* Dr C. E. Nelson, 31 Avondale Road, Southport PR9 0NH. ☎ 01704 538276.

RADLETT (750)
Synagogues:
Radlett (U.S.), P.O. Box 28, Herts. WD7 7PN. *M.* Rabbi Y. Sliw.
Radlett & Bushey Reform Synagogue (RSBG), 118 Watling St., Herts. WD7 7AA.
☎ 01923 856110. *M.* Rabbi Alexandra Wright. *H. Sec.* Karen Young.
Hertsmere Progressive Synagogue (ULPS), High St., Elstree. *M.* Rabbi J. Black. *H. Sec.* Valerie Dickson. ☎ 0181-950 3268.

READING (500)
The community began in 1886 with the settlement of a number of tailors from London. They attracted the help of such personages as Samuel Montague, Claude Montefiore, Sir Hermann Gollancz and Lady Lucas to build and support a synagogue in 1900, and the syn. has been in continuous use ever since. This flourishes today as the centre of the Reading Hebrew Cong., which has a growing membership of 160 families, and is the only Orthodox cong. in Berkshire. The Sir Hermann Gollancz Hall next to the syn. is the venue of many social groups.
The Progressive Community was founded in 1979 and attracts membership from across the Thames Valley.
Orthodox Synagogue, (Reg. Charity No.: 220098). Goldsmid Road, RG1 7YB. ☎ 0118 9571018. *M.* Rabbi David Lister, ☎ 0118 957 3954; *H. Sec.* Mrs Louise Creme, ☎ 0118 957 1018. Internet: www.datanet.co.uk/enterprise/rhc/ E-mail: Secretary@rhc.datanet.co.uk.
WIZO & Judaica Shop. Mrs Pamela Kay ☎ 0118 9573680.
Food Shop. Kosher meat and provisions. Mrs Carol Kay ☎ 0118 575069.
Thames Valley Progressive Jewish Community. (Est. 1979.) (Affiliated to ULPS), 6 Church Street, Reading. For details of services, religious and social events, contact: *Chairman* Ms. D. Adelman ☎ 0118 9867769 or Rabbi Sybil Sheridan ☎ 01628 71058.
University Jewish Society, c/o Reading Hillette, 82 Basingstoke Road, Reading. ☎ 0118 9873282.

REIGATE AND REDHILL (45)
Jewish Community. (Est. 1968.) *Chairman* M. J. Kemper, 59 Gatton Road, Reigate, Surrey. ☎ 017372 42076.

ST. ALBANS (200)
Hebrew Congregation, (Affiliated to the U.S.), Oswald Road. *H. Sec.* H. Turner, 8 Tudor Court, High Street, London Colney, AL2 1JZ. ☎ 01727 825295.
St. Albans Masorti Synagogue, Inquiries: *Sec.* S. Gess. ☎ 01727 48778; *Chairman* P. Curitz.

ST. ANNE'S ON SEA (500)
Hebrew Congregation, Orchard Road, FY8 1PJ. ☎ 01253 721831. *President* P. Davidson. ☎ 01253 723920. *Hon. Secs.* A. Brown & L. Jackson. ☎ 01253-721835. *M.* Rabbi I. Broder. ☎ 01253-781815.
Ladies Guild, *Chairman* Mrs L. Gee. ☎ 01253-726854.
Cemetery: Consecrated section of municipal cemetery at Regents Avenue, Lytham.

SHEFFIELD (ca. 650)
The earliest extant records of the Sheffield Hebrew Congregation date only from 1850, but the congregation had then been in existence for some time, and burial records exist from 1837. There were Jews living in Sheffield at the beginning of the nineteenth century and even earlier. The syn. was at that time in Figtree Lane. Previously there had been one in Holly Lane, and still earlier there had been regular services in private houses.
Representative Council of Sheffield and District Jews. *President* Selwyn M. Burchhardt; *H. Sec.* Tony Kay, 105 Bents Road, S11 9RH. ☎ 0114 236 0970.
Jewish Congregation & Centre, Wilson Road, S11. ☎ 0114 2662930. *R.* Rabbi Y. Golomb. ☎ 0114 2663567. *President* Eric Kalman; *H. Sec.* Mrs M. Shaw, 67 Bents Rd., S11 9RH. ☎ 0114 2362217.
Sheffield and District Reform Jewish Congregation. (Est. 1989) P.O. Box 675, S11 8SP. Services held alternate Friday nights and every fourth Shabbat. For further information please ring 0114 2308433. *Chairman* Dr J. Kinderlerer. ☎ 0114 2301054.
Hebrew Education Board, Psalter House, Psalter Lane, S11 (Est. 1902.) *President* Dr A. Anderson, 5 Kingscroft Close, Dore, S17 3RE. ☎ 0114 2351041.
Jewish Welfare Board, *H. Sec.* M. Ballin. ☎ 0114 2366800.
Sheffield University Jewish Society, c/o The Sabbatical Office, SUSU, Western Bank, S10 2TN.
Sheffield Israel Society. *Chairman* Mrs F. Wilenski, 62 The Glen, Endcliffe Vale Rd., S10 3FN. ☎ 0114 2662210.
Sheffield Housing Association. *Hon. Sec.* Mrs Joyce Flowers, 44 The Glen, S10 3FN. ☎ 0114 2678744.

SOLIHULL (300)
Solihull & District Hebrew Congregation, Monastery Dr, B91 1DW. *M.* Rabbi Y. Pink; *H. Sec.* P. Fiddler, 14 Abbots Close, Knowle B93 9PP. ☎ 01564 775715.
Solihull Jewish Social & Cultural Society, *H. Sec.* E. Lesser, 43 Vicarage Rd., Yardley, Birmingham B33 8PH. ☎ 0121-783 2464.

SOUTH SHIELDS (9)
Hebrew Congregation, *President* Dr M. Anderson, 123 Sunderland Rd., NE33. ☎ 0191 4560965. The synagogue is now closed. Friday evening services at members' homes at 6 p.m. throughout the year.
Cemetery: Consecrated section of the municipal cemetery.

SOUTHAMPTON (105)
The orthodox congregation dates from 1833 when the first synagogue in East Street was founded. The synagogue built in 1864 in Albion Place was demolished in 1963, when the present one was consecrated. There were Jewish residents in Southampton in 1786. Since 1838, when Abraham Abraham was elected to the Town Council, they have shared in civic affairs.
The South Hampshire Reform Jewish Community was formed in 1983 (see Winchester, p.129).
Orthodox Synagogue, Mordaunt Road, Inner Ave. ☎ 01703-220129. *President* S. Ferder. *H. Sec.* C.D. Freeman, 23 Roslin Hall, 6 Manor Rd., Bournemouth BH1 3ES.

Hartley Library, University of Southampton, Highfield, houses the Anglo-Jewish Archives and Parkes Library (see p.55).
Hillel House, 5 Brookvale Road. ☎ 01703 557742.
Cemetery: Consecrated section at the municipal Hollybrook cemetery.

SOUTHEND, WESTCLIFF & LEIGH-ON-SEA (4,500)
Jewish families settled in the Southend area in the late 19th century, mainly from London's East End. In 1906 the first temporary synagogue was built in wood in Station Road, Westcliff. In 1912 one of the present synagogues was built in Alexandra Rd, Southend. In continuous use since, it is now one of the historical sights in the area. A breakaway faction built its own syn. in Ceylon Road, Westcliff, in 1928, but the two congs later reunited. A new syn. was built in Finchley Road, Westcliff in 1969 and the Ceylon Road premises were converted into a youth centre. The com. is growing and Jews from different parts of the world now live in the area.
Southend-on-Sea & District Jewish Representative Council. *Chairman* Derek Baum, M.B.E. ☎ 01702 343789; *Sec.* Jeffrey Barcan, 22 Second Ave., Westcliff-on-Sea, Essex SS0 8HY. ☎ 01702-343192.
Southend and Westcliff Hebrew Congregation, Finchley Rd., Westcliff-on-Sea, Essex SS0 8AD. *M.* Rabbi M. Lew. ☎ 01702 344900. Fax 01702 391131.

Synagogues at:
Finchley Road, Westcliff; 99 Alexandra Road, Southend. *M.* Rev. Rabbi M. Lew; *President* David Gold, 23 Chadacre Road, SS1 3QX. ☎ 01702 586774; *Gen. Sec.* Mrs R. Silver; *Fin. Sec.* Mrs A. Marx. ☎ 01702 344900.

Southend and District Reform Synagogue, 851 London Road, Westcliff. ☎ 01702 75809. *Chairman & Sec.* Mr. N. Klass & Mrs A. Klass, 22 Crowstone Ave., Westcliff. ☎ 01702 338460.
Chevra Kadisha. *Chairman* H. Brown. ☎ 01702 344900. Fax 01702-391131.
Mikva, 44 Genesta Road, Westcliff. ☎ 01702 344900. *Supt.* Mrs S. Caplan, 69 St. Johns Road, Westcliff. ☎ 01702 347410.
Orthodox Jewish Cemetery, Sutton Road, Southend. (Entr. Stock Road.) ☎ 01702 344900.
Reform Jewish Cemetery, Sutton Road, Southend. (Entr. Stock Road).
Myers Communal Hall, Finchley Road, Westcliff. ☎ 01702 344900.
Kashrut Commission, *Chairman* Mrs J. Sheldon. ☎ 01702 344900.
Ladies' Guild (Orthodox). *Chairman* Mrs J. Burns; *Sec.* Mrs B. Franks, 90 Chalkwell Ave, Westcliff, SS0 8NN.
Ladies' Guild (Reform). *Sec.* Mrs R. Brenner, 12 The Drive, Westcliff. ☎ 01702 75809.

EDUCATIONAL, CULTURAL AND YOUTH ORGANISATIONS
B'nai B'rith Youth Organisation. *Chairman* D. Cregor Esq., 162 Lifstan Way, Thorpe Bay, Essex. ☎ 01702-468334.
Coleman & Lilian Levene Talmud Torah (Orthodox), Finchley Road, Westcliff. ☎ 01702 344900. *H.T.* Mrs A. Gilbert.
Emunah Ladies' Society. *Chairman* Mrs F. Sober, 16 Crosby Rd., Westcliff. ☎ 01702-330440. *Sec.* Mrs M. Simons.
Friendship Club. *Chairman* Mrs Z. Jacobson. ☎ 01702 466031.
Hebrew Education Board. *Chairman* Mrs A. Moss. ☎ 01702 344900.
Herzlia Day School, Finchley Road, Westcliff. ☎ 01702 340986. *H. T.* Mrs M. Hass.
JIA. *Chairman* S. Salt Esq., 157 Chalkwell Avenue, Westcliff-on-Sea, Essex. ☎ 01702 76349.
Jewish Lads' & Girls' Brigade. *Chairman* Mrs R. O'Brart, 11 The Drive, Westcliff SS0 8PL. ☎ 01702-714122; *Sec.* Mr R. Rams.

JNF Impact. *Chairman* A. Larholt. *Sec.* L. Barnes, 26 Second Ave., Westcliff, SS0 8HY.
Lecture Board. Mrs S. Greenstein, 62 Chadwick Road, Westcliff SS0 8L. ☎ 01702 343794.
Monday Shalom Club. *Chairman* G. Kalms, 14 Tower Court, Westcliff Parade, Westcliff. ☎ 01702 337152.
Southend District Social Committee (Reform). *Chairman* Mrs S. Kaye.
Talmud Torah (Reform), 851 London Road, Westcliff. *Princ.* Mrs Woods. ☎ 01702 75809.
Women's Zionist Society. *Chairman* Mrs J. Kalms, 6 Leitrim Avenue, Shoeburyness; *H. Sec.* Mrs J. Barnett, 22 Kings Road, Westcliff. ☎ 01702 340731.
Young Marrieds Cultural & Social Group. *Chairman* L. Herlitz Esq., 10 Cliff Road, Leigh-on-Sea, Essex SS9 1JH.
Youth Centre (Orthodox), 38 Ceylon Road, Westcliff. ☎ 01702 346545. *Chairman* A. Witzenfeld; *Sec.* D. Jay, 9 St. Clements Avenue, Leigh-on-Sea.

WELFARE ORGANISATIONS
A.J.E.X. Communal Hall, Finchley Road Synagogue, Westcliff. *Jt. Chairmen* Dr D. Balch, 5 Elderton Rd., Westcliff-on-Sea, SS0 8AG. ☎ 01702 342637. *Chairman* Mrs R. Plaskow, 8 Crosby Rd., Westcliff-on-Sea. ☎ 01702 340995.
B'nai B'rith. *Chairman* Mrs M. Rabinovitch; *Sec.* N. D. Wine, 32 Leasway, Westcliff. ☎ 01702 710607.
Hospital Kosher Meals Service. Rabbi M Lew. ☎ 01702 344900.
Kosher Meals-on-Wheels Service. *H. Sec.* A. Rubin, 14 Drake Rd., Westcliff. ☎ 01702 345568.
Raymond House for Aged, 6 Clifton Terrace, Southend. ☎ 01702 340054 (Residents): 01702 341687 (Matron).
Southend Friends of Ravenswood. J. Freedman, 111 Hampton Gardens, Southend. ☎ 01702-341515.
Southend Aid Society. *Sec.* H. Kanutin, 96 Willingale Way, Thorpe Bay. ☎ 01702 582996.
Southend & District A.J.E.X. *President* Derek Baum, MBE. *Chairman* S. Metselaar; *H. Sec.* J. Barcan, 22 Second Avenue, Westcliff. ☎ 01702 343192.
Southend & Westcliff Community Centre, Victoria Oppenheim House, 1 Cobham Road, Westcliff. ☎ 01702 334655. *Care Services Man.* Mrs P. Turner.

SOUTHPORT (1,382)
The first Synagogue was consecrated in 1893 and the congregation moved to Arnside Road, in 1924. The New Synagogue (Reform) was est. in 1948. The community grew between and during the First and Second World Wars, but is now decreasing.
Jewish Representative Council. *President* Mrs Sonia Abrahamson, 65 Priory Beach Gardens, PR9 2SA. ☎ 01704 540704; *H. Sec.* Ivor Galkoff, Flat 18, Argyle Court, 5 Argyle Road, Hesketh Park. ☎ 01704 538119.
Synagogue, Arnside Road, PR9 0QX. ☎ 01704 532964. M. Rabbi M. L. Rogosnitsky; *President* Dr Cyril Nelson; *Sec.* Mrs Maureen Cohen.
Beth Hasepher, Arnside Road. ☎ 01704 532964.
Manchester House, 83 Albert Road. ☎ 01704 534920 (office); 01704 530436 (visitors).
Mikveh, Arnside Road. ☎ 01704 532964.
New Synagogue, Portland St. PR8 1LR. ☎ 01704 535950. M. ; *Emer. Rabbi* Rabbi S. Kay; *H. Sec.* Tom Nichols.
Jewish Convalescent and Aged Home, 81 Albert Road. ☎ 01704 531975 (office); 01704 530207 (visitors.).

Sharon House Rest Home, 111 Leyland Road, Southport PR9 0JL. ☎ 01704 531386. Visitors 01704 530170. (Under Manchester Beth Din Supervision.)
Southport Nursing and Care Home, 126 Leyland Road, Southport PR9 0JL. ☎ 01704 543898. Visitors 01704 544116. (Under Manchester Beth Din Supervision.).

STAINES & DISTRICT (390)
(Incorporating Slough & Windsor)
Synagogue (affiliated to the U.S.), Westbrook Road, South Street, Middx. TW18 4PR. *H. Sec.* Mrs P. D. Fellman. ☎ 01784 254604.

STOKE-ON-TRENT (30)
Hebrew Congregation, Birch Terr., Hanley. (Est. 1873. Reg. Charity No. 232104) *President* H. S. Morris, 27 The Avenue, Basford, Newcastle, Staffs. ST5 0ND. ☎ 01782 616417; *T. H.* Slann. ☎ 01782 617700.

SUNDERLAND (60)
The first Jewish settlement was in 1755. The first congregation was est. about 1768; and was the first regional community to be represented at the BoD. A syn. was erected in Moor St. in 1862; rebuilt in 1900; and in 1928 the cong. moved to Ryhope Road, The Beth Hamedrash, which was est. in Villiers St. in 1899, and moved to Mowbray Road in 1938, closed in December 1984.
Communal Rav. Rabbi S. Zahn, 11 The Oaks East, SR2 8EX. ☎ 0191 565 0224.
Hebrew Congregation, incorporating Sunderland Beth Hamedrash, Ryhope Road, SR2 7EQ. ☎ 0191-5658093. *President* J. Sadlik; *H. Sec.* T. H. Jackson.
Board of Shechita. *President* J. Sadlik; *H. Sec.* Theo Jackson. ☎ 0191-522 7822.
Centre for Advanced Rabbinics, 2 The Oaks West, Sunderland SR2 8HZ. ☎ 0191-5659290/5671108.
Chevra Kadisha. *President* G. Grantham, 9 The Precinct, SR2 9DN. ☎ 0191-5283502.
Hebrew Board of Guardians. (Est. 1869) Incorporating Guild of Jewish Women. *H. Sec.* Dr B. I. Chazan, 'White Gates', Ashburne Ct., SR2. ☎ 0191-565 0887.
Mikva, Mowbray Road. Contact Mrs Zahn. ☎ 0191-565 0224.
Talmudical College and Yeshiva. ☎ 0191 5650224. (See Gateshead p.105). *Princ.* Rabbi S. Zahn.
Cemetery: Bishopwearmouth Cemetery, Hylton Road, Sunderland.

SWINDON (72)
The community formed by Second World War evacuees has dispersed, but a community was re-formed in 1983.
Jewish Community. (Associated Community of R.S.G.B. Reg. Charity No. 296761). *Chairman* P. Scott, 16 Winterslow Rd., Swindon, Wilts. ☎ 01793-723451. *Sec.* Mrs A. Scott, 8 Eric Long Ct., Kennedy Drive, Elderne, SN3 6DA. ☎ 01793 524093. Services: Fri. evgs; monthly Sat. mornings. Religion sch., adult educ., social events.

TORQUAY (TORBAY) (20)
Synagogue, Old Town Hall, Abbey Road. Sabbath services 10.30 a.m. on first Sabbath of each month. *Chairman* Dr J. Lyons. ☎ 01803 25511. Inq.: E. Freed, 'Son Bou', 7 Broadstone Park Road, Livermead, Torquay TQ2 6TY. ☎ 01803 607197.
Chevra Kadisha: Cemetery, Colley End Road, Paignton, Torbay. *Chairman* Leon Fredman, JP. ☎ 01803 295130.

WALLASEY (50)
Hebrew Congregation, 27a Falkland Road, L44 8EN. (Est. 1911.) *President* D. Daniels; *T. N. J.* Margetts; *H. Sec.* L. S. Goldman, 28 Grant Road, Wirral, Merseyside, L46 2RY. ☎ 0151-638 6945.

WELWYN GARDEN CITY (290)
Synagogue (Affiliated to U.S.), Handside Lane, Barn Close, Herts AL8 6ST. ☎ 01582-762829. *H. Sec.* Mr S. Hirschfield, 3 Newton Close, Harpenden, Herts. AL5 1SP. ☎ 01582 762829.

WHITLEY BAY (20)
Hebrew Congregation, 2 Oxford Street, Whitley Bay NG26 3TB. *H. Sec.* M. A. Sonn, 2 Grasmere Cres. ☎ 01632 2521367; 01670 367053 (day).

WINCHESTER
South Hampshire Reform Jewish Community. (Reg. Charity No. 1040109. Est.1983). *Chairman* Mrs M. Wilcox, 425 Fair Oak Rd., Fair Oak, Hants SO5 7AE. ☎ 01703 600001. *Sec.* Mrs S. Mansfield, 54 St Matthews Rd., Cosham, Portsmouth. ☎ 01705 324205. Services every second and fourth Friday at the Unitarian Meeting Hall, London Road, Southampton. Saturday morning service once a month, varying venues. Sunday morning Cheder. Social activities, Adult Education Discussions etc.

WOLVERHAMPTON (15 families)
Synagogue, Fryer St. (Est. 1850.) Services Fri. 6.45 pm. *H. Sec.* H. Kronheim, 94 Wergs Road, Tettenhall WV6 8TH. ☎ 01902 752474.
Cemetery: Consecrated section at Jeffcock Road Corporation Cemetery, Wolverhampton.

YORK (25)
A memorial stone was consecrated at Clifford's Tower, York Castle, in 1978 in memory of the York Jewish community massacred there in 1190. A small community resettled and continued to live in York until the 1290 expulsion. There is now a small com. in the city and a Jewish Soc. at York Univ.
York Hebrew Congregation. Enq. B. Sugar, 3 Rawcliffe Grove, YO3 4NR. ☎ 01904 624479.
Contact: A. S. Burton. ☎ 01423 330537.

WALES

CARDIFF (1,200)
Jews settled in Cardiff about the year 1787. The present community was founded in 1840.
Jewish Representative Council. *Chairman* Prof. P.D.J. Weitzman; *H. Sec.* Mrs J. R. Cotsen, 71 Cyncoed Road, CF2 6AB. ☎ 01222 484999.
Israel Information Centre Wales & the West of England, P.O.B. 98, Cardiff, CF2 6XN. ☎/Fax 01222 461780. *Dir.* Jean A. Evans.
Orthodox Synagogue, Brandreth Road, Penylan, Cardiff. ☎ 01222 473728/ 491795. *Sec.* Mrs S. C. Glavin.
New Synagogue, Moira Terrace, CF2 1EJ. (opp. Howard Gdns.). (A Constituent of R.S.G.B.) ☎ 01222 491689. *Sec.* Mrs C. Salmon. ☎ 01222 491689.
Hillel House, 89 Crwys Rd., Cardiff. ☎ 01222 231114. Applications for admission: Mrs P. Freed, 210 Lake Road East, CF2 5NR. ☎ 01222 758614.
Cardiff Jewish Helpline (formerly Cardiff Jewish Board of Guardians). *Chairman* Mr. A. Schwartz, 5 Woodvale Avenue, Cyncoed, Cardiff. ☎ 01222 750990.

Jewish Kindergarten, Penylan Synagogue (as above), Mrs C. Bloom. ☎ 01222 756840.
Kashrus Commission. Rabbi D. Levey at Penylan Synagogue Office. ☎ 01222 473728.
Kosher Butcher & Delicatessen. Visiting butcher A. Gee & Son every Wednesday at Penylan Synagogue. ☎ 01222-491795.
Mikva, Wales Empire Pool Bldgs., Wood Street, Cardiff. ☎ 01222 382296.
South Wales Jewish Retirement and Nursing Home, Penylan House, Penylan Road. ☎ 01222 485327. (Est. 1945.) *President* Prof. P.D.J. Weitzman; *Matron* Mrs Varner. *H. Sec.* Mrs M. Cantor.
Union of Jewish Students, c/o Hillel House. ☎ 01222 231114.
Cemeteries: Old Cemetery - High Fields Road, Roath Park; New Cemetery - Greenfarm Road, Ely; Reform: at Cowbridge Road Entrance, Ely Cemetery.

LLANDUDNO AND COLWYN BAY (45)
Hebrew Congregation, 28 Church Walks, Llandudno LL30 2HL. (Est. 1905). Friday night service held from Pesach to Yom Kippur at 8pm. Winter services at 6.15pm. *Sec.* B. Hyman, 9 Glyn Isaf, Llandudno Junction, Gwynedd LL31 9HT. ☎ 01492 572549. Llandudno serves as the centre for the dwindling coms. of North Wales, including Bangor, Rhyl, Colwyn Bay and Caernarvon.

MERTHYR TYDFIL
Synagogue now closed. The com. was est. before 1850. The cemetery is still being maintained. Apply to the Cardiff Jewish Rep. C. (See p.129)

NEWPORT (Gwent) (10)
Synagogue, (Opened 1871.) 3 Queens Hill Cres., NP9 5HH. ☎ 01633 262308. *Chairman* I. Rocker, 2 Stow Park Circle, NP9 4HE.
Burial Society, c/o Cardiff Orthodox Synagogue, Penylan, Cardiff.
Cemetery: Risca Road, Newport.

SWANSEA (245)
The Jewish community dates at the latest from 1768, when the Corporation granted a plot of land for use as a cemetery. In 1780 a syn. was built. Probably its history is even older, for Jews are known to have been living in the town from about 1730. The syn. in Goat St. was destroyed in an air raid in Feb. 1941, but another was erected in the Ffynone district. The former Llanelli cong. is now part of the Swansea com.
Hebrew Congregation. (Est. 1780.) Synagogue, Ffynone. *Chairman* H. M. Sherman, 17 Mayals Green, Mayals, Swansea SA3 5JR. ☎ 01792 401205.
Chevra Kadisha. *Chairman* D. Sandler. ☎ 01792 206285.
Cemeteries at Oystermouth and Townhill.

SCOTLAND
The Scottish Jewish Archives Centre. (Est. 1987.) Garnethill Synagogue, 127 Hill Street, Glasgow G3 6UB. ☎ 0141 332 4911. To collect, catalogue, preserve and exhibit records of communal interest. To stimulate study in the history of the Jews of Scotland. To heighten awareness in the Jewish communities of Scotland of their local cultural and religious heritages. *Chairman* Dr Jack E. Miller, O.B.E., J.P.; Dr Kenneth Collins, Ph.D.; *H. T.* Michael Miller; *H. Sec.* Mrs Natalie Cohen; *Dir.* Harvey L. Kaplan, M.A., *Archivist* Ben Braber, Ph.D.

ABERDEEN (30)
Refurbished synagogue and community centre opened 1983.
Hebrew Congregation, 74 Dee Street, AB1 2DS. ☎ 01224 582135. (Est. 1893.) *H. Sec.* Sandra Shrago. ☎ 01467 642726.

DUNDEE (22)
Hebrew Congregation, 9 St. Mary Place. (Est. 1874. New synagogue opened 1978.) *Chairman* H. Gillis, Sandy Lodge, Carnoustie, Tayside, DD7 6DB. ☎ 01241 853144.
Dundee Univ. Jewish Society is centred at the synagogue.

DUNOON
Argyll and Bute Jewish Community. Contact Barry Kaye, Edgemont, 34 Argyll Road, Dunoon, PA23 8ES. ☎/Fax 01369-705 118.

EDINBURGH (500)
The Edinburgh Town Council and Burgess Roll, Minutes of 1691 and 1717, record applications by Jews for permission to reside and trade in Edinburgh. Local directories of the eighteenth century contain Jewish names. There is some reason to believe that there was an organised Jewish community in 1780 but no cemetery, and in 1817 it removed to Richmond Ct. where there was also for a time a rival congregation. In 1795, the Town Council sold a plot of ground on the Calton Hill to Herman Lyon, a Jewish dentist, to provide a burying place for himself and members of his family. In 1816, when a syn. was opened a cemetery was also acquired. The present syn. in Salisbury Road was consecrated in 1932 and renovated in 1980.
Hebrew Congregation, 4 Salisbury Road. ☎ 0131-667 3144. (Est. 1816, New Synagogue built 1932.) *M. Rabbi* D. Sedley, 67 Newington Road, Edinburgh EH9. ☎ 0131-667 9360; *H. Sec.* W. Simpson, 3 Hallhead Rd., EH16. ☎ 0131-667 1521.
Board of Guardians. *H. Sec.* I. Shein (as above).
Chevra Kadisha. *H. Sec.* R. I. Brodie, 60 Telford Road, Edinburgh EH4 2LY. ☎ 0131-332 4386.
Edinburgh Friends of Israel. *President* The Earl of Balfour; *H. Sec.* Mrs I. Einan, 4 Afton Terr. ☎ 0131-552 2860.
Friendship Club. *President* W. Caplan, 25 Watertoun Road, Edinburgh EH9. ☎ 0131-667 7984.
Jewish Literary Society. *President* Mrs J. Merrick, 10 Sycamore Gardens EH12 5LA. ☎ 0131-334 0242.
Jewish Old Age Home for Scotland (Edinburgh Cttee). *President* J. S. Caplan; *H. Sec.* Miss A. Lurie, 26 South Lauder Road, 9. ☎ 0131-667 5500.
Ladies' Guild. *President* Mrs H. Rifkind, 37 Cluny Drive, Edinburgh EH10 6DU. ☎ 0131-447 7386.
The Edinburgh Star. Community Journal. Published 3 times a year. Editor, 9 Warrington Crescent, EH3 5LA. ☎ 0131-556 7774.
University Jewish Society. *President* P. Albert, c/o Societies' Centre, Room 6, 21 Hill Place.

GLASGOW (6,700)
The Glasgow Jewish community was founded in 1823 although there are records of Jewish activity in the city for many years prior to that. The first Jewish cemetery was opened in the prestigious Glasgow Necropolis in 1831 and the community was housed in a variety of synagogues in the city centre for many years. The community grew in the 1870s and the Garnethill Synagogue, the oldest Jewish building in Scotland and home of the Scottish Jewish Archives Centre, was opened in 1879. At the same time Jews began settling in the Gorbals district just south of the River Clyde where there was a substantial Jewish community with many synagogues and Jewish shops and communal institutions until the 1950s. None of these now remains. In more recent years the community has been centred in the southern suburbs such as Giffnock and Newton Mearns where most Jewish institutions are now situated.

Details of Jewish history in Glasgow in the early days (1790–1919) can be found in a new book 'Second City Jewry' by Dr Kenneth Collins, available from the Glasgow Jewish Representative Council.
Jewish Representative Council, Resource Centre, 222 Fenwick Rd., Giffnock, G46 6UE. ☎ 0141-620 1700. Fax 0141-638 2100. *Chairman* Dr Kenneth Collins; *H. Sec.* E. Borowski. ☎ 0141-638 1214 (Home), 0141-330 5159 (Office). Fax 0141-638 1100. E-mail: gjrc@ort.org
West Scotland Kashrut Commission, *Chairman* M. Livingstone; *H. Sec.* H. Tankel. ☎ 0141-423 5830.
Hebrew Burial Society, 43 Queen Square, G41 2BD. ☎ 0141-423 4420. *Chairman* S. Sankar. *Enquiries* M. Sunderland.
Mikvah, Giffnock & Newlands Syn., Maryville Avenue, Giffnock. *Enquiries*: Mrs C. Fletcher, Dip. Ed. ☎ 0141-620 3156.
United Synagogue Council, Queen's Park Syn., Falloch Road. ☎ 0141-632 1743.

SYNAGOGUES
Garnethill Synagogue, 125/7 Hill Street, G3. ☎ 0141-332 4151. (Est. 1875.) *M.* A. Soudry; *Chairman* G. Levin; *H. Sec.* Mrs V. Livingston.
Queen's Park Synagogue, Falloch Road, G42. ☎ 0141-632 2139. *M.* Rabbi M. Fletcher. *Sec.* Mrs G. Fox. *Chairman* H. I. Tankel.
Giffnock and Newlands Synagogue, Maryville Avenue, Giffnock. ☎ 0141-638 6600. *M.* Rabbi P. T. Greenberg, Rabbi A.M. Rubin; *R. Rev.* E. Levy; *Chairman* Dr B. Groden; *Sec.* Mrs G. Gardner.
Glasgow New Synagogue, 147 Ayr Road, Newton Mearns G77 5ND. *M.* Rabbi P. Tobias; *Sec.* P. Kraven. ☎ 0141-639 1838.
Langside Hebrew Congregation, 125 Niddrie Road, G42. ☎ 0141-423 4062. *M. Chairman* J. Levingstone; *H. Sec.* N. Barnes.
Netherlee and Clarkston Hebrew Congregation, Clarkston Road, Clarkston. *M.* Rabbi A. Jesner; *Chairman* M. Livingstone; *Sec.* Mrs B. J. Mann. ☎ 0141-644 3611.
Newton Mearns Synagogue, 14 Larchfield Court, G77 5BH. ☎ 0141-639 4000. *M. Rev.* Philip Copperman; *Chairman* S. Barmack; *Hon. Sec.* H. Hyman. ☎ 0141-639 3399.

EDUCATIONAL AND COMMUNAL ORGANISATIONS
Board of Jewish Education, 28 Calderwood Road, G43 2RU. ☎ 0141-637 7409. *Chairman* A. Gurevitz; *Jt. H. Sec.* L. Osborne, N. Allon.
Calderwood Lodge Jewish Primary School, 28 Calderwood Road, G43 2RU. ☎ 0141-637 5654. H.M. D. Wolfson, B.A.
Glasgow Israel Committee, 222 Fenwick Rd., Giffnock G46 6UE. ☎ 0141-620 2194. *Chairman* K. Davidson.
Glasgow Jewish Continuity and Renewal, 43 Queen Square, G41. *Chairman* Dr D. Shapiro. *Exec. Officer* D. Kaplan. ☎ 0141-423 1080. Fax 0141-422 1899.
Glasgow Kollel. *Dir.* Rabbi M. Bamberger. ☎ 0141-638 6664.
Glasgow Maccabi, May Terrace, Giffnock, G46 6DL. ☎ 0141-638 7655. *Chairman* Mrs D. Minster; *Sec.* Mrs J. Statt.
Israel Scottish Information Service, Jewish Resource Centre. ☎ 0141-620 0940.
Jewish Choral Society. *Co-Chairmen* Mrs J. Tankel; Mrs D. Mandelstam; *H. Sec.* Mrs A. Sakol. ☎ 0141-639 1756.
Jewish Learning Centre, Jewish Resource Centre. Contact Rabbi M. Fletcher. ☎ 0141-620 3156.
Jewish Male Voice Choir. *Chairman* S. Smullen; *Sec.* G. Kitchener. ☎ 0141-638 2982.
Jewish Resource Centre, 222 Fenwick Rd., Giffnock G46 6UE. ☎ 0141-620 2194. *Admin.* Mrs D. Zolkwer.

Jewish Students' Society 6 Dalmeny Ave., Giffnock.
Jewish Youth Forum, *Contact* Lee Freedman. ☎ 0141-638 0903.
Lubavitch Foundation, 8 Orchard Dr, Giffnock. ☎ 0141-638 6116. *Dir.* Rabbi Chaim Jacobs.
Maccabi Youth Centre, May Terrace, Giffnock G46. *Chairman* Mrs D. Minster. ☎ 0141-638 7655. *H. Sec.* G. Landa.
Northern Region Chaplaincy Board. *Chairman* S. Woldman; *H. Sec.* S. Marks. ☎ 0141-639 4497; *Chaplain* Rabbi D. Cohen.
Teenage Centre. (Atid), at Jewish Resource Centre. Contact David Kaplan ☎ 0141-423 1080.
Yeshivah, Giffnock Syn., Maryville Avenue. *Chairman* Dr K. Collins. ☎ 0141-638 2030. *H. M.* Rabbi A.M. Rubin.

WELFARE ORGANISATIONS
Cosgrove Care, 6 St. John's Road, G41. *Chairman* Mrs J. Dover; *Dir.* Mrs L. Goldberg; *H. Sec.* Mrs L. Markson. ☎ 0141-429 2327.
Jewish Housing Association, Barrland Court, Barrland Drive, Giffnock, G46 7QD. *Dir.* Mrs Joan Leifer. ☎ 0141-620 1890. Fax 0141-620 3044.
Jewish Blind Society Centre, May Terrace, Giffnock, G46 6DL. ☎ 0141-620 1800. Fax 0141-620 1088. *Chairman* A. Moms. *Sec.* Mrs C. Blake.
Jewish Care Scotland (founded 1868), May Terrace Giffnock, G46 6DL. ☎ 0141-620 1800. Fax 0141-620 1088. *Chairman* A. Tankel. *Dir.* Mrs E. Woldman.
Jewish Hospital and Sick Visiting Association. ☎ 0141-638 6048. *Chairman* M. Hartley.
Newark Lodge, Jewish Old Age Home for Scotland, 43 Newark Drive. ☎ 0141-423 8941. *Chairman* A. Jacobson; *Dir.* M. Maddox.
Senior Citizens Club, *Chairman* B. Mann, *Sec.* Mrs V. Mann. ☎ 0141-644 3611.

NORTHERN IRELAND

BELFAST (550)
There was a Jewish community in Belfast about the year 1771, but the present community was founded in 1865.
Hebrew Congregation, 49 Somerton Rd. (Est. 1872; Syn. erected at Carlisle Circus, 1904, present building consecrated, 1964.) *President* Mr. R. Appleton; *Chairman* D. Warm; *H. Sec.* Mrs Norma Simon, 42 Glandore Ave., Belfast, BT15 3FD. ☎ 01232 779491; Mrs G. Taylor, 35 Waterloo Park, N. Belfast.
Jewish Community Centre, 49 Somerton Rd. ☎ 01232 777974.
Wizo. *Chairperson* Mrs N. Lantin; *H. Sec.* Mrs N. Simon, Mrs M. Black.
Belfast Jewish Record. *H. Sec.* Mrs N. Simon, 42 Glandore Ave., Belfast BT15 3FD.

ISLE OF MAN (ca. 35)

Hebrew Congregation. Contact: Leonard Simons, 118 Slieau Dhoo, Tromode Park, Douglas, I. of M. ☎ 01624 673525. *Visiting M.* Rev. M. Weisman, M.A. (Oxon.). No regular services.
Cemetery: Consecrated section of the Douglas Cemetery, Glencrutchery Rd.

CHANNEL ISLANDS

JERSEY (120)
A syn. existed in St. Helier, the capital of the island, from 1843 until about 1870. The present com. was founded in 1962.
Jersey Jewish Congregation. The syn. is on the corner of Route des Genets and Petite Route des Mielles in the Parish of St. Brelade. Sabbath service at 10.30 a.m. *President* D. B. Regal; *Sec.* S. J. Regal, 'Armon', rue de la Croix, St. Ouen; *Visiting M.* Rev. M. Weisman, M.A. Nine families of the Jersey Cong. live in Guernsey.

REPUBLIC OF IRELAND (1,300)

Jews lived in Ireland in the Middle Ages, and a Sephardi community was established in Dublin in 1660, four years after the Resettlement in England. In the eighteenth century there was a community also at Cork. The Dublin congregation declined in the reign of George III, and was dissolved in 1791, but was revived in 1822. The community received its largest influx of members at the turn of the century, the immigrants coming from Eastern Europe, Lithuania in particular. There are now some 1,300 Jews in the country. (See Hyman: The Jews of Ireland, 1972, repr. 1996.)
Chief Rabbi: Rabbi Gavin Broder. Office: Herzog House, Zion Rd., Dublin, 6. ☎ 4923751. *Sec.* J. Charry.
Jewish Community Office, Herzog House, Zion Rd., Dublin, 6. ☎ 492-3751. Fax 492-4680. *Gen. Sec.* N. Caine.
Jewish Representative Council of Ireland, Herzog House, Dublin, 6. *Chairman* A. Benson.
General Board of Shechita & Kashrut Commission. (Est. 1915.) Herzog House, Zion Rd., Dublin, 6.
Irish-Jewish Museum. (Est. 1984.) 3-4 Walworth Rd., off Victoria St., Portobello, Dublin 8. ☎ 453-1797, *Curator* R. Siev. Times: May to September: 11am to 3.30pm on Sundays, Tuesdays and Thursdays; October to April: 10.30am to 2.30pm on Sundays only. The Museum was opened by Irish-born Chaim Herzog, late former President of Israel, on 20th June, 1985 and contains memorabilia of the Irish Jewish Community and a former synagogue is on view.
Jewish Board of Guardians. (Est. 1889.) *H. Sec.* D. Stern, 14 Wasdale Grove, Dublin 6. ☎ 490 5139.
Jewish Home of Ireland, Denmark Hill, Leicester Rd., W6. *Admin.* ☎ 497-2004.
Joint Israel Appeal, Herzog House, Zion Rd., Dublin, 6. ☎ 492-2318. *H. Sec.* L. Bloomfield.
Jewish National Fund, Herzog House, Zion Rd., Dublin, 6. ☎ 492-2318. *H. Sec.* A. Schwartzman.

CORK (30)
Hebrew Congregation, 10 South Terrace. (Est. 1880). *Sec.* F. Rosehill.

DUBLIN (1,300)
Chief Rabbi: Rabbi Gavin Broder.

SYNAGOGUES
Dublin Hebrew Congregation, 37 Adelaide Rd. ☎ 661 2408. (Est. 1836. Present syn. opened 1892; enlarged 1925.) *H. Sec.* Dr S. Menton. ☎ 269-4044.
Terenure Hebrew Congregation, Rathfarnham Rd., Terenure, 6. ☎ 490-8037. *H. Sec.* W. Stein.
Synagogue Machzikei Hadass, 77 Terenure Rd. North, 6. (Est. ca. 1890.)☎ 493-8991. *H. Sec.* D. Ross.
Jewish Progressive Congregation, P.O. Box 3059, 6. (Est. 1945.) *H. Sec.* Mrs J. Finkel. ☎ 490-7605.
Talmud Torah, Stratford Schools, Zion Rd., Rathgar 6. ☎ 492-2315. Fax 492-4680. *H. Sec.* Mrs M. Adler.

Cemeteries: Aughavannagh Rd., Dolphin's Barn, 8. ☎ 454-0806. Inq. to caretaker. The old Jewish cemetery at Ballybough (☎ Ballybough 836-9756) may be visited on application to the caretaker. There is a Progressive cemetery at Woodtown, Co. Dublin.

OTHER COUNTRIES

*Denotes the organisation(s) from which further information about the Jewish community in that country can be obtained. For more detailed information about Jewish communities overseas consult **The Jewish Travel Guide** (Vallentine Mitchell). Population figures taken from 'The Jewish communities handbook 1991' (IJA and WJC).

AFGHANISTAN (50)

Jews have lived in Afghanistan since antiquity. Just over 100 years ago they reportedly numbered 40,000. Since 1948 there has been a mass emigration to Israel, and only a few families remain in Kabul and Herat.

ALBANIA

After the recent emigration to Israel very few Albanian Jews remain in the country.

ALGERIA (150)

It is believed that there were Jews in Algeria as early as the fourth century, BCE. The fortunes of the community varied under the Turkish regime, which began in 1519. After the French conquered Algeria the community was reorganised and in 1870 most Jews were granted French citizenship. However, there have been anti-Jewish excesses even in the present century. After Algeria's bitter fight for independence, the Jews, like other French nationals, lost their possessions when they left the country. About 120,000 at independence in 1962, they remain less than 150 today: almost all fled to France.
Communal Centre and Synagogue: 6 Rue Hassena Ahmed, Algiers. ☎ (213-2) 62 85 72.
American Joint Distribution Committee, 11 Ali Boumdemdjel, Algiers. ☎ (213-2) 63 29 49.

ANTIGUA (West Indies)

A few Jewish residents live permanently on the island. Corr.: Mrs. E. Lygum, Weatherills Estate, P.O.B. 62. ☎ (46)1 0710.

ARGENTINA (240,000)

The early Jewish settlers in Argentina were Marranos, who were gradually absorbed in the general population. The present community grew through immigration (beginning in 1862) from Germany, the Balkans, and North Africa. From Eastern Europe immigrants began to arrive in 1889, many of them going to the agricultural settlements est. by the Jewish Colonization Assn. (see p.72). The com. is est. to number 300,000, incl. 60,000 Sephardim, who have their own separate institutions, according to D.A.I.A., the representative org. of Argentine Jews. The Jewish pop. of Greater Buenos Aires is estimated at 220,000. A survey conducted by the Hebrew Univ. of Jerusalem estimates the Jewish pop. at 240,000, of whom 210,000 are Ashkenazim and 30,000 are Sephardim. This source estimates 180,000 Jews live in Gtr. Buenos Aires.

There are nine other major coms. in Parana, Rosario, Cordoba, Bahia Blanca, Posadas, Resistencia, Tucuman, Mendoza and La Plata. There is a small but very active community in Mar del Plata, south of Buenos Aires. Very few Jewish families remain on the former J.C.A. settlements. There are about 100 syns. (80 Orthodox, one Reform, the rest Conservative or Liberal), and a well-organised network of communal and educ. instits. There are communal offices in **Cordoba** at Alvear 254, and in **Rosario** at Paraguay 1152.

BUENOS AIRES
Congreso Judio Latinoamericano, Larrea 744, 1030. ☎ 961-44532. Fax 963-7056.
Representative Organisation of Argentine Jews: D.A.I.A., Pasteur 633, 5th floor.
Amia Central Ashkenazi Community, Pasteur 633.
Central Sephardi Community: E.C.S.A., Larrea 674.
Latin American Rabbinical Seminary (Conservative), Jose Hernandez 1750.
Argentine Zionist Organisation & Jewish Agency (Sochnut), Cangallo 2471.

ARMENIA (500)

Jews have lived in Armenia for many hundreds of years and the various communities were spread around different parts of the country. There was a synagogue in Yerevan, but in the 1930s it was destroyed. Nowadays, nearly all the Armenian Jews live in Yerevan, with only a few families living in Vanadzor (Kirovakan) and Gjumri (Leninakan), while others are scattered in other small towns and villages. When 'perestroyka' was introduced in 1989, the Jewish community organised itself and in 1991 was registered as a non-formal organisation. Perestroyka opened the doors, so that a large number of the population emigrated to Israel. In 1991 a Jewish Sunday school was opened both for children and adults. In 1992 the Israeli embassy in Moscow financed the school. Over 60 per cent of the population is over 60 years of age and there are about 40 children below the age of 16 years.
President: Mr Willi Weiner, ☎ (7-8852) 525882; *Dir. of Education:* Dr George Fajvush ☎ (7-8852) 735852; *Rabbi:* Gersh Bourstein, ☎ (7-8852) 271115.

ARUBA (50)

Beth Israel Synagogue. Dedicated in 1962, this syn. serves the needs of the com. in this island in the Antilles in the Caribbean, of some 35 Jewish families. Jews from Curaçao settled in Aruba early in the nineteenth century, but did not stay there long, and the present com. dates from 1924.

AUSTRALIA (92,000)

The earliest org. of Jews in Australia was in 1817 when 20 Jews in New South Wales formed a burial society. In 1828 a congregation was formed in Sydney and the first specially erected syn. was opened in 1844. The first Jewish service was held in Melbourne in 1839, four years after the beginning of the colonisation on the banks of the River Yarra, and a syn. was opened in 1847. Congregations were est. at Ballarat (1853) and Geelong (1854). In South Australia, a permanent congregation was formed in Adelaide in 1848. A congregation in Brisbane was est. in 1865. In Western Australia the first congregation (now ended) was formed at Fremantle in 1887, and the present Perth congregation est. in 1892, with Kalgoorlie in 1895. In Tasmania a syn. was opened in Hobart in 1845 and another at Launceston in 1846. Organised Jewish coms. were est. in other States a few years later.

In Australia's public life Jews have played a distinguished part, many having risen to high office in the Federal and State Parliaments or on the Judicial bench. Two Governors-General of Australia have been Jews, Sir Zelman Cowen and the late Sir Isaac Isaacs. Sir John Monash, the Commander of the Australian Expeditionary Forces in the First World War, was a Jew. The Executive Council of Australian Jewry represents the central Jewish organisations in each State.

The Australian census has an optional question on religious affiliation. In 1981, 62,127 people declared themselves Jews by religion. If a proportionate number of 'no religion/religion not stated' replies are regarded as Jewish, the number of Jews rises to 79,345. Recent demographic res. indicated that there are probably about 92,000 people in Australia who are religiously or ethnically Jewish. The main Jewish coms. are in Melbourne (50,000); Sydney (35,000); Perth (4,200); Brisbane (1,500); Adelaide (1,250); The Gold Coast, Queensland (1,000); Canberra (500); Hobart (100).

AUSTRALIA 137

MAIN JEWISH ORGANISATIONS
Executive Council of Australian Jewry, GPO Box 5402 CC, Melbourne, Victoria, 3001. *President* I. Leibler. ☎ 61-3-98288570. Fax: 61-3-98288584.
***N.S.W. Jewish Board of Deputies**, 146 Darlinghurst Rd., Darlinghurst, N.S.W., 2010. ☎ 2-360-1600. Fax: 2-331-4712. *Exec. Dir.* Mrs M. Gutman.
Jewish Community Council of Victoria, 306 Hawthorn Rd., South Caulfield, Victoria 3162. *President* Mr. Geoff Green; *Communal Affairs Director* Mrs. Helen Brustman. ☎ 3-92725566.
Asia Pacific Jewish Association, GPO Box 5402 CC, Melbourne, Victoria 3001. ☎ 3- 9828-8570. Fax: 3-9828-8584. Email: aija@ozemail.com.au *Chairman* Dr. E. Franklin. (See p.67).
Jewish National Fund of Australia, Beth Weizmann, 308 Hawthorn Road, Caulfield, Victoria, 3162. ☎ 3-92725566. Fax: 3-92725570. *President* K. Rathner.
Jewish Museum of Australia, 26 Alma Rd., St. Kilda, Victoria 3182. ☎ (03) 9534 0083.
Zionist Federation of Australia, Beth Weizmann, 308 Hawthorn Road, Caulfield, Victoria, 3162. ☎ 3-9272-5644. Fax: 3-9272-5640. *President* Mrs A. Zablud.
Association of Rabbis & Ministers of Australia and N.Z., c/o 12 Charnwood Grove, St. Kilda, Victoria, 3182. ☎ 3-9537-1433. Fax: 3-9525-3759. *President* Rabbi P. Heilbrunn.
Australian Federation of Sephardim, 40-42 Fletcher St., Bondi Junction, N.S.W., 2022. ☎ 2-389-3355. Fax: 2-369-2143. *President:* A. Gubbay.
Australian Union for Progressive Judaism, 78-82 Alma Rd., St. Kilda., Victoria, 3182. ☎ 3-9510-1488. Fax: 3-9521-1229.
Federation of Australian Jewish Welfare Societies, 146 Darlinghurst Rd., Darlinghurst, N.S.W., 2010. ☎ 2-331-5184. Fax: 2-360-5574. *President* N. Whitmont.
National Council of Jewish Women of Australia, 111-113 Queen St., Woollahra, N.S.W. 2025. ☎ 2-363-0257. Fax: 2-362-4092.
Australian Federation of Wizo, 308 Hawthorn Rd., Caulfield, Victoria 3162. ☎ 3-9272-5599. Fax: 3-9272-5540.
B'nai B'rith District 21of Australia, N.Z., PO Box 443, Kay's Cross, N.S.W. 2011. ☎ 2-556-1079. Fax: 2-597-2755. *President* H. Mueller.
Australasian Union of Jewish Students, Beth Weizmann, 308 Hawthorn Road, Caulfield, Victoria, 3161. ☎ 3-9272-5566. Fax: 3-9272-5560; Shalom College, PO Box 1, Kennington, N.S.W. 2033. ☎ 2-931-9660. Fax: 2-663-4868.

MAIN SYNAGOGUES AND COMMUNAL CENTRES
SYDNEY
New South Wales Jewish Board of Deputies, 146 Darlinghurst Rd, Darlinghurst, NSW 2010. ☎2-9360 1600. Fax 2-9331 4712.
AJWS-Jewish Community Services, Level 3, Leyland House, 332-342 Oxford St, Bondi Junction, NSW 2022. ☎2-9369 1400. Fax 2-9369 5455.
The Great Synagogue (Ashk. Orth.), Elizabeth St. (Office: 166 Castlereagh St.), NSW 2000. ☎2-267 2477. Fax 2-264 8871.
Central Synagogue (Orth.), 15 Bon Accord Ave, Bondi Junction, NSW 2022 (Temporary: 19 Hollywood Ave., Bondi Junction, NSW 2022). ☎2-9389 5622. Fax 2-9389 5418.
North Shore Synagogue (Orth.), 15 Treatts Rd, Lindfield, NSW 2070. ☎2-416 3710. Fax 2-9416 7659.
North Shore Temple Emanuel (Lib.), 28 Chatswood Ave., Chatswood, NSW 2067. ☎2-9419 7011. Fax 2-9413 1474.
Sephardi Synagogue (Orth.), 40-42 Fletcher St, Bondi Junction, NSW 2025. ☎2-9389 3355. Fax 2-9365 3856.

Temple Emanuel (Lib.), 7 Ocean St, Woollahra, NSW 2025. ☎2-9328 7833. Fax 2-9327 8715.
Yeshiva Synagogue (Orth.), 36 Flood St, Bondi NSW 2026. ☎2-9387 3822. Fax 2-9389 7652.

MELBOURNE
Melbourne Hebrew Congregation (Ashk. Orth.), One Toorak Rd., South Yarra, Victoria 3141. ☎ 3-9866-2255.
St. Kilda Hebrew Congregation, 12 Charnwood Gr., St. Kilda, Victoria 3182. ☎ 3-9537-1433.
Temple Beth Israel (Lib.), 76 Alma Rd., St. Kilda, Victoria 3182. ☎ 3-9510-1488.
Beth Weizmann, 308 Hawthorn Rd, Caulfield, Victoria 3182. ☎ 3-9272-5566.
Caulfield Hebrew Congregation, 572 Inkerman Rd., Caulfield, Victoria 3161. ☎ 3-9525-9492.

PERTH
Perth Hebrew Congregation, Cnr. Plantation St. and Freedman Rd., Menora, W.A. 6050. ☎ 9-271-0539.
Temple David Congregation (Lib.), 34 Clifton Crescent, Mt. Lawley, 6050. ☎ 9-271-1458.
Jewish Centre, 61, Woodrow Ave., Mt. Yokine, W.A. 6060. ☎ 9-276-8572.

ADELAIDE
Hebrew Congregation, Synagogue Pl., 13 Flemington St., Glenside, S.A. 5065. ☎ 8-338-2922.
South Australian Liberal Jewish Congregation, 41 Hackney Rd., S.A. 5069. ☎ 8-362-8281.
Jewish Community Council, 13 Flemington St. *President* Norman Schueler.

BRISBANE
Brisbane Hebrew Congregation (Orth.), 98 Margaret St., Brisbane, Qld. 4000. ☎ 7-3229-3412.
Temple Shalom (Lib.), 15 Koolatah St., Camp Hill, Qld. 4152. ☎ 7-398-8843.

CANBERRA
National Jewish War Memorial (A.C.T. Jewish Community Centre), Canberra Ave. and National Circuit, Forest, P.O. Box 3105, A.C.T. 2603. ☎ 6-295-1052.

AUSTRIA (12,000)

The story of Austrian Jewry is punctuated by accounts of expulsion and re-immigration, of persecution on false accusations of ritual murder and other pretexts and recovery. After the 1848 Revolution the Jews gained equality, and their economic and cultural importance grew. But antisemitism had not ended; it culminated in the violence of the years preceding the Second World War. Austria's Jewish population in 1934 was 191,481 (with 176,034 in Vienna), the number today is about 12,000, almost all of them in Vienna. Other coms. are in Graz, Innsbruck, Linz and Salzburg.

*Jewish Community Centre, Israelitische Kultusgemeinde, Seitenstettengasse 4, 1010 Vienna. ☎ 53 1040. Fax: 533 1577. *President* Paul Grosz; *Dir.* Dr. A. Hodik.
Chief Syns. Stadttempel, Seitenstettengasse 4, (Trad.); Machsike Hadass, D. Friedmann-Pl.1, 1010, (Orth.); Khal Israel, Tempelgasse 3, 1010. (Orth.); Ohel Moshe, Lilienbrunnpasse 19, 1020 (Orth.); Misrachi, Judenplatz 8, 1010.
Chief Rabbi: Rabbi Paul Chaim Eisenberg. ☎ 53 104-17.

Jewish Welcome Service, A-1010 Vienna, Stephansplatz 10. ☎ 533 88 91. Fax: 533-8891. *Dir.* Dr. L. Zelman.

BAHAMAS (200)

Freeport Hebrew Congregation. 30 families. Friday night services held most weeks of the year.
Luis De Torres Synagogue, East Sunrise Highway, P.O. Box F-41761, Freeport. ☎ (242) 373 2008. *President and Marriage Officer* Geoff Hurst, P.O. Box F-42515, Freeport; ☎ (242) 373-4025. Fax (242) 373-2130. Email: hurst@gbonline.hi.net; *Sec.-Tr.* Edi Turner, P.O. Box F-42515 Freeport.

BARBADOS (55)

A Jewish com. was formed in Barbados by refugees from Brazil after its reconquest by the Portuguese about the year 1650. In 1802 by Local Govt. Act, all political disabilities of the Jews were removed, but were not confirmed by Westminster until 1820. Barbados was the first British possession to grant full political emancipation to its Jews; Gt. Britain herself doing so more than 50 years later. With the economic decline of the West Indies the fortunes of their Jewish inhabitants also declined. In 1929, only one practising Jew remained, but in 1932 a gp. of Jews settled on the island from Europe. In December, 1987, the Old Synagogue in Bridgetown, one of the two oldest houses of worship in the Western Hemisphere (the other is in Curaçao), reopened for services for the first time in nearly 60 years, following restoration with the island community's support. An appeal fund was launched with Sir Hugh Springer, the Governor-General, as patron. There is a Jewish cemetery by the syn. In 1985, the Barbadian Govt. vested the syn. in the Barbadian Nat. Trust.
*Jewish Community Council, P.O.B. 256, Bridgetown. *President* Benny Gilbert.

BELGIUM (30,000)

Jews have lived in Belgium since Roman times. After the fall of Napoleon the Belgian provinces were annexed by Holland. In 1816 a decree by the Dutch King ordered the erection of two syns. in Maastricht and Brussels. But Belgian Jews had to wait until 1830, when Belgium became independent, to see their status formally recognised. The Constitution accorded freedom of religion in 1831. Before the Second World War the Jewish population was 80,000. Today there are flourishing communities in Antwerp, Brussels, Ostend, Liège, Charleroi and Waterloo totalling (together with the smaller communities) about 30,000 Jews.

ANTWERP

Synagogues and rel. orgs.: Shomre Hadass (Israelitische Gemeente), Terlistr. ☎ 31-41-47. Rabbi D. Lieberman. Syns.: Bouwmeesterstr., Romi Goldmuntz, Van den Vesplei, etc.
Machsike Hadass (Orth.) Jacob Jacobstr. 22. *Rab.* Rabbi Ch. Kreiswirth. Main syn.: Oostenstr. 42-44.
Sephardi Syn.: Hovenierstr. 31. Rabbi A. Mugrabi.
Central Jewish Welfare Organisation, Jacob Jacobsstr. 2. ☎ 232 3890.
Home for the Aged and Nursing Home, Marialei 6-8.
Residentie Apfelbaum-Laub., Marialei 2-4. ☎ 218.9399.
Holiday camp, Villa Altol, Coxyde-on-Sea, Damesweg 10. ☎ 058 512661.
Other orgs.: Zionist Fed. Pelikaanstr. 108; Mizrachi, Isabellalei 65; Romi Goldmuntz Centre, Nervierstr. 12; B'nai B'rith–Nervierstr 12AAT 14.

BRUSSELS

*Comité de Coordination des Organisations Juives de Belgique (C.C.O.J.B.). Av.

Ducpétiaux 68, 1060 Brussels. ☎ 537 1691.
Consistoire Central Israélite de Belgique, 2 rue Joseph Dupont, 1000 Brussels. ☎ 02 512 21 90.
Cercle Ben-Gurion, 89 Chausée de Vleurgat, 1050 Brussels.
Centre Communautaire Laic Juif, 52 Rue Hotel des Monnaies, 1060 Brussels.
Zionist Offices, 66-68 Avenue Ducpétiaux, 1060 Brussels.
Synagogues: 32 rue de la Régence; 67a rue de la Clinique; 73 rue de Thy; 126 rue Rogier; 11 Ave. Messidor; 47 rue Pavillon (Sephardi); Brussels airport, Zaventem.

BERMUDA (125)

Jewish Community of Bermuda, P.O. Box HM 1793, Hamilton, HMHX Bermuda. Contact Diana Lynn, 17 Biological Lane, Ferry Reach, GE01, Bermuda. ☎ 441-297 2267. Fax 809 297 8143. Email dlynn@bbsr.edu
The small community drawn from a dozen countries has never had a synagogue or communal building. A lay leader conducts a Friday service each month at the Unity Foundation, 75 Reid Street, Hamilton; a visiting Rabbi conducts High Holy day services and children's classes are held regularly.

BOLIVIA (640)

Although there have been Jews in Latin America for many centuries, they are comparative newcomers to Bolivia, which received its first Jewish immigrants only in 1905. They remained a mere handful until the 1920s, when some Russian Jews made their way to the country. After 1935, German Jewish refugees, began to arrived in Bolivia. Also from Rumania and mostly from Poland. Today some 640 Jews live there, mostly in the capital of La Paz (about 430), Cochambamba (120) and Santa Cruz (85), Tarija and other cities (5).

COCHABAMBA
Syn.: Calle Junin y Calle Colombia, Casilla 349.
Asociación Israelita de Cochabamba, P.O.B. 349, Calle Valdivieso. *President:* René Jacobowitz.

LA PAZ
Syns.: Circulo Israelita de Bolivia, Casilla 1545, Calle Landaeta 346, P.O.B. 1545. Services Sat. morn. only. *President* Rene Doerfler Elias.
Comunidad Israelita Synagogue, Calle Canada Stronguest 1846, P.O.B. 2198, is affiliated to the Circulo. Fri. evening services are held. There is a Jewish sch. at this address. Circulo Israelita, P.O.B. 1545 is the representative body of Bolivian Jewry. All La Paz organisations are affiliated to it.
Two Homes for Aged: Calle Rosendo Gutierrez 307, and Calle Diaz Romero 1765.
Israel Tourist Information Office: Centro Shalom, Calle Canada Stronguest 1846, La Paz Country Club, Quinta J.K.G. Obrajes. Calle 1, esquina calle Hector Ormachea Castilla 1545, La Paz.

SANTA CRUZ
Centro Cruceño P.O.B. 469, WIZO, Casilla 3409. *President* Sra Guicha Schwartz.

BOSNIA HERCEGOVINA (1,100)
Sarajevo Jewish Community, Dobrovoljacka 83. ☎ 22 023. Fax.: 3871 271851.

BRAZIL (250,000)
The early history of Brazilian Jewry was affected by the struggles for power between the Portuguese and Dutch. The Inquisition, revived in Brazil, increased the number of Marrano Jews. The Dutch, after their victory in 1624, granted full religious freedom to the Jews, but 30 years afterwards the Portuguese reconquered the land and reintroduced the Inquisition. In 1822 Brazil declared its independence of Portugal and liberty of worship was proclaimed. It is believed that about 250,000

Jews are living in Brazil, distributed as follows: Sao Paulo State, 90,000; Rio de Janeiro State, 80,000; Rio Grande do Sul (Porto Alegre) 25,000; Parana State (Curitiba) 2,408; Minas Gerais State (Bel Horizonte) 1,656; Pernambuco State (Recife) 1,276.

RIO DE JANEIRO
*Federacão Israelita, R. Buenos Aires 68, AN15.
Fundo Communitario, R. Buenos Aires 68, AN15.
Orthodox Rabbinate, R. Pompeu Loureiro No.40. ☎/Fax 2360249.
Chevre Kedishe, Rua Barao de Iguatemi 306 (Orthodox).
Congrecão Beth El, Rua Barata Ribeiro 489 (Sephardi).
Associacão Religiosa Israelita, Rua Gen. Severiano 170 (Liberal).
Synagogues: Agudat Israel, Rua Nascimento Silva, 109, Beth Aron, Rua Gado Coutinho, 63, Kehilat Yaacov Copacabana, Rua Capelao Alvares da Silva 15; Templo Uniao Israel, Rua Jose Higino, 375-381.
Associacão Feminina Israelita, Av. Almte. Barroso, 6/14°.
Organizacão Sionista Unificada, Rua Decio Vilares, 258.
Museu Judaico, Rua Mexico, 90/1° andar-Castelo.

SAO PAULO
Federacao Israelita do Estado de São Paulo, Av. Paulista 726, 2nd floor. ☎ 288 6411.
Synggogues and religious centres: Centro Judaico Religioso de Sao Paulo (Orthodox). ☎ 220 5642; Beit Chabad, Rua Chabad 56/60; Communidade Israelita Sefaradi, Rua da Abolicao 457; Congregacão Israelita Paulista, "Einheitsgemeinde" (Liberal), Rua Antonico Carlos 653.
Zionist Offices, Rua Correa Mello 75.

BULGARIA (6,500)
Bulgarian Jewry dates from the second century C.E. Before the Second World War there were 50,000 Jews in Bulgaria. From 1948-49 to about 1954/55, 45,000 emigrated to Israel. Today the number is about 6,500 of whom about 3,000 live in Sofia.
Central Jewish Religious Council and Synagogue, 16 Exarch Joseph St., Sofia 1000. ☎ 359-2/831-273. *President* Joseph Levy.
Organization of the Jews in Bulgaria "Shalom", 50 Al. Stambolijski St., Sofia 130. ☎/Fax: 359-2/870-163. *President* Eddy Schwartz. Publishes newspaper "Evrejski Vesti" and research compendium "Annual". Jewish museum in the Synagogue: Sofia, 16 Exarch Joseph St. Joseph Caro permanent exhibition in the city Museum and a memorial stone in the town of Nikopol. Publishing house "Shalom", Jewish Sunday School, Jewish Resource Centre, Memorial stone dedicated to the Salvation of the Bulgarian Jews near the Parliament. B'nai Brith, Maccabi and other Jewish organizations.

BURMA (Myanmar)
About 25 Burmese Jews live in Rangoon (Yangon), the capital.
Musmeah Yeshua Synagogue (est. 1896), 85 26th St., P.O. Box 45, Rangoon. Man. Tr. J. Samuels. ☎ 951-75062.
Israel Embassy, 49 Pyay Rd. ☎ 951 22290/01. Fax: 951-22463.

BYELORUS
GOMMEL
Syn.: 13 Sennaya St.
Jewish Cultural Society, 1A Krasnoarmeyska St., 24600. *Chairman* V. F. Iofedov.

MINSK
Syn.: 22 Kropotkin St. ☎ (017-2) 55-82-70.

ORSHA
Syn.: Nogrin St.

RECHITSA
Syn.: 120 Lunacharsky St.
There are also Jewish communities in Bobruisk, Mozyr, Pinsk, Brest, Grodno, Vitebsk and Borisov.

CANADA (356,300)

Jews were prohibited by law from living in Canada so long as it remained a French possession. Nevertheless, Jews from Bordeaux David Gradis, a wealthy merchant and shipowner, and his son Abraham Gradis, in particular had a large share in the commercial development of the colony.

Jews played some part in the British occupation of Canada. Half a dozen Jewish officers, including Aaron Hart, whose descendants played important roles in Jewish and Canadian life for several generations, were suppliers to the expeditionary force which occupied Quebec.

A number of Jews settled at an early date in Montreal, where the Spanish and Portuguese Synagogue, Shearith Israel (still flourishing), was established in the 1770s and a cong. of "German, Polish and English" Jews was granted a charter in 1846. A burial society was formed in Toronto in 1849. Montreal Jews were also among the fur traders in the Indian territories. In the 19th century, Jewish immigrants arrived in Canada in some numbers, and in 1832–a quarter of a century earlier than in Britain the Lower Canada Jews received full civil rights.

A fresh era in the history of Canadian Jewry opened at the close of the century, when emigration on a large scale from Eastern Europe began. Montreal, Toronto, and to a lesser degree, Winnipeg, became the seats of Jewish coms. of some importance.

On the history of the Jews in Canada generally, see A. D. Hart, The Jew in Canada, 1926; L. Rosenberg, Canada's Jews, 1939, and B. G. Sack, The History of the Jews in Canada, 1945. The early colonial period in North America is covered in Sheldon and Judith Godfrey, Search out the land, 1995.

NATIONAL INSTITUTIONS
*Canadian Jewish Congress. (Est. 1919, reorganised 1934.)
National Office: 1590 Docteur Penfield Avenue Montreal, Quebec H3G 1C5. ☎ (514) 931-7531. Fax: 931-0548. Website: http://www.cjc.ca. *Nat. President* Goldie Hershon; *Nat. Exec. Dir.* Jack Silverstone.
Atlantic Region: Lord Nelson Hotel, 1515 South Park St., Suite 305, Halifax, Nova Scotia B3J 2L2. ☎ (902) 422-7491. Fax: 425-3722. *Exec. Dir.* Jon Goldberg.
Quebec Region: 1590 Docteur Penfield Ave., Montreal, H3G 1C5. ☎ (514) 931 7531. Fax: 931-3281. *Exec. Dir.* Jack Jedwab.
Ontario Region: 4600 Bathurst St., Willowdale, M2R 3V2. ☎ (416) 635 2883. Fax: 635-1408. *Exec. Dir.* Manuel Prutschi.
National Capital District: Ottawa Jewish Community Council, 151 Chapel Street, Ontario K1N 7Y2. ☎ (613) 789 7306. Fax: 789-4593. *Exec. Dir.*
National Capital Office: Ottawa Jewish Community Council, 151 Chapel Street, Ottawa, Ontario K1N 7Y2. ☎ (613) 789 5253. Fax: 789-8447. *Dir.* Eric Vernon.
Manitoba Region: Winnipeg Jewish Community Council, 370 Hargrave St., Winnipeg, R3B 2K1. ☎ (204) 943-0406. Fax: 956-0609. *Exec. Dir.* Robert Freedman.

Alberta Region (Calgary): Calgary Jewish Community Council, 1607, 90th Ave. S.W., Calgary, T2V 4V7. ☎ (403) 253-8600. Fax: 253-7915. *Exec. Dir.* Joel Miller.
Alberta Region (Edmonton): Jewish Federation of Edmonton, 7200, 156th Street, Edmonton, T5R 1X3. ☎ (403) 487 5120. Fax: 481-1854. *Exec. Dir.* Lesley Jacobson.
Saskatchewan Region (Regina): c/o 4715 McTavish St., Regina, S4S 6H2. ☎ (306) 569-8166. Fax: (306) 569-8166.
Saskatchewan Region (Saskatoon), c/o 715 McKinnon Ave, S7H 2G2. ☎ (306) 343-7023. Fax (306) 343-1244.
Pacific Region: 950 West 41st Ave., Vancouver V5Z 2N7. ☎ (604) 257-5101. Fax: 257-5131. *Exec. Dir.* Erwin Nest.
Canada-Israel Committee, 130 Slater St., Suite 300, Ottawa K1P 6E2. *Exec. Dir.* Rob Ritter. ☎ (613) 234 8271. Ontario Office: 2221 Yonge St. #502, Toronto M4S 2B4. ☎ (416) 489 8889.
Canadian Association for Labour Israel. (Est. 1939) 7005 Kildare Rd., #14 Côte St. Luc, Quebec H4W 1C1.
Canadian Jewish Historical Society, 7489 Briar Rd., Côte St. Luc, Quebec, H4W 1K9. ☎ (514) 848 2066. *President.* Dr I. Robinson.
Canadian ORT, 3101 Bathurst St #604, Toronto, Ontario M6A 2A6.
Emunah Women of Canada. Nat. *President* Mrs. M. Novick, 5253 Decarie Blvd., #110, Montreal H3W 3C3. ☎ (514) 4485 2397.
Hadassah-Wizo of Canada, 1310 Greene Av. #650, Montreal H3Z 2B8. (Est. 1917.) Exec. V. *President* Mrs. L. Frank. Chapters: 220, in most Jewish centres. Toronto office: 638A Sheppard Ave W, #209, M3H 2S1. ☎(416) 630 8373.
Jewish Immigrant Aid Services of Canada. (Est. 1919.) 4600 Bathurst St., Willowdale, Ont., M2R 3VR. *Exec. Dir.* ☎ (416) 630 9051.
Jewish National Fund. 1980 Sherbrooke St. W., Montreal, H3H 1E8. ☎ (514) 934 0313.
Labour Zionist Movement (Est. 1939), 272 Codsell Ave., Downsview, Ont. M3H 3X2.
Mizrachi Organization of Canada. Nat. *Exec. Dir.* Rabbi M. Gopin, 159 Almore Ave., Downsview, Ont. M3H 2H9. ☎ (416) 630 7575.
National Council of Jewish Women of Canada, 1588 Main St., #118, Winnipeg, Manitoba R2V 1Y3. ☎ (204) 339 9700.
Canadian Zionist Federation. (Est. 1967.) 5250 Decarie Blvd., #550, Montreal, H3X 2H9. ☎ (514) 486 9526.
United Israel Appeal. *Exec. V. President* S. Ain, 4600 Bathurst St., Willowdale, Ont. M2R 3V3. ☎ (416) 636 7655. Fax (416) 635-5806.

CAYMAN ISLANDS (40)
There are approx. 40 Jewish residents in the 3 Cayman Islands, nearly all living on Grand Cayman. They are joined by about 30 others who are regular visitors. Services in private homes. *Contact:* Harvey De Souza, P.O. Box 72, Grand Cayman, Cayman Islands, British West Indies.

CHILE (25,000)
The number of Jews in Chile is about 25,000. The great majority live in the Santiago area. Communities also in Arica, Chillan, Chuquicamata, Concepción, Iquique, La Serena, Puerto Montt, Punta Arenas, Rancagua, San Fernando, Santa Cruz, Temuco, Valdivia, Vina del Mar/Valparaiso.

SANTIAGO
*Comité Representativo de las Entidades Judias de Chile (CREJ),** Miguel Claro 196. ☎ 235 8669. Fax 235 0754.
Comunidad Israelita de Santiago, Tarapaca 870. (Ashkenazi). ☎ 633 1436. Fax 638 2076.
Comunidad Israelita de Santiago Congregacion Jafetz Jayim (Orthodox) Miguel Claro 196. ☎ 2745389.

Comunidad Israelita Sefaradi de Chile, R. Lyon 812. ☎ 209 8086. Fax 204 7382.
Sociedad Cultural, Bne Jisroel, Mar Jónico 8860, Vitacura. ☎/Fax 201 1623 (German).
MAZsE, (Hungarian) Pedro Bannen 0166. ☎ 2742536.
B'nai Brith, Ricardo Lyon 1933. ☎274 2006. Fax 225 2039.
Zionist Federation Offices, Rafael Cañas 246. ☎251 8821. Fax 251 0961.
Estadio Israelita Maccabi, Club, Las Condes 8361. ☎ 235 9096. Fax 251 0105.
Wizo Chile, M. Montt 207. ☎ 235 9096. Fax 251 105.

CHINA (50)

In recent years, Jewish tourists from a number of countries, including Britain and the U.S., have visited the ancient city of Kaifeng, 300 miles south of Peking, and met people who claim descent from a sizeable com. which lived there for centuries and dispersed in the 19th century. Some experts believe the Kaifeng Jews to have originated from Persia or Yemen. Few are left of the coms. formed by other immigrants from Asia at the end of the 19th century and by the Russian and German refugees of the First and Second World Wars.

COLOMBIA (7,000)

The Jewish population is about 7,000 with the majority living in Bogota. There are also coms. in Barranquilla, Cali and Medellin.
 *Centro Comunitario Israelita de Bogotá, Carrera 29 126-31, Apartado 12372 Bogotá. ☎ 274 9069.

COMMONWEALTH OF INDEPENDENT STATES (ie former U.S.S.R)

Before World War I, Russian Jewry was the largest Jewish community in the world. For centuries, until the Revolution of 1917, the Jews were cruelly persecuted under the antisemitic policy of the Tsars. The subsequent Soviet regime virtually destroyed the former religious life and organisation of the Jewish communities. According to the official Soviet 1989 census the Jewish population was 1,449,000 but recent mass emigration will have reduced that total. The break up of the Soviet Union following August 1991 is reflected in the new entries under the separate republics, e.g. Byelorus, Latvia, Moldova, Ukraine, etc. Population figures are difficult to estimate but some 400,000 Jews have left the country since 1989.

RUSSIA (1,450,000) (Russian Federation)

MOSCOW
Synagogues: Central ul. Archipova 8; Marina Roshcha, 2nd Vysheslavtsev per.5-A.

ST. PETERSBURG
Synagogue: 2 Lermontovsky Prospekt. ☎ 216-11-53.
Jewish Association 'LEA', Ryleeva 29-31, 191123. ☎ 812-2756104. Fax: 812-2756103.
Jewish Tourist and Research Center HA-IR), Stachek 212-46, 198262. ☎ (812) 184 12 48. Fax (812) 310 61 48.
Other centres of Jewish population include those of Astrakhan, Berdichev, Beregovo, Birobidjan, Irkutsk, Krasnoyarsk, Kuybyshev, Kursk, Malakhavka, Nalchik, Novosibirsk, Ordzhonikidze, Penza Perm, Rostov Saratov, Sverdlovsk, Tula.

COSTA RICA (2,500)

Most of the Jewish population of 2,500 live in San José, the capital, where there are a synagogue and a Jewish primary & secondary school. There is also a country club.

*Centro Israelita Sionista de Costa Rica, Calle 22 y 24. P.O.B. 1473, 1000 San José, Costa Rica. ☎ 233-9222. Fax: 223-5801. *President* J. Kierszenson;. *Sec.* F.A. Cordero.

CROATIA (2,500)

(Former constituent republic of Yugoslavia)
There are nine Jewish coms. in Croatia with a total Jewish population of 2,500 affiliated members.

ZAGREB
Jewish Com. and Synagogue. *President* Prof. Dr. Ognjen Kraus; *Sec. Gen.* Dunja Špraje; Palmotićeva St. 16., P.O.B. 986; ☎ 434 619; 425 517. Fax: 434 638.
The Com. Centre was rebuilt in 1992 after being seriously damaged in an explosion. Services are held on Friday eves and holy days. It houses a Jewish kindergarten, Judaica and Hebraica Library, art gallery, auditorium with daily progammes and other facilities. Here are the headquarters of the Fed. of Jewish Coms. in Croatia, Maccabi Sports Club, Jewish Ladies Assn., the Cultural Society and Union of Jewish Students in Croatia.
The com. publishes an occasional newspaper Bilten and a youth magazine Motek.
There is an impressive monument to Jewish victims of Holocaust in the Jewish cemetery of Mirogoj and a monument to Jewish soliders fallen in the First World War.
There is a plaque in Praska St. 7 on the site of the pre-war Central Syn. of Zagreb. Before 1941 the com. numbered over 12,000 Jews. Today there are 1,500 members.
Lavoslav Shwarz Old People's Home. *President* Dr Branko Breyer; *Man.* Paula Novak, Bukovacka c. 55; ☎ 210 026; 219 922.

DUBROVNIK
Jewish Com. and Syn., Zudioska St. 3 (Jewish Street).
This is the second oldest syn. in Europe, dating back to the 14th century damaged in the 1991-2 war. There are 47 Jews in the city and services are held on Jewish holidays.

OSIJEK
Jewish Com. and Syn. *President* Ing. Darko Fisher; Braće Radića St. 13; ☎ 24 926.
There are 150 Jews in the city and the com. is quite active. It suffered some damage during the 1991-92 war.

RIJEKA
Jewish Com. and Syn.: *President* Josip Engel; *V. Presidents* Dr. Josip Musafia; Ivana Filipovića St. 9; P.O.B. 65. ☎ 425 156.
There are 80 Jews in Rijeka. Services are held on Jewish holidays.

SPLIT
Jewish Com. and Syn.: *President* Eduard Tauber, Zidovski prolaz 1 (Jewish Passage). ☎ 45 672.
There are 200 Jews in Split and the com. is very active one with daily meetings in the com. The syn. is over 350 years old and services are held on Jewish holidays.
There is an impressive cemetery dating back to the 16th century.

There are smaller Jewish coms. in Cakovec, Virovitica, Slavonski Brod and Daruvar. In many towns in north Croatia there are old Jewish cemeteries and former syn. buildings.

CUBA (1,000)

Marranos from Spain settled in Cuba in the sixteenth century, but a real immigration of Jews did not start until the end of the nineteenth century. The majority of the 1,000 Jews live in Havana.
*Comission Coordinadora de las Sociedades Hebreas de Cuba, Calle Bel Vedado, Havana. ☎ 32-8953.

CURAÇAO (450)

A Sephardi Jewish settlement was est. in 1651, making it one of the oldest coms. in the New World. The Mikve Israel-Emanuel Syn. building, which dates from 1732, is the oldest in continuous use in the western Hemisphere; there is a small Jewish museum in the synagogue compound. About 450 Jews live in Curaçao. The cemetery (Bet Hayim) at Blenheim (est. 1659) is the oldest in the Americas.
Synagogues: Sephardi-Mikve Israel-Emanuel, Hanchi di Snoa 29, P.O. Box 322. ☎ 4611067. Fax 4654141. *M.*
Ashkenazi: Shaarei Tsedek, Leliweg 1A, P.O. Box 498. ☎ 375738. *M.* Rabbi R. Poupko.
Israel Consulate: Dr P. Ackerman, Blauwduiffweg 5. ☎ 365068. Fax 370707.

CYPRUS (50)

At the beginning of the present era and earlier, Cyprus was an important and large Jewish centre. An unsuccessful revolt against the Romans in 117, however, was followed by a ruthless suppression and the end of the great period of Jewish history in Cyprus. A new period of prosperity and immigration started in the 12th century but came to an end with the coming of the Genoese and later the Venetians as the island's rulers. By 1560 only 25 families remained in Famagusta, mostly physicians. Attempts at agricultural settlement in the 19th century were unsuccessful. The Jewish population now numbers about 50. The cemetery is at Larnaca.
Jewish Committee has offices in Nicosia c/o S. Ammar, P.O. Box 3807 Nicosia. ☎ 441085.

CZECH REPUBLIC

The break up of Czechoslovakia is reflected by the separate entries here for the Czech lands and for Slovakia on p.180. Records show that Jews were settled in Bohemia in the 11th century and in Moravia as early as the 9th cent. There were flourishing Jewish coms. in the Middle Ages. The Jewish pop. of Czechoslovakia in 1930 was 356,830. The coms. were decimated in the Holocaust.
Today the Jewish population of the Czech Republic is est. at 10,000. Of these 3,000 are registered as members of the Jewish com., with some 1,400 in Prague. There are today 10 Jewish coms. in Bohemia and Moravia in the regional cities of Prague, Plzen, Usti nad. Labem, Karlovy Vary, Liberec, Teplice, Brno, Ostrava, Olomouc. There are regular Shabbat and holiday services held in all these places. There is a kosher kitchen and restaurant in Prague with rabbinical supervision of the chief rabbi of Prague and Bohemia and Moravia (Rav. K. Sidon).
Federation of Jewish Communities in the Czech Republic. Maiselova 18, 11001, Prague. ☎ 2481-1090. Fax: 2481-0912. Email: fedzid@vol.cz. *President* Jan Munk; *Exec. Dir.* Dr. Thomas Kraus.

PRAGUE

Jewish Community of Prague, Maiselova 18, 11001. Tel/Fax: 2318-664. *Chairman* Jiri Danicek.
B'nai B'rith Lodge, Maiselova 18, 11001.
Society of Jewish Culture, Maiselova 18, 11001. *President* Dr. B. Nosek.
Old-New Synagogue (Altneu), Cervena ul. 1, Praha 1 - Stare Mesto.

Jubilee Synagogue, Jeruzalemska 7, Praha 1 - Nove Mesto.

DENMARK (9,000)

The history of the Jews in Denmark goes back to the early years of the seveteenth century. Nearly all of Denmark's 9,000 Jews today live in Copenhagen. Jews have had full civic equality since 1814.

COPENHAGEN
Chief Rabbi: Rabbi Bent Lexner, Oestbanegade, 9, DK 2100. ☎ 39 299520. Fax 39 292517.
*Det Mosaiske Troessamfund i Kobenhavn (Jewish Congregation of Copenhagen), Ny Kongensgade 6, 1472DK. PO Box 2015, 1012 DK. ☎ (33)-128-868. Fax: (33) 123-357.
Synagogues: Krystalgade 12, 1172 DK.
Community Centre, Ny Kongensgade 6.

DOMINICAN REPUBLIC

The Jewish community which settled in Santo Domingo in the sixteenth century has completely disappeared. The present Jewish community, formed shortly before the Second World War, numbers about 150 in Santo Domingo and Sosua.

SANTO DOMINGO
Synagogue, Avenida Ciudad de Sarasota, 5. ☎ 533-1675.

ECUADOR (1,000)

The Jewish population in Ecuador is about 1,000, mainly resident in Quito and Guayaquil.
*Asociación Israelita de Quito, Avenida 18 de Septiembre 954, P.O.B. 17-03-800. ☎ 502-734.
*Comunidad de Culto Israelita, Cnr. Calle Paradiso and El Bosque, Guayaquil.

EGYPT (240)

The history of the Jewish community in Egypt goes back to Biblical times. Following the establishment of the State of Israel in 1948 and the subsequent wars, only about 200 Jews remain, about 150 in Cairo and 50 in Alexandria. There is now a small Israeli and Amer. Jewish com. in Maadi, Cairo. Services are conducted occasionally.

CAIRO
*Jewish Community Headquarters, 13 rue Sebil el Khazendar, Midan el Gueish, Abbasiya. ☎ 824613. *President* Emil Rousseau. ☎ 824885.
Great Synagogue Shaar Hashamayim, 17 Adly Pasha St. ☎ 3929025. Dir. J. Jaffe.
Ben-Ezra Synagogue, 6 Haret il-Sitt Barbara, Masi-Girgas (St. Georges), Old Cairo. ☎ 847695.
Heliopolis Synagogue "Vitali Madjur", 5 rue Misalla, Palmyra, Heliopolis.
Maadi Congregation Meir Enaim, 55 rue 13, Maadi.

ALEXANDRIA
Great Synagogue Eliahu HaNabi, 69 rue Nebi Daniel, Ramla Station. *President* J. Picciotto.

ESTONIA (3,000)
TALLINN
Jewish Community of Estonia. Karu Str. 16. *Contact* Cilja Laud, POB 3576 Tallinn

EE0090. ☎/Fax 438566.
Syn., 9 Magdaleena St. ☎ 557154.
Jewish Cultural Centre. *Edr.* Eugenia Gurin-Loov, POB 3576.
WIZO Estonia. *Contact* Revekka Blumberg, POB 3576. ☎ 43-646 1777. Fax: 43-8566.
There are Jewish communities in Kohtla-Jarve, Narva and Tartu.

ETHIOPIA

The indigenous Jews of Ethiopia, known as Falashas, have probably lived in the country for about 2,000 years. Their origin is obscure but they are believed to be the descendants of members of the Agau tribe who accepted pre-Talmudic Judaism brought into Ethiopia (Abyssinia) from Jewish settlements in Egypt, such as that at Elephantine (Aswan). They were estimated to number half-a-million in the 17th century but by the 1970s the population had shrunk to less than 30,000. In 1975 the Israel Govt. recognised their right to enter under the Law of Return. Towards the end of 1984 the Israel Govt. undertook Operation Moses which entailed transporting about 8,000 Ethiopian Jews from refugee camps in Sudan to Israel. It is estimated that approximately 3,000 died from famine and disease before they could reach Israel. A further dramatic mass emigration to Israel was completed in 1991 and very few remain. A useful book on the subject is David Kessler's The Falashas, the Forgotten Jews of Ethiopia (3rd ed., London 1996), obtainable from Frank Cass Publishers.
Jewish Community, P.O.B. 50 Addis Ababa.

FIJI ISLANDS

Many Jews, mostly from Britain and some from Australia, settled in the islands in the 19th and early 20th centuries. About 12 Jewish families now live in Suva. *Corr.* K. R. Fleischman, G.P.O. Box 905, Suva or Cherry Schneider, P.O.B. 882, Suva.

FINLAND (1,500)

The settlement of Jews in Finland dates from about 1850. The number living there today is about 1,500, with 1100 in Helsinki, the rest in Turku and other parts of the country.
*Synagogue and Communal Centre: Malminkatu 26, 00100 Helsinki 10. ☎ 6941302, 6941297. Fax 6948916.
Synagogue and Communal Centre: Brahenkatu 17, Turku. ☎ 2312557.

FRANCE (600,000)

The first Jewish settlers in France arrived with the Greek founders of Marseilles some 500 years B.C.E. After the destruction of the Second Temple, Jewish exiles established new communities, or reinforced old ones. Rashi and Rabenu Tam are the best known of hundreds of brilliant medieval French rabbis and scholars. In 1791 the emancipation of French Jewry was the signal for the ghetto walls to crumble throughout Europe. During the Second World War, under the German occupation, 120,000 Jews were deported or massacred; but the post-war influx from Central and Eastern Europe and particularly from North Africa, has increased the numbers of French Jewry to about 600,000 (the fourth largest in the world), of whom 380,000 are in Paris and Greater Paris. There are Jewish coms. in about 150 other towns.

PARIS

*Consistoire Central: Union des Communautés Juives de France. The principal Jewish religious org. in France. It administers the Union des Communautés Juives de France, 19 rue St. Georges, 9°. *President* Jean Kahn; *Dir. Gen.* Leon

Masliah. ☎ 49708800. Fax.: 42810366.
Association Consistoriale Israélite de Paris, 17 rue St. Georges, 9°. The principal Jewish religious org. for the Paris area. *President* Moïse Cohen; V. *President* Maitre J. H. Gahnassia. ☎ 40 82 26 26.
Alliance Israélite Universelle, 45 rue La Bruyère, 75009 Paris. This org. works through its network of schools in France, but also in 7 countries, especially in North Africa, Asia and North America. It houses the 'College des Etudes juives' and a library, which includes more than 120,000 books in the field of Hebraica-Judaica. *President* Prof. A. Steg; *Dir.* Jean-Jacques Wahl. ☎ 0142 80 35 00.
American Jewish Joint Distribution Committee, Rue De Miromesnil 33, Paris 75008. ☎ 33-14268-05-68. *Dir.* Alberto Senderey.
Association Culturelle Israélite Agudas Hakehilos, 10 rue Pavée, 4°. ☎ 488721 54.
B'nai B'rith Dist. 19-Continental-Europe, 38 rue de Clichy, Paris, 9°. ☎ 40 82 91 11. *President* M. Honigbaum.
Centre de Documentation Juive Contemporaine, 17 Rue Geoffroy l'Asnier, 4°. (Est. 1943.) This org. has gathered and organised data of Jewish life under the Hitler regime in Europe. Founder The late Isaac Schneersohn; *President* Baron Eric de Rothschild.
Communauté Israélite de la Stricte Observance, 10 rue Cadet, 75009. ☎ 42 46 36 47.
*Conseil Représentatif des Institutions Juives de France (Crif), 19 rue de Teheran 8°. (Est. 1943.) The secular mouthpiece of French Jewry linking 64 of the most important Jewish orgs. ☎ 45 61 00 70. Fax 43 59 06 11. *President* Henri Hajdenberg; *Drice* Mme. J. Keller.
Conseil Représentatif du Judaisme Traditionaliste, c/o Eric Schieber, 6 rue Albert Camus, le Montigny 75010 Paris. 16i. Rep. org. of Orthodox Jewry. ☎ 45 04 94 00. *President* I. Frankforter; Sec. Gen. E. Schieber.
Fédération des Sociétés Juives de France, 68 rue de la Folie Mericourt 11°. Social, cultural and philanthropic in outlook and links many gps. with East European background. ☎ 48 05 28 60. *President* Mordechai Lerman.
Fédération des Organisations Sionistes de France, 17 bis, rue de Paradis 75010, Paris. ☎ 48 24 03 44. D. M. Kalifa.
Fonds Social Juif Unifié (F.S.J.U.), 19 rue de Tehéran, 8°. French Jewry's central organisation in the cultural, educ. and social fields. ☎ 45 63 17 28. *President* Baron David de Rothschild; *Dir.* David Saada.
Keren Kayemeth Leisrael, 11 rue de 4 Septembre 75002. ☎ 42868888.
Mouvement Juif Libéral de France, 11 rue Gaston-de-Caillavet 15°. ☎ 45 75 38 01. (Affil. to World Union for Prog. Judaism). *President* R. Benarrosh; *Ms.* Rabbi D. Farhi; Rabbi M. Konig.
Mouvement Loubavitch, 8 rue Lemartine 9°. ☎ 45 26 87 60.
ORT, 10 Villa D'Eylau, 16°. ☎ 45 00 74 22.
Renouveau Juif, 18 passage du Chantier 12°. ☎ 43 40 40 55. Est. 1979 by Henri Hajdenberg. Advocates stronger pro-Israel stand.
Siona, 52 rue Richer 9°. ☎ 42 46 01 91. Sephardi Z. movement est. by Roger Pinto.
Union des Juifs pour la Résistance et l'Entr'aide, 14 rue de Paradis, 10°. Social, cultural and political org. of extreme Left-wing political views, founded as an armed Resistance group in 1943 under German occupation. *President* Charles Lederman. ☎ 47 70 62 16.
Union Libérale Israélite, 24 rue Copernic, 75116. Org. of Liberal Judaism. *President* C Bloch. ☎ 47 04 37 27. Fax 47 27 81 02.
Union des Sociétés Mutalistes Juives de France, 58 rue du Chateau d'Eau 10°. ☎ 42 06 62 88. East European background.
Wizo, 54 rue de Paradis, 10°. French women Zionists' centre. ☎ 48 01 97 70. *President* Nora Gailland-Hofman.

GERMANY

SYNAGOGUES
Chief Rabbi of France: Rabbi Joseph Sitruk, Consistoire Central, 19 rue Saint-Georges, 9°. ☏ 49 70 88 00. Fax: 40 16 06 11.
Synagogues of the Consistoire de Paris, 44 rue de la Victoire, 9°; 15 rue Notre-Dame-de-Nazareth, 3°; 21 bis rue des Tournelles, 4°; 28 rue Buffault, 9°N Sephardi; 14 rue Chasseloup-Laubat, 15°; 18 rue Sainte-Isaure, 18°; 75 rue Julien Lacroix, 20°; 9 rue Vauquelin, 5°; 70 Avenue Secretan, 19°; 13 rue Fondary, 15°; 6 bis rue Michel Ange, 16°; 14 Place des Vosges, 4°; 84 rue de la Roquette; 120 Boulevard de Belleville 20°; 120 rue des Saule, 18°; 19 Blvd. Poissonniére; 18 rue St. Lazare, 9° (Algerian).
Orthodox Synagogues: 10 rue Cadet, 9°; 31 rue de Montévidéo, 16°; 10 rue Pavee, 4°; 6 rue Ambroise Thomas, 9°; 3 rue Saulnier, 9°; 32 rue Basfroi, H°; 25 rue des Rosiers, 4°; 17 rue des Rosiers, 4°; 24 rue de Bourg Tibourg, 4°; 80 rue Doudeauville, 18°; 5 rue Duc, 18°; 18 rue des Ecouffes, 4°.
Conservative Syn., Adath Shalom, 22 bis, rue des Belles Feuilles, 75116 Paris. ☏ 45 53 84 09.
Liberal Synagogues, 24 rue Copernic, 16°; 11 rue Gaston de Caillavet 15°.
There are also many syns. in the Paris suburbs and in the Provinces.

GERMANY (62,000)

A large Jewish community has existed continuously in Germany since Roman times. Despite recurring periods of persecution, the Jewish communities contributed much of lasting value to culture and civilisation. Hitler and the Nazi regime destroyed the community, which numbered more than half a million before 1933, 160,000 of whom lived in Berlin. Today there are about 62,000 in Germany (incl. 10,500 in Berlin, 6,300 in Frankfurt and 6,300 in Munich). There are 79 other coms. in Germany, and the communities of the former German Democratic Republic have now been integrated in the Zentralrat der Juden in Deutschland.
*Zentralrat der Juden in Deutschland (Central Council for Jews in Germany), Oranienburger Str. 3, 10117 Berlin. ☏ 030/2828714. Fax 0301 2386607.
Central Welfare Org. of Jews in Germany, Hebelstr. 6, 60318 Frankfurt. ☏ 069-944371-0. Fax: 069-494817.
Conference of German Rabbis, Landesrabbiner Joel Berger, Hospitalstr. 36, 70174 Stuttgart 1. ☏ 0711-2283630. Fax 0711-22836186.
B'nai B'rith Lodges, Berlin, Cologne, Dusseldorf, Frankfurt, Hamburg, Munich and Saarbrucken.
*Bundesverband Jüd. Studenten, Joachimstaler Str. 13, 10719 Berlin, and at Jewish Student Organisations at Aachen, Cologne, Frankfurt, Stuttgart, Hanover, Hamburg, Heidelberg and Munich.
Hochschule Für Jüdische Studien (University for Jewish Studies), Friedrichstr. 9, 69117 Heidelberg. ☏ 06221-22576. Fax: 06221-167696.
Jewish Agency for Israel, Hebelstr. 6, 60318 Frankfurt. ☏ 069-9433340. Fax: 069-490473.
Jewish National Fund, Feldbergstr. 5, 60323 Frankfurt. ☏ 069-720521. Fax: 069-7240254.
Jewish Women's League (Frauenbund), c/o ZWST, Hebelstr. 6, 60318 Frankfurt.
Jewish Restitution Successor Organisation, Sophienstr. 26, 60481, Frankfurt.
Magbith (Keren Hayessod-United Jewish Appeal), 60323 Frankfurt, Friedrichstr. 27. ☏ 069-729062.
Makkabi, Gailenbergstr. 13, 87541 Hindelang. ☏ 08324-8386. Fax: 08324-2421.
ORT, Hebelstr. 6, 60318 Frankfurt. ☏ 069-449081.
Wizo, Joachimstalerstr. 13, 10719 Berlin.
Youth Aliyah, Hebelstr. 6, 60318 Frankfurt.
Zentralarchiv zur Erforschung der Geschichte der Juden in Deutschland, Bienenstr. 5, 69117 Heidelberg. ☏ 06221-164141. Fax: 06221-181049.

Zionist Organisation in Germany, Hebelstr. 6, 60318 Frankfurt. ☎ 069-498-0251.
Fax: 069-490473.
Zionist Youth, Falkensteiner St. 1, 60322 Frankfurt. ☎ 069-556963.

GIBRALTAR (600)

In 1473 there was a suggestion that the promontory should be reserved for Marranos. The present Jewish community was formed of immigrants from North Africa shortly after the British annexation in 1704, but Jews had no legal right to settle in the city until 1749, by which year however, the Jewish residents numbered about 600, a third of the total number of residents, and possessed two syns.

During the siege of 1779 to 1783 the size of the Jewish population was reduced, a large proportion removing to England. After the siege the numbers rose again, being at their highest in the middle of the nineteenth century, when they rose above two thousand. (For the history of the Jews of Gibraltar, see A. B. M. Serfaty, 'The Jews of Gibraltar under British Rule,' 1933.)
*Managing Board of the Jewish Community, 10 Bomb House Lane. ☎ 72606. *President* D. Benaim. Fax: 40487. *Admin.* Mrs. E. Benady.
Synagogue Shaar Hashamayim, Engineer Lane. ☎ 78069. Fax: 74029. (Est. before 1749; rebuilt 1768.) *H. Sec.* J. de M. Benyunes, P.O. Box 174.
Synagogue Nefusot Yehudah, Line Wall Rd. (Est. 1781.) *H. Sec.* I. Beniso. ☎ 74791. Fax: 40907.
Synagogue Es Hayim, Irish Town. (Est. 1759.) *H. M. & Sec.* S. Benaim. ☎ 75563.
Synagogue, Abudarham, Parliament Lane. (Est. 1820.) *H. Sec.* D. J. Abudarham. ☎ 78506. Fax: 73249.
Mikveh, Mrs O. Hassan. ☎ 77658.
Joint Israel Appeal. *H. Sec.* E. Benamor. ☎ 77680. Fax: 40493.

GREECE (4,800)

There have been Jewish communities in Greece since the days of antiquity. Before 1939, 77,200 Jews lived in Greece (56,000 in Salonika, now known as Thessaloniki.). Today there are fewer than 5,000, all Sephardim, of these about 2,800 live in Athens; some 1,100 in Thessaloniki; and the rest in some 12 provincial towns.

ATHENS
*Central Board of Jewish Communities, 2 Sourmeli St., GR 104 39. *Sec. Gen.* Moissis Konstantinis. ☎ (01) 8839953. Fax: 823-4488. Email: hhkis@netor.gr
American Joint Distribution Committee, 4 Nikis St., 105 63 Athens. Tel/Fax: (01) 32-31-034.
B'nai B'rith, 15 Paparigopoulou St., 105 61 Athens. ☎ 323-04-05.
Jewish Community Office, 8 Melidoni St., 105 53 Athens. ☎ (01) 3252823. Fax: 3220-761. *Director* A.M. Sasson.
Synagogue, Beth Shalom, 5 Melidoni St., 105 53 Athens. *M.* Rabbi Jakob Arar. ☎ (01) 325 2773.
Jewish Museum of Greece, 36 Amalias Ave., 105 58 Athens. Tel/Fax: (01) 32 31 577. *Director*: S. Rozanis.
Communal Centre, 9 Vissarionos St., 106 72 Athens. ☎ (01) 36 37 092. Fax: 360 8896.

THESSALONIKI
Jewish Community Office, 24 Tsimiski St., 54624. ☎ 031 275701. Fax: 031-229063.
Monastirioton Synagogue, 35 Sigrou St., 54630. ☎ 524968.
Synagogue Yad Le Zicaron, 24 Vasileos Irakliou St., 54624. ☎ 223231.
Centre of Historical Studies of Thessaloniki Jews, 'Simon Marks', 24 Vasileos

Irakliou St., 54624. ☎ 031 223231. Fax: 031-229063.

Other communities:
Corfu Jewish Community, 5 Riz. Voulefton St., 49100. *President* Raphael Soussis. ☎ 0661 30591. Fax: 0661-31898.
Halkis Jewish Community, *President* M. Maissis. 46 Kriezotou Str. GR 34100. ☎ 0221 27297.
Ioannina Jewish Community. 18 Joseph Eliyia Str. GR 452 21. ☎ 0651 25195. *President* M. Eliassa.
Larissa Jewish Community, Platia Evreon Martiron, GR 412 22. ☎ 041 532965. *President* A. Albelansis.
Rodos Jewish Community, 5 Polidorou Str. GR 85100. ☎ 0241 22364. Fax 0251 73039. *President* M. Soriano.
Trikala Jewish Community, *President* I. Venouziou, Kondili-Philippou, 42100. ☎ 0431 25-834.
Volos Jewish Community, 21B Vassani Str. GR 383 33. *President* R. Frezis. ☎ 0421 23079. Fax: 0421-31917.

GUATEMALA (1,500)

Jews have been resident in Guatemala since 1898. The present population is about 1,500, made up of some 300 families all living in the capital.

GUATEMALA CITY
*Comunidad Judia Guatemalteca, 7a. Av. 13-51 Zona 9, Guatemala City, C.A. ☎ (502) 3601509. Email: Comjugua@guate.net. *President* Jaime Camhi.
Centro Hebreo (East European Jews) 7a. Av. 13-51 Zona 9. ☎ 3311975. *President* Ricardo Rich.
Maguen David (Sephardi), 7a. Avenida 3-80 Zona 2. ☎ 2320932. Fax 360 1589. *President* Saúl Mishaan
Consejo Central Sionista de la Comunidad Judia de Guatemala, Apto. Postal 502, Guatemala, C.A. *President* Mano Permuth.

HAITI (150)

There has been a Jewish community in Haiti for the past 80 years, and it now numbers about 150 people.

HOLLAND (25,000)

From the sixteenth century onwards the Jews of Holland had a distinguished historical record. Since 1792 they have had the same constitutional and civil rights as all other citizens. In 1940 there were approximately 140,000 Jews in the country, but as the result of the Nazi occupation only some 25,000 remain, of whom about half are in Amsterdam. Other small coms. are in Amersfoort, Arnhem, Bussum, Eindhoven, Groningen, Haarlem, The Hague, Rotterdam, Utrecht and Zwolle.
Rabbinate Ashkenazic Community: Rabbi F. J. Lewis, Rabbi I. Vorst (both in Amsterdam); Rabbi J. S. Jacobs (Amersfoort).
Rabbinate Sephardic Community: Rabbi B. Drukarch.
Rabbinate Liberal Jewish Congregations: Rabbi D. Lilienthal (Amsterdam); Rabbi A. Soetendorp (The Hague); Rabbi Dr. E. van Voolen (Arnhem).

AMSTERDAM
*Ashkenazi Community Centre and Offices: Van der Boechorststraat 26, 1081 BT. ☎ 646 00 46. Fax: 646-4357.
*Sephardi Communal Centre: Mr. Visserplein, 3, 1011 RD. ☎ 624 53 51. Fax: 625-4680.
Ashkenazi Synagogues: Jacob Obrechtplein; Lekstr 61; Gerard Doustr. 238; Van

der Boechorststraat, 26; Straat van Messina 10, Amstelveen.
East European Jew' Synagogue: G. van der Veenstr. 26-28.
Portuguese Synagogue, Mr. Visserplein 3.
Liberal Community Centre and Synagogue. J. Soetendorpstraat, 8, 1079. ☎ 6423562. Fax: 642-8135. Amsterdam and Dutch Liberal Rabbinate. ☎ 644-2619. Fax: 642-8135.
Zionist Offices: Joh. Vermeerstr. 24. Netzer-Kadima at the Liberal Community Centre.
Jewish Historical Museum: Synagogue Bldg., J. D. Meyerplein.
Anne Frank House, Prinsengracht 263. Judith Drake Library at the Liberal Community Centre.

HONDURAS (150)

There has been a Jewish community in Honduras for the past 50 years.
Tegucigalpa Community. *Sec.* H. Seidel.
Israel Embassy S. Cohen, Ambassador; H. Schiftan, Consul. ☎ 32-4232/32-5176. Telex: 1606 Memistra.
San Pedro Sula, Syn. and Com. Centre. *Sec.* M. Weizenblut.

HONG KONG (3,000)

The Hong Kong com. dates from about 1857. The Ohel Leah synagogue was built in 1901.
The Jewish Community Centre, 1 Robinson Place, 70 Robinson Road, Mid-levels. A new facility with 2 Kosher restaurants and banquet facilities (under Mashgiach supervision), library/function facilities. Meals on the Sabbath. Take-away and Kosher food delivery available. Full programme of activities and classes. ☎ (852) 2868-0828. *Information:* ☎ (852) 2801-5440. Fax 2877-0917. *Gen. Man.* Mildred Houston.
Synagogues:
Ohel Leah Syn. and Mikvah, 70 Robinson Rd. ☎ (852) 8015440. Fax: 852 877 0917. *M.* Rabbi S. Lopin. Friday night, Saturday and weekday services are held. ☎ (852) 2589-2615. Fax (852) 2548-4200.
Lubavitch in the Far East. 1A Kennedy Heights, Midlevels. Holds regular morning services and Shabbat and holiday services in the Furoma Hotel. Rabbi M. Avtzon (852) 2523 9770. Fax: (852) 2845 2772.
Shuva Israel Beit Medrash and Community Center (Seph), 61 Connaught Road Central, 2/F, Fortune House, Central. Rabbi Y. Eliyahu. ☎ (852) 2851-6218. Fax: (852) 2851-7482.
Shuva Israel Synagogue (Seph) (Shabbat and Holidays), 16-18 McDonnel Road, 1-B, Midlevels. ☎ (852) 2851-6128. Fax: (852) 2851-7482.
The United Jewish Congregation (Lib/Ref) (Est. 1991). Friday eve. services at the Jewish Community Centre. ☎ (852) 2589-2623. Fax (852) 2523-3961.
Zion Congregation (Orth). A newly formed congregation in Kowloon. 21 Chatham Road. Rabbi N. Meoded. ☎ (852) 2366-6364.

Israel Consulate-General, Admiralty Centre, Tower II, Room 701, 18 Harcourt Road. ☎ (852) 25296091. Fax: 28550220.
The Jewish Historical Society. Publishes monographs on subjects of Sino-Judaic interest. Information from Dennis Leventhal. ☎ (852) 2547-2550. Fax: (852) 559 2890.
The Jewish cemetery is situated in Happy Valley. ☎ (852) 2589-2615. Fax: (852) 2548-4200.
The Jewish Women's Assn. is affiliated to WIZO and ICJW. *Chair* Mrs R. Cohen ☎ (852) 2845-2885. Fax (852) 2537-4457.

United Israel Appeal is affiliated to Keren Hayesod. *Information* Mr. S Myers. ☎ (852) 2973 0073. Fax: (852) 2869-9812.

HUNGARY (85,000)

Jews have lived in this part of Europe since Roman times. Tombstones with Hebrew inscription have been found originating from the 3rd century. Before World War II, Hungary's Jewish population was about 800,000, of whom some 250,000 lived in Budapest. Some 600,000 perished in the Holocaust. The estimated Jewish population now is 85,000 and some 80,000 live in Budapest and the remainder in the provincial Jewish communities, all affiliated to the Central Board of the Federation of the Jewish Communities in Hungary.

BUDAPEST

*Federation of the Jewish Communities in Hungary (Magyarországi Zsidó Hitközségek Szövetsége) and the Budapest Jewish Community, 1075 Budapest VII Sip utca 12. ☎ 1-3226-475. Fax 342-1790. *Man. Dir.* Gusztav Zoltai; *Dir. Foreign Rel.* Ernö Lazarovits.
Main Synagogue, Budapest VII Dohany utca 2 (Conservative). Chief Rabbi Robert Frölich.
Central Rabbinate, Budapest VII Sip utca 12. *Dir.* Robert Deutsch, Chief Rabbi.
Orthodox Synagogue, Budapest VII Kazinczy utca 27. *President* Herman Fixler.
Rabbinical Seminary, Budapest VIII, József körut 27. *Dir.* Chief Rabbi Dr. Jozsef Schweitzer, Chief Rabbi of Hungary.
There are 20 other syns. and prayer houses in Budapest.
The main provincial coms. are at Debrecen, Miskolc, Szeged, Pécs, Györ.

INDIA (5,600)

The settlement of Jews in India goes back at least to the early centuries of the Christian era. The Indian Jews of today may be divided into four groups: (i) those who arrived in this and the last century mainly from Baghdad, Iran, Afghanistan, etc., known as "Yehudim," forming communities in Bombay, Pune and Calcutta; (ii) Bene Israel, who believe that their ancestors arrived in India after the destruction of the First Temple, and who maintained a distinct religious identity while using local language and dress over the centuries; their main centre is the Bombay area; (iii) the Cochin Jews, in Cochin and the neighbouring centres of the Malabar Coast, in Kerala State in South India, who have records dating back to the fourth century, but who believe that there was a Jewish settlement in Craganore as early as 78 C.E.; (iv) European Jews who came within the last 50 years or so. Since 1948 there has been steady emigration to Israel. According to the 1971 census the Jewish pop. was 6,134. Today, it is estimated at 5,618.
The largest com. is in Maharastra State (4,354), mainly in the Bombay area. Smaller coms. are in Calcutta, Madras, New Delhi and Pune Ahmedabad. In Manipur there are 464 and in Gujarat 217.
*Council of Indian Jewry, c/o The Jewish Club, Jeroo Bldg., Second Fl., 137 Mahatma Gandhi Rd., Bombay, 400023. ☎ 271628. *President* N. Talkar. ☎ 8515195, 861941; *V. Presidents* A. Talegawkar, A. Samson; *Sec.* Mrs. J. Bhattacharya. ☎ 6320589.

INDONESIA

Of the 16 Jews living in Indonesia, 15, made up of five families, live in Surabaya where there is provision for prayers. One lives in Jakarta.

IRAN (25,000)

Jews have lived in the country at least since the time of the Persian king, Cyrus, in the sixth century B.C.E. Some 60,000 Iranian Jews emigrated to Israel in the late 1940s and early 1950s, and there has been an increasing trickle of emigration since. The situation of those who remain estimated to be in the region of 25,000 has become precarious under the new revolutionary regime on account of its anti-Israel stance. Most live in Tehran, some thousands in Shiraz, and the rest in Isfahan, Hamedan, Kermanshah and Abadan.

TEHRAN
*Central Jewish Committee of Iran–Tehran, 385 Skeikh-Hadi St. ☎ 372556.
Synagogues, Haiim, Ghavamol-Saltaneh St.; Etefagh, Anatole France St.; Yousef-Abad, Yousef-Abad St.; Abrishami, (Kakh-Shomali).

IRAQ (200)

The Jewish community in Iraq (anciently known as Babylonia) is the oldest in the Diaspora. Strong hostility exists towards the Jewish remnant of about 200, mainly elderly, that is now left. They mostly live in Baghdad and a few in Basra.

ISRAEL (5,619,000)

Palestine was administered until May 14, 1948, by Gt. Britain under a Mandate approved by the Council of the League of Nations, the preamble to which incorporated the Balfour Declaration. On November 20, 1947, the Assembly of the United Nations recommended that Palestine should be reorganised as two States, one Jewish, the other Arab, together with an internationalised Jerusalem and district combined in an economic union. On the surrender of the Mandate by Britain on May 14, 1948, the Jewish territory, with a Jewish pop. of 655,000, took the name of Israel and set up a Provisional Govt., with Dr. Chaim Weizmann as *President* and David Ben-Gurion as Prime Minister. On July 5, 1950, the 'Law of Return' was proclaimed, conferring on every Jew the right to live in Israel.

The signing of a declaration of a set of principles by Israel and the PLO under the leadership of Yasser Arafat on September 13, 1993, concluded an era of forty-five years of strife between Israel and her Arab neighbours and recognised the aspirations of Palestinian Arabs for territory proposed for them by the UN in 1947. A peace treaty with Jordan was agreed in 1994. Prime Minister Rabin was assassinated in November 1995.

Key events in this history include:
The invasion of the Jewish state by the Arab armies in 1948 concluded by a series of armistices in 1949 and the recognition of Israel by the UN on May 11, 1949; the annexation of Arab Palestine by Jordan in 1950; the absorption by Israel of Jews from Arab lands and the establishment of Palestinian refugee camps in the Arab states; seizure by Egypt of the Suez Canal Zone and the (Franco-British and Israeli) Sinai-Suez campaign of 1956; Egypt's closure of the Straits of Tiran in May 1967 and the Six-Day War of June 1967 which saw the Israeli capture of Jerusalem and occupation of Gaza, Sinai, the Golan and the West Bank and the first National Unity Coalition (1967-70).; the Yom Kippur War of October 1973 and the ensuing negotiations leading to partial Israeli withdrawals in Sinai and the Golan; the Likud election victory of 1977 and the visit to Israel by Egyptian President Anwar Sadat in November 1977 which led to the Camp David Agreement of March 26, 1979, the establishment of diplomatic relations between Egypt and Israel, and the Israeli withdrawal from the whole of Sinai in April 1982; Israel's 'Operation peace for Galilee' in Lebanon in June 1982 and withdrawal in 1985, a war which caused great divisions in Israel; the Intifada of the Palestinians in Gaza and the West Bank starting in 1988; the US-inspired five-point peace plan of 1989 and its failure in

1990; the Gulf War (January 1991) following the Iraqi invasion of Kuwait when the PLO supported Iraq and Israel sustained scud missile attacks without retaliation; the launching of negotiations for a comprehensive Middle East 'peace settlement' between Israel, the Arabs, and representatives of the Palestinians at a meeting in Madrid in October 1991.

It is these negotiations, conducted in public at a series of venues in Europe and the United States, and in secret in Norway since the Labour victory in the elections of June 1992, that came to fruition on the eve of the New Year 5754. Since then, a peace treaty with Jordan has also been signed. Further agreements for the transfer of controls in parts of the West Bank were signed in September 1995. In the interim, the continuing 'peace process' has repeatedly been put under threat by the actions of terrorists intent on destabilising the new situation. Anticipated stages of the process have yet to be achieved and it remains to be seen whether the principles of 'land for peace' on the Israeli side and 'reocgnition of Israel and peace' on the Palestinian can prevail as the basis for long-term accord between Israel and Palestine, and peace in the Middle East.

The assassination of the Prime Minister in November 1995, however, suggests that hostility to the peace process remains the greatest of all dangers to the Israeli polity. The continuing Hamas 'suicide attacks', devastating to Israeli citizens alongside the dispute over Israeli settlements within the occupied territories, and the military conflict in southern Lebanon, resurgent early in 1996 and again in late 1997, make an uncomfortable prelude to the celebrations marking the jubilee of the state this year.

Government

The Provisional Government of Israel was replaced by a permanent one after the election of the First **Knesset** (Parliament) in January, 1949.

Israel's Basic Law provides that elections must be 'universal, nationwide, equal, secret and proportional'. A general election must be held at least every four years. The Knesset is elected by a form of proportional representation in which members are selected in strict proportion to the votes cast for each party. Any candidate who obtains one per cent of the total votes cast is assured of a Knesset seat.

Mainly as a result of the voting system, no single party has so far been able to form a government on the basis of its own Knesset majority. Until the election in 1977, the dominant political force was a coalition of the Left, which formed governments with the help of various smaller parties, usually those with a religious programme. In the elections of 1977 and 1981 an alliance of the Right was able to form an administration with the help of religious parties. One feature of the political situation has been that the religious parties, in particular, have been able to exercise an influence out of proportion to their members.

Within recent years, however, there has been a marked polarisation of attitudes among sections of Israeli society and this was reflected by the proliferation of small parties which contested the 1984 election. The 1984 election produced an inconclusive result, with only three seats separating the two big party blocs. The two big parties formed Israel's second National Unity Government to cope with the urgent economic and other problems. The office of Prime Minister was held in rotation, first by Mr. Shimon Peres, the Labour Alignment leader, and then by Mr. Yitzhak Shamir, the Likud leader. The 1988 election was also inconclusive and was followed by another Coalition Government, with Mr. Shamir continuing as Prime Minister and Mr. Peres as Vice-Premier.The national unity government broke up in March 1990 when the Likud declined to go along with a U.S. plan to promote peace talks. Mr. Shamir constructed a centre-right religious government supported by 66% of the 120 members of the Knesset. The elections of 1992 produced a Labour coalition led by Yitzhak Rabin. Demographic changes brought about by the influx of settlers from Eastern Europe and political and economic pressures contributed in large part to this outcome. While political power rests constitutionally

in the Knesset, the President of Israel, essentially a symbolic and representational figure, can in certain circumstances exercise a degree of de facto power based on his prestige. In particular, he can emerge as the voice of the Nation's conscience. The President is elected for a five-year period, renewable only once. President Herzog was re-elected in 1988 and Ezer Weizman was elected in 1993.
The Knesset elections held in May 1996 included provision for the first time for direct voting for the Prime Ministership. This was won by Binyamin Netanyahu with 50.4% of the vote. Shimon Peres, the Labour leader, had 49.5% of the vote. Party votes were as follows:

Labour	34 (1992:44)			
Likud	32 (40)	Democratic Front for Peace and		
Shas	10 (6)	Equality (Arab)	5	(3)
National		United Torah Judaism	4	(-)
Religious	9 (6)	Third Way	4	(2)
Meretz	9 (12)	United Arabs	4	(2)
Yisrael ba'Aliyah	7 (-)	Moledet	2	(3)

Likud and its allies form the current government.

The Presidents of Israel: Chaim Weizmann 1949-1952; Yitzhak Ben Zvi 1952-1963; Zalman Shazar 1963-1973; Prof. Ephraim Katzir 1973-1978; Yitzhak Navon 1978-1983; Chaim Herzog 1983-1993; **Ezer Weizman** 1993- .
The Prime Ministers of Israel: David Ben-Gurion 1948-1953 and Nov. 1955-1963; Moshe Sharett Dec. 1953–1955; Levi Eshkol 1963–1969; Golda Meir 1969–74; Yitzhak Rabin 1974–1977 and 1992–95; Menachem Begin 1977–1983, Yitzhak Shamir Oct. 1983–Sept. 1984, Oct. 1986–June 1992; Shimon Peres Sept. 1984–Oct. 1986, Nov. 1995–May 1996; **Benjamin Netanyahu** May 1996–
Judiciary: The *President* appoints judges on the recommendation of an independent committee.
Defence Forces: Unified command of Army, Navy and Air Force. Small regular force; compulsory military service for persons aged between 18 and 29 followed by annual service in the Reserve.
Area: Following 1949 armistice agreements – approx. 20,750 sq. km. Following withdrawal from Sinai in April 1982, approx. 28,161 sq. km. (including Golan Heights, West Bank and Gaza Strip).
Neighbouring countries: Egypt, Jordan, Syria, Lebanon.
Population: Sept. 1988: 4,455,000 (incl. 3,653,100 Jews). These figures include 17,000 Druse on the Golan Heights but not the other territories occupied in the Six-Day War (est. at 1,381,000).
Main Towns: Jerusalem (the capital), Tel Aviv, Haifa, Ramat Gan, Petach Tikvah, Netanya, Holon, Bnei Brak, Rehovot, Hadera, Nazareth, Rishon le-Zion, Beersheba, Ashkelon, Ashdod, Bat Yam, Tiberias, Eilat.
Industry: Main products: Cement, fertilisers, metal products, polished diamonds, ceramics, tyres and tubes, plywood, textiles, clothing and footwear, citrus by-products, electrical and electronic applicances, micro-electronics, chemicals, canned fruit, military equipment.
Agricultural Products: Citrus, fruit, vegetables, eggs, milk, wheat, barley, tobacco, groundnuts, cotton, sugarbeet, beef, fish, flowers, wine.
Minerals: Potash and bromine, magnesium, phosphate, petroleum, salt, glass, sand, clay, gypsum, granite, copper, iron, oil, natural gas.
With the exception of Jerusalem and Haifa, the country's largest port, the main centres of population are concentrated in the flat and fertile western coastal plain. Tel Aviv, the centre of Israel's largest metropolitan area, is the chief commercial and

158   ISRAEL

industrial centre. Fast-growing Beersheba is the capital of the arid northern Negev, while Eilat, the country's southernmost port, has been transformed from an isolated military outpost into a bustling Red Sea township linked to the northern centres by a modern highway and giving access now to Jordan as well. In the north lie the largely Arab centre of Nazareth, the popular health resort of Tiberias, overlooking the Lake, and Safad. Round Tel Aviv are clustered a number of towns, including Ramat Gan, Holon and Bnei Brak. Throughout the country and along the border areas are dotted kibbutzim and settlements.

President of State Ezer Weizman; *Knesset Speaker* D. Tichon.

ISRAELI EMBASSIES AND LEGATIONS
Israel now enjoys diplomatic relations with 160 countries and many of these ties have come into being or have been renewed following the peace agreements of 1993.

Permanent Delegation to U.N. 800 2nd Ave., New York, N.Y. 10017. ☎ (212) 449-5400. Fax: (212) 490 9186. Ambassador Gad Yaacobi; *Dep.* Ambassador David Peleg. European H.Q. of U.N. Geneva, 9 Chemin de Bonvent, Geneva; Ambassador N.Y. Lamdan. ☎ 7980500; Vienna, 20 Anton Frankgasse, 1180 Vienna. ☎ 470-4742. Ambassador Yoel Sher.
Embassy to European Communities. 40 Ave. de L'Observatoire, Brussels 1180. ☎ 373-55500. Ambassador E. Halevi.
Permanent Delegation to Council of Europe, 3 Rue Rabelais, 75008 Paris. ☎ 4076-5500. Ambassador A. Gabai.
Albania (see Italy).
Andorra (see Spain).
Angola. Emb. BP 5791, Largo 4 de Fevereire, Hotel Presidente Meridien, Luanda. ☎ 397331. Ambassador Tamar Golan.
Antigua and Barbuda (see Dominican Republic).
Argentina. Emb.: 701 Mayo Ave., Buenos Aires. ☎ 342-1465. Ambassador Itzhak Aviran.
Armenia (see Georgia).
Australia. Emb.: 6 Turrana St., Yarralumla, Canberra, 2600. ☎ 273 2045. Ambassador Shmuel Moyal. ☎ 273 1309.
Austria. Emb.: Anton Frankgasse, 20, Vienna 1180. ☎ 4704377. Ambassador Yoel Sher. ☎ 470 4741.
Azberbaijan. Emb: Stroiteley Prospect 1, Baku. ☎ 385282. Ambassador Eleizer Yotvath.
Bahamas. Consulate, PO Box 7776, Nassau NP. ☎ 3264421. Hon. Consul. Raphael Seligman.
Barbados. Consulate, PO Box 256, Bridgetown. Hon. Consul Bernard Gilbert.
Belarus. Emb.: Partizanski Prospekt 6A, Minsk 220002. ☎ 303479. Ambassador Eliahu Valk.
Belgium. Emb.: 40 Ave. de l'Observatoire, Brussels 180. ☎ 3749080. Ambassador.
Belize (see San Salvador).
Benin (see Côte d'Ivoire).
Bolivia. Emb.: Edificio 'Esperanza', Ave., Mariscal, Santa Cruz; Edificio 'Esperanza', 10 Pizo, Calle 1309, La Paz. ☎ 391126. Ambassador Yair Rekanati.
Botswana (see Zimbabwe).
Brazil. Emb.: Avenida das Nacoes, Lote 38, Brasilia. ☎ 244-7675. Ambassador Yaacov Keinan.
Bulgaria. 1 Bulgaria Sq., NDC Building, 7th Floor. ☎ 5432-01. Ambassador David Cohen.
Burkina Faso (see Côte d'Ivoire).
Burundi (see Zaire).
Kingdom of Cambodia (see Thailand).

ISRAEL 159

Cameroon. Emb.: P.O. Box 5934, Yaounde. ☎ 201644. Ambassador.
Canada. Emb.: 50 O'Connor St., Ottawa. ☎ 5676450. Ambassador David Sultan.
Cape Verde (see Senegal).
Central African Republic (see Cameroon).
Chile. Emb.: Av. Bosque, Las Condes San Sebastian 2812, Santiago De Chile. ☎ 246-1570. Ambassador Pinchas Avivi.
China. Emb.: West Wing Offices, 1 Jianguo Menwai Da Ji, Beijing 100004. ☎ 505-2970. Ambassador Ora Namir.
Colombia. Emb.: Edificio Caxdac Calle 35, No. 7-25, Bogota. ☎ 2321067. Ambassador Avraham Hadad.
Congo (see Zaire).
Costa Rica. Emb.: Calle 2 Avendas 2 y 4 San Jose. ☎ 221-0684. Ambassador Shlomo Tal.
Republic of Côte D'Ivoire. O.1. B.P. 1877, Abidjan 01. ☎ 21 31 78. Ambassador Yaakov Revah.
Cyprus. Emb.: 4 Gripari St., P.O.B. 1049, W. Nicosia. ☎ 445195. Ambassador Shemi Tzur.
Czech Republic. 2 Badeniho St., Prague 7. Ambassador Rephael Gvir.
Denmark. Emb.: Lundevangsvej 4, Hellerup, Copenhagen. ☎ 396 26288. Ambassador Avraham Sitton.
Dominica (see Dominican Republic).
Dominican Republic. Emb.: Pedro Henriques Unena 80. ☎ 5418974. Ambassador Pinchas Lavie.
Ecuador. Emb.: Av. Eloy Alfaro 969 Y, Amazonas, PO Box 2138, Quito. ☎ 565509. Ambassador Yaacov Paran.
Egypt. Emb.: 6 Shariah Ibn-el Maleck, Giza, Cairo. ☎ 3610 528. Ambassador David Sultan.
El Salvador. Emb.: 85 Av. Norte 619, Colonia Escalon, Centro de Gobierno, PO Box 1776, San Salvador. ☎ 2985331. Ambassador Yosef Livne.
Eritrea. Emb.: PO Box 55600, 10 Wodejio Ali St., Asmara. ☎ 120137. Ambassador Ariel Kerem.
Estonia (see Latvia).
Ethiopia. P.O. Box 1266, Addis Ababa. ☎ 610 999. Ambassador Avi Abraham Granot.
Fiji (see Australia).
Finland. Emb.: 5a Vironkatu, Helsinki. ☎ 1356177. Ambassador Ali Yihye.
France. Emb.: 3 Rue Rabelais, Paris 8. ☎ 42564747. Ambassador Aviezer Pazner.
Gabon (see Cameroon).
Gambia (see Senegal).
Georgia. Emb.: Achmashenebeli Ave. 61, Tbilisi 380002. ☎ 964 457. Ambassador Lili Hahamy.
Germany. Emb.: 2 Simrock-allee, 5300 Bonn 2. ☎ (228) 8230. Ambassador Avraham Primor.
Ghana (see Côte d'Ivoire).
Gibraltar. Con.: 3 City Mill Lane. ☎ 59555956. Hon. Con. M. E. Benaim.
Grenada. Emb.: (see Jamaica).
Greece. Emb.: Marathonoromu No. 1. Paleo Psychico, Athens. ☎ 6719-530. Ambassador Ran Coriel.
Guatemala. Emb.: 13 Ave 14-07, Zona 10, Guatemala City. ☎ 371-305. Ambassador Shlomo Cohen.
Guinea Bissau (see Senegal).
Guyana (see Venezuela).
Equatorial Guinea (see Cameroon).
Haiti (see Panama).
Honduras (see Guatamala).
Hong Kong. Cons.: Admiralty 701, Tower 2, 18 Harcourt Rd., Central. ☎

25296091. Con.-Gen. Zohar Raz.
Hungary. Fulank, Utca 8, Budapest. ☎ 1767771. Ambassador Joel Alon.
Iceland. Emb.: (see Norway.) H. Con.-Gen. Pall Arnor Palsson.
India. Emb: 3 Aurangzeb Rd., New Delhi 10011. ☎ 3013238. Ambassador Yehoyada Haim. Cons.: Bombay 400 026, Kailas 50, G. Deshmukh Maro Cumballa Hill. ☎ 386 2793. Consul Walid Mansour.
Ireland. Emb.: Carrisbrook House, 122 Pembroke Rd, Ballsbridge, Dublin 4. ☎ 6680303. Ambassador Zvi Gabay.
Italy. Emb.: Via Michele Mercati 12, Rome. ☎ 36198500. Ambassador Yehuda Milo.
Jamaica. Con.: 7-9 Harbour St., Kingston. ☎ 922-5990. Hon. Consul Joseph Mayer-Matalon.
Japan. Emb.: 3 Niban-Cho, Chiyoda-ku, Tokyo. ☎ 3264-0911. Ambassador Moshe Ben Yaakov.
Jordan. Emb.: Forte Grand Hotel, Amman. ☎ 698541. Ambassador Shimon Shamir.
Kazakhstan. Emb: Dgeltoxan St. 87, Almaty. ☎ 507215. Ambassador Israel Mey-Ami.
Kenya. Emb.: Bishop Rd., Fair View Hotel, P.O. Box 30354, Nairobi. ☎ 722182. Ambassador Menashe Zipori.
Kirghizstan (see Kazakhstan).
Kiribati (Republic of) (see Australia).
Korea (South). Emb.: 823-21 Daekong Building, Yoksam-Dong Kangnam-Ku. ☎ 5643448. Ambassador Arie Arazi.
Laos (see Vietnam).
Latvia. Emb.: 2 Elizabetes St., LV 1340 Riga. ☎ 00 371 2 320739/320980. Fax: 00 371 830170. Ambassador Oded Ben-Hur.
Lesotho (see Swaziland).
Liberia. Emb.: Gardiner Avenue, Sinkor, POB 2057, Monrovia. ☎ 262073/262861. Fax: (977) 4415.
Liechtenstein. Con-Gen. G. Yarden (see Switzerland.)
Lithuania (see Latvia)
Luxembourg (see Belgium).
Macao (see Hong Kong).
Macedonia (see Greece).
Madagascar (see Kenya).
Malawi (see Zimbabwe).
Malta (see Italy).
Marshall Islands (see Australia).
Mauritius (see Kenya).
Mexico. Emb.: Sierra Madre 215, Mexico City 10 D.F. ☎ 540-63-40. Ambassador Moshe Melamed.
Micronesia (see Australia).
Moldova (see Ukraine).
Monaco (see France). Con.-Gen. Joseph Amihoud.
Mongolia (see China).
Morocco. Bureau de Liaison, Souissi, 52 Boulevard Mehdi Ben-Barka, Rabat. ☎ 657680. Head of Liaison Office, David Dadonn.
Mozambique (see Zimbabwe).
The Union of Mayanmar. Emb.: 49 Pyay Rd., Yangon. ☎ 22290. Fax: 22463. Ambassador Gad Natan.
Namibia (see Zimbabwe).
Nauro (see Australia).
Nepal. Emb.: Bishramalaya Hse., Lazimpat, Katmandu. ☎ 411811. Ambassador Esther Efrat Smilg.
Netherlands. Emb.: Buitenhof 47, The Hague, 2513 AH. ☎ 3760500. Ambassador Yossi Gal.

ISRAEL 161

Netherlands Antilles. Curaçao Consulate, Blauwduiffweg 5, Willemstad, Curaçao. ☎ 373533. Hon. Consul Paul Ackerman.
New Zealand. Emb.: PO Box 2171, DB Tower, 111 the Terrace, Wellington. ☎ 4722362. Ambassador Nisan Koren-Krupsky.
Nicaragua (see Guatamala).
Nigeria. Emb.: 636 Adeyemo Elakija St., Victoria Island, Lagos. ☎ 2622055. Ambassador Gadi Golan.
Norway. Emb.: Drammensveien 82, Oslo 2. ☎ 2447924. Ambassador Michael Shiloh.
Oman. Israel Trade Representation Office, PO Box 194, Aladhaiba, P.C. 130 Muscat. Hd. of Mission Oded Ben Haim.
Republic of Palau (see Australia).
Panama. Emb.: Edificio Grobman, Calle Manuel Icaza, Quinto Piso, Panama City 5. ☎ 2648022. Ambassador Yaakov Brakha.
Papua, New Guinea (see Australia).
Paraguay. Emb.: Piso 8, Edificion San Rafael, Calle Yergos No. 437 C/25 De Mayo. ☎ 495097. Ambassador Yoav Bar-On.
Peru. Emb.: Sanches 125, 6 Piso Santa Beatriz, Lima. ☎ 4334431. Ambassador Mario Joel Salpak.
Philippines. Emb.: Tratalgar Plaza 23 Floor, 105 H.V. Dela Costa St., Saleeldo Village, Makati, Manila. ☎ 892-5329. Fax: 819-0561. Ambassador A. Shetibel.
Poland. Interests Office: Ul. L. Krzywickiego 24, Warsaw. ☎ 250923. Ambassador Gershon Zohar.
Portugal. Emb.: Rua Antonio Enes 16-4°, Lisbon. ☎ 570-251. Ambassador B. Oron.
Qatar. Israel Trade Representation Office, Rm 512 Sheraton Hotel, Doha. ☎ 854-444. Hd. of Mission Shmuel Ravel.
Romania. Emb.: 5 Rue Burghelea, Bucharest. ☎ 6132633. Ambassador A. Millo.
Russia. Emb.:56 Bolshaya Ordinka, Moscow. ☎ 2306700. Ambassador Aliza Shenhar.
Rwanda (see Zaire).
St. Christopher, St. Kitts and St. Nevis (see Dominican Republic).
St. Lucia (see Jamaica).
St. Vincent and the Grenadines (see Jamaica).
San Marino. Con.-Gen. (see Italy).
Sao Tome and Principe (see Cameroon).
Senegal. Emb.: B.P. 296, Dakar. ☎ 231044. Ambassador Arieh Avidor.
Seychelles (see Kenya).
Singapore. Emb.: 58 Dalvey Rd., Singapore 1025. ☎ 235 0966. Ambassador D. Megiddo.
Slovakia (see Austria).
Slovenia (see Austria).
Solomon Islands (see Australia).
South Africa. Emb.: 339 Hilda St., Hatfield, Pretoria. ☎ 3422-693. Ambassador Elazar Granot.
Spain. Emb.: Calle Velazques 150, Madrid 28002. ☎ 4111357. Ambassador Ehud Gol.
Suriname (see Venezuela).
Swaziland. Emb.: Mbabane Hse., Warner St., P.O.B. 146, Mbabane. ☎ 42626. Ambassador.
Sweden. Emb.: Torstenssonsgatan 4, Stockholm. ☎ 6630435. Ambassador Gideon Ben-Ami.
Switzerland. Emb.: Alpenstrasse 32, Berne. ☎ 431042. Ambassador Gavriel Padon.
Tajikistan (see Uzbekistan).
Tanzania (see Kenya).
Thailand. Emb.: 75 Sukumvit Soi 19, Ocean Tower II 25th Floor, Bangkok 10110.

162   ISRAEL

☎ 2604854. Ambassador Mordechai Lewi.
Togo (see Côte d'Ivoire).
Tonga (see Australia).
Trinidad and Tobago (see Venezuela).
Tunisia. Interests Office. ☎ 795-695. Hd. Shalom Cohen.
Turkey. Emb.: Mahatma Gandhi Sok 85, Gaziosmanpasa, Ankara. ☎ 4463605. Ambassador Zvi Elpeleg.
Turkmenistan. Emb.: Ambassador Shmuel Meirom (resident in Jerusalem).
Tuvalu (see Australia).
Uganda (see Kenya).
Ukraine. Emb.: GPE - S, Lesi Ukrainki 34, 252195, Kiev, Ukraine. ☎ 2949753. Ambassador Zvi Magen.
United Kingdom. Emb.: 2 Palace Green, Kensington, W8 4QB. ☎ 0171-957 9500. Opening Hours: Mon.-Thur. 09.00-18.00 and Fri. 09.00-14.00. Ambassador Dror Zeigerman-Eden (see also p.21).
United States of America. Emb.: 3514 International Dr., Washington, D.C., 20008. ☎ 364 5500. Ambassador Eliahu Ben-Elissar.
Uruguay. Emb.: Bulevar Artigas 1585/89, Montevideo. ☎ 404164. Ambassador Yair Ben Shalom.
Uzbekistan. Emb.: Lachuti Street, No. 16a, Tashkent. ☎ 567823. Ambassador.
Vanuata (see Australia).
Vatican, Rooms 405-8, Via Barnata Onioni 6, Hotel Rivoli, Rome 00197. ☎ 807-6978. Ambassador Samuel Hadas.
Venezuela. Emb.: Avenida Franciso de Miranda, Centro Empresarial, Miranda 4 Piso Oficina 4-D, Los Ruices, Caracas. ☎ 2394-511. Ambassador Yosef Hasseen.
Vietnam. Emb.: PO Box 003, Thai Hoc, 68 Hguyen, Hanoi. ☎ 433140. Ambassador Uri Halfon.
Western Samoa (see Australia).
Zaire. Emb.: 12 Av. des Aviateure, Kinshasa. ☎ 21955. Ambassador S. Avital.
Zambia (see Zimbabwe).
Zimbabwe. Emb.: Three Anchor House, 6th floor, 54 Jason Moyo Ave, PO Box CY3191, Causeway. ☎ 756808. Ambassador Gershon Gan.

Main Political Parties

ISRAEL LABOUR PARTY
Est. 1968 by the merger of Mapai, Achdut Avoda and Rafi. Its programme: 'To attain national, social and pioneering aims, in the spirit of the heritage of the Jewish People, the vision of socialist Zionism and the vaiues of the Labour movement'. *Chairman* Ehud Barak. Ad.: 110 Hayarkon St., Tel Aviv. ☎ 209222.

LIKUD PARTY
Centre-Right Political Party. Dedicated to the principles of free enterprise and a united Land of Israel. *Chairman* Binyamin Netanyahu. Ad.: Metsudat Ze'ev, 38 King George St., Tel Aviv. ☎ (03) 5252922.

MAPAM
Founded in 1948. Allied with the Labour Party until the 1994 election. Formed an electoral coalition with RATZ and Shinui to form the MERETZ coalition in the current Labour government. Member of the Socialist International and of the Party of European Socialists. *Chair*: Chanan Erea; *Int. Sec.*: Monica Pollack. ☎ 6972175. Ad.: 4 Itama Ben Avi Str., Tel Aviv, 61016. ☎ 6972111. Fax: 6910504.

NATIONAL RELIGIOUS PARTY
Created through the merger of Mizrachi and Hapoel Hamizrachi in 1956. Its motto 'The People of Israel in the Land of Israel, according to the Torah of Israel'.

Ad.: 166 Ibn Gvirol St., Tel Aviv. ☎ 03-5442151. *Sec.* General Zevulun Orlev.

AGUDAT ISRAEL
Founded in 1912 in Katowice, Poland. Its principle is that only the Torah unites the Jewish people. *Political Sec.* M. Porush. Central Off.: Haherut Sq., Jerusalem. (☎ 384357), and 5 Bardechefsky St., Tel Aviv. (☎ 5617844).

HISTADRUT-GENERAL FEDERATION OF LABOUR IN ISRAEL
93 Arlosoroff St., Tel-Aviv. 62 098
☎ 03-692 1111, 692 1630. Telex: 342 488 HISTD IL. Fax: (972) 3 69 69 906. *Chairman* Haim Ramon MK. *Sec.-Gen.* Israel Kessar.
Histadrut is the largest labour organisation in Israel (69% of civilian work force). Membership is individual and open to all men and women 18 years of age and above who live on the earnings of their own labour without exploiting the work of others. 1994 membership totalled over 1.5 million including not only workers but also housewives, the self-employed, professionals as well as the unemployed, students and pensioners. Workers interests are protected through a number of occupational and professional unions affiliated to the Histadrut. In addition the Histadrut offers a wide range of social secunty and welfare services which include: a sick fund (health insurance), pensions' funds, old age welfare installations, strike fund, etc. The sick fund runs its own hospitals, medical clinics and dispensaries, rest and convalescent homes. The Histadrut operates a nation-wide network of educational facilities: workers' colleges vocational and secondary schools, apprenticeship classes, courses for new immigrants, etc. It maintains institutes of labour studies for trade union activists from developing countries. It is also widely engaged in the fields of culture as well as sports. Attached to the Histadrut is a very active women's organisation "Na'amat". Members of collective and cooperative settlements as well as practically all other cooperatives belong to the Histadrut. The Federation also owns or has a major interest in large industrial, transport, building and marketing enterprises. It is linked to a bank 'Bank Hapoalim' (the largest in the country), publishing house and daily newspaper.

Educational and Research Institutions

HEBREW UNIVERSITY OF JERUSALEM
Founded in 1918 and opened in 1925 on Mount Scopus. When, contrary to the provisions of the Armistice Agreement after the War of Independence in 1949, access to Mount Scopus was denied by Jordan, the University functioned in scattered temporary quarters until a new campus was built on Givat Ram, and a medical campus in Ein Kerem, both in Jerusalem. After the Six-Day War of June 1967, the Mount Scopus campus was rebuilt and expanded. Today the University serves some 24,000 students in its seven Faculties: Humanities, Social Sciences, Science, Law, Medicine, Dental Medicine and Agricultural and Environmental Quality Sciences (the latter located in Rehovot). There are 12 Schools: Education, Business Administration, Applied Science, Nutritional Sciences, Nursing, Occupational Therapy, Pharmacy, Public Health, Social Work, Veterinary Medicine, Library & Archive Studies, and School for Overseas Students. The Jewish National and University Library is on the Givat Ram campus and there are about 100 research centres. The Magnes Press/Hebrew University publishes scientific and academic works. *Ch. Bd. of Govs.* A. Grass; *President* Prof. Menachem Magidor; *Rector* Prof. Menachem Ben-Sasson. Ad.: Mount Scopus, Jerusalem, 91905. ☎ (02)5 882917. Fax: (02) 5883021. Website: www.huji.ac.il

ISRAEL INSTITUTE OF TECHNOLOGY (Technion)
Established in 1924 as a small technical institute, it now has 10,600 students and includes among its 19 departments: Civil engineering, architecture, mechanical engineering, electrical engineering, science, aeronautical engineering, agricultural

engineering, materials engineering, industrial design and chemical technology. All departments have been transferred to the new Technion City on Mount Carmel. The main buildings include the Winston Churchill Auditorium and the Shine Student Union. It also has a graduate school, evening school, extension division and Research & Development Foundation. *President* Prof. Z. Tadmor. Ad.: Technion City, Mount Carmel, Haifa. ☎ (04) 228141. Fax: 324-653.

WEIZMANN INSTITUTE OF SCIENCE
The Institute at Rehovot engages in research in Mathematical Sciences, Chemistry, Physics, Biology, Biochemistry and Science Teaching. *President* Prof. H. Harari; *Chancellor* Lord Sieff of Brimpton. Ad.: P.O.B. 26, Rehovot 76100, Israel. ☎ 972-8-9343111. Fax: 972-8-9466966.

BAR-ILAN UNIVERSITY
Since its founding in 1955, Bar-Ilan has grown to become Israel's second-largest university, comprising a modern 70-acre campus in Ramat Gan, outside tel Aviv, with five regional colleges across Israel. Over 6,000 courses are taught in the faculties of natural and social sciences, humanities, Jewish studies and law, by 1,300 academic faculty to 22,000 students. Today, Israel's largest schools of education and social work and the premier Jewish studies faculty, opreate at Bar-Ilan. Additionally, the university is home to world-class scientific research institutes in physics, medicinal chemistry, mathematics, brain reseach, economics, strategic studies, developmental psychology, musicology, archaeology, bible, Jewish law and philosophy, and more. Some 40 prominent universities around the world maintain academic cooperation agreements with Bar-Ilan. The university bridges the gap between religious and secular Israelis. Every day, Israelis of widely varying backgrounds and religious beliefs work and study together in harmony through Bar-Ilan. The university teaches tolerance of diversty, and pluralism in thought and religious belief.. The unique Bar-Ilan formulae blend tradition with modern technologies and scholarship, and teach the compelling ethics of Jewish heritage. *Chancellor* Rabbi Prof. Emanuel Rackman; *President* Prof. Moshe Kaveh; *Rector* Prof. Yehuda Friedlander. *Cor.* BIU, Ramat Gan, Israel 52900. ☎ 972-3-531-8111. *Student information:* 972-3-531-8274; Fax 972-3-535-1522. Internet: http//:www.biu.ac.il. British Friends of Bar-Ilan (London) ☎ 0171-436 9706. Fax 0171-436 2483.

BEN-GURION UNIVERSITY OF THE NEGEV, BEERSHEBA
Founded 1965, the university comprises the following faculties: Humanities and Social Sciences, Natural Sciences, Engineering, Health Sciences and School of Management. *President* Prof. Avishay Braverman. Ad.: P.O. Box 653, Beersheba, 84105. ☎ (07) 6461219.

CENTER FOR JEWISH ART
POB 4262, Jerusalem 91042. ☎ 02-6586605. Fax: 02-6586672. E-mail: cja@vms.huji.ac.il. *Director* Dr. A. Cohen-Mushlin; *Academic Chairman* Prof. Bezalel Narkiss.

DEVELOPMENT STUDY CENTRE
Founded in Rehovot in 1961, its main object is interdisciplinary research & training activities related to regional development in Israel and the developing world, and training new immigrants for better employment. Ad.: P.O.B. 2355 Rehovot, Israel 76122. ☎ 08-9474111. Fax: 08-9475884.

HAIFA UNIVERSITY
Established in 1963, the university comprises 38 departments housed in 4 faculties. The Faculty of Humanities, The Faculty of Social Sciences and Mathematics and the Faculty of Law and 1 school, the School of Education. Its 13,100 students

ISRAEL 165

include many Arab and Druze students. *President* Prof. Y. Hayuth; *Rector* Prof. G. Gilbar. Ad.: Mount Carmel, Haifa 31905. ☎ (04) 8240111. Fax: (04) 8342101. Email: RYRECTOR@uvm.haifa.ac.il

ISRAEL OCEANOGRAPHIC AND LIMNOLOGICAL RESEARCH COMPANY
(Est. 1967) To develop knowledge and technology for use of marine and fresh water sources. *Ch., Bd. Dirs.* Admiral (Res.) Abraham Botzer; *Dir.-Gen.* Dr. Yuval Cohen. Ad.: Tel Shikmona, P.O.B. 8030, Haifa 31080. ☎ 04-8515202. Fax: 04-8511911.

JERUSALEM ACADEMY OF JEWISH STUDIES
53 Katzenellenbogen St., Har Nof, P.O.B. 5454, Jerusalem 91053. ☎ 6522817. Fax: 652287. UK office (Reg. Charity No. 262716), 1007, Finchley Rd., London NW11 7HB. ☎ 0181-458 8563. Fax: 0171-431 3593.

JERUSALEM COLLEGE OF TECHNOLOGY
Est. in 1969 to train engineers and applied scientists within a rel. framework. The College has depts. in Electro-Optics and Applied Physics, Electronic Engineering, Computer Sciences, Management Accounting, Technology Management and Marketing, Applied Mathematics and Teacher Training. The complex includes a Bet Midrash for Jewish studies; one-year yeshiva programme for English-speaking students. The College awards a Bachelor's degree in Technology and Applied Science, Managerial Accounting & Information Systems. *President* Prof. Y. Bodenheimer; *Rector* Prof. Y. Zeisel. Ad.: 21 Havaad Haleumi St., Jerusalem. ☎ 9722-751111. Fax: 9722 422075.

THE LOUIS GUTTMAN ISRAEL INSTITUTE OF APPLIED SOCIAL RESEARCH
Founded in 1946 to advise governmental, public and private bodies on research in social psychology, sociology, psychology and related disciplines. *Scientific Dir.* Prof. S. Kugelmass. Ad.: 19 Washington St., Jerusalem, 91070. ☎ 231421.

MIKVEH ISRAEL AGRICULTURAL SCHOOL
The first agricultural school in Israel, it was founded by Charles Netter of the Alliance Isralite Universelle in 1870. The curriculum, in addition to training in agriculture, comprises instruction in the humanities, Jewish subjects, science, etc. Ad.: Mikveh Israel, Doar Holon. ☎ 03-842050. Zip code 58910.

ORT ISRAEL NETWORK
Est. 1948, ORT Israel manages Scientific and Technological Colleges and schools for around 80,000 young and adult students yearly. *Dir. Gen.*: I. Goralnik. Head office: 39, King David Blvd., Tel-Aviv 61160. Tel: 03-5203222.

TEL AVIV UNIVERSITY
The university sponsors studies and research in all the arts and sciences and includes among its faculties a department of space and planetary sciences, its observatory, at Mitzpe Ramon in the Negev, being the first in Israel. A science based industry utilising the university's manpower and equipment has been established. Its Graduate School of Business Administration was the first established in the country. There is a one year course which prepares new immigrants for entry into Israeli universities. *President* Prof. Yoram Dinstein; *Rector* Prof. Dan Amir. Ad.: Ramat Aviv, Tel Aviv. ☎ 5450111.

THE ZINMAN COLLEGE OF PHYSICAL EDUCATION AT THE WINGATE INSTITUTE
(Est. 1944.) Teachers College for Physical Educators. Offers four-year Bachelor of

Education course, including Teachers' Diploma. Specializations in early childhood, special education, sports for the handicapped, posture cultivation, cardiac rehabilitation, physical activity for the elderly, public health, behaviour analysis, dance and movement, leisure and reaction education, nautical education, scouting education. Joint M.A. programme with Haifa University.
Faculty of 200, student body of 900 full-time students, 1,500 in part-time in-service courses. Ad.: P.E. College at Wingate Institute, Netanya, Israel 42902. ☎ 972-9-639295. Fax: 972-9-653456. Email: zinman@wincol.macam98.ac.il. Internet: http://www.zinman.macam98.ac.il.

Commercial Organisations

BANK OF ISRAEL
Set up by the Knesset in 1954. Its functions include those usually discharged by central banks. It issues the currency and acts as Government banker, and manages the official gold and foreign reserves. *Gov.* Prof Jacob A. Frenkel. Ad.: Rechov Eliezer Kaplan, Kiryat Ben-Gurion, Jerusalem, 91007. ☎ (2) 6552211. Fax: (2) 6528805.

ISRAEL-AMERICA CHAMBER OF COMMERCE AND INDUSTRY
Exec. Dir. Nina Admoni. Ad.: 35 Shaul Hamelech Blvd., Tel Aviv. ☎ 6952341. Fax: 6951272.

ISRAEL-BRITISH CHAMBER OF COMMERCE
(Est. 1951.) 65 Allenby Rd., 65134 Tel Aviv; PO Box 4610, Tel Aviv. ☎ (03) 525 2232. Fax: (03) 620-3032. *Exec. Dir.* F. Kipper.

THE ISRAEL PRO BONO ZEDEK FREE LEGAL AID CENTRE and
ISRAEL LEGAL REFERRAL SERVICE
PO Box 2828, Jerusalem. ☎ (02)-5820126. Fax (02)-5243228. The Israel Pro Bono Zedek Free Legal Aid Centre provides free legal advice and consultations by volunteer lawyers who are members of the Israel Bar Association and by volunteer Rabbinical court pleaders.

MANUFACTURERS' ASSOCIATION OF ISRAEL
Jerusalem: ☎ (02) 252449. Haifa: ☎ (04) 524202. Tel Aviv: ☎ (03) 5198787. *President* D. Propper.
Other Organisations

ASSOCIATION OF JEWISH RELIGIOUS PROFESSIONALS FROM THE SOVIET UNION AND EASTERN EUROPE (SHAMIR)
6 David Yellin St., Jerusalem. ☎ 02-5385384. Fax: 02-5385118. *Sec.* Martelle Urivetsky.

ASSOCIATION FOR THE WELLBEING OF ISRAEL'S SOLDIERS
(Ha'aguda Lemaan Hechayal) The Association for the Wellbeing of Israel's Soldiers was founded in 1942, during the Second World War, at a time when the young men of pre-state Israel were being drafted into the allied armies and the Jewish Brigade. The slogan back then was "The Heart of the People is with its Soldiers", and this sentiment continues to guide the Association's activity today. *Head Off.:* P.O. Box 21707, Tel Aviv 61217. *Overseas Dept*: 60 Weizman St., Tel Aviv 62155. ☎ 03 5465135. Fax (03) 5465145.

BETH HATEFUTSOTH
The Nahum Goldmann Museum of the Jewish Diaspora, which opened in Tel-Aviv in 1978, tells the story of the Jewish people from the time of their expulsion from

ISRAEL 167

the Land of Israel 2,500 years ago to the present. History, tradition and the heritage of Jewish life in all parts of the world are brought to life in murals, reconstructions, dioramas, audio-visual displays, documentary films and interactive multi-media presentation. Ad: Tel-Aviv University Campus, Ramat-Aviv, P.O.B. 39359. Tel-Aviv 61392. ☎ 03-6462020. Fax 03-6462134. Email: bhmuseum@post.tau.ac.il. Website: http://www.bh.org.il.

CHIEF RABBINATE
The Chief Rabbinate consists of two joint Chief Rabbis and a Chief Rabbinical Council of 17. *Chief Rabbis* Rabbi Israel Meir Lan (Ashkenazi) and Rabbi Eliyahu Bakshi Doron (Rishon Lezion, Sephardi). Ad.: Hechal Shlomo, 58 King George St., Jerusalem. ☎ 247-112. Fax 259-641. There are District Rabbinical Courts (Batei Din) in Jerusalem, Tel Aviv, Haifa, Petach Tikvah, Rehovot, Tiberias-Safad, Beersheba and Ashkelon.

ISRAEL MOVEMENT FOR PROGRESSIVE JUDAISM
☎ 02-203484. Fax: 02-203343.

ISRAEL MUSEUM
Hakirya, Jerusalem. ☎ 02-708811. Comprises Bezalel National Art Museum (Jewish art of all ages); Irene and Davide Sala Wing for Israel communities, traditions and heritage; Samuel Bronfmann Biblical and Archaeological Museum; Shrine of the Book (Dead Sea scrolls, etc.); Rockefeller Museum (archaeology of the land of Israel).

JEWISH AGENCY FOR ISRAEL
Founded 1929; Reconstituted 1971. Constitutents are the World Zionist Organisation, United Israel Appeal, Inc. (USA), and Keren Hayesod. By reasons of its record and world-wide org. the Jewish Agency has come to be widely regarded as the representative org. of Jews the world over particularly in regard to the development of Israel and immigration to it. The governing bodies of the Jewish Agency are: the Assembly, which lays down basic policy, the Bd. of Governors, which manages its affairs between annual Assembly meetings, and the Executive, responsible for day-to-day operations. Jewish Agency, P.O. Box 92, Jerusalem. ☎ 972 2 6202450. Fax: 972 26202303. Email: ilanr@jaizo.org.il *Ch. Exec.* Avraham Burg; *Ch. Bd.* Charles Goodman; *Dir.-Gen.* Shimshon Shoshani; *Act. Sec.-Gen.* Ilan Rubin.

KEREN KAYEMETH LEISRAEL (Jewish National Fund)
P.O. Box 283, Jerusalem, Israel. *World Chairman* Moshe Rivlin. *Head of Fund Raising* Avinoam Binder. The work of the JNF is to improve the quality of life for Israeli citizens by means of afforestation, ecology, water conservation and site preparation, and development for upbuilding the land to ensure its future.

NATURE RESERVES AUTHORITY (NRA)
Set up by a decision of the Knesset in 1963, the NRA has opened many areas of scenic beauty and nature reserves and been responsible for nature conservancy in Israel. Ad.: 78 Yirmeyahu St., Jerusalem. ☎ 02 387471. Fax 02-374887.

WOMEN'S INTERNATIONAL ZIONIST ORGANISATION (Wizo)
(Reg. Charity No.: 580057321). 250,000 women, 100,000 of them in Israel, are members of this org. which maintains 800 institutions and services in Israel. *World President* Mrs M. Modai; *V. President and Chairman Exec.* Mrs H. Glaser. Ad.: 38 David Hamelech Blvd., Tel Aviv. 64237. ☎ 03-6923717. Fax: 972-3-6958-267.

WORLD ZIONIST ORGANISATION
Founded by Theodor Herzl at the First Zionist Congress in Basle in 1897, it was

the moving spirit in the events leading up to the establishment of the State of Israel in 1948. The 'Jerusalem Programme,' adopted by the 27th Zionist Congress in Jerusalem in 1968 reformulates the aims of the Zionist Movement as: The unity of the Jewish people and the centrality of the State of Israel in its life, The ingathering of the exiles in the historic Jewish homeland by aliya; The strengthening of the State of Israel, which is founded on the prophetic ideals of justice and peace; Preserving the uniqueness of the Jewish people by promoting Jewish and Hebr. educ. and upholding Jewish spiritual and cultural values; Defending the rights of Jews wherever they live. The supreme body of the W.Z.O. is the Zionist Congress, to which delegates are elected by members of Z. Federations abroad and by the Z. parties in Israel. The two governing bodies elected by the Congress are: the Executive, and the Zionist General Council to which the Executive is responsible and which decides Z. policy between Congresses. *Ch. of Executive* Yehiel Leket. P.O. Box 92, Jerusalem 91920. ☎ 202222. Fax: 252-353.

YAD VASHEM
Har Hazikaron (Mount of Remembrance), Jerusalem. ☎ 02-6751611. P.O.B. 3477 Jeruselem 91034. Website: www.yad-vashem.org.il.
Holocaust memorial and museum. Includes exhibitions, Hall of Remembrance and children's memorial, also archives and a library.

British Settlements
The following are some of the settlements populated by large groups of immigrants from the United Kingdom and Ireland associated with the JIA Israel (see below), which represents the Israeli Office of the Zionist Federation of Great Britain and Ireland. In some cases groups from Britain themselves established these settlements; in others, they joined existing settlements as 'reinforcement' groups. Several of the entries have been revised extensively for this edition.
Beit Chever (Kfar Daniel) established in 1951 near Ben Shemen by Machal ex-Servicemen, mainly from Britain and South Africa. The 80 settlers there specialise in mixed farming.
Kfar Blum, established in 1943 north of Lake Hula, in Upper Galilee. Named after the late Leon Blum, it was the first kibbutz of British and American Habonim who joined forces with Latvian immigrants. Specialises in mixed farming and fish-breeding. Population over 700.
Kfar Hanassi was founded in 1948 in an abandoned Arab village called Mansura, located near the Jordan River on the Syrian border. The kibbutz was placed there to halt westward advancement by the Syrian Army in any attempt to cut Northern Gallilee in half. Two years later, the kibbutz was moved two kilometres westward to its present site, six kilometers from Rosh Pina. Until the Six Day War the kibbutz had been a border settlement. The kibbutz was named in honour of Israel's first president, Chaim Weizmann ('Kfar Hanassi' means 'Village of the President'). Most of the first settlers came from the Habonim Youth Movement in Britain, where they had spent the war years on training farms and had then joined the illegal immigration by sea to Israel. Many were refugees from Europe, brought over to Britain by the youth transports. There was also a smaller group from France and Australia among the first settlers. In the late 1950s the kibbutz was reinforced by another group from 'Habonim' Britain and it also absorbed individuals from America, South Africa and Israel. Most of the younger members (30-50) are Israelis, born on kibbutzim, and their spouses.
Affilation United Kibbutz Movement: Takam. Kfar Hanassi is a non-Orthodox kibbutz. There are services on high holy days and all Jewish festivals are celebrated communally, based upon old tradition and new kibbutz tradition (especially agricultural festivals).

Population 700, including 450 adults (300 of whom are members, the rest are candidates, volunteers and Ulpan students) and 250 children.
Kibbutz institutions Main decisions in the kibbutz are decided in the general assembly and by polls. On a day-to-day basis, the kibbutz is run by committees, such as those for education, health, transport, housing, culture and finance. Members are usually chosen to serve on a committee for a period of two years.
Agriculture Avocado orchards, citrus groves, field crops (such as corn, cotton or beans), medicinal herb crops, juniper nursery, poultry, sheep.
Industry Foundry for high-quality aluminium casting and stainless-steel ball valves (the kibbutz main branch); guest houses offering bed and breakfast; catamaran trips on the River Jordan; Galilee herbal remedies; hydroelectric plant.
Ad. Kibbutz Kfar Hanassi, Upper Galillee 1, 12305. ☎ 972-6-6914901. Fax 972-6-6914017.

Kfar Mordechai, founded near G'dera in 1950, is named after the late Mordechai Eliash, first Israeli Minister to Britain. Sponsored by the British Zionist Federation, Kfar Mordechai was the first middle-class settlement established for immigrants from Britain. Population about 60 families, half of them from Britain. Sugar is produced from locally grown beet. The moshav holds annual summer camps for local children.

Kibbutz Amiad is located in the southern part of Upper Galilee on the Tiberias–Kiryat Shmona road. It is near the route of the ancient coast road which ran from Syria to Egypt. Amiad was founded in 1946 by a settlement group of Jewish youth who had served together in the Jewish underground defence force (Palmach) which operated during the British Mandate in Palestine. Upon completion of their military service, they received agricultural training in Kibbutz Geva and in 1946 they founded their own community. The site was chosen for its strategic value: it overlooks the main road to Upper Galilee. This strategic importance grew during the War of Independence when the kibbutz housed an Israeli army base. Over the years the founders have been joined by Jewish immigrants from England and Holland. Near the kibbutz are the ruins of a medieval inn which are called 'Joseph's Well'. According the Arab tradition, this is the site of the well into which Joseph was thrown by his brothers. In addition, flint tools from the early Canaanite period have been found near the kibbutz.
Affiliations United Kibbutz Movement; Upper Galilee Regional Council.
Population Approximately 400, including 225 members and 150 children.
Agriculture Admiad farms approximately 15,000 dunams of land (3,750 acres) and has another 20,000 dunams (5,000 acres) of natural pastureland at its disposal. Major branches are orchards, both deciduous and subtropical, bananas, citrus, field crops, chickens and cattle.
Industry The kibbutz factory manufactures plastic and metal irrigation and water-filtering equipment for agriculture, industry and municipalities which is marketed world wide. Other commercial initiatives include a winery, graphic design studio, engineering consultants – plastics, and a bed and breakfast motel.
Ad. Kibbutz Amiad, Mobile Post Galil Elyon 1, 12335. ☎ 972-6-6933550. Fax 972-6-6933866.

Kibbutz Bet Rimon is situated in the hills of Lower Galilee. Established in 1980 by members of British Bnei Akiva. Mixed farming with a large dairy herd. Manufacturers of light agricultural tools and parchment for Torah scrolls, Mezuzot and other religious items. Guest house and seminar centre on the kibbutz. A new community neighbourhood is being established beside the kibbutz for non-kibbutz residents. Population about 100.
Ad. Kibbutz Bet Rimon, D.N. Hamovil Natzeret Illit, 17950. ☎ 972-6-6509611. Fax 972-6-6412583.

Kibbutz Beit Ha'emek, established in 1949, near Nahariya, Western Galilee, is the third kibbutz of British Habonim. The original settlers were Hungarian members of the movement and these were later joined by British and Dutch Habonim. The settlement grows avocado, cotton, citrus fruit and bananas. Its activities include poultry, dairy and sheep farming. It has factories involved in the biochemical industry.

Kibbutz Kadarim, in central Galilee overlooking the Kinneret, is an intimate rural community based on the principles of personal freedom, social justice and communal participation. Established in 1980 with a core population of Israeli, Australian and New Zealand youth movement members, Kadarim today has a population of 50 adults, and 40 young children under the age of ten. Approximately 25 per cent of current members are Olim from Habonim-Dror Australasia. Kadarim is a unique community, a partnership in which members retain their individual freedom: in particular, the right to make independent choices about their work-lives and finances. At the same time, a sophisticated system of communal services are provided to all members – and their children – with particular emphasis on high-quality education and healthcare, communal cultural events and social security. Kadarim is presently absorbing new couples and families, and is currently pursuing the option of home-ownership within the kibbutz framework.

Kadarim's businesses at present include manufacturing (Kapro spirit levels and measuring tools), agriculture (mango and citrus groves, a chicken run and beef cattle), and a newly opened bed and breakfast tourist facility. Many members also pursue their chosen professions outside the kibbutz, in teaching, medicine, alternative therapies, engineering, law, social work and computers. ☎ 06-986222. Fax. 06-986208. Email kapro@inter.net.il

Kibbutz Lavi was founded in 1949 by members of 'British Bachad – The Organization of Religious Pioneers' and today is one of the 17 Religious Kibbutzim in Israel. It is located in Lower Galilee, ten minutes west of Tiberias. Over 125 families live in Lavi (total population 650) where they share a communal life based on Torah (Judaism) and Avoda (working and settling the Land of Israel).

Kibbutz Lavi is world famous for its two major businesses: the well-known Kibbutz Hotel Lavi, one of the pioneers of the kibbutz hospitality idea 30 years ago, which hosts tens of thousands of guests each year; and Kibbutz Lavi Furniture Industries, the world's largest manufacturer of synagogue furniture. Kibbutz Lavi is also involved in educational tourism through the Kibbutz Lavi Education Center, which offers programmes and seminars for groups interested in enriching their understanding of Judaism, the kibbutz way of life and the Galilee region. In addition, Kibbutz Lavi has a large dairy and poultry farm, orchards and numerous field crops. Email lavi@lavi.co.il

Kibbutz Yassu'r was founded in January 1949 in western Galilee, ten kilometres east of Acco. The first kibbutz of British members of Hashomer Hatzair. Population of about 350. Economy based on mixed farming, 'Tree of Knowledge' (educational assembly kits factory), 'Magi' sock factory and tourist services. Ad. D.N., Misgav, 20150. ☎04-9960111. Fax 04-9960113.

Kibbutz Zikim, established in 1949 near the northern border of the Gaza Strip by Romanian members of Hashomer Hatzair. British members of the movement have since joined the settlement. The kibbutz concentrates on arable farming and has large vineyards, in addition to citrus groves and banana plantations. Has foam rubber mattress factory. Population about 250.

Massuoth Yitzhak, near Ashkelon, a Hapoel Hamizrachi moshav shitufi established in 1949. Population nearly 300, including 20 families from Britain. Specialises in mixed farming.

Moshav Habonim (Kfar Lamm) near Atlit, was set up in 1948 by Machal members from Britain and South Africa. Specialises in mixed farming and has factory making building insulating material. Runs summer camp for children. Population about 200.

Kibbutz Mevo Hama. Founded on Golan Heights overlooking Lake Kinneret by

British and Australian Habonim after Six-Day War. In addition to beef cattle, ranching and cotton farming, they run a factory, specialising in plastic products.

Kibbutz Mishmar David. Two British Habonim garinim joined to revive this small kibbutz in Jerusalem corridor. Mixed farming and large offset print shop. Originally founded 1948. Population about 140.

Kibbutz Machanayim. Re-established in early 1950s in Upper Galilee near Rosh Pina with members of British Dror movement. Specialises in fruit orchards and mixed farming, particularly flowers. Has a precision tool factory. About 310 members.

Kibbutz Alumim is situated in the north-western Negev, approximately two miles south of Kibbutz Saad; closest towns are Sederot and Netivot. It is an hour's drive from Tel Aviv, one and a half hour's from Jerusalem, and half an hour from both Ashkelon and Beer Sheva. Alumim was established in 1966, by graduates of Bnei Akiva youth movement, and is a member of the Religious Kibbutz Movement (HaKibbutz HaDati). Initially intended as a border settlement, its status changed when Israel captured the Gaza Strip in the 1867 Six Day War.

Alumim's livelihood comes mainly from agriculture: field crops, citrus orchards, avocado plantations, a dairy herd of aproximately 200 milking cows, and rearing chickens for meat. Alumim has no industry but recently opened up several kibbutz branches to outside customers – for example, the garage, carpentry shop, electrical shop and the metalwork shop (now 'Shelah Systems', building computerised automated materials handling systems). There are comfortable, air-conditioned guest rooms and, as a religious kibbutz, all religious facilities are provided.

Alumim has a population of approximately 450, with about 75 families and various temporary groups such as Aliyat HaNoar, Nahal Army groups and youth groups visiting from abroad. Kibbutz Alumim had two large influxes of British Bnei Akiva graduates, in the early 1970s and mid-1980s, and they now comprise about 20 per cent of the population, taking on many of the leading communal roles. Kibbutz Alumim, although past its thirtieth birthday, is young in spirit, financially and socially stable, and set to face the challenges of the twenty-first century.

Ad. Kibbutz Alumim, D.N. HaNegev 85138. ☎ 07 994 9711. Fax 07 994 9700. Guest Rooms Office 07 994 9805. Correspondence to Shmarya Meller, Kibbutz Secretary.

Kibbutz Adamit. Founded after Yom Kippur War by young members of Hashomer Hatzair from various Western countries. Right on Lebanese border. Farming.

Moshav Sde Nitzan was founded in 1973 by a group of immigrants from English-speaking countries including England, US, Canada, New Zealand, Australia and South Africa. We started with 20 families as a small farming community in the western Negev. We are now celebrating our twenty-fifth anniversary having grown to 74 families, 14 of whom joined us during the last three years. About 50 per cent of original families are still here. The original families were joined over the years by Israeli families. Our main occupation is still agriculture, primarily flowers for export. We also have mango orchards and recently planted 1,600 dunam to citrus. The moshav is, in fact, a small village of independent families. In the future we are planning to open a section of up to 100 lots for non-farming families. Our area of the country is entirely kibbutzim and moshavim and very underpopulated. We have a school complex shared by all the moshavim taking children from 18 months through high school. We also have a regional medical centre, including, in addition to medical doctors and visits from specialists, a pharmacy, a dental clinic and a physical therapy wing. Closest city is Beersheva.

Kibbutz Tuval was established in January 1981 by immigrants from British and South African Habonim-Dror as well as graduates of the Israeli Scout Movement. In the course of its history, the kibbutz has maintained a mix of Anglo-Saxons and Israelis, and this has very much shaped the unique quality of the communi-

ty. The kibbutz today has 40 members and has recently taken a decision to enlarge its ranks by establishing a 'Community Village' which will run in parallel with the kibbutz. The plan is for 27 families to join the community in the summer of 1998, and an additional 32 families in 1999. The primary sources of income are a dairy herd, chicken houses, a kiwi-fruit plantation and the Tuval Seminar Centre and guest houses, providing educational workshops for both English- and Hebrew-speaking groups.
Ad. Kibbutz Tuval, D.N. Bikat Bet HaKerem, 25166. ☎ 972-9907-907. Fax 972-4-9907-900.

UJIA Israel (incorporating the British Olim Society). Head Office; 76 Ibn Gvirol St., POB 16266, Tel Aviv 61162. ☎ 03-6965244. Fax 03-6968696. Email 100264,300@compuserve.com
Our organisation, JIA Israel, is the result of the recent merger between the British Olim Society and the Israel office of the Joint Israel Appeal. Our head office is in Tel Aviv with branch offices in Jerusalem, Karmiel and Ashkelon. Not only do we cater to the needs of British immigrants but also we service the Australian, New Zealand, Irish, Scandinavia and German.
JIA Israel is active in four main departments:
Campaign Support Services The strengthening of ties between communities in Britain and Israel is a central goal of JIA Israel. By cultivating British Jewry's involvement in projects in Israel through Project Renewal and Partnership 2,000 and through guest services and missions, this objective is largely achieved.
Immigrant (Oleh) and Absorption Services These include counselling services which not only deal with pre-Aliya questions but help steer the Oleh through the complexities of Israeli bureaucracy. We are experts on all points of status, immigrant rights and housing. Through our experienced employment counsellors, Olim are helped to find jobs in Israel. We offer our immigrants loans and mortgages at attractive rates. We provide our own social worker. For the young we have launched YES, the Young English Speakers group, in conjunction with other immigrant organisations which offers regular social get-togethers on diverse and interesting themes.
Israel Experience Statistics have shown that British youngsters who have been part of the JIA Israel Experience Programme are far less likely to marry out. Each year close to 1,000 of them work in one of the settlements along the northern confrontation line as part of Partnership 2,000, or they are involved in community work in Ashkelon or Dimona.
The BOS Charitable Trust is essentially aimed at helping the disadvantaged and less fortunate. In addition, the BOS Charitable Trust is involved in a host of attractive projects, the most notable of these being, perhaps, the Job Clubs which are courses aimed at teaching immigrants, mainly from the ex-Soviet Union, how best to go about finding work in Israel. To date, over 4,000 immigrants have attended 164 courses in 24 cities and towns throughout the country. Job Clubs have three permanent centres, in Netanya, Haifa and Ashdod.
English Speaking Residents Association (ESRA). P.O.B 3132, Herzliya 46104. ☎ 972-9-580632 or 972-9-581583. Fax 972-9-9543781. Email: esra@trendline.co.il. (Non-profit organisation no. 550037451.) A voluntary organisation assisting absorption of English-speaking immigrants, by means of social, cultural and educational projects, practical help in finding employment, support and advice on emotional, social and legal problems. The ESRA Community Fund initiates and supports welfare and educational projects for disadvantaged Israelis and immigrants from distressed countries. Office also in Ra'anana. Publ. ESRA magazine. *Contact*: Janna Short.
Israel Britain and the Commonwealth Association (IBCA), Industry House, 29 Hamored St., 68125, Tel-Aviv. Fax (03) 5104646. Branches in Haifa and Jerusalem. The main aims of the Association are to encourage, develop, and extend social, cultural and economic relations between Israel and the British

Commonwealth. *Chairman* L. Harris; *Vice-Chairman* Dr. A. Lerner; *Hon. Sec.* Madelaine Mordecai; *Contact* Freida Peled.

ITALY (34,500)

The Jewish community of Italy, whose history goes back to very early times, increased considerably at the time of the Dispersion in C.E. 70. During the Middle Ages and the Renaissance there were newcomers from Spain and Germany. Rich syns. as well as rabbinical schools, yeshivot, and printing houses were set up and became known in many countries. During the first years of fascism Italian Jews did not suffer; only after 1938 (under Nazi pressure) were racial laws introduced and, during the German occupation from 1943 to 1945 nearly 12,000, especially from Rome, were murdered or banished. The number of persons registered as Jews now is around 35,000. The most important communities are those of Rome (15,000), Milan (10,000), and Turin (1,630), followed by Florence, Trieste, Livorno and Venice and other centres.

ROME
*Central organisation: Unione delle Comunità Ebraiche Italiane, 00153 Roma, Lungotevere Sanzio 9. ☎ 5803670. Fax: 5899569. *President* Tullia Zevi.
Community: Lungotevere Cenci, 00186. ☎ 6840061. Fax: 68400684. Rabbinical office. Fax: 68400655.
Chief Rabbi, Dr. Elio Toaff. ☎ 6875051/2/3..
Jewish Agency, Corso Vittorio Emanuele 173, 00185. ☎ 68805290. Fax: 6789511.
Synagogues, Lungotevere Cenci; Via Catalana; Via Balbo 33.
Syn. of Libyan refugees-Via Padova 92. ☎ 44233334.

MILAN
Community, Via Sally Mayer, 2, 20146. ☎ (02) 48302806. Fax: 02/48304660.
Synagogue, Via Guastalla, 19, 10122. ☎ (02) 5512029. Fax: (02) 5512101.
Zionist Fed., Via E de Amicis 49. ☎ (02) 8357558.

JAMAICA (350)

The Jewish settlement here, first composed of fugitives from the Inquisition, goes back before the period of the British occupation in 1655. During the eighteenth century there was an Ashkenazi influx from England. Jewish disabilities were abolished in 1831. There were formerly congregations at Port Royal, Spanish Town (two syns.) and at Montego Bay (1845-1900). The Ashkenazi and Sephardi communities in Kingston merged into one in 1921, the last of eight which once flourished.
*United Congregation of Israelites, Synagogue Shaare Shalom, Duke St. (Syn. built 1885, rebuilt 1911.) *Spiritual Leader* Rev. Dr Ernest H. de Souza,C.D., J.P., DHumL(Hon). ☎ 876-927-7948. Fax: 876-978-6240.

JAPAN (2,000)

The first Jewish community in Japan (at Yokohama) dates back to 1860 and old Jewish cemeteries exist in Yokohama, Kobe and Nagasaki. Jews were among the early foreign settlers. In 1940, 5,000 Jewish refugees from Germany and Poland arrived in Kobe, subsequently leaving for the U.S.A. and Shanghai. There are now about 2,000 Jews in Japan. About 1,000 live in the Tokyo area. There is a cong. of about 40 families in Kobe.
*Jewish Community of Japan, 8-8 Hiroo 3-chome, Shibuya-Ku, Tokyo (150). ☎ 3400-2559. Fax: 03-3400-1827. M. Rabbi Carnie Rose. Kosher meals available on Shabbat and during the week. Advance notification requested.

KENYA (165 families)

Jewish settlement in East Africa dates from 1903, when the British Government offered the Zionist Organisation a territory in the present Kenya for an autonomous Jewish settlement. The offer was refused but not unanimously and shortly afterwards a few Jews settled in the colony. Later, a number of Central European Jewish refugees settled here. The Jewish population in today's independent Kenya is about 165 families, most of whom are Israelis. See 'Jews of Nairobi 1903-1962', by Julius Carlebach.
*Nairobi Hebrew Congregation, P.O. Box 40990, 219703. ☎ 222770. (Est. 1904.) M. vacant. *Chairman* V. Aharoni; H. Tr. C. Szlapak; *Hon Sec.* Ms A. Zola.

LATVIA (17,000)

REZHITSA
Syn.: Kaleyu St.

RIGA
Syn.: 6/8 Peitavas St. ☎ (013-2) 22-45-49.
Jewish Library, LOEK, 6 Skolas St., 226050. ☎ (013-2) 28-95-80.

LEBANON (100)

In the civil war which broke out in 1975 most of the 2,000 Jews left the country. About 100 remain in Beirut.

LIBYA (50)

About the time that Libya became an independent State in 1951 there was a mass emigration of most of its 37,000 Jews to Israel, and only very few remain in Tripoli.

LITHUANIA (11,000)

Jewish Community of Lithuania, 4 Pylimo, Vilnius 2001. ☎ 2-613-003. Fax: 2-227-915.

KAUNAS
Syn.: 11, Ozhesklenes St.
Jewish Community Offices, 26B Gedimino St. ☎ 203-717.

VILNIUS
Syn.: 39 Pylimo St. ☎ (2) 61-25-23.
Lithuanian Jewish State Museum, P.O.B. 1537, Vilnius 232040.
There are also communities in Druskininkai, Klaipeda, Panevezys and Shiauliai.

LUXEMBOURG (1,000)

There are today about 1,000 Jews in Luxembourg, the majority in Luxembourg City. Since the French Revolution they have enjoyed the same rights as other citizens. Before 1933 there were 1,800 Jews in the country; by 1940 the influx of German and other refugees had brought the Jewish population to about 5,000. The main syn. was destroyed by the Nazis.
Synagogue: 45 Avenue Monterey, Luxembourg City 2163.
Chief Rabbi, Joseph Sayagh, 34 rue Alphonse Munchen, 2172. *Chairman* Aach Guy, 45 Av. Monterey.
Esch/Alzette: Synagogue, 52 Rue du Canal. *Chairman* R. Wolf, 19 rue du Nord 4260 Esch/Alzette.

MALTA (50)

There have been Jews in Malta since the period of the Romans, although their number has never been large. During the period of the Knights of St. John and the Spanish Expulsion of 1492, there were few, apart from slaves. A new community, originating from North Africa, arose at the end of the eighteenth century. The synagogue in Spur St., Valetta, opened in 1912, was demolished in 1979 as part of a development scheme.
Jewish Community of Malta. P.O. Box 42, Birkirkara, Malta. *President* A. Ohayon; *Sec.* S. L. Davis, O.B.E., Melita, Triq Patri Guze Delia, Balzan BZN 07. ☎ 445924.

MAURITIUS

There is no permanent Jewish community. The Jewish cemetery contains the graves of 125 refugees from Europe. They were part of a group of 1,700 Jews denied entry to Palestine and interned on the island during 1940-1945. *Corr.* P.M. Birger. P.O. Box 209, Port Louis, Mauritius. ☎ 2080821. Fax: 2083391.

MEXICO (48,000)

The Jewish presence in Mexico dates back to the Spanish Conquest, although it was not until the final years of the nineteenth century and the beginning of the twentieth that a mass immigration of Jews from Syria, the Balkanic Countries and eastern Europe, fleeing from persecution and poverty, laid the foundations of the modern Jewish Mexican community. Today's Jewish population is about 40,000, the majority in Mexico City. The cit has eight Jewish day-schools and several Yeshivot attended by up to 75 per cent of Mexican Jewish children. there are communities in Gudalajara, Monterrey and Tijuana.

MEXICO CITY
*Central Committee of the Jewish Community in Mexico, Cofre de Perote 115, Col. Lomas Barrilaco, 11010 Mexico DF. ☎ 540-7376, 520-9393. Fax 540-3050. *Exec. Dir.* Mauricio Lulka.
Synagogues: Askenazi, Acapulco 70, Col. Roma, ☎ 211-0575; Bet El (Conservative) Horacio 1722, Polanco. ☎ 281-2592; Beth Israel (Conservtive, English speaking), Virreyes 1140, Lomas. ☎ 7520-8515; Sephardic, Tehuantepec 188, Col. Roma. ☎ 574-3788; Monte Sinaí (Damascan), Fuente de la Huerta 22, Tecamachalco. ☎ 589-8322; Maguén David (Aleppo), Lafontaine 229, Polanco. ☎ 203-9964.
Jewish Sport Center, Avila Camacho 620, Lomas de Sotelo. ☎ 557-3000.

MOLDOVA (65,000)

CHISINAU
Syn.: Yakimovsky Per, 8, 277000. ☎ (042-2) 22-12-15.
Towns with Jewish populations include: Tiraspol, Baltsy, Bondery, Soroky, Ribnitsa and Orxey.

MOROCCO (10,000)

The Jews of Morocco have a history dating back to the times before it became a Roman province. Under Moslem rule they experienced alternate toleration and persecution. The expulsion from Spain and Portugal brought many newcomers to Morocco. In the nineteenth century many of the oppressed Jews sought the protection of Britain and France. The former French Protectorate removed legal disabilities, but the economic position of most Jews remained very precarious. During the Vichy period of the second World War Sultan Mohamed V protected the community. Before the est. of the independent kingdom of Morocco in 1958 many emigrated to Israel, France, Spain and Canada, and the present Jewish pop. is est. at 10,000 under the protection of King Hassan II.

CASABLANCA
*Community Offices, 12 rue Abou Abdallah Al Mahassibi. ☎ 222861.Fax: 266953.
Synagogues: Temple Beth El, 61 rue Jaber Ben Hayane. ☎ 267192; Em Habanim, 14, rue Ibn Rochd; Hazan, rue Roger Farache; Tehilla Le David, Blvd. du 11 Janvier; and Benisty rue Ferhat Hachad.
International Organisations: American Joint Distribution Committee, 3 rue Rouget de Lisle. ☎ 274717. Fax: 264089; Ittihad-Maroc, 13 rue Addamir Al Kabir. ☎ 2003-72. Fax: 2003-09; Ose, 151 bis, blvd. Ziraoui. ☎ 267891. Fax 278924; Lubavitch-Maroc, 174 blvd. Ziraoui. ☎ 269037; Ozar Hatorah (Religious School Organisation), 31 rue Jaber Ben Hayane. ☎ 270920.
There are also coms. in Fez, Kenitra, Marrakech, Meknès, Rabat, Tangier, Tetuan, El Jadida and Agadir.

MOZAMBIQUE
Jewish Community of Mozambique, c/o Natalie Tenzer-Silva. P.O. Box 232, Maputo. ☎ 494413.

NEW ZEALAND (4,000)
The settlement of Jews in New Zealand dates from the establishment of British sovereignty in 1840. In the first emigrant ships were a number of Jews from England. But still earlier a few Jewish wayfarers had settled in the northern part of New Zealand, including John Israel Montefiore, a cousin of Sir Moses Montefiore, who settled at the Bay of Islands in 1831, Joel Samuel Polack, one of the earliest writers on the country, in which he travelled in 1831-37, and David Nathan, who laid the foundations of the Jewish community in Auckland in the early 1840s.

The Wellington Jewish com. was founded by Abraham Hort, under the authority of the Chief Rabbi, on January 7, 1843, when the first Jewish service was held. Communities were later est. in Christchurch and Dunedin and other parts of the South Island. From the earliest times Jewish settlers have helped to lay the foundation of the commercial and industrial prosperity of the country.

The number of Jews in New Zealand is estimated at 3,300. Most live in Auckland and Wellington.

Jews have occupied most important positions in New Zealand including that of Administrator, Prime Minister and Chief Justice. There have been six Jewish mayors of Auckland and two of Wellington. See History of the Jews in New Zealand by L. M. Goldmann 1959. During the last 15 years approximately 400 Soviet Jews have settled in New Zealand, mainly in Wellington and Auckland, but many have since emigrated to Australia.
*United Synagogues of N.Z. President S. Goldsmith, 11 Rotherglen Ave., Christchurch.
*New Zealand Jewish Council. President Mr D. Zwartz. P.O. Box 4315 Auckland. ☎ 309-9444. Fax: 373 2283.
Council of Christians & Jews, PO Box 68-224, Newton, Auckland. ☎ (09) 638-7710.
Council of Jewish Women of N.Z., PO Box 27-156, Wellington. *President*: Mrs. S. Payes. ☎ (04) 567-1679.
*Zionist Federation of N.Z. M. Nathan, P.O.B. 4315 Auckland.

Wizo Federation. *President*: Mrs M. Murray ☎ (09) 486 2435.
New Zealand Jewish Chronicle (monthly), PO Box 27-211, Wellington. ☎ (04) 385-0720. Fax: (04) 384-6542. *Edr.* Anna Veritt.

WELLINGTON (1,000)
Hebrew Congregration. *President* D. Lewis. 80 Webb St. ☎ 4845 081.
Beth-El Synagogue, opened 1870 rebuilt 1929, resited in Jewish Community Centre and opened 1977.
Jewish Community Centre, 80 Webb St., P.O. Box 11-173. Moriah Kindergarten open daily.
Moriah College. (Primary Day Sch.) (Est. 1987.) P.O. Box 27233. ☎ 4842401.
Liberal Jewish Congregation (Temple Sinai). *President* V. Josephs, P.O. Box 27 301. ☎ 4850 720.
Zionist Society. *President* D. Young. P.O. Box 27 156.

AUCKLAND (1,600)
Hebrew Congregation. *President* R. Max. P.O. Box 68 224. ☎ 372 908.
Beth Israel Synagogue, 108 Greys Ave. P.O. Box 68 224. ☎ 373-2908 (Est. 1841).
Beth Shalom, The Auckland Congregation for Progressive Judaism, 180 Manukau Rd., Epsom. *President* P. Marks. P.O. Box 26052 Epsom.
Kadimah College and Kindergarten, Greys Ave.
Zionist Society, (Est. 1904). P.O. Box 4315.
There are smaller coms. in Christchurch (130), Hamilton (50) and Dunedin (60).

NORTH YEMEN
Since 1948 the vast majority of Yemeni Jews (who then numbered about 50,000) have emigrated to Israel. It is est. about 1,200 remain in Sa'ana.

NORWAY (2,000)
The Jewish population of Norway is estimated to be about 2,000. There are two organised communities, Det Mosaiske Trossamfund Oslo (about 1,000 members) and Det Mosaiske Trossamfund Trondheim (about 100 members).
The community in Oslo is very active, with regular synagogue services (Friday night and Saturday as well as all holidays), a kindergarden, afternoon classes for children of school-going age, regular meetings and seminars for members of different age-groups, a home for the elderly as well as a shop which supplies kosher food.
*Det Mosaiske Trossamfund (Jewish Community): *President* R. Katz, Bergstien 13 0172 Oslo ☎ 22696570. Fax 22466604.
Synagogue and Community Centre, Bergstien 13, Oslo 0172. ☎ 22696570.
Synagogue and Community Centre, Ark. Cristiesgt. 1, Trondheim. ☎ 7352 6568. *President* Julius Paltiel.

PAKISTAN
Two Jewish families remain in Pakistan's port of Karachi. The Magen Shalom Syn. built in 1893, at Jamila St. and Nishta Rd. junction, was reported closed in 1987.

PANAMA (9,250)
The community has been in existence for nearly 150 years and numbers nearly 9,250, with 8,420 in Panama City.
*Consejo Central Comunitario Hebreo de Panama, Apartado 55-0882-Paitilla, Panama, Panama City. ☎ (507) 263-8411. Fax (507) 264-7936. *Contact* Sion Harari *(President)*.
Beth El, (Cons), Apartado 3087, Panama 3, Panama City.

Congregation Shevet Ahim, (Orth.), Apartado 6222, Panama 2, Panama City.
Kol Shearith Israel, (Reform), Apartado 4120, Panama City.
There are smaller coms. in Colon (100) and David (100).

PARAGUAY (900)

The community, which has been in existence since 1912, numbers about 900.
Consejo Representativo Israelita del Paraguay (CRIP), General Diaz 657. Asuncion, P.O.B. 756. ☎ 41744.

PERU (5,000)

Marranos were prominent in the early development of Peru. Many Jews suffered martyrdom during the centuries that the Inquisition prevailed. The present Jewish population is about 5,000 nearly all living in Lima. There are an Ashkenazi community and a Sephardi community.
*Synagogue and Communal Centre, Húsares de Junin 163 (Jesus Maria), Lima. ☎ 241-412, 31-2410.
Sociedad de Beneficencia (Sefaradim), Enrique Villar 581, Lima.
Sociedad de Beneficencia Israelita de 1870, Esq Jose Gálvez 282 Miraflores.

PHILIPPINES (25)

Jewish Association of the Philippines, H.V. de la Costa, crn. Tordesillas, Salcedo Village, Makati, Metro Manila. ☎ 815 0265; 815 0263. Fax: 840-2566.
Postal Ad.: MC P.O. Box 1925, Makati, Metro Manila, 1259 Philippines.

POLAND (6,000)

Jews first settled in Poland in the twelfth century. Casimir the Great, the last Polish King of the Piast dynasty (1303-1370), was a staunch protector of the Jews. Periods of Jewish freedom and prosperity have alternated with periods of persecution and sometimes, expulsion. Jewish learning flourished in the land from the sixteenth century onwards.

Mystic Chasidism, based on study of the Cabala, had its wonder rabbis. Famous Talmudic scholars, codifiers of the ritual and other eminent men of learning were produced by Polish Jewry. Of the 3,500,000 Jews in Poland in 1939 about three million were exterminated by Hitler. Many put up an heroic fight, like those of the Warsaw Ghetto in 1943. Under half a million fled to the West and to the Soviet Union. Until 1968 the Jewish population was estimated at about 50,000. Large-scale emigration followed the anti-Jewish policy pursued by the regime from then on under the guise of 'anti-Zionism'. Today's Jewish pop. is estimated at between 6,000 and 8,000.

WARSAW

Synagogue and Religious Organisation: Zwiazek Religijny Wyznania Mojzeszowego (Religious Union of Mosaic Faith), Warsaw 00-105. ul. Twarda 6. ☎ 20-43-24. 20-06-76.
Secular Organisation: Towarzystwo Spoleczno-Kulturalne Zydów w Polsce (Social and Cultural Association of Jews in Poland), Zarzad Glowny (Central Board), Warsaw, 00-104, Plac., Grzybowski 12/16, ☎ 20-05-57, 20-05-54.

CRACOW

Religious Organisation: Zwiazek Religijny Wyznania Mojzeszowego, Kongregacja (Religious Union of Mosaic Faith, Congregation) Cracow, 31-066, ☎ 56-23-49. ul. Skawinska 2.
Secular Organisation: Towarzystwo Spoleczno-Kulturalne Zydów w Polsce (Social

and Cultural Association of Jews in Poland), (Cracow Section), Krakow, 31-014, ☎ 22-98-41.ul. Stawkowska 30.
Jewish organisations also exist in the following 16 towns: Bielsko-Biala, Bytom, Chzranów, Dzierzoniów, Gliwice, Katowice, Legnica, Lódz, Lubin, Przyrów, Swindnica, Szczecin Walbrzych, Wroclaw, and Zary.

PORTUGAL (400)

Until the civil war of 1373 Jews lived in tranquillity, and were prominent in court circles. But as a result of the internecine strife the Jewish Quarter of Lisbon was sacked by Castilian forces. In 1496 Manoel signed an order expelling the Jews from Portugal. But instead of being allowed to leave they were forcibly baptised. Despite the Inquisition Marranos survived in the provinces. A new community was established in Lisbon by British Jews from Gibraltar during the Napoleonic era. In 1910, after the Revolution, Jews were again granted freedom of worship. The present Jewish population is about 400 centred in Lisbon. There is a synagogue in Oporto built in Moorish style. The Kadoorie family of Hong Kong has been associated with it.

LISBON
*Communal Offices, Rua Alexandre Herculano, 59, Lisbon 1250. ☎ 385 86 04. Fax 388 4304.
Jewish Centre, Rua Rosa Araujo 10. ☎ 357 20 41.
Synagogues: 59 Rua Alexandre Herculano (Sephardi). ☎ 388 15 92. Avenida Elias Garcia 110-1º Lisbon 1050 (Ashkenazi).

PUERTO RICO (1,500)

Some 1,500 Jews live in Puerto Rico, which is an associated Commonwealth of the U.S.A. A syn. is maintained as well as an afternoon school, adult educ. classes and other orgs.
*Shaare Zedeck Synagogue (Conservative) and Community Centre, 903 Ponce de León Ave. Santurce, P.R. 00907-3390. ☎ (809) 724 4110. Rabbi A. Winter. ☎ 724 4111.
Temple Beth Shalom (Reform), 101 San Jorge & Loiza St., Santurce, P.R. 00911.

ROMANIA (14,000)

Jews have been resident in the territory that now forms Romania since Roman times. Today they number 14,000, of whom some 5,000 live in Bucharest, and the rest in 68 communities. There are 61 syns., four of them in Bucharest, 18 Talmud Torahs and 11 kosher restaurants. A newspaper in Hebrew, Romanian and English, with a circulation of 6,000, is published fortnightly.

BUCHAREST
Chief Rabbi:
*Federation of Jewish Communities, Strada Sf. Vineri 9. ☎ 613-25-38. Fax: 312-0869.

SINGAPORE (240)

The Jewish community of Singapore dates from about the year 1840. The street in which Jewish divine service was first held in a house is now known as Synagogue St. The first building to be erected as a syn. was the Maghain Aboth, opened in 1878. This was rebuilt and enlarged in 1925. A second syn., Chesed El, was built in 1905. The Jewish community consists mainly of Sephardim (of Baghdad origin) but with some Ashkenazim. The first Chief Minister of Singapore was the late David Marshall, appointed in 1956. The affairs of the community are managed by

the Jewish Welfare Board, which is elected annually.
*Jewish Welfare Board, 24/26 Waterloo Street, 187950. ☎ 337 2189. Fax: 336 2127. *President* Jacob Ballas. *H. Sec.* Mrs R. Elias
Synagogue Maghain Aboth, 24 Waterloo Street, 187950. ☎ 337 2189. Fax: 336 2127. Open daily except Monday mornings. *Community Rabbi* Mardoche Abergel. ☎ 7379112.
Synagogue Chesed El, 2 Oxley Rise, 238693. Open Mon. only.
United Hebrew Congregation (Reform), 65 Chulia St., OCBC Centre #31-00 East Lobby, 049513. *Pres.* K. Lewis. ☎ 536-8300.

SLOVAKIA (6,000)

Written evidence of Jewish settlement in Slovakia goes back to the 13th c. but there may have been Jews in the area as far back as Roman times.

BRATISLAVA
Central Union of Jewish Religious Coms. (UZZNO), H. Chairman Prof Pavel Traubner, PhD.; *Exec. Chairman* Fero Alexander. Ad.: Kozia 21/II, 81447 Bratislava, Slovakia. ☎ +421-7-5312167. Fax: 421-7-5311106.
Synagogue, Heydukova 11-13, Services: Monday, Thursday, Friday, Saturday.
Bratislava Jewish Com., Kozia 18, 81103 Bratislava. ☎ 421-7-5316949.
Bnai Brith "Tolerance" in Bratislava. *President* Prof. Pavel Trubner, PhD. Ad.: Krizna 32, 81107, Bratislava.
Pension Chez David (Kosher), Accommodation and Restaurant, Mikvah. Fax: +42-7-5312642. ☎ +421-7-5313824, 5316943. Mausoleum of Chatham Sopher, Orthodox and Neological Jewish cemeteries.

KOSICE
Jewish Religious Community, Zvonarska 5, 04001 Kosice. Kosher restaurant, Mitvah. *President* Dr.Ivan Kolin. ☎/Fax: +421-95-6221047.
Synagogue: Puskinova St.
There are Jewish coms. in Galanta, Dunajska Streda, Presov, Banska Bystrica, Nove Zamky, Komarno, Zilina, Michalovce, Lucenec.

SLOVENIA (78)

LJUBLJANA
Syn.: ☎ 315-884.

SOUTH AFRICA (100,000)

The Jewish Community began as an organised body at Cape Town on the eve of the Day of Atonement, Friday, September 26, 1841. Its first title was 'The Society of the Jewish Community of the Cape of Good Hope', but there had been Jewish residents at the Cape long before the foundation of the Hebrew Congregation. In fact, Jews have been connected with the Cape of Good Hope from the earliest days of South African history.

Jewish pilots accompanied the Portuguese navigators. During the 17th and 18th centuries when the Dutch East India Co. ruled the Cape, there were no professing Jews but it is probable that some individuals were of Jewish origin. After the British occupation in 1806, freedom of religion was extended to all Cape inhabitants and Jews eventually held official positions in the administration.

For further particulars see the 'History of the Jews in South Africa', by Louis Herrman (Victor Gollancz, 1930), The Jews in South Africa: A History, ed. by G. Saron and L. Hotz (Oxford Univ. Press, 1956), The Vision Amazing, by Marcia Gitlin (Johannesburg 1950), South African Jewry, 1976-77, ed. by Leon Feldberg (Alex White, 1977), South African Jewry, ed. by Marcus Arkin (Oxford Univ. Press

1984), Jewish Roots in the S.A. Economy, by Mendel Kaplan (Struik 1986), Chapters from S.A. History, Jewish and General, by Nathan Berger (Kayor, Vol. 1, 1982; Vol. 2, 1986), Jewry and Cape Society, by Milton Shain (Historical Publication Society, 1983), Tiger Tapestry, by Rudy Frankel (Struik, 1988), The Jews of S.A. - What Future? by Hoffman and Fischer (Southern, 1988), Founders and Followers Johannesburg Jewry 1887-1915, Mendel Kaplan (Vlaeberg 1991), The Roots of Antisemitism in South Africa, by M. Shain (Wits U.P. 1994); The Jewish population in South Africa, by A. Dubb (Kaplan Centre, 1994).

The Jews being scattered throughout the territory of the Republic, the organisation of Jewish religious life varies with the density of the Jewish population, which is about 100,000. Over recent years several thousand members of the community have emigrated, especially to Israel, Canada, Australia and the U.S., but the com. has been strengthened by the arrival of some Jews from Zimbabwe and Israel. In all, there are about 50 organised Jewish coms.

The largest coms. are in Johannesburg (58,000), Cape Town (17,500), Durban (3,720) and Pretoria (1,550).

The South African Jewish Board of Deputies is the representative institution of South African Jewry. The B.o.D. for the Transvaal and Natal was founded in 1903, and a similar organisation at the Cape in 1904. The two were united in 1912. The headquarters of the Board is in Johannesburg, and there are provincial committees in Cape Town, Pretoria, Durban, Bloemfontein and Port Elizabeth.

COMMUNAL INSTITUTIONS
*S.A. Jewish Board of Deputies, Anerley Office Park, 7 Anerley Rd., Parktown 2193, PO Box 87557, Houghton 2041. ☎ 486-1434. Fax: 646-4940. *National Dir.* S. Kopelowitz.
S.A. Zionist Federation, P.O. Box 29203, Sandringham 2131. ☎ 485-1020. Fax: 640-6758. Dir. General R. Silverman.
S.A. Board of Jewish Education, P.O. Box 46204, Orange Grove 2119. ☎ 485-1214. Gen. Dir. M. Zimerman.
S.A. Jewish Ex-Service League. See Board of Deputies.
Union of Orthodox Synagogues of South Africa, 24 Raleigh St., Yeoville 2198, Johannesburg. ☎ 648-9136. Fax: 648-4014. Rabbi C. K. Harris, B.A. M.Phil., Chief Rabbi of S. Africa. S.A. Rabbinical Association.
S.A. Union for Progressive Judaism, P.O.B. 1190, Houghton 2041. ☎ 728-4796.
S.A. Yiddish Cultural Federation. See Board of Deputies.
Bnai B'rith, P.O. Box 8425 Johannesburg, 2000. ☎ 648-3804.
Jewish Family and Community Council, 5 Becker St., Yeoville 2198. ☎ 648-9124.
Kollel Yad Shaul, 22 Muller St., Yeoville, 2198, Johannesburg. ☎ 648-1175.
Lubavitch Foundation of S.A., 55 Oaklands Rd., Orchards 2192 Johannesburg. ☎ 640-7561.
ORTSA, 93 Iris Rd., Norwood, Johannesburg. ☎ 728-7154.
Union of Jewish Women of S.A., 1 Oak St., Houghton, Johannesburg, 2198. ☎ 648-1053.
Mizrachi Organisation of S.A., P.O. Box 29189, Sandringham 2192. ☎ 640 4420.
Zionist Revisionist Organisation of S.A., 2 Elray St., Raedene, 2192. ☎ 485-1020. Telegrams: Nezorg.

JOHANNESBURG
United Hebrew Congregation (est. 1915.)
Beth Din, 24 Raleigh St., Yeoville. ☎ 648-9136.
United Progressive Jewish Congregation (est. 1946). ☎ 484-3003.
Adath Jeshurun Congregation, P.O. Box 5128, 41 Hunter St., Yeoville 2198. ☎ 648-6300. Mikva. (Affil. to Union of Orth. Hebr. Congs., London).
Main synagogues. Glenhazel Hebrew Cong., Long Ave., Glenhazel, 2192. Tel: 640-5016 (Orth.) Sydenham/Highlands North Heb Cong., 24 Main St.,

Rouxville, 2192 (Orth) ☎ 640-5021. Temple Emanuel, 38 Oxford Road, Parktown, 2193 (Reform). ☎ 646-6170.

CAPE TOWN
Western Province Zionist Council, Leeusig, Leewen St., Cape Town 8001. ☎ 245-020. Fax: 232-615. PO Box 4176. Cape Town 8000.
The Jacob Gitlin Library, Leeusig, 4 Leeuwen St., 8001. ☎ 245020. Fax 232615. P.O. Box 4176, Cape Town 8000.
Union of Orthodox Synagogues of S.A., and Beth Din, 191, Buitenkant St., ☎ 461-6310. Fax: 461-8320. *Exec. Dir.* R. Glass.
Main synagogues. Great Syn. Government Ave. (Orth.), Temple Israel, Upper Portswood Rd., Green Point (Reform).

SOUTH KOREA
About 25 Jewish families live in Seoul the capital. Religious services are held on Friday evenings at the 8th U.S. Army Religious Retreat Centre. ☎ 7904-4113.

SPAIN (12,000)
Jews were settled in Spain in Roman times. They made an outstanding contribution to culture and civilisation in medieval times. Persecution by the Church culminated in the Inquisition and the Expulsion in 1492. Today there are about 12,000 Jews in Spain, of whom 3,000 live in Barcelona, 3,500 in Madrid 1,500 in Malaga, and the rest in Valencia, Seville, Alicante, Majorca and the Canary Islands. The Jewish com. in Melilla has 900 members and that in Ceuta 700. Ancient syns. of pre-Inquisition times (now put to other uses) exist in Cordoba, Seville and Toledo. The Madrid com. was legally recognised in 1965 and the city's first syn. since the Expulsion was consecrated in 1968. Synagogues and Community Centres:
Madrid, 28010-Calle Balmes, No. 3.
Barcelona, 08021-Calle Avenir, No. 24.
Alicante, Da Lilo Plon-Avda Santander 3, Playa de San Juan.
Ceuta, Calle Sargento, No. 8. Coriat.
Majorca. The first synagogue in 600 years was opened in 1987 in Calle Monserior Palmer, Palma. Fri. evg. and High Holy-day services. *President* J. Segal. ☎ 700243. About 300 Jews live in Majorca.
Malaga, 29001-Calle Duquesa de Parcent, No. 8.
Marbella. Sr Amselem, Jazmines, 21, Urbanización El Real.
Melilla, 29804-Calle General Mola, No.19.
Seville, 41003-Bustos Tavera, 8. ☎ 427-5517.
Valencia. 46026-S. Serfaty, Avda. Ausiás March, 42 Pta. 35.
Tenerife 38002-Jewish Community, P. Abecasis, Villalba Hervas, Santa Cruz de Tenerife.
Las Palmas de Gran Canaria, 35006, S. Zrihen, c/Nestor de la Torre, 34.

SRI LANKA
Corr. Mrs. A. Ranasinghe, 82 Rosmead Place, Colombo 7. ☎ 695642. Fax: 941-698091.

SURINAM (300)
Surinam is one of the oldest permanent Jewish settlements in the Western Hemisphere. The Sephardi Cong. was est. about 1661, but earlier settlements in 1632, 1639 and 1652 have been reported. Some 225 Jews are members of the two synagogues, where Sephardi services are conducted.
Neve Salom Synagogue, Keizerstr. 82, Paramaribo.

Sedek Ve Salom Synagogue, Herenstr. 20, Paramaribo. Temp. not in use due to restoration. *President* René Fernandes, Commewijnestraat 21, Paramaribo. ☎ 400236; P.O. Box 1834, Paramaribo. ☎ 597-411998; Fax: 597-471154.

SWEDEN (18,000)

In 1774, the first Jew was granted the right to live in Sweden. In 1782 Jews were admitted to three Swedish towns, Stockholm, Gothenburg and Norrköping, and the Karlskrona com. was founded soon afterwards. After the emancipation of the Jews in Sweden in 1870, coms. were founded in Malmö and several other towns. Today there are some 18,000 Jews in Sweden, 9–10,000 of them in Stockholm. Others are in Gothenburg, Malmö, Borås, Västerås.

STOCKHOLM
*Judiska Församlingen (Jewish community), Wahrendorffsgatan 3, Box 7427 103 91 Stockholm. ☎ 08-679 2900. Fax: 08-6112413.
Jewish Centre, Nybrogatan 19. ☎ 08-6626686.
Synagogues: Wahrendorffsgatan 3 (Great Synagogue, Conservative); Adas Jeshurun, Riddargatan 5 (Orthodox); Adas Jisroel, St. Paulsgatan 13 (Orth).

SWITZERLAND (17,600)
The Jews were expelled from Switzerland in the fifteenth century, and it was not until early in the seventeenth century that they received permission to settle in the Lengnau and Endingen coms. In 1856 immigration increased, most of the immigrants coming from Southern Germany, Alsace and Eastern Europe. The Jewish pop. is now about 17,600 The largest coms. are in Zurich (6,252), Basle (2,005) and Geneva (3,901). The Swiss Federation of Jewish Communites comprised in 1997 19 coms. with a total membership of 14,000.
*Federation of Jewish Communities, Gotthardstr. 65, 8002 Zurich. ☎ (01) 2015583.Fax: (01) 202-1672.
American Joint Distribution Committee. European Headquarters: 75 Rue de Lyon, 1211, Geneva 13. ☎ (022) 344 90 00.
OSE, Rue de Mont-Blanc 11, 1201, Geneva. ☎ (022) 732 33 01 and (022) 731 59 10.
World Jewish Congress, Rue de Varembé 1, 1211 Geneva. ☎ (022) 734 1325.
Hias, 75 rue de Lyon, 1203 Geneva. ☎ 022 345-9350.
B'nai B'rith, 10 rue St Léger, 1205, Geneva. ☎ (022) 310-46-86.
Basle Synagogues: (Orth.): Leimenstr. 24, ☎ (061) 27998 50. Rabbi Dr. I. M Levinger, ☎ (061) 271 60 24. Ahornstr. 14. Rabbi B.-Z. Snyders, Rudolfstr. 28. ☎ (061) 302 53 91. Communal Centre, Leimenstr. 24. ☎ (061) 279 98 50.
Berne Synagogue, Kapellenstr. 2. ☎ (031) 381 4992. Rabbi Michail Diamond.
Fribourg Synagogue, 9, Av. de Rome. ☎ (026) 332 1670.
Geneva Synagogues: Geneva Syn. (Orth. Ashk.), 11 Place de la Synagogue. ☎ (022) 789-0725. Chief Rabbi M.A. Guedj; Machsike Hadass (Orth. Ashk.) 2 Place des Eaux Vives, Rabbi Avraham Schlesinger. ☎ (022) 735 22 98. Hekhal Haness (Seph.), 54 Route de Malagnou. ☎ (022) 736 96 32. Liberal Syn. (Ref.), 12 Quai du Seujet. ☎ (022) 732 32 45. Rabbi François Garai. ☎ (022) 738 19 11.
Youth Communal Centre: Rue St. Leger 10. ☎ (022) 310 41 93.
Jewish Community of Geneva, Rue St. Leger 10. ☎ (022) 310 46 86.
Lausanne Synagogue: 1 Ave. Juste-Olivier (corner Ave. Florimont). ☎ (021) 312 673. Chief Rabbi H. Krief. Communal Centre: 3 Ave. Georgette. ☎ (021) 312 67 33.
Zurich Synagogues: (Orth. Ashk.) Freigutstr. 37. ☎ (01) 201 49 98; Erikastr. 8. ☎ (01) 463 57 98. Rabbi Dr. Zalman Kossowsky, Lavaterstr. 33. ☎ (01) 201 16 59, (01) 202 52 22 (01) 281 30 15 Beth Chabad Manessestr. 98. Minyan Sikna Sallenbachstr. 40. Minyan Wollishofen, Etzelstr. 6. ☎ (01) 202 45 07. (Lib.)

Fortunagasse, 13. ☎ (01) 221 11 53. **Communal Centre:** Lavaterstr. 33. ☎ (01) 201 16 59.

SYRIA (1,500)

The remnants of this historic Jewish community resident in Damascus, Aleppo and Kamishli, have been estimated at 1,500 following recent aliyah.

DAMASCUS
President of Rabbinical Court Rabbi Ibrahim Hamura, Ecole Ben-Maymoun, Kattatib. Al-Ittihad Al-Ahlieh School (Alliance Israélite), rue El Amine.

TAIWAN (180)

More than 30 Jewish families live on the Island, most of them in Taipei, the capital.
Taiwan Jewish Community Centre. Information: F. Chitayat. ☎ 861-6303. Mailing address: Donald Shapiro, Trade Winds Company, P.O.Box 7-179, Taipei 10602, Taiwan. ☎ 886-2-3960159. Fax: 886-2-3964022. Sunday School. Jewish services at the Ritz Hotel, 155 Minchuan East Road, Taipei, held Friday evenings, Saturday morning, Saturday afternoon. Torah study Saturday afternoons. Holiday services contact Dr. F. Einhorn at 592-2840 or the Ritz Hotel 597-1234.

THAILAND (250)

The community consists of approx. 250 persons, including citizens of the country and expatriates.
Jewish Association of Thailand, Beth Elisheva Synagogue, Mikveh, Jewish Centre, 121 Soi Sai Nam Thip 2, Sukhumvit 22, Bangkok. ☎ 258-2195. Fax 663-0245.
Even-Chen Synagogue, The Bossotel Inn, weekly classes & activities. 55/12-14 Soi Charoengkrung, 42/1 New Road, Bangkok. ☎ 630 6120. Fax: 237 3225.
Ohr Menachem-Chabad, Kaosarn Rd., Banglampoo. Daily services. *M.* Rabbi Y. Kantor. ☎/Fax 282-6388.

TRINIDAD AND TOBAGO

Jewish links go back to 1658 when Portuguese Jews from Livorno and Amsterdam settled there. Most of them left by the end of the 17th century. Portuguese Jews from Venezuela and Curaçao settled in Trinidad in the 19th century. The names of many Catholic families are traceable to 'conversos' of the earlier period. In the mid-1930's some 800 Jews sought temporary refuge in Trinidad and Tobago from Nazi persecution in Germany and Austria and later from other parts of Nazi occupied Europe. Those with German and Austrian passports were subject to internment between 1940 and 1943. Numbers have dropped since with only a few Jews living there now. *Corr* Hans Stecher, c/o The Home Office, Northern Entrance, West Mall, Westmoorings, Port of Spain, Trinidad, W.I. (Caribbean).

TUNISIA (3,000)

The history of the community goes back to antiquity. After Tunisia became a French protectorate in 1881 Jews obtained equal rights with the Moslems, and the continuance of these rights was promised by the authorities of the independent State established in 1957. The Jewish population fell from nearly 100,000 in 1950 to 25,000 in June 1967, and to some 3,000 today. There are coms. in Tunis, Sfax, Sousse and Jerba island, where the ancient El Ghriba synagogue in Hara Sghire village is a listed building.

TUNIS
Grand Rabbinat de Tunisie, 26 Rue Palestine. Communal Offices, 15 Rue du Cap Vert.
Synagogues: 43 Ave. de la Liberté: 3 Rue Eve Nöelle.
American Joint Distribution Committee, 101 Ave. de la Liberté.

TURKEY (25,000)
During the Spanish Inquisition, the Ottoman Empire was one of the principal lands of refuge. With the proclamation of the Turkish Republic, the Jews were granted full citizenship rights. Today their number is estimated at about 25,000 of whom about 23,000 live in Istanbul, 2,000 in Izmir, and 100 each in Ankara, Adana, Edirne and Kirklareli.

ISTANBUL
Chief Rabbinate: Rabbi David Asseo, Yemenici Sok. No. 23 Tünel, Beyoğlu. ☎ (212) 2938794-95. Fax (212) 244-1980. *Sec. General* Lina Filiba.
Communal Centre, Büyük Hendek Sokak No. 61, Galata. ☎ (212) 2441576. Fax: (212) 249-3001.
Synagogues: Neve Shalom, 61 Büyük Hendek Sokak, Galata. ☎ (212) 293-7566; Beth Israel, Efe Sok. 4, Şişli, ☎ (212) 2406599; Etz Ahayim, Muallim Naci Sok. 40/1. ☎ (212) 2601896. (Ashkenazi), 37 Yüksekkaldirim sok, Galata. ☎ 243-6909; (Italian), 29, Şair Ziya Paşa Yokusu, Galata. ☎ (212) 2937784; Hemdat Israel, Izzettin Sok 65 Kadiköy ☎ (216) 336 5293; Heset Leavraam, Pancur Sok, 15, Büyükada ☎ (216) 382-5788 (summer); Caddebostan, Taş Mektep Sokak Göztepe. ☎ (216) 356-5922.
There are ten charitable and social institutions, six youth clubs, a high school and two elementary schools in Istanbul and an elementary school in Izmir. Synagogues also in Izmir and Ankara.

UKRAINE (600,000)
KIEV
Syn.: 29 Shchekovichnaya St. ☎ (044) 416-13-83.
Assoc. of Jewish Organisations, Kurskeya ul. 6, 252049.
Jewish Historical Society, ul. Belgorodskaya 6, apt. 34. ☎ 044-277-1751.
Makor Centre for Jewish Youth Activities, 10/1 Karl Marx St., Apt. 10, 252001. ☎ 044-229-6141. Fax: 044-229-8069.
Other towns with Jewish centres include Bershad, Chernigor, Chernovtsy, Kharkov, Kremenchug, Odessa, Simferopol, Uzhgorod and Zhitomir.

UNITED STATES OF AMERICA (5,950,000)
Though there had been individual Jewish settlers before 1654 in the territory which is now the United States, it was not until that year that Jewish immigrants arrived in a group at New Amsterdam (renamed New York in 1664) 23 of them, who came from Brazil by way of Cuba and Jamaica. The story of the growth of Jewry in the U.S.A. is the story of successive waves of immigration resulting from persecution in Russia, Poland, Romania, Germany and other countries. Today the Jewish population is est. at 5,950,000, of whom 1,720,000 live in the New York Metropolitan Area.

For general information about the American Jewish Community write to: UJA - Federation Resource Line, 130 E 59th St., New York City, 10022.

REPRESENTATIVE ORGANISATIONS
American Jewish Committee, 165 E. 56th St., New York City, 10022.
American Jewish Congress, Stephen Wise Hse., 15 E. 84th St., New York City, 10028.

186   UNITED STATES OF AMERICA

Anti-Defamation League of B'nai B'rith, 823 United Nations Plaza, New York City, 10017.
B'nai B'rith International, 1640 Rhode Island Av., N.W. Washington, D.C., 20036.
Conference of Presidents of Major Jewish Organizations, 110 E 59th St., NYC 10022.
Consultative Council of Jewish Organizations, 420 Lexington Av., Suite 1733, NYC 10170. ☎ 212-808-5437.
Co-ordinating Board of Jewish Organizations, 1640 Rhode Island Ave., N.W. Washington, D.C., 20036.
Jewish Labour Committee, Atran Centre, 25 E. 21st St., New York City, 10010.
Jewish War Veterans of the United States of America, 1811 R St., N.W. Washington, D.C. 20009.
National Jewish Community Relations Advisory Council, 443 Park Ave. S., I Ith floor, New York City, 10016.
National Council of Jewish Women, 15 E. 26th St., New York City, 10010.
National Conference on Soviet Jewry, 10 E. 40th St., Suite 907, New York City, 10016.
National Council of Young Israel, 3 W. 16th St., New York City, 10011.
North American Jewish Students Network, 501 Madison Ave., 17th Fl., New York City, 10022.
United Jewish Appeal, 99 Park Ave. New York City, 10016.
World Confederation of Jewish Community Centers, 15 E. 26th St. New York City, 10010.
World Jewish Congress, 501 Madison Ave., 17th Fl., New York City, 10022. ☎ 755 5770.

RELIGIOUS ORGANISATIONS
Agudath Israel of America, 84 William St., New York City, 10038.
Agudath Israel World Organization, 84 William St., New York City, 10038.
Association of Orthodox Jewish Scientists, 1373 Coney Island Ave., Brooklyn, New York, 11219.
Central Conference of American Rabbis, 192 Lexington Ave., New York City, 10016 (Reforrn).
Jewish Reconstructionist Federation, Church Road and Greenwood Ave., Wyncote PA, 19095.
Lubavitcher Headquarters, 770 Eastem Parkway, Brooklyn, N.Y. 11213. New York Board of Rabbis, 10 E. 73rd St., New York City, 10021.
Rabbinical Alliance of America, 3 W. 16th St., 4th Fl., New York City, 10011. (Orthodox.)
Rabbinical Assembly (Cons.), 3080 Broadway, New York City, 10027.
Rabbinical Council of America, 275 7th Ave., New York City, 10001. (Modern Orthodox).
Reconstructionist Rabbinical Association, Church Road and Greenwood Ave., Wyncote, PA, 19095.
Synagogue Council of America, 327 Lexington Ave., New York City 10016.
Union of American Hebrew Congregations, 838 Fifth Ave., New York City, 10021. (Reform).
Union of Orthodox Jewish Congregations, 333 Seventh Ave., New York City, 1000
Union of Orthodox Rabbis, 235 E. Broadway, New York City, 10002.
Union of Sephardic Congregations, 8 W 70th St., New York City, 10023.
United Synagogue of America, 155 Fifth Ave., New York City, 100 10. (Conservative.)
World Union for Progressive Judaism, 838 Fifth Ave., New York City, 10021.

WELFARE AND REFUGEE ORGANISATIONS
American Association for Ethiopian Jews, 2028 P. St., N.W. Washington DC., 20036.

UNITED STATES OF AMERICA 187

American Federation of Jews from Central Europe, 570 7th Ave., New York City, 10018.
American Jewish Joint Distribution Committee (I.D.C.), 711 Third Ave. New York City, 10017.
American ORT Federation, 817 Broadway, New York City, 10003.
Council of Jewish Federations, 730 Broadway, New York City, 10003.
HIAS, 333 7th Ave., New York City, 1000.
Jewish Conciliation Board, 235 Park Ave. S., New York City, 10003.
JWB, 15 East 26th St., New York City, 10010.
U.J.A. Federation of New York, 130 E. 59th St., New York City, 10022.

ZIONIST ORGANISATIONS and others concerned with Israel
American Associates of Ben-Gurion University of Negev, 342 Madison Ave., Suite 1924, New York City, 10173.
American Committee for Weizmann Institute, 515 Park Ave., New York City, 10022.
American Friends of the Hebrew University, 11 E. 69th St., New York City, 10021.
American Friends of Tel Aviv University, 360 Lexington Ave., New York City, 10017.
American Friends of Haifa University, 41 E. 42nd St., 828, New York City, 10017.
American-Israel Cultural Foundation, 485 Madison Ave., New York City, 10022.
American-Israel Public Affairs Committee, 500 N. Capitol St., N.W. Washington, D.C. 20001.
American Jewish League for Israel, 30 E. 60th St., New York City, 10022.
American Red Magen David for Israel, 888 7th Ave., New York City, 10106.
American Technion Society, 271 Madison Ave., New York City, 10016.
American Zionist Federation, 515 Park Ave., New York City, 10022 from whom information on Zionist organisations and activities can be obtained.
American Zionist Youth Foundation, 515 Park Ave., New York City, 10022.
Americans for Progressive Israel, 150 Fifth Ave., Suite 911, New York City, 10011.
ARZA–Assn. of Reform Zionists of America, 838 5th Ave., New York City, 10021.
Bar-Ilan University in Israel, 853 Seventh Ave., New York City, 10019.
Bnei Akiva of North America, 25 W. 26th St., New York City, 10010.
Betar Zionist Youth Movement, 9 E. 38th St., New York City, 10016.
Dror-Young Kibbutz Movement-Habonim, 27 W. 20th St., New York City, 10011.
Emunah Women of America, 370 7th Ave., New York City, 10001.
Hadassah, Women's Zionist Organization of America, 50 W. 58th St., New York City, 10019.
Hashomer Hatzair, 150 Fifth Ave. Suite 911, New York City, 10011.
Herut–U.S.A., 9 E. 38th St., New York City, 10016.
Theodor Herzl Foundation, 515 Park Ave., New York City, 10022.
Jewish National Fund, 42 E. 69th St., New York City, 10021.
Labor Zionist Alliance (formerly Poale Zion United Labour Org. of America), 275 Seventh Ave., New York City, 10001.
Mercaz, Conservative Zionists, 155 Fifth Ave., New York City, 10010.
Mizrachi-Hapoel Hamizrachi (Religious Zionists of America), 25 W. 26th St., New York City, 10010.
National Committee for Labor Israel–Histadrut, 33 E. 67th St., New York City, 10021.
PEC Israel Economic Corporation, 511 Fifth Ave., New York City, 10017.
Pioneer Women Na'armat, The Women's Labour Zionist Organisation of America, 200 Madison Ave., New York City, 10016.
State of Israel Bonds, 730 Broadway, New York City, 10003
Women's League for Israel, 515 Park Ave., New York City, 10022.
World Confederation of United Zionists, 30 E. 60th St., New York City 10022.
World Zionist Organization, American Section, 515 Park Ave., New York City, 10022.

EDUCATIONAL AND CULTURAL ORGANISATIONS
American Friends of the Alliance Israélite Universelle, 135 William St., New York City, 10038.
American Jewish Historical Society, 2 Thornton Rd., Waltham, Mass., 02154.
Annenberg Research Institute, formerly Dropsie College, 250 N. Highland Ave., Merion. Pa., 19066.
Leo Baeck Institute, 129 E. 73rd St., New York City, 10021. Brandeis University, Waltham Mass., 02254.
Centre for Holocaust Studies, Documentation & Research, 1610 Ave. J., Brooklyn, New York 11230.
Central Yiddish Culture Organization, 25 E. 21st St., New York Clty, 10010.
Gratz College, 10th St., & Tabor Rd., Phila., Pa., 19141.
Theodor Herzl Institute and Foundation, 515 Park Ave., New York City, 10022.
Hebrew Arts School, 129 W. 67th St., New York City, 10023.
Hebrew College, 43 Hawes St., Brookline, Mass., 02146.
Hebrew Union College-Jewish Institute of Religion, 3101 Clifton Ave., Cincinnati, Ohio, 45220; 1 W. 4th St., New York City, 10012, 3077 University Mall, Los Angeles, Calif. 90007; 13 King David St., Jerusalem Israel 94101.
Herzliah Jewish Teachers' Seminary, Touro College, Jewish Peoples, University of the Air, 30 W. 44th St., New York City, 10036.
Histadruth Ivrith of America, 1841 Broadway, New York City, 10023.
JWB Jewish Book Council, 15 E. 26th St., New York City, 10010.
Jewish Education Service of North America, 730 Broadway, New York
Jewish Publication Society, 1930 Chestnut St., Philadelphia, Pa., 19103.
Jewish Museum, 1109 Fifth Ave., New York City, 10028.
Jewish Theological Seminary of America, 3080 Broadway, New York City, 10027.
Memorial Foundation for Jewish Culture, 15 E. 26th St., New York City 10010.
Mesivta Yeshiva Rabbi Chaim Berlin Rabbinical Academy, 1593 Coney Island Ave., Brooklyn, N.Y.
National Foundation for Jewish Culture, 330 7th Ave., 21st. Fl., New York City, 10001.
National Yiddish Book Center, Weinberg Building, Amherst, MH. 01002-3375. ☎ (800) 535-3595; Fax: (413) 256-4700.
Reconstructionist Rabbinical College, Church Road and Greenwood Ave., Wyncote, PA, 19095.
Shomrei AdamahNA Jewish Resource Center for the Environment, Church Road and Greenwood Ave., Wyncote, PA, 19095.
Simon Wiesenthal Centre, 9760 W. Pico Blvd., Los Angeles, Ca., 90035.
Torah Umesorah–National Society for Hebrew Day Schools, 160 Broadway, New York City, 10038.
United Lubavitcher Yeshivoth, 841 Ocean Parkway, Brooklyn, N.Y., 11230.
Yeshiva University, 500 W. 185th St., New York City, 10033; 9760 W. Pico Blvd., Los Angeles, Ca., 90035.
Yivo Institute for Jewish Research, 555 West 57th St., 11th Floor, New York City 10019 (Temporary removal) ☎ (212) 535-6700.

URUGUAY (35,000)

Jewish immigration to Uruguay began in the early 20th century, with a large influx in the 1920s. Some 10,000 European Jews fled to Uruguay with Hitler's rise to power and large numbers came after the Second World War. In the 1940s, 50,000 Jews were est. to be living in the country. At present there are about 35,000, mostly in Montevideo, the capital. Some 12,000 emigrated to Israel before the State was established, during the War of Independence and since.

MONTEVIDEO
*Central and representative org.: Comite Central Israelita del Uruguay, Rio Negro

1308 Piso 5 Esc. 9. ☎ 90 6562. Fax: 91 6057.
Communities: Comunidad Israelita del Uruguay, Canelones 1084 Piso 1°; Comunidad Israelita Sefaradi, 21 de Setiembre 3111 (office), Buenos Aires 234 (syn.); Nueva Congregacion Israelita, Wilson Ferreira Aldunate 1168; Comunidad Israelita Hungara, Durazno 972. Each com. maintains its own syns. There are 3 Jewish schs. and an ORT training centre.
Zionist Organisation of Uruguay, H. Gutierrez Ruiz 1278 Piso 4°.
There are also communities at Maldonado and Paysandu.

VENEZUELA (20,000)

The first community was established in the coastal town of Coro by Sephardi Jews early in the 19th century. Today the Jews in Venezuela number some 21,000, most of whom live in Caracas and the rest mainly in Maracaibo.

CARACAS
*Confederation de Asociaciones Israelitas de Venezuela** (CAIV). Representative organisation of Venezuelan Jewry, Av. Marques del Toro, San Bernardino.
Ashkenazi Synagogue and Centre, Union Israelita de Caracas, Av. Marques del Toro, San Bernardino. ☎ 51-52-53. M. Rabbi P. Brener.
Tifaret Yisrael, (Sephardi), Av. Mariperez, Los Caobos. ☎ 781 1942. M. Rabbi A. Cohen.
B'nai B'rith and Hillel Foundation, 9na Transversal entre 7a, Av. Avila, Altamira. ☎ 32 65 96.
Zionist Federation, Qta Berta, Av. Los Proceres, San Bernardino. ☎ 51-48-52.

VIRGIN ISLANDS (500)

Jews have lived in the Virgin Islands since the seventeenth century and played an important part under Danish rule. Since 1917 the Virgin Islands have been U.S.A. territory. There are some 120 families in the community and the number of affiliated and non-affiliated Jews is about 350. The 150th anniversary of the rebuilding of the synagogue, situated in Crystal Gade, St. Thomas, was celebrated in 1983.
Jewish Community, M. Rabbi S. T. Relkin.

YUGOSLAVIA (3,500)

(Federal Republic, Serbia and Montenegro)
Jews have lived in this territory since Roman times. In 1941 there were about 34,000 Jews in the territory of present Yugoslavia and some 29,000 perished in the Holocaust.

BELGRADE (BEOGRAD)
*Federation of Jewish Communities of Yugoslavia,** Ulica Kralya Petra 7la, 11000 Belgrade. P.O.B. 841 Belgrade. ☎ 624-359/621-837. Sec. M. Grinvald.
Jewish Community of Belgrade, 7 Jula 71 al II. ☎ 624 289; 622 449. Fax: 3811 626674. President Aca Singer.
Synagogue, Marsala Birjuzova 19.
Jewish Historical Museum, 7 Jula 71 a/l. ☎ 622 634.
Communities also in Novi Sad, Niš, Pančevo, Priština, Sombor, Zemun and Zrenjanin.

ZAIRE (100)

Before the Congo obtained independence from Belgian rule in 1960, there were about 2,500 Jews, with eight communities affiliated with the central community in Elisabethville. Now these are about 85 in Kinshasa (formerly Leopoldville), 4 in Lubumbashi (formerly Elisabethville), and six others in Likasi, Kannga and

Kisangani. There are also some temporary Israeli residents.
Chief Rabbi of Zaire: Rabbi Moishe Levy. 50, W. Churchill Ave., Box 15, 1180 Brussels, Belgium.

ZAMBIA (35)

(See also Jews of Zambia Project, p.72).
***The Council for Zambia Jewry Ltd.**, P.O. Box 30020, Lusaka 10101. *Chairman* M. C. Galaun. ☎ 229190. Fax: 221428.
Lusaka Hebrew Congregation, P.O. Box 30020. (Est. 1941.) *Chairman* M. C. Galaun.

ZIMBABWE (900)

Jews came to Rhodesia (Zimbabwe) even before the British South Africa Company received its charter in 1889. Daniel Montage Kisch arrived in the territory in 1869, becoming chief adviser to King Lobengula.

In the 1880s the number of Jewish pioneers, most of them of East European origin, gradually increased. Among those who took a leading part in the development and admin. of the country was Sir Roy Welensky, Prime Minister of the former Central African Federation (1956-1963).

Most of the Jewish settlers came from Russia or Lithuania but others settled from the Aegean Island of Rhodes. Many came up from the South, some through the east coast Portuguese territory of Beira. Joe van Praag, who became Mayor of Salisbury, walked from Beira. During the 1930s, a small influx of German refugees settled mainly in Salisbury (now Harare) and Bulawayo. Post World War II, others joined them mostly from the United Kingdom and South Africa.

Today, most of Zimbabwe's Jews live in Harare and Bulawayo with a very few residing in the smaller districts around the country about 596 in Harare, 303 in Bulawayo and 11 in other centres. There are three synagogues in Harare and one in Bulawayo and each city has its own Jewish primary day school.

Zimbabwe Jewish Board of Deputies (Head office), 54 Josiah Chinamono Ave., PO Box 1954, Harare. ☎ 702506. *President* M.C. Ross. *Sec.* Mrs E. Alhadeff; PO Box 1456, Bulawayo. ☎ 67383. *Sec.* Mrs G. Stidolph.
Central African Zionist Organisation, 44 Jason Moyo St., PO Box 1162, Bulawayo. ☎ 67383. *President* A. Leon.
Womens' Zionist Council of Central Africa, P.O. Box 1162, Bulawayo. ☎ 67383/4. *President* Mrs. Rhebe Tatz.
***Synagogues.** *Harare*: Harare Hebr. Cong., Lezard Ave., PO Box 342. (Est. 1895.) ☎ 727576; Sephardi Hebr. Cong., 54 Josiah Chinamono Ave., PO Box 1051. (Est. 1932.) ☎ 722899. *Bulawayo*: Bulawayo Hebr. Cong., Jason Moyo St, PO Box 337. ☎ 60829. *President* A. Feigenbaum.

JEWISH STATISTICS

In view of the large movements of population in recent years and in many countries the difficulty of obtaining exact figures, the compilation of Jewish population statistics can only be based on estimates received from a variety of sources.

The current happily substantial exodus of Russian Jewry has compounded the problem of maintaining reliable figures but for the time being we can only repeat previous figures pending formal revisions from our informants, most notably the IJPR who have furnished the principle figures on Table I (1991), and the World Jewish Congress (1995).

Estimates of the present world Jewish population give a total of about 15,000,000, including 1,450,000 in the former Soviet Union. Some 3,636,490 are in Europe, about 6,888,757 in North and South America, some 4,550,000 in Asia, including 4,500,000 in Israel, about 146,770 in Africa and about 96,320 in Oceania. Based on the 1991 census in Australia, W. D. Rubinstein has provided new figures for the state centres. Figures for the USA have been revised in the light of Kosman & Scheckner (AJYB 1993). The number of Jews in Moslem countries is about 71,600.

The number of Jews in the world before the outbreak of war in 1939 was estimated at a figure slightly under 17,000,000, of whom about 10,000,000 lived in Europe, 5,375,000 in North and South America (which seems to have been an overestimate), 830,000 in Asia, 600,000 in Africa, and less than 33,000 in Oceania. The difference between the pre-war and post-war figures is accounted for principally by the enormous losses suffered by the Jewish people between 1939 and 1945. Although estimates of Jews murdered by the Nazis and their collaborators vary, the number is commonly accepted to be 6,000,000.

From the seizure of power by Hitler until the outbreak of war in 1939, 80,000 refugees from Central Europe were admitted to Britain. During the six years of war, a further 70,000 were admitted and since the end of the war about 70,000 displaced persons as well as refugees from a number of other countries. Probably some 80 per cent of these were Jews. Many of these were, however, only temporary residents.

Table III has been revised in the light of new figures made available by the Community Research Unit of the Board of Deputies collected in the course of two studies: Synagogue Membership Study for 1989; and, Small Communities Study, prepared May 1990. Data in both cases apply to 1989, the most recent available, although the unit has been expecting to publish revised figures by the end of 1993. Figures for the larger centres are based on Waterman & Kosmin: "British Jewry in the eighties", 1986.

Table I
POPULATION OF THE PRINCIPAL COUNTRIES

Afghanistan 50	Barbados 55
Albania 50	Belgium 30,000
Algeria 150	Bermuda 125
Argentina 240,000	Bolivia 640
Armenia 500	Bosnia Hercegovina 1,100
Aruba & Curacao 500	Brazil 250,000
Australia 92,000	Bulgaria 6,500
Austria 12,000	Canada 356,000
Bahamas 200	Cayman Islands 40

Table I continued

Chile	25,000	Luxembourg	1,000
Colombia	7,000	Malta	50
Costa Rica	2,500	Mexico	48,000
Croatia	2,500	Moldova	65,000
Cuba	1,000	Morocco	10,000
Czech Republic	10,000	New Zealand	4,000
Denmark	9,000	New Caledonia	120
Dominican Rep.	150	Norway	2,000
Ecuador	1,000	Pakistan	17
Egypt	240	Panama	9,250
El Salvador	100	Paraguay	900
Estonia	3,000	Peru	5,000
Ethiopia	1,000	Philippines	25
Fiji	40	Poland	6,000
Finland	1,500	Portugal	400
France	600,000	Puerto Rico	1,500
Germany	62,000	Romania	14,000
Gibraltar	600	Singapore	300
* Great Britain and		Slovakia	6,000
N. Ireland	300,000	South Africa	100,000
Greece	4,800	Spain	12,000
Guatemala	1,500	Surinam	300
Haiti	150	Sweden	18,000
Holland	25,000	Switzerland	17,500
Honduras	150	Syria	1,500
Hong Kong	3,000	Tahiti	130
Hungary	85,000	Taiwan	180
India	5,600	Thailand	250
Indonesia	16	Trinidad	10
Iran	25,000	Tunisia	3,000
Iraq	200	Turkey	25,000
Ireland	1,300	U.S.A.	5,950,000
¶ Israel	5,619,000	Uruguay	35,000
Italy	35,000	†Former U.S.S.R.	1,449,117
Jamaica	350	Venezuela	20,000
Japan	2,000	Virgin Islands	500
Kenya	330	Yemen, North	1,000
Latvia	17,000	Yugoslavia (Serbia)	3,500
Lebanon	100	Zaire	100
Libya	50	Zambia	35
Lithuania	11,000	Zimbabwe	900

¶ Israel Statistical Abstract 1996. Including Eastern Jerusalem and West Bank Settlements.

* According to a report by the Board of Deputies' demographic unit in 1991.

† 1989 census.

Table II
MAJOR CENTRES OF JEWISH POPULATION

EUROPE

Amsterdam	15,000	Malaga	1,500
Antwerp	15,000	Malmo	1,950
Athens	2,800	Marseilles	70,000
Barcelona	3,000	Metz	2,500
Basle	2,000	Milan	10,000
Belgrade	1,627	Minsk	45,000
Berlin	10,000	Moscow	200,000
Bordeaux	6,000	Munich	4,000
Brussels	23,000	Nancy	2,000
Bucharest	11,000	Nice	25,000
Budapest	80,000	Odessa	120,000
Cisinau	50,000	Oslo	900
Cologne	1,260	Paris, Greater	350,000
Copenhagen	8,500	Prague	1,400
Dublin	1,300	Riga	15,000
Dusseldorf	1,710	Rome	15,000
Florence	1,290	Rotterdam	1,500
Frankfurt	5,000	St. Petersburg	100,000
Geneva	3,900	Salonika	1,100
Gothenburg	2,500	Sarajevo	1,090
Grenoble	5,000	Sofia	3,200
Hamburg	1,415	Stockholm	9,500
Helsinki	850	Strasbourg	18,000
Istanbul	23,000	Sverdlovsk	20,000
Izmir	1,000	The Hague	2,500
Kaunas	5,500	Toulouse	25,000
Kazan	10,000	Turin	1,630
Kharkov	80,000	Vienna	1,000
Kiev	110,000	Vilnius	4,500
Lille	3,000	Warsaw	2,000
Lisbon	300	Wrocklaw	1,500
Lodz	1,500	Zagreb	1,500
Lvov	25,000	Zhitomir	20,000
Lyons	30,000	Zurich	6,252
Madrid	3,500		

ASIA

Ankara	100	Shiraz	3,000
Bombay	4,354	Tashkent	50,000
Damascus	1,000	Teheran	20,000
Sa'ana	1,000	Tokyo	750

Table II - continued

ISRAEL

Acco	28,900	Kiryat Gat	27,400
Afula	24,200	Kiryat Motzkin	29,300
Ashdod	72,900	Kiryat Ono	22,000
Askelon	55,700	Kiryat Yam	31,700
Bat Yam	132,800	Lod	33,200
Beersheba	114,600	Nahariya	29,400
Bnei Brak	107,400	Netanya	114,400
Dimona	25,400	Or Yehuda	19,900
Eilat	24,200	Petach Tikva	132,100
Givatayim	45,900	Ramat Gan	115,600
Hadera	43,200	Ramat Hasharon	35,800
Haifa	203,400	Ramle	36,800
Herzlia	70,200	Ra'anana	48,000
Hod Hasharon	23,700	Rehovot	71,900
Holon	143,600	Rishon le Zion	120,100
Jerusalem	346,100	Tel Aviv-Jaffa	308,700
Kfar Saba	52,800	Tiberias	30,800
Kiryat Atta	35,100	Upper Nazareth	21,900
Kiryat Bialik	32,400	West Bank Settlements	140,000

AMERICAS

Alameda (Ca.)	30,000	Miami	202,000
Atlanta	50,000	Middlesex Co. (N.J.)	40,000
Baltimore	94,000	Milwaukee (Wisc.)	29,000
Bergen County (N.J.)	83,700	Minneapolis (Min.)	22,000
Boca Raton-Delray (Florida)	50,000	Montgomery & Prince Georges	105,000
Boston	210,000	Montreal (Que.)	100,000
Buenos Aires	220,000	New Haven (Con.)	26,000
Calgary (Alberta)	5,500	New York (Greater)	1,450,000
Camden (New Jersey)	28,000	Newark & Essex County (N.J.)	79,000
Caracas	18,000	Orange County (Ca.)	75,000
Chicago	248,000	Ottawa (Ont.)	9,000
Cincinnati	22,000	Palm Beach County (Florida)	209,000
Cleveland	70,000	Philadelphia	254,000
Dallas	24,000	Phoenix	50,000
Denver	45,000	Pittsburgh (Pa.)	45,000
Detroit	94,000	Rio de Janeiro	80,000
Edmonton (Alberta)	3,700	Rockland County (N.Y.)	57,000
Elizabeth & Union County (N.J.)	30,000	St. Louis (Mis.)	53,500
Englewood & Bergen Co. (N.J.)	100,000	San Diego	36,400
Fort Lauderdale (Florida)	284,000	San Jose (Ca)	32,000
Halifax (N.S.)	1,500	San Francisco	128,000
Hamilton (Ont.)	4,600	Santiago	21,000
Hartford (Con.)	27,500	Sao Paulo	90,000
Hollywood (Florida)	60,000	Seattle	19,500
Houston	40,000	Toronto (Ont.)	175,000
Kansas City	22,000	Vancouver (B.C.)	18,000
Lima	5,000	Washington (D.C.)	160,000
London (Ont.)	1,900	Windsor (Ont.)	2,500
Los Angeles	490,000	Winnipeg (Man.)	16,000
Mexico City	50,000		

Table II continued

AFRICA

Alexandria	100
Bulawayo	350
Cape Town	28,600
Durban	6,420
Fez	1,500
Harare	625
Johannesburg	63,620
Kinshasa	300
Port Elizabeth	2,740
Pretoria	3,750
Rabat	1,500
Tangier	1,000
Tunis	2,200

OCEANIA

Adelaide	1,250
Auckland	1,600
Brisbane	1,500
Canberra	500
Christchurch	60
Dunedin	40
Hamilton	50
Hobart	100
Melbourne	50,000
Noumea (New Caledonia)	100
Perth	4,200
Sydney	35,000
Wellington	1,000

Table III
JEWS IN BRITAIN AND NORTHERN IRELAND

Aberdeen	30
Amersham	50
Basildon	12
Bedford	35
Belfast	550
Birmingham	3,000
Blackpool	1,500
Bognor Regis	40
Bournemouth	3,000
Bradford	170
Brighton & Hove	8,000
Bristol	375
Cambridge	1,000
Canterbury	160
Cardiff	1,200
Chatham & Rochester	50
Chelmsford	145
Cheltenham	70
Chester	35
Colchester	100
Coventry	140
Crawley	50
Darlington	40
Dundee	22
East Grinstead	35
Eastbourne	63
Edinburgh	500
Exeter	150
Gateshead	1,430
Glasgow	6,700
Grimsby (Great)	45
Guildford	100
Harlow	190
Harrogate	150
Hastings	33
Hemel Hempstead	270
High Wycombe	35
Hull	1,120
Leamington (Warwick)	132
Leeds	8,250
Leicester	670
Liverpool	3,000
Llandudno, Colwyn Bay & Rhyl	45
London (Greater London Area)	215,000
Maidenhead (Royal Windsor &)	1,240
Manchester & Salford	27,000
Margate & Thanet	200
Middlesbrough	65
Milton Keynes	182
Newcastle upon Tyne	1,110
Newport	10
Northampton	185
Norwich	170
Nottingham	1,050
Oxford	700
Peterborough	105
Plymouth	100
Portsmouth	385
Preston	25
Radlett	750
Reading	500
Reigate & Banstead	45
St. Albans	200
St. Anne's (Fylde)	500
Sheffield	650
Solihull	300
S. Shields (S. Tyneside)	9
Southampton & Winchester	105
Southend & Westcliff	4,500
Southport (Sefton)	1,382

Staines & Slough 390
Stoke-on-Trent 30
Sunderland 60
Swansea 245
Swindon (Thamesdown) 72
Torquay (Torbay) 20
Wallasey (Wirral) 50

Welwyn (Hatfield) 290
Whitley Bay (Blyth Valley) 20
Wolverhampton 85
York 25

Isle of Man 35
Jersey & Guernsey 150

HISTORICAL NOTE ON BRITISH JEWRY

There were probably individual Jews in England in Roman and (though less likely) in Anglo-Saxon times, but the historical records of any organised settlement here start after the Norman Conquest of 1066. Jewish immigrants arrived early in the reign of William the Conqueror and important settlements came to be established in London (at a site still known as Old Jewry), Lincoln and many other centres. In 1190 massacres of Jews occurred in many cities, most notably in York. This medieval settlement was ended by Edward I's expulsion of the Jews in 1290, after which date, with rare and temporary exceptions, only converts to Christianity or secret adherents of Judaism could live here. The Domus Conversorum, the House for Converted Jews (on the site of the present Public Record Office in Chancery Lane, London) had been established in 1232. Perhaps the most notable Jews in medieval England were the financier, Aaron of Lincoln (d.c. 1186), and Elijah Menahem of London (d. 1284), financier, physician and Talmudist.

After the expulsion of the Jews from Spain in 1492 a secret Marrano community became established in London, but the present Anglo-Jewish community dates in practice from the period of the Commonwealth. In 1650 Menasseh ben Israel, of Amsterdam, began to champion the cause of Jewish readmission to England, and in 1655 he led a mission to London for this purpose. A conference was convened at Whitehall and a petition was presented to Oliver Cromwell. Though no formal decision was then recorded, in 1656 the Spanish and Portuguese Congregation in London was organised. It was followed towards the end of the seventeenth century by the establishment of an Ashkenazi community, which increased rapidly inside London as well as throwing out offshoots before long to a number of provincial centres and seaports. The London community, has, however, always comprised numerically the preponderant part of British Jewry.

Britain has the distinction of being one of the few countries in Europe where during the course of the past three centuries there have been no serious outbreaks of violence against Jews and in which the ghetto system never obtained a footing, though in 1753 the passage through Parliament of a Bill to facilitate the naturalisation of foreign-born Jews caused such an outcry that it was repealed in the following year. A short-lived outbreak of anti-semitism in 1772, associated with the so-called 'Chelsea murders' is also notable for its rarity.

Although Jews in Britain had achieved a virtual economic and social emancipation by the early nineteenth century they had not yet gained 'political emancipation'. Minor Jewish disabilities were progressively removed and Jews were admitted to municipal rights and began to win distinction in the professions. The movement for the removal of Jewish political disabilities became an issue after the final removal of political disabilities from Protestant dissenters and then Roman Catholics (1829), and a Bill with that object was first introduced into the House of Commons in 1830. Among the advocates of Jewish emancipation were Macaulay, Lord John Russell, Gladstone (from 1847) and Disraeli. The latter, who was a Christian of Jewish birth, entered Parliament in 1837. Jewish MPs were repeatedly elected from 1847 onwards, but were prevented from taking their seats by the nature of the various oaths required from all new members. Owing to the opposition in the House of Lords it was not until 1858 that a Jew (Lionel de Rothschild) was formally admitted to Parliament, this being followed in 1885 by the elevation of his son (Sir Nathaniel de Rothschild) to the Peerage. Meanwhile, in 1835, Sir David Salomons was the first Jew to become Sheriff of London, and in 1855 Lord Mayor of London. The first to be a Member of the government was Sir George Jessel, who became Solicitor-General in 1871, and the first Jewish Cabinet Minister was Herbert Samuel in 1909.

During the 19th century British Jews spread out from those callings which had hitherto been regarded as characteristic of the Jews. A further mark of the organisational consolidation of the community can be seen in the growth and strength of many of the communal institutions mentioned elsewhere in this book, such as the Board of Deputies (founded 1760), the Board of Guardians (founded 1859), and the United Synagogue (founded 1870), as well as the development of the office of Chief Rabbi and the longevity of the Jewish Chronicle which marked its 150th anniversary in 1991. Equally significant by the middle of the century was the appearance of a number of newer Jewish communities which had been formed in many of the new industrial centres in the North of England and the Midlands, the intellectual activities and the overseas connections of which received thereby a powerful impetus.

There has always been a steady stream of immigration into Britain from Jewish communities in Europe, originally from the Iberian Penninsula and Northern Italy, later from Western and Central Europe. The community was radically transformed by the large influx of refugees which occurred between 1881 and 1914, the result of the intensified persecution of Jews in the Russian Empire. The Jewish population rose from about 25,000 in the middle of the 19th century to nearly 350,000 by 1914. It also became far more dispersed geographically. The last two decades of the nineteenth century saw a substantial growth in the number of communities both in England and in Scotland, and in consequence the 'provinces' became more significant both in numbers and in the influence upon the community as a whole. The impact of this immigration on the Anglo-Jewish community was intensified because very many of the Jews who left Eastern Europe on their way to North America or South Africa passed through Britain. From 1933 a new emigration of Jews commenced, this time from Nazi persecution, and again many settled in this country. Since the end of the Second World War and notably since 1956, smaller numbers of refugees have come from Iran, Arab countries and Eastern Europe.

One of the main features of the years after 1914 was the gradual transfer of the leadership of the community from the representatives of the older establishment of Anglo-Jewry to the children and grandchildren of the newer wave of immigrants. Another feature was the growth of Zionist movements, firstly the Chovevei Zion (Lovers of Zion) and later, under the inspiration of Theodore Herzl, the English Zionist Federation. Under the leadership of Chaim Weizmann and his colleagues in this country, the Zionist Movement obtained, in 1917, the historic Balfour Declaration from the British Government. In 1920 the first British High Commissioner in Mandate Palestine was Viscount Samuel. It was after the withdrawal of the British Government from the Mandate that the State of Israel was proclaimed in 1948.

A mark of British Jewry's full participation in public life is reflected in the number of Jewish signatories to the proclamation of accession of Queen Elizabeth II in 1952 which included seven Jewish Privy Councillors. In the highest offices of the State, in Parliamentary and municipal life, in the Civil and Armed Services, in the judiciary and the universities, in all professions and occupations, the Jewish subjects of the Crown – both at home and overseas – play their full part as inheritors of the political and civic emancipation that was achieved last century. There were 21 Jewish Members in the House of Commons elected on May 1, 1997.

In its internal life and organisation, British Jewry has constructed the complex fabric of religious, social and philanthropic institutions enumerated in this book. The Jews in Britain are now estimated to number about 300,000 (see the relevant note in the statistical tables) of whom some 215,000 reside in Greater London and the remainder are spread in some 80 regional communities.

UNITED KINGDOM LEGISLATION CONCERNING JEWS

(Prepared (July 1996) by His Honour Judge Aron Owen.)

HISTORICAL BACKGROUND

In the Middle Ages, hostility towards Jews was a common feature in many European countries. In England, during the reign of Edward I (1272–1307), the *Statutum de Judeismo* was passed in 1275. This statute forbade usury and included an order continuing to oblige Jews to wear a distinguishing badge and imposing upon them an annual poll tax.

In 1290, Edward personally decreed the expulsion of Jews from England. During the reign of Charles I (1625–49) the number of Jews in England steadily increased. Menasseh ben Israel (1604–57) of Amsterdam made a direct appeal to Cromwell to authorize readmission. His 'Humble Addresses' presented to the Lord Protector in October 1655 urged the revocation of the edict of 1290 and entreated that the Jews be accorded the right of public worship and the right to trade freely. No formal announcement was ever made of the Jews' 're-admission' but, from about 1657, the edict of 1290 ceased to have effect.

The Religious Disabilities Act 1846 extended to Jews the provisions of the Toleration Act 1688. Under the 1846 Act, British subjects professing the Jewish religion were to be subject to the same laws in respect of their schools, places for religious worship, education and charitable purposes, and the property held with them, as Protestant dissenters from the Church of England.

PRESENT POSITION

Today, English Law does not regard Jews as a separate nationality or as different from any other British citizen. They have no special status except in so far as they constitute a dissenting religious denomination.

Provision for that special religious position of Jews has, from time to time, been made in legislation (see, for example, the 1846 Act mentioned above). A discussion of the subject will be found in Halsbury's *Laws of England*, fourth edition 1975, Volume 14, paragraphs 1423 to 1432.

Some of the various statutory provisions in force today are set out briefly below. Further information and details can be obtained from the Board of Deputies (5th Floor, Commonwealth House, 1-19 New Oxford St., WC1A 1NF. ☎ 0171-543 5400). Legal advice should be sought by those wishing to know the impact of specific legislation upon their own particular circumstances.

1. The *Representation of the People Act 1983* (which is a consolidation of several previous Acts) enables a voter in a parliamentary of local election, 'who declares that he is a Jew' and objects on religious grounds to marking the ballot paper on the Jewish Sabbath, to have, if the poll is taken on a Saturday, his vote recorded by the presiding officer. This right does not apply to Jewish Holy-days other than the Sabbath. A person unable by reason of 'religious observance' to go in person to the polling station may apply to be treated as an absent voter and to be given a postal vote for a particular parliamentary or local election.

2. The *Education Act 1994* permits Jewish parents to have their children attending state or state-aided voluntary schools withdrawn from any period of religious instruction and/or worship where such instruction or worship is not in the Jewish faith. In order to take advantage of these provisions of the Act, a written request must be submitted to the head teacher of the school.

3. The *Oaths Act 1978*. A Jew may take an oath (in England, Wales or Northern Ireland) by holding the Old Testament in his uplifted hand, and saying or repeating after the officer administering the oath the words: 'I swear by Almighty God that ...' followed by the words of the oath prescribed by law. The officer will administer the oath in that form and manner without question, unless the person about to take the oath voluntarily objects thereto or is physically incapable of so taking the oath.

Any person who objects to being sworn (whether in that way or in the form and manner usually administered in Scotland) is at liberty instead to make a *solemn affirmation* which will have the same force and effect as an oath. The form of the affirmation is as follows: 'I ... do solemnly, sincerely and truly declare and affirm that ...' followed by the words of the oath prescribed by law. The form of affirmation omits any words of imprecation or calling to witness.

4. *Marriage Act 1949*. English law expressly recognizes the validity of marriages by Jews in England if the ceremonies of the Jewish religion have been complied with.

The Secretary of a synagogue has statutory powers and duties in regard to keeping the marriage register books, and the due registration of marriages between persons professing the Jewish religion under the provisions of the Marriage Act 1949. He has no authority unless and until he has been certified in writing to be the Secretary of a synagogue in England of persons professing the Jewish religion by the President of the Board of Deputies.

When the West London Synagogue was established, acting on the advice of the Chief Rabbi and other recognized Jewish ecclesiastical authorities, the President of the Board of Deputies refused to certify the secretary of the new congregation. Accordingly, by the Marriage Act 1949, it is enacted that the Secretary of the West London Synagogue of British Jews, if certified in writing to the Registrar-General by twenty householders being members of that synagogue, shall be entitled to the same privileges as if he had been certified by the President of the Board of Deputies. These privileges are also accorded to a person whom the Secretary of the West London Synagogue certifies in writing to be the secretary of some other synagogue of not less than twenty householders professing the Jewish religion, if it is connected with the West London Synagogue and has been established for not less than one year.

The Marriages (Secretaries of Synagogues) Act 1959 gives similar rights to Liberal Jewish synagogues.

5. The *Family Law Act 1996* contains important specific provisions in relation to Jewish religious divorce.

Section 9, subsections (3) and (4) provide as follows:
'(3) if the parties –
  (a) were married to each other with usages of a kind mentioned in Section 26(1) of the Marriage Act 1949 (marriages which may be solemnized on authority of superintendent registrar's certificate), and
  (b) are required to co-operate if the marriage is to be dissolved in accordance with those usages.
the court may, on the application of either party, direct that there must also be produced to the court a declaration by both parties that they have taken such steps as are required to dissolve the marriage in accordance with those usages.
(4) A direction under subsection (3) –

(a) may be given only if the court is satisfied that in all the circumstances of the case it is just and reasonable to give it; and
(b) may be revoked by the court at any time.'

The effect of these provisions is that where parties, who have been married in accordance with the usages of Jewish law (i.e., *Chuppah* and *Kiddushin*), seek a divorce then, before such a Jewish husband and wife would be granted the civil decree of divorce by the English court, they could be required to declare that there has been a *Get*, i.e., the Jewish religious divorce. There would thus be a barrier to such a Jewish husband or wife obtaining a civil divorce and being able to remarry unless and until there has been a prior *Get*.

It is hoped that these new statutory provisions will go some way towards alleviating the plight of an *Agunah*. The usual case of an *Agunah* (literally 'a chained woman') is that of a wife whose husband refuses to give her a *Get* so that she is unable to remarry in accordance with orthodox Jewish law. Under the above provisions of the Family Law Act 1996 such a husband would himself be unable to obtain a civil decree of divorce and remarry.

6. *Shechita*. Animals and birds slaughtered by the Jewish method (*shechita*) for the food of Jews by a Jew duly licensed by the Rabbinical Commission constituted for the purpose do not come within the provision of the Slaughterhouses Act 1974 or the Slaughter of Poultry Act 1967 relating to the methods of slaughter of animals and birds. The right to practice *shechita* is thus preserved.

In March 1995 both Acts (the Slaughterhouses Act 1974 and the Slaughter of Poultry Act 1967) were repealed and replaced by secondary legislation in the form of a Statutory Instrument. This implements the European Community's Directive (93/119/EC) on the protection of animals at the time of slaughter. There is specific provision that the requirement for animals and poultry to be stunned before slaughter or killed instantaneously does not apply in the case of animals subject to particular methods of slaughter required by certain religious rites. *Shechita* is accordingly safeguarded.

7. The *Sunday Trading Act*, which came into operation on 26 August 1994, has removed many of the difficulties caused by the Shops Act 1950. All shops with a selling and display area of less than 280 square metres may be open at any time on Sundays. Shops with a selling and display area of 280 square metres or more are still subject to some restriction, with an opening time limited to a continuous period of six hours between 10 a.m. and 6 p.m.

There is, however, a special exemption for 'persons observing the Jewish Sabbath' who are occupiers of these 'large' shops. Provided such an individual (and there are parallel conditions for partnerships and companies) gives a signed notice to the Local Authority that he is a person of the Jewish religion and intends to keep the shop closed for the serving of customers on the Jewish Sabbath, he may open it as and when he wishes on a Sunday.

The notice given to the Local Authority must be accompanied by a statement from the minister of the shopkeeper's synagogue or the secretary for marriages of that synagogue or a person designated by the President of the Board of Deputies, that the shopkeeper is a person of the Jewish religion. There are severe penalties for any false statements made in connection with this intention to trade.

Large shops which were previously registered under Section 53 of the Shops Act 1950 may continue to trade on Sundays without new notification. But occupiers of food stores and kosher meat shops over 280 square metres who, even if closed on Shabbat, did not previously require exemption, may well have formally to notify their Local Authority that their premises will be closed on Shabbat to enable them to open on Sunday.

Jewish shopkeepers who close their premises for the 25 hours of Shabbat may open after Shabbat.

8. Discrimination against a person on account of his being a Jew is unlawful under the *Race Relations Act 1976*.

9. *Friendly Societies Act 1974*. A Friendly Society may be registered for the purpose, *inter alia*, of ensuring that money is paid to persons of the Jewish persuasion during *Shiva* (referred to in the Act as 'the period of confined mourning').

10. By the *Places of Worship Registration Act 1855*, as amended by the *Charities Act 1960*, the Registrar-General may certify a synagogue. The effect of Certification is freedom from uninvited interference by the Charity Commissioners and, if exclusively appropriate to public worship, from general and special rates.

11. By the *Juries Act 1870*, the minister of a synagogue who has been certified, is free from liability to serve on a jury, provided he follows no secular occupation except that of a schoolmaster.

THE SCOTTISH POSITION

(Prepared by Sheriff G. H. Gordon, Q.C., LL.D.)

Jews do not appear in Scots legislation as a unique group, except in relation to United Kingdom statutes which treat them as such, of which the only one still in force is the Representation of the People Act 1983. European Regulations apply in Scotland as they do in England.

The Education (Scotland) Act 1944 provides by section 9 that every public and grant-aided school shall be open to all denominations, and that any pupil may be withdrawn by his parents from instruction in religious subjects and from any religious observance in any such school.

The oath is administered by the judge in Scots courts, and the witness repeats the words (which begin 'I swear by Almighty God') after him with his right hand upraised. No books are used. A Jewish witness is in practice allowed to cover his head if he wishes to do so. Anyone who indicates a wish to affirm is allowed to do so.

Section 8 of the Marriages (Scotland) Act 1977 provides that a religious marriage may be solemnized by the minister or clergyman of any religious body prescribed by Regulations, or by any person recognized by such a body as entitled to solemnize marriages. The bodies prescribed by the Marriage (Prescription of Religious Bodies) (Scotland) (Regulations) 1977 (S.I.No. 1670) include 'The Hebrew Congregation', whatever that denotes. In practice Orthodox marriages are solemnized by ministers authorized to do so by the Board of Deputies.

The Law Reform (Miscellaneous Provisions) (Scotland) Act 1980 includes regular ministers of any religious denomination among those persons who although eligible for jury service are entitled to be excused therefrom as of right.

The Race Relations Act 1976 applies to Scotland, but the Sunday Trading Act 1994 does not, nor does the Places of Worship Registration Act 1855.

LISTED SYNAGOGUES AND OTHER JEWISH MONUMENTS IN THE UK

The following list has been compiled by the Working Party on Jewish Monuments in the UK and Ireland (see p.5).

LONDON
Grade I
Bevis Marks, EC3

Grade II*
New West End, St Petersburgh Place, W2
Hampstead, Dennington Park Road, NW6

Former synagogues:
Spitalfields Great, Brick Lane, E1 (former chapel, now a mosque)
Princelet Street, E1 (former synagogue behind Huguenot house)

Grade II
In use as synagogues:
Sandy's Row, E1 (former chapel)
West London Reform, Upper Berkeley Street, W1
New London, Abbey Road, NW8
Spanish & Portuguese, Lauderdale Road, W9

Former synagogues:
Mile End & Bow, Harley Grove, E3 (former chapel, now a Temple)
East London, Rectory Square, E1
New, Egerton Road, N16 – and attached school
Dollis Hill, Parkside, NW2

Other building types:
Stepney Jewish Schools, Stepney Green, E1
Soup Kitchen for the Jewish Poor, Brune Street, E1

ENGLISH REGIONS
Grade I
Lincoln, Jews' Court, Steep Hill

Grade II*
Birmingham, Singers Hill, Blucher Street
Brighton, Middle Street
Liverpool, Old Hebrew Congregation, Princes Road
Manchester, Spanish & Portuguese, 190 Cheetham Hill Road (Manchester Jewish Museum)
Plymouth, Catherine Street

Grade II
Bradford, Bowland Street Reform
Brighton, Devonshire Place (former)
Cheltenham, St James's Square
Exeter, Mary Arches Street
Falmouth, Smithick Hill (former)
Hull, Linneaus Street

Leeds, Chapeltown Road, LS7 (former) - plus boundary wall; Shadwell Lane, Moor Allerton, LS17 (industrial school, former)
Liverpool, Greenbank Drive
Manchester, 19 Cheetham Hill Road (former chapel); Withington, Queenston Road, West Didsbury; South Manchester, Wilbraham Road, M14; Sha'are Sedek, Old Landsdowne Road, West Didsbury
Newcastle-upon-Tyne, Leazes Park (former)
Nottingham, Shakespeare Street (former chapel)
Ramsgate, Montefiore Synagogue and mausoleum, Honeysuckle Road
Reading, Goldsmid Road
Rochester-Chatham Memorial Synagogue, High Street
Sheffield, Wilson Road
Southampton, mortuary chapel, Southampton Old Cemetery, Cemetery Road

Scotland
Glasgow, Garnethill, Hill Street, G3; Queen's Park, Falloch Road, G42

PRIVY COUNSELLORS, PEERS, MPs, etc.

PRIVY COUNSELLORS

Balcombe, Sir John (Lord Justice).
Barnett, Lord.
Brittan, Sir Leon, Q.C.
Cowen, Sir Zelman, A.K., G.C.M.G. G.C.V.O., Q.C.
Dell, Edmund.
Diamond, Lord.
Freeson, Reginald.
Kaufman, Gerald B., M.P.
Lawson, Lord.
Millett, Sir Peter.
Oppenheim-Barnes, Baroness.
Rifkind, Sir Malcolm, Q.C.
Sheldon, Robert, E., M.P.
Woolf, Lord Justice.
Young, Lord.

PEERS

Bearsted of Maidstone, 5th Viscount.
Greenhill of Townhead, 2nd Baron, M.D.
Marks of Broughton, 2nd Baron.
Morris of Kenwood, 2nd Baron.
Nathan, 2nd Baron.
Rothschild, 4th Baron, M.A. (Oxon.).
Samuel of Mt. Carmel & Toxteth, 3rd Viscount.
Swaythling, 4th Baron.

LIFE PEERS

Barnett of Heywood & Royton, Baron, P.C.
Bellwin of Leeds, Baron.
Beloff of Wolvercote, Baron, F.B.A.
Clinton-Davis of Hackney, Baron.
Diamond of Gloucester, Baron, P.C.
Ezra of Horsham, Baron, M.B.E.
Grade of Elstree, Baron.
Haskel of Higher Broughton, Baron.
Hayman of Dartmouth Park, Baroness
Jakobovits of Regent's Park, Baron.
Janner of Braunstone, Baron, Q.C.
Kissin of Camden, Baron.
Lawson of Blaby, Baron, P.C.
Lester of Herne Hill, Baron, Q.C.
Levine, Baron Peter.
Levy of Mill Hill, Baron.
Menuhin of Stoke d'Abernon, Baron, O.M.
Miller of Hendon, Baroness.
Mishcon of Lambeth, Baron, D.L.
Oppenheim-Barnes of Gloucester, Baroness, P.C.
Peston of Mile End, Baron.
Rayne of Prince's Meadow, Baron.
Saatchi, Baron Maurice.
Serota of Hampstead, Baroness.
Sieff of Brimpton, Baron, O.B.E.
Sterling of Plaistow, Baron, (Sir Jeffrey Maurice Sterling C.B.E.).
Weidenfeld of Chelsea, Baron.
Weinstock of Bowden, Baron.
Wigoder of Cheetham, Baron, Q.C.
Winston of Hammersmith, Baron
Wolfson of Marylebone, Baron.
Wolfson of Sunningdale, Baron.
Woolf of Barnes, Lord Justice, P.C.
Young of Graffham, Baron, P.C.

MEMBERS OF PARLIAMENT

Bercow, John (C.), Buckingham.
Bradley, Peter (Lab.), The Wrekin.
Caplin, Ivor (Lab.), Hove.
Cohen, Harry (Lab.), Leyton.
Ellman, Louise (Lab.), Liverpool Riverside.
Fabrikant, Michael (C.), Lichfield.
Hamilton, Fabian (Lab), Leeds North East.
Harris, Dr Evan (Lib.), Oxford West & Abingdon.
Hodge, Margaret (Lab.), Barking.
Howard, Michael, Q.C. (C.), Folkestone & Hythe.
Kaufman, Rt. Hon. Gerald, P.C. (Lab.), Manchester, Gorton.
King, Oona (Lab.) Bethnal Green and Bow.
Letwin, Oliver (C.), Dorset West.
Lewis, Ivor (Lab.), Bury South.
Lewis, Dr Julian (C.), New Forest East.
Merron, Gillian (Lab.), Lincoln.
Roche, Barbara (Lab.), Hornsey & Wood Green.
Sheldon, Rt. Hon. Robert, P.C. (Lab.), Ashton-under-Lyne.
Steen, Anthony (C.), Totnes.
Steinberg, Gerry (Lab.), Durham City.
Winnick, David (Lab.), Walsall North.

MEMBER OF EUROPEAN PARLIAMENT

Newman, Eddie (Lab.), Manchester C.

BARONETS

Cahn, Sir Albert Jonas.
Jessel, Sir George, M.C.
Levy, Sir Ewart M.
Richardson, Sir Leslie R.
Tuck, Sir Bruce A. R.
Waley-Cohen, Sir Stephen.

KNIGHTS

Abeles, Sir Peter, A.C.
Alliance, Sir David.
Balcombe, Rt. Hon. Sir John (Lord Justice Balcombe), P.C.
Beecham, Sir Jeremy.
Berman, Sir Franklin.
Blom-Cooper, Sir Louis.
Bondi, Sir Hermann, K.C.B., F.R.S.
Brittan, Rt. Hon. Sir Leon, P.C., Q.C.
Burgen, Sir Arnold, F.R.S.
Calne, Sir Roy, F.R.S.
Caro, Sir Anthony.
Chinn, Sir Trevor, C.V.O.
Cohen, Sir Edward.
Cohen, Sir Ivor Harold.
Colman, Sir Anthony (the Hon. Mr Justice).
Copisarow, Sir Alcon.
Cowen, Sir Zelman, A.K., C.G.M.C., G.C.V.O.
Djanogly, Sir Harry.
Elton, Sir Arnold.
Elyan, Sir Isadore Victor.
Falk, Sir Roger Salis.
Feldman, Sir Basil.
Frankel, Sir Otto Henberg, F.R.S.
Gainsford, Sir Ian.
Gilbert, Sir Martin, C.B.E.
Godfrey, Sir Gerald (the Hon. Mr Justice, Hong Kong Supreme Court).
Gold, Sir Arthur Abraham, C.B.E.
Goldberg, Sir Abraham, F.R.S.E.
Goldberg, Prof. Sir David.
Golding, Sir John.
Goldman, Sir Samuel, K.C.B.
Gombrich, Sir Ernst H.J., O.M., C.B.E.
Green, Sir Allan, K.C.B.
Greengross, Sir Alan.
Grierson, Sir Ronald.
Halpern, Sir Ralph.
Hamburger, Sir Sidney Cyril, C.B.E.
Harris, Sir William Woolf, O.B.E.
Hirsch, Sir Peter Bernhard, F.R.S.
Hoffenberg, Prof. Sir Raymond.
Hoffmann, Sir Leonard (the Hon. Mr. Justice).
Isaacs, Sir Jeremy.
Jacob, Sir Isaac Hai, Q.C.
Jacobs, Sir David Anthony.
Japhet, Ernest I., Hon. K.B.E.
Joel, Hon. Sir Asher Alexander, K.B.E., AO.
Kalms, Sir Stanley
Katz, Prof.. Sir Bernard, F.R.S.
Kaye, Sir Emmanuel, C.B.E.
Kingsland, Sir Richard, AO, C.B.E., D.F.C.
Klug, Sir Aaron, P.R.S.
Kornberg, Prof. Sir Hans Leo, F.R.S.
Krusin, Sir Stanley Marks, C.B.
Landau, Sir Dennis.
Lawrence, Sir Ivan.
Leigh, Sir Geoffrey.
Levine, Sir Montague.
Lewando, Sir Jan Alfred, C.B.E.
Lightman, Sir Gavin.
Lyons, Sir Isidore Jack, C.B.E.
Millett, Sir Peter, (Lord Justice).
Moser, Sir Claus Adolph, K.C.B., C.B.E., F.B.A.
Ognall, Sir Harry Henry (the Hon. Mr. Justice).
Oppenheim, Sir Alexander, O.B.E.
Phillips, Sir Henry Ellis Isidore C.M.G. M.B.E.
Pliatzky, Sir Leo, K.C.B.
Porter, Sir Leslie.
Rieger, Sir Clarence Oscar, C.B.E.
Rifkind, Sir Malcolm, P.C.
Rix, Sir Bernard.
Robinson, Sir Albert E.P.
Roth, Prof. Sir Martin, F.R.S.
Rothschild, Sir Evelyn de.
Samuelson, Sir Sydney, C.B.E.
Seligman, Sir Peter Wendel, C.B.E.
Sherman, Sir Alfred.
Sherman, Sir Lou, O.B.E.
Sheilds, Sir Neil Stanley, M.C.
Shock, Sir Maurice.
Singer, Sir Hans.
Smith, Sir David, A.K. C.V.O., A.O.
Solomon, Sir Harry.
Sternberg, Sir Sigmund.
Stone, Sir Alexander.
Tumin, Judge Sir Stephen.
Turnberg, Sir Leslie.
Weinberg, Sir Mark.
Woolf, Sir John.
Wolfson, Sir Brian.
Zissman, Sir Bernard.
Zunz, Sir Jack.

DAMES

Heilbron, Dame Rose, D.B.E. (The Hon. Mrs. Justice).
Markova, Dame Alicia, D.B.E.
Porter, Dame Shirley, D.B.E.
Prendergast, Dame Simone, D.B.E., J.P., D.L.
Serota, Baroness, D.B.E.

FELLOWS OF THE ROYAL SOCIETY

Anderson, Prof. Ephraim Saul, C.B.E.
Bondi, Prof. Sir Hermann, K.C.B.
Born, Prof. Gustav Victor Rudolf.
Brenner, Prof. Sydney, C.H.
Burgen, Sir Arnold.
Calne, Sir Roy.
Cohen, Prof. Sydney, C.B.E.
Devons, Prof. Samuel.
Domb, Prof. Cyril.
Dunitz, Prof. Jack David.
Fersht, Prof. Alan.
Frankel, Sir Otto (Herzberg).
Glynn, Prof. Ian Michael.
Goldstone, Prof. Jeffrey.
Hirsch, Prof. Sir Peter Bernhard.
Horn, Prof. Gabriel.
Huppert, Dr. Herbert.
Josephson, Prof. Brian David.
Katz, Prof. Sir Bernard (Vice-President 1965 and 1968-76).
Kennard, Dr. Olga, O.B.E.
Klug, Sir Aaron (President 1995-), O.M.
Kornberg, Prof. Sir Hans Leo.
Mahler, Prof. Kurt.
Mandelstam, Prof. Joel.
Mandelstam, Prof. Stanley.
Mestel, Prof. Leon.
Milstein, Dr. César, C.H.
Nabarro, Prof. F. R. Nunes.
Neumann, Prof. Bernard H.
Orgel, Prof. L. E.
Orowan, Prof. Egon.
Pepper, Dr. Michael.
Perutz, Prof. Max F., O.M.
Pontecorvo, Prof. Guido.
Raphael, Prof. Ralph Alexander.
Roitt, Prof. Ivan.
Roth, Sir Martin.
Rothschild, Dr. Miriam, C.B.E.
Sciama, Dr. Denis.
Shoenberg, Prof. David, M.B.E.
Sondheimer, Prof. Franz.
Tabor, Prof. David.
Weizkrantz, Prof. Lawrence.
Woolfson, Prof. Michael Mark.
Young, Prof. Alec David, O.B.E.

Foreign Members

Calvin, Prof. Melvin.
Feynman, Prof. Richard Phillips.
Katzir, Prof.. Ephraim, form. President of Israel.
Kornberg, Prof. Arthur.

FELLOWS OF THE BRITISH ACADEMY

Beloff, Lord.
Cohen, Prof. Gerald Allan.
Cohen, Laurence Jonathan.
Cohn, Prof. Norman.
Daube, Prof. David.
Gellner, Prof. Ernest Andre.
Gombrich, Prof. Sir Ernst Hans Josef O.M., C.B.E.
Goodman, Prof. Martin.
Hajnal, Prof. John.
Hobsbawm, Prof. Eric John.
Israel, Prof. Jonathan Irvine, D.Phil., F.R.H.S.
Koerner, Prof. Stephan.
Lewis, Prof. Bernard.
Lukes, Prof. Steven.
Marks, Prof. Shula.
Moser, Sir Claus A., K.C.B., C.B.E.
Prais, Sigbert J., Ph.D., Sc.D.
Prawer, Prof. Siegbert Salomon, D.Litt.
Schapera, Prof. Isaac, Ph.D., D.Sc.
Segal, Prof. Judah Benzion, M.C.
Supple, Prof. Barry.
Ullendorff, Prof. Edward (Vice-President 1980-82).
Vermes, Geza, D. Theol.
Yamey, Prof. Basil Selig, C.B.E.

Corresponding Fellows

Blau, Prof. J.
Levi-Strauss, Prof. Claude.
Politsky, Prof. H.J.
Samuelson, Prof. Paul Antony.

VICTORIA CROSS

Lieutenant Frank Alexander De Pass*.
Captain Robert Gee, M.C.*.
Leonard Keysor*.
Acting Corporal Issy Smith*.
Jack White*.
Lieut.-Cmdr. Thomas William Gould R.N.V.R.

GEORGE CROSS

Errington, Harry.
Lewin, Sgt. Raymond M., R.A.F.*.
Latutin, Capt. Simmon*.
Newgass, Lieutenant-Commander Harold Reginald, R.N.V.R.*.

ORDER OF MERIT

Gombrich, Sir Ernst Hans Josef, C.B.E.
Klug, Sir Aaron, P.R.S.
Menuhin, Baron, Sir Yehudi, K.B.E.
Perutz, Prof. Max F.
Freud, Lucian.

COMPANIONS OF HONOUR

Brenner, Prof. Sydney, F.R.S.
Milstein, Dr César, F.R.S.

NOBEL PRIZE WINNERS

Peace

Tobias Asser*; Alfred Fried*; Rene Cassin; Henry Kissinger, Menachem Begin*; Elie Wiesel; Yitzhak Rabin*, Shimon Peres.

Physics

Albert Abraham Michelson*; Gabriel Lippmann*; Albert Einstein*; Niels Bohr*; Enrico Fermi; James Franck*; Gustav Herts*; Otto Stern; Isidor Isaac Rabi; Felix Bloch*; Max Born*; Igor Tamm; Emilio Segre; Donald A. Glaser; Robert Hofstadter*; Lev Davidovic Landau*; Richard Feynman; Julian Schwinger; Hans Bethe; Murray Gell-Mann; Dennis Gabor*; Brian Josephson; Ben R. Mottelson; Aage Bohr; Burton Richter; Arno Penzias; Sheldon Glashow; Steven Weinberg; Leon Lederman; Melvin Schwartz; Jack Steinberger; Georges Charpak.

Chemistry

Adolph Baeyer*; Henri Moissan*; Otto Wallach*; Richard Willstatter*; Fritz Haber*; George de Hevesy*; Melvin Calvin; Max Ferdinand Perutz; William Stein; Herbert Brown; Paul Berg; Walter Gilbert; Roald Hoffmann; Aaron Klug; Dudley Herschebach; Herbert Hauptman; Sidney Altman; Rudolf Marcus.

Medicine

Paul Ehrlich*; Elie Metchnikoff; Robert Barany*; Otto Meyerhoff*; Karl Landsteiner*; Otto Warburg*; Otto Lowei*; Joseph Erlanger*; Sir Ernst B. Chain*; Herbert Gasser; Hermann Joseph Muller*; Tadeus Reichstein*; Selman Abraham Waksman*; Sir Hans A. Krebs*; Fritz Albert Lipmann*; Joshua Lederberg; Arthur Kornberg; Konrad Bloch, Francois Jacob-Andre Lwoff; George Wald; Marshall W. Nirenberg; Salvador Luria*; Sir Bernard Katz; Julius Axelrod; Gerald Maurice Edelman; David Baltimore; Howard Martin Temin; Baruch S. Blumberg; Rosalyn Yalow; David Nathans; Baruj Benacerraf; Cesar Milstein; Joseph L. Goldstein; Michael Brown; Rita Levi-Montalcini; Stanley Cohen; Gertrude Aeilion; Harold Vermus; Gary Becker.

Literature

Paul Heyse*; Henri Bergson*; Boris Pasternak*; Shmuel Yosef Agnon*; Nelly Sachs*; Saul Bellow; Isaac Bashevis Singer*; Elias Canetti*; Jaroslav Seifert; Joseph Brodsky*; Nadine Gordimer.

Economics

Paul Samuelson; Simon Kuznets; Kenneth Arrow; Leonid Kantorovich*; Milton Friedman; Herbert Simons; Lawrence Klein; Franco Modigliani; Robert Solow.

* Deceased.

Who's Who

AARON, Martin, M.B.A., F.S.C.A., M.I. Mgt., F.R.S.A.; b. London, Jan. 25, 1937; Fdr. & Chairman, Jewish Assoc. for the Mentally Ill; form. Tr., Ravenswood Foundation; Fdr. and form. Chairman, Jewish Soc. for Mentally Handicapped; Memb. Council of CONCERN for the Mentally Ill; form. Adv.C., Royal Soc. for Mentally Handicapped Children & Adults; Adv. C., Nat. Assn. for Mental Health; form., Lond. Borough of Brent, Adv. Planning Cttee. Ad.: 24 Brookland Rise, London NW11 6DP ☎ 0181-209 0352.

ABIS, Barrington Gerald, J.P.; b. Ipswich Nov. 28, 1939; Exec. Off, Leeds Jewish Rep. C., Admin. Sec., Leeds Kashrut Authority, Beth Din, Admin. Dir., Leeds Judean Club; and S. H. Lyons Tr. Member Leeds Racial Equality; Mem, West Yorkshire Crime Prevention Panel; Form. Com. Rel. C., Weetwood & Chapeltown North Police Com. Forums; P/Pres. B'nai B'rith Men's Lodge 1055; AJY; North area C., P.R.O., Publ. Rel & Gp. Defence Cttee. Ad.: 151 Shadwell Lane, Leeds LS17 8DW. ☎ 0113-2697520.

ABRAHAMSON, Hon. Abraham Eliezer, B.A.; b. Bulawayo, Oct. 13, 1922, m. Anita née Rabinovitz; M.P. (Bulawayo East, 1953-64); Min. of Treasury, Local Govt. and Housing (1958), Min. of Labour, Social Welfare and Housing (1958-62); H.L.P. (President 1956-58, 64-79) Central African Jew BoD, Life Member C.A.Z.O. (1989-); Member World Exec. WJC, served on Nat. Exec. S.A. Jewish BoD (1991-); Chairman, S.A.Z. Fed. (1991-94), President (1994-); Exec., S.A.Z. Fed (1986); V. Chairman 1988-90. Ad.: 4 Oxford Gdns., 188 Oxford Rd., Illovo 2196, Johannesburg. ☎ 880 1964. Fax: 447 2596.

ABRAMSKY, Chimen, B.A. (Jerusalem), M.A. (Oxon); b. Minsk, Mar. 5, 1917; form. President, Jewish Hist. Soc. of England; form. Goldsmid Prof. of Heb. and Jewish Studies; form. Reader in Jewish hist., Univ. Coll., London; Sr. Fel., St. Antony's Coll., Oxford. Publ.: Karl Marx and the Engl. Labour Movement (jt. auth.); Essays in honour of E H. Carr (ed.), two Prague Haggadot (auth.), First Illustrated Grace After Meals, Jews in Poland (jt ed.), many articles and monographs on modern Jewish hist., etc. Ad: 5 Hillway, N6 6QB. ☎ 0181-340 8302.

ABSE, Dannie, F.R.S.L., M.R.C.S. L.R.C.P.; b. Cardiff, Sept. 22, 1923; writer (poems and novels) and physician. Ad.: Green Hollows, Craig-yr-Eos Rd., Ogmore by-Sea, Glamorgan.

ABSE, Leo; b. Cardiff, Apr. 22, 1917; Solicitor; form. M.P. (Lab.) for Torfaen (1983-87); Pontypool (1958-83). Member, Home Office Adv. Cttees. on the Penal System, 1968, on adoption, 1972; first Ch., Select Cttee. on Welsh Affairs, 1980; Member, Select Cttee. on Abortion, 1975-76, Sec. British-Taiwan Parly Gp, 1983-87. Sponsor or co-sponsor of Private Member's Acts relating to divorce, homosexuality, family planning, legitimacy, widow's damages, industrial injuries, congenital disabilities and relief from forfeiture; sponsored Children's Bill, 1973, later taken over by Govt to become Children's Act, 1975, sponsored Divorce Bill, 1963, later taken over by Govt to become Matrimonial and Family Proceedings Act, 1985; initiated first Commons debates on genetic engineering, Windscale, in vitro pregnancies. Led Labour anti-devolution campaign in Wales, 1979. Member C. Inst. for Study and Treatment of Delinquency, 1964-; Chairman, Winnicott Clinic of Psychotherapy, 1988- (Trustee, 1980-). P. Nat. C. for the Divorced and Separated, 1974-1992; V. President, British Assoc. for Counselling, 1985-1990; Chairman, Parly Friends of WNO, 1985-87; Member of C. Univ. of Wales, 1981-87; UWIST. Regents' Lectr, Univ. of Calif, 1984. Ord. of Brilliant Star (China), 1988. Chairman Cardiff Poale Zion (1951-54). Club: Savile. Publ.: Private Member: a psychoanalytically oriented study of contempo-

rary politics, 1973; (contrib.) In Vitro Fertilisation: past, present and future, 1986; Margaret, daughter of Beatrice: a psychobiography of Margaret Thatcher, 1989, Wotan my enemy, 1994 (Awarded JQ Literary price for non-fiction, 1994). Ad.: 54 Strand-on-the-Green, W4 3PD. ☎ 0181-994 1166.
ALDERMAN, Geoffrey, M.A., D.Phil. (Oxon.), F.R.Hist.S, FRSA, MIQA; b. Hampton Court, Middx., Feb. 10, 1944, m. Marion née Freed; Pro.-V.-C. & Prof. Middlesex University (1994–); form. Prof of Politics & Contemporary History, Royal Holloway Coll. (Lond. Univ.), Vis Lect., Oxford Hebrew Centre; Publ.: British Elections: Myth and Reality, The Railway Interest, The Jewish Vote in Great Britain since 1945, The Jewish Community in British Politics, Pressure Groups and Government in Britain, Modern Britain 1700-1983, The Federation of Synagogues 1887-1987, London Jewry & London Politics, 1889-1986; Modern British Jewry. Ad.: Middlesex University, Trent Park, Bramley Rd., London N14 4YZ. ☎ 0181-362-5963.
ALONY, Dayan Zalman Joseph, b. Penza, Russia, Oct. 10, 1915; Emer.Rosh Beth Din. Fed. of Syns., Lond; form. Dayan, Jewish Coms., Ireland; Chairman, Shechita. Kashrus Cttee., Eire; President, Assn of Jewish Clergy and Teachers. Publ.: Degel Yosef on Law and Ethics (1949), etc.
ALTMAN, Manfred, Dr. (LLD Marburg), Hon. Fel. Univ. Coll., London; b. Salzburg (Austria); Company Director. Chairman, Institute of Jewish Studies, University College, London (since 1988; a Governor and its H. Sec. 1959-1988). Member C. of Frs. Hebrew Univ. (1951-). Member Jewish Memorial C., Member C. and Arts Cttee. Ben Uri Art. Soc., London. Form: Member C. Brit. Israel Chamber of Commerce, Member Exec. Keren Kayemet/Jewish National Fund UK and various Zionist Cttees, H. Sec. Brigadier Kisch Memorial Cttee; Co-Founder Kfar Kisch, Israel. Publ. on int. law, on export marketing from Israel, on Youth Educ., historical and biographical studies. Ad.: c/o Inst. of Jewish Studies, University College, London, Gower Str., WC1E 6BT. ☎ 0171-380 7171. Fax: 0171-209 1026.
ALVAREZ, Alfred, M.A. (Oxon); b. London, Aug. 5, 1929; poet, author and critic; poetry critic, The Observer (1956-66), Gauss Seminarian, Princeton Univ. (1958); Vis. Prof., Brandeis Univ. (1960-61), State Univ. of N.Y., Buffalo (1966). Publ.: The Shaping Spirit, The School of Donne, Under Pressure, Beyond All This Fiddle, Beckett, The Savage God (lit.crit.); Life after Marriage, The Biggest Game in Town, Offshore, Feeding the Rat, Rain Forest, Night (non-fiction); Lost, Apparition, Penguin Modern Poets 18, Autumn to Autumn (poems); Hers Hunt, Day of Atonement (novels); The New Poetry, Faber Book of Modern European Poetry (anthologies). Ad.: c/o Aitken & Stone Ltd., 29 Fernshaw Rd., SW10 OTG. Fax: 0171-794 5929.
AMIAS, Rev. Saul, M.B.E.; b. London, Mar. 9, 1907; M. Emer. Edgware Syn.; Fdr., H. Princ., Rosh Pinah Jewish Primary Schs.; Fdr. & President, Jewish Assn. of Cultural Socs.; Life President, Ajex Edgw. Br.: Member, BoD, AJA, JMC, Nat. C. for Soviet Jewry, C.C.J., President, C.C.J. Edgw. Br. V. President Nat. Peace C.; V. President, United Nats. Assn., Edgw. & Stanmore Br.; Emer. Brigade Chaplain, Jewish Lads' & Girls' Bde.; Chaplain, Royal Masonic Hospital; form. Chaplain to Forces, broadcaster; form. President, Union of Anglo-Jewish Preachers. Ad.: 34 Mowbray Rd., Edgware, Middx. HA8 8JQ. ☎ 0181-958 9969.
ANDERSON, Michael John Howard, M.A. (Oxon.), M.Ed.(L'pool), Dip. Soc. Work (B'ham), C.Q.S.W.; b. Sheffield, May 7, 1948; Form. Dir., Manchester Jewish Soc. Services (1986-91); Sec. Regional Jewish Welfare Fed.; Head, Soc. Work Courses, Manch. Poly. (1985-87); Sr. Lect., Social Work. L'pool Poly. (1977-85). Ad.: 31 Woodland Loop, Edgewater, Western Australia 6027.
APFEL, Rabbi Joseph, M.B.E.; b. Poland, March 15, 1909; Av Beth Din, Leeds Beth Din.; Rab. Com. for Licensing Shochetim; Standing Cttee., Conference of European Rabbis; form. M. and R., Passauerstrasse Syn., Berlin (1933-38). Publ.:

Our Sages Say, The Jewish Sabbath, Yad Yoseph etc. Ad.: 4 Maple Croft, Shadwell Lane, Leeds 17. ☏ 0113-2686395.
APPLE, Rabbi Raymond, A.M., R.F.D., M.Litt., B.A., LL.B.; b. Melbourne, Dec. 27, 1935; Sr. M., Great Syn., Sydney (1972-); Sr. Rabbi. Australian Defence Force; Member, Sydney Beth Din; H.V. President, New South Wales Bd. of Jewish Educ.; Jt. H.M. Mandelbaum House, Sydney Univ.; Lect. in Judaic Studies, Sydney Univ.; Lect., Jewish Law, N.S.W. Univ.; President, Assn. of Rabbis & Mins. of Australia & New Zealand (1980-84; 1988-1992); Jt.P., Australian Council of Christians & Jews (1996-); President, Australian Jewish Hist. Soc.(1985-89); M., Bayswater Syn. (1960-65), Hampstead Syn. (1965-1972); form. Rel. Dir., AJY. Publ.: The Hampstead Syn., 1892-1967; Making Australian Society: The Jews; Francis Lyon Cohen – the passionate patriot etc. Ad.: The Great Syn., 166 Castlereagh St., Sydney 2000, N.S.W., Australia. ☏ 9267 2477. Fax: 9264 8871. Email: greatsyn@magna.com.au
ARGOV, Shlomo, B.Sc., MSc. (Econ.); b. Jerusalem, Dec. 14, 1929; Israeli Ambassador at Court of, St. James's (1979-82); Ambassador to Holland (1977-79), Asst. Dir.-Gen., Israeli Foreign Min. (Dir. Israel Information Services) (1974-77); Ambassador to Mexico (1971-74) Min. Israeli Embassy, Washington, USA (1968-71). Ad.: c/o Foreign Ministry, Jerusalem, Israel.
ARKUSH, Rabbi Shmuel; b. Birmingham May 5, 1951; Dir. Lubavitch in the Midlands; Dir. Operation Judaism; H.T. B.J.E.B. Talmud Torah; Chaplain of the Midlands Region Chaplaincy Bd. (1980-85). Ad.: 95 Willows Rd., Birmingham B12 9QF. ☏ 0121-440 6673; Fax: 0121-446 4199.
AUERBACH, Mrs. Geraldine Yvonne (née Kretzmar), BA(Rand), STC (UCT); b. Kimberly, South Africa, 1940; Founding Festival Dir. Bnai Brith Jewish Music Festival (UK, est. 1984); Founding Chairman The Jewish Music Heritage Trust Ltd. (UK, est. 1989); Founder and MD Jewish Music Heritage Recordings (UK, est. 1984); Founder and former MD (1984-1991) Jewish Music Distribution (UK, est. 1984). Ad.: PO Box 232, Harrow, Middx. HA1 2NN. ☏ 0181-909 2445. Fax: 0181-909 1030. Email: geraldine@jmht.org
AVIDAN, Rabbi Hillel, M.A.; b. Lond., July 16, 1933, m. Ruth; M., Bet David Reform Cong. (1992- (Johannesburg); Chairman Southern African Assoc. Progressive Rabbis (1995–); F.M., West Central Lib. Syn. (1985-92); M. Ealing Lib. Syn. (1986-92); and Chairman, ULPS Rabbinic Conference (1990-92), form. M., Wimbledon & Distr. Ref Syn. (1974-81), Chairman, RSGB Assembly of Rabbis, (1978-80), Teacher Reali High Sch., Haifa; Libr. Haifa Univ. Publ.: Feasts and Fasts of Israel, (Contrib) Judaism & ecology; Renewing the vision. Ad.: Bet David, PO Box 78189, Sandton, 2146, South Africa. ☏ 783-7117; Fax: 883-8991.
BAKER, Adrienne, Ph.D., B.Sc.; b. Manchester, Feb. 15, 1936; Family Therapist & University Lecturer; Senior Lect: School of Psychotherapy, Regent's College, London; Publ.: The Jewish Woman in Contemporary Society: Transitions and Traditions (1993). Ad: 16 Sheldon Ave., Highgate, London N6 4JT. ☏ 0181-340 5970 (home), 0171-487 7406 (college).
BAKER, William, B.A. (Hons.), M.Phil., Ph.D., M.L.S.; b. Shipston-on-Stour, Warwicks., July 6, 1944; Form. Housemaster, Polack's House, Clifton Coll., Lect. in English, Ben-Gurion Univ. (1971-77), Hebrew Univ., Jerusalem (1973-75); Vis. Prof., Pitzer Coll., Claremont, Ca. (1981-82); Sr. Lect., West Midlands Coll. (1978-85); Edr., George Eliot-G. H. Lewes Newsletter; Publ.: George Eliot and Judaism, Harold Pinter (co. auth.), Some George Eliot Notebooks, Vols. I-IV, The George Eliot-G. H. Lewes Library, The libraries of G. Eliot and G. Lewes, Antony & Cleopatra. The Merchant of Venice. Ad:
BALCOMBE, Rt. Hon., Sir (Alfred) John, P.C., M.A. (Oxon.); b. London, Sept. 29, 1925, m. Jacqueline née Cowan; Lord Justice of Appeal (1985-95); High Court Judge (1977-85); Q.C. (1969). Pres. The Maccabaeans; Hon. Fel. Hebrew Univ. (1996). Publ.: Exempt Private Companies, (edr.) Title 'Estoppel' - Halsbury's Laws of England (4th ed.) Ad.: 1A Lingfield Rd., SW19 4QA. Fax

0181-944-0527.
BAND, David; b. Lond., April 8, 1931; HM, Michael Sobell Sinai (Primary) Sch. (1981-90); HM, Solomon Wolfson Bayswater Jewish Sch. (1969-81); Educ. Adviser, Provincial Synagogue Hebrew Classes (under Jewish Memorial C. auspices). Ad.: 23 Woodhill Crescent, Kenton, Middx HA3 0LU.
BARD, Basil Joseph Asher, C.B.E., Ph.D., B.Sc., A.R.C.S., D.l.C.; b. London, Aug. 20, 1914; Scientist; Barrister-at Law; Industrial Consultant (Ret.); V. President (President, 1977-83), AJA, President, JMC (1982-90); Gov., and Honorary Fellow Hebrew Univ. (since 1984); form. Chairman Admin. Com. (1990-94) (UK Friends); Life Gov. Hebrew University (1994-); various com. offices (since 1944); Consultant to United Nations Development Org. (1972-74); Man. Dir., Nat. Res. Development Corp. (1969-73), form. Member of various Govt. Cttees., Min. of Supply (1941-43); Min. of Aircraft Production (1943-45). Gold Medallist and Life Member Licencing Executives Soc. (1973-). Hon. Member Fdn. for Science and Technology, (1990). Ad.: 23 Mourne House, Maresfield Gdns., Hampstead, NW3 5SL. ☎ 0171-435 5340.
BARNETT, Rt. Hon. Lord, Life Peer, Joel Barnett, P.C., J.P.; b. Manchester, Oct. 14, 1923; Accountant and Chairman/Dirs. of Companies; form. V. Chairman B.B.C. Govs.; Mem. European Union Select Cttee.; Chairman European Union Sub. Cttee. on Finance, Trade & Industry; Chairman British Screen Finance Ltd; Tr. Victoria & Albert Museum; Chairman Educ. Broadcasting Society Tr.; Chairman, Public Accounts Cttee.; House of Commons (1979-83); Chief Sec. to H.M. Treasury (1974-79), Member of Cabinet (1977-79), form. Chairman, form. Mem Public Exp. Cttee., M.P (Lab.) for Heywood & Royton (1964-83); Chairman, Building Socs. Ombudsman's C. (1986-96); Gov., Birkbeck Coll., Lond. Univ., Fel., Centre for Study of Public Pol., Strathclyde Univ., Hon. Doctorate, Strathclyde, Member, Halle Cttee. Publ.: Inside the Treasury. Ad.: 7 Hillingdon Rd., Whitefield, Manchester, M25 7QQ; Flat 92, 24 John Islip St., SW1.
BARON COHEN, Gerald, B.A., F.C.A.; b. Lond., July 13, 1932, m. Daniella née Weiser; Chartered Acct.; President, First Lodge of England, B'nai B'rith, Nat. T., B'nai B'rith, Distr. 15, V. Chairman Hillel Foundation; V. Chairman, U.J.S.; Edr.; Mosaic; Dep. Edr., New Middle East, Chairman Bamah-Forum for Jewish Dialogue (Jewish Unity Working Group). Ad.: 70 Wildwood Rd., NW11 6UJ. ☎ 0181-458 1552. Fax: 0181-455 1693.
BARRON, Rabbi Moshe, M.A.; b. Manchester Oct. 24, 1946; M. Richmond Synagogue; M. Bayswater and Maida Vale Synagogue (1976-84) M. South Eastern Hebrew Congregation Johannesburg; Founder Lecturer/Tutor Jewish Students University Programme Johannesburg (1972-76) Ad.: 67 Houblon Rd., Richmond, Surrey TW10 6DB. ☎ 0181-948 1977.
BAUM, Derek, M.B.E.; b. Westcliff-on-Sea, Essex, June 9, 1927; Ret. Co. Chairman Estate Agents/Property Developers. M. Consultant & Adv. and Exec. Cttees Chief Rabbinate C.; H. Life-President, Southend & Westcliff Hebrew Cong. (1997-); T. (1968-82); Pres. (1982-97); Pres. Southend & Distr. AJEX. (since 1966); Chairman S. & D. Jewish Rep. Council (since 1997); T. (1986-97); V.Pres. S & D Jewish Youth Centre; V.Pres. & T. Royal British Legion (S. & D.). Chairman Bd. Govs Herzlia Day School. (1984-88); H.Sec. Nat. AJEX (1964-70); Nat. V.Chairman AJEX (1970-74); Found. AJEX Housing Assn.; Chairman Southend AJEX (1960-62), (1964-66); Member BoD (1968-80) R.A.F (1945-48). Ad.: Flat 1, 33 Clifftown Parade, Southend-on-Sea, Essex SS1 1DL. ☎ (01702) 343789.
BAUM, J. David, MA, MSc, MD, FRCPCH; b. Birmingham 23 July 1940; m. Angela née Goschalk; Professor of Child Health (1985-) and Founding Dir, Institute of Child Health, (1988). University of Bristol; Royal Postgrad. Med. Sch. (1967); Lec. then Clinical Reader in Paed., Oxford (1972): Professor Fellow, St. Catherine's College, Oxford (1977); Vis. Prof. University of Colorado Med. Center (1969); Chm., Adv. Cttee., Winnicott Res. Unit, Cambridge (1991-);

President past Foundling Chm., Nat. Assoc. for Care of Children with Life Threatening Diseases and their families (1990-95); Chm. British Assoc. of Community Child Health (1990-94); Trustee, MusicSpace; Patron, Bristol Family Conciliation Service; Children's Hospice South West; Guardian, Helen House, Oxford. Inventor, Silver Swaddler (1968); co-inventor, Human Milk Pasteuriser (1976). Guthrie Medal, BPA (1976). President Royal College of Paediatrics and Child Health (1996). Publ. Extensive contributors to the medical literature. Ad.: 19 Charlotte Street, Bristol BS1 5PZ. ☎ 0117-926 0448. Fax 0117-925 5051. Email: David.Baum@Bristol.ac.uk

BAYFIELD, Rabbi Anthony Michael, M.A. (Cantab.); b. Ilford, July 4, 1946; Chief Exec. Reform Synagogues of Great Britain; Dir. Reform Foundation Trust; Dir., Sternberg Centre for Judaism; Dir. Manor House Trust; form. Chairman, C., Ref & Lib. Rabbis; Tr., Michael Goulston Educ. Fnd., Lect., Leo Baeck Coll.; Edr., 'Manna'; Rabbi, North-West Surrey Syn. (1972-82); Chairman, Assembly of Rabbis, RSGB (1980-81). Publ.: Churban, The Murder of the Jews of Europe (1981); Dialogue with a Difference (Ed. with Marcus Braybrooke) (1992); Sinai, Law & Responsible Autonomy (1993). Ad: The Sternberg Centre for Judaism, 80, East End Road, N3 2SY. ☎ 0181-346 2288. Fax: 0181-343 0901.

BELLOW, Saul; b. Lachine, Canada, June 10, 1915; novelist; Nobel Prize for Lit. (1976); Prof. in the Cttee. on Social Thought; Chicago Univ. Publ.: Him with His Foot in His Mouth, The Adventures of Augie March, Henderson the Rain King, Herzog, Mr. Sammler's Planet, Humboldt's Gift, To Jerusalem and Back, The Dean's December, The Victim, Mosby's Memoirs and other stories etc. Ad.: Chicago Univ., 1126 E. 59th St., Chicago, 111., 60637, USA.

BELLWIN, Lord, Life Peer; Irwin Norman Bellow, J.P., LL.B., D.L.; b. Leeds, Feb. 7. 1923; form. Min. of State for Local Govt.; form. Parl. Under-Sec., Environment; form. Member, Com. for New Towns; form. V. President, Internat New Towns Assn. (Inta); form Leader, Leeds City C., form. V. Chairman, Assn. Met. Auths., form Member Nat. Sports C.; President, Leeds JBS; Life V. President Leeds Jew Rep. C.; H. President, Moor Allerton Golf Club; President, Soc. of Jewish Past Captains (Golf); form. President, Assn. of Jewish Golf Clubs Socs. of Gt. Britain; form. President, English Basket Ball Assn.; Patron Yorks. Kidney Res. Assn.; Deputy Lieutenant, W. Yorks. Ad.: Woodside Lodge, Ling Lane, Scarcroft, Leeds LS14 3HX. ☎ 0113-2892908. Fax: 0113-2892213.

BELOFF, Lord, (Sir Max Beloff), FBA, MA., DLitt. (Oxon.), Hon. LLD (Pittsburgh), Hon. DCL (Bishops Canada), Hon. DLitt (Buckingham & Bowdoin, US), H Dr (Univ. Aix-Marseille III), Hon. LLD (Manchester). FR Hist.S, FRSA; b. London, July 2, 1913; m. Helen née Dobrin; form. Princ., Univ. Coll. at Buckingham; form. Gladstone Prof. of Govt. and Public Admin., Oxford Univ. Publ.: Books on historical and political subjects including Britain and European Union (1996). Ad.: c/o House of Lords, SW1A 0PW. ☎ 0171-219 6669. Fax: 0171-219 5979.

BENADY, S., C.B.E., Q.C., M.A. (Cantab.); b. Gibraltar, May 21, 1905; barrister; Life President (President, 1956-73) Gibraltar Jewish Com.; Fd. & L.President Gibraltar Oxford & Cambridge Assoc.; Leader, Gib. Bar; Sqdn.-Leader; R.A.F., Second World War. Ad.: 124 Main St., Gibraltar. ☎ 78549.

BENEDICTUS, David Henry, B.A. (Oxon.); b. Lond., Sept. 16, 1938; Author, playwright, theatre dir., Ed. Readings BBC Radio (1989-94) plus Radio 3 Drama from 1992; Commissioning Ed., Channel 4 (1984-86); Judith E. Wilson Vis. Fell., Cambridge Univ. (1981-82); Producer 'Something Understood' (with Mark Tully); Macbeth for BBC Radio 4; Publ.: The Fourth of June, You're a Big Boy Now, This Animal is Mischievous, Hump, or Bone by Bone Alive, The Guru and the Golf Club, A Word of Windows, The Rabbi's Wife, Junk, A Twentieth Century Man, The Antique Collector's Guide, Lloyd George, Whose Life is it Anyway, Who Killed the Prince Consort? Local Hero, The Essential London Guide, Floating Down to Camelot, The Streets of London, The Absolutely Essential

London Guide, Little Sir Nicholas, The Odyssey of a Scientist, Sunny Intervals and Showers, The Stamp Collector, The Essential London Entertainment Guide, How to Cope when the Money Runs Out, Poets for Pleasure (audio books). Ad.: 19 Oxford Rd. Teddington, Middx. TW11 0QA. ☎ 0181-977 6522.

BENZIMRA, Maurice; b. Gibraltar, Feb. 21, 1928; Form. Sec., Spanish and Portuguese Jews. Cong., London. Ad.: 119 Poynter House, St. Anne's Rd., W11 4TB. ☎ 0181-603 3255.

BERCOW, John, B.A., M.P.; b. Edgware, Jan. 19, 1963; Public Affairs Consultant; M.P. for ?–?; Lambeth Councillor (1986-90); Special Adviser to Treasury Ministers (1995), to National Heritage Secretary (1995-96). Ad.: House of Commons, SW1A 0AA. ☎ 0171-219 3000.

BERENBLUM, Isaac, M.D., M.Sc.; b. Bialystok, Poland, Aug. 26, 1903; Emer. Prof, form. Jack Cotton Prof and Hd. of Dept. of Experimental Biology Weizmann Instit., Rehovot (1950-71); form. Pathologist at Dunn Sch. of Path., Oxford Univ., in charge of Oxford Univ. Research Centre of British Empire Cancer Campaign; Res. Fel., Cancer Dept., Leeds Sch. of Medicine; Beit Memorial Res. Fel., Oxford Univ., Israel Prize for Biology, 1974; Alfred P. Sloan Award & Gold Medal, Gen. Motors Cancer Res. Foundation, Washington D.C. (1980), etc.; Member, Israel Academy of Sciences and Humanities. Publ.: Man Against Cancer, Cancer Research Today, etc. Ad.: 3 Kossover Street, Rehovot 76408, Israel. ☎ 08-9473788

van den BERGH, Rabbi Martin, B.Ed.; b. Hilversum, Holland, Dec. 2, 1952; M. Wembley Synagogue; Senior Hospital Chaplain Visitation Cttee (1995-); form. M., Withington Cong., Span. & Port. Jews, Manchester; Tr., S. Manch. Teenage Centre; Chairman Manchester Jewish Visitation Board, (1990-94); Asst. M., Withington Cong. (1974-77), Sheffield United Hebrew Cong. (1977-78) Fdr. Chairman & H. President, Span. & Port. Cong., Israel (1981-83). Ad.: Wembley Synagogue, Forty Lane, Wembley HA9 8JW. ☎ 0181-904 7407.

BERKELEY, Leslie David, J.P.; b. Manchester, Nov. 4, 1934; Comp. Man. Dir., Fdr. Member, Brit.-Israel Chamber of Commerce, Manch. Br.; Fdr., Tr., Whitefield Hebrew Cong.; Member Disability Appeals Tribunal, Ch, Brit. Frs., Israeli War Disabled, Manch. Br.; Member, Soc. Security Appeals Trib., Member of the Valuation and Community Charge Tribunal; Exec., Manch. Chamber of Commerce (1980-83); V. Chairman, Frs., Anti-Tuberculosis League of Israel (1960-70); form. Cllr., Radcliffe Borough; Grammar Schs. Gov.

BERKOVITCH, Rev. Mordechai, B.A. (Ed.), Dip. Counselling, F.I.B.A.; b. Sunderland, Feb. 15, 1934; Dir., Jewish Studies, Carmel Coll. (1984-92); H. Vis. M., Nightingale House (Home for Aged Jews); M., Kingston, Surbiton & Distr. Syn. (1972-84); Hon. Dir. Welfare Chief Rabbi's Cabinet (1980-1985), Penylan Syn., Cardiff (1968-72), Central Syn., Birmingham (1956-68). Ad.: 2/2 Harosmarin, Gilo, Jerusalem 93758. ☎ 026764 341.

BERKOVITS, Rabbi Berel, LL.B.; b. London, June 3, 1949; (1990-); Dayan of Federation of Synagogues, form. Registrar Lond. Beth Din; Lect., Law Dept., Buckingham Univ. (1977-83). Publ.: Commentary of Ramban on Torah, Vols. 2-4 (Edr. & Translator), Talmud Torah, Oxford Dictionary of Law (Contrib.). Pesach in the Modern Home. Ad.: 65 Watford Way, NW4 3AQ. ☎ 0181-202 2263.

BERMANT, Chaim Icyk, M.A., M.Sc., M.Litt.; b. Breslev, Poland, Feb. 26, 1929; Writer; Features Ed., 'Jewish Chronicle' (1964-66). Publ.: Jericho Sleep Alone, Ben Preserve Us, Berl Make Tea, Diary of an Old Man, Israel, Troubled Eden, The Cousinhood, Now Dowager, Roses are Blooming in Picardy, The Last Supper, The Walled Garden, Point of Arrival, The East End, Coming Home (1977 Wingate-'Jewish Chronicle' Award); The Second Mrs. Whiteberg, The Squire of Bor Shachor, The Jews, Now Newman was Old, Ebla (jointly with Dr. M. Weitzman), Belshazzar the Cat, The Patriarch, On the Other Hand, House of Women, Dancing Bear, What's the Joke?, Titch, The Companion, Chief Rabbi

Lord Jakobovits, Murmurings of a Licensed Heretic, etc. Ad.: The Jewish Chronicle, 25 Furnival St., EC4A 1JT.
BERNSTEIN, Marver H., M.A., Ph.D. D.L.; b. Minnesota, Feb. 7, 1919; President, Brandeis Univ. (1972-83); Prof., Georgetown Univ. (since 1983) H.Chairman (form. Chairman), B'nai B'rith Hillel Comm.; President, Nat. Foundation for Jewish Culture (1982-86); President, Amer. Profs. for Peace in Middle East (1985-89); Dir., Amer. Jt. Distribution Cttee. (1978-88), Dir, Fdn. for Jewish Studies; form. Dean, Woodrow Wilson School of Public and Internat. Affairs Princeton Univ. Publ.: The Politics of Israel, The Job of the Federal Executive, etc. Ad.:
BINSTOCK, Rabbi Ivan Alan, B.Sc.; b. London, Oct. 27, 1950; Dayan London Beth Din; Rabbi, St. Johns Wood Syn. (1996-); form. Rabbi, Golders Green Syn.; Deputy Princ. North West London Jewish Day School; M. New Syn. (1978-80), Finsbury Pk Syn. (1974-78), R. South-east London Distr. Syn. (1972-74). Ad.: St. Johns Wood Synagogue, 37-41 Grove End Rd., London NW8 9NG. ☎ 0171-286 3838. Fax: 0171-266 2123.
BIRAN, Mrs. Jane, J.P., B.A., M.I.P.M. (née Dillon); b. Lond., Sept. 10, 1938, m. Yoav Biran; Dep. Dir, Overseas Dev. Dept., Dir. U.K. Desk Jerusalem Fd.; form. Dir., Bipac; form. Edr., Zionist Year Book; V. President, Brit. Na'amat; Publ.: Anglo-Jewry An Analysis; Effectiveness of Fringe Benefits in Industry, The Violent Society (contrib.). Ad.: The Jerusalem Foundation, 11 Rivka St., Jerusalem 91012. ☎ 026 675 1706.
BIRK, Ellis Samuel, B.A. (Cantab); b. Newcastle upon Tyne, Oct. 30, 1915; Solicitor; V.P. Jewish Care; V. President, Central C. Jewish Communal Services; Gov., Hebrew Univ., Exec., Frs. of Hebrew Univ, V. President, AJY; London Exec., JPR; Jt. President, Redbridge Jewish Youth and Com. Centre. Ad.: Flat 1, 34 Bryanston Sq., London W1H 7LQ. ☎ 0171-402 4532.
BLACK, Gerald David, L.L.B., Ph.D; b. Montreal, Jan 9, 1928; m. Anita, née Abrahams; Chairman Balfour Society for Children (1964-); Member of Council of Jewish Historical Society (1992-); Tr. of London Museum of Jewish Life and Jewish Museum (1983-). Publ.: Lender to the Lords, Giver to the Poor (1992); Living up West: Jewish Life in London's West End (1994); JFS: The History of the Jews' Free School (1997). Ad.: 54 St. Johns Ct., Finchley Rd., London NW3 6LF. ☎ 0171-624 8320.
BLASHKI, Arnold Roy, O.B.E., A.M.M., B.A., LL.B. (Melb.); b. St. Kilda, May 26 1918; Barrister-at-Law, State P. and Nat. President, Australian Legion of Ex-Servicemen; form. H. Sec., Victorian Jewish BoD, H. Sec. Victorian Branch AJA; President, Mt. Scopus Coll. Assn.; form T. Australian Legion of Ex-Service Men and Women; form. H. Sec., Exec. C. of Australian Jewry; Fed P, Victorian Jew Ex-Service Assn.; Chairman Australian Veterans and Services Assoc. (Victims). Ad.: 44A Clendon Rd., Toorak, Vic. 3181. ☎ 03 98221694.
BLECH, Harry, C.B.E.; b. London Mar. 2, 1910; Fdr. conductor Laureate, London Mozart Players (and Haydn-Mozart Soc.), Fel., Royal Academy of Music; Trinity Coll. of Music; Royal Manchester Coll. of Music. Ad.: 70 Leopold Rd., SW19 7JQ. ☎ 0181-946 8135.
BLOCH, Lionel Herbert, LL.B. (Hons.); b. Bucharest, Sept. 7, 1928; Hon. Solicitor, Israel Embassy; form. Exec., British Z. Fed. and WJC; form. T., B'nai B'rith, First Lodge of England. Ad.: 'Halcyon', Ormond Ave., Richmond, Surrey TW10 6TN.
BLOM-COOPER, Sir Louis, Q.C., Dr. Jur. (Amsterdam), LL.B. (Lond.); Hon. D. Litt. (Loughborough), H.D. Litt. (Ulster); b. London, March 27, 1926; Judge, Courts of Appeal, Jersey & Guernsey (1989-96); Chairman, Mental Health Act Commission (1987-94); Independent Commissioner for the Holding Centres (NI) (1993-99); National Chairman Victim Support (1994-). Ad.: 2 Ripplevale Grove, London Nl 1HU. ☎ 0171-607 8045
BLUE, Rabbi Lionel, O.B.E., B.A., M.A. (Oxon.); b. London, Feb. 6, 1930; Lect.,

Leo Baeck Coll., form. Convener Beth Din, RSGB; V.-Chairman, Standing Conference Jews, Christians, Moslems in Europe, form. Rel. Dir. (Europe) World Union for Progressive Judaism; Chairman Assembly of Rabbis RSGB, M., St George's Settlement Syn., Middlesex New Syn. Templeton Prize 1993. Publ.: Funeral Service, Forms of Prayer, Vol. I Daily and Sabbath Prayer Book (co-ed.); Vol. III, Days of Awe Prayer Book (co-ed.); Vol.II Shavuoth, Passover & Succoth (co-ed.), To Heaven with Scribes and Pharisees; Bright Blue, A Backdoor to Heaven; Kitchen Blues, Bolts from the Blue, Blue Heaven; The Blue Guide to the Here and Hereafter (co-auth), Blue Horizons; Bedside Manna. How to get up when life gets you down (co-auth.); Tales of body and soul. Ad: c/o Leo Baeck College, Sternberg Centre, 80 East End Rd., London N3 2SY.

BLUMENFELD, Jeffery, B.A. (Hons.); b. London, Dec. 1949; Director, Jewish Marriage C.; Chairman Chief Rabbi's Steering Group on Social and Moral Education (1994-); Act-Chairman JMC Legal Group (1993-); form. Dir. US Youth & Com Services Dept.; Edr., Resources Bulletin, Sch. Assemblies C. (1978-80). Ad.: 23 Ravenshurst Ave., NW4 4EE. ☎ 0181-203 6311. Fax: 0181-203 8727.

BLUMENFELD, Simon; b. London, Nov. 25, 1907; author and journalist. Publ.: Jew Boy, Phineas Kahn, Doctor of the Lost, etc. Ad.

BONDI, Sir Hermann, K.C.B., M.A., F.R.S.; b. Vienna Nov. 1, 1919; Master, Churchill Coll., Cambridge (1983-90); Chairman, Natural Environment Res. C. (1980-84), Chief Scientist Dept of Energy (1977-80); Chief Scientific Adv., Min. of Defence (1971-77); form Dir.-Gen. European Space Research Org.; Prof. of Applied Maths, King's Coll., Lond. Univ., form. Chairman, Nat. Cttee for Astronomy; form. Sec., Royal Astronomical Soc., (1956-64); President, I.M.A. (1974-75), President, Brit Humanist Assn. (since 1982); G. D. Birla International Award for Humanism, New Delhi, 1990. Publ.: Scientific works, Science Churchill and Me (autobiography). Ad.: Churchill College, Cambridge CB3 0DS.

BOTEACH, Rabbi Shmuel, b. Miami, Nov. 19, 1966; Rabbi and Director of Oxford University and London L'Chaim Societies. Publ.: Dreams (1991); Moses of Oxford: A Jewish Vision of a University and Its Life (1994); The Wolf Shall Lie with the Lamb (1993); Why Me - The Good God and the People Who Suffer (1994); Wrestling with the Divine: a Jewish Response to Suffering (1995); The Jewish Guide to Adultery: How to turn your marriage into an illicit affair (1995), Wisdom, Knowledge and Understanding (1996). Ad.: O.U L'Chaim Society, Albion House, Albion Place, St. Ebbes, Oxford OX1 1QZ. ☎ 01865-794462. Fax: 01865-794622; (Home) 5 Wigmore St., London W1H 9LA. ☎ 0171-493 3132. Fax: 0171-493 4757.

BOWER, Marcus H., M.A., LL.M. (Cantab.); b. Belfast, Aug. 22, 1918; Barrister; Chairman, Leo Baeck College (1992-96); V. Chairman, European Board of World Union for Progressive Judaism (1990-96); Chairman RSGB (1987-90); form. Dir., Northern Engineering Industries plc.; Dir., Port of Tyne Auth. Chairman, Northern Counties Inst. of Dirs., Mem. Gov. Body, Newcastle Univ.; Mem. BBC Regional Adv. Council; Ad.: 14 Camelot Cl., SW19 7EA. ☎ 0181-947 5173.

BRAYNIS, Mrs. Vera (née Krichefski); b. Jersey; past Exec. Dir., Children & Youth Aliyah for Gt. Britain; Fdr. and H. President Assn. of Jewish Women's Orgs.: President, League of Jewish Women (1964-67), V. President Intern. C. of Jewish Women (1969-74) and 1st European Chairman. Chief Rabbi's Award for Contribution to Society 1995. Ad: 16 Heathside, Finchley Rd., NW11 7SB.

BRICHTO, Rabbi Sidney, M.A., D.D.; b. Philadelphia, July 21, 1936; Dir.: Joseph Levy Charitable Foundation; Sr. V. President ULPS, Chairman Adv. Com. Israel Diaspora Tr; Bd. Dir. IJPR; Gov. Oxford Centre for Hebrew & Jewish Studies; Hon. Sec. European J. Publ. Soc.; form. Exec. V. President & Dir. ULPS (1964-89); form. Chairman, C. of Ref. and Lib. Rabbis; M., Lib. Jewish Syn. (1961-64).

Ad.: The Joseph Levy Charitable Foundation, 37/43 Sackville St., London W1X 2DL. ☎ 0171-333 8111. Fax: 0171-333 0660.
BRICKMAN, Rev. Stanley Ivan, b. London, March 29, 1939; Cantor, Hampstead Synagogue (1987-); Chairman Assn. of Ministers (Chazanim), Chaplain Royal Free Hospital; London Regional V. President, Cantorial Council of America (1994-); Cantor: Gt. Synagogue, Sheffield (1960-65); Ilford Synagogue (1966-69); New London Synagogue (1969-71); Singers Hill Synagogue, Birmingham (1971-83); Great Synagogue, Cape Town (1983-86); Publ.: Friday evening service with Zemirot for children (Birmingham 1976); Recording; Synagogue Liturgy Music with Singers Hill Choir, 1981. Ad.: 9 Marlborough Mans., Cannon Hill, Hampstead, London NW6 1JP. ☎ 0171-431 0575.
BRIER, Norma, BA(Hons), MSc, CQSW; b. London, Dec. 23, 1949; Exec. Dir. (Services) Norwood Ravenswood (1996-); Exec. Dir. Ravenswood Foundation (1989-96); Dir. of Com. Services – Ravenswood and Jewish Society for Mental Handicap (1985); Lect. in Soc. and Soc. Work/Counselling (Harrow College) (1982); Psychiatric Soc. Worker (1972); Soc. Worker (Camden) (1968). Ad.: Norwood Ravenswood, Broadway House, 80-82 The Broadway, Stanmore, Middx HA7 4HB. ☎ 0181-954 4555. Fax: 0181-420 6800.
BRIER, Sam, M.A.; b. London, July 19, 1946; Exec. Dir. (Resources), Norwood Ravenswood; form. Area Dir., Soc. Services Dept., Lond. Borough of Harrow. Ad.: Norwood Ravenswood, Broadway House, 80-82 The Broadway, Stanmore, Middx HA7 4HB. ☎ 0181-954 4555. Fax: 0181-420 6800.
BRITTAN, Rt. Hon. Sir Leon, P.C., Q.C., MA (Cantab), Hon. D.C.L., Newcastle, Durham, Hon. LL.D., Hull, Edinburgh, Bradford, Bath; b. London, Sept. 25, 1939; Vice-President Commissioner of the European Communities (1989-) Called to Bar, Inner Temple (1962); Conservative candidate for North Kensington in the Gen. Elections (1966 & 1970); MP (Con) for Cleveland and Whitby (1974-83); MP (Con) for Richmond, North Yorkshire (1983-88); Vice-Chairman, Employment Cttee. of Parl. Conservative Party (1974-76); Opposition Spokesman on Devolution and House of Commons Affairs (1976-78); Opposition Spokesman on Devolution and Employment (1978-79); Minister of State, Home Office (1979-81); Chief Sec. to the T. (1981-83); Home Sec. (1983-85); Sec. of State for Trade and Industry (1985-86); Chairman, Cambridge Univ. Conservative Assn. (1960); President, Cambridge Union (1960); Debating tour of USA for Cambridge Union (1961); Chairman, Bow Group (1964-65); Editor of Crossbow (1966-67); Member, Cttee. of the Brit. Atlantic Group of Young Politicians (1970-78); Vice-Chairman, Nat. Assn. of School Governors and Managers (1970-78); Chairman, Soc. of Conservative Lawyers (1986-89); Distinguished Visiting Fellow at Policy Studies Instit. (1988)'; Bencher of the Inner Temple (1983); Publ.: The Conservative Opportunity (contributions), Millstones for the Sixties (jointly), Rough Justice, Infancy and the Law, How to Save your Schools, A New Deal for Health Care (1988), Defence and Arms Control in a Changing Era (1988), Europe: Our Sort of Community (1989 Granada Guildhall Lecture), Discussions on Policy (1989), Monetary Union: the issues and the impact (1989), Hersch Lauterpacht Memorial Lectures, University of Cambridge (1990), European Competition Policy (1992), Europe: the Europe we need (1994). Ad.: Commission des Communautés Européens, rue de la Loi 200, 1049 Brussels, Belgium.
BROCH, Mrs. Hazel (née Rubinstein); b. Dublin, Jan. 29, 1936; H. Life V. President (form. P.) Leeds Jewish Rep. C. and Chairman of its Speakers' Panel; Co-ord. Chairman of the Leeds Emunah Council; H.V. President, Tzfia Goren Emunah; Fdr. Chairman, Leeds Ladies Com. Chevra Kadisha (Chairman 1996/7); H.L.P. Yorkshire and Humberside Chaplaincy Board; Eastern Div; Educ. Off. of the Beth Hamedrash Hagadol Syn.; Exec. Member of the Leeds C.C.J.; Northern Jewish woman of the year 1989; Ad.: 4, Sandmoor Ct., Harrogate Rd., Leeds LS17 7JY. ☎ 0113 2662117.

BRODIE, Rev. Gabriel, b. Bratislava, July 7, 1924; M., Manchester Great & New Syn., Sec. Manch. Yeshiva, Chairman Jerusalem Academy Study Gps., Hon Chaplain Jewish Meals on Wheels, 45 Aid Society. Ad.: 43 Stanley Rd., Salford M7 4FR. ☎ 061-740 2506.
BRODIE, Jeffrey, B.A. (Hons.); b. Manchester, Oct. 3, 1950; Admin., Manch Kashrus Authority; Registrar, Manch. Beth Din, Exec. Director Yeshivas Shaarei Torah; Gov. Prestwich Jewish Day Sch.; Tr., Keren L'David Educ. Tr. Ad.: 56 Stanley Rd., Salford, 7.
BROOKES, Kenneth Joseph Alban, Eur.Ing., B.Sc. (Eng.) Met., C. Eng., F.I.M. F.C.I.J.; b. London, Aug. 5, 1928; Technical Consultant, Author & Journalist; Past-P., Chartered Inst. of Journalists; Vice Chairman, CI of J, Freelance Div.; News Edr., Internat. Journal of Refractory Metals and Hard Materials. Consultant Edr., Metalworking Production; Consultant Edr., Metal Powder Report; UK Edr., Metal Times; Contributing Editor, Chinamac (Hong Kong). Publ.: World Directory and Handbook of Hardmetals and other Hard Materials etc. Ad.: 33 Oakhurst Ave., East Barnet, Herts. EN4 8DN. ☎ 0181-368 4997. Fax: 0181-368 4997.
BROWN, Malcolm Denis, M.A.; b. Sheffield, March 24, 1936; m. Barbara née Langford; Research historian; President, Jewish Historical Society of England (1996-98); Asst. Keeper of Manuscripts, British Museum; Archivist, Anglo-Jewish Archives (1965-66); Asst. ed. Jnl of Warburg and Courtauld Insts (1962-64); Lect. Extra-Mural Dept., Univ. of London (1969-81); Chairman Publications Cttee, Jewish Hist. Soc. of England (1988-96). Publ.: David Salomons House: Catalogues of Mementoes, Commemorative Medals and Ballooniana (1968, 1969 and 1970). Ad.: c/o The Jewish Historical Society of England, 33 Seymour Place, London W1H 5AP. ☎ 0171-723 5852. Email: jhse@dircon.co.uk
BROWN, Rabbi Dr. Solomon, O.B.E., B.A., Ph.D., H.C.F.; b. London, 1921; Sr M., (Ret.) United Heb Cong., Leeds, M., Hornsey and Wood Green Syn. (1943-47); HM, Redmans Rd. Talmud Torah (1942-47); Sr Jewish Chaplain in Germany, Austria and Trieste (1947-50). Publ.: Waters of Life. Ad.: 21 Sandhill Dr., Leeds LS17 8DU. ☎ 0113 2685320
BULL, John, Cllr., J.P.; D.L., Commandeur de l'Ordre National du Mérite; b. London, Nov. 8, 1927, m. Helen née Baran; Antique Dealer; Lord Mayor, City of Westminster (1984-85); V. President, Chairman, Trades Adv. C.; V. President, North London C.F.I. (1976); B.o.D; Freeman, City of London; Fel., Instit. Dirs.; Gen. C. of Income Tax (1976). Ad.: 85 Mayflower Lodge, Regent's Park Rd., N3 3HX; ☎ 0181-346 6657.
BURG, Rabbi Yosef, D. Phil.; b. Dresden, Jan. 31, 1909; Chairman, Yad Vashem, Martyrs' & Heroes' Remembrance Auth., Jerusalem; Mem. Knesset (1949-88); Govt. Minister (1951-86); form. Rel. Affairs M, State of Israel; Leader, Nat. Rel. Party; M. of Interior, Soc. Welfare, Health, Police and Posts; Dep. Speaker, First Knesset (1949-51); Bible commentator on Israel Radio. Ad.: 6 Ben Maimon Blvd, Jerusalem.
BURKE, Allan, F.C.C.S., A.C.I.S.; b. Manchester, Dec. 7, 1914; form. Gen-Sec., Anglo-Israel Chamber of Commerce, Fdr. Edr., Anglo-Israel Trade-Journal; Lieut.-Cdr., R.N. (1939-46); Volunteer, Israel's War of Independence (1948), Commodore, Chief of Naval Operations, Inspector Gen.; Frigate Flotilla Cdr. Ad.: 194 Turnpike Link, Park Hill Village, E. Croydon, Surrey, CR0 5NZ. ☎ 0181-688 1562.
BURMAN, Michael Alfred, B.Sc. (Hons), P.G.C.E., F.R.G.S.; b. Southport Sept. 20, 1944; m. Barbara née Schiltzer; Admin. Dir. ULPS; Gov. Akiva School; Educ. Consultant, Progressive Jewish Day Schools. Ad: The Montagu Centre, 21 Maple Street, London W1P 6DS. ☎ 0171-580 1663. Fax: 0171-436 4184.
BURMAN, Rickie Amanda, M.A. (Cantab), M.Phil.; b, Liverpool, July 5, 1955, m. Daniel Miller; Director, Jewish Museum (1995-); Curator London Museum of

Jewish Life (1984-95); Res. Fell. in Jewish History; Manchester Polytechnic (1979-84); Museum Co-ord; Manchester Jewish Museum (1981-84), Publ. on history of Jewish women in England. Ad.: The Jewish Museum, Raymond Burton House, 129-131 Albert St., London NW1 7NB. ☎ 0171-284 1997. Fax 0171-267-9008.

BURTON, Raymond Montague, C.B.E., M.A. (Cantab.), F.R.S.A.; b. Leeds, 1917; P. Burton Group, p.l.c. (1978-84), V. President Jewish Museum; V. President, Weizmann Instit Foundation; C., C.C.J.; Tr. Master Worshipful Comp. of Loriners (1976); Major, R.A. (1945). Ad.: c/o Trustee Management Ltd., 27 East Parade, Leeds, LS1 5SX.

CALLMAN, His Honour, Judge Clive Vernon, B.Sc. (Econ.); b. June 21, 1927; Circuit Judge, South-Eastern Circuit (1973-), Dep. High Court Judge, Royal Courts of Justice (1975-); Dep. Circuit Judge (1971-73); Senator, London Univ. (1978-94), Gov. Council (1994-); Member Careers Adv. Bd. (1979-92), Gov., Birkbeck Coll. (1982-); Gov. L.S.E. (1990-), C., AJA (1956)-; Gov. Hebrew Univ. of Jerusalem (since 1992); Court City Univ. (1991-), C., West London Syn. (1981-87); Member, Adv. Cttee. for Magistrates' Courses (1979-); Edr. Bd., Media Law & Practice (1980-95); Professional Negligence (1985); Journal of Child Law (1988-94), Child and Family Law Q. (1995-); Exec., Soc. of Labour Lawyers (1958), Chairman, St Marylebone Lab. Party (1960-62). Ad.: 11 Constable Close, NW11 6UA. ☎ 0181-458 3010.

CANNON, Raymond; b. London. Nov. 13, 1933; Solicitor; First Chairman, US Educ. Bd.; form. Chairman, Govs., J.F.S. Comprehensive Sch.; form. T., US Burial Soc.; V.Chairman, Lond. Bd. Jew Rel. Educ., Foundation Chairman, Govs. Michael Sobell Sinai Sch., Chairman, Govs. Solomon Wolfson Jewish Sch; Gov., llford Primary Sch. Ad.: 2 Harewood Pl., Hanover Sq. W1R 9HB. ☎ 0171-629 7991. Fax: 0171-499 6792.

CANSINO, H. Manuel, M.B.E.; b. Manchester, July 12, 1914; V. President, London Bd. of Shechita; V. P. Bd. Elders, Span. and Port. Cong.; C. AJA, C., Jewish Lads' & Girls' Brigade; C., Adv. Cttee., Jew Eccl. Officers; C., Jew Autistic Soc. Ad.: 117a Hamilton Terr., NW8 9QU. ☎ 0171-624 5050.

CAPLAN, Leonard, Q.C.; b. Merthyr Tydfil, June 28, 1909; Master of Bench, Gray's Inn; T., Gray's Inn (1979); Member, Senate of Inns of Court and Bar (1976-82); Sometime Dep. High Court Judge, President, Medico-Legal Soc. (1979-81); Chairman, Coll Hall (Univ. of London) (1956-67); C., AJA; form. Chairman, Mental Health Review Tribunal, S.E. Region. Publ.: The Great Experiment. Ad.: 1 Pump Court, Temple, E.C.4. ☎ 0171-353 2622.

CAPLAN, The Hon. Lord (Philip Isaac), Q.C., L.L.D. (Hon.) (Glasgow), F.R.P.S., A.F.I.A.P.; b. Glasgow, Feb. 24, 1929; Senator of the College of Justice, Scotland (1987); Sheriff Princ., North Strathclyde (1983-1989); Member, Sheriff Courts Rules C. (1983-1989) Memb. Advi. Coun. on Messengers-At-Arms, and Sheriff Officers (1987-88); Com., Northern Lighthouse Bd. (1983-1989); Hon. V. President, Scottish Assn. for Study of Delinquency; Hon. President, Family Mediation Scotland (1994-); Sheriff, Lothian & Borders, Edinburgh (1979-83); V. President, Sheriffs' Assn. (1982-83); Chairman, Plant Variety & Seeds Tribunal (Scotland) (1978-79). Chairman James Powell, U.K. Trust, (1992-); Gov. UK College of Family Mediators (1996-). Ad.: Court of Session, Parliament House, Edinburgh.

CAPLAN, Ivor Keith, M.P.; b. Brighton, Nov. 8, 1958, m. Maureen, née Whelan; M.P. for Hove & Portslade (1997-); Leader, Hove B.C. (1995-97); Dep. Leader Brighton & Hove UA (1996-). Ad.: House of Commons, SW1 1AA. ☎ 0171-219 3414, or 01213 292933 (constituency).

CAPLAN, Simon, M.A. (Oxon.), P.G.C.E.; b. Hamburg (Brit. Army Hospital), Apr. 28, 1955; Community Consultant; Jerusalem Fellow (1990-93); Dir., Jews' Coll., London 1985-90; Dir., Jewish Educ. Development Tr. 1985-90. Ad.: Rehov Zeev Bacher 10/9, Jerusalem 93119.

CAPLIN, Maxwell, O.B.E., F.R.C.P.; b. Lond., Feb. 6, 1917, m. Nancy née Leverson; Ret. Consultant Physician; Lond Chest Hospital (1983); Consultant in Occupational Health, Royal Brompton Nat. Heart and Lung Hospitals and Nat. Heart & Lung Instit. (1983-1991); Honorary Senior Lecturer, Univ. of Lond. (1979-83); Consultant Member Lond. Medical Appeal Tribunal (1977-89); Medical Referee Dept. of Health (1979-90); Chairman Lond. N E Cttee. for Employment of Disabled People (1980-86); Patron, form. Chairman, later President, Greater Lond. Assn. of Disabled People (1982-89). Other professional and vol. offices. Publs: Medical Writings. Ad: 498 Finchley Rd, NW11 8DE. ☎ 0181-455 3314.
CARLEBACH, Rabbi Felix F., M.A.; b. Lübeck, Apr. 15, 1911; form. M., S. Manchester Syn, (1946-86); Dep. to HM, Jew Secondary Sch, Leipzig (1933-39); Asst. M. Adass Yisroel Syn., Hendon (1939-41); M.& H.M., Palmers Green and Southgate Syn. (1941-46). Ad: 2A Elm Rd., Manchester, 20. ☎ 0161-445 5716.
CARLOWE, Melvyn, B.Soc. Sci.; b. Abingdon Oxon., Apr. 13, 1941; Chief Exec. Jewish Care, form. Exec. Dir. JWB (1972-89) Hon. Sec. Central C. for Jewish Soc. Service (1994-); Tr. Third Sector Trust (L.S.E.); President, World Conf. of Jewish Com. Services; Exec. N. Lond. Hospice Group; Member London & Quadrant Honorary Cttee, N.E. Thames. Ad.: 221 Golders Green Rd., NW11 9DQ. ☎ 0181-458 3282. Fax: 0181-455 7185.
CARTER, Emmanuel, B.Com., F.C.C.A., F.T.I.I.; b. London, May 18 1925; Elder US form. V. President, US; Exec., Chief Rabbinate C., Dir. US Trs. Ltd. Fel., Chartered Assn.; Certified Accts., form. Lect., Accounting. Lond. Sch of Econ. Ad.: 37 Deansway, N2 ONF. ☎ 0181-883 7759. Fax: 0171-281 2166 (BARWIN).
CASHDAN, Eli, M.A.; b. June 1, 1905; Barrister-at-Law; Translator of the Centenary (3rd) Ed. of the Singer's Prayer Book, form. Lect. in Bible and Tutor Jews' Coll., form. Senr. Jewish Chaplain, R.A.F. Publ.: Contrib. to Soncino Bible and Soncino Talmud. Ad.: 46 Wykeham Rd. N.W.4. ☎ 0181-202 6857
CASS, Frank, b. London, July 11, 1930, m. Audrey née Steele; Publisher; Chairman & Managing Director, Vallentine Mitchell; Chairman & Managing Director, Frank Cass & Co. Ltd.; Chairman of British Jerusalem Book Fair Committee (1979-); Friends of Jerusalem Award (1989); Joint President Sinclair House, Redbridge Youth & Community Centre; Member of Board of Jewish Care. Ad.: Newbury House, 890–900 Eastern Avenue, Newbury Park, Ilford, Essex IG2 7HH. ☎ 0181-599 8866. Fax: 0181-599 0984.
CESARANI, David, D.Phil.; b. London, Nov. 13, 1956; Dr., Inst. of Contemporary History and Wiener Library (1993-95, 1996-); Parkes-Wiener Prof. of 20th Century Jewish History and Culture, University of Southampton (1996-) ; Alliance Prof. of Modern J. Studies, Univ. Manchester (1995-96); Montague Burton Fel. in Jewish Studies, Univ. of Leeds, (1983-86); Barnett Shine Senior Res. Fel., Queen Mary College, Univ. of London, (1986-89). Publ.: ed. Making of Modern Anglo-Jewry (1990); Justice Delayed (1992); co-ed. The Internment of Aliens in Twentieth Century Britain (1993); ed. The Final Solution (1994); The Jewish Chronical and Anglo Jewry (1994); co-ed. Citizenship, Nationality and Migration in Europe (1996); ed. 'Lest We Forget', CD-ROM Interactive History of the Holocaust. Ad.: Institute of Contemporary History, 4 Devonshire St., London W1N 2BH.
CHARING, Rabbi Douglas Stephen; b. London, Nov. 16, 1945; Dir., Jewish Educ. Bureau, Leeds; Tutor, Geneva Theological Coll., Adv., Theol. & Rel. Studies Bd., Dir. Concord MultiFaith/Multi-Cultural Res. Centre (Leeds), Inter-Euro. Com. on Church & Sch, form. Gov. Centre for Study of Rel. & Educ. (Salford); M., Sinai Syn., Leeds; C. for Nat. Academic Awards; Lect., Manchester Police Coll. Member Brd. of Dir. British Friends of the Anne Frank Centre; Exec. M. Coun. for Religious Freedom; Publ.: Glimpses of Jewish Leeds; Comparative

Religions (co-auth.), The Jewish World Visiting a Synagogue, Modern Judaism (audio-visual), Jewish Contrib., The Junior R.E. Handbook, World Faiths in Education, Praying Their Faith (contributor), Religion in Leeds (contributor), A Dictionary of Religious Education In the Beginning (Audiovisual), etc. Ad.: 8 Westcombe Ave., Leeds LS8 2BS. ☎ 0113 2663613. Fax: 0113 2697318.
CHERNETT, Jaclyn, A.L.C.M.; b. St. Neots, June 6, 1941; m. Brian Chernett; Dir. Masorti Assoc. (1984-86); Co-chairman, Assembly of Masorti Synagogues (1992-95); Co-Chairman Edgware Masorti Synagogue (1984-92); Hon. Life President, Edgware Masorti Synagogue; V. President, World Council of Synagogues. Publ.: Conference papers, Work in progress on research in the musical development of Biblical cantillation. Ad.: 4 Brockley Close, Stanmore, Middx. HA7 4QL. ☎ 0181-958 5090. Fax: 0181-958 7651.
CHEYETTE, Bryan, Ph.D.; b. Leicester, Jan. 15, 1959; m. Susan née Cooklin; Lecturer in English Literature, School of English and Drama, Queen Mary and Westfield College, University of London (1992-); British Academy Postdoctoral Fellow, School of English, University of Leeds (1989-92); Montague Burton Fellow in Jewish Studies, School of English, University of Leeds (1986-89); editorial board, Jewish Quarterly and Patterns of Prejudice. Publ. Constructions of 'the Jew' in English Literature and Society: Racial Representations, 1875-1945 (1993); (editor), Between 'Race' and Culture: Representations of 'the Jew' in English and American Literature (1996); (editor), H.G. Wells, 'Tono-Bungay' (1997); published widely on British-Jewish Literature. Ad.: School of English and Drama, Queen Mary and Westfield College, Mile End Road, London E1 4NS. ☎ 0171-775 3356. Fax: 0181-980 6200. E-mail: b.cheyette@qmw.ac.uk.
CHINN, Rosser, b. Penrhiwceiber, Wales, May 10, 1906; H. President, JNF for Gt. Britain and Ireland; V. President, IJPR; H. President, Z.F.; H. Member, Bd. Govs., Tel Aviv Univ. Ad.: 17 Connaught Pl., W2 2EL. ☎ 0171-705 1212.
CHINN, Sir Trevor, C.V.O.; b. London, July 24, 1935; Chairman, Lex Service PLC; P., UJIA; Chairman, V.Pres., Jewish Assoc. for Business Ethnics; Exec., Variety Club of Gt. Brit., Chief Barker (1977-78); H.V. President, Z. Fed.; Dep. Ch., Royal Academy Trust; Tr., Community Security Tr. Ad.: 17 Connaught Pl., W2 2EL. ☎ 0171-705 1212.
CLINTON-DAVIS, Lord (Life Baron, UK), Stanley Clinton Clinton-Davis (cr. 1990); LL.B.; b. London, Dec. 6, 1928; Solicitor; Pres. Inst. of Travel Management, the British Airline Pilots' Assoc. (BALPA) and the Aviation Environment Federation; J.Pres. of Society of Labour Lawyers; V.Pres. of Chartered Institute of Environmental Health and of the Individual Members Group of the Local Government International Bureau; V.Chairman of the Parliamentary Environment Group; Mem. of the B. of Vice Presidents of The Society for International Trade; Serves on the Advisory Cttee of the CIS Environment Trust and the Adv. Bd. of the Centre of European Law at King's College London; Mem. of The London Criminal Courts Solicitors' Assoc.'; H. Fel. of The Chartered Institution of Water and Environmental Management; Opposition Spokesman on Transport (1990-97) and Dep. Opp. Spokesman on Trade & Industry and Spokesman on Foreign Affairs, H. of Lords; Member Com. of European Communities (Transport, Environment, Nuclear Safety) (1985-89); Chairman Adv. Cttee. on Protection of the Sea (ACOPS), Consultat. S J Berwin & Co.; M.P. (Lab.), Hackney Central (1970-83); Parl. Under Sec. for Companies, Aviation and Shipping, Dept. of Trade (1974-79); Opposition Spokesman for Trade (1979-81); Dep. Opposition Spokesman for Foreign Affairs (1981-83); Exec., Labour Fin. & Industry Cttee.; V. President, Poale Zion; form. B.oD.; Cllr., Hackney Bor (1959-71), Mayor (1968-69); President, Association of the Metropolitan Authorities (1992); President, UK Pilots (Marine) (1991-); Honorary Member of the Council of Justice (1989-); President, Hackney Multiple Sclerosis Soc.; President, Hackney Haifa Cttee. Pres., Refugee C.; Tr. Bernt Carlsson Tr.; Member of the Panel of Judges of the UNEP-Sasakawa

Environmental Prize; Order of Leopold 11 for Services to EC, 1990; Fel. of Queen Mary and Westfield College and King's College, London Univ.; Honorary Doctorate, Polytechnical Univ. of Bucharest (1993); Fel. of the Royal Society of Arts (1993); Publ., Good Neighbours? Nicaragua, Central America and the United States (jt. auth.). Ad.: House of Lords, London SW1A 1AA. ☎ 0171-533 2222. Fax: 0171-533 2000.

COCKS, Lady Valerie (née Davis); b. London, July 10, 1932; Dir., Trade Union Friends of Israel; Lab. Frs. of Israel (1978-88), Parliamentary Wives for Soviet Jewry; Community Centre in Israel Project; Hon. Sec. All-Party Friends of Israel Group (H of Lords). Ad.: 136 Marsham Ct., Marsham St., SW1. ☎ 0171-789 2539.

COFNAS, Rabbi Jerachmiel; b. Poland, 1915; M., New Syn., Birmingham, Exec., Initiation Soc., Chairman, Birm. Mikva Cttee. Ad.:

COFNAS, Rabbi Mordechai Leib; b. Birmingham, Dec. 9, 1943; Rabbi, Childwall Syn., Liverpool; Princ. L'pool Yeshiva & Midrasha; Rav, L'pool Kashrut Comm.; form. Sr. M., Cardiff United Syn.; M., Sunderland Hebrew Cong. Ad.: Childwall Synagogue, Dunbabin Rd., Liverpool, L15 6XL. ☎ 0151-722 2079.

COHEN, Arnold Judah, F.C.A., A.T.I.I.; b. London, Dec. 17, 1936; m. Sara née Kaminski; Chartered Accountant; President, Fed. of Synagogues; form. Tr. Fed. of Synagogues. Publ.: An Introduction to Jewish Civil Law (1991). Ad.: 807 Finchley Rd., NW11 8DP.

COHEN, (Bernard) Martin; b. London, Jan. 31, 1933; Administrator, Lobbyist; Chairman, Jewish Defence & Group Relations Cttee., BoD (1991-94); Member, United Synagogue Council; Harrow Councillor (1962-68, 1971-80); Chairman, Public Works & Services Cttee. (1971-74); Gen. Sec., Labour Friends of Israel (1972-80); V. Chairman, Jewish Defence & Group Relations Cttee. (1988-91). Ad.: 486 Kenton Road, Kenton, Harrow, Middlesex HA3 9DL. ☎ 0181-204 6300.

COHEN, Rabbi Isaac, B.A., Ph.D.; b. Llanelli, 1914; Chief Rabbi, Jewish Coms. in Ireland and Ab Beth Din (1958-79) now engaged in research in Talmudic law in Jerusalem; Jt. P. Union of Immigrant Western Rabbis; President, Frs., Hesder Yeshiva, Shiloh, Member of Standing Cttee., Conf of European Rabbis, and Exec. of Israel Assoc. for the Conference; Edr., Irish Jewish Year Book; Rabbi, Edinburgh Hebrew Cong.; M., United Hebrew Cong. Leeds; Harrow & Kenton Cong; and Off. Chaplain to H.M. Forces. Ad.: 1 Epstein St., Kiryat Ha Yovel, Jerusalem, 96664. ☎ 02-6412536.

COHEN, Isaac Norman, M.B.E., B.A., B.Com., B.Sc. (Econ); b. Cardiff, Oct. 30 1924, m. Naomi; Tr. Machzike Hadath Comm.; form. Sr. W., Penylan Syn., Cardiff; Member, Chief Rabbinate C.: Gov. Body, Univ. of Wales, form. Chairman, Cardiff JIA Cttee. Ad.: 17 Riverside Drive, 300 Golders Green Rd., London NW11 9PU. ☎ 0181- 381 4305. Fax 0181-381 4302.

COHEN, Rabbi Jeffrey M., B.A., M. Phil., A.J.C., PhD.; b. Manchester, Feb. 19, 1940; M., Stanmore & Canon's Pk. Syn.; Chief Examiner, Mod. Hebrew, Jt. Matric Bd. (1973-1987), Lect., Liturg. Studies, Jews' Coll. (1980-1992), Rabbinical Adv. and Gov., Immanuel College; member, Chief Rabbi's cabinet, Executive Lond. Division of JIA; Chaplain to Mayr or Harrow (1994-95); form. M. Kenton Syn.; Sr. M., Newton Mearns Syn., Glasgow; Lect. in Hebrew, Glasg. Univ., Princ. Glasg. Heb Coll., Dir. Glasg. Bd. of Jewish Educ.; Dir., Jew Educ., King David Schs., Manchester; Member, Rev. Cttee., Singers Prayer Bk; Publ.: Understanding The Synagogue Service, A Samaritan Chronicle, Festival Adventure, Understanding the High Holyday Services, Yizkor, Horizons of Jewish Prayer, Moments of Insight, Blessed Are You, (Contrib. ed., Judaism section) Penguin Encyclopedia of Religions, Prayer & penitence, Dear Chief Rabbi (ed.); 1001 Questions on Pesach, Following the Synagogue Service, 1001 Questions and Answers on Rosh Hashanah and Yom Kippur. Ad.: Stanmore & Canon's Pk. Synagogue, London Rd., Stanmore, Middx. HA7 4NS. ☎ 0181-954 2210. Fax:

0181-954 4369.
COHEN, Joseph, B.A.; b. London Oct. 1, 1920; Exec. Dir., Brit. Technion Soc. (1957-1986); C., United Syn.; Member BoD. Ad.: 10 Leeside Cres., NW11 0DB. ☎ 0181-455 0738.
COHEN, Laurence Jonathan, M.A., D.Litt., F.B.A.; b. London May 7 1923; m. Gillian née Slee; Emeritus Fel., form. Fel, and Sr Tutor, Queen's Coll., Oxford; form. Brit. Academy Reader in Humanities, Oxford; form. Vis. Prof., Columbia, Yale, Northwestern Univs.; form. Vis. Lect., Hebrew Univ.; form. Vis. Fel. Australian Nat. Univ.; form. President, Internat. Union of History and Philos. of Science; Sec. General, Int. Council of Scientific Unions (1993-96); form. President, British Soc for Philos. of Science. Publ: Principles of World Citizenship; Diversity of Meaning; The Implications of Induction; The Probable and the Provable; The Dialogue of Reason; Introduction to the Philosophy of Induction and Probability; An Essay on Belief and Acceptance, etc. Ad.: Queen's Coll., Oxford, OX1 4AW. ☎ 01865 279120.
COHEN, The Hon. Leonard Harold Lionel, O.B.E., M.A. (Oxon.); b. London, Jan. 1, 1922; m. Eleanor née Henriques; High Sheriff, Berks. (1987-88) Dir.-Gen. Accepting Houses Cttee. (1976-82); Barrister-at-Law; Chairman Jewish Chronicle Trust Ltd.; Tr., Lionel Cohen Lect.; Bencher of Lincoln's Inn, Chairman, Community Trust for Berkshire (1988-94); form. President, JWB (1961-66) and J.C.A. Charitable Foundation (1976-92); form. Master, Skinners Company; form. H. Colonel 39th (City of London) Signals Regiment (Volunteers); Chairman, C., Royal Free Hospital Med. Sch. (1982-92). Ad.: Dovecote House, Swallowfield Pk., Reading, RG7 ITG. ☎ 01118-9884775.
COHEN, Judge Maxwell, O.C., Q.C. LL.D., D.C.L.; b. Winnipeg, March 17, 1910; Emer. Prof of Law McGill Univ. Sch. in Res., Ottawa Univ.; Judge Ad Hoc, Internat. Court of Justice, The Hague; Chairman Canadian-Jewish Cong.; Canadian Z. Fed. Jt. Cttee. on Mid-East Aff. (1952-66); Chairman, Min. of Justice Special Cttee. on Hate Propaganda (1960-95); Chairman For. Aff. Cttee., C.J.C. (1965-67); Chairman, Cong. Select Cttee. on Canadian Constitution (1980-82), Chairman C.J.C. Cttee. Constitutional and Charter Review (1992-); Canadian Co-Ch. (Canadian/US) Internat. Jt. Com. (1974-79); Dean, Law Faculty, McGill Univ. (1964-69); Dir. Instit. of Air & Space Law McGill Univ. (1962-65). Publ.: The Dominion-Prov. Conference, Law and Politics in Space, The Regime of Boundary Waters - Canadian/US Experience; Lawyers and the Nuclear Debate, articles in acad. and other publ.; various Royal Commissions and Task Force Reports. Ad.: 200 Rideau Terr., Apt. 1404, Ottawa, Canada, K1M 0Z3 ☎ 741 5891. Fax (613) 741-4645.
COHEN, Michael, B.A., M.Phil., Cert. Ed.; b. Oxford, Nov. 3, 1941; Educ. Consultant to Broughton Jewish Cassel Fox Primary School (Manchester), American Endowment School (Budapest), Prague Jewish Community; form. Exec. Dir. Bd. of Religious Educ. US; form. HM, Mt. Scopus Coll., Melbourne, Dir., Jewish Studies North-West Lond. Jewish Day Sch; Principal of Leibler Yavneh Coll., Melbourne (1993-95). Ad.: 50 Princes Park Ave., NW11 0JT ☎ 0181-458 4537.
COHEN, Lieut-Colonel Mordaunt, T.D., D.L.; b. Sunderland, Aug. 6, 1916; Solicitor Reg. Chairman, Industrial Tribunals (1976-89); Chairman (1974-76); Dep. Lieut., Tyne & Wear; Chairman, Provincial Cttee., BoD (1985-91); H. Dir., Central Enquiry Desk (since 1990), BoD; H. Life President, Sunderland Hebrew Cong. (since 1988); form. Member, Chief Rabbinate C., Tr. Ajex Charitable Tr.; V. President, and Nat. Chairman AJEX (1993-95); Chairman Edgware School (1991-96); H. Life President, Sunderland Ajex; Tr. Colwyn Bay Synagogue Trust, Alderman Sunderland Co. Borough C. (1967-74); Cllr., Tyne & Wear County C. (1973-74), Chairman Sund. Educ. Cttee. (1970-72), Ch. Govs., Sund. Polytechnic (1969-72), Court, Newcastle upon Tyne Univ. (1968-72); Chairman, Mental Health Review Tribunal (1967-76); Dep. Chairman, Northern Traffic

Coms. (1972-74), President, Sund. Law Soc. (1970); War service, R.A. (1940-46) (dispatches, Burma campaign), T.A. (1947-55), C.O. 463 (M) HAA Regt. (1954-55); Territorial Decoration (1954). Ad.: 1, Peters Lodge, 2 Stonegrove, Edgware, Middlesex HA8 7TY.
COHEN, Judge Myrella, Q.C., LL.B., H. LLD (Sunderland), FRSA, (Mrs. Mordaunt Cohen); b. Manchester, Dec. 16, 1927; Tr., Jewish Law Publ. Fund; Circuit Judge and Dep. High Court Judge (1972-95); Sr. Judge, Harrow Crown Ct. (1989-95); Recorder Kingston-upon-Hull (1971); Dep. President (and Chairman UK branch), Int. Assoc. of Jewish Lawyers and Jurists; Member, Parole Bd. (1983-86); V. President North of England Cancer Research Campaign; L.M. the Council of the League of Jewish Women; Recorder, Kingston upon Hull (1971); Hon. Mem. WIZO Emunah; Past President, & H. Member Sunderland Soroptimist International; Patron: Sunderland Family Conciliation Service; Suzy Lampugh Trust; Sunderland C. for Disabled; North East Distaff Cttee. Ad.: 1, Peters Lodge, 2 Stonegrove, Edgware, Middlesex HA8 7TY.
COHEN, Mrs Ruth (née Goodman); b. London, July 11, 1936; S.V. Pres. World Union for Progressive Judaism; Chairman European Region of WUPJ; V. Pres. (form. chairman) Reform Synagogues of Great Britain; V.Pres. (form. chairman) NW Reform Synagogue. Ad.: 80 East End Rd., London N3 2SY. ☏ 0181-349 4731. Fax: 0181-343 0901. Email ruth_cohen_wupj@compuserve.com
COHEN, Shimon David; b. Cardiff, May 24, 1960; Dir. Andrew Lloyd Webber's office; Non-Exec. Dir. Jewish Chronicle Newspaper Ltd; Dir. IJPR; Exec. Memb. AIA; Tr. Jakobovits Charitable Trust; Mem., Inst. of Public Relations; form. Senior Cons. Lowe Bell Communications (1990-96); form. Exec. Dir. The Office of The Chief Rabbi, (1983-90); Youth Officer, Stanmore Syn. (1981-83); Sec. Nat. Chaplaincy Bd. (1983-90); Jewish Youth Leader of the Year 1979. Ad.: 10 Eaton Mews, South London SW1W 9HP. ☏ 0171-235 6019. Fax: 0171-245 9154.
COHEN, Sydney, C.B.E., M.D., Ph.D., F.R.C. Path., F.R.S.; b. Johannesburg, S. Africa, Sept. 18, 1921; Emer. Prof, Chemical Pathology, Guy's Hospital Med. Sch.; H. Consultant, Chemical Patholobst, Guy's Hospital; Chairman, Malaria Immunology Cttee., W.H.O. (1978-83); Med. Res. C. (1974-76); Chairman, Tropical Med. Res. Bd. (1974-76). Publ.: Immunology of Parasitic Infections. Ad.: 4 Frognal Rise, London NW3 6RD.
COHEN, Mrs. Zina (née Masie); b. London; form. Chairman Shechita Cttee., BoD (1986-91); Central Enquiry Desk, BoD. (1981-). Ad.: Central Enquiry Desk, Board of Deputies. ☏ 0171-543 5421/2.
COHN, Norman, M.A. (Oxon.), D.Litt. (Glas.), F.B.A. b. London, Jan. 12, 1915, m. Vera Broido; Prof., Sussex Univ., and Dir., Columbus Centre (1966-80), form. Prof of French, Univ. of Durham. Publ.: The Pursuit of the Millennium, Warrant for Genocide, Europe's Inner Demons, Cosmos, chaos and the world to come, Noah's Flood. Ad.: Orchard Cottage, Wood End, Ardeley, Herts. SG2 7AZ. ☏ 01438 869247.
COHN-SHERBOK, Dan, B.A., B.H.L., M.A., M.Litt., Ph.D(Cantab), D.D.; b. Denver, Col., Feb 1, 1945; Form. Rabbi in synagogues in the USA, England, S. Africa, Australia (1971-75); University Lect. in Theology, Univ. of Kent (1975-); Chairman, Dept. of Theology, Univ. of Kent (1980-2); Vis. Prof., Univ. of Essex (1993-94); Vis. Prof. Univ. Middlesex (1994-), Lampeter (1994-). Publ.: The Jews of Canterbury (1984); Exploring Reality (ed.) (1986); On Earth as it is in Heaven; Jews, Christians, and Liberation Theology (1987); The Jewish Heritage (1988); Jewish Petitionary Prayer (1989); Holocaust Theology (1989); Rabbinic Perspectives on the New Testament (1990), Issues in Contemporary Judaism (1990), Islam in a World of Diverse Faiths (ed.) (1990): The Salman Rushdie Controversy in Interreligious perspective (ed.) (1990); The Canterbury Papers, Religous and Modem Society (ed.) (1990); Tradition and Unity; Essays in Honour of Robert Runcie (ed.) (1991), A Traditional Quest; Essays in Honour of Louis

Jacobs (ed.) (1991); Dictionary of Judaism and Christianity (1991); The Blackwell Dictionary of Judaica (1992); Israel: The History of an Idea (1992); The Crucified Jew: Twenty Centuries of Christian Anti-Semitism (1992); Many Mansions: Interfaith and Religious Intolerance (ed); The Jewish Faith (1993); Not a Job for a Nice Jewish Boy (1993); Atlas of Jewish history (1993); Judaism and other Faiths (1994); The future of Judaism (1994); Jewish and Christian Mysticism (1995); Beyond Death (ed.) (1995); A Short History of Judaism (1995); Jewish Mysticism (1995); A Popular Dictionary of Judaism (1995); Modern Judaism (1996); The Hebrew Bible (1996); God and the Holocaust (1996); Fifty Key Jewish Thinkers (1996); Medieval Jewish Philosophy (1996); After Noah (1997); The Jewish Messiah (1997), etc. Ad.: Univ. of Kent Canterbury CT2 7NY. ☎ 01227 764000. Fax: 01227-827848.

COLEMAN, Dr Dena, Ph.D., M.A., B.Sc., P.G.C.E.; b. London, Sept., 1952 m. Gordon Coleman; Headteacher of Hasmonean High School. 2-4 Page St., London NW7 2EU. ☎ 0181-203 4294. Fax: 0181-202 4527. and Holders Hill Road, London NW4 1NA. ☎ 0181-203 1411. Fax: 0181-202 4526.

COLEMAN, Rabbi Dr. Shalom, C.B.E., M.A., B.Litt., Ph.D., J.P., A.M. (Order of Australia); b. Liverpool, Dec. 5, 1918; Rabbi Emer., Perth Hebrew Cong., H. Life President, Assn. of Rabbis & Mins. of Australian & N. Zealand; H. President, Maimonides Coll., Toronto, form. M. South Head Syn., Sydney; United Heb Inst., Bloemfontein. Publ.: Hosea Concepts in Midrash and Talmud, What Every Jew Should Know, What is a Jewish Home? What is a Synagogue? Life is a Corridor (An Autobiography) 1992; etc. Ad.: Unit 1, 72 Spencer Ave., Yokine, Western Australia 6060. ☎ 375 3222.

COLLINS, John Morris, M.A. (Oxon.); b. Leeds, June 25, 1931; H.L. V. President, Leeds Jewish Rep. C. (form. P 1986-89); Crown Courts Recorder (since 1980); Dep. Circuit Judge (1970-80); Called to the Bar, Middle Temple (1956), past P. Leeds Lodge, B'nai B'rith; BoD (1971-93); President, Beth Hamedrash Hagadol Syn. Leeds, (1992-95). Publ.: Summary Justice (1963). Ad.: 14 Sandhill Oval, Leeds, LS17 8EA. ☎ 0113 2686008.

COLLINS, Kenneth Edward, Dr. MBChB, M.R.C.G.P., M.Phil., Ph.D.; b. Glasgow, Dec. 23, 1947; Co. Chairman: Scottish Jewish Archives Cttee., Chairman: Glasgow Bd., of Jewish Educ. (1989-93), President: Glasgow Jewish Rep. C.; Chairman Glasgow Yeshiva. Publ.: Aspects of Scottish Jewry (ed.) (1987), Go and Learn (1988); Second City Jewry, (1990), Glasgow Jewry (1994). Ad.: 3 Glenburn Road, Giffnock, Glasgow G46 6RE. ☎ 0141-638 7462.

CONNICK, (Harold) Ivor, LL.B.; b. London, Jan. 25, 1927; Consultant, Dir., Land Securities plc and A. Beckman plc; V. P. Brit. ORT; Chairman, Central Board World ORT Union; Pres. Westminster Syn.; Board JIA (1985-93); Chairman, Professions Div., JIA (1979-83); Dep. Chairman UDS Group PLC (1983), Director (1975-83). Ad.: 54 Fairacres, Roehampton La., SW15 5LY. ☎ 0181-876 7188. Fax: 0181-878 6198.

CONWAY, Edward Sidney, M.A. (Liverpool), B.A. (Wales), Ph.D. (Lond.), Dip. Ed. (Wales); b. Llanelli May 3, 1911; Adv. Head, I.L.E.A (1976-79); Educ. Consultant, Frs. of Z.F. Educ. Tr. J.E.D.T. (1978-84), Inst. Jewish Educ. (1985-7), Friends Hebrew Univ. (1981-84), Spiro Inst. (1982-4); HM, J.F.S. Comprehensive School (1958-76); Princ., Jewish Orphanage (1951-58); HM, Liverpool Hebrew Schools (1944-51). Publ.: The Future of Jewish Day Schools, Going Comprehensive, Comprehending Comprehensives. Ad.: 193 Golders Green Rd., NW11 9BY. ☎ 0181-458 2117.

COOPER, Rabbi Chaim Joshua, M.A., Ph.D.; b. London, Aug. 9, 1912; Rabbi Emet. Hull Hebrew Cong; form. Com. Rabbi, Hull; Chief M., Adelaide Hebrew Cong. (1958-59); M., Kingsbury Distr. Syn. (1951-57). Ad.: 36 Parkfield Dr., Hull, HU3 6TB. ☎ 01482-561180.

COPISAROW, Sir Alcon Charles, D.Sc.; b. St. Annes-on-Sea, Lancs., June 25, 1920; Council IJA and AJA; Form. Lieut. Royal Navy (1943-47); Min. of Defence

(1947-54), British Embassy, Paris (1954-60); Chief Scientific Officer, Min. of Technology (1964-66), Senior Partner McKinsey and Co Inc. (1966-76); Subsequently: Chairman Tr., The Prince's Youth Business Trust; Tr., Duke of Edinburgh's Award; C. Royal Jubilee Trusts; Press Council, Gov., Benenden School; Dep. Chairman G. English Speaking Union; Tr. Found. for Manufacturing & Industry; Patron, Conseil National des Ingénieurs et des Scientifiques de France; Chairman & Man. Tr., The Athenaeum; form. Chairman Humanitarian Trust of Hebrew Univ. Ad.: 25 Launceston Place, London W8 5RN.

CORNEY, Hyam, B.A. (Hons.); b. Lond., May 20, 1938; Deputy Edr, Jewish Chronicle; form. Foreign edr. Home News edr. Exec. Dir., Publ. Rel., Israel & Foreign Affairs Cttees., BoD; Lond. Corres 'Jerusalem Post'; Edr., 'Jewish Observer & Middle East Review', Information Dir., JNF Ad.: 25 Furnival St., EC4A 1JT. ☎ 0171-415 1616.

COROB, Sidney, D.Sc. Tech. (h.c.) C.B.E.; b. London, May 2, 1928; Chairman, Corob Holdings Ltd.; H.V. President, Frs. of the Sick; V. President Magen David Adom in Brit.; Chairman, Brit. Technion Soc.; V. President C.C.J.; T., Westmount Housing Assn.; H.T., Westmount Charitable Tr.; V. Chairman Central C for Jewish Soc. Service; Chairman Int. Centre for Learning Potential, Jerusalem. Ad.: 62 Grosvenor St., London W1X 9DA..

CORREN, Asher, M.I.B.M.; b. Warsaw, Nov. 2, 1932; Form. Exec. Dir. Nightingale House; form Member of Wandsworth Health Authority; form. Member of Exec. Cttee, Alzheimer's Disease Soc., Member of Exec. Cttee., St Wilfrid's Home for Aged Chelsea. Ad.: Nightingale House, 105 Nightingale Lane, SW12 8NB. ☎ 0181-673 3495. Fax: 0181-675 2258.

COSGROVE, The Honourable Lady, Q.C., LL.D.(Hon), LL.B. (née Hazel Josephine Aronson), b. Glasgow, Jan 12, 1946; m. John A. Cosgrove; Senator of the College of Justice, Scotland; Dep. Chairman of the Boundary Commission for Scotland; Temporary Judge of the Court of Session and the High Court (1992-96); Sheriff of Lothian & Borders at Edinburgh (1983-96); Chairman, Mental Welfare Commission for Scotland (1991-96); Mem., Parole Baord for Scotland F(1998-91); Sheriff of Glasgow & Strathkelvin (1979-83); Advocate, Scottish Bar (1968-79); Jr. Counsel, Dept. of Trade (1977-79). Ad.: Parliament House, Edinburgh EH1 1RQ.

COWEN, The Rt Hon Sir Zelman, PC, AK, GCMG, GCVO KStJ, GCOMRI (Italy); QC, BA, LLM (Melbourne), MA, DCL (Oxon), LLD Hon (HK, Queensland, Melbourne, Australian Nat Univ, West Australia, Tasmania, Turin), DLitt Hon (New England, Sydney, James Cook Univ of N Queensland, Oxford); DHL Hon (Hebrew Union Coll, Cincinnati, Redlands Univ, Calif), D Univ Hon (Newcastle, Griffith Univ), PhD Hon (Hebrew Univ, Jerusalem, Tel Aviv Univ); b. Melbourne, Oct. 7, 1919; m. Anna née Wittner; Chairman Australian National Academy of Music (1995-); Nat. President, Australia-Brit. Assn. (1993-95); P. Order of Australia Association (1992-95); Chairman (1992-94) and Bd. Member (1992-96), John Fairfax Holdings Ltd.; Dir., Sir Robert Menzies Memorial Foundation (Aus.) Ltd. (1991-); Hon. Professor Griffith Univ., Queensland (1991-); Professorial Assoc., Univ. of Melbourne (1990-); Member Bd. of Gov. Weizmann Inst. (1990-); Provost, Oriel Coll., Oxford (1982-90); Pro-V. Chancellor, Univ. of Oxford (1988-90); Chairman, Victoria League for C'wealth Friendship (1987-89); Tr. Winston Churchill Memorial Tr. (UK) (1987-89); Lee Kuan Yew Distinguished Visitor Singapore (1987); Sir Robert Menzies Memorial Tr. (UK) (1984-); Chairman, Press C. (1983-88); Gov.-Gen. of Australia (1977-82), V. Chancellor Queensland Univ. (1970-77); V. Chancellor, New England Univ., N.S.W. (1967-70), Professor, Public Law & Dean, Law Faculty, Melbourne Univ. (1951-66), Emer. Prof (1967); H. Fellowships at New Coll. Oxford, Trinity Coll., Dublin, Oriel Coll., Oxford, Robb & Wright Coll., Univ. of New England, St. John's Coll., Univ. Qld, Univ. House, Australian Nat. Univ.; H. Master of Bench, Gray's Inn; Academic Gov., Bd. of Govs., Hebrew

Univ., Tel Aviv Univ.; Chairman, Van Leer Instit., Jerusalem (19788-95), Hon. Chairman (1995-); Chairman, Australian V. Chancellors' Cttee. (1977); P. Australian Instit. Urban Studies (1973-77); Law Reform Com., Australia (1976-77), Chairman, Australian Studies Centre Cttee., Lond (1982-1990); Menzies Scholar in Residence, Virginia Univ. (1983), Foreign H. Member, Amer. Academy of Arts & Sciences (1965); Fel. Royal Soc. of Arts; H. Fel., Australian Nat. Univ. Coll. of Educ., Academy of Soc. Sciences, Academy of Technolog. Sciences, Academy of Humanities, Soc. of Accountants, Coll. of Rehabilitation Med., Royal Australian Instit. of Architects, Royal Australian Coll. of Med. Admin., Royal Australian Coll. of Obstetricians & Gynaecologists, Instit. of Chartered Accountants in Australia, Hon. Fel. Australian Coll. of Physicians, Australia for Educational Admin.; Hon. Fel. Australian Coll. Pathologists; Fel. ANZAAS (1983); Member, New South Wales Bar Assoc. (life). Knight, Order of Australia; Knight Grand Cross, Order of St Michael and St. George; Knight Grand Cross, Royal Victorian Order; Assoc. Knight, Order of St. John; Knight Grand Cross Order of Merit of Italian Republic, Knight Bachelor. Publ.: (ed. jtly.) Dicey Conflict of Laws; (with P B. Carter) Essays in the Law of Evidence; (with L. Zines) Federal Jurisdiction in Australia, (with D. M. da Costa) Matrimonial Causes Jurisdiction; The British Commonwealth of Nations in a Changing World; Isaac Isaacs; Individual Liberty and the Law; The Virginia Lectures, Reflections on Medicine, Biotechnology and the Law; A Touch of Healing, Australia and the United States: Some Legal Comparisons; American-Australian Private International Law; The Private Man (ABC Boyer Lectures); etc. Ad.: 4 Treasury Place, East Melbourne, Victoria 3002, Australia. ☎ 61-3-96500299. Fax 61-3-96500301.

CRAFT, Maurice, B.Sc.(Econ.) Ph.D., D.Litt.; b. London, May 4, 1932; Prof. Education, Goldsmiths Coll., Univ. London; Res. Prof of Education, Univ. Greenwich (1993-97). Foundation Dean of Humanities & Social Science, Hong Kong Univ. of Science and Technology (1989-93); Prof of Educ. Nottingham Univ. (Dean of Faculty of Education, and Pro-Vice-Chancellor) (1980-89); Goldsmiths' Prof of Educ., London Univ. (1976-80); Prof of Educ., La Trobe Univ., Melbourne (1974-75), Sr. Lect. in Educ., Exeter Univ (1967-73); Publ. include: Teacher Education in Plural Societies (Edr.); Ethnic Relations and Schooling (Jt. Edr.); Change in Teacher Education (Jt. Edr.); Education and Cultural Pluralism (Edr.); Teaching in a Multicultural Society: the Task for Teacher Education (Edr.); Linking Home and School (Jt. Edr.); Ad.: Dept. of Educational Studies, Goldsmiths College, New Cross, London SE14 6NW. ☎ 0181-852 7611.

CREEGER, Morton. b. Luton, Beds., Sept 22, 1941; Dir. Brit. ORT (1973-85); Director, Community Security Trust (1995-); form. Dir. Ronson Foundation (1985-95); Governor, Charles Kalms Henry Ronson Immanuel College (1990-95); Governor, King Solomon High School, Redbridge (1991-); Dir. King Solomon High School, Redbridge Ltd (1993-); Vice-Chairman, and Non-Exec. Director, Camden and Islington Community Services NHS Trust (1992-95); Council Member, Association for Research into Stammering in Childhood (1994-); Fellow, Institute of Charity Fund-raising Managers (1994-). Heron International, 19 Marylebone Road, London NW1 5JL. ☎ 0171-486 4477. Fax: 0171-935 7257.

CREWE, Ivor Martin; b. Manchester, Dec. 15, 1945; Univ. teacher; Vice-Chancellor (1995-), Pro V. Chancellor (Academic) (1992-95) Univ. of Essex, Prof. of Government, Univ. of Essex; Dir. SSRC Data Archive (1974-82); Ed./co-ed. British Journal of Political Science (1977-82, 1984-92); Chairman, Dept. of Govemment (1985-89). Publ.: Survey of Higher Civil Service (HMSO 1969) (with A. H. Halsey), Decade of Dealignment (CUP 1983) (with Bo Särlvik); SDP: The Birth, Life and Death of the Social Democratic Party (with Tony King). Ad.: Vice Chancellor's Office, Univ. of Essex, Colchester, Essex CO4 3SQ.

CRIVAN, Harry Edward, M.B.E., B.Sc.; F.E.I.S.; b. Edinburgh, Nov. 9, 1907; Member C. Langside College, Glasgow (1991-94), President, Glasgow Jewish Rep. C. (1971-74); Co.-Chairman, C.C.J., Scotland (1979-85); Ex. Comm. Scottish Refugee C.; T., Scottish C. for Racial Equality (since 1982); Exec., Strathclyde Com. Rel. C. (since 1973); President, Scottish Rtd. Teachers' Assn. (since 1979); C., Strathclyde Univ. Graduates Assn. (since 1978). Publ.: Casting of Steel, Iron & Steel for Operatives (Consulting Edr.). Ad.: Flat 14, Barrland Ct., Barrland Drive, Giffnock, Glasgow, G42. ☎ 0141-423 5311.
CUTLER, Rabbi Shlomo, b. Liverpool, Dec. 21, 1927; M., Mill Hill Syn. (1959-93); form. M., Luton Syn. Ad.: 38 Selvage Lane, NW7. ☎ 0181-959 6131.
DAICHES, David, C.B.E., M.A. (Edin.), M.A. and D.Phil. (Oxon.), Docteur h.c. (Sorbonne), D.Litt. (Edin., Sussex, Glasgow), D. Univ. (Stirling), Dottore ad honorem (Bologna), etc.; b. Sunderland, Sept. 2, 1912; Dir., Instit. for Advanced Studies in the Humanities, Edinburgh Univ. (1980-86); Prof of Eng., Univ. of Sussex (1961-77); Dean of School of Eng. and Amer. Studies, Univ. of Sussex (1961-68); form. Lect. in English, Univ. of Cambridge, and Fellow of Jesus Coll.; form. Prof of English, Cornell Univ.; form. Fellow of Balliol Coll., Oxford; Second Sec. British Embassy, Washington (1944-46). Publ.: The Authorised Version of the Bible, a study of its origins and sources, A Study of Literature, Robert Burns, Literary Essays, Two Worlds, Milton, A Critical History of English Literature, Was: a Pastime from Time Past, Moses, Glasgow, Edinburgh, God and the Poets, A Weekly Scotsman and other poems, etc. Ad.: 22 Belgrave Crescent, Edinburgh EH4 3AL.
DAICHES, Lionel Henry, Q.C., M.A., LL.B. (Edin.); b. Sunderland, Mar. 8, 1911; Sheriff-substitute of Lanarkshire at Glasgow (1962-67); Advocate of the Scots Bar; Fel., Internat. Acad. of Trial Lawyers; Major, Judge-Advocate General's Branch (1943-46); form. President, Edinburgh Jewish Lit. Soc. and Edinburgh Lodge of B'nai B'rith. Publ.: Russians at Law. Ad.: 10 Heriot Row, Edinburgh, EH3 6HU. ☎ 0131-556 4144.
DANGOOR, Naim Eliahou, B.Sc.(London); b. Baghdad, 1914; Company Chairman; editor and publisher – The Scribe, Journal of Babylonian Jewry. Ad.: 20 Queen's Gate Terrace, SW7 5PF.
DAUBE, David, D.C.L. (Oxon.), Ph.D., F.B.A., Hon. LL.D. (Edin., Leics., Cantab.), Dr. h.c. (Paris), D.H.L. (H.U.C.), Dr. Jur. h.c. (Munich), Dr. Phil. h.c. (Goettingen); b. Freiburg Feb. 8, 1909; Dir., Hebraic & Roman Law Collections, Prof., Sch. of Law, California Univ., Berkeley (1970-81); Emer. Prof (since 1981); Emer. Regius Prof, Oxford Univ. (since 1970), Regius Prof, Civil Law & Fel., All Souls (1955-70), Emer. Fel. (1980); Law Lect., Cambridge (1946-51); H. Fel., Oxford Centre for Postgraduate Hebrew Studies (1973); Acad. Bd., IJA (since 1953); President, Jewish Law Assn. (1983-85); Fdr. P. B'nai B'rith, Oxf. (1961); Fel., Amer Acad. for Jewish Res. (1979); Lionel Cohen Lect., Jerusalem (1970). Publ.: The Aramaic Gospels, Studies in Biblical Law, The New Testament and Rabbinic Judaism, Forms of Roman Legislation The Exodus Pattern in the Bible, The Sudden in the Scriptures, Collaboration with Tyranny in Rabbinic Law, Roman Law, Civil Disobedience in Antiquity, Ancient Hebrew Fables, Ancient Jewish Law, Duty of Procreation, Typology in Josephus, Appeasement or Resistance and Other Essays on New Testament etc. Ad.: School of Law, Univ. of California, Berkeley, Ca. 94720-2499, U.S A.
DAVIDSON, Lionel, b. Hull, Mar. 31, 1922; author. Publ.: The Night of Wenceslas, The Rose of Tibet, A Long Way to Shiloh, Making Cood Again, Smith's Gazelle, The Sun Chemist, The Chelsea Murders, Under Plum Lake, Kolymsky Heights. Ad: c/o Curtis Brown Ltd., 28-29 Haymarket, London SW1Y 4SP.
DAVIS, Frank, J.P.; b. London, June 8, 1920, m. Irene née Lipman; Member, Lloyd's; Mayor of Finchley (1963-64); Nat. Exec. TAC (1955-88); V. President, Maccabi Assn.; Fdr., Wingate Football Club; Chairman, Wingate Charity Tr.;

Nat. Exec. AJA; Gov., Christ's Coll.; Gov., Tel Aviv Univ.; Nat. Insurance Appeals Tribunal; Dept. Soc. Security Appeals Trib. Dep. Chairman Lond. West Central Magistrates' Div.; BoD (Finchley) (1958-70); Cllr., Finchley and Barnet. (1956-71 and 1990-), Member Hon. Soc. of Grays Inn; Dep. Mayor L.B. Barnet (1993-4). Ad.: 20 Connaught Drive, NW11 6BJ.

DAVIS, Sydney, O.B.E.; b. London, Nov. 8, 1921; Vice President, Ajex; form. Nat. Chairman, Ajex; form. Gen. Sec., Ajex; form. Gen. Sec. Ajex Charitable Trust; Management Cttee (form. Admin.) Ajex Housing Assn.; Tr. Ajex 1984 Trust; Nat. Exec, C.C.J. Ad.: Ajex House, East Bank, N16 5RT. ☎ 0181-800 2844.

DEECH, Ruth Lynn (née Fraenkel), M.A. (Oxon), M.A. (Brandeis); Barrister; b. London, April 29, 1943, m. Dr John Deech; Principal, St Anne's College, Oxford; Chairman, UK Human Fertilisation & Embryology Authority; Lecturer in Law, Oxford University (1970–91); Governor, Oxford Centre for Hebrew and Jewish Studies (1994-); Trustee, Jewish Continuity (1994-); Chairman, Stuart Young Foundation Academic Panel (1991-); Chairman Oxford University Admissions Committee (1993-); Senior Proctor, Oxford University (1985-86); Vice-Principal, St Anne's College (1988-91); Non-executive Director, Oxon Health Authority (1993-94); Governor, Carmel College (1980-90); Member, Committee of Inquiry into Equal Opportunities on the Bar Vocational Course (1993-94); Hon. Bencher, Inner Temple (1996); Rhodes Trustee (1996). Ad.: St Anne's College, Oxford, OX2 6HS. ☎ 01865 274800. Fax: 01865 274895.

DEMMY, Lawrence, M.B.E.; b. Manchester, Nov. 7, 1931; Comp. Dir. C. Internat. Skating Union. Ad.: Oak Cottage, 112 Beverley Rd., Kirkella, Hull. ☎ 01482 650232.

DEUTSCH, André, C.B.E.; b. Budapest, Nov. 15, 1917; Publisher, Chairman Aurum Press Ltd. Ad.: 10 Museum St., WC1A 1JS ☎ 0171-379 1252.

DIAMOND, Aubrey Lionel, LL.M., D.C.L., Q.C.; b. London, Dec. 28, 1923; Solicitor, H. Fel., Lond. Sch. of Economics; H. Fel., Queen Mary and Westfield Coll.; Hon. D.C.L., City Univ., Hon. M.R.C.P., Prof. of Law Notre Dame Univ.; Dir., Instit. of Advanced Legal Studies, Lond. Univ. & Prof. of Law (1976-86, now Emer.); Law Com. (1971-76); L.S.E. (1957-66). Publ.: The Consumer, Society and the Law (with Lord Borrie), Introduction to Hire Purchase Law, Instalment Credit (ed.) Sutton and Shannon on Contracts, 7th ed. (co-ed.), Commercial and Consumer Credit, A Review of Security Interests in Property (H.M.S.O.). Ad.: 7 Albemarle St., London W1X 4NB. ☎ 0171-493-9002.

DIAMOND, Rt. Hon. Lord, Life Peer, John Diamond, P.C., F.C.A., LL.D. (h.c.); b. Leeds, April 30, 1907; Chartered Accountant Dep. Chairman of Cttees., House of Lords (1974); Chairman, Royal Comm. on the Distrib. of Income and Wealth (1974-79), Chairman, Industry and Parliament Trust (1976-81); Tr. SDP (1981-82); House of Lords, SDP Leader (since 1982); Leader, Parl. Del. to Israel (1984); M.P. for Gloucester (Lab.) (1957-70), Chief Sec., H.M. Treasury (1964-70); Privy Counsellor 1965; Member of Cabinet, (1968-70); form. M.P. for Blackley, Manchester (Lab.) (1945-51); form. Parl. Pte. Sec. to M. of Works; form Member of Gen. Nursing C. and Chairman of its Finance Cttee. (1947-53); form. Chairman, Cambridge and Bethnal Green Boys' Club; form. T., Fabian Soc.; form. Dir., Sadler's Wells Trust. Publ.: Public Expenditure in Practice. Ad.: 'Aynhoe', Doggetts Wood La., Chalfont-St.-Giles, Bucks. HP8 4TH. ☎ 01494 3229.

DOMB, Cyril, M.A., Ph.D. (Cantab.), M.A. (Oxon), F.R.S.; Em. Prof. of Physics. Bar-Ilan Univ. (since 1989); Academic President, Jerusalem Coll. of Tech (1985-94); form. Prof. of Theoretical Physics, King's Coll., Lond. Univ. (1954-81); I.C.I. Fel. Clarendon Lab., Oxford; Univ. Lect. in Maths, Cambridge; President, Assn. of Orthodox Jewish Sci. Professionals. Publ.: Scientific writings, Clerk Maxwell and Modern Science (ed.), Phase Transitions and Critical Phenomena Vols. 1-3, 5, 6 (ed. with M. S. Green), Vols. 7-17 (ed. with J. L. Lebowitz), Memories of Kopul Rosen (ed.), Challenge, Torah Views on Science and its problems (ed. with A. Carmell), Maaser Kesafim, Giving a Tenth to Charity (ed.). Ad.:

Physics Dept., Bar-Ilan Univ., Ramat Gan, 52900, Israel. ☎ (03) 5138465. Fax: (03) 5353298.

DONN, Leslie, J.P.; b. Salford, Mar. 19, 1920; Magistrate; P.S.D. Bury (1963-90) Chairman (1988-90), and Chairman (1977-83) Juvenile Panel; Cllr. (1958-74), Chairman (1965-66), Whitefield U.D.C., form. President, C. of Manch. and Salford Jews; Founder & Trustee, 1st President Whitefield Heb Cong.; Tr (until 1983) Prestwich Hebrew Cong., Fdr Bury & Whitefield Jewish Primary Sch. Ad.: 119 Higher Lane, Whitefield, Manchester M45 7WZ. ☎ 0161-773 0000. Fax: 0161-773 7355.

DOVER, Dr. Oskar, M.B., Ch.B., M.R.C.G.P.; b. Danzig, Oct. 31, 1929; form. President, Merseyside Jewish Rep. C.; Tr. (form. Sr. Warden) Liverpool Old Hebrew Cong., Tr., Liverpool Jew Youth & Com. Centre, form. Chairman & Foundation Gov., now Tr. King David High Sch., L'pool; Gov. Alice Elliott Sch., form. Chairman, Harold House C. Ad.: 17 Blackwood Ave., Liverpool L25 4RN.

DU PARC BRAHAM, Donald Samuel, F.R.G.S., I.R.R.V., A.C.I.Arb., F.R.S.A.; b. London, June 29, 1928; Lord Mayor, city of Westminster (1980-81); Master of Guild of Freeman of City of London (1989/90); Master of Worshipful Comp. of Horners (1991/1992); President, Regent's Park & Kensington North Conservative Assoc. (1996-); Chairman, London Central European Constituency C. (1988-93); Chairman, Central London Valuation Trib. (1977-); Chairman, Parkinson's Disease Soc. (1990-1991); Pat., Central London Br. Parkinson's Disease Soc. of UK; Member Nat. Exec., C.C.J.; Member, Bd. Man. W. Hampstead Syn.; Member, Jewish Cttee for H.M. Forces; Member, Wiener Library Endowment Appeal Cttee., Member, C. of the Anglo-Jewish Assoc.; Nepalese Order of Gorkha Dakshina Bahu. Ad.: 11 Jerusalem Passage, St. John's Sq., London EC1V 4JP.

DUNITZ, Alfred Abraham, J.P., C.C.; b. London, May 15, 1917; form. Tr. of the Burial Soc. (1978-87); Chairman Burial Soc. (US), (1987-88); Member Exec. Hillel House, Exec. Jewish Memorial Council of AJA; Tr. Jewish Cttee. H.M. Forces; Chairman The Friends of Jewish Servicemen; Worshipful Company of Carmen (Livery Company); The Court of Common Council City of London; Freeman, City of London, Chairman Friends of Ramat Gan (1990-94); Exec. of the JWB, (1983-85), Restored Exeter Synagogue (fd. 1763) 1980; rest. Aberdeen Syn., (1982); Chairman of the House Committee of the JWB Homes at Hemel Hempstead (1978-1985); Eastern Region Council of the C.B.I., (1973-76), Restored and maintains disused cemeteries. Ad.: 14, Sherwood Rd., Hendon, NW4 1AD. ☎ 0181-203 0658.

DUNITZ, Prof. Jack David, F.R.S., B.Sc., Ph.D.(Glasgow), Hon. D.Sc. (Technion, Haifa), Hon. Ph.D. (Weizmann Instit.), b. Glasgow, March 29, 1923; m. Barbara née Steuer; Scientist and teacher; Prof. Chemical Crystallography at the Swiss Federal Inst of Technology (ETH), Zurich, Switzerland (1957-90); Member Academia Europaea, Foreign Member Royal Netherlands Acad. of Arts and Sciences, Foreign Associate, US National Academy of Science, Member Leopoldina Academy; Member Academia Scientarium Artium Europaea; Numerous visiting professorships. Publ.: X-ray Analysis and the Structure of Organic Molecules (1979), Reflections on Symmetry in Chemistry ... and Elsewhere (with E. Heilbronner), (1993). Ad.: Obere Heslibachstr. 77, CH-8700 Küsnacht, Switzerland.

DUNNER, Rabbi Josef Hirsch; b. Cologne, Jan. 4, 1913; Rav., Adath Yisroel Syn., Rav Ab Beth Din, Union of Orthodox Hebrew Congs.; Princ., Beth Jacob Teachers' Training Seminary, form Rav., Königsberg Hebrew Cong. Ad.: 69 Allerton Rd., N16 5UF. ☎ 0181-800 3347.

DUNNETT, Jack, M.A., LL.M. (Cantab.); b. Glasgow, June 24, 1922; Solicitor; M.P. (Lab.) for Nottingham East (1974-83), Central Nottingham (1964-74), form. P.P.S., Min. of Transport and Foreign Office; form. Cllr., M.C.C. and G.L.C., and Ald., Enfield Borough C.; Chairman, Notts. County F.C. (1968-87);

Football League Man. Cttee. (1977-89), Football Assn. (1977-89); P. Football League, (1981-86 and 1988-9); V. President Football Assn. (1988-89). Ad.: Whitehall Ct., SW1A 2EP. ☎ 0171-839 6962 .
DWEK, Joe C., B.Sc., B.A., F.T.I.; b. Brussels, May 1, 1940; Chairman, Bodycote Internat. Plc.; C.B.I. Council and Deputy CBI Regional Council; Director Manchester Business Sch.; Court of Manchester Univ. and UMIST.; Vice President, Z.F.E.T. Ad.: 140 Kingsway, Manchester M19 1BB. ☎ 0161-257 2345. Fax: 0161-257 2353.
EBAN, Abba, M.A.(Cantab.), Litt.D., LL.D. (Hon.); b. Cape Town, 1915; Chairman Knesset Foreign Affairs & Defence Cttee. (1984-88); Foreign Min., State of Israel (1966-74); Dep. Prime Min. (1963-66), Educ. Min. (1960-63), P. Weizmann Inst. of Science, Rehovot (1958-66); Israeli Amb. to US (1950-59); Perm. Rep. of Israel at United Nations (1949-59); Browne Res. Fel. (Oriental Languages), Pembroke Coll., Cambridge (1938); Vis. Prof, Columbia Univ. (1974); Fel., Instit. Advanced Study, Princeton (1978). Publ.: Maze of Justice, Voice of Israel, My People, My Country; An Autobiography, The New Diplomacy, Heritage: Civilization and the Jews, etc. Ad.: Bet Berl, Kfar Sava, nr. Tel Aviv, Israel.
EHRENTREU, Dayan Chanoch; b. Frankfurt-am-Main, Dec. 27, 1932; Rosh Beth Din, Lond. Beth Din; Av Beth Din, Manchester Beth Din (1979-84); Princ., Sunderland Kolel (1960-79). Ad.: London Beth Din. ☎ 0181-343 6270. Fax: 0181-343 6257.
EILON, Samuel, D.Sc. (Eng.), Ph.D., D.I.C., F.I.MeCh.E., F.I.E.E., F.Eng.; b. Tel Aviv, Oct. 13, 1923; Emeritus Prof. and Sr. Res. Fel. at Imperial College, London; form. Chief Ed., Omega, The Int Jl. of Management Science; Member, Monopolies and Mergers Comm.; form Prof of Man. Science, and Hd of Dept., Imperial Coll., Lond.; form. Dir. of ARC, Compari Int., Spencer Stuart and Associates; management consultant to many industrial companies; form. Assoc. Prof, Technion, Haifa. Publ.: 300 scientific papers, 15 books. Ad.: Imperial College, Exhibition Rd., SW7 2BX. Fax: 0181-455 0561.
EIMER, Rabbi Colin, B.Sc. (Econ.); b. Lond., March 8, 1945; M., Southgate & Distr. Reform Syn.; Chairman, Assembly of Rabbis, RSGB (1981-83); Dir. Vocational Studies, Leo Baeck Coll., form. M., Bushey Ref. Syn., Lib. Jew Union Syn., Paris. Ad.: 65 Derwent Rd., N13 4QA. ☎ 0181-886 3726. Fax: 0181-882 7539.
EKER, Mrs. Rita (née Shapiro); b. London, Oct. 15, 1938; Co-Chairman, Women's Campaign for Soviet Jewry (the 35s); V. Chairman, Nat. C. for Soviet Jewry; Co-ord. Medical Campaign for Soviet Jewry, Co-Chairman of One to One and organiser of the One to One Treks in Israel. Ad.: Pannell House, 779/781 Finchley Rd., NW11 8DN. ☎ 0181-458 7148/9.
ELLENBOGEN, Gershon, M.A. (Cantab.) F.C.I. Arb.; b. Liverpool, Jan. 7, 1917; Barrister; V. President & Hon. M. The Maccabaeans; C., Frs. of Hebrew Univ.; C., AJA; former Deputy Circuit judge. Publ.: Legal Works. Ad.: 9 Montagu Sq., W1H 1RB.
ELLENBOGEN, Myrtle (Mrs. Gershon, form. widow of David E. Franklin, née Sebag-Montefiore); b. London, Oct. 18, 1923; Exec. Anglo-Israel Assoc., (1989), form. Chairman, Nat. Women's Div., CBF-WJR.; form. Chairman, Children's Central Rescue Fund, Gov. and Hon. Fel. of Hebrew Univ. of Jerusalem, President, Women Frs. (since 1984), Brit. Frs., Hebrew Univ.; form. Gov., now Fel. of the Purcell Sch. for Musically Gifted Children (1968-88); Alice Model Nursery (Chairman 1984-87; 1958-66); Member, ILEA (1967-73); Chairman, Union of Jewish Women's Loan Fund (1966-72), Chairman, Hampstead & St. John's Wood Group, form. Chairman, Imp. Cancer R.F. (1987-89); Member, Exec. Cttee. Anglo-Israel Assn.; V. Chairman, AJA Educ. Cttee. (1990-93). Publ.: Sir Moses Montefiore 1784 to 1885 (with Michael Bor). Ad.: Flat 83, Apsley House, 23-29 Finchley Rd., London NW8 0NZ. ☎ 0171-586 0464.

ELLIS, Harold, C.B.E., M.A., D.M., M.Ch., F.R.C.S.; b. London, Jan. 13, 1926; Emer. Prof. of Surgery, Lond. Univ.; Prof. & Chairman, Surgery Dept. Charing Cross & Westminster Med. Sch Form. V. President, Royal Coll. of Surgeons; Consultant Surgeon to the Army, resident surgical posts in Oxford, Sheffield & Lond. (1948-62). Publ.: Clinical Anatomy (8th ed.), Maingot's Abdominal Operations, (9th ed.), Famous Operations, etc. Ad.: Dept. of Anatomy, United Medical & Dental School (Guy's Campus), London Bridge, SE1 9RT.
ELYAN, Sir (Isadore) Victor, M.A., LL.B.; b. Dublin, Sept. 5, 1909; Barrister, Sr. Magistrate and Judge; Colonial Legal Service, Gold Coast (1946-54); High Court Judge and Judge of Appeal; Basutoland, Bechuanaland, Swaziland (1955-64); Chief Justice of Swaziland (1964-70); Prof of Law, Dean of Law Faculty, Durban-Westville Univ. (1973-76). Publ.: High Commission Territories Law Reports 1955-60 (ed.) Ad.: P.O.B. 22001 Fish Hoek, Cape, South Africa.
EMANUEL, Aaron, C.M.G., B.Sc. (Econ.); b. London, Feb. 11, 1912; form. Asst. Under-Sec. of State Dept of the Environment; Chairman, W. Midlands Econ. Planning Bd. (1968-72) Consultant, O.E.C.D. (1972-81). Ad.: 119 Salisbury Rd., Birmingham, B13 8LA. ☎ 0121-449 5553.
EMANUEL, Rabbi Charles, B.A. M.H.L. (H.U.C.); b. New York, Dec. 15, 1944; M., North Western Ref. Syn.; form M., Sinai Syn., Leeds. Ad.: North Western Reform Synagogue, Alyth Gdns., NW11 7EN. ☎ 0181-455 6763. Fax: 0181-458 2469.
ENGEL, Ian, M.A., F.C.A.; b. Lond., March 24, 1931; Chartered Accountant; Fin. & Admin. Dir., World ORT Union (since 1979); V. President (Tr. since 1963, Life Gov. since 1966), Ravenswood Norwood; Tr. & Exec. the Sir Georg Solti Music and Arts Fund; Tr. Ian Karten Tr. Ad.: Well Cottage, 22D East Heath Rd., NW3 1AJ.
EPSTEIN, Arnold Leonard, LL.B., Ph.D; b. Liverpool, Sept. 13, 1924; Prof., Emeritus, Social Anthropology, Sussex Univ.; Chairman, Assn. of Soc. Anthropologists of Brit. Commonwealth (1978-81); V. President, Royal Anthrop. Instit. (1981-83), form. Prof & Head, Anthrop. Dept., Australian Nat. Univ. Canberra; Chairman, Brighton & Hove Br. Ben Gurion Univ. Foundation, (1991-). Publ.: Politics in an Urban African Community, The Craft of Social Anthropology (ed.)., Ethos and Identity: Three Studies in Ethnicity; Urbanization and Kinship, The Experience of Shame in Melanesia; Scenes from African Urban Life; In the Midst of Life: Affect and Ideation in the World of the Tolai. Ad.: 5 Viceroy Lodge, Kingsway, Hove BN3 4RA. ☎ 01273 735151/739995. Fax: 01273 739995.
EZRA, Lord (Sir Derek Ezra), Life Peer, M.B.E.; b. Feb. 23, 1919; Chairman, Nat. Coal Bd. (1971-82). Ad.: House of Lords, SW1
FAITH, Mrs. Sheila (née Book), J.P.; b. Newcastle upon Tyne, June 3, 1928, m. Dennis Faith; Dental Surgeon; Member Parole Bd., (1991-94); MEP (Conservative) for Cumbria and Lancashire North (1984-89) Memb. Euro Parl. Transport Cttee (1984-87), Energy Res. & Technological Cttee (1987-89); M.P. (C.) for Belper (1979-83) Memb. House of Commons Select Cttee on Health and Social Servs (1979-83), Memb. Exec. Cttee Cons Med. Soc. (1981-84); Sec. Cons Backbench Health and Social Servs Cttee (1982-83); Northumberland C.C. (1970-74); Memb. Health and Social Services Cttees, LEA rep on S. Northumberland Youth Employment Bd; Vice-Ch Jt Consult Cttee on Educ, Newcastle (1973-74); Memb. Newcastle City C. (1975-77), (Memb. Educ Cttee); JP: Northumberland (1972-74), Newcastle (1974-78), Inner London (1978-); President Cumbria and Lancashire N. Cons Euro Constitutency C. (1989-95); Memb. Newcastle upon Tyne CAB, served as Chairman of several sch. governing bodies and mangr. of community homes. Ad.: 55 Montagu Ct., Montagu Ave., Gosforth, Newcastle-upon-Tyne NE3 7JL. ☎ 0191-285 4438; 73 St James's St., London SW17.
FASS, Richard Andrew, F.C.A.; b. London, Sept. 24, 1945; Chartered Accountant; Man. Dir. Jewish Chronicle Ltd; Member Kessler Fdn.; BoD.; Assoc. Dir. North

West London Mental Health Tr. Ad.: Jewish Chronicle, 25 Furnival St., London EC4A 1JT. ☎ 0171-415 1500. Fax: 0171-415 0278.

FEALDMAN, Barry; b. Liverpool, May 3, 1913; form. Art Critic, 'Jewish Chronicle'; Curator & Sec., Ben Uri Art Gallery (1950-76). Ad.: 34 Queens Ave., N3 2NP. ☎ 0181-346 7393.

FEIBUSCH, Hans Nathan, Hon. D.Litt. (Oxon.); b. Frankfurt-am-Main, Aug. 15, 1898; artist, painter, mural painter sculptor, lithographer, Grand Cross of Merit, W. Germany, 1988; mural paintings, in Stern Hall, West London Syn., St John's Wood Syn., Chichester Cathedral, many churches, Dudley Town Hall, Civic Centre, Newport Gwent, Bath, etc.; statues outside St. John's Wood Church, outside St. Alban's Church Holborn and at Ely Cathedral; Greater Lond. C. 80th Year Exhibition, Holland Park (1978); one-man exhibitions, Berlin (1980) Frankfurt (1986), Brighton (1988); comprehensive exhibitions Chichester (1995), Berlin (1996). Publ.: Books on art. Ad.: 30 Wadham Gdns., NW3 3DP. ☎ 0171-286 7420; 0171-586 1456.

FEIGENBAUM, Clive Harold, F.B.O.A., F.S.M.C.; b St. Albans, Sept. 6, 1939; Company Dir.; Jt. Chairman, Herut Org., Gt. Brit., BoD. Ad.: St. Margarets, Mount Park Rd., Harrow, Middx. HA1 3JP. ☎ 0181-422 1231.

FEINSTEIN, Mrs. Elaine (née Cooklin), M.A. (Cantab), Hon.D.Litt. (Leic.), F.R.S.L.; b. Bootle, Oct. 24, 1930; m. Dr Arnold Feinstein; Writer; Cholmondley Prize for Poetry (1990). Publ.: The Circle, The Amberstone Exit, The Crystal Garden, Children of the Rose, The Ecstasy of Dr. Miriam Garner, Some Unease and Angels (poems), The Shadow Master, The Silent Areas, Selected Poems of Marina Tsvetayeva, The Survivors, The Border, Bessie Smith, (biog.), A Captive Lion: a life of Marina Tsvetayeva, Badlands (poems), Mother's Girl, All you need, Loving Brecht (novel), Lawrence's Women (biog.). Dreamers (novel), Selected poems. Ad.: c/o Gill Coleridge & White, 20 Powis Mews, W11. ☎ 0181-221 3717.

FELDMAN, David Maurice, M.A., Ph.D.; b. Lond., Feb. 16, 1957; Historian; Senior Lecturer in History Birkbeck Coll., (1993-); form. Lecturer in Economic & Social History Univ. of Bristol, form. Lect. & Fell., Christ's Coll., Cambridge (1987-90), Junior Res. Fell., Churchill Coll., Cambridge (1983-87); Publ.: Englishmen and Jews, Social relations and political culture 1840-1914 (1993), Metropolis London (ed. with G. Stedman Jones). Ad.: 44 Victoria Park, Cambridge CB4 3EL. ☎ 01223 312272.

FELDMAN, Rabbi Hyman Israel; b. Llanelli, March 28, 1930; Rav, Golders Green Beth Hamedrash, H. Princ., Menorah Primary Sch. Menoral Foundation Sch.; Edr., Kashrus News; Princ., Gateshead Jewish Boarding Sch. (1960-63). Ad.: 125 The Ridgeway, London NW11 9RX. ☎ 0181-455 5068.

FELSENSTEIN, Denis R., B.A. (Hons), P.G.C.E. (Distinction), Ac. Dip., M.A (Ed); b. London, May 16, 1927; form. Hd. Immanuel Coll., form. Dep. Hd. J.F.S.; Hd.Brooke House, Div. Inspector Camden/Westminster and Senior Staff Inspector (Secondary), ILEA. Publ.: Comprehensive Achievement 1987, part-author Combatting Absenteeism 1986, numerous articles. Ad.: 24, Ossulton Way, London N2 0DS. ☎ 0181-455 2705.

FELSENSTEIN, Frank, B.A. (Hons.), Ph.D.; b. Westminster, July 28, 1944; m. Carole; Reader in English, Univ. of Leeds; Vis. Prof., Vanderbilt U., U.S.A. (1989-90). Publ.: Anti-Semitic Stereotypes: A Paradigm of Otherness in English Popular Culture, 1660-1830 (1995); The Jew as Other: A Century of English Caricature, 1730-1830, exhibition catalogue (Jewish Theological Seminary, New York, 1995); Hebraica and Judaica from the Cecil Roth Collection: exhibition catalogue (Brotherton Library, 1997). Ad.: School of English, Univ. of Leeds, Leeds LS2 9JT. ☎ 0113-233 4761. Fax: 0113-233 4774.

FERSHT, Alan Roy, M.A., Ph.D., F.R.S.; b. Lond., Apr. 21, 1943; Herchel Smith Prof., Organic Chem., Cambridge; Dir., Cambridge C. for Protein Eng.; Fel., Gonville & Caius Coll.; Prof., Biological Chem., Imperial Coll., Lond. and

Wolfson Res. Prof. Royal Soc., (1978-88); Scientific Staff, M.R.C. Lab., Molecular Biology, Cambridge (1969-77). Publ.: Enzyme Structure and Mechanism. Ad.: University Chemical Laboratory, Lensfield Road, Cambridge, CB2 1EW. ☎ 01223 336341. Fax: 01223 336445.

FIERSTONE, Clive A., BA (Hons), MA; b. London, October 5, 1948; Registrar Jews' College London. Ad.: 44a Albert Road Hendon, NW4 2SJ. ☎ 0181-203 6427. Fax: 0181-203 6420.

FINE, Rabbi Yisroel, B.A.; b. Swansea, Nov. 11, 1948; M., Cockfosters and N. Southgate Syn., form. M., Wembley Syn., United Hebrew Cong., Newcastle upon Tyne; Chairman of the Rabbinical C. of the United Synagogue; Hon. Princ. Wolfson Hillel Primary Sch.; Educ. Portfolio, Chief Rabbi's Cabinet. Ad.: 274 Chase Side, N14 4PR. ☎ 0181-449 1750.

FINESTEIN, Israel, Q.C., M.A. Cantab.; LL.D. Hull; b. Hull, April 29, 1921, m. Marion née Oster; P. BoD, (1991-94); V. President, (1988-91); Mem (1945-72); form. Crown Court Judge, (1972-87); President, Mental Health Rev. Trib. (1983-). Member, President of Israel's Standing Conference on Israel and Diaspora (1976-90); Gov. and V-Chairman, Jerusalem Int. Centre to Advance the Study of Jewish Civilisation; Memb. C. IJA; A founder Member of Hillel Fd., P. since 1981; Chairman of Hillel Union of Jewish Students Educ. Cttee. (1981-91); Exec. Cttee. of C.C.J.; V. President, Norwood Child Care; President, (1983-90); Gov. JFS and Exec. Cttee. Jews' College V. President, Central C. for Jewish Soc. Services and lecturer in Council's leadership training courses, Council United Synagogue and Jewish Chaplaincy Bd.; Jewish Memorial Council, Fdr. Member of Yad Vashem Cttee.; Chairman (1992-95) and V.P. UK Branch of Intl. Assoc. Jewish Lawyers; Chairman Jewish Law Publication Fund; V. President, AJY; V. President, Jewish Museum, London and form. Chairman (1989-92) and V. President, Jewish Historical Soc. and form. P. (1973-75, 1993-87), V. President, Conference J. Material Claims Against Germany (1991-94); Member, Exec. Member Fdn. for J. Culture; Ed. Bd. of Christian-Jewish Relations (IJA), V. President, World Jewish Congress (1991-94); V. President, European Jewish Congress, form. President, Cambridge University Jewish Soc. and Chairman, InterUniversity Jewish Federation; Universities Zionist C. and Zionist Youth C.; V.Chairman, Standing Conference of Jewish Youth, Exec. Cttees. of London Bd. and Central Bd. of Jewish Religious Educ. Cttee. of British ORT and JWB Publ. James Picciotto's Sketches of Anglo-Jewish History (Edr.); Short History of Anglo-Jewry; Jewish Society in Victorian England. Ad.: 18 Buttermere Ct., Boundary Rd., NW8.

FINKELSTEIN, Ludwik, O.B.E., M.A., D.Sc., Dr. Univ. h.c., F.Eng., F.I.E.E., C. Phys., F.Inst.P., Hon. F.Inst. M.C.; b. Lwow, Dec. 6, 1929; Prof. of Measurement & Instrumentation, City Univ.; form. Pro-V. Chancellor; form. Prof of Instrument & Control Engineering, City Univ.; form Dean, School of Engineering, City Univ. Scientific Staff N.C.B.; President, Instit. of Measurement & Control (1980), Hartley Medallist; Res. Fel. Jewish History and Thought, Leo Baeck Coll.; Publ.: Works in Mathematical Modelling, Measurement, etc. Ad.: City University, Northampton Sq., EC1V 0HB. ☎ 0171-477-8139. Fax: 0171-477 8568.

FINKLESTONE, Joseph; Author, journalist and radio-television broadcaster. Columnist, the Guardian and regular contributor to The Independent; Middle East correspondent of the London Evening Standard and London correspondent of Jerusalem Report; Broadcaster BBC World Service and Television; form. Asst. Editor, Foreign, Home, Diplomatic Editor, Jewish Chronicle; form. Chief Lond. Correspondent, Maariv, Israel; Member, Middle East group, Royal Instit. of Internat. Affairs; Winner, David Holden Award for outstanding internat. journalist of the year in Brit. Press Awards (1981); Chairman, Guild of Jewish Journalists and first recipient of its award for excellence. Edr. British Z.F. Zionist Review. Publ.: Dangers, Tests and Miracles, the remarkable life story of Chief Rabbi Moses Rosen of Romania (1990), Anwar Sadat: visionary who dared

(1996). Ad.: 9 Beulah Close, Edgware, Middlesex HA8 8SP. ☎ 0181-958 5257. Fax 0181-958 5534.

FISHER, Dayan Michael; b. Grodno, Poland, Aug. 11, 1912; Rav Rashi (ret.), Fed. of Syns.; V. President, Mizrachi Fed. Ad.: C/o Federation of Synagogues, 65 Watford Way NW4 3AQ. ☎ 0181-202 2263.

FISHMAN, William J., B.Sc. (Econ.), Dip. Lit.; D.Sc.(Econ.) (London); b. London, April 1, 1921; Barnett Shine Sr. Res. Fel. in Labour Studies, Queen Mary and Westfield Coll, London Univ. (1972-86), & Vis. Prof. (1986); Princ., Tower Hamlets Coll. for Further Educ. (1955-69); Vis. Fel., Balliol Coll., Oxford Univ. (1965), Vis. Prof., Columbia Univ. (1967), Wisc Univ. (1969-70). Publ.: The Insurrectionists, East End Jewish Radicals, Streets of East London, East End 1888, East End and Docklands; Recordings - CDs. Ad.: 42 Willowcourt Ave., Kenton, Harrow, Middx. HA3 8ES. ☎ 0181-907 5166.

FIXMAN, Sydney; b. Manchester, Apr. 5, 1935; Dir., Instit. for Jewish Music Studies & Performance; Music Lect., Lond. Univ. Instit. of Educ.; Fdr., Conductor, Ben Uri Chamber Orchestra, Jewish Youth Orchestra, Music Dir., West Lond. Syn.; form. Guest Conductor, leading orchestras in Brit. & abroad (seasons in Israel: 1976-89); Conductor, B.B.C. (TV & Radio). Publ.: (ed.) Psaume Tehillim (Markevitch); Recordings, CDs. Ad.: 5 Bradby House, Hamilton Tce., NW8 9XE.

FORSTER, Donald, C.B.E.; b. London, Dec. 18, 1920; Chairman Soc. Jewish Golf Captains (1994-); Man. Dir. & Chairman B. Forster & Co. Ltd. (1946-85); Chairman, Merseyside Development Corp. (1984-87); Chairman Warrington/Runcorn Devel. Corp (1981-85), President, Manchester JIA (1981-83); President, Assn. Jewish Golf Clubs & Socs. (1973-83), H.L.P. Whitefield Golf Club; Pilot (Flt.-Lieut.) R.A.F. (1940-45); Rep. England, 1954 Maccabiah (tennis). Ad.: The Dingle, South Downs Drive, Hale, Cheshire WA14 3HR.

FRANKEL, William, C.B.E., LL.B.; b. London, 1917; Barrister-at-Law; Edr., 'Jewish Chronicle' (1958-77); Director (formerly Chairman), Jewish Chronicle Ltd; Emer. Gov., Oxford Centre for Hebrew Studies; Gov. Cambridge Centre for Modern Hebrew Studies; Vice President, IJPR; Tr. Israel Diaspora Trust; London Museum of Jewish Life; New London Synagogue. Publ.: Friday Nights (Ed.), Israel Observed. Ad.: 30 Montagu Square, W1H 1RJ. Fax: 0171-935 3052.

FRANKENBERG Ronald Jonas, B.A. (Cantab), M A. (Econ.), Ph.D. (Manc.); b. London, Oct. 20, 1929; Emer. Prof. of Sociology and Social Anthropology, Dir., Centre for Med. Soc. Anthropology, Keele Univ.; Prof., Assoc., Brunel Univ., Prof., Dean, Zambia Univ. (1966-69); form Manchester Univ. Publ.: Village on the Border, Communities in Britain; Time, Health and Medicine (1992). Ad.: Keele University, Staffs., ST5 2BG; 19 Keele Rd., Newcastle-under-Lyme, Staffs. ST5 2JT. ☎ 01782 628498. Fax: 01782 634802. Email: sra@keele.ac.uk

FRANSES, Rabbi Simon J.; b. Larissa, Greece, May 25, 1943; M., Middlesex New Syn., Chairman of the Assembly of Rabbis RSGB (1989-91); Asst. M., Edgware & Dist. Reform Syn. (1971-74); M., Glasgow New Syn. (1974-87); Member of Children's Panel for Strathclyde Region (1977-87). Ad.: 39 Bessborough Rd., Harrow, Middx. HA1 3BS. ☎ 0181-864 0133.

FREEDLAND, Michael Rodney; b. London, Dec. 18, 1934; journalist and broadcaster, Exec. Ed. & Presenter (LBC), 'You Don't Have to be Jewish' (1971-94). Publ.: Al Jolson, Irving Berlin, James Cagney, Fred Astaire, Sophie, Jerome Kern, Errol Flynn, Gregory Peck, Maurice Chevalier, Peter O'Toole, The Warner Brothers, Katharine Hepburn, So Let's Hear the Applause-The Story of the Jewish Entertainer, Jack Lemmon, The Secret Life of Danny Kaye, Shirley MacLaine, Leonard Bernstein, The Goldwyn Touch: a Biography of Sam Goldwyn, Jane Fonda, Liza With A Z, Dustin Hoffman, Kenneth Williams, A Biography; Andre Previn; Music man; Sean Connery: a biography; All the Way: a biography of Frank Sinatra; With Morecambe and Wise, There's No Answer To That; with Walter Scharf composed and conducted by Walter Scharf. Ad.: Bays

Hill Lodge, Barnet Lane, Elstree, Herts. WD6 3QU. ☎ 0181-953 3000; 0181-953 7599.

FREEDMAN, Harry, M.A. (London), B.A.; b. London 1950; Dir., Assembly of Masorti Synagogues; Lay minister Exeter Synagogue (1981-87); Dir. & Lecturer Masorti Academy (1994-); Editorial Advisory Committee, Jewish Bible Quarterly, Judaism Today. Ad.: 1097 Finchley Road, London NW11 0PU. ☎ 0181-201 8772. Fax: 0181-201 8917. E-mail: masorti.uk@ort.org

FREEDMAN, Jeromé David, F.C.A.; b. 1935; Chartered Accountant, Finance Director and Deputy Chairman, DAKS Simpson Group plc; Chairperson, Union of Liberal and Progressive Synagogues (ULPS); form. Hon. Tr. ULPS (1990-95); Board of Management, Chartered Accountants' Benevolent Association (CABA); Director, CABA Trustees Ltd. Ad.: 5 Thanescroft Gardens, Croydon, Surrey CR0 5JR. ☎/Fax: 0181-688 2250.

FREESON, Rt. Hon. Reginald, P.C.; b. London, Feb. 24, 1926; Dir. Labour & Trade Union Friends of Israel (1992-94); Urban renewal and housing consultant, Member Housing Centre Trust; Member Town & Country Planning Assn.; Member Labour Finance & Industry Group; Fabian Soc.; Labour Campaign for Electoral Reform; Cooperative Party; Centre for Social Policy Studies in Israel UK Advisory Group; Anglo-Jewish Assc.; Commonwealth Parl. Assoc.; Life Memb. National Tr. & Youth Hostels Assoc. Pol. Sec. Poale Zion (1987-94); Editor, 'Jewish Vanguard' (1988-); Chairman, DOE inner area studies (1974-77); Journ; M.P. (Lab.) for Brent East (1964-87); Chairman, House of Commons Select Cttee. on the Environment (1981-83); Parl. Assembly C. of Europe (1983-87); form. Min. for Housing Construction & Planning; Parl. Sec., Min. of Housing and Local Govt.; Parl. Sec., Min. of Power, Parl. Private Sec. to M. of Transport, form. Chairman, Brent Borough C.; Leader, Willesden Borough C.; Cllr. and Alderman, Willesden and Brent.; Exec. Member Jewish Welfare Board (1970-74); Dir. JBG Housing Society (1982-83); Jewish Orphanage (1931-41); President Norwood Old Scholars Assoc. (1972-). Ad.: 159 Chevening Rd., NW6 6DZ. Tel/Fax: 0181-969 7407.

FRIEDLANDER, Rabbi Albert Hoschander, Ph.D., D.D., M.H.L. Ph.B.; b. Berlin, May 10, 1927; M. Emer. Westminster Syn., Dean and Sr. Lect., Leo Baeck Coll.; Vis. Fel. University of Berlin; Ed., European Judaism periodical; f.PEN; V. President, World Union for Progressive Judaism; International President, World Conference of Religions for Peace, F. Exec., Leo Baeck Inst.; form. M., Wembley Lib. Syn.; Jewish Chaplain, Columbia Univ. and M., East Hampton and Wilkes-Barre. Publ.: Out of the Whirlwind, Six days of destruction (with E. Wiesel), Five scrolls Thread of Gold, Riders Towards the Dawn, etc. Ad.: Kent House, Rutland Gardens, SW7 IBX. ☎ 0171-584 3953.

FRIEDMAN, Milton, B.A., M.A., Ph.D; b. Brooklyn, July 31, 1912; Economist; Nobel Prize in Economics, (1976); Sr. Res. Fel., Hoover Instit. Stanford Univ.; Paul Snowden Russell Distinguished Service Prof. Emer., Chicago Univ.; many honorary degrees. Publ.: Writings on economics. Ad.: Hoover Institution, Stanford, California 94305-6010 USA. ☎ (415) 723-0580.

FRIEDMAN, Rosemary (née Tibber); b. London, Feb. 5, 1929; m. Dennis Friedman, FRCpsych; Writer. Exec. Cttee Society of Authors (1989-92); Exec. Cttee P.E.N. (1993-). Sole judge, Authors' Club First Novel Award 1989; Judge, Betty Trask Fiction Award 1991; Chair of judges, Jewish Quarterly Literary Prizes 1993 and Macmillan Silver Pen Award 1996. Publ.: Vintage, Golden Boy, An Eligible Man, To Live in Peace, A Second Wife, Rose of Jericho, A Loving Mistress, Proofs of Affection, The Long Hot Summer, The Life Situation, The Ideal Jewish Woman and Contemporary Society (Confrontations with Judaism, Ed. Philip Logworth); Home Truths (play, UK tour 1997); Juvenile: Aristide, Aristide in Paris; Works before 1975 with pen name Robert Tibber: Practice Makes Perfect, The General Practice, The Commonplace Day, The Fraternity, Patients of a Saint, We All Fall Down, Love on My List, No White Coat. Ad.: 2 St

Katherine's Precinct, Regent's Park, NW1 4HH. ☏ 0171-935 6252, Fax: 0171-486 2398.

FROSH, Sidney, J.P.; b. London, Aug. 22, 1923; President, US (1987-92), Chairman, Beth Hamedrash & Beth Din. Man. Bd., Chairman, Chief Rabbinate C. (1987-92); Chairman, Min. Placement Cttee., Chairman, Singer's Prayer Book Publ. Cttee. (1987-92); V.P. Norwood Child Care; V. President, Cen. C. for Jewish Comm. Services; Chief Rabbinate C.; V. Chairman & T., Lond. Bd. of Jewish Rel. Educ. (1968-78), Gov., J.F.S. Ad.: 50 Lodge Close, Edgware, Middx. HA8 7RL. ☏ 0181-952 9097. Fax: 0181-951 0823.

GABAY, Isaac, M.B.E.; b. Gibraltar, May 14, 1931; Exec. Head Chef, House of Commons; Head Chef, Hurlingham Club, (1954-62); Head Chef, Army and Navy Club (1962-72). Ad.: 119 Preston Hill, Harrow, Middlesex HA3 9SN. ☏ 0181-204 1943.

GAFFIN, Jean (née Silver), O.B.E., J.P., M.Sc., B.Sc. (Econ.); b. London, Aug. 1, 1936; m. Alexander; Exec. Dir. National Council for Hospice and Specialist Palliative Care Service (1991-); Chief Exec. Arthritis Care (1988-91); Exec. Sec., British Paediatric Assoc. (BPA) (1982-87); Organising Sec., Child Accident Prevention Cttee (1979-82); Lecturer II/Senior Lecturer, Social Policy and Administration, Polytechnic of the South Bank (1973-79); Chairman, OFTEL's Advisory Committee on Telecommunications for Disabled and Elderly People – DIEL (1993-); Council, Open Section, Royal Society of Medicine (Sec. 1988-90, President 1997); Mem. UK Xeno-Transplantation Interim Regulatory Authority; Magistrate, Wimbledon Bench (1977-80), Harrow Bench (1981-). Publ. include: (Editor) The Nurse and the Welfare State (1981); with D. Thoms, Caring and Sharing: the Centenary History of the Co-operative Women's Guild (1983, second ed. 1993); Women's Co-operative Guild 1884-1914, in Women in the Labour Movement, ed. L. Middleton (1977); The Administrative Framework of the Health and Social and Social Services, in A Textbook for Health Visitors, ed. G. Owen (1977, revised second ed. 1983). Ad.: 509 Kenton Rd., Harrow, Middx HA3 0UL. ☏ 0181-206 0327.

GAINSFORD, Doreen; b. London, May 9, 1937; Public & Press Relations Off.; form. Chairman, 35's (Women's Campaign for Soviet Jewry). Emigrated to Israel, March, 1978, Coord, JIA Project Renewal, Ashkelon; Chairman, 35's Israel Campaign for Soviet Jewry (Israel); Dir., Mini Gifts (Israel). Ad.: Beit Brodetsky 36 Brodetsky Str., ☏ Aviv 69051, Israel. ☏ 03-6427897, 6427901, 6410792. Fax: 03-6411111.

GALE, Rev. Norman Eric, B.A., Ph.D.; b. Leeds, Nov. 9, 1929; form. M., Hampstead Syn. (1988-95); M., Ealing Syn. (1968-88); M., Harrogate Hebrew Cong. (1958-68); form. Chairman, U.S. Rabbinical C.; Memb. Chief Rabbi's Cabinet (Welfare Portfolio 1990-93); H. Chaplain, Nat. Assn. of Jewish Friendship Clubs; H. Dir., Jewish Prison Chaplaincy; Chaplain, Wormwood Scrubs Prison; Exec. Member JAMI. Ad.: Flat 6, Orford Ct., Marsh Lane, Stanmore, Middx HA7 4TQ. ☏ 0181-954 3843.

GARAI, George, Ph.D. (Lond.); b. Budapest, Aug. 31, 1926; Journalist; Gen. Sec., Z. Fed. of Gt. Brit. & Ireland (1982-92); Dir., Public Rel., Z. Fed. (1975-82); Edr. Staff, 'Jewish Chronicle' (1966-75); Edr., 'Australian Jewish Times' (1960-66). Ad.: Balfour House, 741 High Rd., London N12 0BQ.

GARBACZ, Bernard, F.C.A.; b. Westcliff, Dec. 30, 1932; W., Kingsbury Syn. (1965-72); President, B'nai B'rith First Lodge of England (1976-78); Fdr. Tr, Jewish Education Development Tr. (1980-91); Receiver and Manager, Jewish Secondary Schools Movement (1979-82); Chairman, Bd. of Govs., Hasmonean Boys' Grammar Sch. (1979-82); Chairman, J. Marriage C. (1989-91), T. then V.-Chairman, Brit-Israel Chamber of Commerce (1980-92); T., Jews Coll. (1971-84); V.Chairman, Hillel Foundation, (1980-92); H. President, Univ. Jewish Chaplaincy Bd.; Dir., Central Middlesex Hospital N.H.S. Tr. (1991-96), Chairman Dmatek Ltd. (1995-). Publ.: Anglo Jewry Research Project 1985

(Garbacz Report on Communal Funding). Ad.: 1 Chessington Ave., N3 3DS. ☎ 0181-349 0871. Fax: 0181-349 2755.
GASTWIRTH, Rabbi Ephraim Levy, B.A., M.Litt.; b. London, 1920; Ret. Rabbi & Chaplain, Heathlands, Manchester; M., Sale Hebrew Cong. (1979-82), Blackpool Hebrew Cong. (1976-79); Princ., Judith Lady Montefiore Coll (1968-76); Dir. of Jewish Studies, Carmel Coll. (1964-66); M., Sunderland Hebrew Cong. (1960-64); M., S. Hampstead Syn. (1956-60). Ad.: 3 Falcon Ct., Park St., Salford, M7 4WH. ☎ 0161-792 4239.
GEE, George Maxwell, F.R.S.A., J.P.; b. Gillingham, Jan. 12, 1921; P. U.S. (1981-84), V. President (1973-81), U.S. Jt. T. (1961-73), Elder U.S. (1984-); Chairman, Affil. Syns. Cttee. (1973-77), Member, U.S. Placement Cttee. (and form. Chairman; Member (form. Chairman & Jt. T.) Chief Rabbinate C. (1961-), Member of Chief Rabbinate Conf. (1966 and 1990); C., Jews' Coll. (1971-90); Singer's Prayer Book Publ. Cttee. (since 1983); Chairman, Beth Hamedrash and Beth Din Man. Bd. (1981-84); President, Jewish Deaf Assn. (1979-), V. President, JNF Educ. Tr. (1984-96); Chairman Cttee. for Jewish H.M. Forces (1971-); T., Frs., Jewish Servicemen & Women; form. Chairman, Dayan Steinberg Member Scholarship Fund (1970-90); Tr., Nathan & Adolph Haendler Char., form. Chairman, U.S. Investment Cttee. (1961-81), Enquiry Cttee. for review of ministers' salaries, status, etc. (1971); U.S. Tr. Affiliated Syns. Cttee.; form. Chairman Building Cttee.; C., World Conf of Syns. & Kehillot (1981-84); Shechita Bd. (1971-77); Kashrus Com. (1971-81); form. Member, Nat. Exec., Ajex; C., AJA; TAC; Lond. Bd. Jewish Rel. Educ.; BoD; Freeman, City of Lond. (1953); Past P & Fdr, Insulating Glazing Assn., Nat. Exec., Fdr. Member, Glass & Glazing Fed.; form. Chairman, Nat. Jt. Indus. C. (London) (Glass Indus.); P.M., Worshipful Comp. Glaziers & Painters of Glass; form. Chairman, Glaziers Tr for preserv. & restor. of glass of hist. interest (1976-84); Chairman of Trustees, London Stained Glass Repository (1989-); L. Member, Royal Engineers O.C.A. Ad.: 23 Denewood Rd., N6 4AQ. ☎ 0181-340 0863. Fax: 0181-348 8797.
GEE, Malcolm J., B.A., F.C.A., F.C.C.A.; b. London, Sept. 3, 1937; Partner, Levy Gee, Chartered Accountants. Ad.: 66 Wigmore St., W1H 0HQ. ☎ 0171-467 4000. Fax: 0171-467 4040.
GILBERT, Sir Martin, C.B.E., M.A.; b. London, Oct. 25, 1936; historian; Official Biographer of Winston Churchill (since 1968); Fel., Merton Col., Oxford; Vis. Prof, Hebrew Univ. (1980, 1995-); Vis. Prof, Tel Aviv Univ. (1979); Vis. Prof. UCL (1995-6); Publ: Winston S. Churchill (6 vols.), Churchill, A Life; The Appeasers (with Richard Gott), Britain and Germany Between the Wars, The European Powers 1900-1945, The Roots of Appeasement, Exile and Return a Study in the Emergence of Jewish Statehood, The Holocaust – the Jewish Tragedy, Churchill a Photographic Portrait, In Search of Churchill, Auschwitz and the Allies, The Jews of Hope, The Plight of Soviet Jewry Today, Shcharansky, Portrait of a Hero; Jerusalem - Rebirth of a City, Jerusalem in the Twentieth Century, First World War, Second World War, The Day the War Ended, The Boys – Triumph over Adversity, and many other historical works, 12 history atlases, including the Jewish History Atlas Jerusalem illustrated history atlas and the Atlas of the Holocaust. Ad.: Merton Coll., Oxford.
GINSBURG, Major the Rev. Alec., Hon C.F.; b. Aberavon, Aug. 21, 1920; Chaplain to H.M. Forces; form Sr. M. & Braham Lect., Old Hebrew Cong. Liverpool; form. M., Hove Hebrew Cong., St. Annes, Terenure and Plymouth Syns.; Lect. Classical Hebrew & Semitics Exeter Univ. (1964-74); Lect., Jew Homilies. Irish Sch. Ecumenics, Dublin (1974-76); (perm.) Ecumenical Panel, King Edward VII Hospital, Midhurst, Sussex; Jew Chaplain Hq. CMF (Udine. Italy), CF (J) Hq. British Troops (Klagenfurt) Austria, 1947, Sr. Jewish Chaplain, Hq. Brit. Troops, Egypt & Middle East (1947-50), Jewish Chaplain, Hq. B.A.O.R. (1950-55), UK Hq. Lond. Distr. (1956-62); Mentioned: London

Gazette, 8 Jan. 1961 on promotion 3rd Class, 8 June, 1962 as Hon. Chaplain Third Class; Rank: Major on retirement; Chap., Dartmoor, Exeter Prisons (1962-74), H.T., Dublin Univ Jewish Soc. Publ.: Judaism and Freemasonry. Ad.: 15 Courtenay Gate, Kingsway, Hove, E. Sussex, BN3 2WJ. ☎ 01273-739440
GINSBURG David, M.A.; b. Lond., Mar. 18, 1921; Comp. Dir., Economist Market and Marketing Res. Consultant; Broadcaster; Fel., Royal Soc. of Med.; M.P. (Lab. 1959-81, SDP 1981-83 Dewsbury), Sec., Research Dept. Labour Party(1952-59); Sr. Research Off., Govt. Social Survey (1946-52). Ad.: 3 Bell Moor, East Heath Rd., NW3 1DY. ☎ 0181-435 8700.
GINSBURY, Rabbi Philip Norman, M.A.; b. London, Mar. 26, 1936; M., South London Syn.; Lect. Bible, Jewish Coll.; Ed. Le'Ela journal; form. M., Streatham Distr. Syn., Brixton Syn.; Chairman South London Rabbinical Council. Publ. Jewish Faith in Action (1995). Ad.:146 Downton Ave., SW2 3TT. ☎/Fax: 0181-674 7451.
GLANVILLE, Brian Lester, b. London, Sept. 24, 1931; writer. Publ.: Along the Arno, A Bad Streak, The Bankrupts, Diamond, etc. Ad.: 160 Holland Park Ave.,W11.
GLATTER, Robert, F.C.A.; b. Antwerp, Belgium, Mar. 14, 1937; Chartered Accountant, Non-Exec. Director Bank Leumi (UK) plc.; V.-Chairman, British-Israel Chamber of Commerce; V. President B'nai B'rith Hillel Foundation; Exec. Member and Tr., Weizmann Instit. Foundation; Tr., Volcani Foundation; Tr., Brady-Maccabi Endowment; Fd., form. Gov., Tr. Carmel Colls.; V. President, Akiva School; President, Maccabi Union of G.B.; Form Chairman, North Western Reform Syn. 1986-88; Chairman, RSGB Cttee. for Educ. and Youth; Chairman, RSGB Israel Action Cttee.; Chairman, V.-Chairman, Tr., V. President Maccabi Union of G.B.; Dep. Chairman, Maccabi Europe; Member, Maccabi World Union; Chairman and Dep. Chairman, Maccabiah Organ. Cttee., Tr. Bd. for Jewish Sport; T., Manor House Tr.; Chairman, Funders Cttee., Assn. Jewish Sixth formers. Ad.: 12 York Gate, NW1 4QS.
GLINERT, Lewis H., B.A. (Oxon), Ph.D.; b. London June 17, 1950; m. Joan née Abraham; University Lecturer; Prof. in Hebrew, Univ. of London (School of Oriental and African Studies); Dir. Centre for Jewish Studies, S.O.A.S.; Vis. Prof. of Hebrew Studies, Chicago U. (1987/8); Asst. Prof. of Hebrew Linguists, Haifa U. (1974-77). Publ.: The Grammar of Modern Hebrew (1989); The Joys of Hebrew (1992); Hebrew in Ashkenaz (1993); Modern Hebrew: An Essential Grammar (1994); Mamma Dear (1997). Ad.: School of Oriental & African Studies, Russell Sq., London WC1H 0XG. ☎ 0171-323 6252. Fax: 0181-436 3844. E-mail: lg@soas.ac.uk
GOLD, Sir Arthur Abraham, C.B.E.; b. Lond., Jan. 10, 1917; Engineer; President, European Athletic Assn.; V.President, Commonwealth Games C. for England; Chairman, Drug Abuse Adv. Group, Sports C.; P. Counties Athletic Union; Life V. President (H.Sec., 1962-77) Brit. Amateur Athletic Bd.; President, Amateur Ath. Assn.; V.President Brit. Olympic Assn.; Member, Sports C.; Exec. Central C. of Physical Recreation; Athletics Team Leader, Olympic Games, Mexico 1968, Munich 1972, Montreal 1976; Commandant, C'wealth Games Team Brisbane 1982, Edinburgh 1986, Auckland 1990; British Olympic Team 1988, 1992; President, Lond. Ath. Club (1962-63); President, Middlesex C.A.A.A. (1963 and 1993). Ad.: 49 Friern Mount Drive, N20 9DJ. ☎ 0181-445 2848.
GOLD, Rev. Sidney, B.A.; b. London Dec. 6, 1919; Emer. M (Chief M., 1960-85) Birmingham Hebrew Cong., form. M., Highgate Syn., Regent's Park & Belsize Park Syn., Bayswater Syn., Member Chief Rabbi's Cabinet (1979-83); P. Union of Anglo-Jewish Preachers (1977-78), form. V.Chairman B'ham C.C.J.; Chairman B'ham Inter-Faith C.; President, B'ham J.I.A Cttee. Publ.: Children's Prayer Book for High Festivals (jt. author). Ad.: 12 Dean Park Mans., 27 Dean Park Rd., Bournemouth BH1 1JA ☎ 01202 551578.
GOLDBERG, Sir Abraham, M.D., D.Sc., F.R.C.P., F.R.S.E.; b. Edinburgh, Dec. 7,

1923; Regius Prof (Materia Med., 1970-78), Emer. Regius Prof. Practice of Med., Glasgow Univ. (1978-89); Chairman, Cttee. on Safety of Medicines (1980-86); Chairman, Biological Res. Cttee., Scottish Home & Health Dept., Glasg. (1978-83); H. Consultant, Western Infirmary, Glasg.; Chairman, Grants Cttee., Med. Res. C. (1972-76), Fdn. P. Faculty of Pharmaceutical Medicine of Royal Colleges of Physicians (UK), (1989-91); Vis. Prof, Tel Hashomer Hospital, Israel (1966), Henry Cohen Lect., Hebrew Univ. (1973); Lord Provost's Award for Public Service to Glasgow (1989); Chairman Glasgow Friends of Shaare Zedek Hospital, Jerusalem. Publ.: Diseases of Porphyrin Metabolism (jt. auth.), Recent Advances in Haematology (jt. edr.). Ad.: 16 Birnam Cres., Bearsden, Glasgow G61 2AU.

GOLDBERG, Rabbi David J., M.A. (Oxon.); b. London, Feb. 25, 1939; Sr. Rabbi, Liberal Jewish Syn. M. Wembley & Dist. Lib. Syn. (1971-75) Associate Rabbi L.J.S. (1975-87); Chairman, ULPS Rabbinic Conference (1981-83, 1986-). Publ.: The Jewish People: their History and their Religion (with John D. Rayner); The Promised Land: a History of Zionist Thought; On the Vistula Facing East (ed.). Ad.: Liberal Jewish Synagogue, 28 St. John's Wood Rd., NW8 7HA. ☎ 0171-286 5181.

GOLDBERG, David Jonathan, M.A. (Jewish Communal Service) Brandeis; Cert. Youth and Community Studies, London; b. London, June 27, 1961. Exec. Director, Zionist Fed. of Great Britain & Ireland; H. Chair, Association of Jewish Communal Professionals (1992-); H. Sec., Bushey Youth Scene (1996-); Senior Youth and Community Work, Redbridge JYCC (1983-90); Chairman - Redbridge Jewish Youth Council (1980-82); Chairman - National Magen David Adom (1979-81). Ad. Chiltern Avenue, Bushey, Herts WD2 3QA. ☎ 0181-950 0080.

GOLDMAN, William; b. London, April 4, 1910; Novelist. Publ.: A Start in Life, A Tent of Blue, East End My Cradle, In England and in English, A Saint in the Making, The Light in the Dust, Some Blind Hand, The Forgotten Word, etc. Ad.: 12 Quintock House, Broomfield Rd., Kew Gdns., Richmond, Surrey TW9 3HT. ☎ 0181-948 4798.

GOLDREIN, Neville Clive, C.B.E., M.A. (Cantab.); b. Hull; m. Dr Sonia Goldrein née Sumner; Solicitor; Member (Leader, 1980-81, V. Chairman, 1977-80) Merseyside County C. (1973-86); Leader, Conservative Group (1980-86); Lancashire County Council (1965-74); Crosby Borough C. (1957-71); Mayor of Crosby (1966-67); Dep. Mayor (1967-68); North-West Economic Planning C. (1972-74); Governor Merchant Taylors' Schools, Crosby (1965-74); Chairman, St John Amb. (South Sefton) (1965-87); Area President, St. John Amb., Sefton (1965-87); C., L'pool Univ. (1977-81); Vice-Chairman, Crosby MENCAP (1966-); C. L'pool Chamber of Commerce (1986-); Chairman, Rivers Cttee (1989-93; Chairman, Police Liaison Cttee; Chairman Environment and Energy Cttee (1993-); British Assoc. of Chambers of Commerce, Mem. Local & Regional Aff. Cttee; Chairman L'pool Royal Court Theatre (Liverpool) Foundation; Chairman, Crosby Conservative Association (1986-89); Chairman (Appeals), Crosby Hall Educ. Trust (1989-91); Bod (1965-85, and 1992-); Sr.W., L'pool Old Hebrew Cong. (1968-71). Ad.: Torreno, St Andrew's Rd., Blundellsands, Liverpool L23 7UR. ☎/Fax: 0151-924 2065. E-mail: goldrein@aol.com

GOLDSCHMIDT, Mrs. Ruth P., (née Lehmann), Dipl. O.A.S., F.L.A.; b. Altona, Germany, Feb. 11, 1930; Libr., Jews' Col. (1955-73); Publ.: Nova Bibliotheca Anglo-Judaica, Anglo-Jewish Bibliography (1937-70, and 1971-1990), Sir Moses Montefiore a bibliography, A Bibliography of Anglo-Jewish Medical Biography, Britain and the Holyland 1800-1914, a select bibliography, etc. Ad.: 6 Tchernichowski St., 92 581, Jerusalem. ☎ 02-5632364.

GOLDSMITH, Walter Kenneth, F.C.A, C.B.I.M., F.R.S.A.; b. Lond, Jan. 19, 1938; Chairman, Ansoll Estates Ltd (1990-); Chairman (1987-1991), V. President

(1992-), Brit Overseas Trade Group for Israel; Dir.-Gen., Inst. of Dirs. (1979-84); Dep. Chairman, Isys Ltd. (since 1987); Dir., Bank Leumi (UK) plc (since 1984); Tr., Israel Diaspora Tr. (1982-92); Tr., Leo Baeck Coll. (1987-89) Chairman Wembley & Dist. Lib. Syn. (1974-76) C. & Exec., U L.P.S. (1965-66); Chairman, Youth Section, World Union for Progressive Judaism (1960-61). Ad.: c/o Ansoll Estates, 2-6 Friern Park, N. Finchley, N12 9BY. ☎ 0181-445 1006. Fax: 0181-446 7520.

GOLDSTEIN, Rabbi Andrew, B.Sc.; b. Warwick, Aug. 12, 1943; M., Northwood and Pinner Liberal Syn.; Chairman, ULPS Rabbinic Conf (1979-81); Chairman, ULPS Educ. Cttee. (1970-88); Dir., Kadimah Holiday School, (1970-89); Chairman, ULPS Prayerbook Editorial Cttee, Chairman ULPS Conference Cttee. Publ.: My Very Own Jewish Home, Jerusalem, Tradition Roots, Britain and Israel, Mishnah Kadimah, Exploring the Bible, Parts 1 & 2. Ad.: 10 Hallowell Rd., Northwood, Middx. HA6 1DW. ☎ 01923 822818. Fax 01923 824454.

GOLDSTEIN, Rabbi Henry; b. London, March 10, 1936; M., South-West Essex Reform Syn., M., Finchley Reform Syn. (1967-73); Princ. 'KEDEM' Adult Educ. C. (1989-90; 1994-96); Ch, RSGB Rabbis' Assembly (1973-75); Chaplain, Chelmsford Gaol. Ad.: 15 Chichester Gardens, Ilford, Essex, IG1 3NB. ☎ 0181-554 2297.

GOLDSTEIN, Michael, M.B.E.; b. London, April 5, 1919; form. Gen. Sec., AJY (1951-77); form. Chairman, Greater Lond. Conf of Vol. Youth Orgs. Ad.: Flat 12, Broadway Close, Woodford Green, Essex, IG8 OHD. ☎ 0181-504 2304.

GOLDWATER, Raymond, LL.B.; b. Hove, Sept. 28, 1918; Solicitor; Elder, US; V. President, AJY; form. Ch, Rel Adv. Cttee., AJY; form Chairman, London Student Counsellor Bd.; form C., Jews' Coll.; form. Lond. Bd., Jewish Rel. Educ.; form. Chairman, Youth & Com. Services Dept. & Jt. T., Bequests & Tr. Funds, US; Chairman, I.U.J.F. & Lond. Jewish Graduates' Assn. Publ.: Jewish Philosophy and Philosophers (Edr.). Ad.: 451 West End Ave., Apt 5E, New York, NY 10024. ☎ 212-873-8221.

GOLOMB, Rev. Maurice Joseph, b. Brisbane, Queensland, Sept. 28, 1931; M., Hammersmith & West Kensington Syn. (since Aug. 1991); M., Enfield & Winchmore Hill Syn. (1967-91); US Kabronim Minister, Waltham Abbey/Bushey Jewish Cemeteries (since 1990); Member, Rabbinical C., US; Exec. Initiation Society., Hospital Visitation Cttee.; Sofer; Mohel. Ad.: 11 Orchard Terr., Enfield, Middx. EN1 1EL. ☎ 0181-363 1359.

GOLOMBOK, Ezra, B.Sc., Ph.D.; b. Glasgow, Aug. 22, 1922; Dir. Israel Information Office, Glasgow; Edr., Jewish Echo; Edr., Scottish Nat. Orchestra Scene; form. Convener, Public Relations Cttee., Glasgow Jewish Rep. C. Ad.: 222 Fenwick Rd., Giffnock, Glasgow G46 6UE. ☎/Fax: 0141-620 0940. Email: exra@isrinfo.demon.co.uk

GOMBRICH, Sir Ernst Hans Josef, O.M., C.B.E., Ph.D. (Vienna), F.B.A., F.S.A.; b. Vienna, March 30, 1909; Dir., Warburg Inst. (1959-1976) and Prof. of the History of the Classical Tradition, Univ. of London; Slade Prof of Fine Art, Univ. of Oxford (1950-53), Univ. of Cambridge (1961-63), and Prof of the Hist. of Art, Univ. Coll., London (1956-59); Premium Erasmianum (1975); Internat. Balzan Prize (1985); Britannica Award 1989, Goethe Preis, (1994); 18 hon. degrees. Publ.: The Story of Art, Art and Illusion, The Sense of Order, Aby Warburg, etc. Ad.: 19 Briardale Gdns., NW3 7PN. ☎ 0171-435 6639.

GOODMAN, Lewis, O.B.E.; b. Breslau, Dec. 9, 1926; V. President, West London Syn.; V.Chairman, Ben Uri Art Soc.; Exec. Anglo-Israel Assoc.; V. President, Brit.Israel Chamber of Commerce. Ad.: 57 Acacia Rd., NW8 6AG. Fax 0171-586 5906.

GOODMAN, Martin David, M.A., D.Phil. (Oxon.) F.B.A., F.S.A.; b. Aug. 1, 1953; m. Sarah Jane Goodman; Professor of Jewish Studies, University of Oxford; Fellow of the Oxford Centre for Hebrew and Jewish Studies and Wolfson College; Lecturer in Ancient History, University of Birmingham (1977-86); Fellow of

Oxford Centre for Hebrew and Jewish Studies (1986-); Senior Research Fellow, St Cross College (1986-91); Reader in Jewish Studies, University of Oxford (1991-96); President, British Association for Jewish Studies (1995); Sec. European Association for Jewish Studies (1995-); Joint Editor of Journal of Jewish Studies (1995-). Publ.: State and Society in Roman Galilee, A.D. 132-212 (1983); Johann Reuchlin, On the Art of the Kabbalah (translation with S.J. Goodman) (1983 and 1993); E. Schürer, The History of the Jewish People in the Age of Jesus Christ, rev. ed. (with G. Vermes and F.G.B. Millar), volume 3 (1986 [part 1], 1987 [part 2]); The Ruling Class of Judaea: the origins of the Jewish Revolt against Rome, A.D. 66-70 (1987); The Essenes according to the Classical Sources (with Geza Vermes) (1989); Mission and Conversion: proselytizing in the religious history of the Roman Empire (1994). Ad.: Oriental Institute, Pusey Lane, OX1 2LE. ☎ 01865-278208. Fax: 01865-278190. E-mail: martin.goodman@orinst.ox.ac.uk

GOODMAN, Mervyn, M.R.C.S. (Eng.), L,R,C.P. (Lond), F.R.C.G.P., F.R.S.H, D.Obst.R.C.O.G.; b. Liverpool, Jan. 8, 1928; Adj. Med Pract, BAMS; Freeman, City of London; Fel., BMA; Fel. Roy. Soc Med; C. L'pool Branch, Jewish Historical Society of England; BoD; C. Gov. Norman Pannell Primary School; member, Court of Univ. of L'pool; form. General Medical Practitioner, Clinical Teacher, Dept Gen Pract, Univ of L'pool; President (now Hon. Life V.P.), Merseyside Jewish Rep. C; L'pool Z. Cent C.; L'pool Jewish Med Soc.; L'pool Univ. Jew Students' Soc., Mersey Reg C. BMA; L'pool Div BMA; C. Merseyside Cttee for Adult Jew. Educ.; C. M'side Amalgamated Talmud Torah; C. L'pool Graduates Soc.; Gov. King David Primary School; Liverpool Local Med. Cttee; L'pool Area Med Cttee; V. Ch Cameron Fund; Council, BMA; Tr. & Summer School Dir. IUJF. Publ.: Medical Epedemiology, Practice Organisation and Therapeutics; Local Jewish Demography. Ad.: 1, Hornby Lane, Liverpool L18 3HH. ☎/Fax 0151-722 7125.

GOODMAN, Mrs. Vera (née Appleberg); b. London; BoD (1973-94), Exec. Cttee. (1985-91), form Chairman, Publ. Rel. Cttee.; Bd. of Elders, Span. & Port Jews' Cong. (1977-80; 1990-94); Life V. President (Chairman, 1976-79) Richmond Park Conservative Women's Constit. Cttee.; Nat. C. for Soviet Jewry (1977-80), Greater Lond. Conservative Women's Gen. Purposes Cttee. (1979-85) Conservative Rep., Nat. C. of Women (1974-79); form. Central Lond. C., Conservative Frs. of Israel; Rep., Union of Jewish Women at U.N.A.; Central C., Conservative Party; Conservative Women's Nat. Cttee, Exec.; European Union of Women (Brit. Section); Chairman, Sephardi Women's Guild; Brit. C., World Sephardi Fed., V. Chairman, Govs., Russell Sch., Petersham (1974-82). Ad.: 87 Ashburnham Rd., Ham, Richmond, Surrey, TW10 7NN. ☎ 0181-948 1060.

GORDIMER, Nadine; b. Springs, S. Africa, Nov. 20, 1923; Author; Nobel Prize for Literature (1991); W. H. Smith Literary Award (1961), James Tait Black Member Prize (1972), Booker Prize (1974), Grand Aigle d'Or (1975), Premio Maleparte (1985), Nelly Sachs Prize (1985), Bennett Award, New York (1986). Publ.: Soft Voice of the Serpent, The Lying Days, Six Feet of the Country, A World of Strangers, Friday's Footprint, Occasion for Loving, Not for Publication, The Late Bourgeois World, A Guest of Honour, Livingstone's Companions, The Conservationist, Burger's Daughter A Soldier's Embrace, July's People, Something Out There, A Sport of Nature, (1990), My Son's Story, Jump (1991), None to Accompany Me (1994), The Essential Gesture (1988 nonfiction), Writing and Being (1995, essays), etc. Ad.: c/o A. P. Watt Ltd, 20 John St., London WC1N 2DR. ☎ 0171-405 6774. Fax: 0171-831 2154.

GORDON, Gerald Henry, C.B.E., Q.C., M.A., LL.B., Ph.D. (Glasgow), LL.D. (Edinburgh), LL.D. (Hon., Glasgow); b. Glasgow, June 17, 1929; Sheriff of Glasgow and Strathkelvin; Personal Professor of Criminal Law (1969-72), Professor of Scots Law (1972-76), Dean of Faculty of Law 91970-73), all at University of Edinburgh. Publ. Criminal Law of Scotland (1st edn. 1968; 2nd edn. 1978), with Second Cumulative Supplement, 1992; Renton & Brown's Criminal Procedure (ed.) (4th edn. 1972, 5th edn., 1983, 6th edn. 1996). Ad.: Sheriff Court, PO Box 23, Carlton Place, Glasgow G5 9DA. ☎ 0141-429 8888.

GORDON, Lionel Lawrence, B.Sc. (Econ.); b. London, Aug. 31, 1933; Market Research Dir.; Chairman, Jewish Chronicle Ltd.; Dir. Jewish Chronicle Trust Ltd.; Ad.: The Hyde, 5 Orchard Gate, Esher, Surrey, KT10 8HY. ☎ 0181-398 5774. Fax: 0181-398 1866.

GOULD, Samuel Julius, M.A. (Oxon.); b. Liverpool, Oct. 13, 1924; Prof. of Sociology, Nottingham Univ. (1964-82); form R., Social Instits., Lond. Sch. of Econ. & Pol. Sci.; Chairman, Trs., Social Affairs Unit, Lond. (since 1981); Res. Dir., Instit. for Pol. Res. (1983-85), Bd. of Dirs., Centre for Pol. Studies; Res. Bd. & Pol. Planning Group, IJA; BoD. Publ.: Dictionary of the Social Sciences (jt edr.), Jewish Life in Modern Britain (jt edr.), The Attack on Higher Education Jewish Commitment: A study in London; Ad.: c/o The Reform Club., Pall Mall London SW1.

GOULDEN, Simon Charles, B.Sc. (Eng.), D.M.S., C.Eng., M.I.C.E., M.I.M.; b. London, Mar. 1, 1949; Chief Exec. Agency for Jewish Education; form. Exec. Dir., Jews' College; Acting Chairman, United Synagogue Bd. of Religious Educ.; Member, Ecumenical Standing Conference on Disability; Princ. Engineer London Borough Haringey (1976-1986). Ad.: 735 High Rd., London N12 0US. ☎ 0181-343 6266.

GOURGEY, Percy Sassoon, M.B.E., F.R.S.A.; b. Bombay, June 2, 1923; Journalist; form. Nat. Chairman, Poale Zion; V. Pres. Z Fed.; Chairman Socialist Societies Section of the Labour Party.; Exec. Cttee., BoD, V. Chairman, Erets Israel Cttee., BoD; Hon. Fel. WZO (1996); form. Chairman Jews in Arab Lands Cttee., Z. Fed.; form. ed. Jewish Advocate, Bombay; Co-Fdr. and first ed. The Scribe (London), ex-Lieutenant RINVR; Parl. C.; Member, Royal Instit. of International Affairs, Chatham House, London, Contr. to Encyclopaedia Judaica, etc. Publ.: The Jew and his Mission, Ideals, India, Israel in Asia, Indian Jews and the Indian Freedom Struggle, The Indian Naval Revolt of 1946, etc. Ad.: 4 Poplar Ct., Richmond Rd., E. Twickenham, Middx. TW1 2DS. ☎ 0181-892 8498.

GRADON, Kenneth Jacob; b. Berlin, July 20, 1919; V. President, Maccabi World Union; P. (Chairman 1967-74), European Maccabi Confed.; Hon. President, Union of Maccabi Assns. in Gt Brit.; Internat. Maccabiah Cttee., form. Chairman Bd. Govs. P. and Tr. of Jew Secondary Schs. Movement; President, B'nai B'rith First Lodge of England (1966-67). Ad.: 4 Meadway Gate, NW11 7LB. ☎ 0181-458 3645.

GRAHAM, Stewart David, Q.C., M.A., B.C.L. (Oxon.). F.R.S.A.; b. Leeds, Feb. 27, 1934; Barrister; form. Chairman, Law, Parl. & Gen. Purposes Cttee., BoD; form. Member, Insolvency Rules Adv. Cttee.; form. Chairman now Mem., C. & Exec. Cttee. of Justice; Senior Vis. Fellow, Centre for Commercial Law Studies, QMW College; Member C. Insurance Ombudsman Bureau; Assoc. Memb. British & Irish Ombudsman Assoc. Publ.: Works on bankruptcy and insolvency (Jt. Edr.). Ad.: 133 London Rd., Stanmore, Middx., HA7 4PQ. ☎ 0181-954 3783.

GRAUS, Eric; b. Bratislava, April 22, 1927; President, Likud-Herut Movement of Gt Britain; Exec., World Likud Movement; Jt. Chairman, Nat. Z. C.; Mem. Bd. Gov. Jewish Agency. Ad.: 143/5 Brondesbury Pk, NW2 5JL. ☎ 0181-451 0002/3.

GREEN, Sir Allan David, K.C.B., Q.C., (K.C.B. 1991); b. March 1, 1935; Form. Dir. of Pub. Prosecutions, First Sr. Treasury Counsel, Central Criminal Court. (1985-87), Sr. Prosecuting Counsel (1979-85), Jr. Prosecuting Counsel (1977-79); Bencher, Inner Temple (1985); Q.C. (1987), Member, Legal Group Tel Aviv Univ. Tr.; Served R.N. (1953-55). Ad.: 1, Hare Court, Temple, EC4Y 7BE.

GREEN, David Robert; b. London, April 26, 1951; Glass Processor; Jt. Dep. Chairman and Jt. Tr. Jewish Care. Ad.: Powerbreaker House, South Road, Harlow, Essex CM20 2BG. ☎ 01279 434561. Fax: 01279 432870.

GREENBAT, Alan, J.P., b. London, April 1929; Hon Consultant, Office of the Chief Rabbi; Sec. Rabbinical Commission for the Licensing of Shochetim; Borough Chairman Inner London Youths Courts; Exec. & V.Chairman National Council of Voluntary Youth Services (1981-91); Exec. Dir. Office of the Chief Rabbi (1990-91); Dir. Assoc. for Jewish Youth (1980-89); Dir. Victoria Community Centre (1961-80); V.Pres. AJY (1989-96); V.Pres. London Union of Youth Clubs (1984-94); V.Principal Norwood Home for Jewish Children (1955-61). Ad.: Adler House, 735 High Road, London N12 0US. ☎ 0181-343 6301. Fax: 0181-343 6310.

GREENBERG, Rabbi Philip T., B.A., M.Phil., F.J.C.; b. Liverpool, June 28, 1937; Rabbi, Giffnock & Newlands Syn., Glasgow; Rav. Glasgow Shechita Bd. (1993-); Chairman Va'ad HaRabbonim, Glasgow; H. Chaplain, Calderwood Lodge Jewish Sch., Glasg.; M., Nottingham Syn. (1968-72), Highams Park & Chingford Syn. (1959-68); Head, Mishna Stream, Hasmonean Boys' Sch. (1972-81). Ad.: 20 Ayr Rd., Glasgow, G46 6RY. ☎ 0141-638 0309.

GREENGROSS, Dr. Wendy, M.B., B.S.(Lond.), L.R.C.P., M.R.C.S., D.Obst., R.C.O.G.; Dip. Med. Law & Eth.; b. London, Apr. 29, 1925; Medical Practitioner; Broadcaster; Medical Consultant; Marriage Guidance C.; V. President, AJY Fel., Leo Baeck Coll.; Tr., Leonard Cheshire Foundation; President, Ranulf Assn.; Member Govt. Enquiry into human fertilisation and embryology; Chairman, Ethics Cttee, Wellington Humana Hospital Publ.: Sex in the Middle Years; Sex in Early Marriage; Marriage, Sex and Arthritis; The Health of Women; Entitled to Love; Jewish and Homosexual; Living, Loving and Aging. Ad.: 2 Willifield Way, NW11 7XT. ☎ 0181-455 1153.

GREENWOOD, Jeffrey Michael, M.A., LL.M.; b. London, Apr. 21, 1935; Solicitor; Chairman Wigmore Property Investment Tr. plc; Consultant Nabarro Nathanson; Chairman Central Council for Education and Training in Social Work; V. President and Dir. Jewish Care; Exec., Anglo-Israel Assn.; Tr & Exec., English Frs., Jerusalem Coll. of Tech; Dir., Bank Leumi (UK) plc; Dep. Chairman Jewish Chronicle Ltd.; M. Council JHSE. Ad.: 50 Stratton St., W1X 6NX. ☎ 0171-518 3323. Fax: 0171-629 7900.

GROSBERG, Percy, M.Sc., Ph.D.; b. Cape Town, Apr. 5, 1925; Sr. Res. Off, S. African Wool Textile Res. Instit.(1949-55); Res. Prof., Chair of Textile Engineering, Leeds Univ., (1960-90); Member Bd. Gov. and currently Marcus Sieff Prof. Shenkar Coll. of Textile Tech. & Fashion, Ramat Gan; Form. Chairman, Leeds Frs., Bar-Ilan Univ. Publ.: Scientific writings. Ad.: Apt 25, 55 Shlomo Hamelech, Netanya 42267. ☎ 09-8628652.

GROSS, Solomon Joseph, C.M.G.; b. London, Sept. 3, 1920; Ret., Dir., British Steel (1978-90), Plc and other comps.; Dir., Reg. Affairs, B.T.G. (1983-84); Under-Sec., Dept. of Industry (1974-80); Min., Brit. Embassy, Pretoria (1969-73); Brit. Dep. High Com. in Ghana (1966-67). Ad.: 38 Barnes Ct., Station Rd., New Barnet, EN5 1QY.

GRUNEWALD, Rabbi Hans Isaac; b. Frankfurt-am-Main, March 15, 1914; Com. Rabbi of Munich (ret.); Member, Standing Cttee, Conf of European Rab. Union of Orth. Jewish Congs. of Continental Europe, form. Chief Rabbi, Hamburg, Niedersachsen and Schleswig Holstein; President, B'nai B'rith Hebraica Lodge, Munich, President, B'nai B'rith Bialik Lodge, Tel Aviv; President, Z. Org., Munich; Jt. Chairman, C., C.C.J., Munich. Publ.: Die Lehre Israels, (1970); Einblicke, (1989); Ad.: 36 Monarch Ct., Lyttelton Rd., N2 0RA. ☎ and Fax: 0181-455 0811.

GRUNEWALD, Rabbi Jacob Ezekiel, B.A.; b. Tel Aviv, Oct. 26, 1945; M., Pinner and Distr. Syn. Ad.: 65 Cecil Park, Pinner, Middx., HA5 5HL. ☎ 0181-723 0654.

GRUNFELD, Judith, Ph.D. (née Rosenbaum), Mrs. Isidor; b. Budapest; Chairman, Beth Jacob Cen. Admin. HM Avigdor School (1934-54); form Princ., Beth Jacob Training Seminary, Cracow. Publ.: Shefford; Contr. Sages & Saints (edr. Leo

Jung) and Jewish Leaders (edr. Leo Jung). Ad.: 214 Green Lanes, N4 2HA. ☎ 0181-800 1043.

GUBBAY, Lucien Ezra, M.A. (Oxon), MICE; b. Buenos Aires, 1931, m. Joyce née Shammah; Consulting Engineer; President of the Board of Elders (1996-) and form. Parnas of Beth Holim, Spanish & Portuguese Jews' Cong.; Dir. Industrial Dwellings Soc (1885) Ltd. Publ.: Ages of Man (1985), The Jewish Book of why and what (1987), Origins (1989), Quest for the Messiah (1990), The Sephardim (1992). Ad.: 26 Linden Lea, London N2 0RG. ☎ 0181-458 3385 (eve); Fax: 0171-372 5476.

GUTERMAN, Henry, M.L.I.A. (Dip.), A.M.C.T.; b. Berlin, Jan. 22, 1926; President, Jewish Rep. C. Greater Manchester & Region, (1986-89), Vice-President and Mem. BoD. (1992-); Chairman, Def. & Publ. Rel. Cttee. (1978-86); Exec., Manch. C. for Com. Rel.; Bd., Com. Rel. Housing Assn.; V. President Disabled Living (1986-); Exec., Manchester Zionist Central Council (1986-); Vice-Chairman CCJ Manchester Branch (1994-); Bd., South-east Lancashire Housing Assoc Ltd. (SELHAL); Exec., Outreach for Jew Youth; Bd., Heathlands Jewish Homes for Aged; Vice-Chairman Manchester Action Cttee. on Health Care for Ethnic Minorities, (M.A.C.H.E.M.) (1984-); Mem. Man. North Manchester Jewish Youth Project (1995-); V.Chairman, Tameside Com. Health C. (1974-77); Chairman, Northwest Cttee. Against Racism (1972-75) C. Nat. League of Hospital Frs. (1968-77) Ad.: 42 Lidgate Grove, Didsbury, Manchester, M20 6TS. ☎ 0161-434 4019; 0161-876 4543 (off.) Fax 0161-877 4340.

HALBAN, Peter Francis, B.A. (Princeton); b. New York, June 1 1946; Book Publisher; Dir., Peter Halban Publishers Ltd. (1986-present), Dir. Mishkenot Sha'ananim (Cultural Centre) Jerusalem (1975-8). Memb. C. European Jewish Publication Soc., (1994-); Memb. Exec. Institute for Jewish Policy Research (1994-). Ad.: Office: Peter Halban Publishers, 42 South Molton St., W1Y 1HB. ☎ 0171-491 1582. Fax: 0171-629 5381.

HAMBURGER, Sir Sidney Cyril, C.B.E., J.P., D.L., Hon. LL.D. (Manch.), M.A.(Salford); b. Manchester, July 14, 1914; Dep. Lieut, H Greater Manch.; Nat. P. (form. Chairman), Trades Adv. C. (since 1984), V. President, Beth Hatefutsoth; Jt. Life President, JIA (Manchester) 1987; V. President, King David Sch. (1991); President, Citizens Advice Bureaux/Greater Manchester (1990); V. President, British Lung Foundation (North West) 1987; President, Motability North West 1989; Chairman, Citizens' Advice Bureau, Greater Manch. (1985-90); C. Anglo-Israel Assn. (1984); Chairman, Manchester Cttee. For Soviet Jewry (1984-94); Chairman, North Western Reg. Health Auth. (1972-83) Chairman, Age Concern, Salford (1983) Chairman Northeast Manch H.M.C. (1971-74); Cllr. & Alderman, Salford City C., 194671; Mayor of Salford (1968-69), L.P Jewish Homes for Aged; Life President, Z. Central C; V. President, Anglo-Israel Friendship League form. President, C. of Manch. & Salford Jews; V. President, Magen David Adom; P. J.I.A Manch., V. President, Mizrachi Fedi., Ch North-West ASH (1975); B'nai B'rith Award (1984); Pro. Ecclesiastical Papal Award (1983); Salvation Army Adv. Bd. (1983); President, Bar-Ilan (Manchester) (1969); Gov., King David School, (1969); Supplementary Benefits Com. (1966-75); N.W. Elec. Consumer C. (1953-70) Coun, Manch. Univ. (1974-83), Ch Hillel House, Manch.; Bd. of Govs, H. Fel., Bar-Ilan Univ. (1979), Gov., Ben-Gurion Univ. (1984). Ad.: 26 New Hall Rd., Salford M7 4HQ. ☎ 0161-834 5452. Fax: 0161-839 5133.

HAMILTON, Fabian, B.A., M.P.; b. April 12, 1955; m. Rosemary née Ratcliffe; M.P., Leeds North-East (1997-); Leeds City Councillor (1987-97); Chair Edcu. Cttee. (1996-97); Chair Economic Development Cttee (1994-96); Chair Race Equality Cttee (1988-94). Ad.: House of Commons, SW1A 0AA. ☎ 0171-219 3493. Fax: 0171-219 4945.

HANDLER, Arieh L.; b. Brun, May 27, 1915; Financial. Consultant; Jewish Agency C. & Member Praesidium Z. Actions Cttee., P. Mizrachi Fed.; Chairman,

Bachad Fellowship (Friends of B'nai Akiva); Chairman, Adv. Body, Torah Dept., Jewish Agency; Exec., BoD; (form. Chairman, Israel Cttee.), Exec. Jewish Child's Day, Youth Aliyah, (form Dir., Y.A.); Exec WZO; V.Chairman, Brit Frs., Boy's Town, Jerusalem, V. President (form. Chairman) Nat. C. for Soviet Jewry; Jt. T., Montefiore Coll.; Jewish Colonial Tr. C.; President, Brit. Frs., Israel Aged, Edr., Jewish Review World Exec. Religious Zionist Movement, T. Mifal Hatorah Aid Foundation; Patron, Jerusalem Institute for the Blind; Member, U.S. Council; President, Midreshet Eretz Yisrael; Member, Jews Coll. C.; Member, Instit. of Bankers; Fel., Instit. of Dirs.; form. Dir., Hapoel Hamizrachi World Org; form. Man. Dir., Migdal London, Man. Dir. JCB, London. Ad.: c/o Reform Club, SW1.
HARDMAN, Rev. Leslie Henry, M.A, H.C.F.; b. Glynneath, Wales, Feb. 18, 1913; Emer. M., Hendon Syn., V. President, Herut Org.; H. President, N.W. Lond. Jewish Ex-Servicemen's Assn.; Chaplain, Napesbury, Shenley, Hospitals, Edgware Hospital (Medical Section); Publ.: The Survivors. Awards: BBC 'Hearts of Gold', 1993; Simon Wiesenthal Museum of Tolerance, 1995. Ad.: 20 St. Peter's Ct., Queens Rd., NW4 2HG. ☎ 0181-202 6977.
HARMATZ, Joseph; b. Rokishkis, Lithuania, Jan. 23, 1925; Dir.-Gen Emeritus World ORT Union; Dir.-Gen., ORT Israel (1967-79); Comptroller ORT Israel (1960-67).
HARRIS, Rabbi Cyril K., B.A., M.Phil.; b. Glasgow, Sept. 19, 1936; Chief Rabbi of South Africa; H. President S.A. Jewish Board of Educ.; H.V.-P. S.A. Zionist Fed., H. P. Mizrachi Org.; H. President S.A. Rabbinical Assoc.; form. M., Kenton Syn. (1958-72), Edgware Syn. (1975-78), St. John's Wood Syn. (1979-87); Sr. Jewish Chap. to H.M. Forces (1966-71); Nat. Dir. Hillel Foundation (1972-75); Chairman, C., U S Rabbis (1978-82); Jt. Chairman, & V. President; Mizrachi (1983-87). Ad.: c/o Union of Orthodox Synagogues of South Africa, 24 Raleigh St., Yeoville 2198, S. Africa. ☎ 648 9136.
HARRIS, Dr Evan, M.P., Ph.D.; b. Sheffield, Oct. 21, 1965; Registrar in Public Health Medicine, M.P. (Lib.Dem.) Oxford West and Abingdon (1997-). Publ. Medical papers. Ad.: House of Commons, London SW1 0AA; 32a North Hinksey Village, Oxford OX2 8NA.
HARRIS, Michael; b. London, Aug. 8, 1928; Public Relations Adviser; Admin. 'Operation Angel'; form. Dir. United Kingdom Jewish Aid, form. Insurance Manager, Freeman of City of London (1976); AJY: Exec (1953-94), V. Pres (1981-), Chairman (1989-93); AJA: Council (1960-); AJEX: Tr. Sutton AJEX (1990-); BoD: Member (for AJY 1948-73) for Sutton & Cheam (1973-); Central J. Lect.. Comm (1982-1994); V.C. (1988-91); Chairman (1991-94), Exec. Comm (1991-94); Educ. Comm (V.C. 1994-97) United Syn. Council (1984-): Israel Comm (1993-) World Confed. JCC's (V.P. (1990-96). Imperial Cancer Research Fund: Life Gov. (1985); Jewish Youth Fund: Adv. Cttee. (1989-95), Nat. Assoc Boys Clubs: C. (1988-); Sutton Synagogue: H. Sec. (1978-84), Warden (1984-88); H. Tr. South London Comm. C. (1990-);North West Jewish Boys Club: H. Sec. (1956-66). Ad.: 40 York Rd., Cheam, Surrey, SM2 6HH. ☎ 0181-643 3228.
HARRIS, Rabbi Michael Jacob, M.A. (Cantab), M.A. (Jerusalem); b. London, Feb. 17, 1964; m. Sara, née Keen; Rabbi, Hampstead Synagogue (1995-); Lecturer in Jewish Law, Jews' College, London (1995-); Co-Chairman, Hampstead Branch, CCJ; Cttee Member, British Friends of Ariel; Consultant, Limmud; Exec. Member, Rabbinic Forum, Keren Haysod-United Israel Appeal; form. Rabbi, Southend and Westcliff Hebrew Cong. (1992-95); Principal, Herzlia Nursery School, Westcliff (1992-95); Hon. Chaplain, Southend and District AJEX (1992-95); Jewish Rep. to Essex Standing Advisory Council on Religious Education (SACRE) and Agreed Syllabus Conference (1992-95). Ad.: Flat 19, Palace Court, 250 Finchley Road, NW3 6DN. ☎/Fax 0171-431 2887.
HASS, Rev. Simon, L.L.C.M.; b. Poland, May 2, 1927; Cantor Central Syn. Gt Portland St., London,W.l. (since 1951); Composer Musical Arranger. Publ.: Many Recordings of Jewish liturgical and classical music. Ad.: "Beit Shirah", 2A

Allandale Ave., N3 3PJ.
HAYMAN, Baroness Helene (née Middleween), M.A.(Cantab); b. Wolverhampton, March 26, 1944; m. Martin Hayman; Parliamentary Under Sec. of State, Dept. of Environment, Transport and the Regions; Labour Mem. of Parliament (1974-79); Chairman, Whittington Hospital (1992-97). Ad.: House of Lords, SW1A 1AA.
HEILBRON, Dame Rose, D.B.E., LL.B., LL.M., Hon. LL.D. (Liverpool), Hon. LL.D. (Warwick), Hon. LL.D. (Manchester); Hon. LL.D. (C.N.A.A.); b. Liverpool, Aug. 19, 1914; Judge of the High Court' Family Division (1974-88); Tr., Gray's Inn (1985); Presiding Judge, Northern Circuit (1979-82); form. Leader, Northern Circuit Recorder and H. Recorder of Burnley; Bencher, Gray's Inn; H. Fel., Lady Margaret Hall, Oxford; H.Fel., Manch. Univ. Instit. of Sci. & Tech.
HELFGOTT, Ben; b. Pabianice, Poland, Nov. 22, 1929; Comp. Dir., Chairman, '45 Aid Soc. (since 1975; 1963-70); Chairman, Yad Vashem Cttee., BoD; Chairman C., Promotion of Yiddish & Yiddish Culture; C., Jewish Youth Fund; Exec., Wiener Libr.; Chairman, Polin-Inst. for Polish Jewish Studies; form. Jt. T., CBF-WJR; Brit. Weightlifting Champion & Record Holder; competed in Olympic Games (1956; 1960); Bronze Medal, Commonwealth Games (1958); Gold Medals, Maccabiah (1950, 1953, 1957). Ad.: 46 Amery Rd., Harrow, Middx. HA1 3UG. ☎ 0181-422 1512.
HELLNER, Rabbi Frank, B.A., B.H.L., M.A., D.D. (Hon.); b. Philadelphia, Pa., Jan. 1, 1935; M. Finchley Progressive Syn. (since 1966); Exec., Barnet Com. Rel. C.; Gov., Akiva Sch.; V. President, Finchley CCJ, Member Leo Baeck Coll. Comp.; Extra-Mural Lect. Birkbech Coll. (Pt.-time); Chairman, ULPS Rabbinic Conference (1970-71); Edr., ULPS News (1978-86); Chaplain to Mayor of L. B. Barnet (1993-94). Publ.: I Promise I Will Try not to Kick My Sister and Other Sermons. Ad.: Finchley Progressive Synagogue, 54 Hutton Grove, N12 8DR. Tel/Fax: 0181-446 4063.
HENIG, Stanley, M.A., (Oxford); Hon. R.N.C.M., (Royal Northern College of Music); b. Leicester, July 7, 1939; Prof of Politics Lancashire Polytechnic; Leader, Lancaster City Council, (1991-); M.P. (Lancaster) (1966-70) Chairman, R.N.C.M. (1986-89); Publ.: Power and Decision in Europe (1981); Political parties in the European Community (1979). Ad.: 10 Yealand Drive, Lancaster LA1 4EW. ☎ 01524 69624
HERMAN, Josef, O.B.E., R.A. Elect; b. Warsaw, Jan. 1, 1911; Artist-Painter; Exhibitions in many cities in UK and in Geneva, Auckland, Melbourne, Basle, Frankfurt etc. Gold Medal for services to the Arts in Wales; Works purchased by public collections in UK, Australia, Canada, Israel, S. Africa. Publ.: Related Twilights, Notes from a Welsh Diary. Ad.: 120 Edith Rd., W14. ☎ 0181-603 5091.
HERSHON, Cyril P., M.A., Ph.D. (Jewish Ed.) M.I.L.; b. Liverpool March 17, 1937; Writer and Broadcaster; University of the West of England; Associate, Université de Montpellier. Ret. (as head of M.L.) Clifton Coll.; Housemaster, Polack's House, Clifton Coll. (1979-86); Court, Bath Univ. Publ.: To Make Them English, When the Rabbi Laughs, Judaism – a GCSE Resource Book, Ripples, The Castles of Cary, Judaism - a National Curriculum handbook, Ashes & Remorse, The Painter and the Poet. Ad.: L.E.S., University of the West of England, Frenchay Campus, Coldharbour Lane, Bristol BS16 1QY. ☎ 0117-9656261.
HERTZBERG, Rabbi Arthur, Ph.D.; b. Lubaczow, Poland; Rabbi Emer., Temple Emanuel of Englewood; form. President, American Jewish Cong.; Hon. V. President, World Jewish Cong., V. President, Member Foundation for Jewish Culture; Prof. of Religion Emer., Dartmouth Coll., Adjunct Prof of Hist. Columbia Univ, Prof of Hist., Hebrew Univ. (1970-71); Fel. Instit. Advanced Studies, Hebrew Univ. (1982); Vis. Prof. of the Humanities, New York Univ. Publ.: The Zionist Idea, Judaism, The French Enlightenment and the Jews, Being Jewish in America, The Jews in America (1989), Judaism, 2nd ed. (1991), Jewish

Polemics (1992). Ad.: 83 Glenwood Rd., Englewood, New Jersey 07631, USA.
☎ 201-568-3259.
HILL, Brad Sabin, A.B., F.R.A.S.; b. New York, Nov. 2, 1953; Librarian and Fel. in Hebrew Bibliography, Oxford Centre for Hebrew and Jewish Studies; form. Hd., Hebrew Section, The British Library (1989-96); Curator of Rare Hebraica, National Library of Canada, Ottawa (1979-89). Publ.: Incunabula, Hebraica & Judaica (1981); Hebraica from the Valmadonna Trust (1989); (ed.) Miscellanea Hebraica Bibliographica (1995). Ad.: 2 Canonbury Square, London N1.
HILTON, Rabbi Michael, M.A., D.Phil., P.G.C.E.; b. London, Feb. 27, 1951; M. Cheshire Reform Congregation (1987-); Homeless Persons off., L.B. Hammersmith & Fulham (1980-82); . Publ.: The Gospels and Rabbinic Judaism (with G. Marshall, 1988.), The Christian Effect on Jewish Life (1994). Ad.: Cheshire Reform Congregation 198 Altrincham Road, Manchester M22 4RZ. ☎ 0161 428 7746.
HOBSBAWM, Eric John Ernest, F.B.A., M.A., Ph.D.; b. Alexandria, Egypt, June 9, 1917; Emer. Prof of Econ. and Soc. Hist., Birkbeck Coll., Lond. Univ.; H. Fel., King's Coll., Cambridge. Publ.: Primitive Rebels, The Jazz Scene, The Age of Revolution, Labouring Men, Industry and Empire, Nations and Nationalism, The Age of extremes, 1914-1991, etc. Ad.: Birkbeck College, Malet St., WC1. ☎ 0171-580 6622.
HOCHHAUSER, Victor, C.B.E.; b. Kosice, Czechoslovakia, Mar. 27, 1923; Impresario for internat. artists orchestras, ballet companies, etc. Ad.: 4 Oak Hill Way, NW3 7LR. ☎ 0171-794 0987. Fax: 0171-431 2531.
HOOKER, Rabbi Bernard, B.A.; b. London, Feb. 4, 1922; Emer. Rabbi, N London Progressive Syn.; M., Jewish Com. of Jamaica (1965-74); form. M., Wembley Lib. Syn. and Lib. Jewish Syn., Birmingham, Sr. Jewish Chaplain to M.E.L.F. (1947). Ad.: 29 Furlong Ct., Ledbury HR8 2X5. ☎ 01531 633788.
HOWARD, Michael, Q.C., M.P.; b. Gorseinon, Wales, July 7, 1941; M.P. (Cons) for Folkestone and Hythe; form. Home Secretary (1993-97); Min. of State Environment Dept., Parl. Under-Sec. of State, Trade & Industry (1985-87); Chairman, Conservative Bow Group (1970-71); form. President, Cambridge Union. Ad.: House of Commons, SW1A 0AA.
HUBERT, Walter I., F.R.S.A., F. Inst. Dir.; b. Schluechtern, Germany, Aug. 13, 1932; First Chairman, Gateshead Foundation for Torah, I.J.A.; Patron, Didsbury Jewish Primary Sch.; H. Life V. President, Brit. Cttee., Peylim of Israei; Gov., Global Bd., & H. Fel., Bar-Ilan Univ.; Gov., Ben Gurion Univ.; V. President, Cancer Res. Cttee., Dir. State of Israel Bonds (UK); V.P; British Herut; form. Chairman, Blackburn Rovers F.C.; First Recipient (1981) Bank Hapoalim Silver Rose Award for new Israeli industry; Jerusalem Educ. Medal (1974); Zurich Jewish Secondary Schs.; "Man of Year" Gold Medal (1978); assoc. with many educ. and charitable instit. in Brit., Israel Switzerland, US & Argentina. Ad.: 24 King David Gdns., 27 King David St., Jerusalem, Israel. ☎ 02 241754.
HURST, Alex; b. Liverpool, Jan. 6, 1935; form. Admin., Merseyside Jewish Welfare C.; form. Sec., L'pool Jewish Housing Assn. Ad.: 440 Allerton Rd., Liverpool L18 3JX. ☎ 0151-427 7377.
HYMAN, Barry S., M.I.P.R.; b. Scotland, June 24, 1941, m. Judith; Public Relations and Media Consultant, Broadcaster, Writer; PR consultant and newsletter editor to Reform Synagogues of Great Britain and the Spiro Institute for Jewish History, Culture and Language; BoD Public Relations Cttee (1988-97); Member of the Institute of Public Relations (1987-); Head of Corporate Affairs, Media Relations, Community Affairs and Company Archive, Marks and Spencer, (1984-94). Publ.: Young in Herts (1996), a history of the Radlett and Bushey Reform Synagogue; (Ed.) Reform Judaism News. Ad.: RSGB, 80 East End Rd., London N3 2SY. ☎ 0181-349 4731.
HYMAN, Mrs. Marguerite Grete (née De Jongh); b. London, Mar. 26, 1913; V. President, (form. Fin. Sec) Union of Lib. & Progr. Syns.; Ad.: 14 The Cedars,

St. Stephen's Rd., W13 8JF. ☎ 0181-997 8258.
INGRAM, Rabbi Chaim Nota, B.A.(Hons.); b. London, May 14, 1952; M./R., The Central Synagogue, Sydney; M., Leicester Hebrew Cong. (1986-92); M./R., United Hebrew Cong., Newcastle Upon Tyne (1982-96); R., Cricklewood Syn, London (1979-82). Publ.: Renana Song Book. Ad: 196 Old South Head Road, Bellevue Hill, Sydney, NSW 2023. ☎/Fax: 02-9365 5716.
ISLER, Dr Ellen, née Skorneck, M.A. (Harvard), Ph.D. (Columbia), b. New York City, 1943; m. Alan Isler; Dir. Gen. World ORT Union; V. President for Institutional Advancement, Hunter College, CUNY (1989-93); Dir. of Operations, JDC (1985-89); Assoc. Dean, Grad. School of Arts and Sciences, Columbia University (1978-84); Vis. Prof. Queens College, CUNY (1973-76); Lect. English Dept, Tel Aviv University (1964-73). Ad.: ORT House, 126 Albert Street, Camden Town, London NW1 7NE. ☎ 0171-446 8500. Fax 0171-446 8650.
ISRAEL, Jonathan Irvine, M.A., D.Phil., F.R.H.S., F.B.A.; b. London, Jan. 22, 1946; Professor, Dutch Hist. & Instits., Lond. Univ., Univ. Coll.; H. Sec., JHSE (1974-79); Wolfson Hist. Prize (1986); Ed. Littman Library of Jewish Civilization (1990-). Publ.: European Jewry in the Age of Mercantilism, 1550-1750, The Dutch Republic and the Hispanic World, 1606-61, Race, Class and Politics in Colonial Mexico, 1610-70, Dutch Primacy in World Trade, (1585-1740), Empires and Entrepots: the Dutch, the Spanish Monarchy and the Jews, 1585-1713, Anglo-Dutch moment: essays on the Glorious Revolution and its world impact. Ad.: 48 Parkside Dr., Edgware, Middx. HA8 8JX. ☎ 0181-958 6069.
ISSERLIN, Benedict Sigmund Johannes, M.A. (Edin.), M.A., B.Litt., D.Phil. (Oxon.); b. Munich, Feb. 25, 1916; form. Reader and Head of Dept. Semitic Studies, Leeds Univ.; form. H. Sec., Anglo-Israel Archaeological Soc.; President, Brit. Assn. for Jewish Studies (1982). Publ.: Writings on Near Eastem Studies, incl. A Hebrew Work Book for Beginners; Ch. on Israelite Art in C. Roth, Jewish Art; Motya, a Phoenician and Carthaginian City in Sicily, I (with J. du Plat Taylor); A Study of Contemporary Dialectal Maltese, I (with J. Aquilina); Contr. Times Atlas of the Bible, and O. Tufnell, Lachish IV. Ad.: c/o Dept. of Arabic and Middle Eastern Studies, Leeds Univ., Leeds, LS2 9JT. ☎ 0113 2751576.
JACKSON, Bernard Stuart, LL.B. (Hons.), D. Phil., LL.D.; b. Liverpool, Nov. 16, 1944; Barrister; Queen Victoria Prof. of Law, Liverpool Univ.; form. Prof. of Law, Kent Univ. (1985-89); Prof. & Head, Law Dept., L'pool Polytechnic (1977-85); Lady Davis Vis. Prof., Hebrew Univ. (1981); Speaker's Lect. in Biblical Studies, Oxford Univ. (1983-86); Gruss Vis. Prof. of Talmudic Legal Studies, Harvard Law School (1992); form. Chairman, Jewish Law Assn.; Edr., The Jewish Law Annual; Sec., J. Law Publ. Fund. Publ.: Theft in Early Jewish Law, Essays in Jewish and Comparative Legal Hist., Semiotics and Legal Theory, Law, Fact and Narrative Coherence, Making Sense in Law, Making Sense in Jurisprudence, (Edr.) Studies in Jewish Legal Hist. in Hon. of David Daube, Modern Research in Jewish Law, Jewish Law in Legal Hist. and the Modern World, Semiotics, Law and Social Science (with D. Carzo), The Touro Conference Volume (Jew Law Assn. Studies I), The Jerusalem Conference Volume (Jewish Law Assn. Studies II), The Boston Conference Volume (Jew Law Assn. Studies IV), The Halakhic Thought of R. Isaac Herzog (Jew. Law Assn. Studies V) The Jerusalem 1990 Conference Volume (Jew. Law Assn. Studies VI) (with S. M. Passamaneck), Legal Visions of the New Europe (with D. McGoldrick), Legal Semiotics and the Sociology of Law, Introduction to the History and Sources of Jewish Law (with N. Hecht & others). Ad.: Faculty of Law, Univ. of Liverpool, POB 147, Liverpool L69 3BX. ☎/Fax: 0151-729 0371.
JACKSON, Rabbi Edward Leo, B.A.; b. Cork, Oct. 28, 1936; M., Hampstead Garden Suburb Syn.; Spec. Adv. to the Chief Rabbi; Rel. Adv., Jewish Marriage C., Member Standing Cttee. Conference of European Rabbis, Co.Chairman, Mizrachi Fed.; form. Chairman, Rabbin C., US; M., Kenton Syn. (1972-80);

Kingston Syn. (1961-72) Jewish Chaplain to Pentonville Prison; form. Asst. M., Hampstead Syn; Member, Chief Rabbi Cabinet; Member, Working Party Internat. Year of the Family. Ad.: 8 Norrice Lea, N2 ORE. ☎ 0181-458 3306.

JACOB, Sir (Jack) Isaac Hai, Q.C., LL.B. (Lond.), Hon. LL.D. (Birmingham, London, Staffordshire), Dr. Juris. (Würzburg); b. Shanghai, China, June 5, 1908; Chairman Univ. Lond. Jewish Students Union, 1931; form. Master Queen's Bench Division, 1957-1975, Sr. Master of the Supreme Court and Queen's Remembrancer (1975-80); H. Bencher, Gray's Inn, form. Dir., Instit. of Advanced Legal Studies (1986-88); Freeman, City of London; Fel.Univ. Coll., Lond., Hon. Fel. Univ. Westminster; Past. Edr. Annual Practice, 1960-66, Gen. Ed. Supreme Court Practice (1967-); Fabric of English Civil Justice (Hamlyn Lectures) (1986); International Perspectives on Civil Justice (1990). Ad.: 31 Totteridge Common, London N20 8LT. ☎ 0181-959 4223.

JACOBI, Rabbi Harry Martin, B.A. Hon.; b. Berlin, Oct. 19, 1925; M. South Bucks Jewish Community; form. M., Zurich Lib. Syn.; M., Wembley Lib. Syn.; Southgate Progressive Syn.; President, Southgate B'nai B'rith Ben-Gurion Lodge (1974-75); Chairman, Frs. of Progressive Judaism in Europe and Israel; Chairman, Rabbinic Bd. ULPS. Ad. 29 Sylvan Court, Holden Rd., London N12 7ED. ☎ 0181-446 1837.

JACOBS, David; b. Manchester, 1951; Dir. Syn. Partnership Division, Reform Synagogues of Great Britain; Co-fdr. Jewish East End Project (1977); Co-fdr. London Museum of Jewish Life (1983); RSGB Youth Development Off. (1975-79); Dir. Victorian Com. Centre (1988-91). Ad.: RSGB,, The Sternberg Centre for Judaism, 80 East End Road, Finchley, N3 2SY.

JACOBS, David Lewis, C.B.E., D.L., Hon. Ph.D, Kingston Univ.; b. London, May 19, 1926; Broadcaster; host and Chairman of BBC radio and television programmes; Dep. Lieutenant for Greater Lond., Rep. Dep. Lieutenant for the R. Borough of Kingston upon Thames; V. President, Stars Org. for Spastics; Form. Chairman, Think British, Campaign; V. President, R. Star and Garter Home, Richmond; Past President, Nat. Children's Orchestra; form. V. Chairman, R.S.P.C.A.; President, Kingston Upon Thames Royal British Legion; V. President, Wimbledon Girls Choir; Chairman, Kingston Theatre Trust; Life Governor Imperial Cancer Research Fd.; Jt. Pres. Thames Community Tr.; Pres. S.W. London Area SSAFFA; Chairman Thames FM; Pres. T.S. Steadfast; Patron Age Resource; Patron Kingston Bereavement Tr.; Pres. Kingston Alcohol Service. Publ.: Jacobs', Ladder (autobiog.), Caroline, Any Questions (with Michael Bowen). Ad.: 203 Pavilion Rd., SW1X 0BJ.

JACOBS, David Michael, b. Bristol, June 4, 1930, m. Marion née Davis; Exec. (form. Gen. Sec.), AJA; Exec. Herut-Likud UK; Vice-P., form. Chairman Guild of Jewish Journalists; H.V. President Chiltern Progressive Syn.; form. Chairman, Beds.-Herts. Progressive Jewish Cong.; form. BoD, Press Officer; Brit. Z. Fed. Publ.: Israel (World in Colour series) 1968, Research & writing for Jewish Communities of the World, (Ed. A. Lerman) 1989. Ad.: 56 Normandy Rd., St. Albans, Herts AL3 5PW. ☎ /Fax: 01727-858454.

JACOBS, Rabbi Irving, B.A., Ph.D. (Lond.); b. London, Aug. 2, 1938; Princ. Jews, College (1990-93); Res. Fell, (1966-69), Lect. (1969-84); Dean (1984-90); First Incumbent, Sir Israel Brodie Chair in Bible Studies; Dir., Midrashah Instit. for Israel Studies (1980-82); form. Min., Sutton and District Hebrew Cong. Publ.: The Midrashic Process. Ad.: 28 Elmstead Ave., Wembley, Middx. ☎ 0181-248 5777.

JACOBS, Rabbi Julian Godfrey, M.A.; Ph.D. (Lond.); b. London, March 6, 1934; M., Ealing Syn.; Chap., Thames Valley Univ.; Chap., Heathrow Airport; M. of Chief Rabbi's Cabinet; Exec. cttee Interfaith Network; form. M., Liverpool Old Hebrew Cong.; M., Blackpool United Hebrew Cong.; Barking & Becontree Syn.; West Hackney Syn.; Richmond Syn. Chap. to Mayor of Ealing (1992-93); Publ.: The Ship has a Captain, From Week to Week, Judaism looks at Modern Issues, A Haftara Companion. Ad.: 12 Ascott Ave., Ealing, W5 5QB. ☎ 0181-567 0527.

JACOBS, June Ruth (née Caller), b. London, June 1, 1930; Professional Volunteer; World President, Int. Council of Jewish Women; Chairman, BOD Standing Conference on Central and Eastern European Jewish Communities; V. Chairman, Jewish Council for Racial Equality and Jewish Black Forum; Co-Chairman, Int. Executive Int. Centre for Peace in Middle East; Life Mem. League of Jewish Women; L. President, Jewish Child's Day; Chairman, Kessler Foundation; Exec. Mem., Council for Jewish Palestinian Dialogue; Exec. Mem., Jewish Youth Fund; Exec. Mem., Board of Deputies; Mem. Intl. Bd. Dir. New Israel Fund; Mem., Inst. of Jewish Policy Research; Sec., Memorial Foundation for Jewish Culture; Exec. European Jewish Congress; Exec. World J. Congress. Ad.: 13 Modbury Gardens, NW5 3QE. ☎ 0171-485 6027. Fax: 0171-284 2809.

JACOBS, Rabbi Louis, C.B.E., B.A., Ph.D., H.D.H.L. (Chicago, New York, Cincinnati), H.Li.D. (Lancaster); b. Manchester, July 17, 1920; M., New London Syn. (since 1964); Vis. Prof, Lancaster Univ.; form. H. Dir., Soc. for Study of Jewish Theology; form. Tutor and Lect., Jews, Coll. (1959-62), form. Minister-Preacher, New West End Syn., London (1954-59); and Rab., Manchester Central Syn. Publ: Jewish Prayer, We Have Reason to Believe, Jewish Values, Principles of the Jewish Faith, A Jewish Theology, Teyku, The Talmudic Argument, A Tree of Life, Helping with Enquiries, Holy Living; God, Torah and Israel, Structure and Form of the Babylonian Talmud, Religion and the Individual, The Jewish religion: a companion etc. Ad.: 27 Clifton Hill, NW8 0QE ☎ 0171-624 1299.

JACOBS, Myrna, née Appleton; b. London, Aug. 18, 1940; m. Laurance D. Jacobs; Headteacher of Immanuel College; Head of Languages, Anna Head High, Berkeley, California (1962-66); Lecturer, Univ. of California Extension (Berkeley & San Francisco) (1964-66); Head of Language Faculty in Borough of Brent, consecutiventy Brondesbury & Kilburn, John Kelly Girls, Preston Manor (1973-89); 1st Deputy Head, Immanuel College (1990-95). Ad.: Immanuel College, 87-91 Elstree Rd., Bushey, Herts WD2 3RH. ☎ 0181-950 0604. Fax 0181-950 8687.

JACOBSON, Dan, B.A.; b. Johannesburg, March 7, 1929; Novelist and univ. Prof. Emer., Univ. Coll. London (1994-); Publ.: A Dance in the Sun, The Beginners, Tbe Rape of Tamar, The Story of Stories: the Chosen People and its God, Her Story, etc. Ad.: c/o A. M. Heath & Co. 79 St. Martin's La., WC2N 4AA ☎ 0171-836 4271.

JAKOBOVITS, Lady, Amelie, (née Munk); b. Ansbach, May 31, 1928; wife of Lord Jakobovits; Fdr. and President, Assoc. of US Women; V. President, Emunah Women's Org.; President, Jewish Marriage C., Dir. of Jewish Care; Fdr. and Patron of Chai Lifeline, L.P. JIA Women's Division; Life V. President, League of Jewish Women; Patron of Dysautonomia Foundation; V. President, Wizo; P. Ladies, Visitation Cttee., US; V. President, Youth Aliyah; Patron 'J' Link; President, 'Chen'. Ad.: 44a Albert Rd., London NW4 2SJ.

JAKOBOVITS, Lord, of Regent's Park, Life Peer (Sir Immanuel Jakobovits), B.A., Ph.D., Hon. D.D. (Univ. Wales), Hon. D.Litt (City Univ., Lond.), D.D. (Lambeth); b. Konigsberg, February 8, 1921; Chief Rabbi of the United Hebrew Congs. of the British Commonwealth (1967-91); Jerusalem Prize 1989, Katz Prize 1990; Templeton Prize 1991; form. Rab., Fifth Ave. Syn. New York City (1958-67); President, Conf European Rabbis; Fdr., JEDT; Gov., Hebrew Univ., Jerusalem, Bar-Ilan Univ., Ramat Gan, Ben Gurion Univ., Beersheba, Haifa Univ.; Fel., Univ. Coll. London, Queen Mary Coll., Lond.; Chief Rabbi, Jewish Coms. in Ireland (1949-58); M., Gt Syn. (1947-49), Temp. M., Brondesbury Syn. (1941-44); Temp. M., S.E. London Syn. (1944-47). Publ.: The Timely and The Timeless, Jewish Medical Ethics, Journal of a Rabbi, If Only My People: Zionism in My Life, Ha-Rav ha-Lord (1995), Dear Chief Rabbi (1995); Editor, Centenary Ed. Authorised Daily Prayer Book 1990, etc. Ad.: 44a Albert Rd., NW4 2SJ. ☎ 0181-203 8667. Fax: 0181-203 8826.

JANNER, Lord (Hon., Greville Ewan), M.A. (Cantab), Hon. Ph.D. (Haifa), Q.C.; b. Cardiff, July 11, 1928; Barrister-at-law; form. M.P. (Lab.) for Leicester West (1970-97); President Inter Party Council Against Anti-Semitism; Chairman, Select Cttee. on Employment (1993-96); Dir., Ladbroke plc (1986-95); Chairman, JSB Group Ltd., including Effective Presentational Skills (1984-); President, BoD (1979-85); P. Commonwealth Jewish C.; Chairman, Trs., Commonwealth Jewish Tr.; Hon. V. President, WJC ; Fdr. and V.Chairman, All-Party Parl. Cttee. for Jews from the FSU; V. Chairman, Brit.-Israel Parl. Group, H. Sec., All-Party Parl. War Crimes Group; Chairman, Holocaust Educ. Tr.; President, Maimonides Foundation; Sec., Parl. Cttee. for East European Jewry; Chairman, All-Party Parl. Industrial Safety Group; P. Ret. Execs. Action Group (REACH); President, Jewish Museum; Bd. Dirs., JIA; Tr., Elsie & Barnett Janner Tr.; Exec., Lab. Frs. of Israel; V. President, AJY, Ajex, Internat. Vol. Service; Fel., Inst. of Personnel and Development; Member N.U.J.; H. Member, Nat. Union Mineworkers (Leics. Br.); form. President, WJC (Europe); form. President, Nat. C. for Soviet Jewry; form. Tr., Jewish Chronicle, form. Dir., Jewish Chronicle; President, Camb. Union & Fdr. & Chairman, The Bridge in Britain; Chairman, Camb. Univ. Lab. Club; form. Chairman, Brady Boys, Club. Lect., contrib. and author 60 books. Ad.: House of Lords, London SW1A 0PW.

JAQUE, Sidney, J.P.; b. Toledo, Ohio, USA, June 23, 1912; Ret. Solicitor; form. Mayor of Holborn (1958), H.L. Patron (form. Chairman), Camden (form. Holborn) Chamber of Commerce, Chairman, Camden Commercial Ratepayers Group (since 1979); Past President, now Hon. Life President Western Marble Arch Syn. (form. Western Syn.); Chairman, Western Charitable Foundation; form. Gov., St. Nicholas Montessori Instit.; form. Gov., J.F.S.; form. Dep. Chairman, West Central Magistrates, Div.; V. President (form. President), Holborn & St. Pancras Conservative Assn.; V.Chairman Frs., Royal Lond. Homoeopathic Hospital, Vice-P., London Youth Tr. Ad.: 56 Sheringham, St. Johns Wood Park, NW8 6RA. ☎ 0171-722 3671.

JOEL, Hon. Sir Asher Alexander, K.B.E., O.B.E., A.O., Hon. D. Litt (Macquarie Univ.), F.R.S.A., Bronze Star (USA), Kt. Cdr. of Rizal (Philippines), Order of Sikatuna (Philippines), Knight of the Order of St. Sylvester; b. Sydney, May 4, 1912; Member, N.S.W. Legislative C. (1957-78); Hebrew University Torch of Learning Award (1978); President Citation, Tel Aviv University (1992); President, Anzac Memorial and Forest in Israel; V. President, JNF; V. President, Australian Jewish Welfare Soc.; Gov., United Israel Appeal; Gov., Australia-Israel Chamber of Commerce & Industry; Gov., Jewish Communal Appeal; Patron, Sydney Jewish Museum, Patron Australian Jewish Historical Soc., Publ.: Without Chains, Free, Australian Protocol and Procedures. Ad.: 120 Clarence Street, Sydney, NSW 2000, Australia. ☎ (02) 9299 2666. Fax: (02) 9290 1740.

JOSEPH, Dr Anthony Peter, MB.BChir. (Cantab), MRCGP, FSG; b. Birmingham, April 23, 1937; General Medical Practitioner; Post-graduate tutor in paediatrics, Univ. of Birmingham (1986-91); form. President JHSE (1994-96); Chairman Birmingham Branch of JHSE (1969-); Corresponding member for Great Britain, Australian Jewish Historical Society (1965-); UK rep. of Society of Australian Genealogists (1965-95); Contributor on Jewish Genealogy to Blackwell Companion to Jewish Culture; Author of papers in many different genealogical publications, including JHSE. Ad.: 25 Westbourne Road, Edgbaston, Birmingham B15 3TX. ☎ 0121-454 0408. Fax: 0121-454 9758.

JOSEPH, Jack, M.D., D.Sc., F.R.C.O.G., F.C.S.L.T. (Hon); b. Glasgow, Dec. 28, 1913; Emer. Prof., Lond. Univ. Publ.: Textbook of Regional Anatomy, Medical works. Ad.: 17 Greenfield Gdns., NW2 1HT. ☎ 0181-458 4373.

JOSEPH, John Michael; b. London, 11 Feb. 1939; Chairman, GET Plc; Chairman, Jewish Blind & Disabled; Chairman, Cavendish Housing Trust Ltd. Ad.: 24 Rosslyn Hill, London NW3.

JOSIPOVICI, Prof. Gabriel David; b. Nice, France, Oct. 8, 1940; Writer; Univ.

Teacher; Prof. of English, School of European Studies, Univ. of Sussex; Asst. Lect. in English, School of European Studies, Univ. of Sussex (1963-5); Lect. in English (1965-73); Reader in English (1973-85); Lord Weidenfeld Vis. Prof., Oxford (1996-97). Publ.: The Inventory, Words, The Present, Migrations, The Air We Breathe, Conversations in Another Room, Contre-Jour, The Big Glass, In a Hotel Garden, Moo-Pak, The World and the Book, The Lessons of Modernism, The Book of God, Text and Voice, Touch. Ad.: 60 Prince Edward's Rd., Lewes, Sussex BN7 1BH.

KALMS, Lady Pamela, M.B.E.; b. London, July 29, 1931; Vol. Services Co-ordinator, Edgware Gen. Hospital; Dir., NHS Wellhouse Tr. (Barnet and Edgware Gen. Hospitals); Tr. and Dir., Ravenswood Foundation. Ad.: Flat 4, 24 St. James's Place SW1A 1NH. ☎ 0171-491 1301.

KALMS, Sir Stanley, Hon. F.C.G.I. (1991), Hon. D.Litt. CNAA/ University of London (1991), Hon. D. Univ. North London (1994); Hon. Fellow London Business School (1995); Hon. D. Econ. Richmond (1996); b. London Nov. 21, 1931; Chairman Dixons Group plc; Dir. Centre for Policy Studies (1991-); Vis. Prof., Busniess Sch., Univ. (formerly Poly.) of North London (1991-); Mem. of Bd. of Funding Agency for Schs – Chairman of the Agency's Finance Cttee (12994-); Gov., Dixons Bradford City Technology Coll. (1988-); Tr. Industry in Educn. Ltd. F(1993-);Gov. of National Institute of Economic & Social Research (1995-); Tr. – The Economic Education Tr. (1993); F. and Sponsor of Centre for Applied Jewish Ethics n Business and the Professions, Jerusalem; Fd. of Stanley Kalms Foundation; Co-Fd. and Sponsor of Immanuel College; form. Chairman of The Jewish Educational Development Tr. (1978-89) and Jews' College (1983-89); Non-Exec. Dir., British Gas (1987-97); Chairman King's Healthcare NHS Trust (1993-96). Ad.: 29 Farm Street, W1X 7RD. ☎ 0171-499 3494. Fax 0171-499 3436.

KAPLIN, Dayan David C., b. London, Oct. 1, 1931; Dayan, London Beth Din, form. Dayan, Fed. of Syn., form. Rav Shomrei Hadath Syn., Hampstead; form Rosh Yeshiva, Yeshivat Etz Chaim; form. Princ. Bet Hatalmud Golders Green, Ed.: Hed Eliyahu; SRIDIM (Standing Cttee. Conference of European Rabbis). Publ.: Keter David, Toldot Noach. Ad.: London Beth Din. ☎ 0171-343 6270.

KATTEN, Mrs. Brenda (née Rosenblit), b. London, Sept. 8, 1936; Chairman, Bnai Brith Hillel Fd.; Chairman UK National Cttee Jerusalem 3000; H. Vice-Pres. Zionist Fed. of Great Britain & Ireland, (Chairman 1990-94); Jt. H. Pres. British WIZO (Chairman 1981-87); Member JC Tr. Ltd., Ad.: c/o Hillel Foundation, 1/2 Endsleigh St., London WC1H 0DS. ☎ 0171-388 0801. Fax: 0171-916 3973.

KATZ, Sir Bernard, M.D., D.Sc., F.R.S.; b. March 26, 1911; Prof. and Head of Biophysics Dept., Univ. Coll., London (1952-78); Nobel Prize for Medicine (1970), V. President, Royal Society (1968-76); Asst. Dir. of Biophysics Res. Lond. Univ.; Res. Fel., Royal Soc. (1946-50) Reader in Physiology (1950-51). Publ.: Scientific writings. Ad.: University Coll., WC1E 8BT. ☎ 0171-387 7050.

KATZ, Dovid, B.A. (Columbia), Ph.D. (Lond.); b. New York, May 9, 1956; Founder of Yiddish Studies at Oxford University; Yiddish linguist and author. Director, Oxford Programme in Yiddish at the Oxford Centre for Postgraduate Hebrew Studies (1978-95); Director, Oxford Institute for Yiddish Studies (1994-97); Academic Director, East European Jewish Heritage Project (1997-). Publ.: Grammar of the Yiddish Language (1987); ed. Origins of the Yiddish Language (1987); ed. Dialects of the Yiddish Language (1988); ed. Oxford Yiddish (vol. 1, 1990; vol. 2, 1991; vol. 3, 1995); Klal-takones fun yidishn oysleyg [Code of Yiddish Spelling] (1992); Tikney takones: fragn fun yidisher stilistik [Amended Amendments: Issues in Yiddish Stylistics] (1993); founder and ed. Yiddish Pen (literary monthly) (1994-96); Yiddish fiction under pseudonym of Heersadovid Menkes: Edra Don (1992); Der flakher shpitz [The Flat Peak] (1993); Misnagdishe mayses fun vilner gubernye [Tales of the Misnagdim of Vilna Province] (1996). Awards: Israel Marshak Award in Modern Yiddish Literature,

Canadian Jewish Congress (1979); John Marshall Medal in Comparative Philology, University College London (1980); Sholem Aleichem Award for Literature, Tel Aviv (1988); Hirsh Rosenfeld Award for Yiddish Literature, Canadian Jewish Congress, Montreal (1994); Chaim Grade Award for Yiddish Literature, Congress for Jewish Culture, New York (1995); Zhitlovsky Award for Yiddish Literature, Zhitlovsky Foundation, New York (1996); Manger Prize in Yiddish Literature, Tel Aviv (1997). Ad.: 2 Bryn Aber, Fairy Glen Road, Capelulo, Gwynedd LL34 6YU. ☎/Fax 01492 622944.

KATZ, Milton, A.B., LL.D.; b. New York City, 1907; Dir. of Internat. Legal Studies and Henry L. Stimson Prof. of Law, Harvard Univ. (since 1954); Emer. Dist. Prof., Suffolk Univ. Law Sch (since 1979); Assoc. Dir., Ford Foundation (1951-54); form. USA Special Rep. in Europe, with rank of Amb. Extraordinary and Plenipotentiary; Chairman, Energy Adv. Crtee., Office of Technology Assessment US Congress (1972-82); Co.-Chairman, Amer. Bar Assn.NAmer. Assn. for Adv. of Science Com. on Science and Law (1978-82); Chairman, Bd. of Tr., Carnegie Endowment for Internat. Peace (197078); Tr., World Peace Foundation P. Citizens, Research Foundation; President, Amer Academy of Arts and Sciences, (1979-82); form. Dir., Nat. Conf of Christians and Jews; Tr., Chairman, Academic Affairs, Brandeis Univ., U.S Legion of Merit; Cmdr.'s Cross West German Order of Merit; Grande Ufficiale Italian Order of Merit. Publ.: Legal, political and foreign policy works. Ad.: 6 Berkeley St., Cambridge, Mass. 02138, USA.

KATZ, Rabbi Steven Anthony, B.A. (Hons.); b. London, Dec. 18, 1948; M., Hendon Ref. Syn., H. Sec. RSGB Assembly of Rabbis; Chaplain, Univ., Coll. Hospital, London. Ad.: Hendon Reform Synagogue, Danescroft Ave., NW4 2NA. ☎ 0181-203 4168.

KATZIR, (Katchalski) Professor Ephraim; b. Kiev, May 16, 1916; Fourth President, State of Israel (1973-78); Chief Scientist, Israel Def. Forces (1966-68); Prof, Weizmann Instit. of Science; Prof Emer., Tel Aviv Univ.; Foreign Member, Royal Society Lond.; Hon. Member, The Royal Institution of Great Britain (1989); Foreign Assoc. Nat. Acad. of Sciences USA; Foreign Hon. Member, Amer Acad. of Arts & Sciences. Many honorary doctorates, honours prizes, medals and awards. Publ.: Papers & reviews in scientific journals & books. Ad.: Weizmann Instit., Rehovot 76100, Israel. ☎ 972-8-9343947. Fax: 972-8-9468256.

KAUFMAN, Rt. Hon. Gerald Bernard, M.A., P.C., M.P.; b. Leeds, June 21, 1930; Journalist; Labour Party Parl. Cttee (1980-92); Opposition Spokesman for Foreign Affairs (1987-92); Member, Nat. Exec. Cttee. of the Labour Party (1991-1992), Chairman, House of Commons Nat. Heritage Cttee (1992-); Opp. Spokesman for Home Affairs (1983-87); form. Min. of State, Dept of Industry; Parl. Under-Sec., Industry; Parl. Under-Sec., Environment; M.P. (Lab.) for Ardwick (1970-83) for Gorton, Manchester (since 1983); Parl. Press Liaison Off, Labour Party (1965-70); Pol. Corr., New Statesman, (1964-65); Pol. Staff, Daily Mirror, (1955-64), Asst. Gen. Sec., Fabian Society (1954-55). Publ.: How to be a Minister, To Build the Promised Land, How to live under Labour (co-author), My Life in the Silver Screen, Inside the Promised Land, Meet me in St Louis, The Left (ed.), Renewal (ed). Ad.: 87 Charlbert Ct., Eamont St., NW8 7DA. ☎ 0171-219 5145. Fax: 0171-219 6825.

KAUFMANN, Georgia Louise, B.A., M.Sc., D.Phil; b. Edgware, Middx, Jan. 10, 1961; Dir. UKJAID (UK Jewish Aid & International Development) (1996-); Fellow of the Institute of Development Studies (IDS) at the University of Sussex (1992-95); Bell-MacArthur Fellow at Harvard Center for Population & Development Studies (1994-95). Ad.: UKJAID, 33 Seymour Place, London W1H 6AT. ☎ 0171-723 3442. Fax 0171-723 3445. Email: ukjaid@ort.org

KAY, Rabbi Sidney, b. Manchester, Oct. 25, 1920; M., Southport New Syn. (1976-84), Emer. Rabbi (since 1985). Ad.: 4 Westhill, Lord St. West, Southport, PR8 2BJ. ☎ 01704 541344. Fax: 01704-541344.

KEMPNER, Mrs. Sheila (née Goldstein); b. London, May 22, 1933; Chairman BoD Women's Issues Action Gp. (1995-); Hon. Sec. Int. Council of Jewish Women; Memb. Thames Customer Service Cttee OFWAT (1993-96); form. President, League of Jewish Women's; V. Chairman, Hillingdon Com. Health C. (1974-82); Member Hillingdon Dist. Health Auth. (1983-87); Member, Women's Nat. Com. (1990-94). Ad.: 11 Water Gdns., Gordon Ave., Stanmore, Middx. HA7 3QE. ☎ 0181-954 9986.
KERSHEN, Anne Jacqueline (née Rothenberg), B.A., M.Phil., F.R.S.A.; b. London, June 8, 1942; Historian; Barnett Shine Res. Fell. Queen Mary & Westfield Coll. Univ. of London (1990-); Director Centre for the Study of Migration, QMW (1994-); Memb. Faculty Leo Baeck Coll. (1992-); Memb. C. J.H.S.E.; Council Memb Jewish Museum; Curator London Museum Jewish Life, (1988-89); Publ.: Uniting the Tailors (1995); 150 years progressive Judaism (ed.) (1990); Off-the-peg: Story Women's Wholesale Clothing industry (ed.) (1988); Trade unionism amongst Jewish Tailors in London, 1872-1915 (1988), (with Jonathan Romain) Tradition and Change, the history of Reform Judaism in Britain, 1840-1995 (1995). Ad.: Dept. of Political Studies, Queen Mary & Westfield College, Mile End Rd., E1 4NS. ☎ 0171-975 5003.
KESSLER, David Francis, O.B.E., B.A.; b. Pretoria, June 6, 1906; Form. Chairman, Jewish Chronicle Ltd.; Fdr. and form. Chairman, Vallentine, Mitchell & Co., Ltd.; C., A.J A., C., Council of Christians and Jews; H. President; CBF-WJR; Hon. Pres. Soc for the Study of Ethiopian Jewry; Major, Royal Artillery, seconded Iraq Levies (1942-44); Political Warfare Exec. (1944-45); Brit. Econ. Mission to Greece (1946). Publ.: The Falashas; The Rothschilds and Disraeli in Buckinghamshire. Ad.: Lovetts, Bragenham Side, Stoke Hammond, Bucks., MK17 9DB. ☎ 01525270/210.
KESTENBAUM, Jonathan, B.A. (Hons.), M.A., M.B.A.; b. Tokyo, Japan, Aug. 5, 1959; Chief Exec. UJIA; Ex. Dir. Office of the Chief Rabbi; Mazkir, Bnei Akiva London (1982-83); IDF, Outstanding Soldier Award (1983); Jerusalem Fellows Researcher (1985-87). Ad.: Balfour House, 741 High Rd., Finchley N12 0BQ.
KING, Oona, M.P.; b. Sheffield, Oct. 22, 1967; m. Tiberio Santomarco; M.P. for Bow & Poplar (Lab.) (1997-). Ad.: House of Commons, SW1A 1AA.
KING-HAMILTON, His Honour Myer Alan Barry, Q.C., M.A.; b. London, Dec. 9, 1904; Additional Judge, Central Criminal Court (1964-79); Chairman, Jt. Standing Cttee. of R.S.G.B and ULPS; President, West Lond. Syn. (1977-83 and 1965-72), Hon. Life President (1994-); President, Maccabaeans (1967-75); Leader Oxford Circuit (1961-64); Recorder of Wolverhampton (1961-64), Gloucester (1956-61), Hereford (1955-56); Dep. Chairman. Oxford Qrt. Sessions (1956-64); Bencher, Middle Temple (1961); V. President, World Cong. of Faiths (since 1970); President, Westlon Hsg. Assn. (1970-95), Hon. Life President (1995); London J.; Hsg. Cttee. (1975-); President, Birnbeck Hsg. Assoc. (1995-); Chairman, Pornography and Violence Research Trust (form. Mary Whitehouse, etc.) (1986-96); Master, Worshipful Comp. of Needlemakers (1969-70); form. President, Cambridge Union Soc.; Squadron Leader R.A.F. Publ.: And Nothing But The Truth (autobiog.) Ad.: 33 Seymour Place, W1H 6AP.
KINGSLAND, Sir Richard, A.O., C.B.E., D.F.C.; b. Moree, New South Wales, Australia, Oct. 19, 1916; President Barnardos Canberra (1995-); Dir. Sir Edward Dunlop Medical Res. Fd. (1995-); Chairman, A.C.T. Health Promotion Fund (1990-94); Tr., Canberra Festival (1988-92); Sec., Australian Veterans Affairs Dept. (1970-81); Chairman, Repatriation Com. (1970-81); Sec., Interior Dept. (1963-70); Nat. Dir., Australian Bicentennial Auth. (1983-89); President, Man. Bd., Goodwin Retirement Villages (1984-88); Nat. C., Australian Opera (1983-96); Chairman, Uranium Adv. C. (1982-84); H. Nat. Sec., Nat. Heart Foundation (1976-90); Member at Large since 1990; form. Chairman, Commonwealth Films Review Bd.; First Chairman, C., Canberra Sch. of Art (1975-84); First Chairman, A.C.T. Arts Development Bd. (1981-84); Tr.,

Australian War Memorial (1966-76); Man. Sydney Airport (1948-49); Dir.-Gen., Org., R.A.A.F. Hq. (1946-48); Dir., R.A.A.F. Intelligence (1944-45); Cdr., R.A.A.F. Base, Rathmines, N.S.W. (1942-43); Cdr., No. 11 Sqdn. R.A.A.F. Papua New Guinea (1941-42); No. 10 Sqdn. R.A.A.F., Brit. (1939-41). Ad.: 36 Vasey Cresc., Campbell, A.C.T. 2612, Australia. ☎ (06) 2478502.

KISSIN, Baron, of Camden, Life Peer (Harry Kissin), LL.D., F.R.S.A.; b. Danzig, Aug. 23, 1912; L.P, Guinness Peat Group plc.; (Chairman, 1972-79); Life President, Lewis & Peat Hldgs. (Chairman 1982-87); Chairman Lewis & Peat Ltd. (1961-72); Dir., Tycon S.P.A. (Italy 1975-95); Chairman, Instit. of Contemporary Arts (1968-75); Dir., Royal Opera House (1972-84) Mem. Royal Opera House Tr. (1974-87, Chairman 1974-80); Bd. Govs., Hebrew Univ., Jerusalem (1980-); Gov. Bezalel Academy of Art & Design (1975-89); Cdr., Ordem Nacional Do Cruzeiro Do Sol (Brazil); Chevalier, Legion d'Honneur (France). Ad.: House of Lords, SW1A 0PW.

KLAUSNER, Menny; b. Frankfurt, Sept. 19, 1926; Comp. Dir.; Chairman, Mizrachi–Hapoel Hamizrachi Fed., UK & Ireland; Chairman, Israel Cttee., BoD; CoChairman, Nat. Z.C.; President, Hendon Adath Yisroel Cong.; T., N.W. Lond. Com. Mikva, T., Mifal Hatora Med. Aid Fund; Gov., Hasmonean Prep. Sch., Hendon; Chairman, Frs. of Ariel Instits., Israel; Netiv Meir Sch., Jerusalem; Actions Cttee., WZO, Adv. Bd., Torah Dept. Youth Aff. Com., World Mizrachi Exec.; Chairman, Mizrachi Fed. (1972-76); V. Chairman & T., Jewish Review, (1966-71); V.Chairman, Tora Vavoda (1948-52). Ad.: 1 Edgeworth Ave., NW4 4EX. ☎ 0181-202 9220, 0171-286 9141.

KLUG, Sir Aaron, O.M., Sc.D., P.R.S.; b. Aug. 11, 1926, m. Liebe (née Bobrow); Nobel Prize for chemistry (1982); Med. Res. C. Laboratory of Molecular Biology, Cambridge; Hon. Fel., Peterhouse, Cambridge; form. Nuffield Fel., Birkbeck Col., Lond.; Lect., Cambridge Univ., Cape Town Univ. Publ.: Papers in scientific journals. Ad.: Peterhouse, Cambridge, CB2 1RT.

KNAPP, Alexander Victor, M.A.(Hons.), Mus.B.(Cantab), Hon. A.R.A.M., L.R.A.M., A.R.C.M., Churchill Fellow; b. London, May 13, 1945; m. Caroline; Joe Loss Lecturer in Jewish Music, City University, London; Vis. Scholar Wolfson College, Cambridge (1983-86); Assistant Dir. of Studies, Royal College of Music, London (1977-83). Publ.: Four Sephardi Songs (1993). Ad.: Music Department, City University, Northampton Square, London EC1V 0HB. ☎ 0171-477 8283. Fax 0171-477 8576. Email a.v.knapp@city.ac.uk

KNOBIL, Henry Eric, F.T.I.; b. Vienna, Nov. 27, 1932; Chairman British-Israel Chamber of Commerce; Chairman, Bd. Gov. Immanuel Coll.; Tr., JEDT; Gov., Shenkar Coll.; Bd. Govs., Carmel Coll. (1980-87). Ad.: Flat 3, 1 Hyde Park St., W2 2JW. ☎ 0171-402 3065.

KNORPEL, Henry, C.B., Q.C., B.C.L., M.A. (Oxon).; b. London, Aug. 18, 1924; Barrister; Bencher, Inner Temple; Counsel to the Speaker, House of Commons (1985-95); Solicitor to D.H.S.S. (1978-85); Princ. Asst. Solicitor (1971-78). Ad.: Conway, 32 Sunnybank, Woodcote Grn., Epsom, Surrey KT18 7DX. ☎ 01372 721394

KOCHAN, Lionel, B.A., M.A. (Cantab), Ph.D. (Lond.), F.R. Hist. Soc.; b. London, Aug. 20, 1922; Bearsted Reader in Jewish Hist., Warwick Univ. (1968-87); form. Reader, Mod. Hist., East Anglia Univ.; P, Jew Hist. Soc. (1980-82). Publ.: Russia and Weimar Republic, Pogrom - November 10, 1938, Making of Modern Russia, Struggle for Germany 1914-45, The Jews in Soviet Russia Since 1917 (ed.), The Jew and His History, Jews Idols and Messiahs - The Challenge from History (1990), The Jewish Renaissance and some of its discontents (1992), Beyond the graven image. Ad.: 237 Woodstock Rd., Oxford OX2 7AD. ☎ 01865 558435

KOCHMANN, Max Michael, J.P.; b. Berlin, May 17, 1921; Chairman, Pafra Ltd. Chairman, Basildon Hebrew Cong.; Chairman, Leo Baeck Housing Association; Chairman, Basildon & District Local Enterprise Agent; Chairman, London Support Group, Centre for German-Jewish Studies, University of Sussex;

Chairman, Chevra Kadisha & Hon. Treas. Belsize Square Synagogue; Life President, British Adhesives & Sealant Association; Chairman, Association of Jewish Refugees (1994-95); Chairman, Otto Schiff Housing Association F(1995); President, Bnai Brith Leo Baeck (London) Lodge (1975-77). Ad.: 3 Furlongs, Basildon, Essex, SS16 4BW. ☎ 01268 524947. Fax: 01268-271358.

KOPELOWITZ, Lionel, M. A. (Cantab.), M.R.C.S. L.R.C.P., M.R.C.G.P., J.P.; b. Newcastle upon Tyne, Dec. 9, 1926; President, BoD (1985-91); V. President, Trades Adv. C.; V. President, Conf J. Material claims against Germany; Exec. Ctte. Member, Member F. J. Culture; Member, Gen. Med. C. (1984-94); C., BMA (1982-94); Fel. (1980); President, WJC Europe (1988-90), World Exec. WJC (1986); C., AJA; President, Nat. C., Soviet Jewry (1985-91); President, Rep. C., Newc. Jewry (1967-73); First President, United Hebrew Cong. Newc. (1973-76); Life President, (President 1964-74) Newc. JWB, H.V. President, Tyneside CCJ; Chairman, Newc. Med. Cttee., (1980-86); Family Prac. Cttee. (1979-85); President, Soc. Family Prac. Cttees. (1978-79); President, Cttee., B.M.A Deputising Services; Gen. Optical C. (1979-94); V. President, British Friends Shaare Zedek Hospital Medical Centre; President, Old Cliftonian Soc. (1991-); Council, United Synagogue (1991-96); Chairman, St. Marylebone Division BMA (1992-) Member Bd. Gov., Clifton College, Bristol; Mem. C., Royal Coll. General Practitioners (1995-). Ad.: 10 Cumberland House, Clifton Gardens, W9 1DX. ☎ 0171-289 6375.

KOPS, Bernard; b. London, 1926; Writer; C., Day Lewis Fellowship (1980-83). Pub.: Yes; From No Man's Land, The Dissent of Dominick Shapiro, By the Waters of Whitechapel, The Passionate Past of Gloria Gaye, Settle Down Simon Katz, Partners, On Margate Sands (novels), Collected Plays, The Hamlet of Stepney Green (play), Erica I Want to Read You Something, For the Record (poetry), Barricades In West Hampstead (poetry), The World is a Wedding (auto- biography), Neither Your Honey Nor Your Sting (history), Playing Sinatra (play), Dreams of Anne Frank (play), Green Rabbi (play), Cafe Zeitgeist (play), etc. Ad.: Flat 1, Maisemore Mans., 35 Canfield Gdns., NW6 3JN. ☎ 0171-624 2940.

KORNBERG, Sir Hans (Leo), M.A., D.Sc. (Oxon) Sc.D. (Cantab), Hon. Sc.D. (Cincinnati), Hon. D.Sc. (Warwick, Leicester, Sheffield, Bath, Strathclyde, Leeds), Hon. D.U. (Essex), Dr. Med., h.c. (Leipzig), Ph.D. (Sheffield), F.R.S., Hon. F.R.C.P. F.l.Biol., F.R.S.A.; b. Herford, Germany, Jan. 14, 1928; Sir W. Dunn Prof of Biochemistry, Cambridge Univ. (1974-95); Master, Christ's Coll. Cambridge (1982-95); H.Fel., Worcester Coll., Brasenose Coll., Oxford, Wolfson Coll., Cambridge; Member, German Acad. Sciences 'Leopoldina', For. Assoc., Nat. Acad. Sci., US; For. H. Member, Amer. Acad. Arts & Sciences; H. Member, Amer. Soc. Biochem. & Mol. Biol.; Japanese Biochem. Soc., German Soc. Biol. Chem. (Warburg Medallist); Fel., Amer. Acad. Microbiol.; Mem. Academia Europea; form. Member American Philosophical Soc.; Hon. Mem. Phi Beta Kappa; Prof. of Biochemistry, Leicester Univ. (1960-75); President, Brit. Assn. Adv. Sci. (1984-85); Academic Gov., Hebr. Univ.; Sci. Gov., Weizmann Inst.; Tr., Nuffield Foundation (1973-93); Gov., Wellcome Trust (1990-95); Gov., Lister Inst. Prev. Med.; Chairman, Royal Comm. on Environmental Pollution (1976-81); Member, (1990-95) Agric. & Food. Res. C. (1981-84); Member Priorities Bd., Res. & Development in Agric. (1984-90); Adv. C., Applied Res. & Development(1982-85), Chairman, Brit. Nat. Cttee. for Problems of Environment (1982-87); P. Internat. Union of Biochem. & Mol. Biol. (1991-1994); President, Biochemical Soc. (1990-95); Ch, Adv. Cttee. on Genetic Modification (1986-95); Dir., UK. Nirex Ltd (1986-95); Chairman, Kurt Hahn Trust (U. of Camb.) (1990-95); Member, Science Res. C. (1967-72) and Chairman, Science Bd. (1969-72). Publ.: Scientific writings. Ad.: The University Professors, Boston University, 745 Commonwealth Ave., Boston, MA 02215. Fax (617) 353-5084.

KOSMIN, Barry A., B.A., M.A., D.Phil.; b. London, Oct. 11, 1946; m. Helen;

Professor of Sociology; Exec. Dir. Research Unit, Board of Deputies of British Jews (1974-86); Fellow, Institute for Advanced Studies, Hebrew University (1980-81); Founding Dir., North American Jewish Data Bank, The Graduate School and University Center of The City University of New York (1986-96); Dir. of Research, Council of Jewish Federations, NY (1986-96); Dir. CUNY National Survey of Religious Identification (1989); Dir. CJF 1990 National Jewish Population Survey (1990). Publ.: Majuta: A History of the Jews in Zimbabwe (1981); British Jewry in the Eighties: A Statistical and Geographical Guide (1986); Highlights of the CJF 1990 National Jewish Research Population Survey (with S. Goldstein, J. Waksberg, N. Lerer, and A. Keysar) (1991); Contemporary Jewish Philanthropy in America (Joint editor with P. Ritterband (1991); One Nation Under God: Religion in Contemporary American Society (with S. Lachman) (1993). Ad.: Director of Research, JPR, Institute for Jewish Policy Research, 79 Wimpole Street, London W1M 7DD.

KOSSOWSKY, Rabbi Zalman, M.Ed., Ph.D.; b. Teheran, Dec. 15, 1940; Rabbi Israelitische Cultusgemeinde, Zurich; form. Rabbi, Kenton Syn. (1986-91); Chaplain, US Naval Reserve; Rabbi, Sydenham Highlands N. Hebrew Cong., Johannesburg (1978-86); Admin., Colorado Kosher Meats, Colorado Springs, US (1974-78), Rabbi, Young Israel, Greater Miami Florida (1972-74); Assoc. Dean, Talmudic Res. Instit., Colorado (1967-72). Publ.: Prayer Book for Friday Evening and Festivals, Prayer Book for the House of Mourning, The Modern Kosher Home. Ad.: Lavaterstrasse 33, Zürich CH-8002 Zürich, Switzerland. ☎ 201 1659. Fax: 202 2287.

KRAIS, Anthony; b. Lond., May 3, 1938; Dir. Special Projects, Jewish Care; Exec. Director, Jewish Blind Soc. (1980-89); Member, Exec. of European Council of Jewish Communities; Bd. Association for the Blind in Israel assisted by Guide Dogs; Tr., Chairman British Frs. Jaffa Inst.; British Friends, Israel Guide Dog Centre for the Blind; Fdr. Member and form. Chairman, Voluntary Movement Group; Memb. Independent Tribunal Service. Ad.: 14 Mayflower Lodge, Regents Park Rd., London N3 3HU ☎ 0181-349 0337.

KRAUSZ, Ernest, M.Sc., Ph.D.; b. Romania, Aug. 13, 1931; Rector, Bar-Ilan Univ. (1986-89), Prof. of Soc. (Dean, Soc. Sci. Faculty (1973-76) Bar-Ilan Univ.; Reader in Sociology, City Univ. Lond. (1971-72); Vis. Prof, Dept. of Social Studies, Newcastle Univ. (1976-77); L.S.E. (1981-82); C., Higher Educ, Israel (1979-81), Planning and Grants Cttee. C. Higher Educ. (1990-96); Mem.C. Israel Science Fd. (1994-); Edr., Studies of Israeli Society (1979-); Dir., Sociological Instit. for Community Studies, Bar-Ilan Univ. Publs.: Leeds Jewry, Sociology in Britain, Jews in a London Suburb, Ethnic Minorities in Britain, Key Variables in Social Research, Social Research Design, On Ethnic and Religious Diversity in Israel, Sociological Research - A Philosophy of Science Perspective, Co-ed. Sociological Papers (1992-). Ad.: Dept. of Sociology Bar-Ilan Univ., Ramat Gan 52900, Israel. ☎ (03) 5344449. Fax: (03) 6350995.

KRITZ, Simon Gedaliah, b. Lond., Sept. 17, 1919; Gen. Sec., Mizrachi Fed. Reg., Midrashah Instit. for Israel Studies Asst. Edr., Jewish Review; Sec., Frs. of Mifal Hatorah; Sec., Mizrachi Palestine Fund Charitable Tr., Sec., Brit. Frs. of Ariel; Gen. Sec., Nat. Z. C.; W., Willesden & Brondesbury Syn., Exec. & C., US; form. Fin. Rep., Willesden Syn.; Central Jewish Lect. & Information Cttee., BoD. Ad.:

KUPFERMANN, Jeannette Anne, B.A. (Hons.), M.Phil. Anthropology, (née Weitz); b. Woking, March 28, 1941; Anthropologist, Feature writer for The Sunday Times, Broadcaster Columnist, The Daily Telegraph, TV Critic, Daily Mail, TV writer: The Quest for Beauty (Channel 4); Everyman Film on Edith Stein (B.B.C.). Publ.: The Mistaken Body, When the Crying's Done: A Journey through Widowhood. Ad.: c/o Sunday Times, 1 Pennington St, E1.

KUSHNER, Tony, Ph.D.; b. Manchester, May 30, 1960; University Lecturer; Marcus Sieff Senior Lecturer, Dept of History, and Director Centre for the Study of Jewish/Non-Jewish Relations Parkes Library University of Southampton;

Historian at Manchester Jewish Museum (1985-86); Member of C., JHSE, Convenor, Working Party on Jewish Archives in the UK; Tr., Anne Frank Educ. Trust, UK; Tr. Searchlight Educ. Trust, UK. Publ.: The Persistence of Prejudice: Antisemitism in British Society During the Second World War, (1989), (jt. ed.,) Traditions of Intolerance, (1989); (jt. ed.,) The Politics of Marginality, (1990); Jewish Heritage in British History: Englishness and Jewishness, (1992); (ed.); (jt. ed.) The Internment of Aliens in Twentieth Century Britain (1993); The Holocaust and the Liberal Imagination (1994). Ad.: Dept. of History, The University, Southampton SO17 1BJ. ☎ 01703-592211

KUSTOW, Michael David, b. London Nov. 18, 1939; Writer, Theatre Dir.; Literary Dir., Amer. Repertory Theatre (1980-82); Associate Dir., Nat. Theatre (1975-80), Dir., Instit. of Contemporary Arts (1968-71); Publ.: Tank, an Autobiographical Fiction. Ad.: c/o Tim Corrie, The Chambers, Chelsea Harbour, Lots Rd., London SW10 0XF.

LACHS, Judge Henry Lazarus, M.A., LL.B. (Cantab.); b. Lond., Dec. 31, 1927; Circuit Judge; President, L'pool Yeshiva; form. Crown Court Recorder; Regional Chairman, Merseyside Mental Health Review Tribunal. Ad.: 41 Menlove Gdns. West, Liverpool, L18 2ET. ☎ 0151-722 5936.

LAMM, Rabbi Norman, Ph.D.; b. Brooklyn, N.Y., Dec. 19, 1927; President, Yeshiva Univ. & President, Rabbi Isaac Elchanan Theol. Semin., New York (since 1976); Erna and Jakob Michael Prof of Jewish Philosophy, Yeshiva Univ. (since 1966); Fdr. Edr., Tradition; Edr., The Library of Jewish Law and Ethics (14 vols.); Rabbi, Cong. Kodimoh, Springfield, Mass. (1954-58); Rabbi Jewish Centre, New York (1958-76). Publ. A Hedge of Roses, The Royal Reach; Faith and Doubt, Torah Lishmah, The Good Society, Torah Umadda and Halakhot ve'Halikhot. Ad.: Yeshiva Univ., 500 W. 185th St., New York, N.Y. 10033. ☎ (212) 960 5280.

LANDAU, Frederic Moses, LL.B.; b. London, Jan. 19, 1905, Barrister, Law & Parl. Cttee., BoD; Elder, US; Exec., JMC. Publ.: Legal writings. Ad.: 5 Langford Cl., NW8 0LN. ☎ 0171-328 1145.

LANGDON, Harold S., B.Com; b. Lond. April 22, 1916; Economist; Chairman, Public Rel. Cttee. (1979-85), BoD; Exec., BoD (1974-91); Life Gov. (Chairman, 1975-78) Leo Baeck Coll.; Chairman, RSGB (1967-70); North Western Reform Syn. (1960-61). Publ.: Contr., A Genuine Search (ed. Dow Marmur). Ad.: 24 Hoop Lane, NW11 8BU.

de LANGE, Rabbi Nicholas, R.M. M.A., D. Phil.; b. Nottingham, Aug. 7, 1944; Reader in Hebrew & Jewish Studies, Cambridge Univ; C., Jewish Hist. Soc. of England; Fel., Wolfson Coll., Cambridge. Publ.: Judaism, Apocrypha Jewish Literature of the Hellenistic Age, Atlas of the Jewish World, various specialised works and literary translations. Ad.: Faculty of Divinity, St John's Street, Cambridge CB2 1TW. ☎ 01223 332597. Fax 01223 332582.

LAPPIN, Elena, b. Moscow, Dec. 16, 1954; form. Editor, "Jewish Quarterly". Freelance editor & author, New York (1990-94); English (ESL) insutructor, Technion, Haifa, Israel (1986-90). Publ.: Jewish Voices, German Words: Growing up Jewish in Postwar Germany and Austria 1(994), Daylight in Nightclub Inferno: new fiction from the post-Kundera Generation (1997). Ad.:

LAQUEUR, Walter; b. Breslau, May 26, 1921; Co-Dir., Wiener Library (1964-1992); Edr., Journal of Contemporary History; Chairman, Research C., Centre for Strategic and International Studies, Washington, USA.; Several honorary degrees. Publ.: Communism and Nationalism in the Middle East, Young Germany, Russia and Germany, The Road to War - 1967, Europe since Hitler, A History of Zionism. etc. Ad.: CSlS, 1800 K St., Washington D.C. 20006, USA. Fax: (202) 686-0048.

LASKY, Melvin J., M.A.; b. New York, Jan. 15, 1920; Co-Edr., Encounter Magazine (Lond.) (since 1958); Edr., Dir., Library Press, New York; Publ., Alcove Press Lond.; Edr. & Publ., Der Monat (Berlin); Dist. Alumnus Award,

New York City Univ. (1978); Michigan Univ. Sesquicentennial Award (1967); US Combat Historian, France & Gemany (1944-45). Publ.: Utopia and Revolution, Festschrift for Raymond Aron, Sprache und Politik, New Paths in American History, The Hungarian Revolution (ed.), Africa for Beginners. Ad.: Encounter, 59 St Martins La., WC2N 4JS. ☎ 0171-836 4194.

LAUTERPACHT, Elihu, C.B.E., Q.C., M.A., LL.B.; b. London, July 13, 1928; Fel., Trinity Coll., Cambridge; Hon. Prof. International Law; Reader, Internat. Law (1980-88); Dir., Res. Centre for Internat. Law, Cambridge Univ. (1983-95); Chairman, East African Common Market Tribunal (1972-75); Dir. of Research, Hague Academy of Internat. Law (1959-60); Legal Adv. to Australian Dept. of Foreign Affairs (1975-77); Consultant, Central Policy Review Staff (1978-80; 1972-74); President, World Bank Admin. Tribunal; Chairman, Asian Development Bank Admin. Tribunal(1993-95); Judge ad hoc, Int. Court of Justice (1993-); Chairman, Dispute Settlement Panel, US-Canada NAFTA (1996), US-Mexico (1997-), US-Costa Rica (1997-); Member Institut de Droit International; Bencher, Gray's Inn (1983); H. Fel., Hebrew Univ. of Jerusalem, 1989; H. Member, Amer. Soc. of Internat. Law, (1993). Publ.: Aspects of the Administration of International Justice (1991); Jerusalem and the Holy Places (1968), The Development of the Law of International Organisations; Ed. International Law Reports. Ad.: Research Centre for Internat. Law, 5 Cranmer Road, Cambridge CB3 9BP. ☎ 01223 335358. Fax: 01223-300406.

LAWRENCE, Sir Ivan, M.A. (Oxon.), Q.C.; b. Brighton, Dec. 24, 1936; barrister; M.P. (C.) for Burton (1974-97); Knighted for political services (1992); Bencher, Inner Temple (1990)' Recorder of the Crown Courts (1983); form. Chairman, HoC Home Affairs Select Cttee; Chairman, Conservative Parlt. Legal Cttee; Chairman, Conservative Parlt. Home Affairs Cttee; Chairman, Joint All-Party Barristers Gp; Vice-Chairman Conservative Friends of Israel; Sec. All-Party Parlt. Cttee for Release of Soviet Jewry; Vice Chairman European Inter-Parl. Cttee for Soviet Jewry; Mem. of Policy Planning Gp. of IJA; Tr. Parlt. Cttee for East European Jewry; Mem. of Parlt. War Crimes Cttee; Chairman, Exec. of Commonwealth Parlt. Assoc.; Mem. of BoD; Mem. Exec. Cttee of Inter-Parlt. Council Against Anti-Semitism; Tr. of Holocaust Educational Trust; Mem. of Commonwealth Jewish Council. Ad.: Dunally Cottage, Walton Lane, Shepperton, Middx. TW17 2J.H.

LAWTON, Clive Allen, B.A., M.A., M.Ed., Cert. Ed., A.D.B. (Ed.); b. London, July 14, 1951; Educ. and organisational consultant; form. Ch. Exec. Jewish Continuity (1993-96); form. Dep. Dir., Liverpool City Local Educ. Auth.; RE Consultant, Liverpool City Educ. Auth.; Member RS Cttee., School's Examination and Assessment Council (SEAC); form. Exec., AJY; Chairman, Shap Working Party on World Rels. in Educ.; Edr., Shap Calendar of World Rel. Festivals; Fdr., Limmud Conf; form. HM, King David High Sch., L'pool; Exec. Dir., Central Jewish Lect. & Information Cttee. & Educ. Off, BoD; Coordinator, Vietnam Working Party; Educ. Off., Yad Vashem Cttee., Exec. C. CCJ; form. V. Chairman, IUJF. Publ.: The Jewish People – Some Questions Answered, The Seder Handbook, I am a Jew, Passport to Israel, Religion Through Festivals; Celebrating Cultures: Islam; Ethics in Six Traditions. Ad.: 363 Alexandra Rd., London N10 2ET. Email: clive@calawton.demon.co.uk

LEDERBERG, Joshua, B.A., Ph.D., Litt.D., M.D.(h.c.), Sc.D.(h.c.), Sc.D.(h.c.) Tel Aviv Univ. (1991); b. New Jersey, May 23, 1925; Prof., Rockefeller U. (1990-); President, The Rockefeller Univ.; Prof., Stanford U. (1959-78); Nobel Prize for Medicine (1958); US Nat. Medal of Science (1989); Gov. Bd., Weizmann Inst.; Tr., Sackler Med. Sch., Tel Aviv. Publ.: Scientific works. Ad.: The Rockefeller Univ., 1230 York Ave., New York, NY 10021 ☎ (212) 327 7809.

LEE, Arnold, b. London, Aug. 31, 1920; Solicitor; form. Chairman, Jews, Coll. Ad.: 47 Orchard Court, Portman Sq., W1H 9PD. ☎ 0171-486 8918.

LEE, John Robert Louis, b. Manchester, June 2, 1942; MP (Cons.), Pendle, (1983-

92) and for Nelson & Colne (1979-83); F.C.A., Fdn. Dir., Chancery Consolidated Ltd., Investment Bankers; Dir., Paterson Zochonis (UK) Ltd., (1975-76); V. Chairman NW Conciliation Cttee., Race Relations Bd. (1976-77); Political Sec. to Rt. Hon. Robert Carr, (1974); Chairman Council, Nat. Youth Bureau, (1980-83); Jt. Sec., Conservative Back Bench Industry Cttee., (1979-80); PPS to Minister of State for Industry (1981-83); to Sec.of State for Trade & Industry, (1983); Parly. Under Sec. of State MOD, (1983-86); Dept. of Employment, (1986-89); Minister for Tourism, (1987-89); Non-exec.; Chairman, Country Holidays Ltd. (1989); Non-exec. Dir., P. S. Turner (Holdings) Ltd (1989-); Non-exec. Dir., Paterson Zochonis, (1990-); Chairman, A.L.V.A. (1990-). Ad.:

LEGUM, Colin, b. South Africa, Jan. 3, 1919, m. Margaret née Roberts; Journalist, author, broadcaster, lect.; Edr., The Africa Contemporary Record; Assoc. Edr., The Middle East Contemporary Survey; Edr., Third World Reports; Assoc. Edr. and Commonwealth Corresp., The Observer, (1949-81); Gen. Sec., S.A. Lab. Party (1946-48); Edr. The Forward and Illustrated Bulletin (Johannesburg); Political Corr. Sunday Express (Johannesburg); Political Asst S.A. Zionist Fed.; Exec. Memb. Poale Zion (S.A.); S.A. Jewish BoD (1938-47);. Member of Johannesburg City C., (1941-47). Publ.: Books on Africa, Middle East and Third World. Ad.: Kob Cottage, 12 Harris Rd., Kalk Bay, Cape 7975, RSA. ☎/Fax: (012) 788 8455.

LEHMAN, Rabbi Israel Otto, M.A. B.Litt., D.Phil., F.R.A.S.; b. 1912; Adjunct Prof. of Jewish Studies, Miami Univ.; Assoc. Oxford Centre for PostGraduate Hebrew Studies; Hon. Fel. of the John F. Kennedy Library; form. Lect., Leo Baeck Coll.; Curator of Manuscripts Emer., Hebrew Union Coll., form. Assist. Keeper, Bodleian Library (1947-56); Fdr., Oxford B.B. Lodge, O.U.J.S. Library. Publ.: Translation of Chief Rabbi's Pentat. into Germ., 'Moses', (ed.), Handbook of Hebrew and Aramaic Manuscripts. etc. Ad.: 3101 Clifton Ave., Cincinnati, Ohio, USA. ☎ 45220-2488.

LEIBLER, Isi Joseph, A.O., (1989), C.B.E., (1977), B.A. (Hons.) (1957); D.Litt. (Hon.), Deakin University, (1990); b.Antwerp, Belgium Oct. 9, 1934; Chairman and Man. Dir., Jetset Tours Pty Ltd. (1965-); Chairman, Governing Bd World Jewish Congress (1995-), V.P World Jewish Congress (1988-1991); President, Asia Pacific Region, World Jewish Congress (1981-); Chairman, Asia Pacific Jewish Assoc. (1980-); Chairman, Australian Institute of Jewish Affairs (1983-), President, Exec. Council of Australian Jewry (1978-1980), (1982-1985), (1987-1989), (1992-95); Member Exec. and Gov. Bd., World Jewish Congress (1978-), Bd. of Gov., Memorial Foundation for Jewish Culture (1979-); Board of Gov., Tel Aviv University (1990-); Dir. and Member, Exec. Cttee., Conference on Jewish Claims Against Germany (1979-). Publ.: Soviet Jewry and Human Rights (1963) Soviet Jewry and the Australian Communist Party (1964), The Case for Israel (1972), The Contemporary Condition of World Jewry (1990), Jewish Religious Extremism: a Threat to the Future of the Jewish people. (1991), The Israel-Diaspora Identity Crisis: A looming disaster (1994). Ad.: 116 Kooyong Rd., Caulfield, Victoria, 3161, Australia. ☎ 98288520. Fax 98288555.

LEIGH, Rabbi Michael, M.A., D.D.; b. London, Nov. 12, 1928; M., Emer. Minister Edgware and Dist. Ref. Syn. (Minister 1963-93); form. Assoc. M., West Lond. Syn. (1958-63); Publ.: Jewish Observance in the Home. Ad.: 64 Lansdowne Rd., Stanmore, Middx. HA7 2SA. ☎ 0181-954 3415.

LERMAN, Antony, B.A. Hons.; b. London Mar. 11, 1946; Exec. Dir. Inst. for Jewish Policy Research, Jt. Ed., Patterns of Prejudice; Ed., JPR Reports; Chairman Jewish Council for Com. Relations (1992-94); Assist Ed., Survey of Jewish Affairs (1982-91); form. Ed., Jewish Quarterly (1985-86). Publ.: Ed., The Jewish Communities of the World (1989), Jt. Gen. Ed. Antisemitism World Report (1992-97) Ad.: 79 Wimpole Street, W1M 7DD. ☎ 0171-935 8266. Fax: 0171-935 3252.

LERNER, Max, A.B. (Yale), M.A., Ph.D.; b. Minsk, Russia, Dec. 20, 1902; author and journalist; form. Prof. of Pol Science, Williams Coll. and Sarah Lawrence Coll., Harvard Univ.; Prof of Amer. Civilisation & World Politics Brandeis Univ.; Welch Prof. of Amer Studies, Notre Dame Univ.; Prof. Graduate Sch. of Human Behaviour, San Diego (since 1974); Publ.: America as a Civilisation (also revised ed.), The Unfinished Country, The Age of Overkill, Education and a Radical Humanism, Ted and the Kennedy Legend: a Study in Character and Destiny, etc. Ad.: 25 East End Ave., New York 10028, USA.

LEVENBERG Schneier, Ph.D.; b. Kursk Russia; Consultant, Jewish Agency, UK, Member, World Z. Cttee. Presidium; Chairman, World Jewish Congress Internat. Affairs Cttee.; Jt. President, Z. Fed.; President, Labour Zionist Movement; Member Israel Cttee., BoD; historian of Jewry. Publ.: Future of Minorities' Rights, The Jews and Palestine; Encyclopaedia Judaica (Divisional Edr.) etc. Ad.: 741 High Rd., Finchley, N12 0BQ. ☎ 0181-446 1477.

LEVENE, Lord Peter, KBE; b. Pinner, Middlesex, December 8, 1941; Chairman & Chief Exec. Canary Wharf Ltd; Prime Minister's Adviser on Efficiency & Effectiveness; Deputy Chairman & Managing Dir. Wasserstein Perella & Co. Ltd; Alderman, City of London (Portsoken) (1984-); form. Managing Dir. United Scientific Holdings plc (1968-85); Chairman (1981-85); Chief of Defence Procurement, Ministry of Defence (1985-91); Chairman Docklands Light Railway Ltd. (1991-94). Ad.: One Canada Square, Canary Wharf, London E14 5AB. ☎ 0171-418 2250. Fax: 0171-418 2082.

LEVIN, Salmond S., O.B.E., LL.B.; b. Limerick, June 17, 1905; form. President, Nat. C., Shechita Bds.; form. President, Lond. Bd. of Shechita; Elder (President, 1977-81), US; Chairman, Lond. Bd. of Jewish Rel. Educ. (1954-68); form. Chairman Govs., J.F.S. (1958-68); Govs., J.F.S. School (1958-68); form. C., Jews, Coll.; form. Gen. Sec., JNF; form. President, Univ. Zionist Fed.; form. Chairman Inter-Faith Cttee. N.C.S.J.; Chairman InterFaith Cttee.; Nat. C., Soviet Jewry. Publ.: Century of Anglo-Jewish Life 1870-1970, Origins of the J.F.S., Story of a Congregation. Ad.: 72 Bridge Lane, NW11 0EJ. ☎ 0181-455 5685.

LEVITEN, Sara-Joy, B.A.; b. 1960; Dir., Youth and Students Division, Reform Synagogues of Great Britain; Nat. Org., FZY (1981-83); AJY Provincial Off. (1983-85); Dir., JPMP (now L'pool Jewish Resource Centre (1984-86); Admin., L'pool Rape Crisis (1987-88). Ad.: RSGB, The Sternberg Centre for Judaism, 80 East End Road, Finchley, N3 2SY.

LEVY, Rabbi Abraham, Knight Commander (Encomienda) Order of Civil Merit (Spain), B.A., Ph.D., F.J.C.; b. Gibraltar, July 16, 1939; m. Estelle; Com. Rabbi, Spiritual Head, S. & P. Cong., Lond.; M., Lauderdale Rd. Syn.; Jt. Eccl. Auth. BoD; Co-President, C.B.F., W.J.R.; Dep.P., Jews, Coll.; Dir., The Sephardi Centre form. Dir. Young Jewish Leadership Instit.; H. Princ., Naima Jewish Preparatory Sch.; Gov., Carmel Coll.; President, Union Anglo-Jewish Preachers (1973-75); V. President, AJA. Publ.: The Sephardim-A Problem of Survival; Ages of Man (jt. auth.). The Sephardim (jt. auth.). Ad.: 2 Ashworth Road, W9 1JY. ☎ 0171-289 2573. Fax: 0171-266 3682.

LEVY, David, B.A. (Com.), F.C.A., b. Manchester, June 27, 1942; Chart. Accountant; Dir , Brian Forbes Search & Selection; Chief Exec. Brideoak Associates, Financial Arbitration Services; Member, Worshipful Comp. of Chartered Accountants; Freeman, City of London. Ad.: 6, The Mews, Gatley, Cheadle, Cheshire SK8 4PS. ☎ 0161-428 7708/0161-477 2622 (Off.).

LEVY, Elkan David, B.A.(Hons.), M.H.L.; b. Preston, Lancs, March 29, 1943; m. Celia, née Fisher; Solicitor; President, United Synagogue (1996-); Chairman, Chief Rabbinate Council; Chairman, Beth Hamidrash Cttee.; Chairman, Ministerial Placement Cttee.; Chairman, Singers Prayer Book Publication Cttee.; Jt. Chairman, Stanmore Council of Christians and Jews; Mem., BoD (1991-); form. Minister, Belmont Synagogue (1969-73); Warden, Stanmore Synagogue

(1980-90); Chairman U.S. Burial Society (1992-96); Mem. United Synagogue Council (1980-92); Mem. London Board of Shechita (1986-96); Mem. Conference to appoint the Chief Rabbi (1989-91). Ad.: United Synagogue, Adler House, 735 Finchley Road, N12 0U. Email elkan.levy@easynet.co.uk

LEVY, Rabbi Emanuel, B.A., b. Manchester, July 31, 1948; M., Palmers Grn. & Southgate Syn.; Hon. Sec. Rabbinical Council of the United Synagogue; Fdn. Gov. JFS School; Memb. Borough of Enfield Educ. Cttee.; Form. Hon. Principal, Herzlia Jewish Day School, Westcliff-on-Sea; form. Rabbi, Southend & Westcliff Hebrew Cong.; Chief Rabbi's Cabinet, Reg. Affairs, to Chief Rabbi's Cabinet Education Portfolio; J. Rep. to Standing Advisory Council for Religious Education (SACRE) for Borough of Enfield: form. Chaplain to Mayor of Southend (1981-82, 1983-84); form. Rabbi, Langside Hebrew Cong., Glasgow; Rabbi, South Broughton Syn, Manchester; Chairman, Rabbinical Council of the Provinces (1986-88); F.P. Southend Community Relations Council, (1986-88). Ad.: 11, Morton Crescent, Southgate, London N14 7AH. ☎ 0181-882-2943.

LEVY, Rev. Isaac, O.B.E., TD., B.A., Ph.D. (Lond.); b. London, Sept. 14, 1910; form. Dir., JNF in Britain; form. M. Hampstead Syn., Hampstead Gdn. Suburb Syn. and Bayswater Syn.; form. Sr. Jewish Chaplain to H.M. Forces and Middle East Forces and Brit. Army of the Rhine, V.Pres. CCJ; Chaplain to Ajex. Publ.: Daiches Memorial Volume (jt Edr.), Guide to Passover, The Synagogue Its History and Function, Journeys of the Children of Israel, All About Israel, Now I Can Tell, Witness to Evil-Belsen 1945. Ad.: 25 Lyndale Ave., NW2 2QB. ☎ 0171-435 6803.

LEVY, Jack Morris, LL.B.; b. Manchester, Aug. 21, 1918; Solicitor; form. President, C. of Manch. & Salford Jews; BoD Ad.: 11 Cherrington Rd., Cheadle, Cheshire. ☎ 0161-428 2315.

LEVY, John David Ashley, B.A. (Hon.) Sociology; b. Lond., Sept. 10, 1947; Dir. Frs. of Israel Educ. Tr.; Dir., F.O.I. Consultants Ltd.; Exec. Dir., Academic Study Group on Israel & Middle East; Hon. Co-ord. UK Society for the Protection of Nature in Israel; form. Information Dir., Z. Fed.; Social Worker, Lond. Borough of Lambeth Ad.: 25 Lyndale Ave., NW2 2QB. ☎ 0171-435 6803. Fax 0171-794 0291. Email: foi_asg@msn.com

LEVY, Michael Abraham, F.C.A.; b. London, July 11, 1944; Comp. Chairman; President of Jewish Care; Hon. V. President JIA; Chairman Fd. for Education; Chairman Chief Rabbis Awards for Excellence; President JFS School; V. Chairman Central Council for Jewish Community Services; Member of Commission on Israel-Diaspora Relations; Patron of British Music Industry Awards; recipient of 1994 B'nai B'rith First Lodge Award; form. Member of the World Board of Gov. of the Jewish Agency - representing Great Britain; form. Chairman of the Youth Aliyah Cttee. of the Jewish Agency Board of Govs.; form. V. President, JIA; form. Nat. Campaign Chairman JIA; form. Chairman, JIA Kol Nidre Appeal; form. V. Chairman British Phonographic Industry; form. V. Chairman Phonographic Performance Limited. Ad.: Chase House, Nan Clarke's Lane, Mill Hill, London NW7 4HH. ☎ 0171-487 5394/5174. Fax 0171-486 7919.

LEVY, Lord Peter Lawrence, O.B.E., B.Sc., F.R.I.C.S.; b. Lond., Nov. 10, 1939; Chartered Surveyor; Chairman, Shaftesbury plc; Chairman IJPR; President, Akiva Sch.; Trustee and Tr. Jewish Youth Fund; Vice President Central Council; Tr., Frs. of Israel Educ. Tr.; V. President Cystic Fibrosis Tr.; V. President, London Federation of Boys Clubs, V. Chairman, JIA (1979-81); Chairman, Young Leadership JIA (1973-77); Professional Div. JIA (1977-79). Ad.: 52 Springfield Rd., NW8 0QN. ☎ 0171-624 4777. Fax: 0171-372 7424.

LEW, Jonathan Michael, B.Com., A.C.M.A.; b. London, Nov. 23, 1937; Accountant; Hon. Off., United Synagogue (1984-85); Chief Exec., United Synagogue (1986-). Ad.: Adler House, 735 High Road, N12 0US. ☎ 0181-343 8989.

LEWIN, Mrs. Sylvia Rose (née Goldschmidt), B.A.(Log.), (Rand); b. Johannesburg, Speech Therapist; H. President (Nat. President 1982-86, 1988) B'nai B'rith Distr 15 (Gt Brit & Ireland). Ad.: White Gables, 156 Totteridge Lane, N20 8JJ. ☎ 0181-446 0404. Fax: 0181-445 8732.
LEWIS, Bernard, B.A. Ph.D., F.B.A., F.R. Hist. S., Hon. Dr. (Hebrew Univ, Tel Aviv Univ., H.U.C., Univ. Pennsylvania, S.U.N.Y., Univ. Haifa, Yeshiva Univ., Brandeis, Bar-Ilan Univ.); b. London, May 31, 1916; Cleveland E. Dodge, Prof of Near Eastern Studies Princeton Univ. (1974-86), now Emer.; Mem. American Philosophical Soc.; American Academy of Arts & Sciences; Corr. Mem. Institut de France, Académie des Inscriptions et Belles-Lettres. Member, Instit. for Advanced Study, Princeton (1974-86); Prof. Near & Middle East Hist., Lond. Univ. (1949-74); Army (1940-41), attached to a Foreign Office dept. (1941-45). Publ.: The Jews of Islam; Semites and Anti-Semites; The Political Language of Islam; books on Turkish and Arabic Studies; Race and Slavery in the Middle East; Islam and the West; Cultures in Conflict; The Middle East: Two Thousand Years of History. Ad.: Near Eastern Studies Dept., 110 Jones Hall, Princeton University, Princeton, N.J., 08544, USA. ☎ (609) 258 5489. Fax: (609) 258 1242.
LEWIS, Ivan, b. Manchester, March 4, 1967; m. Juliette née Fox; M.P. (Lab.), Bury South (1997-); Chief Exec. Jewish Social Services, Greater Manchester (1992-97); Coordinator, Contact Community Care Group (1986-89). Ad.: House of Commons, London SW1A 0AA. ☎ 0171-219 6404.
LEWIS, Dr Julian Murray, b. Swansea, Sept. 26, 1951; M.P. (Con.), New Forest East (1997-); Historian, researcher and campaigner; Dep. Dir. Conservative Research Dept. (1990-96); Dir., Policy Research Associates (1985-); Research Dir. and Dir., Coalition for Peace Through Security (1981-85). Publ.: Changing Direction: British Military Planning for Post-War Strategic Defence, 1942-1947 (1988); Who's Left? An Index of Labour MPs and Left-wing Causes, 1985-1992 (1992); What's Liberal? Liberal Democrat Quotations and Facts (1996). Ad.: House of Commons, London SW1A 0AA. ☎ 0171-219 3000.
LICHFIELD, Nathaniel, B.Sc., Ph.D., F.R.I.C.S., C.Eng.; b. Lond., Feb. 29, 1916; Emer. Prof. of Economics of Environmental Planning, Lond. Univ.; Fdr. Partner, Nathaniel Lichfield & Part. (1962-92); Partner, Dalia & Nathaniel Associates Urban Planning (1992-); Vis. Prof. Hebrew Univ. (1980-); Nottingham Univ (1989-); Consultant to Mins., internat. orgs., cities in Britain and overseas. Publ.: Israel's New Towns: A strategy for their Future (with A. Berlert and Samuel Shaked), etc. Ad.: 13 Chalcot Gdns., Englands Lane, NW3 4YB. ☎ 0171-586 0461.
LIGHTMAN, Sir Gavin Anthony, b. London, Dec. 20, 1939; Justice of the High Court, Chancery Division; Q.C. (1980-94); Bencher of Lincolns Inn (1987); Deputy President of AJA (1986-92); Chairman of Education Cttee of AJA (1988-94); V. President, AJA (1994-); Chairman Education Cttee of Hillel (1992-94); Vice-President (1994-); Chairman, Legal Friends of Univ. Haifa (1986-); Patron Commonwealth J. Assoc. (1994-); The Hammerson Home (1995-); Chairman, The Bar Adv. Bd. of the College of Law (1996-). Publ.: (with G. Battersby) Cases and Statutes on the Law of Real Property (1965); (with G. Moss) Law of Receivers of Companies (1st ed. 1986, 2nd ed. 1994). Ad.: Royal Courts of Justice, Strand, London WC2 2LL. ☎ 0171-936 6671. Fax: 936 7379.
LIGHTMAN, Sidney, F.I.L.; b. Lond. Apr. 5, 1924; journalist, translator; Sec., British & European Machal Assoc.; form. (1981-89) Asst. Foreign Edr., Jewish Chronicle; form. (1966-89) Edr., Jewish Travel Guide. Ad.: 5 West Heath Ct., North End Rd., NW11 7RE. ☎ 0181-455 1673.
LINCOLN, Fredman Ashe, Q.C., M.A., B.C.L., G.C.St.J.; Capt., R.N.V.R., form. Recorder and Dep. Judge, Crown Court; Master of the Bench, Inner Temple; P. R.N.R. Officers Club, form. Member Exec., Bar Council; form. Master, Worshipful Company of Plaisterers; P. Masorti Assn.; V. President, Soc. for Jew

Study Tr., Brit. Maritime Charitable Tr.; National Chairman, Maritime Volunteers Service; form Tr., A.M.A.R.C.; form. V.Chairman and H.Sec., WJC (Brit. Section) and Chairman, Political Cttee.; V. President, Ajex; D.P., World Assn. of Jewish Lawyers and Jurists; First Naval Adviser to Govt. of Israel (Apr.-July, 1948). Publ.: Is Orthodoxy Worth While? The Starra, Secret Naval Investigator, Odyssey of a Jewish sailor, etc. Ad.: 9 Kings Bench Walk. Temple, EC4Y 7DX. ☎ 0171-353 7202.

LIPMAN, Maureen Diane (Mrs. Jack Rosenthal); b. Hull, May 10, 1946; Actress/Writer; One-woman show 'Live & Kidding', Duchess Theatre (1997). Publ.: How Was It For You?; Something To Fall Back On; You Got An 'Ology; Thank you for Having Me; When's It Coming Out?; You Can Read Me Like a Book. Ad.: c/o Anne Hutton, 200 Fulham Road, SW3. ☎ 0171-352 4825.

LITHMAN-IMBER, Mrs. Ethel; b. Lond.; P. (form. Nat. Chairman), Brit. Olim Relatives Assn.; Hadassah Medal for services to Israel (1967); Staff Off, Brit. Red Cross, Second World War; form. Cttee., Guild Jewish Journs.; form. Member, Norfolk County Council SACRE; President Norwich Hebrew Cong. (1997); V. President Norwich Synagogue (1996); Act. Chairman, Norwich CCJ. Publ.: The Man Who Wrote Hatikvah (intro. by Menachem Begin). Ad.: c/o BORA, Balfour House, 741 High Road, N12 0BQ. ☎ 01379-674400.

LIVINGSTON, Edward Colin, M.B., B.S. (Lond.), J.P.; b. London, Mar. 22 1925; Med. Prac.; Barrister; Ombudsman, Central C. for Jewish Community Services; P/T. Chairman, Soc Sec. Appeal Trib., Harrow; Chairman, Harrow Com. Tr; Liveryman. Soc. of Apothecaries; Freeman, City of Lond.; Flt./Lieut (Med. Br.) R.A.F.V.R. (1948-50); P/T.Chairman, Disability Appeal Tribunal, South East Region. Ad.: Wyck Cottage, Barrow Point La., Pinner, Middx. HA5 3DH. ☎ 0181-868 1973.

LOBENSTEIN, Josef H., M.B.E.; b. Hanover, Apr. 27, 1927; Mayor, London Borough of Hackney (1997); Hon. Freeman L. B. Hackney; President, Adath Yisroel Syn. and Burial Soc.; Chairman, N. London Jt. Liaison Cttee.; Vice-President; Union of Orth. Hebrew Cong and Chairman External Affairs Cttee; Exec. Kedassia Kashruth Cttee.; Exec., Agudath Israel World Org.; V. Chairman, Agudath Israel of Great Britain; Executive, National Shechita C.; V.Chairman, Hackney North Conservative Assn., North East Lond. Valuation Tribunal; Mem. City and Hackney Community Health C.; Mem. City and Hackney Community Health C.; form. Gen. Sec., Agudath Israel of Great Britain; Member, BoD; Tr. Jewish Secondary School Movement; Conservative Opposition Leader L. B. Hackney (1974-97); Councillor Metropolitan Borough of Stoke Newington (1962-65); President Hackney and Tower Hamlets Chamber of Commerce. Ad.: 27 Fairholt Rd., N16 5EW. ☎ 0181-800 4746. Fax: 0181-806 7799.

LOEWE, Raphael James, M.C., M.A. (Cantab.), F.S.A.; b. Calcutta, Apr. 16, 1919; form. Goldsmid Prof. of Hebrew (form. Dir., Instit. of Jewish Studies), Univ. Coll., Lond.; form. S. A. Cook ByeFellow, Caius Coll., Cambridge; form. Lect. in Hebrew, Leeds Univ.; Vis. Prof in Judaica, Brown Univ. Providence, R.I. (1963-64); C. (form. P.), JHSE; C., Soc. for Jew Study; Cttee., Lond. Soc. of Jews and Christians; form. Elder and Warden, Span. & Port. Jews, Cong., Lond.; War service, Suffolk Regt., Royal Armoured Corps. Publ.: Women in Judaism, Omar Khayyam (Hebr.), The Rylands Sephardi Haggadah, Ibn Gabirol, etc. Ad.: 50 Gurney Dr., N2 0DE. ☎ 0181-455 5379.

LOWENTHAL, Ernst Gottfried, Dr.; b. Cologne, Dec. 28, 1904; Journalist; H. Prof, West Berlin Senate (1985); Dr.Leopold-Lucas Prize, Tuebingen Univ. (1986); Conference on Jewish Material Claims against Germany (1953-62); Head of Dept., Jewish Trust Corp. for Germany (1951-53); Dir. of Div., Jewish Restitution Successor Org. and Jewish Cultural Reconstruction, inc. (1949-51); Field Dir., Gemmany, Jewish Relief Unit (1946-49); Sr. Staff Member, Jewish Refugees Cttee., London (1939-46); Adviser, Juedischer Central-Verein Berlin (1929-38), and Reichsvertretung (1933-39); Asst. Edr. C.V. Zeitung, (1929-38);

Edr. Zeitschrift f d. Geschichte d. Juden in Deutschland, (1930-38); Judische Sozialarbeit, (1956-65) Bd., Leo Baeck Instit. (Lond., New York). ORT Germany.
LUBOFSKY, Rabbi Ronald, B.A.; b. Lond., July 7, 1928; Rabbi Emer. St. Kilda Hebrew Cong.; Sr. Lect./Head of Dept. of Jewish Studies, Victoria Coll.; form. President, Assn. of Rabbis of Australian and N.Z.; P, Jewish Museum of Australia, President, CCJ, Australia; Rep., Australian Jewry on Govt. Bicentennial Auth.; Standing Cttee. of Bio-ethics, Monash Univ.; past President, Mount Scopus War Memorial Coll., Melbourne; form. M., Great Syn., Sydney, and Cockfosters Syn., London. Ad.: 7 Balaclava Rd., East St. Kilda, 3183, Melbourne, Vic. ☎ 613 5259405. Fax.: 613 5259921.
LUCAS, Gerald Ephraim, b. London, Oct. 20, 1946; m. Angela née Daltroff; Exec. Dir., B'nai B'rith Hillel Foundation. Ad.: Hillel House, 1/2 Endsleigh Street, London WC1H 0DS. ☎ 0171-388 0801. Fax 0171-916 3973.
LUCAS, Mrs Stella (née Waldman), J.P.; b. London, July 30, 1916; V. President Jewish Care; Chairman, Stepney Girls' Club and Settlement; President, First Women's Lodge B'nai B'rith (1975-77), V. President Assn. of US Women; President, Dollis Hill Ladies, Guild; V. President (Chairman, 1978-84); Frs. of Hebrew Univ. (Women's Group); Exec. Off., Internat. C. of Jewish Women (1963-66); Chairman, Union of Jewish Women (1966-72); Chairman, Women Frs. of Jewis, Coll. (1957-66); Central Council for Jewish Soc. Services; BoD; Chairman, Brodie Instit.; Convenor BoD Central Enquiry Desk; Fdr. 'All Aboard Shops'. Ad.: 51 Wellington Ct., Wellington Rd., NW8 9TB. ☎ 0171-586 3030.
LYONS, Bernard, C.B.E., J.P., D.L., Hon. LL.D. (Leeds); b. Leeds, Mar. 30, 1913, m. Lucy; President (Chairman 1972-82), U.D.S. Group plc; L.P. Leeds Jewish Rep. C.; Chairman, Yorks. & N.E. Conciliation Cttee.; Race Rel. Bd (1968-70); Community Rel. Com. (1970-72); Dep. Lieutenant Yorks., W. Riding (1971); Leeds City C (1951-65). Publ.: The Thread is Strong; The Narrow Edge; The Adventures of Jimmie Jupiter; Tombola. Ad.: Upton Wood, Fulmer, Bucks. SL3 6JJ. ☎ 01753-662404. Fax: 01753-662413.
LYONS, Edward, Q.C., LL.B. (Leeds); b. Glasgow, May 17, 1926, m. Barbara; Recorder; M.P. (SDP) Bradford West (1981-83); M.P. (Lab.) Bradford West (1974-81); Bradford East (1966-74); Parl. Pr. Sec. Treasury (1969-70); Bencher, Lincoln's Inn; Nat. Cttee., SDP (1984-89). Ad.: 4 Primley Park Lane, Leeds, LS17 7JR. ☎ 0113 2685351 and 59 Westminster Gardens, Marsham Street, SW1P 4JG. ☎ 0171-834 1960.
LYONS, Sir Isidore Jack, C.B.E., Hon. D.Univ. (York); b. Leeds, Feb. 1, 1916; Life V. President, JIA; Dep. Chairman, Youth Aliyah; Member of Court, York Univ.; H.V. President, Leeds Musical Festival; Ch of Trs., London Symphony Orchestra; Life Tr. Shakespeare Birthplace Trust; Chairman, Henry Wood Rehearsal Hall; H. Fel., Royal Acad. of Music; Chairman, Foreign and Commonwealth Office US Bicentennial sub-cttee.
MACCOBY, Hyam Zoundell, M.A. (Oxon.); b. Sunderland, March 20, 1924; Emer. Fellow Leo Baeck Coll., Lond.; Edr. Bd., European Judaism; Publ.: Revolution in Judaea, Judaism on Trial, The Sacred Executioner, The Mythmaker, Early Rabbinic Writings, Judas Iscariot and the myth of Jewish evil (awarded Wingate Prize 1992-3), Paul and Hellenism, The Disputation (TV & Stage play), A Pariah People, etc. Ad.: Leo Baeck College, 80 East End Rd., N3 2SY. ☎ 0181-349 4525.
MAGONET, Rabbi Professor Dr Jonathan David, M.B., B.S., Ph.D., (Heid.); b. London, Aug. 2, 1942; Princ., Leo Baeck Coll.; V. President, World Union for Progressive Judaism; Chairman, Yth Section, WUPJ. (1964-66); Co-Editor European Judaism (1992-). Publ.: Returning: Exercises in Repentance, Forms of Prayer, Vol. I, Daily and Sabbath (co-ed.); Vol. II, Pilgrim Festivals (co-ed.); Vol. III, Days of Awe Prayerbook (co-ed.); Form and Meaning- Studies in Literary Techniques in the Book of Jonah, Guide to the Here and Hereafter (co-ed.); A Rabbi's Bible (1991); Bible Lives (1992), How To Get Up When Life Gets You

Down (1993) (co-ed.); The Little Blue Book Of Prayer (1993) (co-ed.); A rabbi reads the Psalms (1994). Kindred spirits (co-ed. 1995); Jewish explorations of sexuality (ed. 1995); The Subversive Bible (1977). Ad.: 18 Wellfield Ave., N10 2EA. ☏ 0181-444 3025.

MAILER, Norman, b. Long Branch, N.J., Jan. 31, 1923; Writer; Pulitzer Prize for non-fiction and Nat. Book Award for Arts and Letters (1969), Ed., Dissent, (1953-69). Publ.: The Naked and the Dead, Barbary Shore, The Deer Park, Advertisements for Myself, Deaths for the Ladies, The Presidential Papers, The armies of the night, Existential Errands, Marilyn, The Fight, The Executioner's Song, Of Women and Their Elegance, Pieces and Pontifications, Ancient Evenings, Tough Guys Don't Dance, Harlot's ghost, Oswald's tale, Portrait of Picasso as a young man etc. Ad.: c/o Rembar, 19 W. 44th St., New York, NY 10036 USA.

MALITS, Rabbi Malcolm Henry, M.A., D.Litt.; b. Birmingham, Jan. 26, 1919; Emer. R.; M., Allerton Hebrew Cong. Liverpool (1964-90); Chaplain Ajex (Masonry), Past Prov. Grand Chap. for West Lancashire. Ad.: 12 Glenside, Liverpool L18 9UJ. ☏ 0151-724 1967.

MANKOWITZ, Wolf, M.A. (Cantab.) b. London, 7 Nov. 1924; m. Ann Margaret Seligmann; Author; Univ of New Mexico: adjunct prof of English 1982-86, adjunct prof of theatre arts 1987-88; hon consul Republic of Panama in Dublin 1971: Plays incl: Belle (musical, 1961), Pickwick (musical 1963, rev. 1993/94), Passion Flower Hotel (musical, 1965), Samson and Delilah (published as The Samson Riddle, 1978), Casanova's Last Stand (1980), Iron butterflies (1986); Films Make Me an Offer (1954), A Kid for Two Farthings (1954), The Bespoke Overcoat (1955), Expresso Bongo (1960), The Millionairess (1960), the Long and The Short and The Tall (1961), The Day the earth Caught Fire (1961), TheWaltz of the Toreadors (1962), Where The Spies Are (1965), Casino Royale (1967), The Assassination Bureau (1969), Bloomfield (1970), Black Beauty (1971), Treature Island (1972), The Hebrew Lesson (and dir, 1972), The Hireling (1973), Almonds and Raisins (1984); Television Dickens of London (1976); Books novels: Make Me An Offer (1952), A Kid for Two Farthings (1953), Laugh till You Cry (1955), My Old Man's a Dustman (1956), Cockatrice (1963), The Biggest Pig in Barbardos (1965), Penguin Wolf Mankowitz (1967), Raspberry Reich (1979), Abracadabra! (1980), The Devil in Texas (1984), Gioconda (1987), The Magic Cabinet of Professor Smucker (1988), Exquisite Cadaver (1990), A Night with Casanova (1991); short stories: The Mendelman Fire (1957), The Blue Arabian Nights (1973), The Day of the Women and the Night of the Men (fables, 1977); biographies: Dickens of London (1976), The Extraordinary Mr Poe (1978), Mazeppa (1982); miscellaneous: Wedgwood (a history, 1957), 12 Poems (poetry, 1971): Ad.: The Bridge House, Ahakista, Co Cork.

MARCUS, Mark Hyman, B.A. (Com.); b. Manchester, Feb. 22, 1933; Exec. Dir., B'nai B'rith Distr. 15; Dir. Provincial & London Divisions, J.I.A Ad.: B'nai B'rith Hillel House, 1-2 Endsleigh St., WC1H ODS. ☏ 0171-387 5278/5954. Fax: 0171-387 8014. Email: bnaib@ort.org

MARGOLYES, Miriam, B.A. (Cantab.), L.G.S.M&D; b. Oxford, May 18, 1941; Actress. Ad.: c/o Jonathan Altaras Associates Ltd, 2 Goodwins Court, WC2N 4LL ☏ 0171-497 8878 Fax.: 0171-497 8876.

MARINER, Rabbi Rodney John, B.A. (Hons.), Dip. Ed.; b. Melbourne, Australia, May 29, 1941; M., Belsize Sq. Syn.; Convener, Beth Din, RSGB; Assoc. M., Edgware & Distr. Ref. Syn. (1979-82); Asst. M., North Westem Ref Syn. (1976-79). Publ.: Prayers For All The Year: Part 1, Shabbat; Part 2, Festivals; Part 3, New Year; Part 4, Atonement. Ad.: 37a Alexandra Gardens, London N10 3RN.

MARKOVA, Dame Alicia, D.B.E., Hon. D.Mus. (Leics. and East Anglia Univs.); b. London, Dec. 1, 1910; Prima Ballerina Assoluta; P.: English National Ballet (since 1989); V. President, Royal Academy of Dancing (since 1958); Dir.,

Metrop. Opera Ballet, New York (1963-69), Gov., Royal Ballet, Prof. of Ballet and Performing Arts., Univ. of Cincinnati; President, Lond. Ballet Circle (since 1981), President, All England Dance Competition (1983); President, Arts Educ. Schs (1984); Lond. Festival Ballet (1986). Publ.: Giselle and I, Markova Remembers. Ad.: c/o Barclays Bank, P.O. Box 40, SW3 1QB.

MARKS, John Henry, M.D., F.R.C.G.P., D.Obst., R.C.O.G.; b. London, May 30, 1925; m. Shirley, née Nathan; Chairman, C. BMA (1984-90); Chairman, Rep. Body BMA (1981-84); Gen. Med. C. (1979-84, 1989-94); V. President, Lond. Jewish Med. Soc. (1983-84). Publ.: The Conference of Local Medical Committees and its Executive: An Historical Review. Ad.: Brown Gables, Barnet La., Elstree, Herts., WD6 3RQ. ☎ 0181-953 7687.

MARKS, Kenneth Anthony, b. London, July 28, 1931; Company Director; Non-Exec. Dir., Bank Leumi (UK) Ltd; Non-Exec. Dir. Owen and Robinson plc; Non-Exec. Dir. Focus D.I.Y.; Non-Exec. Dir., Courts plc; Dir., Kenneth Marks Associates Ltd. (Consultants); V. President British-Israel Chamber of Commerce; Gov., Shenkar College, Israel. Ad.: 279 Dover House Rd, Roehampton, SW15 5BP.

MARKS, Shula Eta (née Winokur), O.B.E., F.B.A., B.A.(UCT), Ph.D.(London), Hon. D.Litt.(UCT), Hon. D.Soc.Sci. (Natal); b. Cape Town, Oct. 14, 1936; m. Isaac Meyer Marks; Historian; Prof. History of Southern Africa, SOAS (1993-); Dir. Institute of Commonwealth Studies, Univ. of London (1983-93); Lecturer and Reader, History of Southern Africa, Jointly SOAS and ICS (1963-83); Chair, Society for Protection of Science and Learning (1993-). Publ.: Reluctant Rebellion: The 1906-1908 Disturbances in Natal (1970); The Ambiguities of Dependence in South Africa (1986); 'Not Either an Experimental Doll': The Separate Lives of Three South African Women (1987); Divided Sisterhood: Class, Race and Gender in the South African Nursing Profession (1944). Ad.: Dept. of History, School of Oriental and African Studies, Thornhaugh St., WC1H 0XG. ☎ 0171-637 2388, 0171-323 6046 (Home 0181-69936611). Email smi@soas.ac.uk

MARMUR, Rabbi Dow, b. Sosnowiec, Poland, Feb. 24, 1935; Sr. Rabbi, Holy Blossom Temple, Toronto; V. President Canadian Zionist Fed.; form. President, Toronto Board of Rabbis; form. Chairman, C. of Reform and Lib. Rabbis; M., North Western Reform Syn. (1969-83); South-West Essex Reform Syn. (1962-69). Publ.: Beyond Survival; The Star of Return; Walking Toward Elijah; On being a Jew; Reform Judaism (Edr.); A Genuine Search (Edr.) Ad.: 1950 Bathurst St., Toronto, Ontario, M5P 3K9, Canada. ☎ (416) 789 3291. Fax: (416) 789 9697.

MASSEL, Abraham David, B.A. (Admin.); b. Manchester, May 10, 1927; m. Eva; Asst. Dir. Central Enquiry Desk BoD (1995-); Exec. Dir., BoD (1973-95); Sec., C. of Manchester and Salford Jews (1957-59); Sec. Jewish Defence & Group Rel. Cttee. (1959-73); Sec. Jewish Tribunal (Shops Act 1950), (1973-95). Ad.: 43 Green Lane, NW4 2AG. ☎ 0181-203 4467.

MAY, Michael, M.Sc. (econ.); b. Jerusalem, Dec. 16, 1945; Exec. Director, European Council of Jewish Communities; Form. Dir., Institute of Jewish Affairs, London; Dir. Jewish Film Fdn.; form. Assoc. Ed., J. Quarterly; Member BoD Foreign Affairs Cttee.; Member Adv. C., S.T.I.B.A. (Dutch) Foundation for the Fight Against Anti-Semitism; Member Adv. Bd., Intern. Centre for Holocaust Studies, N.Y.; former Dir. Jewish Book Council; Member Gov. Bd., World Jewish Congress (1983-91); Dir., Jewish Literary Trust (1984-91); Co.-Fdr. & Tr. Limmud Conf. (1980-84); Ad.: 74 Gloucester Place, W1H 3HN. ☎ 0171-224 3445. Fax: 0171-224 3446. E-mail: ecjc@ort.org.

MAYER, Daniel, b. Paris, April 29, 1909; Member (President, 1983) French Constitutional C.; form. M. of Labour, War-time Member of C.N.R. (Resistance Nat. C.); Deputy for Seine; Sec.-Gen.; Socialist Party, S.F.I.O.; President, Internat. Fedn. of Human Rights; Conseil Supérieur de la Magistrature; President, Ligue des Droits de l'Homme. Ad.: Conseil Constitutionnel, 2 rue de

Montpensier, Paris, 1e.

MAZAR, Benjamin, Ph.D.; b. Grodno (Russia), 1906; form. P. and Rector, Hebrew Univ., Jerusalem, and Prof Ancient Jewish Hist. and Archaeology; President, Israel Exploration Soc.; Co-Edr., Encyclopaedia Biblica. Conducting Excavations in Jerusalem (Temple area), Bet'o Shearim, Ein Gedi, etc. Publ.: Hist of Archaeological Excavations in Pal. Hist. of Pal., The Mountain of the Lord Canaan and Israel, etc. Ad.: 9 Arbanel St., Jerusalem. ☎ 639854

MEHDI, Sion, b. Jerusalem, July 14, 1932; Exec. Dir, Children & Youth Aliyah, Gt. Brit. & Eire (1985-); Chairman, Exec., Victoria Com Centre; Norwood Child Care Youth & C. Serv. Cttee. (1995-); Chairman, Educ. & Youth Cttee.; BoD (1982-88; 1991-94); Form. H. Sec. Assoc. of Jewish Communal Professionals; Member Council Zionist Fed; Commonwealth Jewish Councils, British Sephardi C.; BoD (1979-); Member Central Jewish Lecture & information Cttee. (1988-91); The Exec. Cttee., AJY (1958-95); V. Chairman (1990-94), Sec. (1994-), The Herut Movement of G.B.; Member, C. The United Syn. (1989-93), Member, U.S. Bd of Religious Educ. (1989-92); Brent Cross Teenage Centre; Gov., Simon Marks Jewish Primary School (1989-94); Chairman, Cttee. for Welfare of Iranian Jews in Gt. Brit.; H. Sec. Jewish Child's Day, H. Sec., Persian Heb Cong., Frs. of Jewish Youth, Sephardi Fed. of Gt. Brit & C'wlth, AJY (1969-85); Exec. Dir., Iranian Jew Centre, Man Bd., Finchley (United) Syn.; Nat. C., A. F. C., Ta'ali. Ad.: 17 Arden Rd., N3 3AB. ☎ 0181-346 3121. Fax: 0181-343 7383.

MELINEK, Rabbi A., B.A., Ph D.; b. London, Sept. 15, 1912; form. Edr., L'Eylah; form. M., Willesden Brondesbury Stoke Newington Syns.; Lect. Jews, Coll., Member, Court of the Univ. of Kent. Publ.: Life and Times of Abarbanel. Ad.: 6 Elm Close, NW4 2PH. ☎ 0181-202 9826.

MENUHIN, Lord Yehudi, O.M., K.B.E.; b. New York, April 22, 1916; violinist and conductor; Hon. D. Mus. (Oxon., Cantab., Sorbonne, Dr. of Law h.c., Toronto, Tokyo and 17 other degrees from Brit. and Foreign univs.); Gold Medal, Royal Philharmonic Soc. (1962) Jawaharlal Nehru Award for lnternat Understanding (1970), Sonning Music Prize, Denmark (1972); Handel Medal, New York City; City of Jerusalem Medal, Buber Rosenzweig Medal (1989-Bonn), Glenn Gould Prize (Canada 1990); many other internat. awards; debut at age of seven and has since played with most of the world's orchestras; has made many visits to Israel; Fdr., Yehudi Menuhin Sch. of Music, Stoke d'Abernon, Surrey (1963), Menuhin Academy Gstaad; initiated annual Music Festival, Gstaad, Switzerland and in Bath (1959-68), Artistic Dir., Windsor Festival (1969-72); Soloist and Conductor, Menuhin Festival Orchestra; many recordings; P. and Assoc. conductor of the Royal Philharmonic Orchestra; P. of Young Musicians Symphony Orchestra; Founder and Conductor of Asian Youth Orchestra; Principal Guest Conductor of English String Orchestra; Conducts Berlin Philharmonic Orchestra each year. President, Royal Philharmonic Orchestra, President, Trinity Coll. of Music (1971); Freedom of Edinburgh, Bath; Grand Officer, Legion of Honour (France), Order of Leopold (Belgium); Order of Merit (West Germany), Royal Order of Phoenix (Greece); Cdr., Order of Orange-Nassau (Holland), H. Citizen, Switzerland (1970); Epée d'Academicien, Academie des Beaux Arts, Paris (1988); Patron, Zemel Choir, Lond. Publ.: The Violin: Six lessons; Theme and Variations; Violin and Viola; Unfinished Journey (autobiogr.), The Music of Man; Conversations with Menuhin (by Robin Daniels), The King, the Cat and the Fiddle, Life Class. Ad.: c/o Sym Music Co., P.O. Box 6160, London SW1W 0XJ.

MICHAELS, Rabbi Maurice Arnold, M.A.; b. Woolmer's Park, Herts., Aug. 31, 1941; Assoc. Rabbi, Edgware and Dist. Reform Syn.; Life Gov. of Leo Baeck Coll.; Previous: Chairman and V. President, RSGB; Chairman, Leo Baeck Coll.; Chairman, S. W. Essex Reform Syn.; Chairman, Redbridge Business Educ. Partnership; Gov. of Redbridge Coll.; Gov. of Akiva School; Gov. of Jewish Joint Bur. Soc.; Tr., Redbridge Racial Equality Council; Tr., Limmud; Member, World

Union for Progressive Judaism Gov. Body; Member, Redbridge Jewish Cttee; Council Member, Redbridge Campaign Against Racism and Fascism; Dir., Harlow Enterprise Agency; Man. Cttee., West Essex Business Educ. Partnership; V. Chairman, Harlow & Dist. Employers' Group; Member, BoD; Member, Nat. Council Zionist Fed.; Member, Nat. Council Soviet Jewry. Ad.: 18 Exeter Gardens, Ilford, Essex IG1 3LA. ☎ 0181-554 2812.

MIDDLEBURGH, Rabbi Charles H., B.A. Hons., Ph.D.; b. Hove, Oct. 2, 1956. Minister, Kingston Liberal Synagogue (1977-83); Rabbi, Harrow and Wembley Progressive Synagogue (1983-97); Dir. Union of Liberal and Progressive Synagogues (1997-); Assoc. Ed. Siddur Lev Chadash (1989-95); Co-Ed., Mahzor Ruach Chadashah (1996-); Chairman, ULPS Rabbinic Conference (1988-90, 1993-95); Lect. and Principal, ULPS Evening Institute F(1980-92). Lect. Aramaic, Bible, Practical Rabbinics, Leo Baeck College (1985-). Ad.: The Montagu Centre, 21 Maple St., W1P 6DS. ☎ 0171-580 1663. Fax: 0181-436 4184.

MILLER, Arthur, b. New York, Oct. 17, 1915; Novelist and Playwright; President, Internat. P.E.N. Publ.: Focus, All My Sons, Death of a Salesman, After the Fall, A View from the Bridge, The Crucible, Incident at Vichy, The Price, The American Clock Playing for Time, Timebends, The ride down Mount Morgan, etc. Ad.: c/o Kay Brown, I.C.M., 40 West 57th St., New York, N.Y. 10019.

MILLER, Harold, b. London, 1917; Member BoD; form. Chairman, Z.F.; V. President, form. Chairman, Brit Poale Zion; Elected to Fel. of WZO, 1993; Member of Board of Deputies. Ad.: 71 Francklyn Gdns., Edgware, Middlesex ☎ 0181-958 5418.

MILLER, Rabbi Israel, M.A., D.D. (Yeshiva Univ.); b. Baltimore, Md., April 6, 1918; Sr. V. President Emeritus, Yeshiva Univ.; H. President, Amer. Z. Fed.; President, Conference Jewish Material Claims against Germany; V. President, Amer.-Israel. Publ Affairs Cttee. (198390); V.-Chairman, Amer. Z. Youth Foundation; Sec., Memorial Foundation for Jewish Culture; V.P , Jewish Com. Relations C. of New York; V. President, Nat. Jewish Welfare Bd. (1970-78); Chairmam., Conf of Presidents. of Major Amer. Jewish Orgs. (1974-76); Chairman, Amer. Jewish Conference on Soviet Jewry (1965-67); Chairman, Com. on Jewish Chaplaincy, NJWB (1962-65). Ad.: 2619 Davidson Ave., Bronx, N.Y. 10468. ☎/Fax (718) 364 4842.

MILLER, Dr. Jack Elius, O.B.E., F.R.C.G.P., J.P., O.ST.J.; b. Glasgow, March 7, 1918; form. Treasury Med. Off.; H.V.P (President 1968-71), Glasg. Jewish Rep. C.; H. V. President, Garnethill Syn.; Chairman, Soviet Jewry Com. (1968-78); Chairman, WJC Scotland (1954-63); H. President (Chairman 1950-57, 1960-65), Ajex Scotland (1997); BoD (1979-88), Nat.T. BMA (1972-81); Fel., BMA, Royal Soc. of Med, Royal Coll. of G.Ps.; Gold Medallist, BMA; Freeman of the City of London; Chairman, Scottish Gen. Med. Services Cttee (1969-72); Gen. Med. Services Com.; H. V. President, Scottish Marriage Guidance C. & Glasg. M.G.C.; Race Rel. Bd., Scottish Conciliation Cttee. (1968-75); H. V. President, Prince and Princess of Wales Hospice, Glasg.; Chairman, Epilepsy Assn. of Scotland, Strathclyde Br. (1983-88); Chairman, Working Party on Priorities of the National Health Service; (1985-87); Sharpen, Report (1988); Edr., Glasg. Doctors, Handbook. Ad.: 38 Fruin Ave. Newton Mearns, Glasgow G77 6HJ. ☎ 0141-639 7869.

MILLER, Maurice Solomon, M.B.Ch.B., J.P.; b. Glasgow, Aug. 16, 1920; Med. practitioner; M.P. (Lab.) for East Kilbride (1974-87); M.P. for Kelvingrove (Glasgow) (1964-74), form. H.Sec., Lab. Frs. of Israel, Parl. Br. Publ.: Window on Russia. Ad.:

MILLETT, Sir Peter Julian (the Rt. Hon. Lord Justice), P.C., M.A. (Cantab.); b. London, June 23, 1932; Lord Justice of Appeal (1994-), Judge of the High Court Chancery Div. (1986-94); Q.C. (1973-86), Member, Insolvency Law Review Cttee. (1976-82); Stndg. Jr. Counsel, Trade & Industry Dept. (1967-73);

Bencher, Lincoln's Inn, Called to Bar, Middle Temple; form. Chairman, Lewis Hammerson Home (1981-1991); President, West London Syn. (1991-95); Hon. Fel. Trinity Hall (1994). Publ.: (contrib.) Halsbury's Law of England, Encyclopaedia of Forms and Precedents. Ad.: 18 Portman Cl., W1H 9HJ. ☎ 0171-935 1152.

MIRVIS, Rabbi Ephraim Yitzchak, B.A.: b. Johannesburg, Sept. 7, 1956; Rabbi Finchley Synagogue (1996-); M. Western Marble Arch Syn. (1992-96); form. Chief Rabbi, Jewish Coms. of Ireland (1984-92); M. Dublin Hebrew Cong. (1982-84); Lect. Machon Meir, Jerusalem (1980-82). Ad.: 69 Lichfield Grove, London N3 2JJ ☎ 0181-346 3773.

MISHCON, Baron of Lambeth in Greater London, Life Peer (Victor Mishcon), D.L. Q.C.; b. London Aug. 14, 1915; Solicitor; Official Opposition Spokesman in House of Lords on Legal Affairs (1983-92); Dep. Lieut. for Greater Lond.; Chairman, L.C.C (1954-55); form. Chairman, Gen. Purposes Cttee., G.L.C. L.C.C. and various L.C.C. Cttees., Member, Govt. Com. of Inquiry into Lond. Transport (1953-54), Member Dept. Cttee. of Inquiry into Homosexual Offences and Prostitution (1954-57); Member, Nat. Theatre Bd. (1965-90) and South Bank Theatre Bd.; President Brit. C. of Shaare Zedek Hospital, Jerusalem; H. President, Brit. Technion Cttee; V. President, (form. P), AJY; Hon. Solicitor, JIA; Patron, and (1968-88) Chairman, Instit. of Jewish Studies; V. Chairman, CCJ (1977-79); form. V. President, BoD.; Cdr., Royal Swedish Order of North Star, Star of Ethiopia; Star of Jordan; LL.D (Hon.) Birmingham Univ. 1991; Hon. Fellow, U.C.L.; Q.C. (Hon.) 1992. Ad.: House of Lords, SW1A 0PW.

MISHON, Philip, O.B.E., b. Lond., March 23, 1924; Comp. Dir.; Chairman, Trs., UK Frs. for Further Educ. in Israel; V. President (Nat. Chairman, 1966-68) A.J.E.X. Appointed Tr. 1993; J.D. Cttee., BoD; CCJ; J.L.G.B.; President, Ajex Golf Soc. Ad.: 53 Bolsover St., W1P 7HL. ☎ 0171-387 6404. Fax: 0171-722 3354.

MITCHELL, Mrs. Eva (née Rose); b. Munster, June 14, 1929; Life V. President, West Lond. Syn. of Brit. Jews (1994-); Exec. Dir., C.B.F.W.J.R. (1979-89); form. Chairman, V. President Chairman, RSGB (1973-76); form. Chairman, Assn. of Jew Women's Orgs. in UK; form. V. Chairman; Nat. C. for Soviet Jewry. Ad.: 15 Avenue Court, Draycott Ave., SW3 3BU. ☎ 0171-584 4746.

MOCKTON, Rev. Leslie, b. Manchester Aug. 5, 1928; M., Waltham Forest Hebrew Cong.; Mayor's Chaplain, Lond. Borough Waltham Forest (1981-82); Hospital Chaplain Forest. Health Care Trust (1992-96); form. M., Highams Pk. & Chingford Syn. (1969-87); form. M. Bradford Hebrew Cong. (1965-69); West End Gt. Syn. (1958-65); Barking & Becontree Hebrew Cong. (1955-58). Ad.: Waltham Forest Hebrew Con., 140 Boundary Rd., Walthamstow E17 8LA. ☎ 0181-520 3572.

MONTAGU, Iris Rachel (née Solomon), the Hon. Mrs. Ewen Montagu; b. London, May 9, 1903; Ad.: 24 Montrose Ct., Exhibition Rd., SW7 2OQ. ☎ 0171-589 9999.

MONTAGUE, Lee, b. Bow, London, Oct. 16, 1927; Actor; many leading roles including Shakespeare and Chekhov, title-role Leon in The Workshop, Raymond Chandler in Private Dick, O'Connor, in Cause Célèbre (London 1977), Ed, in Entertaining Mr. Sloane (New York 1965); Court in the Act (London 1987); films include Moulin Rouge, Mahler, Brass Target, London Affair Silver Dream Racer, Lady Jane, Madame Sousatzka; television appearances include Holocaust, Thank You Comrades, Tussy Marx, Parsons Pleasure, The Workshop, Passing Through, Sharing Time, Kim Dr. Sakharov, Bird of Prey, Much Ado About Nothing, Countdown to War, Incident in Judaea, House of Elliott; Casualty. Best TV Actor of the Year 1960. Ad.: c/o Joyce Edwards, 275 Kennington Rd., London SE11 6BY.

MONTEFIORE, Alan Claude Robin Goldsmid, M.A.(Oxon.); b. London Dec. 29, 1926; Emer. Fellow, form. Fellow and Tutor in Philosophy, Balliol College, Oxford; form. Sr. Lect. in Moral & Political Philosophy, Keele Univ.; President,

Wiener Libr. Publ.: A Modern Introduction to Moral Philosophy, British Analytic Philosophy (co-ed.), Neutrality and Impartiality, The University and Political Commitment (ed), French Philosophy Today (ed)., Goals, No-Goals and Own Goals A Debate on Goal Directed and Intentional Behaviour (co-edr.), The Political Responsibility of Intellectuals (co-edr.), etc. Ad.: 34 Scarsdale Villas, W8 6PR. ☎ 0171-937 7708. Fax: 0171-938 4257.

MONTY, Mrs. Regina Joy (née Dixon); b. London, Sept. 19, 1935; Co-President, Fed. Women Zionists (Brit. WIZO); form. Chairman, V. Chairman & Membership Chairman, FWZ. Ad.: 107 Gloucester Pl., W1H 4BY.

MOONMAN, Eric, O.B.E.; b. Liverpool, Apr. 29, 1929; M.P. (Lab.) for Basildon (1974-79), for Billericay (1966-70); V. President, BoD (1994-); Sr. V. President, BoD (1985-91); Chairman, Media Network; Chairman City of Liverpool Continuing Care Cttee (1996-); Prof Health Management, City Univ., London.; Chairman, Essex Radio plc; Chairman, Academic Response to Racism & Antisemitism (1994-); Consultant, ICRC (Africa) (1992-95); Director Natural History Museum Development Trust (1989-91); (seconded) Chairman, WJC Europe Br. Cttee. on Antisemitism (1985-92); Chairman Community Research Unit, (1985-96); Chairman, Z. Fed. (1975-80); President, Friends of Union of Jewish Students; Co.-Chairman, Nat. Jewish Solidarity Cttee. (1975-79); form. Parl. Pte. Sec. to Sec. of State for Educ. and Science; form. Sr. Res. Fel., Manch. Univ.; form. Leader, Stepney Borough C.; Sr. Adv., Brit. Instit. of Management (1956-62); European Adv. WJC (1973-76); Chairman, Nat. Aliyah and Volunteers C.; Chairman, P.R. Cttee., Z.F. (1983-85; 1972-75); Trustee, Balfour Tr.; CRE Award for Multi Racial Service (1996). Publ.: The Alternative Government, The Manager and the Organisation, Reluctant Partnership, European Science and Technology, etc. Ad.: 1 Beacon Hill, N7 9LY.

MORGAN, Rabbi Fred; b. New York City, March 18, 1948; M. Temple Beth Israel, Melbourne, Australia; Hon. Assoc. Rabbi Sim Shalom Jewish Community Budapest; M. North West Surrey Synagogue (1984-97); Lect. in Midrash and Jewish Thought Leo Baeck Rabbinical College (1987-97); V.-Chairman Assembly of Reform Rabbis (1996-97); Lect. in Judaism, Roehampton Institute (1989-92); Lect. in Religious Studies, Univ. of Bristol (1973-79); Vis. Prof. Eotvos Lorand Univ., Budapest (1992-94). Ad.: Temple Beth Israel, 76-82 Alma Road, St Kilda 3182, Victoria, Australia. ☎61-3-9510 1488. Fax: 61-3-9521 1229. Email: ravmorgan@starnet.com.au.

MORITZ, Ludwig Alfred, M.A., D.Phil. (Oxon.); b. Munich, May 11, 1921, retd.; form. V. Princ. (Admin.) and Reg., Univ. Coll., Cardiff; Lect., Bedford Coll., Lond., Univ. Coll. Cardiff, Prof of Classics, Univ. Coll. of Ghana, Univ Coll., Cardiff; Chairman Cardiff New Syn. (1991-95). Publ.: Classical studies. Ad.: 1 Llanedeyrn Rd., Penylan, Cardiff CF3 7DT. ☎ 01222 485065.

MORRIS, Henry, b. London Mar. 5, 1921; form. Chairman, Jewish Defence & Group Rel Cttee., BoD; V. President (Nat.Chairman 1979-81) Ajex. Ad.: 94 Randall Ave., NW2 7SU ☎ 0181-452 9805; 0181-636 5361.

MORRIS, Norman Harold, F.R.S.A.; b. London, June 8, 1932; Principal N.M. Consultants; form. Exec. Dir., Balfour Diamond Jubilee Tr. (Consult. 1995-); Exec. Consultant Scopus Jewish Educational Tr. (1995-); Freeman, City of Lond.; form. Exec. Sec. Z. Fed.; Dep. Provincial Dir., Z. Fed.; J.P.A.; Printing & Publ. Cttee., Brit.-Israel Chamber of Commerce; Sec., Eastern Cape Z. C. Ad.: Balfour House, 741 High Rd., N12 0BQ. ☎ 0181-3438 8196. Fax 0181-347 7283.

MORRIS OF KENWOOD, Philip Geoffrey, 2nd Baron, J.P.; b. Sheffield, June 18, 1928; form. P. Hotel Caterers and Allied Trades Aid for Israel Cttee.; President, JNF Bridge Tournament. Ad.: Lawn Cottage, Orchard Rise, Kingston, Surrey KT2 7EY. ☎ 0181-942 6321.

MORRIS OF KENWOOD, Lady Ruth (née Janner); b. London, Sept. 21, 1932; Solicitor; President, Nat. Cttee., Va'ad Lema'an Habonim; H. Solicitor, various youth orgs.; Jt. Cttee. for Youth Affairs; V. President, AJY; Exec., W.O.Y.L.; Tr.

Elsie & Barnett Janner Charitable Tr.; Womankind worldwide; form. Man., Brady Girls' Club; form. exec. Member, Victoria Boys' and Girls' Club; Tr., Rowan Educ.; Tr.; form. Member, Gen. Adv. C., Independent Broadcasting Auth. (I.B.A.). Chairman D.S.S. Appeals Tribunal. Ad.: Lawn Cottage, Orchard Rise, Kingston, Surrey KT2 7EY.

MOSER, Sir Claus, K.C.B., C.B.E., F.B.A., B.Sc. (Econ.) Hon. D. (Southampton, Leeds, Surrey, Sussex, York, Keele, City, Wales, Edinburgh, Liverpool London, Brunel, Brighton, Hull, Heriot-Watt, Northumbria, South Bank Univs); b. Berlin, Nov. 24, 1922; Chancellor, Keele Univ. (1986-); Tr. British Museum (1988-); Chairman British Museum Dev. Trust (1994-); Chancellor Open University Israel (1994-); Warden, Wadham Coll., Oxford (1984-93); Chairman, Harold Holt Ltd. (1990-); Dir., Economist Newspaper; Dir., V. Chairman, C.B.F.-W.J.R. Publ.: Writings on statistics. Ad.: 3 Regent's Park Tce., NW1 7EE. ☎ 0171-485 1619.

NABARRO, Eric John Nunes, J.P., F.C.A.; b. London, April 5, 1917; m. Cecily née Orenstein; Chartered accountant; P. of Elders, Spanish and Portuguese Jews, Cong., London (1984-88; 1994-96); T., Heshaim (Beth Hamidrash) (1984-94); H. Member, Nat. Shechita C.; Tr., Ravenswood Foundation (1986-92), Chairman, Sephardi Kashrut Auth. (1968-84); President, Sephardi Welfare Bd. (1979-87); T., BoD (1973-79); V. President (T. 1947-72), Victoria Com. Centre; Capt., Jewish Brigade (1945); T., London Bd. for Shechita (1949-63); Chairman, Kosher School Meals Service (1966-73). Ad.: 11 The Marlowes, NW8 6NB. ☎ 0171-586 1240.

NABARRO, Frank Reginald Nunes, M.B.E., M.A., B.Sc. (Oxon.), D.Sc. (Birmingham), D.Sc. (Hon.) (Witwatersrand, Natal, Cape Town), F.R.S., Hon. F.R.S.S.Af.; b. London March 7, 1916; P. Roy. Soc. S. Africa (1988-92); H. Prof Res. Fel., Physics Dept. Witwatersrand Univ., Johannesburg; Fell. S. African CSIR; Dep. V. Chancellor (1978-80), form. Dean, Faculty of Science; Fd. Mem., S.A. Acad. Sci.; Foreign Assoc. U.S. Nat. Acad. Eng. Publ.: Theory of Crystal Dislocations; Physics of Creep (with H. L. de Villiers). Ad.: 32 Cookham Rd., Auckland Park, Johannesburg 2092, S. Africa. ☎ (11) 726 7745. Fax: (11) 339 8262.

NADDELL, Alexander Walker, K. St. J., K.M.L.J., ERD., J.P., D.L., F.R.C.S., F.R.F.P.S., F.S.A. (Scot.), F.R.S.A.; b. Glasgow, Dec. 25, 1910; Orthopaedic and Neuro. Surgeon; Queen's Household Surgeon; Fel., Royal Soc. of Med. Col. (T.A. Vol. Res.); Distr. Court Judge; Dir. Glasgow Humane Soc.; V. President, Technion Soc., Glasg. Publ.: The Slipped Disc and the Arching Back of Man, Fight Old Age, Migrain, new method of control and care. Ad. 22 Sandyford Pl., Glasgow, G3 7NG. ☎ 0141-221 7571.

NAGLER, Neville Anthony, M.A. (Cantab); b. London, Jan. 2, 1945; m. Judy née Mordant; Director General BoD; Exec. Cttee, Interfaith Network for the UK; form. Asst. Sec. Home Office (1980-91); UK Representative to UN Narcotics Comm., (1983-88); Chairman, Council of Europe Drug Co-op Group (1984-88); Haldane Essay Prize (1979); Princ. H.M. Treasury; Pte. Sec. Chancellor of Exchequer (1971); Fin. Rep. and Warden, Pinner Syn. (1979-91). Ad.: Board of Deputies ☎ 0171-543 5400. Fax: 0171-543 0100. Email bod@ort.org

NATHAN, Clemens Neumann, C.Tex.F.T.I., F.R.A.I., Officers' Cross, Austria; b. Hamburg, Aug. 24, 1933; Comp. Dir., P. (T., 1965-71) Anglo-Jewish Assn.; V. President (President 1983-1989); Jt. Chairman Consultant C. of Jewish Orgs. (Non-Govt. Org. at United Nations); Claims Conf, Memorial Foundation for Jewish Culture; Mem, Jewish Memorial C.; Hon. Fell. Shenkar Coll., Israel; Hon. Fell. SSEES, Univ. London; Director Sephardi Centre; CCJ, Fdr. Member, Internat. Cttee. for Human Rights in Soviet Union (1966); BoD (1979-85); Soc. of Heshaim, Span. & Port. Jews, Cong., Lond. (since 1979), Bd. of Elders (1977-83); Chairman, Sha'are Tikva Cttee. (1975-81); form. V. President, Textile Instit.; Textile Institute Medal for services to the Industry and Institute Cavalieri,

al Merito della Repub. Italiana. Publ.: Technological and marketing works. Ad.: 2 Ellerdale Cl., NW3 6BE. ☎ 0171-794 6537
NATHAN, David, b. Manchester, Dec. 9, 1926; m. Norma née Ellis; Writer; theatre critic, Jewish Chronicle, theatre critic, Daily Herald - Sun, (1960-69); President, Critics', Circle (1986-88), Deputy Ed., Jewish Chronicle, (1978-91). Publ.: Hancock (biography with Freddie Hancock), The Freeloader; The Laughtermakers, A Quest for Comedy; Glenda Jackson, A Critical Profile; John Hurt, An Actor's Progress; The Story So Far; Contributor to Shaw and Politics, Pennsylvania State Univ. Press. T.V.: That Was The Week That Was, etc.; Plays: A Good Human Story (Granada, 1977); The Belman of London (Radio 3, 1982); The Bohemians (Radio 4, 1983); Royal Television Soc. Writer's Award, Highly Commended 1978. Ad.: 16 Augustus Close, Brentford Dock, Brentford, Middx. TW8 8QE. ☎ 0181-568 8987.
NATHAN, Roger Carol Michael, 2nd Baron; Hon. LL.D. (Sussex); b. London, Dec. 5, 1922; H. President (Chairman 1971-77) C.B.F.-W.J.R (since 1977); President, JWB (1967-71); V. Chairman, Cancer Res. Campaign (Chairman Ex. Cttee. 1970-75); Chairman Cttee. on Energy and the Environment (1974); V. Chairman Cttee. on Charity Law and Practice (1976); Member Royal Com. on Environmental Pollution (1979-89); Memb. House of Lords Select Cttee. on Science & Technology (1994-); Member House of Lords Select Cttee. on European Com.; Chairman, Sub-Cttee. (Environment) (to 1992); Chairman, House of Lords Select Cttee. on Murder and Life Imprisonment (1988-89); Chairman Cttee. on Effectiveness and the Voluntary Sector (1989-90); Sol; V. President (Chairman 1975-77); Royal Society of Arts; Fel., Soc. of Antiquaries; Fel., Royal Geographical Soc.; Chairman, Sussex Downs Conservation Board (1992-); President Weald & Downland Open Air Museum (1994-). Master, Worshipful Co. of Gardeners (1964); Capt., 17/21 Lancers (Ment. in Dispatches). Ad.: House of Lords SW1 0PW .
NAVON, Yitzhak, b. Jerusalem, April 9, 1921; Form. Israeli Dep. Prime Min. and Educ & Culture Min.; President, State of Israel (1978-83); Member, Knesset (1965-78; since 1984); form. Chairman, Knesset Foreign Affairs and Defence Cttee.; Dir., Office of Prime Minister (Ben-Gurion) (1952-63). Publ.: Bustan Sephardi, Six Days and Seven Gates. Ad.: The Knesset, Jerusalem, Israel.
NETANYAHU, Benjamin, b. Tel Aviv, Oct. 21, 1946; m. Sara; Prime Minister of Israel (1996-); Deputy Chief of Mission in the Israeli Embassy in Washington (1982); Israel's Ambassador to the United Nations (1984-88); Member of Knesset, Deputy Foreign Minister (1988); Member of Knesset, Deputy Foreign Minister (1988); Senior membr of the Israeli delegation to the Madrid Peace Conference (Oct. 1991); Likud Party Chairman and party's candidate for Prime Minister (March 1993). Publ.: Yoni's Letter: The Letters of Jonathan Netanyahu (ed. 1978); International Terrorism: Challenge and Response (ed. 1979); Terrorism: How the West can Win (ed. 1986); A Place Among the Nations: Israel and the World (1992); Fighting Terrorism: How Democracies Can Defeat Domestic and International Terrorism (1995). Ad.: Prime Minister's Office, 3 Kaplan Street, Hakirya, Jerusalem 91919. ☎ 972-2-705555. Fax 972-2-664838.
NEUBERGER, Rabbi Julia Babette Sarah (née Schwab), M.A. (Cantab.) Hon. Doctorates Univ. Humberside, Ulster, City, Stirling, Oxford Brookes, Teesside, Nottingham; b. London, Feb. 27, 1950, m. Anthony; Chancellor Univ. Ulster (1994-); Council Univ. College, London (1994-); Council Memb. Save the Children Fund (1994-); Vis. Fel., Harvard Memorial Church (1994-); Memb. General Medical Council (1993-); Mem. Medical Res. C. (1995-); Chairman, ULPS Rabbinic Conference (1983-85); Lect., Leo Baeck Coll. Nat. Cttee. SDP (1983-85); Tr., Crusaid; Harkness Fell Harvard University (1991-92); Memb. Human Fertilisation and Embryology Authority (1990-95); T., Runnymede Trust (1990-); Visiting Fel., King's Fund Instit. (1989-91); Memb. C. St. George's House, Windsor (1989-); Chairman, Patients, Assn. (1988-91); Rabbi, S. Lond.

Lib. Syn. (1977-1989); Assoc., Newnham Coll., Cambridge, Presenter, Choices, BBC-1 (1986-87); Chairman, Camden & Islington Com. Health Services NHS Trust (1993-). Publ.: 'Women in Judaism'; The Fact and The Fiction in: 'Women's Religious Experience, (ed. Pat Holden), The Story of Judaism (for children), Judaism, in: Spiritual Care in Nursing (ed. McGilloway and Myco), Days of Decision, Vols. I-IV (ed.); Women's Policy, Defence and Disarmament, Bill of Rights and Freedom of Information, Privatisation, Caring for Dying Patients of Different Faiths (Lisa Sainsbury Foundation, 2nd ed. 1994). Ed. (with Canon John White) A Necessary End (1991); Whatever's happening to women (Kyle Cathie 1991); Ethics and Healthcare: The role of research ethics committees in the UK (Kings's Fund 1992); (ed.) The things that matter (1993), On being Jewish (1995). Ad.: 36 Orlando Road, SW4 0LF. ☎ 0171-622 2995. Fax: 0171-498 5712.

NEWMAN, Aubrey Norris, M.A. (Glasgow), M.A., D.Phil. (Oxon.), F.R.Hist S.; b. London, Dec. 14, 1927; Prof. of history, Leicester Univ.; President, Jewish Hist. Soc. (1977-79, 1992-93); Scholarship Ctee., JMC. Publ.: The United Synagogue 1870-1970, The Stanhopes of Chevening, Parliamentary Diary of Sir Edward Knatchbull, etc. Ad.: 33 Stanley Rd., Leicester. ☎ 0116 270 4065.

NEWMAN, Eddy, M.E.P., b. Liverpool, May 14, 1953. Manchester City Councillor (1979-85); Labour Member of European Parliament for Greater Manchester Central (1984-). Pub.: Respect for Human Rights in the European Union', a report of the European Parliament Committee on Civil Liberties, 1994. Ad.: Graphic House, 308 Moseley Rd, Levenhulme, Manchester M19 2LH. ☎ 0161-256 2525. Fax: 0161-257 3000.

NEWMAN, Rabbi Isaac, M.Phil. P.G.C.E., Dip. Counselling; b. London, Apr. 3, 1924; Chairman, Rabbis for Human Rights (Israel); M. Retd., Barnet Syn.; Sr. Lect., Judaica, & Chaplain, Middlesex Polytechnic, Trent Park; form. H.Sec., Rabbinical C., United Synagogue; Chaplain to R.A.F. Publ.: Talmudic Discipleship. Ad.: 90 Sderot Herzl, Jerusalem. ☎ 02 6525763.

NEWMAN, Rabbi Jeffrey, M.A.(Oxon.); b. Reading, Dec. 26 1941; m. Bracha; Minister Finchley Reform Synagogue (1973-); form. Chairman Rabbinic In-service training, Leo Baeck Rabbinical College (L.B.C.); form. Chairman, Pastoral Skills and Counselling Department L.B.C.; Chairman of Tr. Israel Palestine Centre for Research and Information; Ed. Living Judaism (1969-73); Lect. in Heimler Training. Contributor to various journals on Judaism, Psychology and Spirituality. Ad.: Finchley Reform Synagogue, Fallowcourt Avenue, N12 0BE. ☎ 0181-446 3244. Fax 0181-446 5980.

OPPENHEIM-BARNES, Baroness, Sally, P.C.; b. Dublin, July 1930; Min. of State for Consumer Affairs (1979-82); M.P. (Conservative) for Gloucester (1970-87); form. Chairman, Conservative Party Parl. Prices and Consumer Protection Cttee.; form Nat. V. President, Nat. Union of Townswomen's Guilds; form. Nat. V. President, R.O.S.P.A.; Chairman, Nat. Consumer C. (1987-89); Dir. (non-exec.) Robert Fleming, 1989; Non-Exec. Director. HFC Bank. Ad.: House of Lords.

OPPENHEIMER, Peter Morris, M.A.; b. London, Apr 16, 1938; Economics Lect., Oxford Univ., Student (Fel.) Christ Church Oxford; Dir. Jewish Chronicle Ltd.; Delbanco, Meyer & Co. Ltd.; Chief Economist, Shell Internat. Petroleum Co. (1985-86). Ad.: Christ Church, Oxford OX1 1DP. ☎ 01865 558226. Fax: 01865-516834.

ORGEL, Leslie Eleazer, D.Phil., F.R.S.; b. London, Jan 12, 1927; Sr. Fellow & Res. Prof., Salk Instit. and Adjunct Prof., Univ. of California, San Diego; Member Nat Acad. Sci., form. Fellow of Peterhouse, Cambridge Univ. Publ.: Scientific work. Ad.: Salk Instit., P.O. Box 85800, San Diego, California 92186-5800, USA.

ORLINSKY, Harry M., B.A., Ph.D.; b. Owen Sound, Ont., Can, Mar 14, 1908; Prof. of Bible. H.U.C.-J.I.R., New York (since 1943); Ed., Library of Biblical Studies, President, Soc. of Biblical Lit. (1969-70); Centennial Award for Biblical Scholarship; President, Amer. Friends of Israel Exploration Soc. (1951-79);

President, Internat. Org. for Masoretic Studies; President, Internat. Org. for Septuagint and Cognate Studies (1969-75), President, Amer. Acad. for Jewish Res.; Fel. Guggenheim Form. Soc. of Scholars, Johns Hopkins Univ. (1982); form. Vis. Prof., Hebrew Univ.; Acad. Cttee., Annenberg Res. Instit. (since 1987). Publ.: Works of Bible, lit. and hist., The Pentateuch A Linear Translation, 5 vols.; Revised Standard Version, Old Testament; The Torah, Edr.-in-chief of J.P.S. trans. (1963); The Prophets; The Writings; The So-called Servant of the Lord and Suffering Servant in Second Isaiah; Ancient Israel; Understanding the Bible; The Bible as Law; Tanakh; Essays in Biblical Culture and Bible Translation, etc. Ad.: 1 West 4th St., New York 10012. ☎ 212-674 5300.

OWEN, His Honour Judge Aron, B.A., Ph.D. (Wales); b. Tredegar, Gwent, Feb. 16, 1919, m. Rose née Fishman; Circuit Judge, South-East Circuit (1980-94); Dep. High Court Judge, Family Division; Freeman, City of Lond; C. JHSE; Patron, Jewish Marriage Co. Publ.: Social History of Jews in Thirteenth-Century Europe, Amos and Hosea, Rashi. Ad.: 44 Brampton Grove, NW4 4AQ. ☎ 0181-202 8151.

OZIN, Malcolm John; b. London, Nov. 14, 1934; Managing Dir., Investment & Securities Trust Ltd.; Hon. Jewish Blind & Disabled; Tr. Cecil Rosen Found.; Hon. Sec. Cavendish Housing Trust Ltd. Ad.: 118 Seymour Place, W1H 5DJ. ☎ 0171-262 2003. Email: mjo@jblind.cix.co.uk

PADWA, Rabbi Henoch Ber, b. Busk, Poland, Aug. 1908; m. Raisal née Tauber; Principal Rabbinical Authority of the Union of Orthodox Hebrew Congregations (1956-); Rabbi Shomrei Hadass, Vienna (1922-38); Rabbi of Yad Machane Yehuda, Jerusalem (Aidah HaCharedis) (1940-56). Publ.: Responsa Cheshen HaEphod (1963-91), 3 vols. Ad.: 140 Stamford Hill, London N16 6QT. ☎ 0181-802 6226. Fax: 0181-809 2610.

PATTERSON, David, M.A., Ph.D., D.H.L. (Hon.) (Balt.), D.H.L. (Hon.) (H.U.C.); b. Liverpool, June 10, 1922; Cowley Lect. in Post-Biblical Hebrew, Univ. of Oxford (1956-89); Emeritus President & H. Fel., Oxford Centre for Hebrew & Jewish Studies; Emeritus Fel. St. Cross Coll., Oxford; Vis. Prof. (Scholar in Res. 1981) Northwestern Univ. (1983, 1985 & 1993); Fel., Soc. Humanities (Vis. Prof. 1966-71) Cornell Univ. (1983); Fel., Humanities Res. Centre, Canberra (1979); Prof. Jewish Studies, Mt. Holyoke Coll., Mass. (1987-88); Scholar in Res., Vis. Prof. (1993) Hebrew Union Coll. Cincinnati (1982); Vis. Prof., Univ. of Sydney (1993), Vis. Prof. Smith Coll., Mass. (1994-95); Vis. Prof. Hampshire College, Mass. (1995); form. Lect. in Modern Hebrew, Manchester Univ. (1953-56); Fel., Jew. Academy of Arts and Sciences, U.S.A.; Brotherhood Award, Nat. Conf., Christians and Jews, USA (1979); Stiller Prize, Baltimore Hebrew Univ (1988); Webber Prize for translation of Hebrew Literature 1989; Member Senate of the Hochschule für Jüdische Studien, Heidelberg. Publ.: Abraham Mapu, The Hebrew Novel in Czarist Russia, A Phoenix in Fetters, Tradition and Trauma (with G. Abramson, eds) etc. Ad.: 35 Hayward Rd., Oxford, OX2 8LN. ☎/Fax: 01865 59003.

PAUL, Geoffrey D., O.B.E.; b. Liverpool, March 26, 1929; Ed. (1977-1990) Jewish Chronicle, American Affairs Ed 'JC' (1991-96). Ad. 1 Carlton Close, West Heath Rd., NW3 7UA. ☎/Fax 0181-458 6948.

PEPPER, Michael, B.Sc., M.A., Ph.D., Sc.D., F.R.S.; b. London, Aug. 10, 1942, m. Jeannette; Physics Prof, Cambridge Univ., Fel., Trinity Coll.; Warren Res. Fel., Royal Soc. (1978-86); Vis. Prof Bar-Ilan Univ. (1984). Ad.: Cavendish Laboratory, Madingley Rd., Cambridge, CB3 0HE. ☎ 01223 337330.

PEREIRA-MENDOZA, Vivian Moses, M.Sc. Tech., F.I.E.E., C.Eng.; b. Manchester, Apr. 8, 1917; Ret Educationist & Elec. Eng.; President, Bd. of Elders, Span. & Port. Cong., London (1988-89); V. President, (1986-88); Tr., Manchester Jewish Museum (1989-92); Dir., South Bank Poly., London. (1970-80). Ad.: 20 "Whitegates", Wilmslow Rd., Cheadle, Cheshire SK8 1HG. ☎ 0161-491 2900.

PERES, Shimon, b. Poland, Aug. 16, 1923; form. Prime Min. (1995-96); Foreign Min. (July 1992-95); Nobel Peace Prize, 1994; Prime Min. (Sept. 1984-Oct. 1986); Vice-Premier & Foreign Min. (Oct. 1986-Dec. 1988); Vice-Premier & Finance Min. (Dec. 1988-March 1990); Chairman, Israel Lab. Party (1977-Feb., 1992); Actg. Prime Min. (1977); Defence Min. (1974-77); Inf. Min. (1974); Communications & Transport Min. (1970-74), Absorption Min. (1969-70); form. Rafi Sec.-Gen.; Dep. Defence Min.; Dir.-Gen. of Defence Min.; went to Palestine 1934. Publ.: From These Men, Tomorrow is Now, The Next Phase, David's Sling. Ad.:.

PERSOFF, Meir, M.A. (Lond), F.R.S.A.; b. Letchworth, Aug. 25, 1941; Judaism Edr., Saleroom corr. form. News Edr. (1974-76), Arts Edr. (1980-85), Features Edr. (1976-90), Jewish Chronicle; President, Israel-Judaica Philatelic Soc.; form. Cttee., Jewish Book C.; form. Publ. Cttee., Jewish Marriage C.; Silver Medallist, internat. philatelic exhibitions, Jerusalem, London, Stockholm, Pretoria, Paris, Madrid. Publ.: The Running Stag: The Stamps and Postal History of Israel, edr., Jewish Living, The Hasmonean, etc. Ad.: 25 Furnival St., EC4A 1JT. ☏ 0171-415 1500.

PILCHIK, Rabbi Ely E., M.H.L., D.D.; b. Baranowicze, Poland, June 12, 1913; President, Central Conf of Amer. Rabbis (1977-79); President, Jewish Book C. of Amer. (1957-58). Publ.: Hillel, From the Beginning, Judaism Outside the Holy Land. Retired, now Senior Scholar-Congregation B'nai Jeshrun, Short Hills, N.J.; Author of 15 miniature books of Jewish content. Ad.: 1025 So. Orange Ave., Short Hills, N.J. 07078, USA. ☏ (201) 379 6275.

PINNER, Hayim, O.B.E., F.R.S.A.; Commander Order of Civil Merit (Spain); b. London, May 25, 1925; Dir., Sternberg Charitable Trust; Hon. Sec. CCJ; form. Sec.-Gen., BoD (1977-1991); H.V. President, Z.F.; V. President, Labour Z. Movt.; form Dir B'nai Brith (1957-77); form Exec., TAC; Lab. Frs. of Israel; Exec., CCJ; Member, Adv. C., World Congress of Faiths, Inter-Faith Network; Central Campaign; Exec., JIA; Chairman, Belsen Commemoration Cttee., Imperial War Museum; Freeman, City of Lond.; Hillel Foundation C.; BoD Defence & Eretz Israel Cttee.; World Zion. "Actions Cttee."; Jewish Agency Assembly; Chairman, Poale Zion; P. Z. Del., Lab. Party Confs.; Edr., Jewish Vanguard, Jewish Labour News, B'nai B'rith Journal. Ad.: 62 Grosvenor St., W1X 9DA. ☏ 0171-485 2538

PINNICK, Jeffrey, F.C.A.; b. London Dec. 6, 1935; T., BoD; Chairman, Fin. Cttee., BoD (V. Chairman, 1982-85); V.Chairman, Frs., Boys Town, Jerusalem, Ad.: Woburn House, Tavistock Sq., WC1H 0EP. ☏ 0171-387 3952.

PINTER, Harold, C.B.E.; b. London, Oct. 10, l930; Playwright. Publ.: The Birthday Party, The Caretaker, The Homecoming, Old Times, No Man's Land, Moonlight, Betrayal, and other plays. Ad.: Judy Daish Associates Ltd., 2 St Charles Place, W10 6EG. ☏ 0181-964 8811. Fax: 0181-964 8966.

PLANCEY, Rabbi Alan, b. Edinburgh, Oct. 30, 1941; M., Borehamwood & Elstree Syn.; Chairman, Rabbin. C. U.S. (1987-94); Member Chief Rabbi's Cabinet; H. V.-President & Rel Adv., Jewish Care; Area Chaplain Met. Police; Freeman of the City of London; M., Luton Syn. (1965-69); Youth M., Hampstead Garden Sub. Syn. (1970-76). Ad.: 98 Anthony Rd., Borehamwood, Herts., WD6 4NB. ☏ 0181-207 3759. Fax 0181-207 0568.

PLASKOW, Rev. Michael Lionel, L.T.S.C., A.L.C.M.; b. Palestine, July 8, 1936; R., Woodside Park Syn. (since 1956); Ch, Central Found. School; Jewish Old Boys Group; Cttee. Member, and Memb. Reg. Board Initiation Society; Chairman, Whetstone Police Sector Working Group; Form. Chairman, Assoc. Ministers (Chazanim); Chap. Barnet General & Finchley Memorial Hospitals; Authorised Mohel; Vis. M., Kisharon Sr. Sch., Finchley; Chaplain, Jewish Deaf Assn.; Past. Assist. Grand Chaplain in the Grand Lodge of England (Freemasonry); Norman B. Spencer award 1992 for research into Freemasonry, Freeman City of London (1994). Publ. The Story of a Community Woodside Park 1937-1987. Ad.: 12 Singleton Scarp, Woodside Park, N12 7AR. ☏ 0181-445 2860.

POLONSKY, Antony, B.A.(Rand), M.A., D.Phil (Oxon); b. Johannesburg, Sept. 23, 1940, m. Arlene née Glickman; Walter Stern Hilborn Professor of Judaic and Social Studies, Chair, Department of Near Eastern and Judaic Studies, Brandeis University; Vice-president, Institute for Polish-Jewish Studies, Oxford; Vice-president, American Association for Polish-Jewish Studies, Cambridge, MA; Member Exec Ctte, National Polish American-Jewish American Council; Ed., Polin: A Journal of Polish-Jewish Studies. Publ. Politics in Idependent Poland (1972), The Little Dictators (1973), The Great Powers and the Polish Question (1976), The Beginnings of Communist Rule in Poland (1981), (ed.) The Jews in Poland (1986), (ed.) A Cup of Tears (1989), (ed.) Recent Polish Debates about the Holocaust (1990), (ed.) Polish Paradoxes (1990), (ed.) The Jews of Warsaw (1991), (ed.) The Jews in Old Poland (1992). Ad.: 322 Harvard Street, Cambridge, MA 02139. ☎ (617) 492 9788, 736 2980, Fax (617) 736 2070.
PORTER, Sir Leslie, Ph.D. (Hon) (Tel Aviv Univ.) O.St.J.; b. July 10, 1920; President, Tesco p.l.c (1970-1985); Companion, Brit., Instit. of Management; V. President, Nat. Playing Fields Assn.; Member, Lloyd's; President, Instit., Grocery Distribution (1977-80); Chancellor, Tel Aviv Univ.; President, Frs., Boys Town Jerusalem; Gov., Hong Kong Baptist Coll.; Dr., Sports Aid Foundation; President, Coombe Hill Gold Club; Dyrham Pk. G.C., Frilford Hth. G.C.
PORTER, Dame Shirley (née Cohen), DBE., F.R.S.A., Hon.D. (Tel Aviv); b. Nov. 29, 1930; Form. Leader, Westminster City C. (1983-91); Lord Mayor (1991); V. President London Union of Youth Clubs; Past Master Worshipful Co. Environmental Cleaners; Freeman of the City of London; Dep. Ch., London Festival Ballet, Tidy Britain Group. Publ.: A Minister for London, Efficiency in Local Government. Ad.: PFM Advisory Ltd., 12 Hans Rd., London SW3 1RT ☎ 0171-584 4277.
POSEN, Felix, B.A. (John Hopkins Univ.), D.Phil. (Hon., Hebrew Univ.; b. Berlin, Oct 24, 1928; m. Jane née Levy; Gov. Oxford Centre for Hebrew and Jewish Studies; Gov. Hebrew University; Chairman Jerusalem Fellows; V.-Chairman Mandel Institute, Jerusalem; Tr. Institute of Archaeo-metallurgical Studies, University of London; Member of the Bd of Alma Hebrew College, Tel Aviv; Member of the Bd of the College of Pluralistic Judaism, Jerusalem; Council member of the JPR; Member Cttee Interfaith Mission for Christians, Muslims and Jews. Ad.: 24 Kensington Gate, London W8 5NA ☎ 0171-584 0914. Fax: 0171-584 0904. Email: nesop@dircon.co.uk
PRAG, Derek Nathan, M.A. (Cantab.), H.D.Litt. (Univ. Herts), Hon. MEP; b. Merthyr Tydfil, Aug. 6, 1923; m. Dora née Weiner; MEP (Cons), for Hertfordshire (1979-94); Dep. Chairman Instit. Cttee. (1989-94); Conservative Spokesman, Instit. Cttee. (1982-84) and Pol. Cttee. (1984-87); Dep. Chairman, Cttee. of Enquiry into Racism and Fascism (1984-87); Dep. Chairman European Parl. Delegation for Relations with ASEAN (1979-87); Member, European Parl. Delegation for relations with Israel (1989-94); Chairman, All-Party Disablement Group (1980-94); V. Chairman, European Parl.-Israel Intergroup (1990-94); Chairman, Lond. Europe Soc. (1973-); Dir., Lond. Inf. Off., EEC (1965-73); Head Publ. Div., E.E.C. Jt. Inf Service (1959-67); Inf Off., High Auth., Europe Coal & Steel Cttee (1955-59); Journalist with Reuters News Agency (1950-55) in London, Brussels and Madrid, Dep. Chairman, Conservative Group for Europe (1974-77 and 1991-93); H. Dir., Wyndham Place Tr. (1977-79), Mem. Council (1979-); Commander of the Order of Leopold II (Belgium) (1966); Silver Medal of European Merit, Luxembourg (1974); H. Dir., EEC. Com (1974). Publ.: Businessman's Guide to the Common Market (1973), Europe's international strategy, (1978) etc. Ad.: Pine Hill, 47 New Rd., Digswell, Herts., AL6 0AQ. ☎ 01438-712999. Fax: 01438-840422.
PRAIS, Sigbert J., M. Com., Ph.D., Sc.D. (Cantab.), Hon. D. Litt. (City), F.B.A.; b. Frankfurt am Main, Dec. 19, 1928; Economist, Edr. Adv. Bd., Jewish Journal of Soc.; Vis. Prof. of Econometrics, City Univ.; Sr. Res. Fel., Nat. Instit. of Econ. and

Social Res., London; form. H. Consultant, BoD Statistical and Demographic Res. Unit; Economist, Internat. Monetary Fund; Adv. on Statistics, Govt. of Israel; Lect., Cambridge Univ. Publ.: Productivity and Industrial Structure; The Evolution of Giant Firms; Analysis of Family Budgets; Productivity, Education and Training. Ad.: 83 West Heath Rd., NW3 7TN. ☎ 0181-458 4428.

PRAWER, Siegbert Salomon, M.A., D. Litt. (Oxon.), M.A., Litt.D. (Cantab.), Ph.D., Hon.D.Litt. (Birmingham), D. Phil. hc. (Cologne), F.B.A.; b. Cologne, Feb. 15, 1925; Member of the German Academy of Languages and Literature; Taylor Prof of German, Emer., Oxford Univ.; Hon. Fel. Jesus College, Cambridge; Hon. Fel. Queen's Coll.. Oxford; Hon. Fel., form. President, Brit. Comparative Lit. Assn.; H.Fel., form. H. Dir., Lond. Univ. Instit. of Germanic Studies; Hon. Member of the Modern Language Association of America; V. President of the English Goethe Soc. (1994-), President (1991-94); Memb. of the London Bd. of the Leo Baeck Inst. (1969-96); form. Prof of German, Lond. Univ. and Head of German Dept., Westfield Coll.; Sr. Lect. Birmingham Univ.; Vis. Prof, City Coll., New York, Chicago, Harvard, Hamburg, California, Pittsburgh, Otago (New Zealand), Australian Nat. Univ., Canberra, Brandeis; C., Leo Baeck Instit.; Goethe Medal (1973); Isaac Deutscher Prize (1977); Friedrich Gundolf Prize (1986); Gold Medal of the Goethe Gesellschaft 1995. Publ.: Writings on German, English, Jewish and Comparative Literature. Ad.: The Queen's Coll., Oxford OX1 4AW.

PRENDERGAST, Dame Simone Ruth (née Laski), D.B.E., J.P., D.L., O.St. J.; b. Manchester, July 2, 1930;, President C.B.F. World Jewish Relief; Chairman, Jewish Refugees Cttee. (1981-1991); Pt. time Commissioner for Commission for Racial Equality (1996-); Commandant JLGB (1986-); Co. Patron Fed. Womens Zionists; Chairman, Blond McIndoe Centre for Med Res.; Chairman, Westminster Children's Soc. (1980 90); Court of Patrons, Royal Coll. of Surgeons; Chairman, Greater London Area Conservative & Unionist Assns. (1984-87), Solicitors Disciplinary Tribunal (1986-); Lord Chancellors Advisory Cttee. (Inner London) (1981-91); V. Chairman, Age Concern Westminster (1989-); Member East London & Bethnal Green Housing Assoc. (1990); Tr., Camperdown House Trust (1990-). Ad.: 52 Warwick Sq., SW1V 2AJ.

PRESTON, Rosalind (née Morris), O.B.E.; b. London, Dec. 29, 1935; Professional Volunteer; V. President British WIZO (1993-); Jt. Hon. Sec. CCJ (1997-); Co. Vice Chair Interfaith Network, UK; form. V. President, BoD; form. President, The National Council of Women of G.B. (1988-90). Ad., 7 Woodside Close, Stanmore, Middx. HA7 3AJ. ☎ 0181 954 1411. Fax: 0181-954 6898.

PRIJS, Leo, Pro. Dr.; b. Breslau, June 27, 1920; Prof Univ. (retired); Ph.D. in semitic languages, Basle 1948; Lect. on Bible, Univ. Bar-Ilan, (1956-1959); Lect. in Jewish Studies, Univ. Munich (1962-68); Prof. (1968-86). Publ.: Judische Tradition in der Septuaginta (1948); Grammatikalische Terminologie des Abraham ibn Esra (prize winning work of the Univ. Bern) (1950); Die Jeremia Homilie Pesikta Rabbati Kap. 26 (1966); Judische Religion, eine Einführung (1977); Die Welt den Judentums (1980) (2nd ed. 1982), Worte zum Sabbat (1990); Abraham ibn Esras commentary to Bereshit Chapters 1-3 critical edition and explanation (Hebr) (1990); Catalogue of Hebrew mss. in Frankfurt-am-Main and Stuttgart (1982-93, with Prof. E. Roth); 11 other books and 30 articles in scholarly periodicals; See also: Encycl. Judaica (Engl.), vol. XIII, p. 1091, s.v. Prijs. Ad.: 18 St. George's Road, NW11 0LR. ☎ 0181-455 3176.

PULZER, Peter George Julius, M.A., B.Sc.(Econ.), Ph.D.; b. Vienna, May 20, 1929; Gladstone Prof, Government & Publ. Admin., Fel. All Souls College, Oxford; Official Student (Fel.) in Politics, Christ Church, Oxford (1962-84). Publ.: The Rise of Political Antisemitism in Germany and Austria, Political Representation and Elections in Britain, Jews and the German State: The Political History of a Minority (1848-1933); German Politics 1945-1995; Germany 1870-1945: Politics, State Formation and War. Ad.: All Souls College, Oxford, OX1 4AL. ☎

01865 281408.
RABINOVITCH, Rabbi Nachum L., B.Sc., M.A., Ph.D., b. Montreal, Apr 30, 1928; Rosh Yeshiva, Maale Adumim and Res. Prof, Jews, Coll., Lond.; form. Princ., Jews, College; Rab., Clanton Park Syn., Toronto. Publ.: Hadar Itamar, Probability and Statistical Inference in Ancient and Medieval Jewish Literature; Critical Edn. of Rambam's Mishneh Torah with comprehensive commentary, Yad P'shutah, Vols. 1-6. Ad.: 72 Mizpe Nevo St., Maale Adumim, Israel 90610. ☎ : (02) 5353655.
RABINOWICZ, Rabbi Harry, B.A., Ph.D.; M., Willesden & Brondesbury Syn.; M., St. Albans Hebrew Cong. (1947-49); M., Ilford and Dist. Syn. (1949-51); Dollis Hill (1951-78), Cricklewood (1978-88). Publ.: The Will and Testament of the Biala Rabbi, The World of Chasidism, Legacy of Polish Jewry, Treasures of Judaica, Guide to Life The Jewish Literary Treasures of Engiand and America, Encyclopedia of Hasidism (ed.), Hasidism and the State of Israel, Guide to Hasidism, Hasidic Story Book, Chasidism: The Movement and its Masters, Chasidic Rebbes, The World Apart: History of Hasidism in England, The Prince who turned into a rooster. Ad.: 31 Sherwood Rd., NW4. ☎ 0181-203 2634.
RABINOWITZ, Rabbi Benjamin, B.A., M.Phil., A.J.C.; b. Newcastle upon Tyne June 21, 1945; M., Edgware Syn.; Chaplain, Edgware Hospital (1983-); Tr., Co-Chairman Edgware CCJ (1982-); form. M. Yeshurun Heb Cong., Gatley; Blackpool Hebrew Cong. Ad.: 14 Ashcombe Gdns. Edgware Middx. HA8 8HS. ☎ 0181-958 5320/6126 (Synagogue office).
RABINOWITZ, Rabbi Lippa, b. Manchester, Nov. 15, 1930; Rav, Vine St Syn., Manch.; Princ., Manch. Jewish Grammar Sch., form. Princ. Judith Lady Montefiore Coll., Ramsgate; Lect., Etz Haim Yeshiva, Tangier. Publ.: Eleph Lamateh Chidushim on Sugioth (Israel). Ad.: 57 Waterpark Rd., Salford.
RABSON, Ronald Jeffery, M.A.; Dipl. Arch. F.R.I.B.A.; b. Lond, March 3, 1928; Chartered Architect; form. Chairman & Jt. H. Sec., Lond. Bd. Jewish Rel. Educ.; form. Chairman & Gov., J.F.S. Comp. Sch.; form. Chairman, Instit. of Jewish Educ.; Gov., Michael Sobell Sinai Sch.; Life M., C., US. Ad.: 16 Broadfields Ave., Edgware, Middx, HA8 8PG. ☎ 0181-958 9035. Fax: 0181-905 4035.
RADOMSKY, Rabbi David, B.A., M.A.; b. East London, South Africa, Sept. 4, 1956; Deputy H.T. and Head of Jewish Studies at Immanuel Coll.; Lect., Jews, Coll., (1991-); form. M., Wembley Syn.; Com. M. Jewish Com. in Eire (1985-88); Talmud Lect., Midrashiat Noam Yeshiva High Sch. Pardes Hanna, Israel (1982-85). Ad.: 27 Windsor Ave, Edgware, Middx. HA8 8SR. ☎ 0181-958 3879.
RAJAK, Tessa, née Goldsmith, M.A., D.Phil., b. London, Aug. 2, 1946, m. Harry; Scholar and University Teacher; Hd. Dept of Classics, Univ. Reading; Grinfield Lect. in the Septuagint, Oxford (1994-96). Publ.: Josephus, the historian and his society, The Jews among Pagans and Christians in the Roman Empire (jt. ed). Ad.: 64 Talbot Rd., N6 4RA.
RAPHAEL, David D., D.Phil., M.A., Hon. F.I.C.; b. Liverpool, Jan. 25, 1916; Emer. Prof of Philosophy, Lond. Univ.; Chairman, Westminster Syn. (1987-89); form. Head Humanities Dept., Imperial Coll.; Prof. Phil., Reading Univ.; Prof. Pol. & Soc. Phil., Glasgow Univ.; Sr. Lect., Moral Phil., Glasgow Univ.; Prof., Phil., Otago Univ., Dunedin; form. Princ. Off M. of Lab. and Nat. Service. Publ.: The Moral Sense, Richard Price's Review of Morals, Moral Judgement, The Paradox of Tragedy, Political Theory and the Rights of Man, British Moralists 1650-1800, Problems of Political Philosophy, Adam Smith's Theory of Moral Sentiments (Jt. Edr.), Hobbes: Morals and Politics, Adam Smith's Lectures on Jurisprudence (Jt. Edr.), Justice and Liberty, Moral Philosophy, Adam Smith, etc. Ad.: Humanities Programme, Imperial College, SW7 2BX.
RAPHAEL, Frederic Michael, M.A. (Cantab.), F.R.S.L.; b. Chicago, Aug. 14, 1931; Writer. Publ.: Novels, Obbligato, The Earlsdon Way, The Limits of Love, The Graduate Wife, The Trouble with England, Lindmann, Darling, Orchestra and

Beginners, Who Were You With Last Night?, Like Men Betrayed, April June and November, California Time, The Glittering Prizes, Heaven and Earth, After The War, The Hidden I, A Double Life, Old Scores, Coast to Coast; Short stories, Sleeps Six, Oxbridge Blues, Think of England, The Latin Lover. Non-fiction: Byron, Somerset Maugham, Cracks in the Ice, Of Gods and Men, France: the Four Seasons, The Necessity of Anti-Semitism. Published Screenplays and Drama: Two for the Road, Darling, Oxbridge Blues. Translations: Lorca-Blood Wedding; (with Kenneth McLeish) The Poems of Catullus, The Oresteia of Aeschylus, Sophocles' Aias, Euripides' Medea, Bacchae and Hippolytus. Ad.: c/o Rogers, Coleridge and White, 20, Powis Mews, W11 1JN.

RAPHAEL, Ralph Alexander, C.B.E., B.Sc., Ph.D., D.Sc., A.R.C.S., D.I.C., F.R.I.C., F.R.S.E., F.R.S.; b. Croydon, Jan. 1, 1921; Emeritus Prof., Organic Chemistry Cambridge Univ.; form. Regius Prof. of Chemistry, Glasgow Univ.; form. Prof of Organic Chemistry Queen's Univ., Belfast. Publ.: Scientific writings. Ad.: 4 Ivy Field, High St., Barton, Cambs., CB3 7BJ.

RAPPAPORT, Charles David, M.A. (Cantab.); b. Lond., May 12, 1913; form. Dir., Jewish Colonization Assn (J.C.A.); form. Sec., For. Aff & Israel Cttees. BoD & Rep., Co-ord. Bd., Jewish Orgs. at U.N. (1959-68); Fdr. Member, U.N.A. Human Rights Cttee.; form. Educ. Off., CCJ; Sec., Palestine Cttee. BoD (1947-49). Ad.: 7 Howard Walk, N2 OHB.

RASMINSKY, Louis, C.C., C.B.E., LL.D., D.C.L., D.H.L.; b. Montreal, Feb. 1, 1908; Gov., Bank of Canada (1961-73); President, Industrial Development Bank (1961-73); H. Fel., Lond. Sch. of Economics. Ad.: 1006-20 Driveway, Ottawa, Ontario, K2P 1C8, Canada. ☎ 613-594-0150.

RAYNE, Baron, of Prince's Meadow in Greater London, Life Peer (Sir Max Rayne), Hon. LL.D. (London); b. Feb. 8, 1918; Dir. of Companies; Chairman, London Merchant Securities, plc.; Chairman, Nat. Theatre Bd. (1971-88); Special Tr., St. Thomas' Hospital; Gen. C., King Edward Vll's Hospital Fund for Lond.; Chairman, Lond. Festival Ballet Tr. (1967-75); Fdr. Patron, The Rayne Fdn.; H.V. President, Jewish Care. H.Fel., Univ. Coll., Lond., Darwin Coll., Cambridge, Univ. Col., Oxford, Lond. Sch. of Economics; Royal Coll. of Psychiatrists; King's Coll. Hospital Med. School; King's College London; Westminster School; Officier, Legion d'Honneur, 1987 (Chevalier, 1973); Hon. Fel., UMDS, 1992; Hon. F.R.C.P. 1992. Ad.: 33 Robert Adam St., W1M 5AH. ☎ 0171-935 3555.

RAYNER, Rabbi John D., C.B.E., M.A. D.D.(Hon.); b. Berlin, May 30, 1924; Hon. Life President, Union of Liberal and Progressive Synagogues, M. Emer. (Sr. M. 1961-89), Lib. Jewish Syn.; M., South London Lib. Syn. (1953-57); Chairman, C., Reform and Lib. Rabbis (1969-71, 82-84, 1989-92); V. President and Lect., Leo Baeck Coll.; Co-President, Lond. Soc. of Jews & Christians. Publ.: Guide to Jewish Marriage; Gate of Repentance (co-ed.), Judaism for Today (co-author), Passover Haggadah (ed.), The Jewish People: Their History and Their Religion (co-author), Siddur Lev Chadash (co-ed), An Understanding Judaism, A Jewish Understanding of the World. Ad.: 37 Walmington Fold, N12 7LD. Tel/Fax: 0181-446 6196.

REICHMANN, Eva Gabriele (née Jungmann), Dr. Phil. (Heidelberg), Ph.D. (Lond.); b. Lublinitz, Upper Silesia; Edr., Der Morgen, (Berlin), Bd., Leo Baeck Instit.; C. of Jews from Germany. Publ.: Hostages of Civilisation: A Study of the Social Causes of Antisemitism, Greatness and Doom of German-Jewish Existence (Documents of a Tragic Encounter), etc. Ad.: 2 Strathray Gdns., NW3 4NY. ☎ 0171-794 4343.

REIF, Stefan, B.A., Ph.D. (Lond.), M.A. (Cantab.); b. Edinburgh, Jan. 21, 1944; Dir., Taylor-Schechter Genizah Research Unit, Cambridge Univ.; Sr. Under-Libr., & Head of Oriental Dept., Cambridge Univ. Library; Member, Faculties of Oriental Studies and of Divinity, Cambridge Univ.; President JHSE (1991-92); President Brit. Assoc. for Jewish Studies (1992); T., Cambridge Traditional Jewish Cong.; Gov., Carmel Coll.; Lect., Hebrew and Semitics, Glasgow Univ.

(1968-72); Princ., Glasgow Hebrew Coll. (1970-72); Asst. Prof., Hebrew Language and Lit., Dropsie Coll. (1972-73). Publ.: Shabbethai Sofer and His Prayer Book; Judaism and Hebrew Prayer; Hebrew Manuscripts at Cambridge University library; (ed.) Interpreting the Hebrew Bible, Cambridge Univ. Library Genizah Series, etc. Ad.: Cambridge University Library, CB3 9DR. ☎ 01223-333000. Fax: 01223-333160.
REISS, Simon, b. Berlin, Dec. 31, 1923; Comp. Dir.; V. President Zionist Fed.; President Western Marble Arch Syn.; Mem. BoD; Chairman, Jt. Cttee., Youth Aff; Tr. Balfour Diamond Jubilee Trust; form. Chairman, Yad Vashem Cttee., BoD; President, JIA Fur Trade Cttee. Ad.: Third Floor, 25 Enford Street, Marylebone, London W1H 2DD. ☎ 0171-258 0344. Email: admin@bdjt.win-uk.net
RICHARDSON, Montague, M.A., (Cantab.); b. London, July 4, 1918; form. Welfare & Youth Off., US & Welfare Off., Jewish After-Care Assn.; form. Chairman, Tower Hamlets Soc.; form. V. Chairman Tower H. Soc. Service C.; Chaplain: Aldington, Blantyre House, Canterbury, Cookham Wood Elmley, E. Sutton Park, Maidstone, Rochester, Stanford Hill, Swaleside Prisons & Dover Youth Custody Centre; V. President (form. Chairman) AJY; Tr. and form. Chairman, Tower Hamlets Old People's Welfare Trust; form. Tr., London Museum of Jewish Life; form. Tr., Children's Aid Cttee. Charitable Fund; form. Chairman, Brady Boys' Club; form. V. Chairman Tower H. Adult Educ. Instit.; form. Chairman, Soc. Security Appeal Tribunal; form Exec., Tower H. Racial Equality C.; Chairman, Zekeinim Club. Ad.: Flat 1, 12 Belsize Sq., NW3 4HT. ☎ 0171-794 9684.
RIETTI, Robert, Cavaliere Ufficiale, O.M.R.I., Officer, Knight of the Italian Republic; b. London, Feb. 8, 1923; Actor, broadcaster, writer, director, editor of Drama Quarterly GAMBIT; BAFTA nomination for Special Award (1993); English translations of the entire dramatic works of Luigi Pirandello, (John Calder). Ad.: 40 Old Church Lane, NW9 8TA. ☎ 0181-205 3024. Fax: 0181-200 4688.
RIFKIND, Rt. Hon. Sir Malcolm, Q.C., P.C.; b. Edinburgh, June 21, 1946; form. M.P. for Edinburgh, Pentlands (Con.) (1974-97); Foreign Secretary (1995-97), Min. of Defence (1992-95), Min. of Transport (1990-92); Sec. of State for Scotland (1986-90), Min. of State Foreign & Commonwealth Office (1983-86); Parl. Under-Sec. of State, F.C.O. (1982-83); Parl. Under-Sec. of State, Scottish Office (1979-82); H. President, Scottish Young Conservatives (1976-77); H.Sec., Conservative Frs. of Israel Parl. Group (1974-79); Sec. Conservative Parl. Foreign & Commonwealth Affairs Group (1977-79); Opposition Spokesman on Scottish Affairs (1975-76); Select Cttee. on Overseas Development (1978-79); Edinburgh Town C. (1970-74). Ad.:
RIGAL, Mrs. Margaret H., (née Lazarus); b. London, Nov. 28, 1932; Co.-Chairman, Women's Campaign for Soviet Jewry (the 35s), H.Sec., Jewish Aged Needy Pension Soc.; Co-ord Parl. Wives for the Release of Soviet Jewry; Sec., Interfaith Cttee. for the Rights of Jews, Christians and Muslims in the USSR. Ad.: 14 Pembridge Place, W2 4XB. ☎ 0171-229 8845 .
ROBERG, Rabbi Meir, B.A. (Hons.), M.Phil., Dip.Ed.; b. Wurzburg Germany, June 25, 1937; HM, Hasmonean High Sch.; Chairman, Academic Cttee. Massoret Instit.; Chairman, Assoc. of Head Teachers of Orthodox Jewish Schls.; form. HM Middlesex Reg. Centre; Dep. HM, Yavneh Grammar Sch. Ad.: 34 Green Lane, NW4 2NG. ☎ 0181-203 2632.
ROBINS, Ruth, B.A., TTHD; b. Johannesburg, October 18, 1946; Headteacher JFS. Ad.: 175 Camden Road, London NW1 9HD. ☎ 0171-485 9416. Fax: 0171-284 3948.
ROBSON, Jeremy, b. Llandudno, Sept. 5, 1939; Chairman & Man. Dir., Robson Books Ltd. Publ.: 33 Poems, In Focus (poetry), Poetry anthologies, incl. The Young British Poets (ed.), Poems from Poetry and Jazz in Concert (ed.). Ad.: Robson

Books, 5/6 Clipstone St., W1P 8LE. ☎ 0171-323 1223. Fax: 0171-636-0798.
ROCHE, Barbara Maureen, (née Margolis), B.A. (Oxon.); b. London, April 13, 1954; Barrister; M.P., Hornsey and Wood Green (Lab. 1992-); Shadow Trade & Industry Minister. Ad.: House of Commons, London SW1. ☎ 0171-219 3000.
ROITT, Ivan Maurice, M.A., D.Sc. (Oxon.), F.R.C.Path., F.R.S., Hon. F.R.C.P.; b. Lond., Sept. 30, 1927; Emer. Prof. Immunology UCL. Publ.: Essential Immunology. Ad.: Windeyer Building, UCL., Cleveland Street, W1P 6DB. ☎ 0171-380 9360. Fax: 0171-380 9400.
ROMAIN, Rabbi Jonathan Anidjar, B.A.; Ph.D.; b. Lond., Aug. 24, 1954; M., Maidenhead Syn., Chairman, Youth Assn. of Syns. in Gt. Brit. (1972-74); Director, Jewish Information and Media Science. form. M., Barkingside Progressive Syn. Publ.: The Open and Closed Paragraphs of the Pentateuch, In a Strange Land, Signs and Wonders, The Jews of England, Faith and Practice, I'm Jewish, My Partner Isn't, Tradition and Change, Till Faith Us Do Part, Renewing the Vision. Ad.: 9 Boyn Hill Ave., Maidenhead, Berks. SL6 4ET. ☎ 01628 71058. Fax: 01628 25536.
ROSE, Rabbi Abraham Maurice, M.A.; b. Birmingham, Sept. 7, 1925; Exec. Dir., C. of Young Israel Syn. (Israel) (1975-90); Adm. Dir. & Lect., Jerusalem Academy of Jewish Studies (1973-74); Exec. Dir., Office of the Chief Rabbi (1962-73); Dir., Conf of Europ. Rabbis; form. M., Sutton Syn. (1952-62), Derby Syn. (1948-52). Ad.: Rechov Machal 30/2, Jerusalem 97763. ☎ 5812859. Fax: 5810080.
ROSE, Aubrey, O.B.E., F.R.S.A.; b. London, Nov. 1, 1926; Solicitor; Senior V. President, BoD (1991, 1994); Commissioner & Dep. Chairman Commission for Racial Equality (CRE); Tr. Project Fullemploy; Tr. Commonwealth Human Rights Initiative; Member, Working Group Commonwealth Jewish Coun.; form. Chairman, Defence and Group Rel. Cttee. BoD; Chairman, Working Group on Environment BoD, Publ.: Jewish Communities in the Commonwealth (CJT); Judaism and Ecology (1992); Journey into Immortality, the Story of David Rose (1997); Brief Encounters of a Legal Kind (1997). Ad.: Monkenholt, Hadley Green Road, Barnet, Herts. EN5 5PR. ☎ 0181-449 2166. Fax: 0181-449 1469.
ROSE, Eliot Joseph Benn, C.B.E., b. London, June 7, 1909; Chairman, Penguin Books (1973-80); Editorial Dir., Westminster Press (1970-73); Dir., Internat. Press Instit. Zurich (1952-62); Dir., Survey of Race Relations in Brit (1963-68); Chairman, Inter-Action Tr. (1968-84), Co. Fdr., Runnymede Tr., (Chairman 1980-91); Tr., Writers & Scholar's Educ. Trust; Consultant to Unicef; form. Lit. Edr., 'Observer', Sec., Baldwin Fund for German Jewish Refugees (1939). Publ.: Colour and Citizenship. Ad.: 37 Pembroke Sq., W8 6PE. ☎ 0171-937 3772 .
ROSE, Jeffery Samuel, B.D.S. F.D.S., D.Orth. R.C.S.; b. Harrow, Middx., Dec. 22, 1924; Ret. Consultant Orthodontist, London Hospital (1967-90); Chairman Reform Foundation Tr. (1996-); President Brit. Orthodontic Soc. (1994-95); V. President World Union Progressive Judaism (1995-); form. Chairman, Leo Baeck Coll. (1985-88); Life Gov. (1988); Hon. Fellow (1988); Chairman, Euro. Region, World Union Prog Judaism (1990-95); form. V. President & Chairman RSGB; form. V. President & Chairman, North Western Reform Syn.; President, Brit. Paedontic Soc. (1964-65); President, Brit. Soc. for the Study of Orthodontics (1972-73). President, British Assoc. of Orthodontists (1991-94). Ad.: 9 Meadway Close, NW11 7BA. ☎ 0181-455 5771. Fax: 0181-731 9588.
ROSE, Mrs. Joyce Dora Hester (née Woolf), C.B.E., J.P., D.L. (Herts); m. Cyril Rose, b. London, August 14, 1929; Hertfordshire Family Mediation Service (1996-); S.W. Hertfordshire Hospice Charitable Trust (The Peace Hospice) (1996-); Chairman, Nat. Exec. and Council, Magistrate Assn. (1990-93); Mem. Bd. Dir. Apex Tr. (1994-); Herts Care Tr. (1995-); V. President Magistrates Assn. and V. President Hertfordshire Branch; H. D. Laws, Univ. of Hertfordshire (1992); form. P. (1979-80), Chairman (1982-83), Lib. Party; President, S.W. Herts Const. L.D.; form. Chairman, Watford (Herts.) Bench (1990-94); Dep.

Chairman, Family Proceedings Panels; P. & Chairman, Women's Liberal Fed. (1972-73); V. Chairman, UK Cttee. for Unicef (1968-70); Ad.: Brindmere, 38 Main Ave., Moor Park, nr Northwood, Middx., HA6 2LQ. ☎ 01923 821385. Fax 01923 840515.

ROSEN, Clive H., F.B.C.O.; b. London Apr. 15, 1938; City Univ. 1963. Freeman, City of London 1964; Chairman Z. F. Fund-Raising Cttee. (1996-); Hon. Sports Vision Consult. to Leyton Orient FC (1997-); Hon. Tr. East London and the City Health Authority L.O.C. (1994-96); Chairman, Menorah J.N.F. Committee (1974-1985); Hon. Off. J.N.F. (1979-81, 1983-90); Memb. Zionist Federation National Council, (1989-); Hon. Tr. Z. F. (1994-96); Founding memb. Israel-Judaica Stamp Club; Chairman, J.P.S. (1990-); Ed. consult., The Judaica Collector Journal; Dir. David Elliott (Opticians) Ltd. (1965-). Ad.: 152 Morton Way, London N14 7AL. ☎ 0181-886 9331. Fax 0181-886 5116. Email: clive@london.web.net

ROSEN, Rabbi Jeremy, M.A. (Cantab.); b. Sept. 11, 1942; Rabbi Western Syn. (1985-1991); Rabbi, Western Marble Arch Syn., (1991-1992); Chief Rabbi's Cabinet advisor Interfaith (1987-90); Prof., Jewish Studies F.V.G. Antwerp. (1991-); Tr., Yakar Foundation; Princ., Carmel Coll. (1971-84); Rabbi, Giffnock & Newlands Syn., Glasgow (1968-71). Ad.: c/o Yakar, 2 Egerton Gardens, London NW4 4BA.

ROSENBERG, Mrs. Rosita (née Gould); b. London, Sept. 2, 1933; Dir., ULPS Ad.: The Montagu Centre, 21, Maple St., W1P 6DS. ☎ 0171-580 1663. Fax: 0171-436 4184.

ROSENTHAL, Jack (Morris), C.B.E., B.A., M.A (Hon.), H.D. Litt.; b. Manchester, Sept. 8, 1931; m. Maureen née Lipman; Writer; Brit. Academy of Film and Television Arts Writers Award, 1976; Royal Television Society Writers' Award, 1976, Royal Television Society Hall of Fame (1993). TV plays include: The Evacuees, Ready When You Are, Mr McGill; Barmitzvah Boy (also stage musical), Auntie's Niece; Spend, Spend, Spend; The Knowledge; And A Nightingale Sang; Bag Lady; P'Tang, Yang, Kipperbang, Day to Remember, Wide-Eyed And Legless, London's Burning; Bye, Bye, Baby; Eskimo Day; etc. Feature Films include: Yentl (co. writer), The Chain. Ad.: c/o Casarotto Ramsay Ltd., 60-66 Wardour St., W1V 4ND.

ROTBLAT, Joseph, C.B.E., M.A., D.Sc. (Warsaw), Ph.D. (Liverpool), D.Sc. (Lond.), F.Inst P.; b. Warsaw, Nov. 4, 1908; Prof. of Physics in the Univ. of London at St. Bartholomew's Hospital Med Coll. (1950-76); now Emer.; Asst. Dir., Atomic Physics Instit., Free Univ. of Poland (1937-39); Lect., Liverpool Univ. (1940-49), Dir. of Research in Nuclear Physics, Univ. of Liverpool (1945-49); V. President, Atomic Scientists, Assn. Publ.: Scientific works. Ad.: 8 Asmara Rd., NW2 3ST. ☎ 0171-435 1471.

ROTH, Sir Martin, F.R.S.; b. Budapest, Nov. 6, 1917, m. Constance née Heller; Prof. Emer. of Psychiatry Cambridge Univ.; Fel., Trinity Coll. Cambridge; Mems. WHO Steering Cttee for Epidemiological Studies of Alzheimer Disease; form. Prof. of Psychological Medicine, Newcastle Univ.; first P. Royal Coll. of Psychiatry (1971-75); Member, Medical Research C. (1964-68). Publ.: Clinical Psychiatry (with E. Slater); The Reality of Mental Illness (with J. Kroll, 1986), Handbook of Anxiety, vols. 1-5 (Ed. with R. Noyes & G. Burrows 1990-93), Alzheimer Disease and related disorders (with L. Iversen 1986), Psychiatry, human rights and the law (with R. Bluglass, 1985). Ad.: Trinity College, Cambridge. ☎ 01223-242106. Fax: 01223-412193.

ROTHSCHILD, Edmund Leopold de, C.B.E., T.D., Hon. D.Sc., (Salford Univ.); b. London, Jan. 2, 1916; Hon. LL.D. (Univ. of Newfoundland); Hon. V. President, C.B.F., World Jewish Relief; V. President, CCJ; President, Ajex; Bd. Govs., Technical Univ., Nova Scotia; form. Major, Royal Artillery, 1939-46, (Commanded P. Battery, Jewish Field Regt.). Publ.: Window on the World. Ad.: New Court; St. Swithin's Lane, EC4P 4DU.

ROTHSCHILD, Sir Evelyn de; b. Aug. 29, 1931; Merchant Banker; Dir., Industrial Dwellings Soc. Ltd.; form. President, JBS Ad.: New Court, St. Swithin's Lane, EC4P 4DU. ☎ 0171-280 5000.
ROTHSCHILD, Leopold David de, C.B.E.; b. London, May 12, 1927; Dir., N. M. Rothschild & Sons; Investment Adv. Cttee., JWB; Ad.: New Court, St. Swithin's Lane, EC4P 4DU. ☎ 0171-280 5000.
ROTHSCHILD, Miriam (Hon. Mrs. Miriam Lane), C.B.E., F.R.S., Hon. Doc. (Oxford, Hull, Göteburg, North-Western Univ., Chicago Leicester, Open University); b Ashton, Peterborough., Aug. 5, 1908; d. of the late Hon. N. Charles Rothschild and aunt of Lord Rothschild; zoologist and farmer; Tr., Brit. Museum; H. Fellow, St. Hugh's Coll., Oxford; Romanes Lect. (1985); Vis. Prof, Lond. Univ.; Wigglesworth Medal, RHS Victorian Medal of Honour; Med. Soc. Chem. Oecology; Linnearc Soc.; Mendel Award. Publ.: Catalogue of Fleas in the Rothschild and British Museum Collection, Fleas, Flukes, and Cuckoos, and 300 other zoolog. works; Biography of 2nd Lord Rothschild The Butterfly Gardener, Atlas of Insect Tissues, Animals and Man, Butterfly Cooing like a Dove, Rothschild Gardens, Rothschild's Reserves. Ad.: Ashton Wold, Peterborough, PE8 5LZ.
ROTHSCHILD, Nathaniel Charles Jacob, Lord, M.A. (Oxon.); b. Cambridge, Apr. 29, 1936; Chairman RIT Capital Partners plc; President St. James's Place Capital plc; Chairman of the J. Rothschild Group; President IJPR (1992-); Chairman of the Tr. of the National Gallery (1985-91); Chairman of the Tr. of the National Heritage Memorial Fund (1992-); C., Weizmann Instit. Foundation; Tr., Jerusalem Foundation. Ad.: 27 St. James's Pl., SW1A INR. ☎ 0171-493 8111. Fax: 0171-493 5765.
RUBEN, David-Hillel, B.A., Ph.D.; b. Chicago, July 25, 1943; Professor of Philosophy, London School of Economics (1984-97); University of Glasgow, Lecturer in Philosophy (1970-75); University of Essex, Lecturer in Philosophy (1975-79); The City University, London, Senior Lecturer in Philosophy (1979-84). Publ.: Marxism and Materialism (1979); The Metaphysics of the Social World (1985); Explaining Explanation (1990); Explanation, editor (1993). Ad.: Dept of Philosophy, Logic and Scientific Method, London School of Economics (University of London), Houghton Street, London WC2A 2AE. ☎ 0171-955 7333. Fax: 0171-242 0392.
RUBENS, Alfred, F.S.A., F.R.I.C.S., F.R.Hist.S.; b. London, July, 1903; form. President, JHSE; V. President, Jewish Museum; C., Anglo-Israel Assn.; War Service: Admiralty (1942-43), Intelligence Corps (1943-45). Publ.: Anglo-Jewish Portraits, A Jewish Iconography, A History of Jewish Costume. Ad.: 104 Wigmore St., W1H 9DR. ☎ 0171-486 1884.
RUBENS, Bernice Ruth, Hon. D. Litt. Univ. Wales; b. Cardiff, July 26, 1926; author; film dir.; Fel. Univ. Coll. Cardiff. Publ.: The Elected Member (Booker Prize, 1970), Brothers, Mr. Wakefield's Crusade, Our Father, A Solitary Grief, Mother Russia, Autobiopsy (1993) etc. Ad.: 111 Canfield Gardens, London NW6 3DY. ☎ 0171-625 4845.
RUBENS, Mrs. Frances (née de Pinna Weil); b. London, March 6, 1910; H. V. President (President, 1963-66) Internat. C. of Jewish Women; Chairman, Women's Adv. C., United Nations Assoc. (1973-76); Exec. Cttee. U.N.A. (1973-76); form. Member, Exec Cttee., For. Affairs Cttee., BoD; Chairman, BoD U.N,A. Jewish Affiliates Coordinating Cttee. (1979-83); form. Man. Cttee., Nat. C. of Women, Gt. Britain; form. V.Chairman, N.C.W. Soc. Welfare Cttee.; UK Cttee., Human Rights Year, 1968; UK Co-ordinating Cttee. for Internat. Women's Year, 1975; V. President (Dep. President, 1971-75) AJA; Chairman, Assoc. of Jewish Women's Orgs. in UK (1967-69); H.L. Member, C. of League of Jewish Women; Recipient of B'nai B'rith Award, 1967. Ad.: 104 Wigmore St., W1H 9DR. ☎ 0171-486 1884.
RUBENS, Kenneth David, F.R.I.C.S., F.R.S.A.; b. Lond., Oct. 10, 1929; Chartered

Surveyor; President, World Jewish Relief; President, UK Jewish Aid & Development; Past Chairman, Industrial Dwellings Soc. (1885) Ltd.; Chairman, Jewish Museum, London., Chairman, ORT Trust.; L. Elder Span. & Port. Jews, Cong.; Past Master, Worshipful Company, Painter-Stainers.; Hon. Life Mem., Brit. Property Fed. Ad.: 104 Wigmore Street, W1H 9DR. ☎ 0171-486 1884.
RUBINSTEIN, William David, B.A., Ph.D., F.A.HA., F.A.S.S.A., F.R.Hist.S.; b. New York, Aug. 12, 1946; m. Hilary L. Rubinstein; Professor of History, The University of Wales, Aberystwyth (1995-); Prof. of Social and Economic History, Deakin University, Australia; Ed., Journal of the Australian Jewish Historical Society (1988-95); President, Australian Association for Jewish Studies (1989-91); Member, Committee of Management, Executive Council of Australian Jewry (1983-95). Publ.: Men of Property: The Very Wealthy in Britain Since the Industrial Revolution (1981); The Jews in Australia: A Thematic History (with Hilary L. Rubinstein) (1991); Capitalism, Culture, and Decline in Britain, 1750-1990 (1993); A History of the Jews in the English-Speaking World: Great Britain (1996; The Myth of Rescue (1997). Ad.: Department of History, University of Wales, Aberystwyth, Penglais, Ceredigion SY23 3DY. ☎ 01970 622661. Fax 01970 622676.
RUDMAN, Michael Edward, M.A. (Oxon.), B.A. (Oberlin Coll.); b. Tyler, Texas, USA, Feb. 14, 1939; Artistic Director, Sheffield Theatres (1992-94); Dir. Chichester Festival Theatre (1989-90); Assoc Dir., Nat. Theatre, (1979-88); Dir. Lyttelton Theatre (1979-81), Bd. Dirs. Art. Dir.; Hampstead Theatre (1973-78); Art. Dir., Traverse Theatre Club (1970-73). Ad.: c/o Peter Murphy, Curtis Brown Group, 4th Floor, 28/29 Haymarket, SW1Y 4SP. ☎ 0171-396 6600. Fax: 0171-396 0110.
RUDOLF, Anthony, B.A., (Cantab); b. London, Sept. 6, 1942; Writer, Publisher & Translator; Ad. Ed. Modern Poetry in Translation, Ad. Ed., Jerusalem Review; Adam Lecturer, Kings Coll. London (1990); Ed./Literary Ed. of European Judaism, (1970-75). Publ.: Piotr Rawicz and Blood from the Sky (1996); The Diary of Jerzy Urman (1991); Primo Levi's War against Oblivion, (1990); After the Dream, (1979). Ad.: 8 The Oaks, Woodside Av., N12 8AR. ☎/Fax 0181-446 5571.
RUSSELL, Henry, J.P., M.B., B.S., B.Hy', D.P.H., F.R.S.A.; b. Jerusalem; Physician; Ald. (Lord Mayor 1961-62, Sheriff 1964-65), Newcastle upon Tyne; Freeman, City of Newcastle; form. Chairman, Northern Planning Cttee; form. President, Rep.C., North-East Jewry; form. Chairman, North-East, Lab. Frs. of Israel; Fdr.P., B'nai B'rith Lodge; form. C., Newcastle Univ., form. Chairman, Finance Cttee., Newcastle Area Health Auth.; Vatican Order of Malta. Ad.:
RUSSELL, Cllr. Mrs. Theresa Science, O.B.E., J.P., D.C.L. (Hon.) F.R.S.A.; b. Hull; Rotary Intl. Paul Harris Fel. (1989); Lord Mayor (1965-66), form. Lady Mayoress and Sheriff's Lady, Newcastle upon Tyne; Chairman, N. East Emunah; Chairman, Newc. Inf & Publicity Cttee.; Chairman, North-East Diocesan After-Care Cttee.; Brit. President, Internat. Friendship Force; Gov., Royal Grammar Sch.; Reg. Hospital Area Health Auth.; Fdr. President, B'nai B'rith Lodge; B.B.C. Appeals Cttee. Newcastle B.B.C. Radio Cttee.; Vis. Magistrate; Low Newton Prison, Exec., Northumbria Tourist Bd.; Jewish Woman of Distinction Award (1977); Chairman, Newcastle Children in Danger. Ad.:
SABIN, Albert, M.D., D.Sc. (Hon.), Ph.D. (Hon.), Litt.H.D. (Hon.), L.H.D. (Hon.), LL.D. (Hon.); b Bialystok, Aug. 26, 1906; Scientist; form. President, Weizmann Inst., Rehovot, Emer. Dist. Res. Prof., Univ. of Cincinnati Cincinnati, Ohio; Med. Univ. of S Carolina, Charleston, S. Carolina. Publ.: 380 publs. in scientific jnls. Ad.: Sutton Towers, Apt. 1001, 3101 New Mexico Ave. N.W., Washington DC, 200165902 USA. ☎ (202) 363-8066
SACKS, Chief Rabbi Jonathan Henry, M.A. (Cantab.), Ph.D., Hon. DD (Camb.), Hon. DD. (King's Coll., Lond.), Hon. D. Univ. (Middx.); b. London, March 8, 1948; Chief Rabbi of the United Hebrew Congregations of the Commonwealth

(1991-); Princ., Jews College and holder of the Lord Jakobovits Chair (1984-1990); M. Marble Arch Syn. (1983-1990); M., Golders Green Syn. (1978-1982); BBC Reith Lect. (1990); Ed. L'Eylah (1984-1990). Publ.: Torah Studies (1986); Tradition and Transition (1986); Traditional Alternatives (1989); Tradition in an Untraditional Age (1990); The Persistence of Faith (1991); Arguments for the Sake of Heaven (1991); Orthodoxy Confronts Modernity (1991); Crisis and Covenant (1992); One People: Tradition Modernity and Jewish Unity (1993); Will We Have Jewish Grandchildren? (1994); Faith in the Future (1995); Community of Faith (1995); The Politics of Hope (1997). Ad.: Office of the Chief Rabbi, 735 High Road, London N12 0US.

SAFRAN, Rabbi Alexander, Ph.D. (Vienna); b. Bacau, Romania, Sept. 12, 1910; Chief Rabbi of Geneva (1948-); Lect. in Jewish Thought at Univ. of Geneva; form. Chief Rabbi of Romania and Member of Romanian Senate. Publ.: La Cabale, Israel dans le Temps et dans l'Espace, etc. Ad.: 1 rue Crespin, CH 1206 Geneva. ☎ 346-66-97. Fax: 346-8405.

SAIDEMAN, Seymour Geoffrey, F.C.A.; b. London, April 5, 1939; Consultant; National President B'nai B'rith; form. President, United Syn. (1992-96); Chairman, Chief Rabbinate Council (1992-96); form. Chairman, Board of Man. of the Beth Hamidrash Cttee.; form. Chairman, Ministerial Placement Cttee.; form. Chairman, Singer's Prayer Book Publications Cttee; form. Chairman, London Board of Jewish Rel. Educ. (1984-87); form. Chairman, Governors JFS Comprehensive Sch. (1984-87). Ad.: Hillel House, 1-2 Endsleigh St., WC1H 0DS. ☎ 0171-387 5287. Fax 0171-387 8014. Email: bnai@ort.org

SALAMAN, Esther, A.R.A.M., L.R.A.M., (Mrs. Paul Hamburger); b. Barley, Herts; Singing Consultant, Trinity Coll. Music; form. Prof, Guildhall School of Music and Drama; Prof. singer & teacher of Voice, form. Hon. Org., Jewish Inst. Sunday Concerts; Recitals and Talks on B.B.C. Radio 3; form. Consultant Teacher for Nat. Opera Studio. Master Classes and Demonstrations England and Overseas; H. Music Adv., Spiro Instit. Publ.: Unlocking your Voice, freedom to sing, 1989. Ad.: 114 Priory Gdns., N6 5QT. ☎ 0181-340 3042.

SALASNIK, Rabbi Eli; b. Old City of Jerusalem; Rav. in London since 1950 Chairman, Rabbin. C., East Lond. and West Essex; District Rav Lond. Bd. for Shechita. Ad.: 8 The Lindens, Prospect Hill, Waltham Forest, London E17 3EJ. ☎ 0181-520 1759

SALASNIK, Rabbi Zorach Meir, B.A., F.J.C.; b. Lond., July 29, 1951; M., Bushey & Distr. Syn.; V. Chairman Rabbin. C., US; Community Development Programme, U.S.; Chaplain, Rishon Multiple Sclerosis Aid Gp.; Cttee., Michael Sobell Sinai School; Rabbinical Adv., Agency for Jewish Education; form. M., Notting Hill Syn., Leytonstone & Wanstead Syn. Ad.: 8 Richfield Rd., Bushey Heath, Herts., WD2 3LQ. ☎ 0181-950-6453. Fax: 0181-421 8267.

SAMUEL, David Herbert, 3rd Viscount, of Mount Carmel and of Toxteth, O.B.E., M.A., (Oxon), Ph.D., (Jerusalem); b. Jerusalem, July 8, 1922; Scientist, Prof. Emeritus, Weizmann Inst. of Science, Rehovot, Israel, President, Shenkar Coll. of Textile Tech. and Fashion, Ramat Gan, Israel (1987-94); Vis. Prof. Dept. of Chemistry, Univ. York (1995-97); Vis. Prof. Dept. of Pharmacology, Yale Univ. Sch. of Med. (1983-84); McLaughlin Prof, McMaster Univ. Sch of Health Sciences, Hamilton, Canada (1984); Royal Society Vis. Prof, M.R.C. Neuroimmunology Unit Zoology Dept., Univ. Coll., Lond (1974-75); Dir., Centre for Neurosciences and Behavioural Res. (1978-87), Weizmann Inst. of Science; Dean, Faculty of Chemistry (1971-73); Dep. Chairman, Scientific C. (1963-65); Vis. Prof., Sch. of Molecular Sciences, Warwick Univ. (1967); Res. Fel., Laboratory of Chemical Biodynamics (Lawrence Radiation Lab.) Univ. of California, Berkeley (1965-66); Res. Fel., Chemistry Dept., Harvard Univ., Cambridge Mass. (1957-58); Postdoctoral Fel., Chemistry Dept., Univ. Coll., Lond. (1956); Bd. Israel Centre of Psychobiology; Bd. Tr., Menninger Foundation, Topeka, Kansas USA; Bds. of Bezalel Academy of Arts and Design;

Tel Aviv Museum of Art; C., Anglo-Israel Assn., Lond.; Brit.-Israel Arts Foundation; form. Chairman, US-Israel Educ. Foundation; Chairman, Isr. Bd. Amer.-Israel Cultural Foundation; Advisory Bd.; Chairman, Batsheva de Rothschild Foundation; Academic Adv. Cttee., Everyman's (Open) Univ. Cttee on Teaching of Chemistry, Intl. Union of Pure & Appl. Chemistry (1981-89); Served in British Army (UK, India, Burma, Sumatra) (mentioned in Despatches) (1942-46). Publ.: The Aging of the Brain (D. Samuel et al, edrs.), and over 300 scientific articles. Ad.: Weizmann Institute, Rehovot, Israel. ☎ (972)-8934429; 99553242 (home). Fax: (972)-99552511.

SAMUEL, Edgar Roy, B.A. (Hons.), M. Phil., F.R.Hist.S., F.B.C.Optom., D.C.L.P.; b. London, 1928; Chairman Publ. Cttee J.H.S.E.; Past Dir., Jewish Museum (1983-95); Past President, JHSE (1988-90), Records & Treasures Cttee., Span. & Port. Cong., Lond. Publ.: Contribs. to Transactions of Jewish Hist. Soc.; The Portuguese Jewish Community in London, 1656-1830 (1992). Ad.: 4 Garden Court, 63 Holden Rd., N12 7DG. ☎ 0181-445 1327.

SAMUELSON, Sir Sydney Wylie, C.B.E., Hon. D. Sheffield Hallam U.; b. Paddington, London, Dec. 7, 1925, m. Doris née Magen; British Film Commissioner; Fel. British Film Institute (1997); Fd., Chairman & Chief Exec., Samuelson Group PLC (1954-1990); Trustee, Chairman Bd. Man. and Fellow, British Academy of Film and Television Arts (1973-); Chairman (1965-85), President (1985-), Israel Association for the Habilitation of the Mentally Handicapped (AKIM) (1965-); Memb., Exec. Cttee, Inter-Parliamentary Council Against Antisemitism; Memb., Beth Hatefutsoth. Ad.: 31 West Heath Ave., NW11 7QJ.

SANDELSON, Neville Devonshire, M.A. (Cantab.); b. Leeds, Nov. 27, 1923; Barrister; Dir., Consultancy Comps.; M.P. for Hillingdon, Hayes and Harlington (Lab. 1971-81, SDP 1981-83). Ad.:

SANDLER, Merton, M.D., F.R.C.P., F.R.C.Path; F.R.C.Psych, C.Biol., F.I.Biol.; b. Salford, Mar. 28, 1926; Emeritus Prof. of Chemical Pathology, Royal Postgraduate Med. Sch., Instit. of Obstetrics & Gynaecology, London Univ.; H. Consultant, Chemical Pathologist, Queen Charlotte's and Chelsea Hospital. Publ.: Scientific writings. Ad.: 12, Model Cottages, East Sheen, SW14 7PH. ☎ 0181-878 1790. Fax: 0181-878 7408.

SARAH, Rabbi Elizabeth, B.Sc. (Soc.); b. 1955; Semichah Leo Baeck Coll. (1989); Rabbi, Buckhurst Hill Reform Syn. (1989-1994); Pt. time Lect. Leo Baeck College (1997-); Dir., Programmes Division, Reform Synagogues of Great Britain and Dep. Dir. of the Sternberg Centre (1994-97); co-ed., Learning to Lose – Sexism and Education (1980), On the Problem of Men (1982); ed., Reassessments of First Wave Feminism (1982); researcher into Rabbi Regian Jonas, 1902-44 (died in Auschwitz, first woman to receive Semichah); contr. to Hear our voice – women rabbis tell their stories (1994), Jewish Explorations of Sexuality (1995), The Dybbuk of Delight (1995), Renewing the Vision (1996); Chair, Leo Baeck Coll. In-service Training Team; Mem. 'The Half-empty Bookcase' Co-ord. Group. Ad.: LBC, The Sternberg Centre for Judaism, 80 East End Road, N3 2SY.

SARNA, Nahum Mattathias, M.A., (Lond.), Ph.D.; b. Lond., March 27, 1923; Vis. Prof. Florida Atlantic Univ. (1995-96); Vis. Prof. Columbia Univ. (1992); Vis. Prof., Yale Univ. (1992-94); Prof, Emer. (1985) Bible Studies, Brandeis Univ., USA; Chairman, Nr. Eastern and Judaic Studies Dept., Brandeis (1969-75); President, Assn. for Jewish Studies (1983-85); Departmental Edr., Encyclopaedia Judaica; Edr., translator, Jewish Publ. Soc. Bible; Ed., Proc. of the American Academy for Jewish Research (1990-); Gen. Edr., Jewish Publ. Soc. Bible Commentary Series; Edr. Bd. Soc. Biblical Lit. Monograph Series; Fel., Instit.. Advanced Studies, Hebrew Univ. (1982-83); Academic Adv. C., Nat. Foundation Jewish Culture; Fel., Amer. Academy; Jewish Res. Member, Israel Exploration Soc., Palestine Exploration Soc.; Biblical Colloquium; Minister's diploma, Jews,

Coll. Lond. Edr. Prc. American Acad. Jewish Research. Publ.: Understanding Genesis, Exploring Exodus, Commentary on the Book of Exodus, Commentary on the Book of Genesis, A New Translation of the Book of Psalms (co-auth.), (Contribs.) Encyclopaedia Britannica, Encyclopaedia Judaica, Encyclopaedia Hebraica, Encyclopaedia of Religion, An Introduction to the Book of Psalms, Songs of the heart, Oxford Companion to the Bible, A new translation of the Book of Job (co-author), etc. Ad.: 7886 Chula Vista Crescent, Boca Raton, Fl. 33433. ☎ (407) 395 0486. Fax (561) 395 7289.

SAVITT, Martin F., Inst.S.M., b. London, 1921; form. V. Chairman, Z. Fed. of Brit. & Ireland; Chairman, For. Aff. Cttee. & Chairman, form. Org. Cttee. for Warsaw Ghetto Memorial mtgs.; BoD; V. President, BoD (1979-85); form. Chairman Jew Def. & Group Rel. Cttee.; form. Chairman Brit-Isr. Chamber of Commerce; Anti-Boycott Co-ord. Cttee.; Chairman, Euro. Com. on Antisemitism; Mem. Holocaust Educ. Tr.; Dir. Material Claims Against Germany; form. Member, Gov. Bd., WJC; V. President, (Ch 1964-66) Ajex; Chairman, Ajex Anti-Defamation Cttee. (1954-58); President, Ajex Housing Assn. Ltd.; Fdr., Jt Cttee. Against Racialism; form. Chairman, All Party & Interfaith Cttee. Racial Justice; form. H. Nat. T., Distr. 15, B'nai B'rith, Com., Anti-Defamation League; Life President, Monash Br., Brit. Legion; Member, Earl Haig Br.; R.A.S.C. Western Desert (1941-42), later in charge transport maintenance, Suez Canal zone. Ad.: 18 Laurel View, N12 7DT. ☎ 0181-445 7017. Fax 0181-446 5499.

SCHINDLER, Rabbi Alexander M., B.S.S., B.H.L., M.H.L., D.H.L., C.C.N.Y. and HUC-JIR; b. Munich, Oct. 4, 1925; Immediate Past President, Union of Ameican Hebrew Congs. (Reform); President, Memorial Foundation for Jewish Culture; V. President, World Jewish Congress; Bd. of Directors, American Joint Distribution Cttee; Chairman, Conf. of Presidents of Major Amer. Jewish Orgs. (1976-79); Hon. Doctorates: HUC-JIR, Lafayette, Univesity of South Carolina, Hamilton, Wittenberg, College of the Holy Cross; Townsend Harris Medal, C.C.N.Y.; Bublick Prize, Hebrew University; servied in Ski Troops US Army, won Purple Heart and Bronze Star. Ad: Union of American Hebrew Congregations, 838 Fifth Ave. New York, N.Y. 10021 ☎ 650-4150. Fax: (212) 650 4169.

SCHLESINGER, John Richard, C.B.E., M.A. (Oxon.); b. London, Feb 16, 1926; Film Dir., Princ. Films directed: Terminus, A Kind of Loving, Billy Liar, Darling, Far from the Madding Crowd, Midnight Cowboy, Sunday Bloody Sunday, The Day of the Locust, Marathon Man, Yanks, Honky Tonk Freeway, Separate Tables (HBO & HTV), An Englishman Abroad (BBC), The Falcon and the Snowman, The Believers, Madame Sousatzka, Pacific Heights, Cold Comfort Farm, The Innocent, A Question of Attribution (BBC), Eye for an Eye. Plays: No, Why, Timon of Athens, I and Albert, Heartbreak House, Julius Caesar, True West. Operas: Les Contes d'Hoffmann, Der Rosenkavalier, Un Ballo in Maschera. Ad.: Duncan Heath, ICM, 76 Oxford St., W1R 1RB.

SCIAMA, Dennis William Siahou, M.A., Ph.D., F.R.S.; b. Manchester, Nov. 18, 1926; Prof., Astrophysics, Internat Sch. for Advanced Studies, Trieste; Consultant, Internat. Centre for Theoretical Physics, Trieste; form. Physics Prof, Texas Univ.; Maths. Lect., Cambridge Univ.; Jr. Res. Fel., Trinity Coll., Cambridge; Sr. Res. Fel. All Souls Coll., Oxford; Extraord. Fel., Churchill Coll. Cambridge. Publ.: The Physical Foundations of General Relativity, Modern Cosmology, The Unity of the Universe, Modern cosmology and the dark matter problem. Ad.: 7 Park Town, Oxford OX2 6SN. ☎ 01865 559441.

SEBAG-MONTEFIORE, Harold, M.A. (Cantab.); b. Dec. 5, 1924; m. Harriet née Paley; Barrister at Law, President, AJA (1965-71), Dep. Circuit Judge (1973-83); Tr., Royal Nat. Theatre Fdn.; Jt. President, Barkingside Jewish Youth Centre (1988-94); Freeman City of London, Chevalier Legion d'Honneur. Ad.: 7B Vicarage Gate, W8 4HH. ☎ 0171-937 1831.

SECHER, Paul, LL.B.; b. Whitehaven, March 1, 1951; Man. Dir., J.S.B. Group

(Training Publishing and Consultancy); Chairman, C'wealth Jewish C. Publ.: Coauth., books & video manual on employment law, health and safety at work, communication skills. Ad.: 37 Fortress Road, NW5 1AD. ☎ 0171-267 7792. Fax: 0171-267 6394.
SEGAL, Anthony Walter, M.B., Ch. B., M.D., M.Sc., Ph.D., D.Sc., F.R.C.P.; b. Johannesburg, Feb. 24, 1944; Charles Dent Prof. of Med Lond. Univ., attached Univ. Coll. & Middlesex Hospital Med.; Sch. Ad.: 48B, Regents Park Rd., NW1 7SX. ☎ 0171-586 8745.
SEGAL, Judah Benzion, M.C., M.A. (Cantab.), D.Phil. (Oxon.), F.B.A., b. Newcastle, June 21, 1912; V. President, RSGB (1985-91); Emer. Prof. of Semitic Languages Sch. of Oriental & African Studies, London Univ.; President, form. Princ., Leo Baeck Coll.; President, NorthWestem Reform Syn.; V. President, Anglo-Israel Archaeological Soc; Lect. in Aramaic, Ain Shams Univ., Cairo (1979); form. with Sudan Gov. (1939-41); Intelligence Off, M.E.F. (1942-44); Capt, Brit. Mil. Admin., Tripolitania (1945-46). Publ.: Hebrew Passover, History of the Jews of Cochin and other Orientalist studies Ad. 17 Hillersdon Ave., Edgware, Middx. HA8 7SG. ☎ 0181-958 4993.
SELBY, The Hon. David Mayer, A.M., E.D., Q.C., B.A., LLB., Hon D. Sydney Univ. (1991), Lieut-Col. (R.); b. Melbourne Mar. 13 1906; Justice of the Supreme Court of N.S.W. (1962-76); Dep. Chancellor, (1971-87); Fel. Senate, Sydney Univ. (1964-89); President, N.S.W Medico-Legal Soc.; V. President, N.S.W. Marriage Guidance C. (1964-89); form. O.C., Rabaul A/A Battery (1941-42; Chief Legal Off., Eastern Command, Acting Justice Supreme Court, Territory of Papua & New Guinea (1961-62), Life Member, Australian Red Cross Soc. (1990); Hon. Dr. Syd. Univ. 1991. Publ.: Hell and High Fever, Itambu. Ad.: 19 Pibrac Ave., Warrawee N.S.W., 2074.
SHAHAR, Tovia, B.A. (Hebrew Univ.); b. Lond., Sept. 14, 1927; form. Sr. Educ. Officer, London Bd. of Jewish Religious Education; Registrar, Central Exam. Bd., Jews' Coll.; Lect., Hebrew Grammar, Jerusalem Teachers Coll.; HM, Moriah Coll., Sydney; Dir., Jewish Studies, Mt. Scopus Coll., Melbourne. Publ.: Medinatenu. Ad.: 9 Durley Rd., N16 5JW. ☎ 0181-800 2603 .
SHAMIR, Yitzhak; b. Ruzinoy, Poland, 1915; form. Prime Min., State of Israel (June 1990-June 1992; Oct. 1983-Sept 1984; Oct. 1986-Mar. 1990); Vice-Premier (1984-86), Foreign Min. (1980-86); Herut Leader; M. K. (since 1973); Member, Betar in Poland emigrated Palestine 1935; joined Irgun Zvai Leumi (1937); later helped reorganise Central Cttee., Lohamei Herut Yisrael. Publ.: Summing Up (1994). Ad.: Beit Amot Misphat, 8 Shaul HaMelech Blvd., Tel Aviv. ☎ Tel Aviv 695-1166.
SHAW, Rabbi Joseph, B.A.; b. London, July 2, 1922; M. Emer. (M., 1952-87) Palmers Grn. & Southgate Syn.; form. M., Sutton & Distr. Syn. (1948-49); Asst. M., Hampstead Syn. (1949-52); Jt. Chaplain to Mayor of Borough of Southgate (1958-59); Chaplain to Mayor of Borough of Southgate (1964-65); Chaplain to Mayor of Lond. Borough of Enfield (1980-81); Jt. Chaplain, Southgate, Palmers Grn. & Distr. Br., Ajex; H. Chaplain, Nat. Assn. of Jewish Friendship Clubs (1985-1993). Ad.: 24 Russell Gdns., NW11 9NL. ☎ 0181-455 5368.
SHAW, Martin, B.A., I.C.F.M.; b. London, Aug. 16, 1949; Ind. Consultant to the Charity and Voluntary Sector (1995-); Exec. Dir. of the Assoc. for Jewish Youth (1989-95), Senior Youth Off., London Borough of Ealing (1986-89); S Youth Off., I.L.E.A. (1983-86), Project Dir. Nat. C. for Voluntary Youth Services (1979-82). Publ.: 'Young People and Decision'. Ad.: 64 The Grove, Edgware, Middx. HA8 9QB. ☎ 0181-958 6885. Email: mshaw@dircon.co.uk
SHAW, Peter; b. Lond., Dec. 17, 1935, m. Leila; Sec., Jewish Youth Fund; Exec. Dir., Jewish Child's Day; Clerk, Finnart House School Trust; Dir. British Friends of the Assaf Harofeh Medical Centre; Bd. Memb. (Chief Exec. 1971-77) Redbridge Jewish Youth & Com. Centre; Exec. C., Bernhard Baron St. George's Jewish Settlement; Tr., The Duveen Trust Org. (1990-96); Sec., Stamford Hill

Assoc. Clubs (1959-71); Dep. Dir., Youth & Hechalutz Dept., WZO (1977-80); Exec. Dir., Norwood Child Care (1980-84); form. Chairman, Jewish Assn. of Professionals in Soc. Work, Chairman, Assn. of Execs. of Jewish Com. Orgs. (1982-84); Chairman, Jewish Programme Materials Project (1980-84). Ad.: 2 Lodge Close, Canons Drive, Edgware, Middx HA8 7RL. ☏ 0181-381 2894. Fax: 0181-446 7370.

SHEFF, Mrs. Sylvia Claire (née Glickman), M.B.E., J.P., B.A.; b. Manchester, Nov. 9, 1935; Ret. Teacher; Asst. Nat. Dir. (Nat. Projects Dir., 1974-85), Conservative Frs. of Israel (1985-89); Fdr. & Dir., Friendship with Israel, Group (European Parl.) (1979-90); P. (Fdr. Chairman, 1972-80), Manch. 35 Group Women's Campaign for Soviet Jewry (1980-); H. Sec., Nat. C. for Soviet Jewry (1987-89); Assoc. Dir. Jewish Cultural & Leisure Centre (1990-93); Del. BoD (1987-). Int. Co-ord. Yeled Yafeh Fellowship of Children of Chernobyl (1990-93). Magistrate (1976-). Ad.: 6, The Meadows, Old Hall La., Whitefield, Manchester M45 7RZ. ☏ 0161-766 4391.

SHELDON, Rt. Hon. Robert Edward, P.C., M.P.; b. Sept. 13, 1923; M.P. (Lab.) for Ashton-under-Lyne (since 1964); Chairman, Public Accounts Cttee.; form. Fin. Sec., Treasury. Ad.: 27 Darley Ave., West Didsbury, Manchester M20 8ZD.

SHELLEY, Ronald Charles, F.C.A.; b. London, March 27, 1929; T., BoD (1991-); Form. Chairman, Central Jewish Lect. & Information Cttee., BoD; V. President (Nat. Chairman, 1975-77) Ajex; Chairman, Ajex Housing Assn. (1987-91); Tr., London Museum of Jewish Life. Ad.: Second Floor, 45 Mortimer St., W1M 7TD. ☏ 0171-323 6626. Fax: 0171-255 1203.

SHERIDAN, Rabbi Sybil Ann, M.A. (Cantab.); b. Bolton, Lancs., Sept. 27, 1953; m. Jonathan Romain; M., Thames Valley Progressive J. Community, Reading; Lect. Leo Baeck College, the Muslim College; form. M., Swindon Jewish Com.; Ealing Lib. Syn. Publ.: Stories from the Jewish World (1987), Creating the Old Testament (contr, 1994), Hear Our Voice (ed) (1994), Christian-Jewish Dialogue (1996, contr.), Renewing the Vision (1996, contr.). Ad. 9 Boyne Hill Ave., Maidenhead, Berks SL6 4ET. ☏ 01628 71058. Fax: 01628 25536.

SHIELDS, Sir Neil (Stanley) M.C.; b. London, Sept. 7, 1919; Chairman, Com. for New Towns (1982-95); Bd., Lond. Transport (1986-93), Chairman, (1988-89) Dep. Chairman (1989-93); Chairman, Lond. Transport Property Bd. (1986-95); Dep. Leader (1952-61), Hampstead Bor C.; Nat. Exec. Chairman London area (1961-63), Conservative Party; C., AJA. Ad.: 12 London House, Avenue Rd., NW8 7PX.

SHINDLER, Colin, B.Sc., M.Sc. Dip.Ed. (Further Education); b. Hackney, London, Sept. 3, 1946; Lect. in Chemistry; Ed., Judaism Today, Political Affairs Sec., World Union of Jewish Students (1970-72); Ed., Jews in the USSR, (1972-75). Ed. Jewish Quarterly (1985-94); Co-ord. European Jewish Publication Soc. (1995-). Publ.: All Party Parl. Exhibition on Soviet Jewry (1974), Exit Visa: Detente, Human Rights and the Jewish Emigration Movement in the USSR (1978), The Raoul Wallenburg Exhibition (1982), Ploughshares into Swords? Israelis and Jews in the Shadow of the Intifada (1991), Israel, Likud & the Zionist Dream (1995). Ad.: 80 Stanhope Ave., London N3 3NA. ☏ 0181-349 1264.

SHINE, Rabbi Cyril, B.A.; b. London, Jan. 24, 1923; M., Central Syn. (1955-90); Domestic Chaplain to Lord Mayor of London (1960-61); Westminster C. Com. Rel. Cttee.; Chairman Central JIA Cttee.; Chaplain, Pentonville Prison; form. M., N. Finchley & Woodside Park Syn., Walthamstow & Leyton Syn. and Peterborough. Ad.: Suite R, 82 Portland Pl., W1N 3DH ☏ 0171-636 3195.

SHIPTON, Sidney Lawrence, LL.B, M.B.A., F.R.S.A., F.Inst.M.; b. London, Jul. 25 1929; Solicitor; Freeman of the City of London; Exec. Member, Council of Christians and Jews; Council, JHSE; Exec. Scopus J. Educ. Tr.; Exec. The Network; Member, Royal Instit. of Internat. Affairs; Co-ord. The Three Faiths Forum; Mem. of the Praesidium of the WZO Zionist General Council and the

Jewish Agency Assembly; V. President Leo Baeck (London) Lodge of Bnai Brith; Hon. V. President Zionist Federation of Great Britain and Chair Constitution Cttee; Hon. V. President Federation of Zionist Youth; Hon. President Hanoar Hazioni; form. Exec. Dir. World Movement for a United Israel (Ta'ali); Exec. Dir., Sephardi Fed. of Brit. & C'wlth; Exec. Dir., WOJAC (British Section); form. Chairman, Israel Cttee. BoD; form. Chairman, Simon Marks Jewish Day Sch.; form Chairman, Assoc. Execs. of Jewish Com. Orgs.; Gen. Sec., Chairman, H. Sec. and H.T. Z. Fed.; Dir., J.N F., Man. Dir., K.K.L. Executor & Tr. Co. Ltd. Ad.: 82 Hurstwood Rd., NW11 0AU. ☎/Fax.: 0181-455 0987.
SHIRE, Michael, B.A. (Hons.), M.A., Ph.D. (Hebrew Union Coll. L.A.); Rabbinic ordination at Leo Baeck Coll. (1996); b. 1957; Dir., Centre for Jewish Education, Reform Synagogues of Great Britain/Union of Liberal and Progressive Synaoguges, and Dir., Education and Training Div., RSGB; Dir. of Education, Temple Beth Hillel, Hollywood (1983-88); Lect. in Education, Leo Baeck Coll. (1988-); Gov., Akiva School (1990-); Ed. Cons. 'Illustrated Atlas of Jewish Civilization'. Ad.: CJE, The Sternberg Centre for Judaism, 80 East End Road, Finchley N3 2SY.
SHOMBROT, Jeffrey, O.B.E., B.Sc. (Eng.), F.I.C.E.; b. London, Apr. 30, 1915; Ret. Consult, form. Supt. Eng. Admiralty and Environment Dept. Ad. Holly Lodge, 7 Aylmer Dr., Stanmore HA7 3EJ. ☎ 0181-954 4316.
SHORT, Mrs. Renee; b. Apr., 1919; M.P. (Lab.) for Wolverhampton, North-East (1964-87;) Member, N.E.C. Lab. Party; form. Chairman, Educ. Cttee.; Chairman, Parl. Select Cttee. for Soc. Services; Patron, Chiropractic Advancement Assn.; President, Nat. Campaign for Nursery Educ; Member, Med. Res. C. (1988) Ethics Cttee. Royal Coll. Physicians; BMA Invitro Fertilisation Ethics Cttee.; P, Action for Newborn; Chairman, CO-ORD; C., N.S.P.C.C.; Hon. Life Member; Inst. Medical Ethics; Working Party on Aids; Hon. Fel., Wolverhampton Polytechnic (1987); Hon. Fel. Royal Coll. Psychiatrists (1988); Hon. MRCP (1989); Ch. Celebrities Guild (1989-92); Member BoD Community Res. Cttee; V. President, Health Visitors Assn.; V. President, Womens National Cancer Control Campaign (WNCCC); V. President, Parl. Scientific Cttee. Publ.: The Care of Long Term Prisoners Ad: 70 Westminster Gdns., Marsham St., SW1P 4JG.
SHUKMAN, Harold, B.A. (Nottingham), M.A., D.Phil. (Oxon.); b. London, March 23, 1931; Fel., St. Antony's Coll., Oxford; Lect., Modern Russian Hist., Oxford; Chairman Edr. Bd., Soviet Jewish Affairs. Publ.: Lenin and the Russian Revolution, Ed. Blackwell's Encyclopedia of the Russian Revolution, trans. Children of the Arbat, by A. Rybakov; Ed. & trans. Memories by Andrey Gromyko; Ed. & trans. Stalin: Triumph & Tragedy by Dmitri Volkogonov; Ed. Stalin's Generals; trans. Lenin (D. Volkogonov); Ed. & trans. Trotsky, Seven Leaders (D. Volkogonov), Rasputin. Ad.: St. Antony's Coll., Oxford, OX2 6JF. ☎ 01865 284747.
SHULMAN, Milton, B.A., LL.B.; b. Toronto; Writer and critic; Evening Standard, theatre and television critic; IPC Critic of the Year Award, 1966; Evening Standard, and Daily Express, film critic (1948-58); Film Critic, Vogue, (1975-87); Regular Member, B.B.C. Radio 4 Stop the Week; Exec. Producer, Granada TV (1958-62); Asst. Controller of Programmes, Rediffusion TV (1962-64); Served in Canada Army (Major, mentioned in dispatches). Publ.: Defeat in the West, How to be a Celebrity, Kill 3, The Ravenous Eye, The Least Worst Television in the World, etc. Ad.: Flat G, 51 Eaton Sq., SW1. ☎ 0171-235 7162.
SHULMAN, Rabbi Nisson E., B.A., M.A., D.H.L.; b. New York, Dec. 12, 1931; Dir., Dept. of Rabbinic Services, RIETS, Yeshiva Univ. (1994-); form. Rabbi St. John's Wood Syn. (1988-94); London; Rab., Central Syn., Sydney; Dayan Sydney Beth Din (1985-88); Rab., Fifth Ave. Syn., New York (1978-85); Rab. & Educ. Dir., Cong. Shaarei Tehila, Los Angeles, & Dean, Yavneh Hebrew Cong. (1971-77); Rabbi & Educ. Dir., Cong. Sons of Israel, Yonkers, N.Y. (1962-71);

Chaplain, Ready Reserves, US Navy (1958-88); Capt., CHC, USNR.; Chap., Active Duty, USN. (1956-58); Co-Chairman, Com. of Med. Ethics; Fel. of Jewish Doctors, New South Wales; Chairman, Med. Ethics Conference; Fel. of Jewish Doctors, Sydney (1985-86); Edr., Proc. of the 1987 Sydney Med. Ethics Conf.; Chairman, Rab. Adv. Bd., JIA, Sydney (1986-88); Nat. V. President, Rab. C. of Amer. (1983-84); V. President, Com. of Syn. Rel. Fed. of Jewish Philanthropies (1984-85); Co-Chairman, Achdut Com., Union of Orth. Jewish Congs. & Rab. C. of Amer. (1980-85); Member, Med. Ethics Com., Fed. of Jew Philanthropies N.Y. (1971-78); Vis. Faculty, Sydney Univ. (1986-88); Fac., Los Angeles City Univ. (1975-77); West Coast Br., Yeshiva Univ. (1971-77); Vis. Fac., Jewish Studies Progressive, Yeshiva Univ., N.Y. (1960-61); Stern Coll. for Women, Yeshiva Univ. (1955-56). Publ.: Authority & Community 16th Century Polish Jewry, (Edr.) Australian Medical Ethics Symposium Proc., The Jewish Holy Days (USN. publ.). Ad.: Apt. 207, 383 E. Grand St., New York City 10002. USA. ☎ (212) 505-3432.

SICHEL, Rev. Leo; b. Nuremberg, Oct. 31, 1922; Emer. M., Reading Hebrew Cong (1959-87); H. Chap., Broadmoor Hospital; form. M., Belfast, Cardiff, Swansea Hebrew Congs. Ad.: 62 Monarch Ct., N.2. ☎ 0181-458 3328.

SIEFF of Brimpton, Lord, Life Peer, (Sir Marcus Joseph Sieff), O.B.E., M.A., Hon. LL.D. (St. Andrews), Hon. Dr. (Babson Coll., Massachusetts), Hon. Lit.D. (Reading Univ.), Hon. F.R.C.S., Hon. Dr. (Stirling), Hon. DLL. (Leicester), D.Phil, (Tel Aviv), (Jerusalem); b. July 2, 1913; H. President, Marks & Spencer p.l.c., Hon. P. (1985-); P. (1984-85), Chairman (1972-84), Jt. Man. Dir. (1967-83), joined 1935; Chancellor Weizmann Inst. Science; Hon. President UJIA; Non-Exec. Chairman, The Independent (since 1986); Chairman, First Internat. Bank of Israel Fin. Tr. Ltd. (1983-88); form. Non-Exec. Dir., Wickes plc.; President, Brit.-Israel Chamber of Commerce (since 1975); Member Nat. Export C. (1965-71), (Chairman, Export Cttee. for Israel), (1965-68); V. President (Exec., since 1975), Policy Studies Instit. (form P.E.P.); form. Tr., Nat. Portrait Gallery, Lond.; Hambro Award, Businessman of the Year (1977); Aims Nat. Free Enterprise Award (1978); B'nai B'rith Internat. gold medallion for humanitarianism (1982); Retailer of the Year Award, Nat. Retail Merchants, Assn. (1982); Brit. Instit. of Man. Gold Medal (1983); H. Fel., Corpus Christi Coll., Cambridge (1975); served Royal Artillery (1939-45). Publ.: Memoirs, Don't Ask the Price, Lord Sieff on Management. Ad.: House of Lords, SW1A 0PW.

SILBERG, Rabbi Sidney, M.A.; b. Leeds June 27, 1934; M., Hendon Syn.; form M., Bournemouth Hebrew Cong. Jesmond Hebrew Cong., Newcastle upon Tyne; Ealing & Acton Syn. Ad.: 19 Alderton Cresc , NW4 3XU. ☎ 0181-202 6407.

SILK, Donald, M.A. (Oxon.); b. Lond., 1928; Solicitor; H.V. President, Z. Fed.; C., Hebrew Univ., Ch, Z. Fed. (1967-71); Chairman, Fed. Z. Youth (1953-55), Tr. Chichester Festival Theatre. Ad.: 69 Charlbury Rd., Oxford OX2 6UX. ☎ 01865 513881.

SILKIN, Jon, B.A. (Hon), (Leeds); F.R.S.L.; b. London, 1930; Poet and Editor. English Literature Dept., Tsukuba Univ., Japan (1991-94); C. Day Lewis Fellowship (1976-77); Visiting poet at Mishkenot Sha'ananim (1980); Publ: The Peaceable Kingdom (1954); Out of Battle (1972); The Penguin book of First World War Poetry (ed. 1979); The Psalms with their Spoils (1980); Selected Poems (1988 and 1994); The Ships Pasture (1986), The Lens-breakers (1992), The war poems of Wilfred Owen (1994), The Life of Metrical and Free Verse in Twentieth Century Poetry (1996). Co-ed. Stand Magazine. Ad.: 13 Queen's Terr., Newcastle on Tyne NE2 2PJ. ☎ 0191-281 2614.

SILVER, Leslie Howard, O.B.E.; b. Lond., Jan. 22, 1925; Chairman Chief Exec. Kalon Group of Comps.; Chairman, Leeds Utd A.F.C.; Yorkshire Businessman of Year (1983); form P , Paintmakers Assn., Paint Res. Assn., Oil & Colour Chemists Assn., Paint Industry Club. Ad.:

SILVERBECK, Michael Harrison, b. Liverpool, Apr. 10, 1940; Chartered Accountant; form. President, Merseyside Jewish Rep C., P. King David Foundation L'pool (1981-87); Chairman, Morris Datnow Hillel Hse (1974-77); T., L'pool Z Central C. (1970-73). Ad.: 7 Queens Dr., Liverpool L18 2DS. ☎ 0151-722 1516.

SILVERMAN, Rabbi Robert Malcolm (Reuven), B.A., Ph.D.; b. Oxford, July 26, 1947; m. Dr Isobel Braidman; M., Manchester Reform Syn.; Hon Fel., Middle Eastern Studies Dept., Univ. Manchester; Chairman, Assembly of Rabbis, RSGB (1991-93); Anglo-Israel Friendship League, Manch.; Chaplain, Progressive Jew. Students, Manch.; form. Second M., Edgware Reform Syn.; M., Mikve Israel Emanuel, Curacao. Publ: Baruch Spinoza. Ad.: 26 Daylesford Rd., Cheadle, Cheshire, SK8 1LF. Fax: 0161-834 0415 or 0161-839 4865.

SINCLAIR, Clive John, B.A., Ph.D. (East Anglia Univ.), F.R.S.L.; b. Lond., Feb 19, 1948; British Library Penguin Writers Fellow (1996); form. Lit. Edr., Jewish Chronicle, Writer-in-Residence Uppsala Univ., 1988. Publ.: The Brothers Singer, Bedbugs, Hearts of Gold, Bibliosexuality, Blood Libels, Diaspora Blues, Cosmetic Effects, Augustus Rex., The Lady with the Laptop. Ad.: 22 Church St., St Albans, Herts. AL3 5NQ.

SINCLAIR, Rabbi Dr Daniel Bernard, LLB, LLM, Dr. Juris, b. London, June 30, 1950; Principal, Jews' College (1994-97); Lect. in Jewish Law, Gold College, Jerusalem (1978-84); Research Fellow, Institute for Research in Jewish Law, Hebrew University, Jerusalem (1978-84); Tutor in Jewish Law, Hebrew University, Jerusalem (1980-84); Visiting Research Associate, Centre for Criminology and the Social and Philosophical Study of Law, Edinburgh University (1984-87); M. of the Edinburgh Hebrew Congregation, Edinburgh (1984-87); Tutor in Jurisprudence, Faculty of Law, Edinburgh University, Edinburgh (1985-87); Senior Research Fellow, Institute for Research in Jewish Law, Jerusalem (1987-); Lect. in Jewish Law and Comparative Biomedical Law, Tel Aviv University (1988-); Lect. in Jewish Law and Philosophy of Halakhah, Pardes Institute, Jerusalem (1988-90); Lecturer in Jewish and Comparative Bioethics, Hebrew University, Jerusalem (1991); Jacob Herzog Memorial Prize, 1980; Asst. Ed. Jewish Law Annual (1990). Publ: Tradition and the Biblogical Revolution (1989), Selected Topics in Jewish Law, vols. 4-5 (1994). Ad.: Jews' College, London, 44 Albert Rd., NW4 2SJ. ☎ 0181-203 6427.

SINCLAIR, Dr. Michael J.; b. London, Dec. 20, 1942, m. Penny; Chairman, Sinclair Montrose Trust Ltd.; Partner, Atlantic Medical Partners U.S.A.; Vice Chairman UJIA; Gov. Carmel College; Chairman of Management Cttee, Sidney and Ruza Last Foundation Home; Member of Council The Caldecott Community. Ad.: 5th Floor, Cheapside House, 138 Cheapside, EC2V 6BJ. ☎ 0171-776 1500. Fax: 0171-776 1592.

SINGER, Rabbi Marcus, B.A.; b. Vienna, Jan. 12, 1926; M., Central Syn., Birmingham. Ad.: 12 Speedwell Rd. Birmingham B5 7PS. ☎ 0121-440 2455.

SINGER, Norbert, C.B.E., B.Sc., Ph.D., Hon. D.Sc (Greenwich), C.Chem., F.R.S.C.; b. Vienna May 3, 1931; Physical Chemist; Fellow Queen Mary & Westfield College; Vis. Prof. Univ. Westminster (1996-); Chairman, Bexley Dist. Health Auth. (1993-94); Chairman Oxleas NHS Tr. (1995-); Chairman Rose Bruford College Gov. Body (1994-); V. Chanc., Univ. Greenwich (1992-93); Dir., Thames Polytechnic (1978-92); Res. Chemist, Morgan Crucibles Co. Ltd. (1954-57); Lect. and eventually Dep. Hd. of Dept. of Chemistry Northern Polytechnic (1958-70); Hd. of Dept. of Life Sciences & Prof., Polytechnic of Central London (1971-1974); Assist. then Dep. Dir., Polytechnic of North London (1974-78); Member of C.N.A.A. & Cttees. (1982-93). Ad.: Croft Lodge, Bayhall Rd.; Tunbridge Wells, Kent TN2 4TP. ☎ 01892 523821.

SITRUK, Rabbi Joseph, b. Tunis, 1945; Chief Rabbi of France; Chief Rabbi Marseilles (1975-87); Rabbi, Strassbourg (1970-75). Ad.: 19 rue St. Georges, 75009 Paris. ☎ 4970 8800.

SKELKER, Philip David, M.A. (Oxon.), F.R.S.A.; b. Sept. 7, 1946; HM, Carmel Coll, HM, King David High Sch., Liverpool (1981-84). Ad.: Carmel College Wallingford, Oxon. OX10 8BT. ☎ 01491 837505. Fax: 01491-825305.
SKLAN, Alexander, B.Sc., Soc. Sci, M.Sc. Econ., C.Q.S.W.; b. London Jan. 13, 1947; m. Cheryl; Assistant Chief Exec. Jewish Care, Dir. of Quality Assurance; Dir. of Social Services Jewish Welfare Board (1979-90); Dir. of Social Services Jewish Care (1990-96); Chairman, Assembly of Masorti Synagogues (1996-). Ad.: Stuart Young House, 221 Golders Green Rd., NW11 9DW. ☎ 0181-458 3282. Fax 0181-455 7185. Email alex@jewishcare.org
SMITH, Rabbi Amnon Daniel, M.A.; b. Hadera, Israel, Oct. 10, 1949; Sr. M., Edgware & Dist. Reform Syn.; Chairman RSGB Assembly of Rabbis; form. M., Wimbledon & Dist. Syn.; form. Assoc. M., West Lond. Syn.; Fdr. Chairman, Raphael Centre - a Jewish counselling service. Ad.: 118 Stonegrove, Edgware, HA8 8AB.
SOBER, Phillip, F.C.A., F.R.S.A.; b. London, April 1, 1931; m. Vivien; Chartered Accountant; Dir. Liberty International Holdings plc (form. TransAtlantic Holdings plc) (Member of Chairman's and Remuneration Cttees., Chairman Audit Cttee.) (1983-); Dir. Capital & Counties plc (1993-); Dir. Capital Shopping Centres plc (Chairman Audit Cttee.) (1994-); Consultant, BDO Stoy Hayward, Chartered Accountants (1990); Gov. and Chairman of Audit Cttee., London Institute Higher Education Corporation (1994); Tr. Jewish Assoc. of Business Ethics; Chairman, Central Council for Jewish Community Services; form. Jt. Tr., Ravenswood; Partner, Stoy Hayward, Chartered Accountants (1958-90); Fell. of the Inst. of Chartered Accountants (1963-); International Partner and Member of Management Cttee., Stoy Hayward, Chartered Accountants (1974-90); Chairman, Accounting Standards Cttee., British Property Federation (1976-83); Member Council, UK Central Council for Nursing, Midwifery and Health Visiting (1980-83); Crown Estate Commissioner (1983-94); Senior Partner, Stoy Hayward, Chatered Accountants (1985-90); Tr., Royal Opera House Tr. (1985-91); President, Norwood Child Care (1989-94); European Regional Dir., Horwarth International (1990-94); Consult. Hunting Gate Group Ltd. (1992-95). Publ.: Articles in professional press on various subjects but primarily on property company accounting. Ad.: 4 Horbury Mews, W11 3NL. ☎ 0171-727 2427. Office BDO Stoy Hayward, 8 Baker Street, W1M 1DA. ☎ 0171-486 5888. Fax 0171-487 4585.
SOETENDORP, Rabbi David Menachem Baruch; b. Amsterdam, July 1, 1945; Rabbi, Bournemouth Reform Syn; V. President, B'mouth Br., CCJ; Chairman Exodus 2000; J. Chaplain, Dorchester & Winchester Prison, Bournemouth Univ.; Contrib., local radio, TV; Contr. 'Renewing the Vision', SPC London; Chairman, AFETUK; Rabbi, South Hants Reform Cong. Publ.: Op Weg Naar Het Verleden. Ad.: 25 De Lisle Rd., Bournemouth, BH3 7NF. ☎ 01202 514788.
SOLOMON, Sir Harry, K.B., F.R.C.P. (Hon.); b. Middlesbrough, March 20, 1937; Company Chairman; Hillsdown Holdings plc (1975-1993): Chairman (1987-1993); Non-Exec. Dir. (from 29.4.93); Fel. of the Royal Coll. of Physicians (Hon.). Ad.: 3 Coach House Yard, Hampstead High St., NW3 1QD. ☎ 0171-431 7739.
SOLOMON, Rabbi Norman, Ph.D (Manc.), M.A. (Cantab.), B.Mus (Lond.); b. Cardiff, May 31, 1933; Fellow, Oxford Centre for Hebrew and Jewish Studies (1995-); Lect. Faculty of Theology, Univ. Oxford; form. Dir., Centre for Study of Judaism & Jewish Christian Relations, Selly Oak Colls.; Chairman BAJS (1994); Edr., Christian Jewish Relations (1986-91); form. M., Birmingham Central Syn., Hampstead Syn., Lond., Greenbank Drive Syn., Liverpool, Whitefield Hebrew Cong., Manchester. Publ: Judaism and World Religion (1991), The Analytic Movement (1993), A Very Short Introducction to Judaism (1996). Ad.: 5 Phoebe Court, Bainton Rd., Oxford OX2 7AQ. ☎/Fax: 01865-316530.

SPENCER, Charles Samuel, b. Lond. Aug. 26, 1920; Fine Art and Theatre Lect.; Exhibition organiser; Lond. correspondent art publ. in Italy, Germany, Greece, etc.; form. Sec., AJA, Maccabi Union, Brady Clubs, Edr., Art and Artists; Member Jewish Relief Unit (1944-46). Publ.: Erté; The Aesthetic Movement: A Decade of Print Making, Leon Bakst and the Ballets Russes, The World of Serge Diaghilev, Cecil Beaton, Film and Stage Designs. Ad.: 24A Ashworth Rd., W9 1JY. ☎ 0171-286 9396. Fax 0171-286 1759.

STEEN, Anthony, M.P.; b. London, July 22, 1939; Barrister, social worker, youth ldr., law lect; M.P. (Con.) for Totnes (1997-), South Hams (1983-97), for Liverpool, Wavertree (1974-83); Party Cttees.; Chairman, Urban & Inner City Cttee., (1987-93); Chairman Deregulation Cttee (1994-); Chairman Sane Plamony; V. Chairman, Health & Soc. Services (1979-80); Chairman 1974 Conservative M.Ps. Gp; V. Ch, Parl. Brit. Caribbean Gp; Race Rel. (1974-79); Select Cttee. Environment (1991-); All Party Group Y.M.C.As.; Fdr., First Dir., Task Force (1964-68); First Dir., Yng. Vol. Force (1968-74); Bd., Vol. Service Overseas, Nat. Playing Fields Assn., Com. Transport; Adv., Canadian Govt. (1970-72) on job creation and economic initiatives; V. Chairman, Task Force Tr.; V. President Internat. Centre Child Studies. Publ.: New Life for Old Cities, Tested Ideas for Political Success Public Land Utilisation Management Schemes (PLUMS) (1988). Ad.: House of Commons, SW1A 0AA. ☎ 0171-219 5045.

STEIN, Cyril, b. London Feb. 20, 1928; V. President, UJIA. Ad.: 94 Wigmore St., London W1H 9DR.

STEINBERG, Gerry, M.P.; b. Durham Apr. 20, 1945; M.P. (Lab.) for Durham City; Member, Parl. Select Ctte. on Educ. Durham Distr. Cllr. (1976-87); form HM, Spennymoor Special Sch., Durham. Ad.: House of Commons, SW1. ☎ 0171-219 6909.

STEINER, Prof. George, M.A., D.Phil.; Hon. D.Litt: East Anglia, 1976; Louvain, 1980; Mount Holyoke Coll., USA, 1983; Bristol, 1989; Glasgow, 1990; Liège, 1990; Ulster, 1993; Kenyon College, 1995; Trinity College, Dublin, 1995; b. Apr. 23, 1929; m. Zara née Shakow; Member, staff of the Economist, in London (1952-56); Extraordinary Fellow, Churchill College, Cambridge, (1969-); Weidenfeld Professor of Comparative Literature, and Hon. Fellow of Balliol College, Oxford (1995-); Inst. for Advanced Study, Princeton (1956-58); Gauss Lect., Princeton Univ. (1959-60); Fellow of Churchill Coll., Cambridge (1961-); Prof. of English and Comparative Literature, Univ. of Geneva (1974-94). Lectures: Massey (1974); Leslie Stephen, Cambridge (1986); W. P. Ker (1986), Gifford (1990), Univ. of Glasgow; Page-Barbour, Univ. of Virginia (1987). Fulbright Professorship (1959-69); Vis. Prof., Collège de France (1992). O. Henry Short Story Award (1958); Guggenheim Fellowship (1971-72); Zabel Award of Nat. Inst. of Arts and Letters of the US (1970); Faulkner Stipend for Fiction, PEN (1983); Pres., English Assoc., 1975; Corresp. Mem., (Federal) German Acad. of Literature (1981); Hon. Mem., Amer. Acad. of Arts and Sciences (1989); FRSL (1964). PEN Macmillan Fiction Prize, 1993. Chevalier de la Légion d'Honneur (1984). Publ: Tolstoy or Dostoevsky, 1958; The Death of Tragedy, 1960; Anno Domini, 1964; Language and Silence, 1967; Extraterritorial, 1971; In Bluebeard's Castle, 1971; The Sporting Scene: White Knights in Reykjavik, 1973; After Babel, 1975 (adapted for TV as The Tongues of Men, 1977); Heidegger, 1978; On Difficulty and Other Essays, 1978; The Portage to San Cristobel of A.H., 1981; Antigones, 1984; George Steiner: a reader, 1984; Real Presences: is there anything in what we say?, 1989; Proofs and Three Parables, 1992; No Passion Spent, 1996; The Deeps of the Sea, 1996; Homer in English (ed.), 1996; Errata: an Examined Life, 1997. Ad: 32 Barrow Rd., Cambridge CB2 2AS. ☎ 01223 61200.

STEPHENS, Judge Martin, Q.C., M.A. (Oxon.); b. Swansea, June 26, 1939; Circuit Judge (since 1986); Recorder (1979-86); form. Chairman, Cardiff Jewish Rep. C. (1986-95). Member Parole Bd., (1995-); Member Main Bd., Judicial St.

Bd. (1997-). Ad.: c/o Swansea Crown Court, St. Helens Rd., Swansea SA1 4PF.
STERLING OF PLAISTOW, Jeffrey Maurice of Pall Mall in the City of Westminster (Cr. 1991); Kt 1985, CBE, 1977; Hon. DBA (Nottingham Trent Univ.); Hon. D.C.L. (Durham); b. Dec. 27, 1934; Paul Schweder and Co. (Stock Exchange (1955-57); G. Eberstadt & Co. (1957-62); Fin. Dir. Gen. Guarantee Corp. (1962-64; Mng. Dir., Gula Investments Ltd. (1964-69); Chairman Sterling Guarantee Trust plc (1969-) (merging with P&O 1985); The Peninsular and Oriental Steam Navigation Company (1980-, Chairman, 1983-); Chairman, orgn. cttee. World ORT Union (1969-73), Mem. Exec. (1966-), Tech. svcs. (1974-), V. President Brit. ORT (1978-); Dep. Chairman and Hon. Tr. London Celebrations Cttee. Queen's Silver Jubilee (1975-83); Chairman Young Vic Co. (1975-83); V. Chairman and Chairman of the Exec. Motability (1977-); Bd. Dirs. Bitish Airways (1979-82); Spl Adv. Sec. of State for Industry (1982-83) and to Sec. of State for Trade & Industry (1983-90); Chairman Govs. Royal Ballet Sch. (1983-); Gov. Royal Ballet (1986-); President of the General Council of British Shipping (1990-91); President, European Community Shipowners' Associations (1992-94); Freeman of the City of London; Hon. Captain Royal Naval Reserve (1991); Elder Brother Trinity House (1991); Hon. Fellow Institute of Marine Engineers (1991); Hon. Fellow Institute of Chartered Shipbrokers (1992); Hon. Member Institute of Chartered Surveyors (1993); Fellow of the ISVA (1995). Ad. Office: 79 Pall Mall, SW1Y 5EJ. ☎ 0171-930 4343.
STERN, David, J.P., F.R.I.B.A.; b. Lond., July 18, 1920; Architect; Dir., Inventerprise; H. President, B.B. Distr. 15. Ad.: 9 Willowdene, View Rd., N6 4DE. ☎ 0181-348 0261.
STERN, Isaac; b. Kreminiecz, Russia, July 21, 1920; Concert Violinist; President, Carnegie Hall; Fd. Mem. Nat. Endowment for the Arts. C., Chairman Emer., Amer.-Israel Cultural Foundation. Ad.: c/o I.C.M. Artists Ltd., 40 West 57th St., New York City, N.Y. 10019, USA.
STERNBERG, Sir Sigmund, K.C.S.G., J.P., O.H., Hon.D. (Essex); b. Hungary, June 2, 1921; Chairman, Martin Slowe Estates, Paul Harris Fel., Rotary Internat.; Officer Brother of the Order of St. John; Chairman, ISYS Ltd; Exec. Cttee., Internat. C.C.J; Gov., Oxford C. Post G. Hebrew St.; Manor House Tr.; Court, Essex Univ.; Co-Chairman Jewish Jain Assoc.; President, Friends of C.R.U.S.E.; Fell. Loe Baeck Coll.; Gov., Hebrew Univ.; Form. Judge Templeton Prize; Chairman, Labour Fin. and Industry Group (1972-1992); Chairman of Exec. Cttee., internat.CCJ; Life President, Sternberg Centre; Chairman of the Manor House Tr.; Hon. Tr. of the Fabian Society Appeal; N.W Metrop. Reg. Hospital Bd. (1965-74); Greek Presidential Decree of Commander of the Order of Honour; Order of Merit of Warsaw Univ. Chairman; St. Charles Group Hospital Man. Cttee. (1972-74). Ad.: Sternberg Centre, The Manor House, 80 East End Rd., N3 2SY.
SUDAK, Rabbi Nachman; b. Feb. 3, 1936; Princ., Lubavitch Foundation (1959-); Lubavitcher Rebbe's Emissary in Britain. Ad.: 37 Portland Ave., N16 6HD. ☎ H. 0181-800 6432. O. 0181-800 0022.
SUFRIN, Rev. Aron Dov, M.A.A.E.H.; b. Manchester, May 19, 1930; Dir. of Educ., Lubavitch Foundation, Lond. Publ.: Teachers Programme, Vols. I & II. Ad.: 361 Cranbrook Rd., Ilford, Essex, IG1 4UG. ☎ 0181-518 0554.
SUMBERG, David Anthony Gerald; b. Stoke-on-Trent, June 2, 1941, m. Carolyn née Franks; Solicitor; Dir. Anglo-Israel Association (1997-); form. M.P. (Cons) for Bury South (1983-97); Parl. Pte. Sec., Attorney Gen. (1986-90); Jt. H.Sec., Parl. Group, Conservative Frs. of Israel, V.Chairman, All-Party Cttee., Release of Soviet Jewry; V. Chairman, All-Party War Crimes Group; Memb. Home Affairs Select Cttee. of the House of Commons, (1991-92); Memb. Foreign Affairs Select Cttee. House of Commons (1992-97); Mem. Lord Chancellor's Adv. Cttee. on Public Records (1992); Tr. Holocaust Educ. Tr. Ad.: 42 Camden Sq., London NW1 9XA. ☎ 0171-267 9590.

SUMRAY, Monty, C.B.E., F.INSTD, F.C.F.I., FRSA; b. London, Oct. 12, 1918; Dir. of FIBI Bank (UK) Plc; V.-P., British-Israel Chamber of Commerce; Chairman, British Footwear Manufacturers Federation Project Survival Cttee.; V. President, Jewish Care; V -P., Stamford Hill branch of AJEX; Member of the Anti-Boycott Co-ordination Cttee.; Fel. of the Clothing & Footwear Instit.; Fel. of the Instit. of Dir.; Pres. London Footwear Manufacturers Assoc; Member of the Footwear Industry Study Steering Group, and Chairman of its Home Working Cttee.; President, British Footwear Manufacturers Federation (1976-77); Mem., Footwear Economic Development Cttee. Chairman, British-Israel Chamber of Commerce; Captain Royal Berkshire Regiment (1939-46); Served in Burma. Ad.: 11 Neville Drive, N2 0QS. ☎ 0181-458 2788.
SUZMAN, Janet; b. Johannesburg, Feb. 9, 1939; Actress/Director; V. Chairman C. of L.A.M.D.A.; Hon. M.A. (Open University); Hon. D.Litt (Warwick Univ., Leicester Univ., QMW); Hon. Assoc. Artist, RSC. Ad.: c/o William Morris (UK) Ltd., 31/32 Soho Sq., W1V 5DG. ☎ 0171-434 2191. Fax: 0171-437 0238.
TABACHNIK, Eldred, Q.C., B.A., LL.B. (Cape Town), LL.M. (London); b. Cape Town, Nov. 11, 1943; m. Jennifer; Board of Deputies (1986–); Hon. Officer (Warden), Richmond Syn. (1980-94); Chairman, British Friends and Boys Team, Jerusalem. Ad.: Board of Deputies, Commonwealth House, 1-19 New Oxford Street, London WC1A 1NF.
TABICK, Rabbi Jacqueline Hazel (née Acker), B.A.(Hons.), Dip. Ed.; b. Dublin, Oct. 8, 1948; Assoc. Rabbi, West London Syn.; Past Chairman, Assembly of Rabbis, RSGB; Past Chairman, Central Educ Cttee., R.S.G.B; Council of Reform & Liberal Rabbis. Ad.: 33 Seymour Pl. W1H 6AT. ☎ 0171-723 4404.
TABICK, Rabbi Larry Alan, B.A., M.A.; b. Brooklyn, N.Y., Nov. 24, 1947; Ed. & trans. Siddur Sha'ar Hadash (1991); Rabbi, Hampstead Ref. Jewish Com; Rabbi Leicester Progressive Jewish Community; Assoc. Rabbi, Edgware & Dist. Ref. Syn. (1986-90); Asst. Rabbi, Middlesex New Syn. (1981-86), Rabbi Hampstead Ref. Jew Com. (1976-81) Ad.: 1 Ashbourne Grove, Mill Hill, NW7 3RS. ☎ 0181-959 3129
TABOR, David, Sc.D. (Cantab.) Hon. D.Sc. (Bath), F.R.S.; b. London, Oct. 23, 1913; Fellow, Gonville and Caius Coll., Emer. Prof., Dept. of Physics, Cambridge Univ. Publ.: Scientific works. Ad.: 8 Rutherford Rd., Cambridge, CB2 2HH. ☎ 01223-841366.
TANKEL, Henry Isidore, O.B.E., M.D., F.R.C.S.; b. Glasgow, Jan. 14, 1926; surgeon; Non-Exec. Dir., Southern Gen. Hosp. NHS Trust (1993); Chairman, Glasgow J. Hsng. Assoc. (1996-); H.V. President Glasgow Jew. Rep. C.; Sec. Glasgow Board for Shechita; Chairman, Scottish Joint Consultants Cttee. (1989-92); Member Scottish Health Service Advisory Cttee. (1989-92); Jt. Con. Cttee. (UK) (1989-92); Chairman, Youth Liaison Cttee.- Glasgow Hospital Med. Services Cttee; Scottish Hospital Med. Services Cttee. Books: Gastroenterology – an intergrated course (contrib 1983); Cancer in the Elderly (contrib 1990). Ad.: 26 Dalziel Drive, Glasgow, G41 4PI . ☎ 0141-423 5830. Fax: 0141-424 3648.
TANN, Rabbi Leonard, B.A.; b. London, Apr. 20, 1945; Chief M., Birmingham Hebrew Cong.; M., Sutton (Surrey) Syn. (1972-82); Hale Syn. (Manch.) (1982-86) . Publ: Books on Philately. Ad.: 61 Wheeleys Rd., Birmingham B15 2LL. ☎ 0121-440 8375.
TANNENBAUM, Mrs. Bernice Salpeter; b. New York City; Chairman Hadassah Magazine; form. Chairman, Amer. Section, WZO; Nat. Chairman, Hadassah International; Nat. President, Hadassah (1976-80); Exec. Nat. Conference on Soviet Jewry; V. President, United Israel Appeal; Exec., WJC Amer. Section; Exec. Bd., Jewish Agency; President, World Confed., United Zionists; Gov. Bd., Hebrew Univ.; Bd., U.I.A. Publ.: It Takes a Dream, The Story of Hadassah; The Hadassah Idea (co.-ed.). Ad.: Hadassah, 50 W 58 Street, N.Y., 10019. ☎ (212)

303-8081.
TAUSKY, Vilem, C.B.E.; b. Prerov, Czechoslovakia, July 20, 1910; Composer & Conductor; Dir. of Opera, Guildhall Sch. of Music; Freeman, City of Lond.; Czechoslovak M.C. & Order of Merit; form. Conductor, B.B.C.; Mus. Dir. Carl Rosa Opera. Ad.: 44 Haven Green Court, W5 2UY. ☎ 0181-997 6512.
TEMKO, Edward J.; b. Washington, DC, USA, Nov. 5, 1952; Journalist, Ed. Jewish Chronicle (1991-); Foreign Corr. United Press International (1976); Associated Press (1977-78), The Christian Science Monitor (1978-1988); World Monitor Television (1984-90). Publ.: To Win or To Die (Biography of Menachem Begin, 1987). Ad.: 25 Furnival St., EC4A 1JT.
TERRET, Norman Harold, J.P.; Compagnon d'Europe; F.Inst.D., MBA.; b. Ayr, Scotland, Jan. 10, 1951; President, CITS Group Hounslow, Middx.; SITA V. President, Marketing; Tr., British Israel Educ. Tr. Ad.: SITA, Lampton House, Lampton Road, Hounslow, Middx., TW3 4ED.
TIBBER, Judge Anthony Harris; b. London, June 23, 1926; Circuit Judge; Ad: c/o Edmonton County Court, Fore St., N18 2TN. ☎ 0181-807 1666.
TILSON THOMAS, Michael; b. Dec. 21, 1944; Conductor; Musical Director, San Francisco S.; Artistic Director, New World S.; Princ. Guest Conductor, London Symphony Orchestra; Artistic Director, Pacific Music Festival, Sapporo. Ad: c/o Columbia Artists Management Inc., 165 W. 57th Street, New York, NY 10019.
TOLEDANO, Dayan Pinchas, B.A., Ph.D.; b. Meknes, Morocco, Oct. 12, 1939; Ab Beth Din Sephardi Communities of G.B.; Rabbi, Wembley Sephardi Cong.; Eccl. Auth., Lond. Bd. of Shechita; V. President, Mizrachi Fed.; V. President, Herut, Gt. Brit., Patron, Mentally Handicapped Soc., Patron, Massoret; Edr., SRIDIM, (Standing Cttee., Conf of European Rabbis). Publ.: Rinah-oo-Tefillah, (co-Edr), Fountain of Blessings, Home Ceremonies, Sha'alou - Le Baruch, Rabbinic response (co-edr.) Ad.: 17 Barn Hill, Wembley Park, Middlesex, HA9 9LA. ☎ 0181-904 7658. Fax: 0171-289 2709.
TRAVIS, Anthony Selwyn; b. Cardiff, June 9, 1932; Emeritus Prof. of Planning - Univ. of Birmingham; Visiting Prof. in Tourism - Glasgow Caledonian Univ.; Director, East-West Tourism Consultancy; form. Programme Co-ordinator EEC PHARE. Tourism Programme for Poland; Dir. Research, Newcastle City Planning Dept. (1962-62); Prof. of Planning, Heriot Watt Univ., Edinburgh (1967-73); Prof and Dir., Centre for Urban and Regional Studies, Univ. of Birmingham. Publ.: 300, including Recreation Planning for the Clyde (1970), Realising Tourism Potential of the S. Wales Valleys (1985). Ad.: 20 Mead Rise, Birmingham B15 3SD. ☎/Fax: 0121-454 1215.
TROPP, Asher, B.Sc.(Econ.), M.A., Ph.D.; b. Johannesburg, Jan. 2, 1925; Prof. of Sociology, University of Surrey (1967-1987). Publ.: The School Teachers (1957); Jews in the Professions in Great Britain 1891-1991 (1991). Ad.: 162 Goldhurst Terrace NW6 3HP. ☎ 0171-372 6662.
TUCKMAN, Fred, O.B.E.; b. Magdeburg, June 9, 1922; Management Consultant; President, AJA (1989-95); M.E.P (1979-89), Conservative Spokesman, Soc. & Employment Affairs (1985-84); Cllr., Lond. Borough of Camden (1965-71); H.Sec., Conservative Bow Group (1958-9); Commanders Cross of the German Order of Merit 1990. Ad.: 6 Cumberland Rd., London SW13 9LY ☎ 0181-748 2392. Fax: 0181-746 3918.
TURNER, Rev. Reuben; b. Karlsruhe, Jan. 8, 1924; H. Princ., Mathilda Marks-Kennedy Sch.; Min., Finsbury Park Syn. (1948-50); Reader, Brixton Syn. (1950-68), Dir. Zion. Fed Syn C. (1967-70); Gen. Sec., Mizrachi-Hapoel Hamizrachi Fed. of Gt. Britain (1970-73). Director JNF Educ. Dept. (1973-91). Publ.: Jewish Living, The Popular Jewish Bible Atlas. Ad.: 13 St. Peter's Court, NW4 2HG. ☎ 0181-202 7023.
ULLENDORFF, Edward, M.A. (Jerusalem), D.Phil. (Oxford), Hon D.Litt. (St. Andrews), Hon. Dr. Phil. (Hamburg); Hon Fell. S.O.A.S., F.B.A.; b. Jan. 25,

1920; Prof Emer., Semitic Languages Lond. Univ. (since 1982); Prof. of Ethiopian Studies (1964-79); form. Prof. of Semitic Languages and Literatures, Manchester Univ. (1959-64); Jt. Edr., Journal of Semitic Studies; V. President, Brit. Academy (1980-82), Schweich Lect. (1967); V. President, Royal Asiatic Soc. (1981-85; 1975-79); served in Brit. Mil. Govt, Eritrea and Ethiopia (1942-46); Asst. Sec. Palestine Govt (1947-48); Res. officer, Inst. Colonial Studies Oxford (1948-49); Reader in Semitic Languages, St. Andrews Univ. (1950-59); Chairman, Assn. of Brit. Orientalists (1963-64); Chairman, Anglo-Ethiopian Soc. (1965-68); Haile Selassie intern. prize for Ethiopian studies (1972). Publ.: The Semitic Languages of Ethiopia, The Ethiopians, Comp. Grammar of the Semitic Languages, Ethiopia and the Bible, Studies in Semitic Languages & Civilizations, The Hebrew Letters of Prester John, The Two Zions, From the Bible to Enrico Cerulli, H. J. Polotsky 1905-91, From Emperor Haile Selassie to H. J. Polotsky, 1995, etc. Ad.: 4 Bladon Close, Oxford, OX2 8AD.

UNTERMAN, Rev. Alan, B.A., B.Phil., Ph.D.; b. Bushey, Herts., May 31, 1942; M., Yeshurun Syn., Gatley, Cheshire; form. Lect., Comparative Rel. & Chaplain to Jewish Students, Manchester Univ.; Lect., Jerusalem Academy of Jewish Studies; Hillel Dir., Victoria, Australia. Publ: Encyclopaedia Judaica (Contribs), Wisdom of the Jewish Mystics, Jews their Religious Beliefs and Practices, Judaism, Penguin Dictionary of Religion (Contribs. on Judaism and Hinduism), Penguin Handbook of Living Religions (Contrib. Judaism), Dictionary of Jewish Lore and Legend. Ad.: 13 South Park Rd., Gatley, Cheshire, SK8 4AL. ☏ 0161-428 8469.

UNTERMAN, Rabbi Maurice Mordecai; b. Poland, Mar. 18, 1917; Emer. M. (M., 1961-82) Marble Arch Syn.; V. President and Hon. Chaplain, Ravenswood Foundation for Mental Health; Special Adviser to Chief Rabbi (1984-91), Co-ordinator Singer's Prayer Book Revision Cttee (1987-91); formerly Jt. Edr. Hamesilah, US journal, Lect., Applied Rabbinics, Jews, Coll., H. Dir., Chief Rabbi's Israel Off; Fdr. member Liaison Cttee. Inter-Community Rels. (1985-95); M., Cardiff United Syn. (1937-46); President, Hove Hebrew Cong. (1953-54); H. Chaplain, Nightingale Hse. (Home for Aged Jews), Dir. Frs. of Bar-Ilan Univ. (1958-61). Ad.: Flat 67, Wellington Ct., Wellington Rd., NW8 9TD. ☏ 0171-722 1331.

URIS, Leon M.; b. Baltimore Aug. 3, 1924; Writer. Publ.: Exodus, Mila 18, and other novels, screenplays and essays. Ad.: c/o Doubleday Publ. Co, 245 Park Ave., New York, 11530, USA.

VEIL, Mme. Simone (née Jacob), b. Nice, July 13, 1927; deported to Auschwitz and Bergen-Bergen Nazi concentration camps (1944-45); m. 1946 Antoine Veil, Inspecteur des Finances. Educ.: Lycée de Nice; Lic. en Droit, dipl. de l'Institut d'Etudes Poliques, Paris; qualified as Magistrate, 1956; Sec. Gen. Superior Coucil of the Magistrature (1970-74); Cons. Adm. ORTF (1972-74); French Health Min. (1974-76), Health and Social Security Min. (1976-79); Member Europ. Parliament (1979-93), President (1979-82); Chairman Liberal Group (1984-89); State Min. Social Affairs, Health and Urban (1993-95); President Haut Conseil à l'Intégration (1997). Dec.: Chevalier de l'Ordre National du Mérite; Médaille Pénitentiaire; Médaille de l'Education surveillée. Dr (h.c.) Universities: Princeton, USA; Weizman Institute, Israel; Bar Ilan, Israel; Yale, USA; Cambridge, GB; Edinburgh, GB; Georgetown, USA; Urbino, Italy; Yeshiva Univ., NY, USA; Sussex, GB; Universitié Libre de Bruxelles, Belgium; Brandeis, USA; Glasgow, GB; Pennsylvania, USA. Recipient of honours and prizes from many countries including France, Israel, Germany, Spain, Brazil, Luxembourg, Greece, Ivory Coast, Morocco, Senegal, Venezuela, Sweden, USA, Italy. Publ.: Les Données Psycho-sociologiques de l'Adoption (with Prof. Launay and Dr Soule). Ad : 1 rue Bixio, 75007 Paris. ☏ 01 45 51 09 68.

VERMES, Geza, M.A., D.Litt. (Oxon), Hon. D.D. (Edinburgh, Durham), Hon. D. Litt. (Sheffield), F.B.A., W. Bacher Medallist, Hungarian Academy of Sciences; b.

Meko, June 22, 1924; m. Margaret Unarska; Prof. of Jew. Studies, Oxford Univ. (1989-91), now Emeritus; Dir. Forum for Qumran Research, Oxford Centre for Hebrew and Jewish Studies (1991); R. in Jew. Studies, Oxford (1965-91), Fel. of Wolfson Coll. (1965-91), now Emer.; form. Lect. and Sr. Lect. Divinity, Newcastle Univ. (1957-65); Chairman, Curators of the Oriental Instit. (1971-74); Chairman, Oriental Studies Board (1978-80); President, British Assn. for Jew. Studies (1975, 1988); President, European Assn. for Jew. Studies (1981-84); Edr. Journal of Jew. Studies (1971-); Vis. Prof. Rel. Studies, Brown Univ. (1971); Riddell Memorial Lect., Newcastle Univ. (1981); Dist. Vis. Prof., Judeo-Christian Studies, Tulane Univ., New Orleans (1982); Igor Kaplan Vis. Prof., Toronto Univ. (1985, 1987); Vis. Prof. Judaic Studies, Univ. of Calif. San Diego (1995); Vis. Prof. Hebr. Studies, Peter Pazmany Univ., Budapest. Publ. Discovery in the Judean Desert, Scripture and Tradition in Judaism, The Dead Sea Scrolls in English, Jesus the Jew, Postbiblical Jewish Studies, The Dead Sea Scrolls: Qumran in Perspective, The Gospel of Jesus the Jew, Jesus and the World of Judaism, History of the Jewish People in the Age of Jesus Christ by E. Schürer (co-ed. and reviser), The Essenes according to the Classical Sources (co-author), The Religion of Jesus the Jew, The Complete Dead Sea Scrolls in English. Ad.: West Wood Cottage, Foxcombe Lane, Boars Hill, Oxford, OX1 5DH. ☎ 01865 735384. Fax: 01865 735 034.

VOGEL, Rabbi Shraga Faivish; b. Salford, Lancs, April 22, 1936; Dir., Lubavitch Foundation Ad.: 15 Paget Rd, N16. ☎ 0181-800 7355.

WAGERMAN, Mrs. Josephine Miriam (née Barbanel), O.B.E., B.A. (Hons.), P.G.C.E., Ac. Dip., M.A.(Ed); b. London, Sept. 17, 1933, m. Peter; Inner Cities Religious C. (Dept. of the Environment) (1994-); Mem. Academic Panel, Stuart Young Awards (1990-); Advisor of the Trustees, Pierre and Maniusia Gildesgame Trust (1996-); Trustee of the Central Foundation Schools London (1996)' Jewish Care Woman of Distinction (1996); Mem. Bd. of Dir. JIA/Continuity (1997-); Chief Exec. Lennox Lewis College (1994-96); Memb.C. Centre for Study of Jewish Christian Relations Selly Oak Colleges (1995-); form. Headteacher, J.F.S.; Member BoD, V. President (1994-); President, Lond. A.M.M.A. (1982-83); form. Member, I.L.E.A Standing Jt. Adv. Cttee., Working Party on Teachers Service Conditions, Hist. & Soc. Studies Adv. Cttee. Ad.: 38 Crespigny Rd., London NW4 3DX. ☎/Fax: 0181-203 7471.

WAGNER, Leslie, M.A. (Econ.); b. Manchester, Feb. 21, 1943, m. Jennifer; Professor, Vice-Chancellor, Leeds Metropolitan Univ. (1994-); V. Chanc. & Chief Exec. University of North London (1987-93); Dep. Sec., Nat. Adv. Body, Publ. Sector Higher Educ. (1982-87); Prof. & Dean, Sch. of Soc. Sciences & Business Studies Central Lond. Poly. (1976-82); Lect. The Open Univ. (1970-76); V. President, United Syn., (1992-93); Member, C., US M. Exec. Comm. of Chief Rabbinate C; C. Cttee of V.Cs and Principals; Chairman, Society for Research into Higher Education (1994-96); Chairman, Higher Education for Capability; Member Council for Industry & Higher Education; Board, Higher Education Quality Council; Chairman Jewish Community, Allocation Bd. (1994-96). Publ.: Choosing to Learn: Mature Students in Education (with others), The Economics of Educational Media, Agenda for Institutional Change in Higher Education (Edr.), Readings in Applied Microeconomics (Edr.). Ad.: Leeds Metropolitan University, Calverey Street, Leeds LS1 3HE. ☎ 0113 283 3100.

WALD, George, Ph.D.; b. New York City, Nov. 18, 1906; Emer. Prof. (Higgins Prof of Biology 1968-77), Harvard Univ., Nobel Prize for Medicine (1967). Publ: General Education in a Free Society (co-author), Twenty-Six Afternoons of Biology (Addison Wesley). Ad: 21 Lakeview Ave., Cambridge, Massachusetts, 02138, USA. ☎ (617) 868 7748.

WALLENSTEIN, Meir, M.A., Ph.D. (Manchester); b. Jerusalem 1903; Prof., Hebrew Lit., Bar-Ilan Univ.; Adv. Mem., Hebrew Language Academy Jerusalem; Mem., Hanhalat Halashon, Brit. Ivrit Olamit Section; form. Reader, Medieval and Mod. Hebrew, Manchester Univ.; Edr., Melilah. Publ.: Hymns from the Judean Scrolls, Unpublished Piyyutim from the Cairo Genizah, A number of publications from "Shocken 37", 17th Century Hebrew Poets in Egypt, Reminiscences, etc. Ad.: Neve Aviv, Kfar Shmaryahu, 46910, Israel. ☎ 0527 8829.

WALSH, David, LLB (Hons); b. Leeds, May 21, 1937; m. Jenny, née Cronin, Solicitor, Director, Peek Plc, Carlisle Group Plc; Mem. Bd. of J.I.A.; form. Chairman, RSGB, now Vice President; form. Chairman, West London Synagogue (1981-85); President, West London Synagogue (1988-91). Ad.: 82 North Gate, Prince Albert Road, London NW8 7EJ. ☎ 0171-586 1118. Fax: 0171-483 2598.

WASSERSTEIN, Bernard Mano Julius, M.A., D.Phil., F.R.Hist. S.; b. London, Jan. 22, 1948; President Oxford Centre for Hebrew & Jewish Studies (1996-); form. Prof. of Hist., Brandeis Univ. (Dean of Graduate Sch. of Arts and Sciences, 1990-92) (1982-96); Lect., Modern Hist., Sheffield Univ. (1976-80); Vis. Lect., Hist. Hebrew Univ. (1979-80); form. Res. Fel., Nuffield Coll., Oxford. Publ.: The British in Palestine, Britain and the Jews of Europe 1939-1945, The Secret Lives of Trebitsch Lincoln, Herbert Samuel, Vanishing Diaspora. Ad.: Oxford Centre for Hebrew and Jewish Studies, Yarnton, Oxon OX5 1PY. ☎ 01865 377946. Fax 01865 541078.

WEBER, Harry, C.B.E.; b. Nov. 10, 1899; form Princ. Exec. Off, Min. of Educ.; V. President, N W. Lond. Jew. Boys, & Girls, Clubs & V. President Old Boys, Assn. Ad.: Sunridge Ct., 76 The Ridgeway, NW11 8PG ☎ 0181-209 1743

WEIDENFELD, Lord, Life Peer (Sir George Weidenfeld), Hon. Ph.D., Ben Gurion Univ.; Holder of the Knight Commander's Cross (Badge & Star) of the German Order of Merit; Holder of the Golden Knight's Cross with Star of the Austrian Order of Merit, Chevalier de l'Ordre National de la Légion d'Honneur, France; b. Vienna, Sept. 13, 1919; Publisher; Chairman, Weidenfeld & Nicolson, Lond.; V. Chairman, Z. Fed. of Great Brit.; Member of English Nat. Opera Bd.; Jt. V.-P. Campaign for Oxford; Vice-Chairman, Oxford University Dev. Programme; Member Bd. Gov Institute of Human Science, Vienna; Member of South Bank Bd., Dir. of the Jerusalem Post; Political adv. to President Weizmann of Israel (1950), Gov. Bezalel Art Academy; Member of South Bank Bd., Lond; Chairman, Bd of Govs., Ben Gurion Univ. of Negev, Gov. V. Chairman, Weizmann Instit. of Science; Gov., Tel Aviv Univ.; Tr., Jerusalem Foundation. Publ.: The Goebbels Experiment, Remembering My Good Friends (auto). Ad.: 9, Chelsea Embankment, SW3 4LE. ☎ 0171-351 0042.

WEIL (Brever-Weil), George; b. Vienna July 7, 1938; Sculptor, painter, jeweller, exhibited UK, US, Israel, Tokyo, Switzerland, South Africa etc.; portrait busts Ben-Gurion, Churchill, General de Gaulle, etc., Specialist in Judaica, including Bar-Ilan collection shown in Mann Auditorium, Tel Aviv; collections in Brit. Museum, Antwerp Museum, Royal Museum of Scotland, etc. H. Mem., Japanese Art Carvers Soc. (1986), only Western Artist so honoured. Ad.: 93 Ha Eshel Street, Herzlia Pituach, Israel.

WEINER, Rabbi Chaim, B.A. (Hebrew Univ. of Jerusalem), M.A. (Hebrew Univ. of Jerusalem), Rabbinical Ordination (Seminary of Judaic Studies Jerusalem (Masorti); b. Sydney, Nova Scotia, Nov. 11, 1958; m. Judy; Rabbi of Edgware Masorti Synagogue; National Dir. of Noam, Masorti Youth Movement, Israel (1987-91); Dir. Gesher, Masorti Teenage Centre, London (1991-96). Ad.: Edgware Masorti Synagogue, Stream Lane, Edgware, Middx HA8 7YA.. ☎ 0181-905 4096. Email chaim. weiner@ort.org

WEISMAN, Malcolm, O.B.E., M.A. (Oxon.), O.C.F.; Barrister-at-Law; Recorder, S.E. Circuit; Hon. President Birmingham J. Graduates Assoc. (1995-96); Chief Rabbi's Award for Excellence (1993); B'nai B'rith Award for Community Service (1980); Asst. Com., Parl. Boundaries (1976-85), Rel. Adv. to Small Coms; Member, Chief Rabbi's Cabinet; Chaplain, Oxford Univ. & new univs.; Fell. Centre for the Study of Theology, Univ. of Essex; Hillel Nat. Student Cllr.; Sr.

Jew. Chaplain to H.M. Forces; Hon. V. President, Monash Branch of Roy. Brit. Legion; Tr. Jewish Music Heritage Tr.; Gov. Carmel College; Edr. Menorah, Chairman and Sec.Gen., Sr. Allied Air Force Chaplains (1980-1992) President (1993); Sec. Allied Air Forces Chaplain Cttee.; Member, Council of Selly Oak Coll. Birmingham (1992), Chaplain to Lord Mayor of Westminster (1992-93), Mayor of Barnet (1994-95); Member, Min. of Def. Advisory Cttee on Chaplaincy; Chaplain R.A.F. Univs. Jew Chaplaincy Bd., Progr. Jewish Students Chaplaincy; Nat. Exec., Mizrachi Fed.; Nat. Exec. Council of Christians and Jews; Ct., Lancaster, East Anglia, Kent, Warwick, Sussex and Essex Univs.; Exec. United States Military Chaplains Assoc.; form. JWB, Ajex Exec.; Jewish Youth Fund; President, Univ. Coll. Jew. Soc.; form. H. Sec., I.U.J.F.; form. V. President, Torah V'avodah Org., Provincial Exec., JIA. Ad.: 25 Enford St., W1H 2DD. ☎ 0171-724 7778.

WEIZMAN, Ezer; b. Tel Aviv, 1924; President of Israel (1993-); Science and Technology Min., State of Israel, Defence Min. (1977-80); Transport Min. (1969-70); Served as fighter pilot in World War II and Israel War of Independence Commander of Israel Air Force 1958-66; Head of General Staff Branch/GHQ (1966-69). Publ.: On Eagles' Wings (autobiog.), The Battle for Peace. Ad.: Presidential Residence, Jerusalem. ☎ (02) 707211. Fax: (02) 660445.

WESKER, Arnold, F.R.S.L., D.Litt (Hon.), Hon. Fell. Queen Mary & Westfield Coll., London; b. London, May 24, 1932, m. Dusty Bicker; Co.P., Internat. Playwrights Cttee. (1980-83); Chairman, Brit. Section, Internat. Theatre Instit. (1978-83); Dir. Centre 42 (1960-70). Publ.: Chicken Soup with Barley, 1959; I'm Talking about Jerusalem, 1960; The Wesker Trilogy, 1960; The Kitchen, 1961; Chips with Everything, 1962; The Four Seasons, 1966; Their Very Own and Golden City, 1966; The Friends, 1970; Fears of Fragmentation (essays), 1971; Six Sundays in January, 1971; The Old Ones, 1972; The Journalists, 1974 (in Dialog; repr. 1975); Love Letters on Blue Paper (stories), 1974, 2nd edn 1990; (with John Allin) Say Goodbye! You May Never See Them Again, 1974; Words – as definitions of experience, 1976; The Wedding Feast, 1977; Journey into Journalism, 1977; Said the Old Man to the Young Man (stories), 1978; The Merchant, 1978; Fatlips (for young people), 1978; The Journalists, a triptych (with Journey into Journalism and A Diary of the Writing of The Journalists), 1979; Caritas, 1981; Shylock (form. The Merchant), 1983; Distinctions, 1985; Yardsale, 1987; Whatever Happened to Betty Lemon, 1987; Little Old Lady, 1988; Shoeshine, 1989; Collected Plays: vols. 1 and 5, 1989, vols. 2, 3, 4 and 6, 1990, vol. 7, 1994; As Much As I Dare (autobiog.), 1994; Circles of Perception, 1996, Denial, 1997; Break, My Heart, 1997. Film scripts: Lady Othello, 1980; Homage to Catalonia, 1990. Television: (first play) Menace, 1963; Breakfast, 1981; (adapted) Thieves in the Night, by A. Koestler, 1984; (adapted) Diary of Jane Somers, by Doris Lessing, 1989; Maudie, 1995. Radio: Yardsdale, 1984; Bluey (Eur. Radio Commn.), Cologne Radio, 1984, BBC Radio 3, 1985. Ad.: Hay-on-Wye, Hereford HR3 5RJ. Fax.: 01497-821 005.

WHITESON, Adrian Leon, O.B.E., M.B.B.S.(Hons.), M.R.C.S., L.R.C.P.; b. London, Dec. 12, 1934, m. Myrna; Med. Practitioner; President of the Brit. Paralympic Assoc., Chairman, World Boxing Council and European Boxing Union Med. Commission; Chief Med. Off., Brit. Boxing Board of Control; Chairman, The Teenage Cancer Tr.; Member, Govt. Review Body for Sport for People with Disabilities. Ad.: Pender Lodge, 6 Oakleigh Park North, Whetstone, London, N20 9AR. ☎ 0171-580 3637. Fax: 0171-487 2504. 58a Wimpole St., W1M 7DE. ☎ 0171-935 3351.

WIEDER, Naphtali, Ph.D.; b. Sziget, Hungary, May 5, 1905; form. Reader in Jewish Studies, Univ. Coll., London; Lect. in Liturgy, Midrash and Talmud, Jews, Coll., Prof. in Talmud, Bar-Ilan Univ. Publ.: Islamic Influences on Jewish Worship, The Judean Scrolls and Karaism, etc. Ad.: 10 Harav Frank St., Jerusalem.

WIESEL, Elie, D.Lett. (h.c.), D.Hum.Lett. (h.c.), D.Hebrew.Lett. (h.c.), Ph.D. (h.c.), D.L. (h.c.); b. Sighet, Sept. 30, 1928; Survivor of Auschwitz and Buchenwald; Fd. Elie Wiesel Foundation for Humanity; Andrew W. Mellon Prof. in the Humanities, Boston Univ.; Dist. Prof., Judaic Studies, City Univ , N.Y. (1972-76); Chairman, US President's Com. on Holocaust (1979-80); Chairman, US Holocaust Memorial C. (1980-86); Bd. Dirs., Internat. Rescue Cttee., Grand-Officier, Legion of Honour; US Congress Gold Medal; Presidential Medal of Freedom (1986); Nobel Peace Prize (1986); Internat. Peace Prize Royal Belgian Acad. Publ.: Night, Dawn, The Jews of Silence, etc.; Ani Maamin, a cantata (music by D. Milhaud), Zalmen, or the Madness of God (produced by Habimah, Nouvelle Comedie, etc.), A Jew Today, Messengers of God, Souls on Fire, The Trial of God (play), The Testament (novel), Five Biblical Portraits, Somewhere a Master, Paroles d'Etranger, The Golem, The Fifth Son, Signes D'Exode, Against Silence (3 vols.), Twilight, L'oublié, From the Kingdom of Memory, Reminiscences, The Forgotten, etc. Ad.: Boston University, 745 Commonwealth Ave., Boston, Mass., 02215. ☎ (617) 353 4566.

WIESENBERG, Rabbi Ernest, B.A. Ph.D.; b. Kosice, Czechoslovakia, Mar 11, 1909; Res. Unit, Taylor-Schechter Collection of tbe Cairo Genizah Cambridge; form. Actg. Rav., Lond Machzike Hadath; Reader, Hebrew Dept., Univ. Coll., Lond.; Rab. and M., Great Syn., Sheffield; M.-Preacher, Windsor Place Syn., Cardiff, Hammersmith and W. Kensington Syn. Publ.: Abraham, MaimonidesÆ Commentary on Genesis and Exodus, The Treatise Sanctification of the New Moon, in Moses Maimonides' Code, etc. Ad.: 30 Hillcrest Ave., NW11 0EN.

WIGODER, Lord, Life Peer (Basil Thomas Wigoder), Q.C., M.A.; b. Manchester, Feb. 12, 1921; Barrister; Recorder, Crown Court. Ad.: House of Lords, SW1A 0PW.

WIGODER, Geoffrey Bernard, M.A., D.Phil. (Oxon.); b. Leeds, Aug. 3, 1922; Edr.-in-Chief, Encyclopaedia Judaica, Dir., Oral History Dept., Instit. of Contemporary Jewry, Hebrew Univ.; Member Planning Team and Adv., Beth Hatefutsoth; Dir., Overseas Broadcasts, Israel Broadcasting Auth. (1960-67). Visit. Prof. of Modern Jewish Studies, Univ. Manchester (1991); Chairman, Interreligious Coordinating Council in Israel. Publ.: The Story of the Synagogue, Jewish-Christian Relations since World War II; Edr., New Standard Jewish Encyclopaedia, Encyclopaedia of Jewish Rel., Jewish Art and Civilisation, Everyman's Judaica Illustrated Dictionary and Concordance of the Bible; Dictionary of Jewish biography; New Encyclopaedia of Zionism and Israel; Oxford Dictionary of the Jewish Religion, etc. Ad.: 11 Rehov Hameyasdim, Jerusalem, 96224.

WINE, Judge Hubert, M.A., LL.B., T.C.D.; b. Dublin, April 3, 1922; Dublin district judge (since 1976), H. President, Jewish Rep. C. of Ireland; Cllr., H.L.P., Dublin Hebrew Cong.; H. President, C. of Ireland for Soviet Jewry; Patron, Criminal Lawyers, Assn., Gt. Brit. & Ireland; Patron, Jewish Adoption Soc., Great Britain & Ireland, H. L. P. Dublin Maccabi Assn., Patron, Irish Frs. of Hebrew Univ.; Patron Israel-Ireland Friendship League; form. Irish Internat. Table Tennis player & Irish champion; form. Capt., Edmondstown Golf Club. Ad.: 19 Merrion Village, Merrion, Dublin, 4. ☎ Dublin 269 5895.

WINNICK, David, M.P.; b. Brighton, June, 1933; M.P. (Lab.), for Walsall North (1979-), Croydon South (1966-70). Ad.: House of Commons, SW1A 0AA.

WINSTON, Clive Noel, B.A. (Cantab.); b. Lond., April 20, 1925; V. President (form. Chairman) ULPS; form. Tr., European Bd. of WUPJ; form., Dep. Solicitor, Metropolitan Police. Ad.: 2 Bournwell Cl., Cockfosters, Herts. EN4 0JX. ☎ 0181-449 5963.

WINSTON, Baron (Life Peer) of Hammersmith in the London Borough of Hammersmith and Fulham, Robert Maurice Lipson, M.B., B.S., L.R.C.P., M.R.C.S., F.R.C.O.G.; b. London, July 15, 1940; Prof., Fertility Studies, Obstetrics & Gynaecology Instit., Lond. Univ.; Dean, Institute of Obstetrics &

Gynaecology (1995-); Consultant Obstetrician & Gynaecologist, Hammersmith Hospital, Lond., Prof. of Gynaecology, Texas Univ. (1980-81); Vis. Prof., Leuven Univ., Belgium (1976-77); Chief Rabbi's Open Award for Contribution to Society (1993). Publ.: Reversibility of Female Sterilization, Tubal Infertility, Infertility: a Sympathetic Approach; Scientific writings on aspects of reproduction. Ad.: 11 Denman Dr., NW11. ☎ 0181-455 7475.

WINSTON-FOX, Mrs. Ruth (née Lipson), M.B.E., J.P., B.Sc.; b. London, Sept. 12, 1912; form. Mayor & Ald., Lond. Borough of Southgate; V. President, Internat C. of Jewish Women (1974-81); Chairman, Inter-Affilliate Travel Cttee. (1975-81); Chairman, Status of Women Cttee. (since 1984, 1970-78); Chairman, ICJW Cttee., Women in Judaism; form. President, League of Jewish Women; Member Exec. Cttee, Jewish Commonwealth C. (1980-); President, B'nai B'rith First Women's Lodge; Co-Chairman, Women's Nat. Com.; Member BoD (1960-); Member of Exec. BoD (since 1982); Chairman, Educ. Cttee. (1974-80); Fdr., H. Org., Jewish Way of Life Exhibition, sponsored by BoD in many parts of Brit. (1978-); V. President, Southgate Old People's Welfare Cttee., Fdr., Ruth Winston House, Southgate Old People's Centre, the first comprehensive day centre in Brit.; Chairman, Jewish Com. Exhibition Centre; P. Relate (Enfield Marriage Guidance C.) (1985-); Lond. Rent Assessment Panel (1976-83) Herts. Adoptions Consultant (1949-77) Ad.: 4 Morton Cres., N14 7AH. ☎ 0181-886 5056.

WISTRICH, Robert Solomon, B.A., M.A. (Cantab, 1970), Ph.D. (London, 1974); b. Lenger (USSR), April 7, 1945; Univ Prof.; First Holder of the Jewish Chronicle Chair in Jewish Studies, University Coll., London; Neuberger Chair of Modern Jewish History, Hebrew University of Jerusalem (since 1985). Publ.: Revolutionary Jews from Marx to Trotsky (1976); Trotsky (1979); Socialism and the Jews (1982), Who's Who in Nazi Germany (1982), Hitler's Apocalypse (1985); The Jews of Vienna in the Age of Franz Joseph (1989); Between Redemption and Perdition (1990); Antisemitism: The Longest Hatred (1991); Weekend in Munich (1995); Co-maker, Understanding the Holocaust (film, 1997). Ad.: 63 Woodstock Road, NW11. ☎ 0181-455 6949.

WOLFSON, Baron (Cr. 1985; Life Peer) of Marylebone in the city of Westminster: (Leonard Gordon Wolfson Kt. 1977), 2nd Bart 1991, Hon. Fel. St. Catherine's Coll. Oxford; Wolfson Coll., Cambridge, Wolfson Coll., Oxford; Worcester Coll.; U.C.L.; L.S.H.T.M., 1985; Queen Mary Coll., 1985; Poly. of Central London, 1991; Imperial CoD., 1985; Patron Royal College of Surgeons, 1976; Hon. F.R.C.P., 1977; Hon. F.R.C.S., 1988; Hon. F.B.A., 1986; Hon. D.C.L; Oxon, 1972; East Anglia, 1986; Hon. L.L.D., Strathclyde, 1972; Dundee, 1979; Cantab, 1982; London, 1982; Hon. D.S.C., Hull, 1977; Wales, 1984; D. Univ. Surrey, 1990; Hon. Dr. Medicine, Birmingham, 1992; Hon. P.H.D., Tel Aviv, 1971; Hebrew Univ., 1978; Weitzmann Inst., 1988, Hon. D.H.L.; Bar-Ilan Univ., 1983; Winston Churchill award British Technion Society 1989; b. London, Nov. 11, 1927; Chairman, since 1972 Wolfson Fodn; Chairman, Great Universal Stores since 1981 (Man. Dir., 1962, Dir., 1952); Burberrys Ltd. since 1978; Tr. Imperial War Museum, 1988; Pr. of Jewish Welfare Bd., 1972-1982. Ad.: 18-22 Haymarket, SW1Y 4DQ.

WOLFSON, Rev. M, b. Liverpool Feb. 22, 1908; Emer. M., Childwall Cong. Ad.: 9 Sinclair Drive, Liverpool, L18 0HN. ☎ 0151-722 5618.

WOOLF, The Lord, The Rt. Hon. Harry, P.C., LL.B., D.L.L. (Hon.), Buckingham 1992, Bristol 1992, Lond. 1993, Anglia 1994, Manchester Metropolitan 1995; b. Newcastle-upon-Tyne, May 2, 1933; Master of the Rolls (1996-); Lord of Appeal in Ordinary (1992-96); Lord Justice (1985-92); High Court Judge (1979-85); Presiding Judge S.E. Circuit (1981-85), Member, Senate Bench & Bar; Master of the Bench, Inner Temple; Pro-Chancellor, Univ. London (1994-); Tr. Jewish Chronicle Trust (1994-); Tr. Jewish Continuity (1994-); Fel. Univ. Coll., Lond.; First Counsel to Treasury (Common Law) (1974-79); Jnr. Counsel to Inland Revenue (1973-74), Recorder of the Crown Court (1972-9);

Chairman, Bd. of Man., Instit. of Advanced Legal Studies (1987-94), H. President, Assn. of Law Teachers, (1985-89); Instit. of Jewish Affairs Legal Section; Int. Jewish Lawyers Assoc. (1993-); Anglo-Jewish Archives (1985-89), Tel Aviv Univ. Tr. (Legal Section) (1995); Chairman, Lord Chancellor's Adv. Cttee. on Legal Educ. (1987-90); President, UK Frs., Magen David Adam (since 1987); President, Central C. for Jewish Soc. Services, (since 1987); Gov. of the Oxford Centre for Hebrew & Jewish Studies (1989-93); Chairman, Bar & Bench Cttee., J.P.A. (1974-76); 15/19th Hussars (1954-56) Captain (1955). Publ.: Protecting the Public: the New Challenge (Hamlyn Lectures, 1989), Zamir and Woolf, Declaring Judgement, 2nd Ed. (1993). Appointed to Inquire into Prison Disturbances (1990), Civil Procedure of Access to Justice (1994); Judicial Review of Administrative Action, 5th ed. (1995, ed. jt. with De Smith). Ad.: Royal Courts of Justice, Strand, WC2A 2LL. ☎ 0171-936 6002.

WOOLFSON, Michael Mark, M.A., Ph.D., D.Sc. F.R.S., F.R.A.S., F.Inst P.; b. London, Jan. 9, 1927; Emer. Prof., Theoretical Physics York Univ., form. Reader in Physics, Manchester Instit. of Sci. & Tech. Publ.: Direct Methods in Crystallography, An Introduction to X-Ray Crystallography, The Origin of the Solar System. Physical and Non-physical Methods of Solving Crystal Structures. Ad.: Physic Dept., Univ. York, York, YO1 5DD. ☎ 01904-432230.

WORMS, Fred Simon, F.C.A.; b. Frankfurt, Nov. 21, 1920; President, B'nai B'rith Hillel Foundation; Gov., Tel Aviv Museum; Tr. Jewish Care Pension Fd.; H. L. President, (form. President) Bnai Brith, Gt. Brit.; Chairman, B'nai B'rith Foundation; Chairman, B.B. Housing Soc.; Chairman, Network of Jewish Housing Assocs.; Gov., Hebrew Univ., Jerusalem; H. President, Maccabi World Union; H. L. President, Union of Jewish Students; Board of Regents, Internat. Centre for Teaching of Jewish Civilisation, Jerusalem; V. President, Brit.-Israel Chamber of Commerce; Council IJPR; H. Fellow Israel Museum; Gov., Pelech Sch., Jerusalem; Bnai Brith Award for Communal Services; Publ.: A Life in Three Cities (1996). Ad.: 23 Highpoint, North Hill, Highgate, N6 4BA. ☎ 0181-458 1181. Fax: 0181-458 6045.

WOUK, Herman, B.A., L.H.D. (Hon.) LL.D. (Hon.), Litt. D. (Hon.) (American Internat. Univ.), Hon. D. (Bar Ilan Univ., Hebrew Univ.); b. New York, May 27, 1915; Writer. Publ.: Non-fiction: This is My God; Novels: Aurora Dawn, Marjorie Morningstar, The Winds of War, War and Remembrance, Youngblood Hawke, Don't Stop the Carnival, The Caine Mutiny, Inside, Outside, City Boy, The Hope (1993), The Glory (1994). Plays: The Caine Mutiny, Court-Martial, etc. TV Screenplays: The Winds of War, War and Remembrance. Ad.: c/o B.S.W. Literary Agency, 3255 N. St. N.W., Washington, D.C., 20007, 2845.

WURZBURGER, Rabbi Walter S.; b. Munich Mar. 29, 1920; form. President, Syn. C. of Amer.; form President, Rab. C. of Amer. Rabbi, Emer. Cong. Shaaray Tefila, Lawrence N.Y., Adjunct Prof. of Philosophy Yeshiva Univ.; Edr., Tradition, (1962-87), Co-Edr., A Treasury of Tradition. Ethics of responsibility, 1994. Ad.: 138 Hards La., Lawrence, New York, N.Y. 11559, USA. ☎ 516-2397181 .

YAMEY, Basil Selig, C.B.E., B.Com., F.B.A.; b. Cape Town, May 4, 1919, m. Demetra Georgakopoulou; Emer. Prof., Lond. Univ.; form. Economics Prof., Lond. Sch. of Economics; Member, Monopolies and Mergers Com. (1966-78); Tr., National Gallery (1974-81); Tr., Tate Gallery (1978-81), Museums & Galleries Com (1983-85); Tr., Instit. of Econ. Aff (1986-91). Dir., Private Bank & Trust Co. Ltd. (1989-94). Publ.: Economics of Resale Price Maintenance, Economics of Underdeveloped Countries (part auth.), The Restrictive Practices Court (part auth.), Economics of Futures Trading (part auth.), Essays on the History of Accounting, Arte e Contabilità, Art & Accounting. Ad.: London Sch. of Economics, Houghton Street, London WC2A 2AE. ☎ 0171-405 7686.

YOUNG, Rt. Hon. Lord, Life Peer; David Ivor Young, P.C., LL.B. (Hons.); b. London, Feb. 27, 1932; Solicitor; Dep. Chairman, Conservative Party (1989-90); President, Jewish Care (1990-); Chairman Oxford Centre for Hebrew and

Jewish Studies (1990-); Exec. Chairman, Cable & Wireless plc (1990-); Dir. Salomon Inc. (1990-); Sec. of State for Trade and Industry (1987-89); Sec. of State for Employment (1985-87), Min. without Portfolio, Min. in Cabinet (1984-85); Chairman, Manpower Services Com. (1982-84), Nat. Economic Development Org (1982-89); Chairman, Admin. Cttee., World ORT Union (1980-84), Gov., Oxford Centre for Post-Graduate Heb Studies; form. President, Brit. ORT; Dir., Centre for Policy Studies (1979-82), Chairman Internat. C., Jewish Soc. & Welfare Services (1982-83). Publ.: The Enterprise Years, A Businessman in the Cabinet (1990). Ad.: 88 Brook St., W1A 4NF.

YOUNG, Emanuel, A.R.C.M.; b. Brighton, Feb. 12, 1918; Conductor, Royal Ballet, Royal Opera House Lond. Guest Conductor, concerts, TV recordings, etc.; form. Cond., Royal Opera House, New Lond. Opera Company. Ad.: 16 Selborne Rd., N14 7DH. ☎ 0181-886 1144.

YUDKIN, Leon Israel, b. Northampton, Sept. 8, 1939; m. Meirah (Mickey) née Goss; University Lecturer, Hebrew Dept., ULL (1996-) and Author; Univ. Lect., University of Manchester (1966-96). Publ.: Isaac Lamdan: A Study in Twentieth-Century Hebrew Poetry (1971); Escape into Siege: A Survey of Israeli Literature Today 91974); Jewish Writing and Identity in the Twentieth Century (1982); 1984 and After: Aspects of Israeli Fiction (1984-); On the Poetry of Uri Zvi Greenberg (in Hebrew, 1987); Else Lasker-Schueler: A Study in German Jewish Literature (1991); Beyond Sequence: Current Israeli Fiction and its Context (1992); A Home Within: Varieties of Jewish Expression in Modern Fiction (1996); Ed. Modern Hebrew Literature in English Translation (1987); Agnon: Texts and Contexts in English Translation (1988); Hebrew Literature in the Wake of the Holocaust (1993); Israeli Writers Consider the 'Outsider' (1993); Co-edited (with Benjamin Tammuz) Meetings with the Angel: Seven Stories from Israel (1973); Ed. of the monograph series 'Jews in Modern Culture'. Ad.: 51 Hillside Court, 409 Finchley Rd., London NW3 6HQ. ☎ 0171-435 5777. Fax 0171-209 1026. Email l.yudkin@uzl.ac.uk

ZAHN, Rabbi Shamai; b. Nuremberg, Germany, July 6, 1920; Communal Rabbi Sunderland; Princ., Sunderland Talmudical Coll. Publ.: Sepher Beth Shammai (Talmudic Discourses) (Israel)); V'Gam Le-Shemona (Commentary on Rambam's Introduction to Pirkei Aboth). Ad.: 11 The Oaks (East), Sunderland, SR2 8EX. ☎ 0191-565 0224.

ZALUD, Rabbi Norman, A.Ph.S., F.R.S.A.; b. Liverpool, Oct. 5, 1932; M., Liverpool Progressive Syn. Ad.: 265 Woolton Rd., L16 8NB. ☎ 0151-722 4389; 0151-733 5871.

ZELLICK, Graham John., M.A., Ph.D. (Cantab.) CI Mgt, F.R.S.A., F.R.S.M., F.Inst.D.; b. London, Aug. 12, 1948; Barrister; Princ., Queen Mary & Westfield Coll., Univ. of London (1991-); Vice-Chancellor Univ. London (1997-), Dep. V. Chancellor (1994-97); Prof of Law, Univ. of London (1991-); Sr. V.-Princ. and Act. Principal QMW (1990-91); Liveryman, Drapers' Co.; Freeman, City of London; Member C. and Chairman Education Cttee, West London Syn. (1990-93); Member, East London and the City Health A. (1995-); Member, South Thames Reg. Health Authority (1994-95); form. Member C. St. Bartholomew's Hospital Medical College and Governor, The London Hospital Medical College; Member of Council Cttee. of Vice-Chancellors & Principals; Drapers' Prof. of Law, (1988-91); Prof. of Public Law (1982-88); Dean of Laws Faculty (1984-88); Hd. of Law Dept., Queen Mary Coll , Lond., (1984-90); Dean of Laws Faculty, Lond. Univ. (1986-88); Member, Lord Chancellor's Adv. Cttee. on Legal Aid (1985-88), Chairman Cttee. of Heads of Univ. Law Schs. (1988-90); Member, Lord Chancellor's Advisory Cttee. on Legal Educ. (1988-90); J.P. (1981-85); Co-Chairman Legal Cttee., All Party Parl. War Crimes Group; Data Protection Tribunal, (1985-96); Academic Adv. Cttee., Jews, Coll. (to 1992); Chairman, Lawyers' Group, Tel Aviv Univ. Tr. (1984-89); Edr., Public Law, (1980-86), European Human Rights Reports (1978-82); Edr. Bd., Brit. Journal of

Criminology (1980-90); Howard Journal of Criminal Justice (1984-87), Civil Law Lbr., Ct. of Govs. N. Lond. Poly. (1986-89), Central Lond. Poly. (1973-77); V. Chairman Nat. Adv. Council, Acad. St. Group for Israel & The Middle East. Publ.: (contrib.) Halsbury's Laws of England, 4th edn., etc. Ad.: Senate House, University of London, Malet St., London WC1E 7HU. ☎ 0171-636 4752. Fax: 0181-580 3605.

ZERMANSKY, Victor David, LL.B. (Hon.); b. Leeds, Dec. 28, 1931, m. Anita née Levison; Solicitor; Past P. Leeds Law Soc. (1988-9), Asst. Recorder; H. L. V-P (President, 1974-77), Leeds Jewish Rep. C.; Life President, Leeds Z.C.; Exec., Leeds Kashrut Auth., Beth Din Admin. Cttee., Beth Hamedrash Hagadol Syn., Immigration Appeals Adjudicator (1970-78). Ad.: 52 Alwoodley Lane, Leeds, LS17 7PT. ☎/Fax: 0113 2673523.

ZIPPERSTEIN, Steven J., B.A., M.A., Ph.D. (UCLA); b. Los Angeles, Dec. 11, 1950; m. Sally, née Goodis; Daniel E. Koshland Prof. in Jewish Culture and History, Stanford University; Dir. Progression Jewish Studies; President, Conferences on Jewish Social Studies; Ed. Jewish Social Studies; Prof. Stanford University (1991-); Assoc. Prof. UCLA (1987-91); Frank Green Fellow in Modern Jewish History, Oxford Centre for Postgraduate Hebrew Studies (1981-87); Research Fellow, Wolfson College, Oxford (1983-87). Publ.: Elusive Prophet: Ahad Ha'am and the Origins of Zionism (1993), awarded National Jewish Book Award; Assimilation and Community: The Jews in Nineteenth-Century Europe, jnt. ed. (1992); The Jews of Odessa: A Cultural History (1985), awarded Smilen Prize in Jewish History. Ad.: Dept. of History, Stanford University, 3775 El Centro Palo Alto, CA94306. Fax (415) 725-0597.

ZISSMAN, Sir Bernard Philip, F.R.S.A.; b. Birmingham Dec. 11, 1934; Chairman, The Communication HUB Ltd; C. Mem. Birmingham, Chamber of Commerce & Industry; Lord Mayor, City of Birmingham (1990-91); Freeman of the City of London (1991); Leader, Conservative Group, Birmingham City Council (1992-95); Hon. Alderman, City of Birmingham (1995); Tr. City of Birmingham Symphony Orchestra (1992-); Chairman, Representative Council of Birmingham & Midland Jewry (1992-); Chairman, Alexandra Theatre (Birmingham) Ltd (1986-93); Chairman, Cttee to establish Birmingham International Convention Centre/Symphony Hall (1982-86); Mem. Birmingham City Council (1965-95); Chairman, Millennium Point Partnership (1995-); Mem. Council Birmingham Hebrew Congregation (1980-). Ad.: 4 Petersham Place, Richmond Hill Rd., Birmingham B15 3RY. ☎/Fax: 0121-454 1751.

Obituaries, November 1996-October 1997

Full Obituary notices may be found in the pages of the Jewish Chronicle, The Times and The Independent, and selective journals in music and the arts

Abramsky, Miriam, Psychiatrist, 6 February 1917-25 April 1997;
Apley, Alan Graham, Orthopaedic Surgeon, 10 November 1914-20 December 1996;
Beloff, Nora, Journalist, 24 January 1919-12 February 1997;
Bernstein, Isidore, Journalist, 31 January 1905-17 February 1997;
Bernstein, Rev. Solomon, 7 September 1907-17 February 1997;
Birk, Baroness Alma, of Regent's Park (née Wilson), Politician, 22 September 1917- 29 December 1996;
Borchardt, Dietrich, Librarian, 14 April 1916-6 June 1997;
Braceiner, Dayan Pesach, May 1911-18 July 1997;
Brenner, Nathan, Community leader, 7 March 1894-7 April 1997;
Buchthal, Professor Hugo, Art Historian, 11 August 1908-10 November 1996;
Bunt, Sidney, Community Leader, 18 November 1925-2 March 1997;
Burman, Charles, Librarian, 1922-March 1997;
Canetti, Jacques, Record Producer, 30 May 1909-7 June 1997;
Charles, Gerda, Novelist, 1920(?)-4 November 1996;
Cohen, Louis, Physicist, 14 October 1925-28 July 1997;
Corcos, Michael, Medical Researcher, 2 December 1919-12 December 1996;
Delbanco, Gustav, Art Dealer, 7 December 1903-25 January 1997;
Dollinger, Revd. Joseph, Cantor, 27 February 1907-16 September 1997;
Donska, Maria, Pianist, 3 September 1912-20 December 1996;
Fishman, Jack, Journalist, 14 June 1920-10 April 1997;
Fleischman, Lawrence A., Philanthropist, 14 February 1925-31 January 1997;
Frankel, Professor Herbert, Economist, 22 November 1903-11 December 1996;
Frankl, Dr Victor, Neurologist, 26 March 1905-2 September 1997;
Freeman, Iris (née Alberge), Writer, 7 July 1927-17 February 1997;
Fuchs, Joseph, Violinist, 26 April 1900-14 March 1997;
Ginsberg, Allen, Poet, 3 June 1926-5 April 1997;
Golomb, Rev. Maurice, 28 September 1931-27 May 1997;
Goldenberg, Hon. H. Carl, Barrister, 1907-22 July 1997;
Gordon, Charles, AJEX Leader, 23 January 1914-22 October 1997;
Grossman, Issy, Kosher Poulterer, 2 September 1911-22 June 1997;
Hassan, Hon. Sir Joshua Abraham, Gibraltar Statesman, 1915-1 July 1997;
Hermlin, Stephan (né Rudolf Leder), Writer, 13 April 1915-6 April 1997;
Herzog, Chaim, President of Israel, 17 September 1918-17 April 1997;
Hornung, Berthold, Architect, 25 March 1925-20 March 1997;
Jacobs, Arthur, Music critic, 14 June 1922-13 December 1996;
Jaffe, Professor Michael, Museum Director, 3 June 1923-13 July 1997;
Janner, Myra, Community Leader, 17 November 1929-9 December 1996;
Kashdan, Alexander, Byzantine scholar, 3 September 1922-29 May 1997;
Kassner, Edward, Music Publisher, 28 February 1920-19 November 1996;
Kersh, Rev. Bernard, 27 January 1915-6 February 1997;
Khariton, Yuli, Nuclear Physicist, 27 February 1904-19 December 1996;
Kopelev, Lev Zinovievich, Writer, 1912-18 June 1997;
Kotlowski, Henry, Community Leader, 31 March 1907-19 September 1997;
Kuczynski, Professor Jurgen, Historian, 19 September 1904-6 August 1997;
Levenberg, Dr Schneier, Zionist Leader, 1907-22 May 1997;
Lucas, Victor, Communal Leader, 19 May 1916-5 May 1997;
Menuhin, Marutha (née Sher), 6 January 1896-15 November 1996;
Nassauer, Rudolf, Writer, 8 November 1924-5 December 1996;

Nathan, Ernest, Community Leader, -11 October 1997;
Pela, David, Journalist, 28 September 1919-6 October 1997;
Perry, Jack, Businessman, 31 March 1915-12 December 1996;
Polikoff, Gary, Community Leader, 30 September 1951-2 September 1997;
Prevezer, Professor Sidney, Solicitor, 9 May 1929-24 April 1997;
Rosten, Leo Calvin, Writer, 11 April 1908-19 February 1997;
Roth, Irene (née Davis), 17 September1904-4 December 1996;
Rubin, Lotte, Community Leader, 1895-24 December 1996;
Saipe, Freda, Community Leader, 30 November 1907-1 January 1997;
Salkind, Alexander, Film Producer, 2 June 1921-8 March 1997;
Samuel, Raphael, Historian, 26 September 1934-9 December 1996;
Sandler, Bernard, Infertility Expert, 18 January 1907-1 October 1997;
Schwarzchild, Martin, Astronomer, 31 May 1912-10 April 1997;
Scott, Ronnie (né Schott), Saxophonist, 28 January 1927-23 December 1996;
Shahar, David, Writer, 17 June 1926-2 April 1997;
Shmeruk, Chone, Professor of Yiddish, 5 January 1921-5 July 1997;
Sieff, Lady Lily, Community Leader, 16 July 1930-28 February 1997;
Silver, Jonathan, Patron of the Arts, 21 October 1949-24 September 1997;
Simmons, Anne, Community Leader, 3 September 1917-11 September 1997;
Slater, Ralph, Businessman, 4 July 1919-24 April 1997;
Solti, Sir Georg (né Stern), Conductor, 1913-September 1997;
Spector, David, Community leader, 23 June 1912-16 February 1997;
Stein, Kitty (née Kitay), Community Leader, 9 November 1899-5 January 1997;
Sufrin, Rev. Aron Dov, 19 May 1930-8 September 1997;
Susser, Rabbi Dr. Bernard, 29 September 1930-18 April 1997;
Taylor, Rt. Hon. Lord Taylor of Gosforth, Lord Chief Justice, 1 May 1930-28 April 1997;
Temkin, Professor Sefton, Historian, 7 June 1917-20 December 1996;
Tobias, Rev. Dr Alexander, 1916-11 December 1996;
Topor, Roland, Writer, 7 January 1938-16 April 1997;
Unterman, Rabbi Avraham, March 1910-9 August 1997;
Weisgall, Hugo David, Composer, 13 October 1912-11 March 1997;
Wolkind, Jack, Community Leader, 16 February 1920-6 March 1997;
Zinneman, Fred, Film Director, 29 April 1907-14 March 1997.

Events of 1997

Anniversaries
300th of the Alderney Road (Ashkenazi) cemetery
200th of the birth of Sir David Salomons
200th of the birth of Heinrich Heine
200th of the death of the Vilna Gaon
200th of the publication of the Tanya in Belarus
Centenary of Solomon Schechter's acquisition of the Cairo Genizah fragments
Centenary of Herbert Bentwich's 'Maccabaean Pilgrimage' to Palestine
Centenary of the First Zionist Congress in Basle
Centenary of the Manchester Soup Kitchen
Centenary of the Hackney, Notting Hill, West Ham & Upton Park Synagogues
Centenary of the death of James Joseph Sylvester
80th Balfour Declaration
75th Potters Bar Golf Club
60th World Jewish Congress
60th Highams Park & Chingford Synagogue
50th UN Partition of Palestine
50th Publication of the Diary of Anne Frank
50th Jewish Women's Week
Salonika celebrated as European Cultural Capital

January
Natan Sharansky's first return visit to Russia
Three-Faiths Forum launched

February
President Weizman's State Visit to Britain
Monument to Raoul Wallenberg unveiled
Memorial Meeting for Hugo Gryn
Helicopter crash in Israel
Mr Boutros Ghali guest of honour at Manchester JIA Dinner
Publication of Chief Rabbi's 'Politics of Hope' in *The Times*

March
Hamas bomb in Tel Aviv
Rededication of Blackburn cemetery
Furore over Chief Rabbi's correspondence with Dayan Padwa
Israeli schoolgirls massacred at Naharayim

April
Judaica Collection exhibition at the Brotherton Library, Leeds
Manchester Jewish Federation launched

May
London Refuge for battered Jewish women and children opened
Fire at Ruislip Synagogue
Exhibition of Jewish carpets at Jewish Museum

June
Racial attacks on several London synagogues
UK Jews stoned at the Kotel

July
15th Maccabiah in Tel Aviv
Hamas attack in Jerusalem
Closure of Newport Synagogue
Swiss banks published list of 'dormant accounts' in newspapers around the world
Taylor–Schechter Genizah exhibition in Israel

August
Reubens, Baker Street restaurant re-opened after restoration
Sale of Carmel College

September
Launch of the new UJIA
Closure of Simmonds Bookshop, Fleet Street
New York Holocaust Musuem opened
Nathan's and Montefiore's 'Don John of Austria' performed in Spitalfields
Hamas bomb in Jerusalem
Sale of Benno Schotz' sculptures in Glasgow
Ben Uri exhibition in Blackpool

October
Papon War Crimes trial in Bordeaux
H.M. The Queen's visit to the 16th-century synagogue in Cochin

November
Death of Sir Isaiah Berlin
Prime Minister Netanyahu's visit to Britain

Publications and Booksellers

The following is a list of notable British and Irish publications of 1996-97 with paperback reprints, available from Jewish and general bookshops.

Antisemitism
Jones, S., Kushner, T., and Pearce, S., eds.: Cultures of ambivalence and contempt: studies in Jewish–non-Jewish relations, Vallentine Mitchell, 1997;

Biography and Autobiography
Aronsfeld, C.C.: A wanderer from my birth, Janus, 1997;
Bernelle, A.: The fun palace: an autobiography, Lilliput Press, 1996;
Bloom, C.: Leaving a doll's house: a memoir, Virago, 1996;
Daiches, D.: Two worlds, Canongate, 1997;
Duchen, J.: Erich Wolfgang Korngold, Phaidon, 1996;
Elon, A.: Founder [Rothschild], HarperCollins, 1997;
Englander, D., ed.: Dictionary of Jewish biography: Jews in Britain 1100–1994, Peter Halban, 1997;
Frankl, V.: Man's search for ultimate meaning, Plenum, 1997;
Frankl, V.: Recollections: an autobiography, Plenum, 1997;
Fry, S.: Making history, Hutchinson, 1997;
Ginsberg, A.: Journals: mid-fifties, 1954–1958, edited by G. Ball, Viking, 1996;
Gold, R.: Good as gold: the rags to riches story of the Gold brothers, Robson Books, 1997;
Helfgott, G.: Love you to bits and pieces: the true story of David Helfgott and the movie *Shine*, Penguin Books, 1997;
Herzog, C.: Living history: the memoirs of a great Israeli freedom fighter, soldier, diplomat, statesman, Weidenfeld & Nicolson, 1997;
Isaacs, E.: Episodes, Walker & Carson, 1997;
Kehoe, L.: In this dark house, Viking, 1996;
Klein, G.W.: All but my life, Indigo, 1997;
Leon, G.: The way it was, Book Guild, 1997;
Litvinoff, E.: Journey through a small planet, Quartet, 1996;
Mertens, P.: Shadowlight, translated by E. Jephcott, Peter Halban, 1997;
Nadel, I.B.: Various positions: a life of Leonard Cohen, Bloomsbury, 1997;
Narkiss, U.: Soldier of Jerusalem, translated by M. Kett, Frank Cass, 1997;
Potok, C.: Gates of November: chronicles of the Slepak family, Secker & Warburg, 1997;
Ridley, J.: The young Disraeli, Sinclair-Stevenson, 1996;
Rothschild, M., Gordon, K., and Rothschild, Lionel de: The Rothschild gardens, Gaia Books, 1996;
Ruby, T. and Frye, P.: Double or nothing: two lives in the theatre, Janus, 1997;
Sebag-Montefiore, D.: The story of Joseph Sebag and Co., and its founding families, Privately published, 1996;
Sheffer, G.: Moshe Sharett: biography of a political moderate, OUP, 1996;
Slovo, G.: Every secret thing, Little Brown, 1997;
Smith, P.: Disraeli, CUP, 1997;
Steiner, G.: Errata: an examined life, Weidenfeld & Nicolson, 1997;

Current Affairs
Gerlis, D.: Those wonderful women in black: the story of the Women's Campaign for Soviet Jewry, Minerva, 1996;
Goldberg, J., and Kosmin, B.: The social attitudes of unmarried young Jews in contemporary Britain, IJPR, 1997;

Graham, S. and Gold, S.: Jewish charity guide, 5th ed., The Guide, 1997;
Green, J.: Words apart: the language of prejudice, Kyle Cathie, 1996;
Jones, C.: Soviet Jewish Aliyah, 1989–92, Frank Cass, 1997;
Keogh, D.: The Jewish community and the Irish State, University of Cork Press, 1997;
Kershen, A., ed.: London, the promised land?: the migrant experience in a capital city, Avebury, 1997;
Kolinsky, E. and Horrocks, D., eds.: Jewish culture in German society today, Berghahn Books, 1997;
Lebor, A.: A heart turned east, Little Brown, 1997;
Lewin-Epstein, N., Roi, Y., and Ritterband, P.: Russian Jews on three continents: emigration and resettlement, Frank Cass, 1997;
Romain, J.: Till faith do us part: the experiences of couples who fall in love across the religious divide, Fount, 1996;
Rose, G.: Love's work, Vintage, 1997;
Sacks, J.: The Politics of Hope, Jonathan Cape, 1997;
Symons, A.: The Jewish contribution to the twentieth century, Polo Publ., 1997;
Twerski, A.J.: The shame borne in silence: Spouse abuse in the Jewish community, Mirkov Publ., 1997;
Wasserstein, B.: Vanishing diaspora: the Jews of Europe since 1945, Penguin Books, 1997;

Arts

Bohm-Duchen, M. and Grodzinski, V.: Rubies and rebels: Jewish female identity in contemporary British art, Lund Humphries, 1996;
Felton, A.: Jewish carpets, Antique Collectors' Club, 1997;
Frojmovic, E. and Felsenstein, F., comps.: Hebraica and Judaica from the Cecil Roth collection: decorated manuscripts and broadsheets in the Brotherton Collection, Brotherton Library, 1997;

History

Ancona, Jacob d': The city of light: an epic journey to China predating Marco Polo's celebrated journey, edited by D. Selbourne, Little Brown, 1997;
Arbel, B., ed.: Intercultural contacts in the medieval Mediterranean: essays in honour of Professor David Jacoby, Vallentine Mitchell, 1996;
Armstrong, K.: The history of Jerusalem: one city, three faiths, HarperCollins, 1997;
Assis, Y-T.: The golden age of Aragonese Jewry: community and society in the crown of Aragon, 1213–1327, Littman Library, 1996;
Frankel, J.: The Damascus Affair, C.U.P., 1997;
Gat, M.: The Jewish exodus from Iraq, 1948-51, Frank Cass, 1997;
Gilbert, M.: Jerusalem in the twentieth century, Pimlico, 1997;
Greene, M.F.: The temple bombing, Vintage, 1997;
Hayward, C.T.R.: The Jewish temple: a non-Biblical sourcebook, Routledge, 1996;
Hundert, G.D., ed.: Jews in early modern Poland (Polin 10), Littman Library, 1997;
Jolles, M.: A short history of the Jews of Northampton, 1159–1996, Jolles Publications, 1996;
Kertzer, D.: The kidnapping of Edgardo Mortara, Picador, 1997;
Leasor, J.: Rhodes and Barnato: architects of empire, Leo Cooper, 1997;
Mann, V.B.: From the court Jews to the Rothschilds, 1600–1800: art, patronage, power, Thames & Hudson, 1996;
Massil, W.I.: Immigrant furniture workers in London 1881-1939 and the Jewish contribution to the British furniture trade, Jewish Museum, 1997;

Pastor, J.: Land and economy in ancient Israel, Routledge, 1997;
Reiter, Y.: Islamic endowments in Jerusalem under the British mandate, Vallentine Mitchell, 1996;
Schreckenberg, H.: The Jews in Christian art: an illustrated history, SCM Press, 1996;
Scottish Jewish Archives: Patterns and images of immigration in Scotland, The Archives Centre, 1997;
Shavit, Y.: Athens in Jerusalem: classical antiquity and Hellenism in the making of the modern secular Jew, Littman Library, 1997;
Sheffy, Y.: British military intelligence in the Palestinian campaign, 1914–1918, Frank Cass, 1997;
Susser, B.: Studies in Anglo-Jewish history, Nos. 1 and 2, 1996;
Wistrich, R.S.: The limits of fraternity: Dreyfus, the Jews, and the French Republic, Littman Library, 1997;

Holocaust

Barkow, B.: Alfred Weiner and the making of the holocaust library, Vallentine Mitchell, 1997;
Bartov, O.: Murder in our midst: the holocaust, industrial killing, and representation, OUP, 1997;
Bierman, J.: Righteous gentile: the story of Raoul Wallenberg, missing hero of the holocaust, rev. ed., Penguin Books, 1997;
Bower, T.: Blood money: the Swiss, the Nazis and the looted billions, Macmillan, 1997;
Cesarani, D., ed.: The Final Solution: origins and implementation, Routledge, 1997;
Cohen, D. and Kagan, J.: With the Bielski partisans, Vallentine Mitchell, 1997;
Cohn-Sherbok, D.: God and the holocaust, 2nd ed., Gracewing, 1996;
Cyprys, R.A.: A jump for life: a survivor's journal from Nazi-occupied Poland, edited by E. Potter, Constable, 1997;
Duttman, A.G.: The memory of thought: an essay on Heidegger and Adorno, Athlone Press, 1997;
Fischer, E.: Aimee and Jaguar, Bloomsbury, 1996;
Fischler-Martinho, J.: Have you seen my little sister?, Vallentine Mitchell, 1997;
Frank, A.: Diary of a young girl, edited by O.H. Frank and M. Pressler, Viking, 1997;
Friedlander, S.: Nazi Germany and the Jews, Vol. 1: The years of persecution, 1933–1939, Weidenfeld & Nicolson, 1997;
Gelissen, R.: Rena's promise: a story of sisters in Auschwitz, Weidenfeld & Nicolson, 1996;
Gilbert, M.: Holocaust journey: travelling in search of the past, Weidenfeld & Nicolson, 1997;
Goldhagen, D.J.: Hitler's willing executioners: ordinary Germans and the holocaust, Abacus, 1997;
Harel, I.: The house on Garibaldi Street, Frank Cass, 1997;
Hertzberg, A.J.: Between two streams: a diary from Bergen-Belsen, I.B. Tauris, 1996;
Josephs, J.: Rosa's child: one woman's search for her past, I.B. Tauris, 1996;
Kanner, M.A., and Kugler, E.R.: Shattered crystals, CIS, 1997;
Lang, B.: Heidegger's silence, Athlone Press, 1996;
Leicht, E.F.: The unsung years, Minerva Press, 1997;
Reilly, J., Cesarani, D., Kushner, T., and Richmond, C., eds.: Belsen in history and memory, Vallentine Mitchell, 1997;
Rubinstein, W.D.: The myth of rescue: why the democracies could not have saved more Jews from the Nazis, Routledge, 1997;

Sierakowiak, D.: Diary of Dawid Sierakowiak, edited by A.Adelson, Bloomsbury, 1996;
Szereszewska, H.: Memoirs from occupied Warsaw, 1940–1945, Vallentine Mitchell, 1997;
Wilkomirski, B.: Fragments: memories of childhood, 1939–1948, Picador, 1996;

Israel

Bregman, A.: Living and working in Israel: how to prepare for a successful longterm stay, How To Books, 1996;
Eshed, H.: Reuven Shiloah: the man behind the Mossad: secret diplomacy in the creation of Israel, translated by D. and L. Zander, Vallentine Mitchell, 1997;
Kaminer, R.: The politics of protest: the Israeli peace movement and the Palestinian Intifada, Sussex Academic Press, 1996;
Karmi, G.: Jerusalem today: what future for the peace process?, Ithaca Press, 1997;
Karsh, E.: Fabricating Israeli history: the new Israeli historiography and its methods, Frank Cass, 1997;
Karsh, E., ed.: From Rabin to Netanyahu: Israel's troubled agenda, Frank Cass, 1997;
Lochery, N.: The Israeli Labour Party: in the shadow of Likud, Ithaca, 1997;
Near, H.: The Kibbutz Movement: a history, Vol. 2: crises and achievements, 1940–77, Littman Library, 1997;
Rein, R.: In the shadow of the holocaust and the inquisition: Israel's relations with Francoist Spain, Vallentine Mitchell, 1997;
Sheffer, G., ed.: U.S.–Israeli relations at the crossroads, Frank Cass, 1997;
Sufott, E.Z.: A China diary, Vallentine Mitchell, 1997;
Wistrich, R.S. and Ohana, D.: The shaping of Israeli identity: myth, memory and trauma, Frank Cass, 1997;

Middle East

Brutton, P.: A captain's mandate: Palestine 1946–68, Leo Cooper, 1996;
Cohen, M.J.: Fighting world war three from the Middle East: allied contingency plans, 1945–54, Frank Cass, 1997;
Deshen, S., and Zenner, W.P., eds.: Jews among Muslims: communities in the precolonial Middle East, Macmillan, 1996;
Engel, A.: The Nili spies, Frank Cass, 1997;
Gelber, Y.: Jewish–Transjordan relations, 1921–48, Frank Cass, 1997;
Joffe, L., ed.: Keesing's guide to the Mid-East peace process, Cartermill, 1996;
Karsh, E., ed.: Between war and peace: dilemmas of Israeli security, Frank Cass, 1996;
Levran, A.: Israeli strategy after Desert Storm: lessons of the Second Gulf War, Frank Cass, 1997;
Liebes, T.: Reporting the Arab–Israeli conflict: how hegemony works, Routledge, 1997;
Ma'oz, Z.: Regional security in the Middle East: past, present and future, Frank Cass, 1997;
Maddy-Weitzman, B., and Inbar, E.: Religious radicalism in the greater Middle East, Frank Cass, 1997;
Nevo, J.: King Abdallah and Palestine: a territorial ambition, Macmillan, 1996;
Quigley, J.: Flight into the maelstrom: immigration to Israel and the Middle East peace, Ithaca, 1997;
Sherman, A.J.: Mandate days: British lives in Palestine, 1918–1948, Thames & Hudson, 1997;
Shlaim, A.: War and peace in the Middle East: a concise history, Penguin Books, 1996;

Vatikiotis, P.J.: The Middle East: from the end of empire to the end of the cold war, Routledge, 1997;

Zionism

Berkowitz, M.: Western Jewry and the Zionist project, 1914–1933, CUP, 1996;
Freeman, G.: Manchester: cradle of Zionism, Representative Council, 1997;
Raider, M.A., Sarna, J.D., and Zweig, R.W., eds.: Abba Hillel Silver and American Zionism, Frank Cass, 1997;
Robertson, R., and Timms, E., eds.: Theodor Herzl and the origins of Zionism, T.&T. Clark, 1997;
Schoeps, J.H.: Theodor Herzl and the Zionist dream, Thames & Hudson, 1997;

Judaism

Ariel, D.S.: What do Jews believe?: the Jewish faith examined, Rider, 1996;
Cohen, J.M.: 1,001 Questions and answers on Rosh Hashanah and Yom Kippur, Horwits, 1997;
Cohen, J.M.: Following the synagogue service, Gnesia, 1997;
Cohn-Sherbok, D.: Fifty key Jewish thinkers, Routledge, 1997;
Cohn-Sherbok, D.: Medieval Jewish philosophy: an introduction, Curzon, 1996;
Eaton, J.: Mysterious messengers: a course on Hebrew prophecy from Amos onwards, SCM Press, 1997;
Feldman, L.H.: In Jewish life and thought among Greeks and Romans: primary readings, edited by R. Meyer, T&T Clark, 1996;
Frank, D.H., and Leaman, O.: History of Jewish philosophy, Routledge, 1996;
Freedman, H., ed.: Reflections of the year: an anthology of the weekly Masorti guide to the weekly Torah readings and to Jewish life, Masorti Publications, 1997;
Grabbe, L.L.: An introduction to first century Judaism: Jewish religion and history in the Second Temple period, T&T Clark, 1996;
Kochan, L.: Beyond the graven image: a Jewish view, Macmillan, 1997;
Levinas, E.: Between us: a collection of essays, Athlone Press, 1997;
Levinas, E.: Proper names, translated by M.B. Smith, Athlone Press, 1997;
Lieu, J.: Image and reality: Jews in the world of the Christians in the second century, T&T Clark, 1996;
Montagu, R.: Judaism, SCM Press, 1997;
Romain, J.: Abraham and his sons, Marshall, 1997;
Romain, J.: Renewing the vision: rabbis speak out on modern Jewish issues, SCM Press, 1996;
Rosenberg, L.: Jewish synagogue, A&C Black, 1997;
Stemberger, G.: Introduction to the Talmud and the Midrash, 2nd ed., translated by M. Bockmuehl, T&T Clark, 1996;
Werblowsky, R.J.Z. and Wigoder, G., eds.: The Oxford dictionary of the Jewish religion, OUP, 1997;
Wittenberg, J.: A Pesach companion, Masorti Publications, 1997;
Wittenberg, J.: The three pillars of Judaism: a search for faith and values, SCM Press, 1996;

Language and Literature

Abraham, P.: Romance reader, Quartet Books, 1996;
Abramson, G., ed.: The Oxford book of Hebrew short stories, OUP, 1997;
Appelfeld, A.: Badenheim, 1939, translated by D. Bilu, Quartet Books, 1997;
Armstrong, K.: In the beginning: a new interpretation of Genesis, Fount, 1997;
Bellow, S.: The actual, Viking, 1997;
Berg, L.: Flickerbook, Granta, 1997;
Berlin, I.: The proper study of mankind: an anthology of essays, Chatto & Windus, 1997;

Bloom, A.: Love invents us, Picador, 1997;
Bloom, H.: Omens of millenium: the gnosis of angels, dreams, and resurrection, Fourth Estate, 1997;
The Book of Ruth, translation L. Zisquit, Osband Press, 1996;
Brodsky, J.: So forth, Hamish Hamilton, 1996;
Brookner, A.: Visitors, Jonathan Cape, 1997;
Campbell, J.: Deciphering the Dead Sea Scrolls, HarperCollins, 1996;
Cartel-Bloom, O.: Dolly City, Loki Books, 1997;
Cohn-Sherbok, D.: Biblical Hebrew for beginners, SPCK, 1996;
Currie, E.: She's leaving home, Little Brown, 1997;
Drosnin, M.: The Bible code, Weidenfeld & Nicolson, 1997;
Du Broff, S.: On Sinai's lofty mountain: a novel, Geiser Productions, 1996;
Elias, G.: Overdone by the sixth sense: poems, Horizon Publications, 1997;
Freud, E.: Gaglow, Hamish Hamilton, 1997;
Goldstein, D.: Jewish legends, Chancellor, 1996;
Grant, L.: The cast iron shore, Picador, 1997;
Grossman, D.: The zigzag kid, translated by B. Rosenberg, Bloomsbury, 1997;
al-Harizi, J.: The book of Tahkemoni, translated by D. Segal, Littman Library, 1997;
Hudson, J.F.: Hadassah, Lion, 1996;
Isler, A.: Op. non cit., Jonathan Cape, 1997;
The Jerusalem Bible, Bravo Ltd., 1997;
Kirsch, J.: The harlot at the side of the road: forbidden tales of the Bible, Rider, 1997;
Levy, S.: Here, there and everywhere: space in Canadian and Israeli drama, Sussex Academic, 1996;
Louvish, S.: Days of miracles and wonders: an epic of the new world disorder, Canongate, 1997;
Lyndon, S. and Baskin, S., eds.: The slow mirror, and other stories: new fiction by Jewish writers, Five Leaves Publications, 1996;
Magonet, J.: The subversive Bible, SCM Press, 1997;
Mayne, S.: Song of Moses and other poems, Menard Press, 1996;
Mendelsohn, E., ed.: Literary strategies: Jewish texts and contexts, OUP, 1996;
Michaels, A.: Fugitive pieces, Bloomsbury, 1997;
Mosley, W.: A little yellow dog, Serpent's Tail, 1996;
Mulisch, H.: The discovery of heaven, Viking, 1997;
Oz, A.: Panther in the basement, translated from the Hebrew, Vintage, 1997;
Pinter, H.: Ashes to ashes, Faber and Faber, 1996;
Phillips, C.: The nature of blood, Faber and Faber, 1997;
Pollack, R.: Godmother night, Abacus, 1996;
Reif, S., ed.: Hebrew manuscripts at Cambridge University Library: a description and introduction, CUP, 1997;
Richler, M.: Barney's version, Chatto & Windus, 1997;
Roth, H.: Mercy of a rude stream, 3: From bondage, Weidenfeld & Nicolson, 1996;
Roth, P.: American pastoral, Jonathan Cape, 1997;
Rubens, B.: The waiting game, Little Brown, 1997;
Samokovlija, I.: Tales of old Sarajevo, edited by Z. Lesic, Vallentine Mitchell, 1997;
Sepher tehillim, edited by E. Cashdan, Minerva, 1997;
Sebald, W.G.: The emigrants, Harvill/Panther, 1997;
Simons, B.: The golem of old Prague, Five Leaves Publications, 1997;
Steiner, G.: No passion spent, Faber and Faber, 1997;
Sutcliffe, W.: New boy, Penguin Books, 1996;
Tal, M.: The lion and the cross, Minerva, 1997;
Vermes, G., ed.: The complete Dead Sea Scrolls, Allen Lane, Penguin Press, 1997;
Wesker, A.: Birth of Shylock and the death of Zero Mostel: the diary of a play, Quartet Books, 1997.

Booksellers

The booksellers listed below specialise in Jewish books. Many also supply religious requisites.

GREATER LONDON

J. Aisenthal, 11 Ashbourne Pde., Finchley Rd., NW11. ☎ 0181-455 0501. Fax: 0181-455 0501.
Blue and White Shop, 6 Beehive La., Gants Hill, Ilford, Essex, IG1 3RD. ☎ 0181-518 1982.
Carmel Gifts, 62 Edgware Way, Middx. ☎ 0181-958 7632. Fax: 0181-958 6226.
Dillons The Bookstore, 82 Gower St., WC1E 6EG. ☎ 0171-636 1577.
Aubrey Goldstein, 7 Windsor Court, Chase Side, N14 5HT. ☎ 0181-886 4075.
R. Golub & Co. Ltd., 305 Eastern Av., Gants Hill, Ilford, Essex IG2 6NT. ☎ 0181-550 6751.
Hebrew Books & Gift Centre, 18 Cazenove Rd., N16 6BD. ☎ 0171-254 3963 (day) & 0181-802 4567 (evg.). Fax: 0171-254 3963.
B. Hirschler, 62 Portland Av., N16 6EA, & 71 Dunsmure Rd., N16 5PT. ☎ 0181-800 6395. Also maps, ceremonial art, etc.
J. Hochhauser, 61 Lordship Pk., N16 5UP. ☎ 0181-800 8804.
Jerusalem the Golden, 146a Golders Green Rd., NW11 8HE. ☎ 0181-455 4960 or 458 7011. Fax: 0181-203 7808.
Jewish Books & Gifts (Sandra E. Breger), 1 Rosecroft Walk, Pinner, Middlesex HA5 1LJ. ☎ 0181-866 6236.
Jewish Memorial Council Bookshop, 25 Enford St., W1H 2DD. ☎ 0171-724 7778. Fax: 0171-706 1710.
John Trotter Books, 80 East End Rd., N3 2SY. ☎ 0181-349 9484. Fax: 0181-346 7430. Email: jt@jt.demon.co.uk
Joseph's Bookstore, 2 Ashbourne Parade, Temple Fortune, Finchley Rd., NW11 0AD. ☎/Fax: 0181-731 7575; Fax: 0181-431 6280.
H. Karnac (Books) Limited, 58 Gloucester Road, SW7 4QY.
Kuperard (London) Ltd., No. 7 Spectrum House, 32-34 Gordon House Rd., NW5 1LP. ☎ 0171-424 0554. Fax: 0171-424 0556. (Also distributors and direct mail exihibitions). Email: Kuperard@bravo.clara.net
Manor House Bookshop, 80 East End Rd., N3 2SY. ☎ 0181-349 9484.
Menorah Book Centre, 16 Russell Parade, Golders Green Rd., NW11. ☎ 0181-458 8289.
Muswell Hill Bookshop, 72 Fortis Green Rd., N10 3HN. ☎ 0181-444 7588.
George & Vera Nador, 63 Cranbourne Rd., Northwood, Middx., HA6 1JZ. ☎ 01923 821152. Hebraica, Judaica, maps. By appointment only.
M. Rogosnitzky, 20 The Drive, NW11 9SR. ☎ 0181-455 7645 or 4112.
Selfridges Departmental Store, Jewish Section of Book Dept., Oxford St., W1A 1AB. ☎ 0171-629 1234.
Stamford Hill Stationers, 153 Clapton Common, E5 9AE. ☎ 0181-802 5222.
Swiss Cottage Books, 4 Canfield Gdns., NW6 3BS. ☎ 0171-625 4632. Fax: 0171-624 9084.
Torah Treasures, 4 Sentinel Sq., NW4 2EL. ☎ 0181-202 3134. Fax: 0181-202 3161.
WH Smith, Brent Cross Shopping Centre, NW4. ☎ 0181-202 4226.
Waterstone's Booksellers Ltd., 68 Hampstead High St., NW3 1QP. ☎ 0171-794 1098.
The Woburn Book Shop, 10 Woburn Walk, WC1H 0JL (near The Place Theatre), ☎ 0171-388 7278.

PUBLICATIONS AND BOOKSELLERS 321

REGIONS

BIRMINGHAM
Lubavitch Bookshop, 95 Willows Rd., B12 9QF. ☎ 0121-440 6673. Fax: 0121-446 4199.

GATESHEAD J. Lehmann (mail order and wholesale), 20 Cambridge Ter., NE8 1RP. ☎ 0191-490 1692. Fax: 0191-477 5955.

GLASGOW J. & E. Levingstone, 47 & 55 Sinclair Dr., G42 9PT. ☎ 0141-649 2962.

LEICESTER Bookshop: Com. Centre, Highfield St. LE2 0NQ. Inq.: J. Markham, 74 Wakerley Rd., LE5 6AQ. ☎ 0116 273762.

LIVERPOOL Book & Gift Centre, Jewish Youth & Community Centre, Dunbabin Rd., L15 6XL. Sun. only, 11 a.m. to 1 p.m.

MANCHESTER & SALFORD
J. Goldberg, 11 Parkside Ave., Salford, M7 0HB. ☎ 0161-740 0732.
Hasefer, 18 Merrybower Rd., Salford M7 0HE. ☎ 0161-740 3013.
B. Horwitz (Wholesale & retail Judaica), 20 King Edward Bldgs., Bury Old Rd., M8. ☎ 0161-740 5897, & 2 Kings Rd., Prestwich. ☎ 0161-773 4956.
Jewish Book Centre (Mr Klein), 25 Ashbourne Gr., Salford, M7 4DB. ☎ 0161-792 1253. Fax: 0161-661 5505.

OXFORD B. H. Blackwell Ltd., 48-51 Broad St., OX1 3BQ. ☎ 01865 792792, has a Jewish book section.

SOUTHEND Dorothy Young, 21 Colchester Rd., SS2 6HW. ☎ 01702 331218 for appointment.

PRINCIPAL FESTIVALS AND FASTS 1997–2005 (5758–5765)

Festival or Fast	Hebrew Date	5758 1997-98	5759 1998-99	5760 1999-2000	5761 2000-01	5762 2001-02	5763 2002-03	5764 2003-04	5765 2004-05
New Year	Tishri 1	Oct. 2	Sept. 21	Sept. 11	Sept. 30	Sept. 18	Sept. 7	Sept. 27	Sept. 16
Day of Atonement	Tishri 10	Oct. 11	Sept. 30	Sept. 20	Oct. 9	Sept. 27	Sept. 16	Oct. 6	Sept. 25
Tabernacles, 1st Day	Tishri 15	Oct. 16	Oct. 5	Sept. 25	Oct. 14	Oct. 2	Sept. 21	Oct. 11	Sept. 30
Tabernacles, 8th Day	Tishri 22	Oct. 23	Oct. 12	Oct. 2	Oct. 21	Oct. 9	Sept. 28	Oct. 18	Oct. 7
Rejoicing of the Law	Tishri 23	Oct. 24	Oct. 13	Oct. 3	Oct. 22	Oct. 10	Sept. 29	Oct. 19	Oct. 8
Chanucah	Kislev 25	Dec. 24	Dec. 14	Dec. 4	Dec. 22	Dec. 10	Nov. 30	Dec. 20	Dec. 8
Purim	Adar[1] 14	Mar. 12	Mar. 2	Mar. 21	Mar. 9	Feb. 26	Mar. 18	Mar. 7	Mar. 25
Passover, 1st Day	Nisan 15	Apr. 11	Apr. 1	Apr. 20	Apr. 8	Mar. 28	Apr. 17	Apr. 6	Apr. 24
Passover, 7th Day	Nisan 21	Apr. 17	Apr. 7	Apr. 26	Apr. 14	Apr. 3	Apr. 23	Apr. 12	Apr. 30
Israel Indep. Day	Iyar 5[2]	Apr. 30	Apr. 21	May 10	Apr. 26	Apr. 17	May 7	Apr. 26	May 12
Feast of Weeks	Sivan 6	May 31	May 21	June 9	May 28	May 17	June 6	May 26	June 13
Fast of Ab	Ab 9	Aug. 2[3]	July 22	Aug. 10	July 29	July 18	Aug. 7	July 27	Aug. 14

1. Ve-Adar 14 in Leap Years.
2. When this date occurs on Friday or Sabbath, Israel Independence Day is observed on the previous Thursday.
3. Ab 10 (Ab 9 being Sabbath).

THE JEWISH CALENDAR

The Jewish Calendar is a lunar one, adapted to the solar year by various expedients. The hour is divided into 1,080 portions or *minims*, and the month between one new moon and the next is reckoned as 29 days, 12 hours, 793 minims. The years are grouped in cycles of 19. The present calendar was fixed by the Palestinian Jewish Patriarch, Hillel II, in 358 C.E. In early Talmudic times the new moons were fixed by the actual observation, and were announced from Jerusalem to the surrounding districts and countries by messenger or beacon.

If the time elapsing between one new moon and another were *exactly* 29½ days, the length of the months could be fixed at alternately 29 and 30 days. But there are three corrections to make which disturb this regularity: (1) The excess of 793 minims over the half day, (2) the adjustment to the solar year, (3) the requirement that the incidence of certain Jewish festivals shall not conflict with the Sabbath. To overcome these difficulties the Jewish Calendar recognises six different classes of years; three of them common and three leap. The leap years, which are the 3rd, 6th, 8th, 11th, 14th, 17th, and 19th of the Metyonic cycle of 19 years, are composed of thirteen months, an additional month being added. It is usually stated that this intercalary month is inserted after the month of Adar which in the ordinary year is of 29 days, but in a leap year has 30 days, but in reality the inserted month precedes the ordinary Adar and always has 30 days. Both the common and the leap years may be either regular, "minimal" , or full. The regular year has an alternation of 30 and 29 days. The "minimal" year gives Kislev only 29 days instead of 30, while in a full year Marcheshvan has 30 instead of 29 days.

Besides the lunar cycle of 19 years there is a solar cycle of 28 years, at the beginning of which the *Tekufah* of Nisan (the vernal equinox) returns to the same day and the same hour.

The chief disturbing influence in the arrangement of the Jewish Calendar is to prevent the Day of Atonement (Tishri 10th) from either immediately preceding or immediately succeeding the Sabbath, and Hoshana Rabba (Tishri 21st) from falling on the Sabbath. Consequently the New Year (Tishri Ist) cannot fall upon Sunday, Wednesday or Friday. A further complication of a purely astronomical character is introduced by the consideration that the Jewish day formally commences six hours before midnight. Hence, if the Molad or lunar conjunction for the month of Tishri occurs at noon or later, the new moon will be seen only after 6 p.m. and the Festival is postponed to the next day. When, after paying regard to these and certain other considerations, the days upon which two successive New Year Festivals fall are determined, the number of days in the intervening year is known and the length of Marcheshvan and Kislev is fixed accordingly.

It is customary to describe the character of a Jewish Year by a "Determinative" consisting of three Hebrew letters. The first of these indicates the day of the week upon which the New Year Festival falls, the second whether the year is regular, "minimal", or full, and the third the day of the week upon which Passover occurs. To this "Determinative" is added the Hebrew word for "ordinary" or "leap".

Authorities differ regarding the manner in which the figure employed for the Jewish Era (this year 5758) is arrived at. It is sufficient to describe it as the "Mundane Era" (dating from the Creation of the World) or the "Adamic Era" (dating from the Creation of Man). The chronology is based on Biblical data.

For the beginning of Sabbaths and Festivals, rules were laid down for the latitude of London by David Nieto, Haham of the Sephardi Community (1702-

1728). The hours for nightfall given here are based on those fixed by Nathan Marcus Adler, Chief Rabbi, in accordance with the formula of Michael Friedlander, Principal of Jews' College, but adjusted to take account of the movement of the Jewish population within the Metropolis since their day.

THE JEWISH YEAR

The times in this calendar for the beginning and ending of Sabbaths, Festivals and Fasts are given in Greenwich Mean Time from January 1 to March 28 and October 25 to the end, and in British Summer Time from March 29 to October 24, 1998.

5758

is known as 758 on the short system, and is a regular common year of 12 months, 51 Sabbaths and 354 days. Its first of Tishri is on a Thursday, and the first day of Passover on a Sabbath.

It is the first year of the 304th minor or lunar cycle (of 19 years each) since the Era of Creation, and the eighteenth of the 206th major or solar cycle (of 28 years each) since the same epoch.

The year began on Wednesday evening, October 1, 1997, and concludes on Sunday, September 20, 1998.

5759

is known as 759 on the short system, and is a full common year of 12 months, 50 Sabbaths and 355 days. Its first of Tishri is on a Monday, and the first day of Passover on a Thursday.

It is the second year of the 304th minor or lunar cycle (of 19 years each) since the Era of Creation, and the nineteenth of the 206th major or solar cycle (of 28 years each) since the same epoch.

The year begins on Sunday evening, September 20, 1998, and concludes on Friday, September 10, 1999.

CALENDAR NOTES

Pent. denotes Pentateuchal readings; **Proph.** denotes Prophetical readings.
Parentheses in either of the above denote Sephardi ritual.
Times for the commencement of the Sabbath during the summer months are, as is the tradition in Britain, given as 20.00. The actual times are given in parentheses.

ABRIDGED JEWISH CALENDAR FOR 1998 (5758-5759)

Fast of Tebet, 5758	Thursday	1998 January 8
New Moon Shebat	Wednesday	28
New Year for Trees	Wednesday	February 11
New Moon Adar, 1st day	Thursday	26
Fast of Esther	Wednesday	March 11
Purim	Thursday	12
Shushan Purim	Friday	13
New Moon Nisan	Saturday	28
Fast of Firstborn	Friday	April 10
First Day Passover	Saturday	11
Second Day Passover	Sunday	12
Seventh Day Passover	Friday	17
Eighth Day Passover	Saturday	18
Holocaust Memorial Day	Thursday	23
New Moon Iyar, 1st Day	Sunday	26
Israel Independence Day	Thursday	30
Minor Passover	Sunday	May 10
Thirty-third day of the (Lag Ba') Omer	Thursday	14
Jerusalem Day	Sunday	24
New Moon Sivan	Tuesday	26
First Day Feast of Weeks	Sunday	31
Second Day Feast of Weeks	Monday	June 1
New Moon Tammuz, 1st day	Wednesday	24
Fast of Tammuz	Sunday	July 12
New Moon Ab	Friday	24
Fast of Ab	Sunday	August 2
Festival of 15th Ab	Friday	7
New Moon Elul, 1st day	Saturday	22
First Day New Year, 5759	Monday	September 21
Second Day New Year	Tuesday	22
Fast of Gedaliah	Wednesday	23
Day of Atonement	Wednesday	30
First Day Tabernacles	Monday	October 5
Second Day Tabernacles	Tuesday	6
Hoshana Rabba	Sunday	11
Eighth Day of Solemn Assembly	Monday	12
Rejoicing of the Law	Tuesday	13
New Moon Marcheshvan, 1st day	Tuesday	20
New Moon Kislev, 1st day	Thursday	November 19
First Day Chanucah	Monday	December 14
New Moon Tebet 1st day	Saturday	19
Fast of Tebet	Tuesday	29

ABRIDGED JEWISH CALENDAR FOR 1999 (5759-5760)

New Moon Shebat, 5759	Monday	1999 January 18
New Year for Trees	Monday	February 1
New Moon Adar, 1st day	Tuesday	16
Fast of Esther	Monday	March 1
Purim	Tuesday	2
Shushan Purim	Wednesday	3
New Moon Nisan	Thursday	18
Fast of Firstborn	Wednesday	31
First Day Passover	Thursday	April 1
Second Day Passover	Friday	2
Seventh Day Passover	Wednesday	7
Eighth Day Passover	Thursday	8
Holocaust Memorial Day	Tuesday	13
New Moon Iyar, 1st Day	Friday	16
Israel Independence Day	Wednesday	21
Minor Passover	Friday	30
Thirty-third day of the (Lag Ba') Omer	Tuesday	May 4
Jerusalem Day	Friday	14
New Moon Sivan	Sunday	16
First Day Feast of Weeks	Friday	21
Second Day Feast of Weeks	Saturday	22
New Moon Tammuz, 1st day	Monday	June 14
Fast of Tammuz	Thursday	July 1
New Moon Ab	Wednesday	14
Fast of Ab	Thursday	22
Festival of 15th Ab	Wednesday	28
New Moon Elul, 1st day	Thursday	August 12
First Day New Year, 5760	Saturday	September 11
Second Day New Year	Sunday	12
Fast of Gedaliah	Monday	13
Day of Atonement	Monday	20
First Day Tabernacles	Saturday	25
Second Day Tabernacles	Sunday	26
Hoshana Rabba	Friday	October 1
Eighth Day of Solemn Assembly	Saturday	2
Rejoicing of the Law	Sunday	3
New Moon Marcheshvan, 1st day	Sunday	10
New Moon Kislev, 1st day	Tuesday	November 9
First Day Chanucah	Saturday	December 4
New Moon Tebet, 1st day	Thursday	9
Fast of Tebet	Sunday	19

JANUARY, 1998   TEBET 3 – SHEBAT 4, 5758
Tekufah Tues Jan 6 16.30   Molad Wed Jan 28 1h 3m 23s

			Tebet
1	Th		3
2	F	Sabbath commences 15.48	4
3	S	Sabbath ends 16.58. **Pent** Vayiggash, Gen **44**, 18-**47**, 27.	5
		Proph Ezek **37**, 15-28	
4	S		6
5	M		7
6	T		8
7	W		9
8	**Th**	**Fast of Tebet** ends 16.58. **Pent** morning and afternoon Ex **32**, 11-14	10
		and **34**, 1-10. **Proph** afternoon only Is **55**, 6-**56**, 8 (none).	
9	F	Sabbath commences 15.57	11
10	S	Sabbath ends 17.06. **Pent** Vay'chi, Gen **47**, 28 to end of Book.	12
		Proph I Kings **2**, 1-12	
11	S		13
12	M		14
13	T		15
14	W		16
15	Th		17
16	F	Sabbath commences 16.07	18
17	S	Sabbath ends 17.16. **Pent** Shemot, Ex **1**, 1-**6**, 1.	19
		Proph Is **27**, 6-**28**, 13; **29**, 22-23 (Jer **1**, 1-**2**, 3)	
18	S		20
19	M		21
20	T		22
21	W		23
22	Th		24
23	F	Sabbath commences 16.19	25
24	S	Sabbath ends 17.27. **Pent** Va'era, Ex **6**, 2-9. **Proph** Ezek **28**,	26
		25-**29**, 21. Benediction of Shebat.	
25	S		27
26	M		28
27	T	Yom Kippur Katan	29
			Shebat
28	W	Rosh Chodesh. **Pent** Num **28**, 1-15.	1
29	Th		2
30	F	Sabbath commences 16.31	3
31	S	Sabbath ends 17.38. **Pent** Bo, Ex **10**, 1-**13**, 16. **Proph** Jer **46**, 13-28	4

Liturgical notes - Jan 8, Selichot, Aneinu. - Jan 27, omit Tachanun in Minchah. - Jan 28, Half-Hallel.

FEBRUARY, 1998   SHEBAT 5 – ADAR 2, 5758
Molad Thurs Feb 26 13h 47m 27s

			Shebat
1	S		5
2	M		6
3	T		7
4	W		8
5	Th		9
6	F	Sabbath commences 16.44	10
7	S	Sabbath ends 17.50. **Pent** Beshallach, Shabbat Shirah, Ex **13**, 17-17. **Proph** Judges **4**, 4-**5**, 31 (**5**, 1-31)	11
8	S		12
9	M		13
10	T		14
11	W	**New Year for Trees**	15
12	Th		16
13	F	Sabbath commences 16.57	17
14	S	Sabbath ends 18.02. **Pent** Yitro, Ex **18-20**. **Proph** Is **6**, 1-7, 6 and 9, 5-6 (**6**, 1-13)	18
15	S		19
16	M		20
17	T		21
18	W		22
19	Th		23
20	F	Sabbath commences 17.09	24
21	S	Sabbath ends 18.14. **Pent** Mishpatim, Parshat Shekalim, Ex **21-24** and 30, 11-16. **Proph** II Kings **12**, 1-17 (**11**, 17-**12**, 17). Benediction of Adar.	25
22	S		26
23	M		27
24	T		28
25	W	Yom Kippur Katan	29
26	Th	Rosh Chodesh first day. **Pent** Num **28**, 1-15	30
			Adar
27	F	Sabbath commences 17.22. Rosh Chodesh second day. **Pent** Num **28**, 1-15	1
28	S	Sabbath ends 18.26. **Pent** Terumah, Ex **25-27**, 19. **Proph** I Kings **5**, 26-**6**, 13	2

Liturgical notes - Feb 10, omit Tachanun in Minchah. - Feb 11, omit Tachanun. - Feb 25, omit Tachanun in Minchah. - Feb 26 and 27, Half-Hallel.

MARCH, 1998   ADAR 3 – NISAN 4, 5758
Molad Sat Mar 28 2h 31m 30s

			Adar
1	S		3
2	M		4
3	T		5
4	W		6
5	Th		7
6	F	Sabbath commences 17.35	8
7	S	Sabbath ends 18.38. **Pent** Tetsaveh, Parshat Zachor, Ex **27**, 20-30, 10 and Deut **25**, 17-19. **Proph** I Sam **15**, 2-34 (**15**, 1-34)	9
8	S		10
9	M		11
10	T		12
11	W	**Fast of Esther** ends 18.38. **Pent** Morning and afternoon Ex **32**, 11-14 and **34**, 1-10. **Proph** afternoon only Is **55**, 6-56, 8 (none)	13
12	Th	**Purim** Pent Ex **17** 8-16	14
13	F	**Shushan Purim** Sabbath commences 17.47	15
14	S	Sabbath ends 18.50. **Pent** Ki Tissa, Ex **30**, 11-**34**. **Proph** I Kings **18**, 1-39 (20-39).	16
15	S		17
16	M		18
17	T		19
18	W		20
19	Th		21
20	F	Sabbath commences 17.59	22
21	S	Sabbath ends 19.02. **Pent** Vayakhel-Pekudei, Parshat Parah, Ex **35** to end of Book and Num **19**. **Proph** Ezek **36**, 16-38 (16-36) Benediction of Nisan	23
22	S		24
23	M		25
24	T		26
25	W		27
26	Th	Yom Kippur Katan	28
27	F	Sabbath commences 18.11.	29
			Nisan
28	S	Sabbath ends 19.14. Rosh Chodesh. **Pent** Vayikra, Parshat Hachodesh, Lev **1-5**, Num, **28**, 9-15 and Ex **12**, 1-20, **Proph** Ezek **45**, 16-**46**, 18 (**45**, 18-**46**, 15 and Is **66**, 1 and 23).	1
29	S		2
30	M		3
31	T		4

Liturgical notes – March 11, Selichot, Aneinu; omit Tachanun in Minchah; Al Hannissim is said in Maariv; Book of Esther is read; Half-Shekel is given. – March 12, Al Hannissim said; Book of Esther read in morning; omit Tachanun, El Erech Appayim and Lamenatse'ach. – March 13, omit Tachanun and Lamenatse'ach. – March 28, Half-Hallel; omit Tsidkatcha Tsedek in Minchah. – March 29 to 31, omit Tachanun.

APRIL, 1998
Tekufah Tues Apr 7 24.00

NISAN 5 – IYAR 4, 5758
Molad Sun Apr 26 15h 15m 33s

			Nisan
1	W		5
2	Th		6
3	F	Sabbath commences 19.22	7
4	S	Sabbath ends 20.27. **Pent** Tsav, Shabbat Haggadol, Lev **6-8**. **Proph** Mal **3**, 4-24	**8**
5	S		9
6	M		10
7	T		11
8	W		12
9	Th		13
10	F	**Fast of Firstborn.** Sabbath and Festival commence 19.34 **First Seder** in evening	14
11	S	**Passover first day.** Sabbath ends 20.39. **Second Seder** in evening **Pent** Ex **12**, 21-51; Num **28**, 16-25. **Proph** Josh **5**, 2-6, 1 (and **6**, 27)	15

			Omer days	
12	S	**Passover second day** ends 20.41. **Pent** Lev **22**, 26-23, 44; Num **28**, 16-25. **Proph** II Kings **23**, 1-9 and 21-25	1	**16**
13	M	**Pent** Ex **13**, 1-16; Num **28**, 19-25	2	17
14	T	**Pent** Ex **22**, 24-23, 19; Num **28**, 19-25	3	18
15	W	**Pent** Ex **34**, 1-26; Num **28**, 19-25	4	19
16	Th	Festival commences 19.44. Eruv Tavshilin. **Pent** Num **9**, 1-14 and **28**, 19-25	5	20
17	F	**Passover seventh day.** Sabbath commences 19.46 **Pent** Ex **13**, 17-15, 26; Num **28**, 19-25; **Proph** II Sam **22**	6	**21**
18	S	**Passover eighth day.** Sabbath and Festival end 20.52 **Pent** Deut **14**, 22-**16**, 17; Num **28**, 19-25; **Proph** Is **10**, 32-**12**, 6	7	**22**
19	S	Issru Chag	8	23
20	M		9	24
21	T		10	25
22	W		11	26
23	Th	**Holocaust Memorial Day**	12	27
24	F	Sabbath commences 19.58	13	28
25	S	Sabbath ends 21.05. **Pent** Shemini. Lev **9-11**, **Proph** Machar Chodesh, I Sam **20**, 18-42. Benediction of Iyar. Ethics I.	14	**29**
26	S	**Rosh Chodesh first day. Pent** Num **28**, 1-15	15	30
				Iyar
27	M	**Rosh Chodesh second day. Pent** Num **28**, 1-15	16	1
28	T		17	2
29	W		18	3
30	Th	**Yom Ha'atsma'ut – Israel Independence Day.**	19	**4**

Liturgical notes - April 1 to 10, omit Tachanun.-April 4, omit Tsidkatcha Tsedek, read from Haggadah and discontinue Barachi Nafshi in Minchah; omit Vihi Noam in Maariv.-April 9, Bedikat Chamets in evening.-April 10, omit Mizmor Letodah and Lamenatse'ach; abstain from Chamets by 10.47; Biur Chamets; discontinue Tal Umatar after Minchah-April 11, discontinue Mashiv Haruach in Mussaf; in the evening commence counting the Omer.-April 11 and 12, Whole Hallel.-April 13 to 18, Half-Hallel.-April 13 to 16, omit Mizmor Letodah.-April 18, read Song of Songs.-April 19 to 24, omit Tachanun.-April 25, omit Tsidkatcha Tsedek in Minchah.-April 26 and 27, Half-Hallel.-April 30, see Order of Service and Customs for Israel Independence Day (publ. Routledge & Kegan Paul, 1964).

MAY, 1998   IYAR 5 – SIVAN 6, 5758

Molad Tues May 26 3h 59m 37s

			Omer days	Iyar
1	F	Sabbath commences 20.00 (20.09)	20	5
2	S	Sabbath ends 21.19. Pent Tazria-Metsora, Lev 12-15. Proph II Kings 7, 3-20. Ethics 2.	21	6
3	S		22	7
4	M	**First fast day** ends 21.17	23	8
5	T		24	9
6	W		25	10
7	Th	**Second fast day** ends 21.22	26	11
8	F	Sabbath commences 20.00 (20.21)	27	12
9	S	Sabbath ends 21.32. Pent Acharei Mot-Kedoshim, Lev 16-20. Proph Amos 9, 7-15 (Ezek 20, 2-20), Ethics 3.	28	**13**
10	S	**Minor Passover**	29	14
11	M	**Third fast day** ends 21.30	30	15
12	T		31	16
13	W		32	17
14	Th	**Lag b'Omer – Scholars' festival**	33	**18**
15	F	Sabbath commences 20.00 (20.32)	34	19
16	S	Sabbath ends 21.45. Pent Emor, Lev 21-24. Proph Ezek 44, 15-31. Ethics 4.	35	**20**
17	S		36	21
18	M		37	22
19	T		38	23
20	W		39	24
21	Th		40	25
22	F	Sabbath commences 20.00 (20.42)	41	26
23	S	Sabbath ends 21.57. Pent Behar-Beckukkotai, Lev 25 to end of Book. Proph Jer 16, 19-17, 14. Benediction of Sivan. Ethics 5	42	**27**
24	S	**Yom Yerushalayim – Jerusalem Day**	43	28
25	M	Yom Kippur Katan	44	29
				Sivan
26	T	Rosh Chodesh. Pent Num 28, 1-15	45	1
27	W		46	2
28	Th		47	3
29	F	Sabbath commences 20.00 (20.51)	48	4
30	S	Sabbath ends and Festival commences 22.08. Pent Bemidbar, Num 1-4, 20. Proph Hosea 2, 1-22, Ethics 6.	49	5
31	S	**Feast of Weeks** first day ends 22.10. Pent Ex 19-20; Num 28, 26-31. Proph Ezek 1 and 3, 12		**6**

Liturgical notes - May 4, 7 and 11, Selichot are said in some communities and, if there be a Minyan who fast, Vay'chal is read.-May 13, omit Tachanun in Minchah.-May 14, omit Tachanun.-May 25, omit Tachanun in Minchah.-May 26, Half-Hallel.-May 27 to 29, omit Tachanun.-May 30, say Av Harachamim in morning service; omit Tsidkatcha Tsedek in Minchah.-May 31, Whole Hallel.

JUNE, 1998   SIVAN 7 – TAMMUZ 6, 5758
Molad Wed June 24 16h 43m 40s

			Sivan
1	M	**Feast of Weeks** second day ends 22.11. **Pent** Deut 15, 19-16, 17; Num 28, 26-31. **Proph** Habak 2, 20-3, 19.	7
2	T	Issru Chag	8
3	W		9
4	Th		10
5	F	Sabbath commences 20.00 (20.58)	11
6	S	Sabbath ends 22.17. **Pent** Naso, Num 4, 21-7. **Proph** Judges 13, 2-25. Ethics 1.	12
7	S		13
8	M		14
9	T		15
10	W		16
11	Th		17
12	F	Sabbath commences 20.00 (21.04)	18
13	S	Sabbath ends 22.24. **Pent** Beha'alotecha, Num **8-12**. **Proph** Zech 2, 14-4, 7, Ethics 2	19
14	S		20
15	M		21
16	T		22
17	W		23
18	Th		24
19	F	Sabbath commences 20.00 (21.07).	25
20	S	Sabbath ends 22.28. **Pent** Shelach Lecha, Num **13-15**. **Proph** Joshua 2. Benediction of Tammuz. Ethics 3.	26
21	S		27
22	M		28
23	T	Yom Kippur Katan	29
24	W	Rosh Chodesh first day. **Pent** Num 28, 1-15.	30
			Tammuz
25	Th	Rosh Chodesh second day. **Pent** Num 28, 1-15.	1
26	F	Sabbath commences 20.00 (21.08).	2
27	S	Sabbath ends 22.28. **Pent** Korach, Num **16-18**. **Proph** I Sam 11, 14-12, 22. Ethics 4	3
28	S		4
29	M		5
30	T		6

Liturgical notes - June 1, Whole Hallel; Book of Ruth is read. -June 2, omit Tachanun. - June 23; omit Tachanun in Minchah. - June 24 and 25, Half-Hallel.

JULY, 1998   TAMMUZ 7 – AB 8, 5758
Tekufah Wed July 8 07.30   Molad Fri July 24 5h 27m 43s

			Tammuz
1	W		7
2	Th		8
3	F	Sabbath commences 20.00 (21.06)	9
4	S	Sabbath ends 22.25. Pent Chukkat, Num 19, 1-22. 1. Proph Judges 11, 1-33. Ethics 5	10
5	S		11
6	M		12
7	T		13
8	W		14
9	Th		15
10	F	Sabbath commences 20.00 (21.02)	16
11	S	Sabbath ends 22.18. Pent Balak, Num 22, 2-25, 9. Proph Micah 5, 6-6, 8,.Ethics 6.	17
12	S	Fast of Tammuz ends 22.11. Pent Morning and afternoon Ex 32, 11-14 and 34, 1-10. Proph Afternoon only Is 55, 6-56, 8 (none).	18
13	M		19
14	T		20
15	W		21
16	Th		22
17	F	Sabbath commences 20.00 (20.55)	23
18	S	Sabbath ends 22.10. Pent Pinchas, Num 25, 10-30, 1. Proph Jer 1-2, 3. Benediction of Ab. Ethics 1.	24
19	S		25
20	M		26
21	T		27
22	W		28
23	Th	Yom Kippur Katan	29
			Ab
24	F	Sabbath commences 20.00 (20.47). Rosh Chodesh. Pent Num 28, 1-15.	1
25	S	Sabbath ends 21.58. Pent Mattot-Massei, Num 30, 2-end of Book. Proph Jer 2, 4-28; 3, 4 (Jer 2, 4-28; 4, 1-2) Ethics 2.	2
26	S		3
27	M		4
28	T		5
29	W		6
30	Th		7
31	F	Sabbath commences 20.00 (20.36)	8

Liturgical notes - July 12, Selichot, Aneinu. - July 23; omit Tachanun in Minchah. - July 24, Half-Hallel.

AUGUST, 1998   AB 9 – ELUL 9, 5758
Molad Sat Aug 22 18h 11m 47s

			Ab
1	S	Sabbath ends 21.46. **Pent** Devarim, Shabbat Chazon, Deut **1**, 1-3, 22. **Proph** Is **1**, 1-27. Fast commences 20.50.	9
2	S	**Fast of Ab** ends 21.38. **Pent** morning Deut **4**, 25-40; afternoon Ex **32**, 11-14 and **34**, 1-10; **Proph** morning Jer **8**, 13-9, 23; afternoon Is **55**, 6-**56** 8 (Hosea **14**, 2-10 and Micah **7**, 18-20).	10
3	M		11
4	T		12
5	W		13
6	Th		14
7	F	Sabbath commences 20.00 (20.24). **Festival of Ab**	15
8	S	Sabbath ends 21.31. **Pent** Va'etchanan. Shabbat Nachamu. Deut **3**, 23-**7**, 11. **Proph** Is **40**, 1-26. Ethics 3.	16
9	S		17
10	M		18
11	T		19
12	W		20
13	Th		21
14	F	Sabbath commences 20.00 (20.11)	22
15	S	Sabbath ends 21.16. **Pent** Ekev. Deut **7**, 12-**11**, 25. **Proph** Is **49**, 14-**51**, 3. Benediction of Elul. Ethics 4.	23
16	S		24
17	M		25
18	T		26
19	W		27
20	Th	Yom Kippur Katan	28
21	F	Sabbath commences 19.57	29
22	S	Sabbath ends 21.00. Rosh Chodesh first day. **Pent** Re'eh. Deut **11**, 26-**16** 17, and Num **28**, 9-15. **Proph** Is **66**, 1-24 (Is **54**, 11-**55**, 5; **66**, 1 and 23; I Sam **20**, 18 and 42). Ethics 5.	30

			Elul
23	S	Rosh Chodesh second day. **Pent** Num **28**, 1-15.	1
24	M		2
25	T		3
26	W		4
27	Th		5
28	F	Sabbath commences 19.42	6
29	S	Sabbath ends 20.44. **Pent** Shof'tim, Deut **16**, 18-**21**, 9, **Proph** Is **51**, 12-**52**, 12. Ethics 6.	7
30	S		8
31	M		9

Liturgical notes - Aug 1, say Av Harachamim in morning service; omit Tsidkatcha Tsedek in Minchah; no 'Ethics' are read; Book of Lamentations is read in Maariv, after which say Ve'attah Kadosh, omitting Vihi Noam and Veyitten Lecha. - Aug. 2 read Kinot; omit Tachanun and Lamenatse'ach; say Aneinu and insert Nachem in Minchah. - Aug. 6; omit Tachanun in Minchah. - Aug 7, omit Tachanun. - Aug. 22 and 23, Half-Hallel. - Aug 22, omit Tsidkatcha Tsedek in Minchah. - Aug. 23 to 31, the Shofar is blown on weekdays.

SEPTEMBER, 1998   ELUL 10, 5758–TISHRI 10, 5759

Molad Mon Sept 21 6h 55m 50s

			Elul
1	T		10
2	W		11
3	Th		12
4	F	Sabbath commences 19.26	13
5	S	Sabbath ends 20.27. Pent Ki-Tetsei, Deut 21, 10-25. Proph Is 54, 1-55 5 (54, 1-10). Ethics 1 and 2.	14
6	S		15
7	M		16
8	T		17
9	W		18
10	Th		19
11	F	Sabbath commences 19.10	20
12	S	Sabbath ends 20.10. Pent Ki-Tavo, Deut 26-29, 8. Proph Is 60. Ethics 3 and 4.	21
13	S		22
14	M		23
15	T		24
16	W		25
17	Th		26
18	F	Sabbath commences 18.54	27
19	S	Sabbath ends 19.53. Pent Nitsavim, Deut 29, 9-30. Proph Is 61, 10-63, 9. Ethics 5 and 6.	28
20	S	Festival commences 18.49	29
			Tishri
21	M	New Year 5759 first day ends 19.49. Pent Gen 21; Num 29, 1-6. Proph I Sam 1-2, 10	1
22	T	New Year second day ends 19.46. Pent Gen 22; Num 29, 1-6. Proph Jer 31, 2-20.	2
23	W	Fast of Gedaliah ends 19.38. Pent Morning and afternoon Ex 32, 11-14 and 34, 1-10. Proph afternoon only Is 55, 6-56, 8 (none)	3
24	Th		4
25	F	Sabbath commences 18.38	5
26	S	Sabbath ends 19.37. Pent Vayelech. Shabbat Shuvah, Deut 31. Proph Hosea 14, 2-10; Joel 2, 15-27 (Hosea 14, 2-10; Micah 7, 18-20).	6
27	S		7
28	M		8
29	T	Fast commences 18.29; service 18.40	9
30	W	Day of Atonement ends 19.28. Pent morning Lev 16; Num 29, 7-11. Afternoon Lev 18 Proph morning Is 57, 14-58, 14. Afternoon Book of Jonah and Micah 7, 18-20	10

Liturgical notes - Sept. 1 to 18, the Shofar is blown on weekdays. - Sept. 13 to 20, Selichot on weekdays. - Sept. 19; omit Vihi Noam in Ma'ariv. - Sept. 20; omit Tachanun. - Sept. 21, Tashlich. - Sept. 23 to 29, Selichot on weekdays. - Sept, 23, Aneinu. - Sept. 26, omit Vihi Noam in Maariv. - Sept 29, omit Mizmor Letodah, Tachanun and Lamenatse'ach; Vidduy said in Minchah.

OCTOBER, 1998 TISHRI 11 – MARCHESHVAN 11, 5759
Tekufah Wed Oct 7 15.00   Molad Tues Oct 20 19h 39m 53s

			Tishri
1	Th		11
2	F	Sabbath commences 18.22	12
3	S	Sabbath ends 19.21. Pent Ha'azinu, Deut 32. Proph II Sam 22.	13
4	S	Festival commences 18.17	14
5	M	**Tabernacles first day** ends 19.16. Pent Lev 22, 26-23; 44; Num 29, 12-16. Proph Zech 14.	15
6	T	**Tabernacles second day** ends 19.14. Pent Lev 22, 26-23, 44; Num 29, 12-16. Proph I Kings 8, 2-21.	16
7	W	Pent Num 29, 17-25.	17
8	Th	Pent Num 29, 20-28.	18
9	F	Sabbath commences 18.06. Pent Num 29, 23-31.	19
10	S	Sabbath ends 19.05. Pent Ex 33, 12-34, 26; Num 29, 26-31. Proph Ezek 38, 18-39, 16.	20
11	S	**Hoshana Rabba.** Festival commences 18.02. Pent Num 29, 26-34.	21
12	M	**Eighth Day of Solemn Assembly** ends 19.01. Pent Deut 14, 22-16, 17; Num 29. 35-30. I. Proph I Kings 8, 54-66.	22
13	T	**Rejoicing of the Law** ends 18.59. Pent Deut 33-34; Gen 1, 1-2, 3; Num 29, 35-30, 1. Proph Joshua 1, (1, 1-9).	23
14	W	Issru Chag	24
15	Th		25
16	F	Sabbath commences 17.51.	26
17	S	Sabbath ends 18.51. Pent Bereshit, Gen 1, 1-6, 8. Proph Is 42, 5-43, 10 (42, 5-21). Benediction of Marcheshvan.	27
18	S		28
19	M		29
20	T	Rosh Chodesh first day. Pent Num 28, 1-15.	30
			Marcheshvan
21	W	Rosh Chodesh second day. Pent Num 28, 1-15.	1
22	Th		2
23	F	Sabbath commences 17.36	3
24	S	Sabbath ends 18.37. Pent Noach, Gen 6, 9-11. Proph Is 54, 1-55, 5. (54, 1-10).	4
25	S		5
26	M		6
27	T		7
28	W		8
29	Th		9
30	F	Sabbath commences 16.23	10
31	S	Sabbath ends 17.24. Pent Lech Lecha, Gen 12-17. Proph Is 40, 27-41, 16	11

Liturgical notes - Oct. 1 to 14, omit Tachanun. - Oct. 3, omit Tsidkatcha Tsedek in Minchah and Vihi Noam in Maariv. - Oct. 5 to 13, Whole-Hallel. - Hoshanot: Oct. 5, Lema'an Amitach; Oct. 6, Even Shetiyah; Oct. 7, E'eroch Shu'i; Oct. 8, Om Ani Choma; Oct. 9, El Lemaoshot; Oct. 10, Om Netsurah. - Oct. 10, Ecclesiastes is read; omit Tsidkatcha Tsedek in Minchah and Vihi Noam in Maariv. - Oct. 12, Mashiv Haruach commenced in Mussaf. - Oct. 17, Barachi Nafshi commenced in Minchah. - Oct. 19, omit Tachanun in Minchah. - Oct. 20 and 21, Half-Hallel.

NOVEMBER, 1998 MARCHESHVAN 12 – KISLEV 11,5759
Molad Thurs Nov 19 8h 23m 57s

			Marcheshvan
1	S		12
2	M		13
3	T		14
4	W		15
5	Th		16
6	F	Sabbath commences 16.10	17
7	S	Sabbath ends 17.13. Pent Vayera, Gen 18-22. Proph II Kings 4, 1-37 (4, 1-23)	18
8	S		19
9	M	**First fast day** ends 17.04	20
10	T		21
11	W		22
12	Th	**Second fast day** ends 17.00	23
13	F	Sabbath commences 15.59	24
14	S	Sabbath ends 17.03. Pent Chaye Sarah, Gen 23-25, 18. Proph I Kings 1, 1-31. Benediction of Kislev.	25
15	S		26
16	M	**Third fast day** ends 16.55	27
17	T		28
18	W	Yom Kippur Katan	29
19	Th	Rosh Chodesh first day. Pent Num 28, 1-15.	30
			Kislev
20	F	Sabbath commences 15.50. Rosh Chodesh second day. Pent Num 28, 1-15	1
21	S	Sabbath ends 16.56. Pent. Tol'dot, Gen 25, 19-28, 9. Proph Malachi 1-2, 7	2
22	S		3
23	M		4
24	T		5
25	W		6
26	Th		7
27	F	Sabbath commences 15.43.	8
28	S	Sabbath ends 16.50. Pent. Vayetsei, Gen 28, 10-32, 3. Proph Hosea 12, 13-**14**, 10 (**11**, 7-**12**, 12).	9
29	S		10
30	M		11

Liturgical notes - Nov. 9, 12 and 16, Selichot are said in some communities and, if there be a Minyan who fast, Vay'chal is read. - Nov. 18, omit Tachanun in Minchah. - Nov. 19 and 20, Half-Hallel.

DECEMBER, 1998   KISLEV 12 – TEBET 12, 5759
Molad Fri Dec 18 21h 8m 0s

			Kislev
1	T		12
2	W		13
3	Th		14
4	F	Sabbath commences 15.38	15
5	S	Sabbath ends 16.46. Pent Vayishlach, Gen 32, 4-36. Proph Hosea 11, 7-12, 12. (Others, Book of Obadiah)	16
6	S		17
7	M		18
8	T		19
9	W		20
10	Th		21
11	F	Sabbath commences 15.36	22
12	S	Sabbath ends 16.45. Pent Vayeshev, Gen 37-40. Proph Amos 2, 6-3, 8. Benediction of Tebet	23
13	S	First Chanucah Light in the evening	24
14	M	**Chanucah first day.** Pent Num 7, 1-17	25
15	T	**Chanucah second day.** Pent Num 7, 18-29	26
16	W	**Chanucah third day.** Pent Num 7, 24-35	27
17	Th	**Chanucah fourth day.** Pent Num 7, 30-41.	28
18	F	**Chanucah fifth day.** Sabbath commences 15.37 Pent Num 7, 36-47.	29
19	S	**Chanucah sixth day.** Rosh Chodesh first day. Sabbath ends 16.47. Pent Mikkets, Gen 41-44, 17; Num 28, 9-15 and 7, 42-47. Proph Zech 2, 14-4, 7 (and Is 66, 1 and 23; I Sam 20, 18 and 42).	30

			Tebet
20	S	**Chanucah seventh day.** Rosh Chodesh second day. Pent Num 28, 1-15 and 7, 48-53	1
21	M	**Chanucah eighth day.** Pent Num 7, 54-8, 4	2
22	T		3
23	W		4
24	Th		5
25	F	Sabbath commences 15.41	6
26	S	Sabbath ends 16.51. Pent Vayiggash, Gen 44, 18-47, 27. Proph Ezek 37, 15-28	7
27	S		8
28	M		9
29	T	**Fast of Tebet** ends 16.47. Pent morning and afternoon Ex 32, 11-14 and 34, 1-10. Proph afternoon only Is 55, 6-56, 8 (none).	10
30	W		11
31	Th		12

Liturgical notes - Dec 5, Tal Umatar commenced in Maariv. - Dec. 13, omit Tachanun in Minchah. During Chanucah say Al Hannissim and Whole-Hallel; omit Tachanun, El Erech Appayim and Lamenatse'ach, and on Sabbath Tsidkatcha Tsedek in Minchah. - Dec 29, Selichot, Aneinu.

JANUARY, 1999   TEBET 13–SHEBAT 14, 5759

Tekufah Wed Jan 6 22.30   Molad Sun Jan 17 9h 52m 3s

			Tebet
1	F	Sabbath commences 15.47	13
2	S	Sabbath ends 16.57. Pent Vay'chi, Gen 47, 28 to end of Book. Proph I Kings 2, 1-12	14
3	S		15
4	M		16
5	T		17
6	W		18
7	Th		19
8	F	Sabbath commences 15.55	20
9	S	Sabbath ends 17.05. Pent Shemot, Ex 1, 1-6, 1. Proph Is 27, 6-28, 13; 29, 22-23 (Jer 1, 1-2, 3)	21
10	S		22
11	M		23
12	T		24
13	W		25
14	Th		26
15	F	Sabbath commences 16.05	27
16	S	Sabbath ends 17.14. Pent Va'era, Ex 6, 2-9, Proph Ezek 28, 25-29, 21. Benediction of Shebat.	28
17	S	Yom Kippur Katan	29
			Shebat
18	M	Rosh Chodesh. Pent Num 28, 1-15.	1
19	T		2
20	W		3
21	Th		4
22	F	Sabbath commences 16.17	5
23	S	Sabbath ends 17.25. Pent Bo, Ex 10, 1-13, 16. Proph Jer 46, 13-28	6
24	S		7
25	M		8
26	T		9
27	W		10
28	Th		11
29	F	Sabbath commences 16.29	12
30	S	Sabbath ends 17.36. Pent Beshallach, Shabbat Shirah, Ex 13, 17-17. Proph Judges 4, 4-5, 31 (5, 1-31).	13
31	S		14

Liturgical notes - Jan 17, omit Tachanun in Minchah. - Jan 18, Half-Hallel. - Jan 31, omit Tachanun in Minchah.

FEBRUARY, 1999   SHEBAT 15 – ADAR 12, 5759
Molad Mon Feb 15 22h 36m 7s

			Shebat
1	M	New Year for Trees	15
2	T		16
3	W		17
4	Th		18
5	F	Sabbath commences 16.42	19
6	S	Sabbath ends 17.48. Pent Yitro, Ex 18-20. Proph Is 6, 1-7, 6 and 9, 5-6 (6, 1-13)	20
7	S		21
8	M		22
9	T		23
10	W		24
11	Th		25
12	F	Sabbath commences 16.55	26
13	S	Sabbath ends 18.00. Pent Mishpatim. Parshat Shekalim, Ex 21-24 and 30, 11-16. Proph II Kings 12, 1-17 (11, 17-12, 17). Benediction of Adar.	27
14	S		28
15	M	Yom Kippur Katan	29
16	T	Rosh Chodesh first day. Pent Num 28, 1-15	30
			Adar
17	W	Rosh Chodesh second day. Pent Num 28, 1-15	1
18	Th		2
19	F	Sabbath commences 17.07	3
20	S	Sabbath ends 18.12. Pent Terumah, Ex 25-27, 19. Proph I Kings 5, 26-6, 13	4
21	S		5
22	M		6
23	T		7
24	W		8
25	Th		9
26	F	Sabbath commences 17.20	10
27	S	Sabbath ends 18.24. Pent Tetsaveh, Parshat Zachor, Ex 27, 20-30, 10 and Deut 25, 17-19. Proph I Sam 15, 2-34 (15, 1-34)	11
28	S		12

Liturgical notes - Feb 1, omit Tachanun. - Feb. 15, omit Tachanun in Minchah. - Feb 16 and 17, Half-Hallel.

CALENDAR 341

Calendar
EVENING TWILIGHT VARIATION FOR REGIONS

This table shows the number of minutes required to be added to, or substracted from, the times for London, in order to determine the time of the termination of Sabbath, Festival, or Fast. For dates between those indicated here, an approximate calculation must be made. Acknowledgement is made to the Royal Greenwich Observatory for valued co-operation in the compilation of this table.

		BIRMINGHAM	BOURNEMOUTH	GLASGOW	LEEDS	LIVERPOOL	MANCHESTER	NEWCASTLE
Jan.	1	+9	+15	0	+4	+11	+8	0
	11	+9	+14	+1	+4	+11	+8	0
	21	+9	+14	+3	+5	+12	+9	+2
	31	+9	+13	+6	+6	+12	+9	+3
Feb.	10	+9	+12	+9	+7	+13	+10	+5
	20	+9	+11	+12	+8	+14	+11	+7
Mar.	2	+10	+10	+16	+10	+16	+13	+10
	12	+10	+9	+20	+12	+18	+15	+13
	22	+10	+7	+22	+12	+18	+15	+14
Apr.	1	+11	+7	+27	+15	+20	+17	+18
	11	+12	+7	+31	+17	+22	+19	+22
	21	+13	+7	+35	+20	+24	+21	+26
May	1	+16	+7	+40	+23	+27	+24	+30
	11	+18	+7	+46	+26	+30	+27	+35
	21	+20	+7	+52	+30	+34	+31	+42
	31	+23	+7	+57	+34	+37	+34	+48
June	10	+25	+7	+63	+38	+40	+38	+55
	20	+26	+7	+64	+40	+41	+39	+58
	30	+26	+7	+62	+38	+40	+38	+55
July	10	+23	+7	+57	+35	+38	+35	+50
	20	+21	+7	+51	+31	+34	+31	+43
	30	+19	+8	+46	+27	+30	+27	+38
Aug.	9	+17	+8	+40	+24	+27	+24	+32
	19	+16	+8	+35	+20	+25	+22	+27
	29	+16	+8	+30	+18	+23	+20	+23
Sept.	8	+14	+8	+26	+15	+20	+17	+18
	18	+13	+8	+23	+12	+18	+15	+15
	28	+13	+10	+20	+12	+18	+15	+14
Oct.	8	+12	+10	+16	+10	+16	+13	+10
	18	+11	+12	+13	+9	+15	+12	+9
	28	+11	+12	+10	+8	+14	+11	+6
Nov.	7	+10	+13	+7	+6	+13	+10	+4
	17	+10	+14	+4	+5	+12	+9	+3
	27	+10	+14	+2	+4	+11	+8	+1
Dec.	7	+10	+15	0	+4	+11	+8	0
	17	+9	+15	0	+3	+11	+7	-1
	27	+9	+15	0	+3	+11	+8	-1
	31	+9	+15	0	+4	+11	+8	0

SIDROT AND HAFTAROT FOR 1999
(5759-5760)

Haftara parentheses indicate Sephardi ritual.

1999	5759		HAFTARA	SIDRA
Jan. 2	Tebet	14	I Kings 2, 1-12	*Vay'chi*
9		21	Isaiah 27, 6-28, 13; and 29, 22-23 (Jer 1, 1-2, 3)	*Shemot*
16		28	Ezekiel 28, 25-29, 21	*Va'era*
23	Shebat	6	Jeremiah 46, 13-28	*Bo*
30		13	Judges 4, 4-5, 31 (5, 1-31)	*Beshallach (Shirah)*
Feb. 6		20	Isaiah 6, 1-7, 6; 9, 5-6 (6, 1-13)	*Yitro*
13		27	II Kings 12, 1-17 (11, 17-12, 17)	*Mishpatim (Shekalim)*
20	Adar	4	I Kings 5, 26-6, 13	*Terumah*
27		11	I Samuel 15, 2-34 (15, 1-34)	*Tetsaveh (Zachor)*
Mar. 6		18	Ezekiel 36, 16-38 (16-36)	*Ki Tissa (Parah)*
13		25	Ezek 45, 16-46, 18 (45, 18-46, 15)	*Vayakhel-Pekudei (Hachodesh)*
20	Nisan	3	Isaiah 43, 21-44, 23	*Vayikra*
27		10	Malachi 3, 4-24	*Tsav (Haggadol)*
Apr. 3		17	Ezekiel 37, 1-14	*Chol Hamo'ed Pesach*
10		24	II Samuel 6, 1-7, 17 (6, 1-19)	*Shemini*
17	Iyar	1	Isaiah 66, 1-24	*Tazria-Metsora (Rosh Chodesh)*
24		8	Amos 9, 7-15 (Ezek 20, 2-20)	*Acharei Mot-Kedoshim*
May 1		15	Ezekiel 44, 15-31	*Emor*
8		22	Jeremiah 16, 19-17, 14	*Behar-Bechukkotai*
15		29	I Samuel 20, 18-42	*Bemidbar (Machar Chodesh)*
22	Sivan	7	Habakkuk 2, 20-3, 19	*2nd Day Shavuot*
29		14	Judges 13, 2-25	*Naso*
June 5		21	Zechariah 2, 14-4,7	*Beha'alotecha*
12		28	Joshua 2, 1-24	*Shelach Lecha*
19	Tammuz	5	I Samuel 11, 14-12, 22	*Korach*

Sidrot and Haftarot

1999	5759	HAFTARA	SIDRA

June 26 Tammuz 12 Micah 5, 6-6, 8 .... Chukkat-Balak

July 3   19   Jeremiah 1, 1-2, 3 .... Pinchas
      10   26   Jeremiah 2, 4-28 and 3, 4
                          (2, 4-28 and 4, 1-2) .... Mattot-Massei
      17 Ab   4   Isaiah 1, 1-27 .... Devarim (Chazon)
      24   11   Isaiah 40, 1-26 .... Va'etchanan (Nachamu)
      31   18   Isaiah 49, 14-51, 3 .... Ekev

Aug. 7   25   Isaiah 54, 11-55, 5 .... Re'eh
      14 Elul   2   Isaiah 51, 12-52, 12 .... Shof'tim
      21   9   Isaiah 54, 1-10 .... Ki Tetsei
      28   16   Isaiah 60, 1-22 .... Ki Tavo

Sept. 4 5760   23   Isaiah 61, 10-63, 9 .... Nitsavim-Vayelech
      11 Tishri   1   I Samuel 1-2, 10 .... 1st Day Rosh Hashana
      18   8   Hosea 14, 2-10 and Joel
                          2, 15-27 (Hosea 14, 2-10 and
                          Micah 7, 18-20) .... Ha'azinu (Shuvah)
      25   15   Zechariah 14, 1-21 .... 1st Day Succot

Oct. 2   22   I Kings 8, 54-66 .... Shemini Atseret
       9   29   I Samuel 20, 18-42 .... Bereshit
                                          (Machar Chodesh)
      16 Cheshvan 6   Isaiah 54, 1-55, 5 (54, 1-10) .... Noach
      23   13   Isaiah 40, 27-41, 16 .... Lech Lecha
      30   20   II Kings 4, 1-37 (4, 1-23) .... Vayera

Nov. 6   27   I Kings 1, 1-31 .... Chayei Sarah
      13 Kislev   4   Malachi 1, 1-2, 7 .... Tol'dot
      20   11   Hosea 12, 13-14, 10 (11, 7-
                        12, 12) .... Vayetsei
      27   18   Hosea 11, 7-12, 12 (Obadiah) ...... Vayishlach

Dec. 4   25   Zechariah 2, 14-4, 7 .... Vayeshev (Chanucah)
      11 Tebet   2   I Kings 7, 40-50 .... Mikkets (Chanucah)
      18   9   Ezekiel 37, 15-28 .... Vayiggash
      25   16   I Kings 2, 1-12 .... Vay'chi

MARRIAGE REGULATIONS (General)

Marriages may be contracted according to the usage of the Jews between persons *both* professing the Jewish religion, provided that due notice has been given to the Superintendent Registrar and that his certificate (or licence and certificate) has been obtained. There is no restriction regarding the hours within which the marriage may be solemnised, nor the place of marriage, which may be a synagogue, private house, or any other building.

The date and place of the intended marriage having been decided, the parties should consult the Minister or Secretary for Marriages of the synagogue through which the marriage is to be solemnised. He will advise of the necessary preliminary steps and the suitability of the proposed date.

Notice of the intended marriage must be given to the local Superintendent Registrar, and the document or documents obtained from him must be handed to the Synagogue Marriage Secretary in advance of the date appointed. In the case of a marriage in a building other than a synagogue, care should be taken that these documents contain the words *"both parties being of the Jewish persuasion"* following the description of the building.

If the marriage is to be solemnised at or through a synagogue under the jurisdiction of the Chief Rabbi, his Authorisation of Marriage must be presented. The minister of the synagogue will explain how this may be obtained.

No marriage is valid if solemnised between persons who are within the degrees of kindred of affinity (e.g., between uncle and niece) prohibited by English law, even though such a marriage is permissible by Jewish law.

A marriage between Jews must be registered immediately after the ceremony by the Secretary of Marriages of the synagogue of which the husband is a member. If he is not already a member he may become one by paying a membership fee in addition to the marriage charges.

The belief that marriage by licence may be solemnised only by civil ceremony at a Registry Office is erroneous. It may take place in a synagogue, or any other building, provided that the place of solemnisation is stated to the Superintendent Registrar when application is made for his licence.

No marriage between Jews should take place without due notice being given to the Superintendent Registrar, and without being registered in the Marriage Register of a synagogue. Marriages in such circumstances are not necessarily valid in English law. (Outside England and Wales other regulations apply and the Minister of the synagogue should be consulted.)

According to the regulations valid among Orthodox Jews, marriages may not be solemnised on the following dates:

1998		1999
8 January	Fast of Tebet	–
11 March	Fast of Esther	1 March
12 March	Purim	2 March
10 April	Day before Pesach	31 March
11-18 April	Pesach	1-8 April
28 April-13 May	Sephirah	18 April-3 May
15-25 May	Sephirah	5-14 May
30 May	Day before Shavuot	20 May
31 May-1 June	Shavuot	21-22 May
12 July-2 August	Three Weeks	1-22 July
20 September	Day before Rosh Hashana	10 September
21-22 September	Rosh Hashana	11-12 September
23 September	Fast of Gedaliah	13 September
29 September	Day before Yom Kippur	19 September
30 September	Yom Kippur	20 September
4 October	Day before Succot	24 September
5-13 October	Succot	25 September-3 October
29 December	Fast of Tebet	19 December

Nor on any Sabbath

Among Reform Jews, marriages are solemnised during the Sephirah, from the Fast of Tammuz until the Fast of Ab (but not on the Fast of Ab itself), on the days that precede Festivals, on the Second days of Festivals, and on Purim, but not on the other prohibited days mentioned above.

CALENDAR
JEWISH CALENDAR FOR THIRTY YEARS

5745–5774

(1984–2014)

INSTRUCTIONS FOR USE

The following Table shows on one line the civil date and the day of the week on which every date of the Jewish year falls during the thirty years which it covers; those dates which occur on Sabbath are printed in *heavier* type. Thus, Tishri 10, 5752, coincided with September 18, 1991, and this was a Wednesday, since September 14 is marked as being Sabbath. The civil dates on which the festivals and fasts (or any other occasion of the Jewish Calendar) occur in any particular year may be ascertained in the same manner. The Table is arranged according to the months of the Hebrew Year, the day of the month being shown in the left-hand column.

YAHRZEIT. – This is always observed on the Jewish date on which the parent died. It has never been customary under the jurisdiction of the Chief Rabbi of the United Hebrew Congregations of the British Commonwealth to observe the Yahrzeit after the death on the anniversary of the burial as is enjoined, in certain circumstances, by some authorities. If the death took place after dark, it must be dated from the next civil day, as the day is reckoned among Jews from sunset to sunset. This date must be located in the Table, according to the month and day, and the civil date of the Yahrzeit in any particular year will be found on the same line in the column beneath the year in question. It should be noted, however, that if a parent died during Adar in an ordinary year, the Yahrzeit is observed in a leap year in the First Adar. (Some people observed it in both Adars.) If the death took place in a leap year the Yahrzeit is observed in a leap year in the same Adar (whether First or Second) during which the death happened. The Yahrzeit begins and the memorial light is kindled on the evening before the civil date thus ascertained.

BARMITZVAH. – A boy attains his Barmitzvah (religious majority) when he reaches his thirteenth birthday, i.e., on the first day of his fourteenth year, this being computed according to the Jewish date on which he was born. The date and year of birth being located in the Table, the corresponding civil date of the first day of his fourteenth year will be found on the same line in the 13th column. If this be a Sabbath, he reads his *Parsha* on that day; if a week-day, he reads it on the following Sabbath. By consulting the Calendar the scriptural portion of the week may be ascertained. It should be noted, however, that if a boy be born in Adar of an ordinary year and become Barmitzvah in a leap year, the celebration falls in the Second Adar. If he were born in a leap year and becomes Barmitzvah in a leap year it is celebrated in that Adar (whether First or Second) during which his birth occurred. If he were born in a leap year and the Barmitzvah is in an ordinary year, it is observed in Adar.

TISHRI (30 days)

5745		46	47	48	49	50	51	52	53	54	55	56	57	58	59	60	61	62	63	64	65	66	67	68	69	70	71	72	73	74
1984		85	86	87	88	89	90	91	92	93	94	95	96	97	98	99	2000	01	02	03	04	05	06	07	08	09	10	11	12	13
Tish	Sept-Oct	Sept-Oct	Oct-Nov	Sept-Oct	Sept-Oct	Sept-Oct	Sept-Oct	Sept-Oct	Sept-Oct	Sept-Oct	Sept-Oct	Sept-Oct	Sept-Oct	October	Sept-Oct	Sept-Oct	Sept-Oct	Sept-Oct	Sept-Oct	Sept-Oct	Sept-Oct	Oct-Nov	Sept-Oct	Sept-Oct	Sept-Oct	Sept-Oct	Sept-Oct	Sept-Oct	Sept-Oct	Sept-Oct
1	27	16	**4**	24	12	**30**	20	9	28	16	6	25	**14**	2	21	**11**	**30**	18	**7**	**27**	16	4	**23**	13	30	**19**	9	29	17	5
2	28	17	5	25	13	1	21	10	29	17	7	26	15	3	22	12	1	19	8	28	17	5	24	14	1	20	10	30	18	6
3	**29**	18	6	**26**	14	2	**22**	11	30	**18**	8	27	16	**4**	23	13	2	20	9	29	**18**	6	25	**15**	2	21	**11**	**1**	19	**7**
4	30	19	7	27	15	3	23	12	1	19	9	28	17	5	24	14	3	21	10	30	19	7	26	16	3	22	12	2	20	8
5	1	20	8	28	16	4	24	13	2	20	**10**	29	18	6	25	15	4	**22**	11	1	20	**8**	27	17	**4**	23	13	3	21	9
6	2	**21**	9	29	**17**	5	25	**14**	**3**	21	11	**30**	19	7	**26**	16	5	23	12	2	21	9	28	18	5	24	14	4	**22**	10
7	3	22	10	30	18	6	26	15	4	22	12	1	20	8	27	17	6	24	13	3	22	10	29	19	6	25	15	5	23	11
8	4	23	**11**	1	19	**7**	27	16	5	23	13	2	**21**	9	28	**18**	**7**	25	**14**	**4**	23	11	**30**	20	7	**26**	16	6	24	12
9	5	24	12	2	20	8	28	17	6	24	14	3	22	10	29	19	8	26	15	5	24	12	1	21	8	27	17	7	25	13
10	**6**	25	13	**3**	21	9	**29**	18	7	**25**	15	4	23	**11**	30	20	9	27	16	6	**25**	13	2	**22**	9	28	**18**	**8**	26	**14**
11	7	26	14	4	22	10	30	19	8	26	16	5	24	12	1	21	10	28	17	7	26	14	3	23	10	29	19	9	27	15
12	8	27	15	5	23	11	1	20	9	27	**17**	6	25	13	2	22	11	**29**	18	8	27	**15**	4	24	**11**	30	20	10	28	16
13	9	**28**	16	6	**24**	12	2	**21**	**10**	28	18	**7**	26	14	**3**	23	12	30	19	9	28	16	5	25	12	1	21	11	**29**	17
14	10	29	17	7	25	13	3	22	11	29	19	8	27	15	4	24	13	1	20	10	29	17	6	26	13	2	22	12	30	18
15	11	30	**18**	8	26	**14**	4	23	12	30	20	9	**28**	16	5	**25**	**14**	2	**21**	**11**	30	18	**7**	27	14	**3**	23	13	1	19
16	12	1	19	9	27	15	5	24	13	1	21	10	29	17	6	26	15	3	22	12	1	19	8	28	15	4	24	14	2	20
17	**13**	2	20	**10**	28	16	**6**	25	14	**2**	22	11	30	**18**	7	27	16	4	23	13	**2**	20	9	**29**	16	5	**25**	**15**	3	**21**
18	14	3	21	11	29	17	7	26	15	3	23	12	1	19	8	28	17	5	24	14	3	21	10	30	17	6	26	16	4	22
19	15	4	22	12	30	18	8	27	16	4	**24**	13	2	20	9	29	18	**6**	25	15	4	**22**	11	1	**18**	7	27	17	5	23
20	16	**5**	23	13	**1**	19	9	**28**	**17**	5	25	**14**	3	21	**10**	30	19	7	26	16	5	23	12	2	19	8	28	18	**6**	24
21	17	6	24	14	2	20	10	29	18	6	26	15	4	22	11	1	20	8	27	17	6	24	13	3	20	9	29	19	7	25
22	18	7	**25**	15	3	**21**	11	30	19	7	27	16	**5**	23	12	**2**	**21**	9	**28**	**18**	7	25	**14**	4	21	**10**	30	20	8	26
23	19	8	26	16	4	22	12	1	20	8	28	17	6	24	13	3	22	10	29	19	8	26	15	5	22	11	1	21	9	27
24	**20**	9	27	**17**	5	23	**13**	2	21	**9**	29	18	7	**25**	14	4	23	11	30	20	**9**	27	16	**6**	23	12	**2**	**22**	10	**28**
25	21	10	28	18	6	24	14	3	22	10	30	19	8	26	15	5	24	12	1	21	10	28	17	7	24	13	3	23	11	29
26	22	11	29	19	7	25	15	4	23	11	**1**	20	9	27	16	6	25	**13**	2	22	11	**29**	18	8	**25**	14	4	24	12	30
27	23	**12**	30	20	**8**	26	16	**5**	**24**	12	2	**21**	10	28	**17**	7	26	14	3	23	12	30	19	9	26	15	5	25	**13**	1
28	24	13	31	21	9	27	17	6	25	13	3	22	11	29	18	8	27	15	4	24	13	31	20	10	27	16	6	26	14	2
29	25	14	**1**	22	10	**28**	18	7	26	14	4	23	**12**	30	19	**9**	**28**	16	**5**	**25**	14	1	**21**	11	28	**17**	7	27	15	3
30	26	15	2	23	11	29	19	8	27	15	5	24	13	31	20	10	29	17	6	26	15	2	22	12	29	18	8	28	16	4

In the left-hand margin figures in **black type** denote major Holy-days; elsewhere they denote Sabbaths. 1st and 2nd, New Year; 3rd, Fast of Gedaliah (if on Sabbath, postponed to Sunday); 10th, Day of Atonement; 15th to 23rd, Tabernacles, etc.; 30th, First day of New Moon of Marcheshvan.

CALENDAR 5745–5774 (1984–2014)

CHESHVAN or MARCHESHVAN (29 or 30 days)

Figures in **black type** denote Sabbaths.
30th, First day of New Moon of Kislev.

CALENDAR 5745–5774 (1984–2014) 349

KISLEV (29 or 30 days)

Kis	5745 1984 Nov-Dec	46 85 Nov-Dec	47 86/87 Dec-Jan	48 87 Nov-Dec	49 88 Nov-Dec	50 89 Nov-Dec	51 90 Nov-Dec	52 91 Nov-Dec	53 92 Nov-Dec	54 93 Nov-Dec	55 94 Nov-Dec	56 95 Nov-Dec	57 96 Nov-Dec	58 97 Nov-Dec	59 98 Nov-Dec	60 99 Nov-Dec	61 2000 Nov-Dec	62 01 Nov-Dec	63 02 Nov-Dec	64 03 Nov-Dec	65 04 Nov-Dec	66 05 Dec	67 06 Nov-Dec	68 07 Nov-Dec	69 08 Nov-Dec	70 09 Nov-Dec	71 10 Nov-Dec	72 11 Nov-Dec	73 12 Nov-Dec	74 13 Nov-Dec
1	25	14	3	22	10	29	18	8	26	15	4	24	12	30	20	10	28	16	6	26	14	2	22	11	28	18	8	27	15	4
2	26	15	4	23	11	30	19	9	27	16	5	25	13	1	21	11	29	17	7	27	15	3	23	12	29	19	9	28	16	5
3	27	**16**	5	24	**12**	1	20	10	**28**	16	6	26	14	2	22	12	30	**17**	8	28	16	**3**	24	**13**	**30**	20	10	29	**17**	6
4	28	17	6	25	13	2	21	11	29	17	7	27	15	3	23	13	1	18	**9**	29	17	4	**25**	14	1	**21**	11	30	18	7
5	29	18	7	26	14	3	22	12	**30**	18	8	28	16	4	24	14	2	19	10	30	18	5	26	15	2	22	12	1	19	**8**
6	30	19	8	27	15	4	23	13	1	19	9	29	17	5	25	15	3	20	11	1	19	6	27	16	3	23	**13**	2	**20**	**9**
7	1	20	**9**	**28**	16	5	**24**	14	2	**20**	10	**30**	18	6	26	16	4	21	12	2	**20**	7	**28**	**17**	4	24	14	3	21	10
8	2	21	10	29	17	6	25	15	3	21	11	1	19	7	27	17	5	22	13	3	21	**8**	29	18	5	**25**	15	4	22	11
9	3	22	11	30	18	7	26	16	4	22	12	2	20	8	28	18	6	23	14	4	22	9	30	19	6	26	**16**	5	23	12
10	4	**23**	12	1	**19**	8	27	17	5	23	13	3	21	9	29	19	7	24	15	5	**23**	10	1	20	7	27	17	6	24	13
11	5	24	13	2	20	**9**	28	18	6	24	14	4	22	10	30	20	8	25	16	6	24	11	2	21	8	28	18	7	25	14
12	6	25	14	3	21	10	29	19	7	25	15	5	23	11	1	21	9	26	17	7	25	12	3	22	9	29	19	8	26	15
13	7	26	15	4	22	11	30	**20**	8	26	16	6	**24**	12	2	22	10	27	18	8	26	13	4	23	10	30	20	9	27	16
14	8	27	16	5	23	12	1	21	9	27	17	7	25	13	3	23	11	28	19	9	27	14	5	24	11	1	21	10	28	17
15	9	28	17	6	24	13	2	22	10	28	18	8	26	14	4	24	12	29	20	10	28	15	6	25	12	2	22	11	29	18
16	10	29	18	7	25	14	3	23	11	29	19	9	27	15	5	25	13	30	21	11	29	16	7	26	13	3	23	12	30	19
17	11	30	19	8	26	15	4	24	12	30	20	10	28	16	6	26	14	1	22	12	30	17	8	27	14	4	24	13	1	20
18	12	1	20	9	27	16	5	25	13	1	21	11	29	17	7	27	15	2	23	13	1	18	9	28	15	5	25	14	2	21
19	13	2	21	10	28	17	6	26	14	2	22	12	30	18	8	28	16	3	24	14	2	19	10	29	16	6	26	15	3	22
20	14	3	22	11	29	18	7	27	15	3	23	13	1	19	9	29	17	4	25	15	3	20	11	30	17	7	27	16	4	23
21	**15**	4	23	12	30	19	**8**	28	16	5	24	14	2	**20**	**10**	30	18	5	26	16	4	22	12	1	18	8	28	**17**	5	24
22	16	5	24	13	1	20	9	29	17	6	**25**	15	3	21	11	1	19	6	27	17	5	23	13	2	19	9	29	18	6	25
23	17	6	25	14	2	21	10	30	18	7	26	16	4	22	12	2	20	7	28	18	6	24	14	3	20	10	30	19	7	26
24	18	7	26	15	3	22	11	1	19	8	27	17	5	23	13	3	21	8	29	19	7	25	15	4	21	11	1	20	8	27
25	**19**	8	**27**	16	4	23	12	2	20	9	28	18	6	24	14	4	22	9	30	20	8	26	16	5	22	12	2	21	9	28
26	20	9	28	17	5	24	13	3	21	10	29	19	7	25	15	5	23	10	1	21	9	27	17	6	23	13	3	22	10	29
27	21	10	29	18	6	25	14	4	22	11	30	20	8	26	16	6	24	11	2	22	10	28	18	7	24	14	4	23	11	—
28	**22**	11	30	19	7	26	15	5	23	12	1	21	9	27	17	7	25	12	3	23	11	29	19	8	25	15	5	24	12	1
29	23	12	31	20	—	27	16	6	24	13	2	22	10	28	18	8	26	13	4	24	12	30	20	9	26	16	6	25	13	2
30	24	—	1	21	—	28	17	7	—	14	3	23	—	29	19	9	—	14	5	25	—	31	—	—	27	17	7	26	—	3

Figures in **black type** denote Sabbaths.
25th to 29th or 30th, Chanucah (opening days); 30th, First day of New Moon of Tebet.

TEBET (29 days)

CALENDAR 5745–5774 (1984–2014)

Figures in **black type** denote Sabbaths.
1st to 2nd or 3rd, Chanucah (final days); 10th, Fast of Tebet.

CALENDAR 5745–5774 (1984–2014) 351

CALENDAR 5745–5774 (1984–2014)

ADAR (29 days); in Leap Year, known as ADAR RISHON — 1st ADAR (30 days)

Adar	5745 1985 Feb-Mar	46 86 Feb-Mar	47 87 March	48 88 Feb-Mar	49 89 Feb-Mar	50 90 Feb-Mar	51 91 Feb-Mar	52 92 Feb-Mar	53 93 Feb-Mar	54 94 Feb-Mar	55 95 Feb-Mar	56 96 Feb-Mar	57 97 Feb-Mar	58 98 Feb-Mar	59 99 Feb-Mar	60 2000 Feb-Mar	61 01 Feb-Mar	62 02 Feb-Mar	63 03 Feb-Mar	64 04 Feb-Mar	65 05 Feb-Mar	66 06 March	67 07 Feb-Mar	68 08 Feb-Mar	69 09 Feb-Mar	70 10 Feb-Mar	71 11 Feb-Mar	72 12 Feb-Mar	73 13 Feb-Mar	74 14 Feb-Mar
1	22	10	2	19	6	26	15	5	22	12	1	21	8	27	17	7	24	13	3	23	10	1	19	7	25	15	5	24	11	1
2	23	11	3	20	7	27	16	6	23	13	2	22	9	28	18	8	25	14	4	24	11	2	20	8	26	16	6	25	12	2
3	24	12	4	21	8	28	17	7	24	14	3	23	10	1	19	9	26	15	5	25	12	3	21	9	27	17	7	26	13	3
4	25	13	5	22	9	1	18	8	25	15	4	24	11	2	20	10	27	16	6	26	13	4	22	10	28	18	8	27	14	4
5	26	14	6	23	10	2	19	9	26	16	5	25	12	3	21	11	28	17	7	27	14	5	23	11	1	19	9	28	15	5
6	27	15	7	24	11	3	20	10	27	17	6	26	13	4	22	12	1	18	8	28	15	6	24	12	2	20	10	29	16	6
7	28	16	8	25	12	4	21	11	28	18	7	27	14	5	23	13	2	19	9	29	16	7	25	13	3	21	11	1	17	7
8	1	17	9	26	13	5	22	12	1	19	8	28	15	6	24	14	3	20	10	1	17	8	26	14	4	22	12	2	18	8
9	2	18	10	27	14	6	23	13	2	20	9	29	16	7	25	15	4	21	11	2	18	9	27	15	5	23	13	3	19	9
10	3	19	11	28	15	7	24	14	3	21	10	1	17	8	26	16	5	22	12	3	19	10	28	16	6	24	14	4	20	10
11	4	20	12	29	16	8	25	15	4	22	11	2	18	9	27	17	6	23	13	4	20	11	1	17	7	25	15	5	21	11
12	5	21	13	1	17	9	26	16	5	23	12	3	19	10	28	18	7	24	14	5	21	12	2	18	8	26	16	6	22	12
13	6	22	14	2	18	10	27	17	6	24	13	4	20	11	1	19	8	25	15	6	22	13	3	19	9	27	17	7	23	13
14	7	23	15	3	19	11	28	18	7	25	14	5	21	12	2	20	9	26	16	7	23	14	4	20	10	28	18	8	24	14
15	8	24	16	4	20	12	29	19	8	26	15	6	22	13	3	21	10	27	17	8	24	15	5	21	11	1	19	9	25	15
16	9	25	17	5	21	13	1	20	9	27	16	7	23	14	4	22	11	28	18	9	25	16	6	22	12	2	20	10	26	16
17	10	26	18	6	22	14	2	21	10	28	17	8	24	15	5	23	12	1	19	10	26	17	7	23	13	3	21	11	27	17
18	11	27	19	7	23	15	3	22	11	29	18	9	25	16	6	24	13	2	20	11	27	18	8	24	14	4	22	12	28	18
19	12	28	20	8	24	16	4	23	12	1	19	10	26	17	7	25	14	3	21	12	28	19	9	25	15	5	23	13	29	19
20	13	R	21	9	25	17	5	24	13	2	20	11	27	18	8	R	15	4	22	13	R	20	10	26	16	6	24	14	1	20
21	14	2	22	10	26	18	7	25	14	4	21	12	28	19	9	27	16	5	23	14	2	21	11	27	17	7	25	15	3	21
22	15	3	23	11	27	19	8	26	15	5	22	13	1	20	10	28	17	6	24	15	3	22	12	28	18	8	26	16	4	22
23	16	4	24	12	28	20	9	27	16	6	23	14	2	21	11	29	18	7	25	16	4	23	13	1	19	9	27	17	5	23
24	17	5	25	13	1	21	10	28	17	7	24	15	3	22	12	1	19	8	26	17	5	24	14	2	20	10	28	18	6	24
25	18	6	26	14	2	22	11	29	18	8	25	16	4	23	13	2	20	9	27	18	6	25	15	3	21	11	1	19	7	25
26	19	7	27	15	3	23	12	1	19	9	26	17	5	24	14	3	21	10	28	19	7	26	16	4	22	12	2	20	8	26
27	20	8	28	16	4	24	13	2	20	10	27	18	6	25	15	4	22	11	1	20	8	27	17	5	23	13	3	21	9	27
28	21	9	29	17	5	25	14	3	21	11	28	19	7	26	16	5	23	12	2	21	9	28	18	6	24	14	4	22	10	28
29	22	10	30	18	6	26	15	4	22	12	R	20	8	27	17	6	24	13	3	22	10	29	19	7	25	15	5	23	11	R
30	3	R	—	—	7	R	—	5	—	R	—	—	9	—	—	7	—	4	—	23	11	—	—	R	—	—	6	—	—	R

Figures in **black type** denote Sabbaths.
13th, Fast of Esther (if on Sabbath, observed the preceding Thursday); 14th, Purim; 15th, Shushan Purim.
NOTE. — In a Jewish leap year, indicated by the letter R (for Adar Rishon) at the foot of a column, the above days are observed in 2nd Adar.
In a leap year, 30th day is First day of New Moon of the 2nd Adar.

CALENDAR 5745–5774 (1984–2014)   353

2nd ADAR — ADAR SHENI, also known as VE-ADAR (29 days)

5745	46	47	48	49	50	51	52	53	54	55	56	57	58	59	60	61	62	63	64	65	66	67	68	69	70	71	72	73	74	2nd Adar
1985	86	87	88	89	90	91	92	93	94	95	96	97	98	99	2000	01	02	03	04	05	06	07	08	09	10	11	12	13	14	
Mar-Apr	Mar-Apr			Mar-Apr			Mar-Apr			March		Mar-Apr			Mar-Apr			Mar-Apr		Mar-Apr			Mar-Apr			Mar-Apr			March	
	12			8			6			3		10			8			5		12			8			7			3	1
	13			9			7			4		11			9			6		13			9			8			4	2
	14			10			8			5		12			10			7		14			10			9			5	3
	15			**11**			9			6		13			**11**			**8**		15			11			10			6	4
	16			12			10			7		14			12			9		16			12			11			7	5
	17			13			11			**8**		**15**			13			10		17			13			**12**			**8**	6
	18			14			12			9		16			14			11		18			14			13			9	7
	19			**15**			13			10		17			**15**			12		**19**			**15**			14			10	8
	20			16			**14**			**11**		18			16			13		20			16			**15**			**11**	9
	21			17			15			12		19			17			14		21			17			16			12	10
	22			**18**			16			13		20			**18**			**15**		22			**18**			17			13	11
	23			19			17			14		21			19			16		23			19			18			14	12
	24			20			18			**15**		**22**			20			17		24			20			**19**			**15**	13
	25			21			19			16		23			21			18		**25**			**21**			20			16	14
	26			22			20			17		24			**22**			**19**		26			22			21			17	15
	27			**22**			21			**18**		25			23			20		27			23			22			18	16
	28			23			**22**			19		26			24			21		28			24			23			19	17
	29			24			23			20		**27**			25			**22**		**29**			**25**			24			20	18
	30			**25**			24			**21**		28			26			23		30			26			**25**			**21**	19
	31			26			25			22		**29**			27			24		31			**27**			26			**22**	20
	1			28			26			23		30			28			25		1			28			27			23	21
	2			**29**			**27**			**24**		31			**29**			26		2			**29**			28			24	22
	3			30			**28**			**25**		1			30			**27**		**3**			30			**29**			**25**	23
	4			31			29			26		2			31			28		4			31			30			26	24
	5			**1**			30			27		3			**1**			**29**		**5**			**1**			**31**			**27**	25
	6			2			31			28		4			2			30		6			2			1			28	26
	7			3			1			29		**5**			3			31		7			3			**2**			**29**	27
	8			4			2			30		6			4			1		8			4			3			30	28
	9			**5**			3			31		7			**5**			**2**		**9**			**5**			4			31	29

Figures in **black type** denote Sabbaths.
13th, Fast of Esther (if on Sabbath, observed on the preceding Thursday); 14th, Purim; 15th Shushan Purim.

NISAN (30 days)

	5745	46	47	48	49	50	51	52	53	54	55	56	57	58	59	60	61	62	63	64	65	66	67	68	69	70	71	72	73	74
	1985	86	87	88	89	90	91	92	93	94	95	96	97	98	99	2000	01	02	03	04	05	06	07	08	09	10	11	12	13	14
Nis	Mar-Apr	Apr-May	Mar-Apr	Mar-Apr	Apr-May	Mar-Apr	Mar-Apr	Apr-May	Mar-Apr	Mar-Apr	April	Mar-Apr	Apr-May	Mar-Apr	Mar-Apr	Apr-May	Mar-Apr	Mar-Apr	Apr-May	Mar-Apr	Apr-May	Mar-Apr	Mar-Apr	Apr-May	Mar-Apr	Mar-Apr	Apr-May	Mar-Apr	Mar-Apr	April
1	**23**	10	31	**19**	6	27	**16**	**4**	23	13	**1**	21	8	**28**	18	6	25	14	3	23	10	30	20	6	26	16	5	**24**	12	1
2	24	11	1	20	7	28	17	5	24	14	2	22	9	29	19	7	26	15	4	24	11	31	21	7	27	17	6	25	13	2
3	25	**12**	2	21	**8**	29	18	6	25	15	3	**23**	10	30	**20**	**8**	27	**16**	**5**	25	12	**1**	22	8	**28**	18	7	26	14	3
4	26	13	3	22	9	30	19	7	26	16	4	24	11	31	21	9	28	17	6	26	13	2	23	9	29	19	8	27	15	4
5	27	14	**4**	23	10	**31**	20	8	**27**	17	5	25	**12**	1	22	10	29	18	7	**27**	14	3	**24**	10	30	**20**	**9**	28	**16**	**5**
6	28	15	5	24	11	1	21	9	28	18	6	26	13	2	23	11	30	19	8	28	15	4	25	11	31	21	10	29	17	6
7	29	16	6	25	12	2	22	10	29	**19**	7	27	14	3	24	12	**31**	20	9	29	**16**	5	26	**12**	1	22	11	30	18	7
8	**30**	17	7	**26**	13	3	**23**	**11**	30	20	**8**	28	15	**4**	25	13	1	21	10	30	17	6	27	13	2	23	12	**31**	19	8
9	31	18	8	27	14	4	24	12	31	21	9	29	16	5	26	14	2	22	11	31	18	7	28	14	3	24	13	1	20	9
10	1	**19**	9	28	**15**	5	25	13	1	22	10	**30**	17	6	**27**	**15**	3	**23**	**12**	1	19	**8**	29	15	**4**	25	14	2	21	10
11	2	20	10	29	16	6	26	14	2	23	11	31	18	7	28	16	4	24	13	2	20	9	30	16	5	26	15	3	22	11
12	3	21	**11**	30	17	**7**	27	15	**3**	24	12	1	**19**	8	29	17	5	25	14	**3**	21	10	**31**	17	6	**27**	**16**	4	**23**	**12**
13	4	22	12	31	18	8	28	16	4	25	13	2	20	9	30	18	6	26	15	4	22	11	1	18	7	28	17	5	24	13
14	5	23	13	1	19	9	29	17	5	**26**	14	3	21	10	31	19	**7**	27	16	5	**23**	12	2	**19**	8	29	18	6	25	14
15	**6**	24	14	**2**	20	10	**30**	**18**	6	27	**15**	4	22	**11**	1	20	8	28	17	6	24	13	3	20	9	30	19	**7**	26	15
16	7	25	15	3	21	11	31	19	7	28	16	5	23	12	2	21	9	29	18	7	25	14	4	21	10	31	20	8	27	16
17	8	**26**	16	4	**22**	12	1	20	8	29	17	**6**	24	13	**3**	**22**	10	**30**	**19**	8	26	**15**	5	22	**11**	1	21	9	28	17
18	9	27	17	5	23	13	2	21	9	30	18	7	25	14	4	23	11	31	20	9	27	16	6	23	12	2	22	10	29	18
19	10	28	**18**	6	24	**14**	3	22	**10**	31	19	8	**26**	15	5	24	12	1	21	**10**	28	17	**7**	24	13	**3**	**23**	11	**30**	**19**
20	11	29	19	7	25	15	4	23	11	1	20	9	27	16	6	25	13	2	22	11	29	18	8	25	14	4	24	12	31	20
21	12	30	20	8	26	16	5	24	12	**2**	21	10	28	17	7	26	**14**	3	23	12	**30**	19	9	**26**	15	5	25	13	1	21
22	**13**	1	21	**9**	27	17	**6**	**25**	13	3	**22**	11	29	**18**	8	27	15	4	24	13	1	20	10	27	16	6	26	**14**	2	22
23	14	2	22	10	28	18	7	26	14	4	23	12	30	19	9	28	16	5	25	14	2	21	11	28	17	7	27	15	3	23
24	15	**3**	23	11	**29**	19	8	27	15	5	24	**13**	1	20	**10**	**29**	17	**6**	**26**	15	3	**22**	12	29	**18**	8	28	16	4	24
25	16	4	24	12	30	20	9	28	16	6	25	14	2	21	11	30	18	7	27	16	4	23	13	30	19	9	29	17	5	25
26	17	5	**25**	13	1	**21**	10	29	**17**	7	26	15	**3**	22	12	1	19	8	28	**17**	5	24	**14**	1	20	**10**	**30**	18	**6**	**26**
27	18	6	26	14	2	22	11	30	18	8	27	16	4	23	13	2	20	9	29	18	6	25	15	2	21	11	1	19	7	27
28	19	7	27	15	3	23	12	1	19	**9**	28	17	5	24	14	3	**21**	10	30	19	**7**	26	16	**3**	22	12	2	20	8	28
29	**20**	8	28	**16**	4	24	**13**	**2**	20	10	**29**	18	6	**25**	15	4	22	11	1	20	8	27	17	4	23	13	3	**21**	9	29
30	21	9	29	17	5	25	14	3	21	11	30	19	7	26	16	5	23	12	2	21	9	28	18	5	24	14	4	22	10	30

In the left-hand margin figures in **black type** denote major Holy-days; elsewhere they denote Sabbaths. 14th, Fast of the Firstborn (if on Sabbath, observed on the preceding Thursday); 15th to 22nd, Passover; 30th, First day of New Moon of Iyar.

CALENDAR 5745–5774 (1984–2014)

Figures in **black type** denote Sabbaths.
18th, 33rd Day Omer, Scholars' Festival.

SIVAN (30 days)

	5745	46	47	48	49	50	51	52	53	54	55	56	57	58	59
	1985	86	87	88	89	90	91	92	93	94	95	96	97	98	99
Sivan	May-Jn	Jn-July	May-Jn	May-Jn	Jn-July	May-Jn	May-Jn	Jn-July	May-Jn	May-Jn	May-Jn	May-Jn	Jn-July	May-Jn	May-Jn
1	21	8	29	17	4	25	14	2	21	11	30	19	6	26	16
2	22	9	**30**	18	5	**26**	15	3	**22**	12	31	20	**7**	27	17
3	23	10	31	19	6	27	16	4	23	13	1	21	8	28	18
4	24	11	1	20	7	28	17	5	24	**14**	2	22	9	29	19
5	**25**	12	2	**21**	8	29	**18**	**6**	25	15	**3**	23	10	**30**	20
6	26	13	3	22	9	30	19	7	26	16	4	24	11	31	21
7	27	**14**	4	23	**10**	31	20	8	27	17	5	**25**	12	1	**22**
8	28	15	5	24	11	1	21	9	28	18	6	26	13	2	23
9	29	16	**6**	25	12	**2**	22	10	**29**	19	7	27	**14**	3	24
10	30	17	7	26	13	3	23	11	30	20	8	28	15	4	25
11	31	18	8	27	14	4	24	12	31	**21**	9	29	16	5	26
12	**1**	19	9	**28**	15	5	**25**	**13**	1	22	**10**	30	17	**6**	27
13	2	20	10	29	16	6	26	14	2	23	11	31	18	7	28
14	3	**21**	11	30	**17**	7	27	15	3	24	12	**1**	19	8	**29**
15	4	22	12	31	18	8	28	16	4	25	13	2	20	9	30
16	5	23	**13**	1	19	**9**	29	17	**5**	26	14	3	**21**	10	31
17	6	24	14	2	20	10	30	18	6	27	15	4	22	11	1
18	7	25	15	3	21	11	31	19	7	**28**	16	5	23	12	2
19	**8**	26	16	**4**	22	12	**1**	**20**	8	29	**17**	6	24	**13**	3
20	9	27	17	5	23	13	2	21	9	30	18	7	25	14	4
21	10	**28**	18	6	**24**	14	3	22	10	31	19	**8**	26	15	**5**
22	11	29	19	7	25	15	4	23	11	1	20	9	27	16	6
23	12	30	**20**	8	26	**16**	5	24	**12**	2	21	10	**28**	17	7
24	13	1	21	9	27	17	6	25	13	3	22	11	29	18	8
25	14	2	22	10	28	18	7	26	14	**4**	23	12	30	19	9
26	**15**	3	23	**11**	29	19	**8**	**27**	15	5	**24**	13	1	**20**	10
27	16	4	24	12	30	20	9	28	16	6	25	14	2	21	11
28	17	**5**	25	13	**1**	21	10	29	17	7	26	**15**	3	22	**12**
29	18	6	26	14	2	22	11	30	18	8	27	16	4	23	13
30	19	7	**27**	15	3	**23**	12	1	**19**	9	28	17	**5**	24	14

	60	61	62	63	64	65	66	67	68	69	70	71	72	73	74
	2000	01	02	03	04	05	06	07	08	09	10	11	12	13	14
Sivan	Jn-July	May-Jn	May-Jn	June	May-Jn	Jn-July	May-Jn	May-Jn	Jn-July	May-Jn	May-Jn	Jn-July	May-Jn	May-Jn	May-Jn
1	4	23	12	1	21	8	28	18	4	24	14	3	22	10	30
2	5	24	13	2	**22**	9	29	**19**	5	25	**15**	**4**	23	**11**	**31**
3	6	25	14	3	23	10	30	20	6	26	16	5	24	12	1
4	7	**26**	15	4	24	**11**	31	21	**7**	27	17	6	25	13	2
5	8	27	16	5	25	12	1	22	8	28	18	7	**26**	14	3
6	9	28	17	6	26	13	2	23	9	29	19	8	27	15	4
7	**10**	29	**18**	**7**	27	14	**3**	24	10	**30**	20	9	28	16	5
8	11	30	19	8	28	15	4	25	11	31	21	10	29	17	6
9	12	31	20	9	**29**	16	5	**26**	12	1	**22**	**11**	30	**18**	**7**
10	13	1	21	10	30	17	6	27	13	2	23	12	31	19	8
11	14	**2**	22	11	31	**18**	7	28	**14**	3	24	13	1	20	9
12	15	3	23	12	1	19	8	29	15	4	25	14	**2**	21	10
13	16	4	24	13	2	20	9	30	16	5	26	15	3	22	11
14	**17**	5	**25**	**14**	3	21	**10**	31	17	**6**	27	16	4	23	12
15	18	6	26	15	4	22	11	1	18	7	28	17	5	24	13
16	19	7	27	16	**5**	23	12	**2**	19	8	**29**	**18**	6	**25**	**14**
17	20	8	28	17	6	24	13	3	20	9	30	19	7	26	15
18	21	**9**	29	18	7	**25**	14	4	**21**	10	31	20	8	27	16
19	22	10	30	19	8	26	15	5	22	11	1	21	**9**	28	17
20	23	11	31	20	9	27	16	6	23	12	2	22	10	29	18
21	**24**	12	**1**	**21**	10	28	**17**	7	24	**13**	3	23	11	30	19
22	25	13	2	22	11	29	18	8	25	14	4	24	12	31	20
23	26	14	3	23	**12**	30	19	**9**	26	15	**5**	**25**	13	**1**	**21**
24	27	15	4	24	13	1	20	10	27	16	6	26	14	2	22
25	28	**16**	5	25	14	**2**	21	11	**28**	17	7	27	15	3	23
26	29	17	6	26	15	3	22	12	29	18	8	28	**16**	4	24
27	30	18	7	27	16	4	23	13	30	19	9	29	17	5	25
28	**1**	19	**8**	**28**	17	5	**24**	14	1	**20**	10	30	18	6	26
29	2	20	9	29	18	6	25	15	2	21	11	1	19	7	27
30	3	21	10	30	**19**	7	26	**16**	3	22	**12**	**2**	20	**8**	**28**

In the left-hand margin figures in **black type** denote major Holy-days; elsewhere they denote Sabbaths.
6th and 7th, Pentecost; 30th, First day of New Moon of Tammuz.

CALENDAR 5745–5774 (1984–2014)

TAMMUZ (29 days)

Figures in **black type** denote Sabbaths.
17th, Fast of Tammuz (if on Sabbath, postponed to Sunday).

CALENDAR 5745–5774 (1984–2014)

AB (30 days)

Ab	5745 / 1985 / July-Au	46 / 86 / Au-Sep	47 / 87 / July-Au	48 / 88 / July-Au	49 / 89 / August	50 / 90 / July-Au	51 / 91 / July-Au	52 / 92 / July-Au	53 / 93 / July-Au	54 / 94 / July-Au	55 / 95 / July-Au	56 / 96 / July-Au	57 / 97 / Au-Sep	58 / 98 / July-Au	59 / 99 / July-Au	60 / 2000 / August	61 / 01 / July-Au	62 / 02 / July-Au	63 / 03 / July-Au	64 / 04 / July-Au	65 / 05 / Au-Sep	66 / 06 / July-Au	67 / 07 / July-Au	68 / 08 / August	69 / 09 / July-Au	70 / 10 / July-Au	71 / 11 / August	72 / 12 / July-Au	73 / 13 / July-Au	74 / 14 / July-Au
1	19	6	27	15	2	23	12	31	19	9	28	17	4	24	14	2	21	10	30	19	6	26	16	2	22	12	1	20	8	28
2	**20**	7	28	**16**	3	24	**13**	**1**	**20**	10	**29**	18	5	**25**	15	3	**22**	11	**31**	**20**	7	27	17	3	23	**13**	2	**21**	9	29
3	21	8	29	17	4	25	14	2	21	11	30	19	6	26	16	4	23	12	1	21	8	28	18	4	24	14	3	22	10	30
4	22	**9**	**30**	18	**5**	26	15	3	22	12	31	**20**	7	27	17	**5**	24	**13**	2	22	**9**	**29**	**19**	**5**	**25**	15	4	23	11	31
5	23	10	31	19	6	27	16	4	23	13	1	21	8	28	18	6	25	14	3	23	10	30	20	6	26	16	5	24	12	1
6	24	11	1	20	7	28	17	5	24	14	2	22	9	29	19	7	26	15	4	24	11	31	21	7	27	17	6	25	13	2
7	25	12	2	21	8	**28**	18	6	25	15	3	23	10	30	20	8	27	16	5	25	12	1	**22**	**8**	**28**	18	7	26	14	3
8	**26**	13	3	22	**9**	29	19	7	26	**16**	4	24	**11**	31	21	9	**28**	17	6	26	13	2	23	9	29	**19**	8	**27**	15	4
9	**27**	14	4	**23**	10	30	**20**	8	**27**	17	**5**	**25**	12	**1**	22	**10**	29	18	**7**	**27**	**14**	3	24	10	30	**20**	9	28	16	5
10	28	15	5	24	11	31	21	9	28	18	6	26	13	2	23	11	30	19	8	28	15	4	25	11	31	21	10	29	17	6
11	29	16	6	25	12	1	22	10	29	19	7	27	14	3	24	12	31	**20**	9	29	**16**	**5**	26	12	1	22	11	30	18	7
12	30	17	7	26	**13**	2	23	11	30	20	8	28	15	4	25	13	1	21	10	30	17	6	27	13	2	23	**12**	31	19	**8**
13	31	18	8	27	14	3	24	12	31	21	9	29	16	5	26	14	2	22	11	31	18	7	**28**	14	3	24	13	1	**20**	**9**
14	1	19	9	28	15	4	25	13	1	22	10	30	17	6	27	15	3	23	12	1	19	8	29	15	4	25	14	2	21	10
15	2	**20**	10	29	16	5	26	14	2	23	11	31	18	7	28	16	4	24	13	2	**20**	9	30	16	**5**	26	15	3	22	11
16	3	21	11	30	17	6	27	**15**	3	24	12	1	19	8	29	17	5	25	14	3	21	**10**	31	**17**	6	27	16	4	23	12
17	4	22	12	31	18	7	28	16	4	25	13	2	20	9	30	18	6	26	15	4	22	11	1	18	7	28	17	5	24	13
18	**5**	23	13	1	**19**	**28**	29	17	5	26	14	3	21	10	31	19	7	27	16	5	23	12	2	19	8	29	18	6	25	14
19	6	24	14	2	20	29	30	18	6	27	15	4	22	11	1	20	8	28	17	6	24	13	3	20	9	30	19	7	26	15
20	7	25	**15**	3	21	30	31	19	7	28	16	5	23	12	2	21	9	29	18	7	25	14	4	21	10	31	20	8	27	**16**
21	8	26	16	4	22	1	1	20	8	29	17	6	24	13	3	22	10	30	19	8	26	15	5	22	11	1	21	9	28	17
22	9	**27**	17	5	23	2	2	21	**9**	30	18	7	**25**	14	4	**23**	**11**	**31**	20	9	**27**	16	6	23	12	2	22	10	29	18
23	**10**	28	18	6	24	3	3	22	10	31	19	8	26	15	5	24	12	1	21	10	28	17	7	24	13	3	23	11	30	19
24	11	29	19	7	25	4	4	23	11	1	20	9	27	16	6	25	13	2	22	11	29	18	8	25	14	4	24	12	31	20
25	12	30	20	8	26	5	5	24	12	2	21	10	28	17	7	26	14	3	23	12	30	19	9	26	15	5	25	13	1	21
26	13	31	21	9	27	6	6	25	13	3	22	11	29	18	8	27	15	4	24	13	31	20	10	27	16	6	26	14	2	22
27	14	1	22	10	28	7	7	26	14	4	23	12	30	19	9	28	16	5	25	14	1	21	11	28	17	7	27	15	3	**23**
28	15	2	23	11	29	8	8	27	15	5	24	13	31	20	10	29	17	6	26	15	2	22	12	29	18	8	28	16	4	24
29	16	3	24	12	30	9	9	28	16	6	25	14	1	21	11	30	18	7	27	16	3	23	13	30	19	9	29	17	5	25
30	17	4	25	13	31	10	10	29	17	7	26	15	2	22	12	31	19	8	28	17	4	24	14	31	20	10	30	18	6	26

Figures in **black type** denote Sabbaths.
9th, Fast of Ab (if on Sabbath, postponed to Sunday); 30th, First Day of New Moon of Elul.

CALENDAR 5745–5774 (1984–2014)

INDEX

A

Abbeyfield (Camden)
  Society 93
Aberdeen (Scotland) ...130
Abridged Calendar
  1998 325
Abridged Calendar
  1999 326
Academic Study Group on
  Israel & Middle East ..24
ACJR 17
Adath Yisroel Burial
  Society 12
Adath Yisroel Synagogue .81
Adath Yisroel Tottenham
  Beth Hamedrash 81
Aden Jews'
  Congregation 85
Adelaide (Australia) 138
Admission of Jewish
  Ecclesiastical Officers,
  Advisory Committee
  for 61
Affiliated Synagogues,
  US 78
Federation 80
Afghanistan 135
Aged Needy Pension
  Society, Jewish 94
Agency for Jewish
  Education 35, 48
Agudas Harabbonim 59
Agudas Hashochtim
  v'Hashomrim 59
Agudas Israel 66
Agudas Israel Community
  Services 66
Agudus Israel Housing
  Assoc. 93
Ahavat Israel Synagogue .81
Ajex 62
  Housing Association ...93
  Military Museum 54
AJR Charitable Trust ...,17
AJY 46
Akim 25
Akiva School 89
Albania 135
Alderney Road
  Cemetery 89
Alexandria 147
Algeria 135
Aliyah Department of
  Jewish Agency 21
Alyn, Friends of 29
All Aboard Shops ...2, 100
All Party Parliamentary
  War Crimes Group 61
Alliance Israelite

Universelle 67, 149
Altmann Library 58
Alyth 86
Choral Society 98
American Jewish
  Committee 185
American Joint Distribution
  Committee 187
Amersham 102
Amsterdam 152
Anglo-German
  Cultural Forum 17
Anglo-Israel Archaeological
  Society 25
Anglo-Israel Association .25
Anglo-Jewish
  Archives 54, 56
Anglo-Jewish Association .3
Anne Frank Educational
  Trust 18
Antigua 135
Anti-Tuberculosis
  League, Friends of 30
Antwerp 139
Arbib Lucas Trust 93
Argentina 135
Argyle & Bute.
  See Dunoon
Armenia 136
Art Museums of Israel,
  Friends of 27
Aruba 136
Asia-Pacific Jewish
  Association 67, 137
Assaf Harofeh Medical
  Centre, Friends 27
Assembly of Masorti
  Synagogues 12, 82-83
Assembly of Rabbis
  (Reform) 12
Association for Jewish
  Youth 46
Association for Soldiers'
  Welfare 166
Association of Adath
  Yisroel Synagogues 11
Association of British
  Settlers 172
Association of Children
  of Jewish Refugees 17
Association of Jewish
  Communal
  Professionals 59
Association of Jewish
  Ex-Berliners 18
Association of Jewish
  Ex-Service Men &
  Women 61
Association of Jewish
  Friendship Clubs ...3, 98

Association of Jewish Golf
  Clubs & Societies 61
Association of Jewish
  Humanists 61
Association of Jewish
  Refugees 17
Association of Jewish
  Sixth-Formers 53
Association of Jewish
  Teachers 35
Association of Jewish
  Women's
  Organisations 3
Association of Ministers
  (Chazanim) of Great
  Britain 59
Association of Orthodox
  Jewish Professionals ...35
Association of Synagogue
  Secretaries (U.S.) 60
Association of United
  Synagogue Women 87
Athens 151
Auckland
  (New Zealand) 177
Australia 136-138
Austria 138
Authorisation of
  marriage - Office of
  Chief Rabbi 7
Avigdor Primary School ..90

B

Bachad Fellowship 50
Bahamas 139
Balfour Diamond Jubilee
  Trust 25
Bank Leumi (U.K.) 25
Bank of Israel 166
Bar-Ilan University 164
  Friends of 29
Barbados 139
Barcelona 182
Barking & Becontree
  Synagogue 78
Barkingside Progressive
  Synagogue 86
Barmitzvah Dates ..346-359
Barnet Synagogue 78
Baronets 207
Basle 183
Basildon 102
Bath 102
Baths, Ritual. See Mikvaot
Bedford 102
Beit Klal Yisrael 86
Belfast 133
Belgium 139
Belgrade 189

INDEX 361

Belmont Synagogue 76
Belsize Square Synagogue 83
Ben Gurion University ..164
 Foundation 26
Ben Uri Arts Society 54
Bereavement Counselling 94
Bermuda 140
Berne 183
Bernhard Baron St. George's
 Jewish Settlement 98
Besht Tellers 98
Betar-Tagar 50
Beth Abraham
 Synagogue 81
Beth Chodos Synagogue .81
Beth Din (U.S.) 7
Beth Din (Federation) ...11
Beth Din (Reform) 12
Beth Din (Sephardi) 10
Beth Hamedrash
 Beis Nadvorna 81
Beth Hamedrash
 D'Chasidey Belz 81
Beth Hamedrash
 D'Chasidey Gur 81
Beth Hamedrash
 D'Chasidey Ryzin 81
Beth Hamedrash D'Chasidey
 Sans-Klausenburg 81
Beth Hamedrash
 D'Chasidey Square 81
Beth Hamedrash
 Divrei Chaim 81
Beth Hamedrash
 Hendon 81
Beth Hamedrash
 Heshaim 84
Beth Hamedrash Imrey
 Chaim D'Chasidey
 Vishnitz-Monsey 81
Beth Hamedrash
 Ohel Naphtoli 81
Beth Hamedrash
 Torah Etz Chaim 81
Beth Hamedrash
 Torah Chaim Liege 81
Beth Hamedrash
 Yetiv Lev 82
Beth Hammidrash
 Library 55
Beth Hatefutsoth 166
Beth Holim 83
Beth Israel (Trisker)
 Synagogue 82
Beth Jacov Movement ...65
Beth Shalom Holocaust
 Memorial 35, 121
Beth Shmuel Synagogue .82
Beth Sholom Synagogue .82
Beth Talmud Centre 82
Beth Yisochor Dov Beth
 Hamedrash 82
Bevis Marks 84

Bikur Cholim Hospital,
 Jerusalem, British
 Committee for 30
Binoh Centre for Special
 Jewish Education 90
Bipac, Britain-Israel
 Public Affairs Centre ...26
Birkath Yehuda Beth
 Hamedrash 82
Birmingham 103
Blackpool 103
Blind, Jewish Homes for .94
Blind Society, Jewish 95
B'nai B'rith 67
B'nai B'rith Hillel
 Foundation 53
B'nai B'rith Housing
 Society 93
B'nai B'rith Jewish
 Music Festival 39
B'nai B'rith Youth
 Organisation 47
Bnei Akiva 50
Bnei Brak Hospital,
 British Committee of ..26
Board for Shechita
 (London) 88
Board of Deputies 1-2
Bodleian Library 55
Bognor Regis 104
Bolivia 140
Bonds, State of Israel 34
Bonn (Sir Max) Memorial
 Youth Centre 49
Booksellers 320-321
Borehamwood &
 Elstree Synagogue 76
Bosnia Hercegovina ...140
Botgi, British Overseas
 Trade Group of Israel ..29
Bournemouth 104
Boys' Town Jerusalem,
 Friends of 30
Bradford 105
Brady-Maccabi Centre ...98
Brady Street Cemetery ..89
Bratislava 180
Brazil 140
Bridge Lane Beth
 Hamedrash 81
Brighton & Hove 105
Brijnet 7
Brisbane 138
Bristol 106
Britain-Israel Public
 Affairs Centre 26
British Academy,
 Fellows of 208
British Aliya Movement ..20
British Association for
 Ethiopian Jewry 68
British Association for
 Jewish Studies 43

British Council for Jews
 in Eastern Europe 19
British Emunah 20
British & European
 Machal 26
British Israel Arts
 Foundation 28
British-Israel Chamber of
 Commerce 28
British-Israel Forum 28
British-Israel
 Parliamentary Group ..29
British Jewry, historical
 note 197
British Library (Hebrew
 Department) 55
British Olim Relatives
 Association (Bora) 20
British Olim Society ...172
British ORT 13
British Overseas
 Trade Group 29
British Settlements in
 Israel 168-172
British Tay-Sachs
 Foundation 14
British Technion
 Society 29
British Video Archive ...37
British Wizo 21
Bromley Reform
 Synagogue 86
Brotherton Library,
 Leeds 55
Brussels 139
Bucharest 179
Budapest 154
Buenos Aires 136
Bulawayo 190
Bulgaria 141
Bullscross Ride
 Cemetery 83, 89
Burial Societies:
 Adath Yisroel 12
 Federation 10, 80
 Liberal & Reform 85
 Sephardi 84
 United Synagogue, ..8, 79
 West End Great 83
Burma 141
Bushey Cemetery 89
Bushey & District
 Synagogue 76
Byelorus 141

C

Cairo 147
Calendar 323
Calendar for 1998 318
Calendar for 1999 319
Calendar for 30
 years 346-359

INDEX

Cambridge 106
Cambridge University
  Library 55
Campaign for the
  Protection of Shechita..61
Canada 142-143
Canberra 138
Canterbury 107
Cape Town 182
Cardiff 129
Casablanca 176
Catford and Bromley
  Synagogue 78
Cayman Islands 143
CBF 13
Celebrities Guild of
  Great Britain 62
Cemeteries (London) .89-90
  Federation 81
  Liberal 87
  Reform 85
  Sephardi 85
  United 79
  West End Great 83
  Western 84
Cemeteries, Disused,
  The Regions 102
Central Council for
  Jewish Community
  Services 14
Central Enquiry Desk
  and Communal Diary ...3
Central Lecture
  Committee, Board
  of Deputies 1
Central Mikvaoth Board .88
Central Synagogue 76
Centre for German-Jewish
  Studies 43
Centre for Jewish Art ..164
Centre for Jewish
  Education (CJE) 35
Centre for Jewish Studies
  (Leeds) 43
  (Univ. London) 43
Centre for Modern
  Hebrew Studies 43
Centre for the Study of
  Judaism and Jewish-
  Christian Relations 36
Ceuta 182
Chabad Lubavitch
  Centre 98
Chai-Lifeline 14
Chamber of Commerce:
  British-Israel 27
  Israel-British 166
Channel Islands 133
Chaplain to the
  Forces 9, 303
Chatham 107
Chelmsford 107
Chelsea Synagogue 78

Cheltenham 107
Chester 107
Chief Rabbinate
  (British) 7
  (Israel) 167
Chief Rabbinate
  Council 7
Chief Rabbi's Office (and
  for the authorisation of
  marriages) 7
Chigwell & Hainault
  Synagogue 76
Child Resettlement Fund:
  Emunah 20
Children and Youth
  Aliyah Committee 21
Children's Country
  Holidays Fund
  (Jewish Branch) 96
Chile 143
Chiltern Progressive
  Synagogue 87
China 144
Chingford. See Highams
  Park & Chingford
Christians and Jews,
  Council of 3
International
  Council of 71
Christians, London
  Society of Jews and ...101
Circumcision 9, 13
City of London
  Regiment Memorial ...88
CJE 36
Clapton Synagogue 79
Clayhall Synagogue 76
Clifton College,
  Polack's House 41
Club 1943 18
Clubs and Cultural
  Societies (London) ...98
Cockfosters and North
  Southgate Synagogue ..76
Cohen Scholarship Trust
  Fund, Alfred Louis 9
Colchester 107
Colombia 144
Commonwealth of
  Independent States ...144
Commonwealth Jewish
  Council 68
  Trust 68
Communal Diary 2
Community Research
  Unit, Board of
  Deputies.............1
Companions of Honour 209
Conference of European
  Rabbis 68
Conference on Jewish
  Material Claims
  against Germany 68

Congregation of Jacob ..80
Conjoint Passover Flour
  Committee 8, 9
Connect: Jewish
  Marriage Bureau 62
Conservative Friends of
  Israel 29
Constituent Synagogues,
  Federation 79
Constituent Synagogues,
  U.S. 76
Consultative Council of
  Jewish Organisations ..69
Copenhagen 147
Cordoba (Argentina) ...135
Cork 134
Costa Rica 144
Council of Reform &
  Liberal Rabbis 13
Council of Christians &
  Jews 3
Council of Jews from
  Germany 18
Counselling Services: See
  Welfare Organisations;
  See also:
  Bereavement 94
  Chai-Lifeline 14
  Get Advisory Service ..14
  Jewish AIDS Trust 14
  Jewish Bereavement
  Counselling 94
  Jewish Care 94
  Jewish Crisis Helpline..96
  Jewish Information
  Services 2, 7
  Jewish Lesbian & Gay
  Helpline 14
  Jewish Marriage
  Council 15
  Jewish Women's Aid ...15
  Miyad 97
  Operation Judaism 64
  Raphael Centre 97
  Tay Sachs Screening
  Centre 17
Court of the Chief
  Rabbi (Beth Din) 7
Coventry 107
Cracow 178
Crawley 108
Cricklewood Synagogue .76
Croatia 145
Croydon Synagogue 79
Cuba 146
Cultural Societies
  (London) 98
Cultural Societies, Jewish
  Association of 99
Curaçao 146
Cyprus 146
Czech Memorial Scrolls
  Centre 62

INDEX 363

Czech Republic 146

D

Damascus 184
Darlington 108
Dames 208
Davar 36
David Ishag Synagogue . . 85
Deaf Association Jewish . 96
Defence Committee (of
 Board of Deputies) 1
Delissa Joseph Memorial
 Fund. See Necessitous
 Ladies Fund
Denmark 147
Deputies, Board of 1-2
Discount Bank Ltd 32
Discount Bank of New
 York 32
Dollis Hill Synagogue . . . 76
Dominican Republic . . . 147
Dror 51
Drugsline 93
Dublin 134
Dundee 131
Dunoon 131
Dunstable. See Luton
Dvar Yerushalayim 36

E

Ealing Liberal
 Synagogue 87
Ealing Synagogue 76
East Grinstead 108
East Ham Cemetery 89
East London Central
 Synagogue 79
East European Jewish
 Heritage Project 19
Eastbourne 108
Eastern Jewry Community
 (London) 85
Ecuador 147
Edgware Adath Yisroel
 Synagogue 83
Edgware Masorti
 Synagogue 83
Edgware Reform
 Synagogue 86
Edgware Synagogue 76
Edgwarebury Cemeteries 89
Edinburgh 131
Edinburgh House 85
Edmonton Cemetery . . . 89
Education and Youth
 Committee, Board of
 Deputies 1
Education and Youth
 Department, Reform
 Synagogues of Great
 Britain 49

Educational
 Organisations 35-46
Educational Organisations
 (London) 89-93
Egypt 147
Elm Park Synagogue . . . 78
Elstree. See Borehamwood
Emunah 20
Enfield & Winchmore
 Hill Synagogue 78
Enfield Cemetery 89
English Speaking Residents
 Assoc. (ESRA) 172
Enquiry Desk, Central . . . 3
Estonia 147
Ethiopia 148
European Association for
 Jewish Studies 69
European Community,
 Israeli representation
 with 158
European Council of
 Jewish Communities . . . 69
European Jewish Forum . 69
European Jewish
 Publication Society . . . 69
European Parliament,
 Members of 206
European Rabbis,
 Conference of 68
European Union of
 Jewish Students 69
Evening Institute of
 ULPS 37
Evening Twilight
 Variation Table 341
Exeter 108
Exhibition Centre,
 Jewish Community 57
Exhibitions, Museums
 & Libraries 54-59
Exodus 2000 19
Ex-Service Men & Women,
 Association of Jewish . . 62
Ezra Youth Movement . . . 51
Ezrath Nashim Hospital . 28

F

Falasha Welfare
 Association 68
Federation of Jewish
 Relief Organisations . . . 29
Federation of
 Synagogues 11, 79-80
Federation of Women
 Zionists 20
Federation of Zionist
 Youth 51
Festivals & Fasts 322
Fieldgate Street
 Synagogue 80
Fiji Islands 148

Finchley Central
 Synagogue 80
Finchley Kosher Lunch
 Service 94
Finchley Progressive
 Synagogue 87
Finchley Reform
 Synagogue 86
Finchley Road
 Synagogue 80, 82
Finchley Synagogue 76
Finland 148
Finsbury Park
 Synagogue 76
Finnart House School
 Trust 14
Food for the Jewish
 Poor 94
45 Aid Society 17
France 148-150
French Synagogue
 (London) 83
Friendly Societies/
 Jewish 63
Friends of Assaf Harofeh
 Medical Centre 27
Friends of Israel:
 Conservative 29
 Labour 33
 Liberal Democrat 33
Friends of the Hebrew
 University 30
Friends of the Kingsbury
 Mikveh 94
Friends of Israel Aged
 (Re'uth) 30
Friends of Israel Cancer
 Association 31
Friends of Israel
 Educational Trust 30
Friends of Israel Free
 Loan Association 26
Friends of Jewish Youth . . 98
Friends of the Sick 94
Friends of Yiddish 36
Friendship Clubs
 Association of Jewish . . . 3
Friendship with Israel
 (European Parliament) . . 70

G

Gan Aviv Kindergarten . . 90
Garden Suburb Beth
 Hamedrash 82
Gateshead 108
General Federation of
 Jewish Labour 163
General Zionist
 Organisation 21
Geneva 183
Genizah Research Unit . . 56
George Crosses, Jewish . 209

INDEX

Germany 150
Germany, Council of
  Jews from 17
Get Advisory Service 14
Gibraltar 151
Glasgow 131-133
Goldbloom (Hebrew Studies
  Department) J.F.S.
  Comprehensive School .91
Golders Green Beth
  Hamedrash
  Congregation 83
Golders Green
  Synagogue 76
Grand Order of Israel &
  Shield of David 63
Greater London Radio ... 6
Greece 151
Greenford Synagogue ... 80
Grimsby 109
Group Relations
  Committee (of Board of
  Deputies) 1
Guatemala 152
Guernsey
  (Channel Islands) 133
Guild of Jewish
  Journalists 59
Guildford 109

H

Habonim-Dror 51
Hackney Cemetery 89
Hackney & East
  London Synagogue 76
Hadassah Medical Relief
  Association United
  Kingdom 31-32
Haendler (Nathan &
  Adolphe) charity 16
Haftarot and Sidrot for
  1999 342-343
Hagadolim Charitable
  Organisation 94
Haifa University 164
  Friends of 27
Haiti 152
Half-Empty Bookcase ... 99
Hamashbir Hamerkazi .. 31
Hammersmith & West
  Kensington Synagogue .76
Hammerson, Lewis, Home
  for Elderly People 96
Hampstead Garden
  Suburb Synagogue 77
Hampstead Reform
  Synagogue 86
Hampstead Synagogue .. 77
Hanoar Hatzioni 52
Harare 190
Harlow 109
Harold Hill Synagogue .. 78

Harold House
  (Liverpool) 114
Harrogate 109
Harrow Progressive
  Synagogue 87
Harry & Abe Sherman Rosh
  Pinah Primary School .. 92
Harry Rosencweig
  Collection (of Jewish
  Music) 55
Hartley Library,
  Southampton 55
Hashomer Hatzair 52
Hasmonean Schools 90
Hastings 109
Hatch End Jewish
  Community 86
Haven Foundation 94
Hebrew University 163
  Friends of 30
Hebreware User Group .. 70
Heimler International ... 70
Helen Lucas Fund. See Arbib
  Lucas Fund
Help Lines: See Counselling
  Services; Welfare
  Organisations
Hemel Hempstead
  Synagogue 78, 109
Hendon Adath Yisroel
  Synagogue 82
Hendon Reform
  Synagogue 86
Hendon Synagogue 77
H.M. Forces Jewish
  Committee for 8, 9
Hereford 109
Hertsmere Progressive
  Congregation 87
Herut Movement
  (Great Britain) 21
Hias 70
High Seas Sailing Club .. 62
High Wycombe 78, 109
Highams Park and
  Chingford Synagogue .. 78
Highgate Synagogue 77
Hillel Brodetsky Library .56
Hillel Foundation 53
Historical note on
  British Jewry 197
Holland 152
Holland Park
  Synagogue 85
Holocaust
  Education Trust 37
  Memorials ... 36, 88, 121
  Stanley Burton Centre .46
  Survivors' Centre 18
Holyland Philatelic
  Society 32
Home for Aged Jews 97
Homes (Jewish Care) .95-96

Homes for Jewish
  Children, Norwood ... 97
Homes for the Blind,
  Jewish 94
Homes for Handicapped
  Jewish Children 97
Honduras 153
Hong Kong 153
Hoop Lane Cemetery ... 89
Hospital Kosher Meals
  Service 94
Hospital Visitors Branch,
  Visitation Committee .101
Hounslow Synagogue ... 78
Hove. See Brighton
Hull 110
Hungary 154

I

IJPR 70
Ilford Congregation
  (Sephardi) 85
Ilford Federation
  Synagogue 80
Ilford Jewish Schools .90, 91
Ilford Synagogue 77
Immanuel College 90
Independent
  Congregations
  (London) 83
Independent Jewish Day
  School 90
India 154
Indonesia 154
Information Committee,
  Board of Deputies 1
Information Services 7
Initiation Society 9
Institute for Jewish Music
  Studies and Performance.99
Institute for Jewish Policy
  Research (IJPR) 71
Research Library 56
Institute of Community
  Relations 62
Institute of Contemporary
  History 56
Institute of Jewish
  Studies 43
International Association
  of Jewish Lawyers
  & Jurists 71
International Council
  of Christians & Jews .. 71
International Council
  of Jewish Women 71
International Council
  on Jewish Social and
  Welfare Services 72
International Jewish
  Genealogical
  Resources 72

INDEX 365

International Jewish
 Vegetarian Society 72
International
 Organisations 66-75
Iran 155
Iranian Jews in Great
 Britain, Committee for .18
Iraq 155
Ireland, Northern 133
Ireland, Republic of ...134
Isle of Man 133
Israel 155-173
 British Immigrant
  Offices 172
 British Settlements 168-171
 Chief Rabbinate 167
 Commercial
  Organisations 166
 Educational and Research
  Institutions 163-165
 Embassies and
  Legations 158-162
 London 21
 Government 156
 Knesset 157
 Political Parties 162
 President 157
Israel Action 32
Israel Aged, Friends of ...30
Israel Britain and the
 Commonwealth Assoc.
 (IBCA) 172
Israel-British Chamber
 of Commerce 166
Israel Cancer Association,
 Friends of 30
Israel Discount Bank Ltd. 32
Israel Discount Bank of
 New York 32
Israel Educational Trust,
 Friends of 30
Israel Embassy (London) ..21
Israel Folk Dance
 Institute 37
Israel Free Loan
 Association, British
 Friends of 27
Israel Government Tourist
 Office 32
Israel Information 21
Israel Institute of
 Technology 163
Israel–Judaica Stamp
 Club 32
Israel Labour Party 162
Israel Museum 167
Israel, Organisations
 concerned with 24-35
Israel Philatelic Agency
 in Great Britain 32
Israel Philharmonic
 Orchestra, British
 Friends of 27

Israel War Disabled,
 British Friends of 27
Israel Zangwill
 Fellowship 37
Israel Zangwill
 Memorial Fund 37
Israeli Embassies and
 Legations 21, 158-162
Istanbul 185
Italy 173
"It's Kosher" 7

J

Jacob Benjamin Elias
 Synagogue 85
J.A.C.S...............99
Jamaica 173
Japan 173
J.A.T. 37
JBD 94
J.B.G. Housing Society ..94
J.C.A. Charitable
 Foundation 72
JCi 7
Jersey 133
Jerusalem Academy Trust
 (JAT) 37
Jerusalem College of
 Technology 165
 Friends of 31
Jerusalem Rubin Academy
 of Music, Friends of ...31
Jewish Aged Needy
 Pension Society.......94
Jewish Agency for
 Israel 21, 167
Jewish AIDS Trust 14
Jewish Appreciation
 Group Tours 99
Jewish Association for
 Business Ethics 63
Jewish Association for
 the Mentally Ill 15
Jewish Association for
 the Physically
 Handicapped 94
Jewish Association of
 Cultural Societies 99
Jewish Association of
 Spiritual Healers 63
Jewish Bereavement
 Counselling Service ...94
Jewish Blind and
 Disabled 94
Jewish Blind Society 95
Jewish Blind in Israel
 Association 33
Jewish Book Council 37
Jewish Book List ..314-319
Jewish Calendar 323
Jewish Calendar for 30
 years 346

Jewish Care 95-96
Jewish Children's
 Holiday Fund 96
Jewish Child's Day 15
Jewish Chronicle
 Newspaper 5, 38
Jewish Colonization
 Association 72
Jewish Committee for
 H.M. Forces 8, 9
Jewish Communal
 Marriage Bureau 62
Jewish Communal
 Professionals
 Association 59
Jewish Community
 Exhibition Centre 56
Jewish Community
 Information (JCi) 7
Jewish Community
 Services,
 Central Council for ...13
Jewish Community
 Theatre 38
Jewish Council for
 Racial Equality 63
Jewish Crisis Helpline ...96
Jewish Deaf Association .96
Jewish Defence and
 Group Relations
 Committee 1
Jewish Documentation
 Centre (Paris) 149
Jewish Education Aid
 Society 38
Jewish Educational
 Development Trust 38
Jewish Ex-Service Men
 and Women,
 Association of 61
Jewish Feminist Group ..63
Jewish Film Foundation .38
Jewish Friendly
 Societies 63
Jewish Friendship Clubs,
 Association of 3
Jewish Genealogical
 Society 38
Jewish Guide Advisory
 Council 47
Jewish Historical
 Society of England 38
Jewish Homes for the
 Blind 94
Jewish Information
 Services 5
Central Enquiry Desk ...3
Jewish Journalists,
 Guild of 59
Jewish Lads' and Girls'
 Brigade 47
Jewish Learning
 Exchange 47

INDEX

Jewish Lesbian and Gay
  Helpline 15
Jewish Marriage Council .15
Jewish Medical Society,
  London 101
Jewish Memorial
  Council 9
Jewish Museum 56
Jewish Music Festival ...39
Jewish Music Heritage
  Trust 39
Jewish National Fund ...21
  Charitable Trust 22
  Education Dept. ...22, 47
  Younger J.N.F. 53
Jewish Nurses & Midwives
  Association 60
Jewish Press (United
  Kingdom) 5-6
Jewish Programme
  Materials Project
  (JPMP) 48
Jewish Radio
  Programmes 6
Jewish Reconstructionist
  Federation 72, 186
Jewish Relief and
  Education Trust
  (JRET) 20
Jewish Representative
  Councils (United
  Kingdom) 2-3
Jewish Research Group ..99
Jewish Resource Centre ..90
Jewish Scout Advisory
  Council 48
Jewish Secondary
  Schools' Movement ...91
Jewish Society for the
  Mentally
  Handicapped 96
Jewish Statistics ...191-196
Jewish Students,
  Union of 54
Jewish Students, World
  Union of 74
Jewish Studies Library,
  UCL 57
Jewish Telephone Crisis
  Line (Miyad) 97
Jewish Vegetarian
  Society 72
Jewish Welfare Board ...96
Jewish Women,
  International
  Council of 71
Jewish Women,
  League of 4
Jewish Women's Aid
  (JWA) 15
Jewish Women's
  Organisations,
  Association of 3

Jewish Youth, Association
  for 46
Jewish Youth Fund 48
Jewish Youth Orchestra ..48
Jewish Youth,
  Organisations concerned
  with 46-53
Jewish Youth Study
  Groups 48
Jews & Christians, London
  Society of 101
Jews' College 44
  Library 57
Jews' Free School 91
Jews of Zambia Project ..72
Jews' Temporary Shelter .96
J.F.S. (Comprehensive
  School) 91
JMC Bookshop 10
Joe Loss Research
  Fellowship 39, 44
Johannesburg 181
John Rylands University of
  Manchester Library ...57
Joint Authority for Jewish/
  Zionist Education 52
Joint Kashrus Committee ..12
Jordan is Palestine
  Committee (United
  Kingdom) 73
Journalists,
  Guild of Jewish 59
JPMP 48
Judaica Philatelic Society .32
Judith Lady Montefiore
  College 84

K

Kadimah-Victoria Youth
  Club 99
Kehal Chasidim
  Synagogue 82
Kedassia: see Joint
  Kashrus Committee
Kenton Synagogue 77
Kenya 174
Kerem Schools 91
Keren Hatorah Library ...58
Keren Kayemeth Le Israel
 167
Keren Yaldenu, British
  Committee of 26
Kesher 39
Kibbutzim, British ..168-171
Kibbutz Representatives .52
Kidmah 52
King Solomon School ..91
Kingsbury Road
  Cemetery 89
Kingsbury Synagogue ...77
Kingston Liberal
  Synagogue 87

Kingston & Surbiton
  Synagogue 78
Kisharon 91
K.K.L. Executor &
  Trustee Co. 22
Knesset 157
Knightland Road
  Synagogue 82
Knights 207
Kol-Chai – Hatch End
  Jewish Community 86
Kosher Meals Services ...94
Kressel Collection
  Oxford (Archive and
  Library) 58

L

Labour Friends of Israel .33
Labour Zionist
  Movement 22
Latvia 174
Lauderdale Road
  Synagogue 84
Lausanne 183
Law of Truth
  Talmudical College 91
League of Jewish
  Women 4
Leamington 110
Lebanon 174
Leeds 110-113
Legislation, United Kingdom,
  concerning Jews ..200-203
Leicester 113
Leo Baeck College 39
  Library 58
Leo Baeck Institute 40
Leopold Muller Memorial
  Library 58
Leytonstone & Wanstead
  Synagogue 80
Liberal Democrat
  Friends of Israel 33
Liberal Jewish Cemetery .89
Liberal Jewish
  Synagogue 87
Liberal & Progressive
  Synagogues,
  Union of 12, 86-87
Libraries, Museums &
  Exhibitions 54-59
Libya 174
Licensing of Shochetim,
  Rabbinical
  Commission for 10
Life Peers 206
Lifeline for the Old 33
Likud (Alliance) Bloc ...162
Likud-Herut Movement .22
Limmud 40
Lincoln 113
Lisbon 179

INDEX 367

Listed Buildings (UK) 204-205
Lithuania 174
Littman Library 40
Liverpool 113-115
Living Memory of the Jewish Community 58
Llandudno 130
London 76-101
London Academy of Jewish Studies 40
London Beth Din - See Beth Din (U.S.)
London Board for Shechita 88
London Diary of Jewish Events 98
London Jewish Academy .36
London Jewish Housing Committee 93
London Jewish Male Choir 99
London Jewish Medical Society 101
London Jewish Music Centre 39, 99
London Museum of Jewish Life 56
London Society of Jews & Christians 101
Loughton and Chigwell Synagogue 80
Lubavitch Foundation ... 91
Lubavitch Lending Library 58
Lubavitch of South London 99
Lubavitch Synagogue 82
Lucas Trust. See Arbib Lucas Trust
Lusaka 190
Luton 115
Luxembourg 174

M

Maccabeans, The 99
Maccabi, Brady, Centre .. 98
Maccabi Associations, Union of 49
Maccabi World Union ... 73
Machal Association 25
Machzikei Hadath Synagogue 80
Madrid 182
Magen David Adom, Friends of 31
Maidenhead 115
Maidstone 115
Maimonides Foundation .63
Majorca 182
Malaga 182
Malta 175

Manchester 115-120
Manor House Centre for Psychotherapy & Counselling 16
Manor House Media 40
Manor House Society ... 99
Manor House Sternberg Centre for Judaism 13
Manufacturers' Association of Israel .. 166
Mapam (United Kingdom) 22
Young 53
Marble Arch Synagogue .78
Margate 120
Margulies Library 57
Marriage Bureau, Jewish Communal 62
Marriage Regulations .. 344
Marriage, Authorisation of 7
Masorti Academy 40
Assembly of Synagogues .. 12, 82-83
Massoret see MST
Mathilda Marks-Kennedy School 92
Mauritius 175
Mazal Tov 16
Medical Aid Committee for Israel .. 33
Medical Society, London Jewish 101
Melbourne 138
Melilla 182
Member of European Parliament 206
Members of Parliament .206
Memorial Foundation for Jewish Culture 73
Memorial to Jewish Servicemen & Women .88
Memorials 88
Menorah Foundation School 92
Menorah Grammar School for Boys 92
Menorah Primary School 92
Mentally Handicapped, Jewish Society for 96
Merthyr Tydfil 130
Mesifta Synagogue 82
Mexico 175
Michael Goulston Educational Foundation .. 41
Michael Sobell House ... 96
Michael Sobell Sinai School 92
Middlesbrough 121
Middlesex New Synagogue (Reform) ... 86

Midrashia, Friends of ... 31
Mikvaot 88, 102
Milan 173
Mile End Road Cemetery 89
Mill Hill Synagogue 77
Milton Keynes 121
Minsk 142
Mishcon Library 57
Miyad 97
Mizrachi-Hapoel Hamizrachi Federation .. 22
Mocatta Library & Museum 57
Mohelim 8, 13
Moldova 175
Monash Branch, Royal British Legion 64
Montagu Jewish Community Trust 64
Montefiore (Judith, Lady) College 84
Montefiore (Sir Moses) Synagogue 84, 109
Montefiore Endowment Committee 84
Montevideo 188
Morocco 175
Moscow 144
Mozambique 176
MST 92
Multiple Sclerosis Aid Group 97
Museum of Jewish East End 56
Museums, Libraries & Exhibitions 54-59
Muswell Hill Synagogue .77

N

Nairobi 174
Naima Jewish Preparatory School 92
Nathan & Adolphe Haendler Charity 16
National Council for Soviet Jewry 20
National Council of Shechita Boards 10
National Life Story Collection 58
National Religious Party 162
National Tay Sachs Centre 17
National Zionist Council .23
Necessitous Ladies' Fund .97
Ner Yisrael Synagogue ... 83
Netherlands. See Holland
Netzer/Reform Synagogues of Great Britain 49
Neveh Shalom Community 85

INDEX

New Essex Masorti
  Congregation 83
New Israel Fund of
  Great Britain 33
New London Synagogue .82
New North London
  Synagogue 83
New Synagogue 77
New West End
  Synagogue 77
New Whetstone
  Synagogue 83
New Wimbledon and
  Putney Synagogue 80
New York 185
New Zealand 176
New Zealand, Zionist
  Federation 172, 176
Newark 121
Newbury Park
  Synagogue 77
Newcastle upon Tyne ..121
Newport (Gwent) 130
Nightingale House 97
Noam (Noar Masorti) ...49
Nobel Prize Winners ...209
North Finchley Synagogue.
  See Woodside Park
  Synagogue
North Hendon Adath
  Synagogue 82
North London Progressive
  Synagogue 87
North-West London
  Jewish Day School 92
North-West Surrey
  Synagogue (Reform) ...86
North-Western Reform
  Synagogue 86
North Yemen 177
Northampton 122
Northern Ireland 133
Northwood and Pinner
  Liberal Synagogue 87
Northwood Synagogue ..77
Norway 177
Norwich 122
Norwood Child Care ...97
Norwood Ravenswood ..97
Notting Hill Synagogue ..80
Nottingham 122

O

Obituary 310-311
Ohel David Synagogue ..85
Ohel Israel Synagogue ...82
Ohel Jacob Beth
  Hamedrash 80
Ombudsman 13
Operation Judaism 64
Operation Wheelchairs
  Committee 34

Organisations Concerned
  with Soviet Jewry ..19-20
Order of Merit 209
ORT 13, 74, 165
ORT House Conference
  Centre 4
Orthodox Hebrew
  Congregations, Union of .11
Otto Schiff Housing
  Association 16
Oxford 123
Oxford Centre for Hebrew
  & Jewish Studies 45
Oxford Institute for
  Yiddish Studies 45
Oxford & St. George's
  Jewish Centre 100

P

Pakistan 177
Palmers Green &
  Southgate Synagogue ..77
Panama 177
Paraguay 178
Pardes House Schools ...92
Paris 148
Parkes Library 55
Parliament, Members of 206
Passover Flour,
  Conjoint Committee 8
Peers 206
Pensions Fund, Jewish
  Memorial Council 9
Persian Synagogue
  (London) 85
Perth (Australia) 138
Peru 178
Peterborough 79, 123
Philatelists, British
  Association of
  Palestine-Israel 32
Philippines 178
Physically Handicapped,
  Jewish Association for
  the 94
Pinner Synagogue 77
Plashet Cemetery 89
Plymouth 123
Poale Agudat Israel 34
Poale Zion 23
Polack's House, Clifton
  College 41
Poland 178
Polish-Jewish Ex-
  Servicemen's
  Association 19
Polish Jewish Refugee
  Fund 19
Populations,
  Jewish 191-196
Porath Yosef Synagogue ..83
Porton Library 58

Portsmouth 123
Portugal 179
Post-graduate Hebrew
  Studies, Oxford Centre
  for 45
Potters Bar
  Synagogue 79, 124
Prague 146
Press................5
Preston 124
Prisoners' Memorial 88
Privy Counsellors 206
Pro-Zion: Progressive
  Religious Zionists 23
Professional
  Organisations 59-60
Progressive Jewish Marriage
  Bureau 16
Progressive Jews for
  Israel 32
Progressive Judaism
  World Union for 74
Progressive Judaism in
  Israel & in Europe,
  Friends of 31
Progressive Synagogues,
  Union of Liberal and ..12
Project SEED Europe ...41
Provincial Hebrew
  Classes Committee 9
Provincial Jewish
  Ministers' Fund 60
Public Schools'
  Committee 9
Puerto Rico 179

Q

QMW Programme for
  Yiddish & Ashkenazic
  Studies 45
Queen's Elm Parade
  Cemetery 89
Quito 147

R

Rabbinic Conference
  (Liberal) 13, 60
Rabbinical Commission
  for the Licensing of
  Shochetim 10
Rabbinical Council of
  East London and West
  Essex 60
Rabbinical Council of
  the Provinces 60
Rabbinical Council of
  United Synagogue 60
Rabbinical Court
  (Reform) 12
Radio Programmes
  (U.K.) 6

Radio Sussex 6
Radlett 77, 86, 124
Rainham Cemetery 89
Rambam Medical Centre,
 British Friends of 28
Ramsgate 84
Raphael Centre 97
Rav Rashi (Federation) . .10
Ravenswood Foundation.
 See Norwood
 Ravenswood
Reading 124
Redbridge Jewish
 Programme &
 Materials Project 100
Redbridge Jewish Youth &
 Community Centre . . .100
Redhill (see Reigate)
Reform Foundation 12
Reform & Liberal
 Association of
 Mohalim 13
Reform Synagogues of
 Great Britain . . 11, 85-86
Reform Synagogue
 Youth/Netzer 49
Refugee
 Organisations 17-19
Refugees, Association of
 Jewish 17
Reigate & Redhill 124
Religious Instruction at
 Schools 43
Religious Organisations
 (U.K.) 7-13
Religious Organisations,
 London 87
Representative Councils . .2
Representative
 Organisations 1-4
Research Unit, Board of
 Deputies 1
Richmond Synagogue . . .77
Riga 174
Rio de Janeiro 141
Rishon Multiple
 Sclerosis Aid Group . . .97
Ritual Baths 88
Romania 179
Rome 173
Romford Synagogue 79
Rosario (Argentina) 135
Rosh Pina Jewish
 Schools 92
Roth Collection 56
Rowan Road Cemetery . .89
Royal British Legion
 Monash Branch 64
Royal Fusiliers
 Memorial 88
Royal Society, Fellows . .208
R.S.G.B. 12
RSGB Students 41

RSY-Netzer 49
Ruislip Synagogue 79
Russia 144

S

Sabbath Observance
 Employment Bureau . . .88
St. Albans 79, 83, 124
St. Anne's-on-Sea 125
St. John's Wood
 Synagogue 77
St. Petersburg 144
Salford. See Manchester
San Jose 145
Sandy's Row Synagogue .83
Santiago (Chile) 143
Santo Domingo 147
Sao Paulo 141
Sarah Herzog Memorial
 Hospital, British
 Friends 28
Sarajevo 140
Scandinavian Zionist
 Federation 172
Scholarships, Jewish
 Memorial Council 9
Schonfeld Square
 Development 93
School of Oriental &
 African Studies 46
 Library 58
Schools & Colleges. See
 Educational Organisations
Schools, Sabbath
 Observance in 89
Scopus Jewish Educational
 Trust 41, 92, 112, 114
Scotland 130-133
Scottish Jewish Archives 130
Sebba Rosh Pina
 Nursery School 92
Sephardi Burial Society . .84
Sephardi Centre 42
 Library 59
Sephardi Communal
 Centre 84
Sephardi Kashrut
 Authority 84
Sephardi Refugees,
 Friends of 85
Sephardi Synagogues 84
Sephardi Welfare Board . .84
Settlement Synagogue . . .86
Shaare Zedek Medical
 Centre, Jerusalem,
 British Council of 27
Shamir Organisation . . .166
SHAPE International
 Jewish Community 73
Sharon Kindergarten 92
Shatnez Centre Trust 64
Shechita Board, London .88

Shechita Boards,
 National Council of . . .10
Shechita Committee,
 Board of Deputies 1
Sheffield 124
Shelter,
 Jews' Temporary 96
Sherman, Harry & Abe,
 Rosh Pinah Jewish
 Primary School 92
Shochetim, Rabbinical
 Commission for the
 Licensing of 9
Shomerim,
 Association of 59
Shomrei Hadath
 Synagogue 80
Sidrot and Haftarot for
 1999 342-343
Silver Street Cemetery . . .89
Simon Marks Jewish
 Primary School 92
Simon Wiesenthal Centre,
 European Office 73
Sinai Synagogue 80
Sinclair House 100
Singapore 179
Singer's Prayer Book
 Publication
 Committee 10
Sir Max Bonn Memorial
 Centre 49
Sir Moses Montefiore
 Synagogue 84, 109
Sixth-Formers,
 Association of Jewish . .53
Slovakia 180
Slovenia 180
Small Communities
 Committee of Jewish
 Memorial Council 10
SOAS 46
 Library 58
Society for Jewish Study .42
Society of Friends of
 Jewish Refugees 19
Society of Friends of the
 Torah 66
Solihull 125
South Africa 180-182
South Bucks Liberal
 Jewish Community . . .102
South Hampshire Reform
 Jewish Community . . .128
South Hampstead
 Synagogue 77
South Korea 182
South London
 Communal Council . . .60
South London Liberal
 Synagogue 87
South London
 Synagogue 77

INDEX

South Shields 125
South Tottenham
  Synagogue 77
South-West Essex
  Reform Synagogue 86
Southampton 125
Southend &
  Westcliff 126-127
Southgate Progressive
  Synagogue 87
Southgate Reform
  Synagogue 86
Southgate Synagogue,
  Palmers Green and 77
Southport 127
Southsea. See Portsmouth
Soviet Jewry, National
  Council for 19
Spain 182
Spanish & Portuguese Jews'
  Congregation ..10, 84-85
  Archive 59
Spec Jewish Youth &
  Community Centre ...100
Spectrum (Radio) 6
Spiro Institute 42
Springboard Education
  Trust 42
Springfield Synagogue ...80
Sri Lanka 182
Staines 79, 128
Stamford Hill Beth
  Hamedrash 80
Stamford Hill
  Community Centre 97
Stanislowa Beth
  Hamedrash 82
Stanley Burton Centre
  for Holocaust Studies ..46
Stanmore & Canons
  Park Synagogue 78
State of Israel Bonds 34
Statistical & Demographic
  Research Unit, Board
  of Deputies 1
Statistics, Jewish ...191-195
Stepney Jewish B'nai
  B'rith Clubs and
  Settlement 100
**Sternberg Centre for
Judaism** 13
  Other organisations
  located at this address:
  Council of Reform &
    Liberal Rabbis 13
  Israel Action 32
  Leo Baeck College .40, 58
  London Museum of
    Jewish Life 58
  Manor House Centre for
    Psychotherapy &
    Counselling 15
  Manor House Media ..41

Manor House Society ..99
Michael Goulston
  Educational
  Foundation 41
Pro-Zion: Progressive
  Religious Zionists ...23
Reform & Liberal
  Association of
  Mohalim 13
Reform Synagogues of
  Great Britain 12, 85
Reform Synagogue
  Youth/Netzer 49
Stockholm 183
Stoke-on-Trent 128
Students Jewish,
  organisations
  concerned with 53-54
Students,
  Union of Jewish 54
Students, World Union
  of Jewish 74
Sukkath Shalom Reform
  Synagogue 86
Sunderland 128
Sunridge Housing
  Association 97
Surinam 182
Sutton Synagogue 79
Swansea 130
Sweden 183
Swindon 128
Switzerland 183
Sydney, Australia 137
Synagogue Française de
  Londres 83
Synagogue Secretaries'
  Association 60
Syria 184

T

Taiwan 184
Tay-Sachs Screening
  Centre 17
Taylor-Schechter
  Geniza Collection.
  See Cambridge
Technion 163
Technion Society, British..28
Tehilla 34
Tehran 155
Tel Aviv University 165
Trust 34
Temporary Shelter, Jews .96
Thailand 184
Thames Valley Progressive
  Jewish Community
  (Reading) 124
Thanet & District Reform
  Jewish Community
  (Margate) 120

The 35s 20
Three Faiths Forum 4
Torah Centre Trust 92
Torquay (Torbay) 128
Tottenham Congregation
  and Talmud Torah 80
Trade Union Friends of
  Israel 34
Trades Advisory Council ..1
Trinidad 184
Tunisia 184
Turkey 185
Tzedek 64

U

UJIA 23, 172
UK Society for the
  Protection of Nature
  in Israel 34
Ukraine 185
ULPS 13, 86-87
  Evening Institute 36
  Youth Dept. 49
Union of Jewish
  Students 54
  Progressive Synagogues
  (ULPS) 13
Union of Maccabi
  Associations 50
Union of Orthodox
  Hebrew
  Congregations 11, 81
United Kingdom Jewish
  Aid and International
  Development
  (UKJAID) 64
United Kingdom
  Legislation
  Concerning Jews .200-203
United Mizrahi Bank
  Ltd. 35
United Nations
  (Jewish Organisations
  with consultative
  status) 66
United Nations, Israel
  Representations at ...158
United States of
  America 185-188
United Synagogue .8, 76-79
United Synagogue
  Secretaries'
  Association 60
United Synagogue
  Women,
  Association of 87
University Centres &
  Orgs. 43-47
University College
  London 46
University Jewish
  Chaplaincy Board 54

INDEX

University Scholarships ...9
Uruguay 188

V

Venezuela 189
Victoria Community
 Centre 99
Victoria Crosses, Jewish 208
Vienna 138
Vilnius 174
Virgin Islands 189
Visitation Committee 8, 101
Hospital Visitors
 Branch 101

W

Wales 129
Waley Cohen Memorial
 Scholarship,
 Sir Robert 9
Walford Road
 Synagogue 83
Wallasey 129
Waltham Abbey
 Cemetery 89
Waltham Forest
 Synagogue 83
Wanstead & Woodford
 Synagogue 79
Warsaw.............178
Watford Synagogue.....78
Waverley Manor 95
Weizmann Institute,
 Rehovot 164
Foundation 35
Welfare Organisations
 (London).......93-97
 (U.K.) 13-17
Wellington
 (New Zealand) 177
Welwyn Garden
 City 79, 129
Wembley Sephardi
 Synagogue 84
Wembley Synagogue 78
West Central Liberal
 Jewish Synagogue 87
West End Great
 Synagogue 83
West Hackney
 Synagogue 80
West Ham Cemetery 89
West Ham & Upton Park
 Synagogue 78
West London
 Synagogue 85
Westcliff. See Southend
Western Charitable
 Foundation 100
Western Marble Arch
 Synagogue 78, 84

Western Synagogue
 Cemetery 89
Westlon Housing
 Association 98
Westlon Trust 98
Westminster Synagogue..84
Westmount Charitable
 Trust 98
Westmount Housing
 Association 98
Whitley Bay 129
Who's Who 210-309
Wiener Library 56
Willesden &
 Brondesbury
 Synagogue 78
Willesden Cemetery 89
Wimbledon Synagogue
 (Reform) 86
Wimbledon, New
 Synagogue
 (Federation) 80
Winchester 129
Windsor 128
Wingate Institute......165
Wingate Youth Trust 54
WIZO 21
Wolfson Hillel Primary
 School 92
Wolverhampton 129
Women, International
 Council of Jewish 70
Women,
 League of Jewish 4
Women Zionists,
 Federation of 21
Women's Campaign for
 Soviet Jewry (The 35s) .20
Women's International
 Zionist
 Organisation 21, 167
Women's Organisations
 (UK)
 Association of Jewish
 Ex-Service Men &
 Women 61
 Association of
 Jewish Women's
 Organisations 3
 Association of
 United Synagogue
 Women 87
Ezrath Nashim
 Hospital 27
Federation of Women
 Zionists 21
Half-Empty Bookcase ..99
Jewish Feminist Group ..63
Jewish Nurses & Midwives
 Association 60
Jewish Women's Aid ...15
League of Jewish
 Women 4

The 35s 20
Women Zionists,
 Federation of 21
Women's Organisations,
 Association of Jewish ...3
Woodford Progressive
 Synagogue 87
Woodside Park
 Synagogue 78
Woolwich Synagogue ...80
Working Party on
 Jewish Archives in
 the United Kingdom &
 Ireland 5
Working Party on Jewish
 Monuments in the UK
 & Ireland 5
World Council of
 Conservative/Masorti
 Synagogues.........73
World Jewish Congress..74
World Jewish Relief 17
World ORT Union 74
World Union for
 Progressive Judaism ...74
World Union of Jewish
 Students 74
World Zionist
 Organisation 23, 167
Youth & Hechalutz
 Department 24

Y

Yad Sarah, Friends of 31
Yad Vashem 168
Committee, Board of
 Deputies............1
Yad Voezer 98
Yahrzeit Dates 346-359
Yakar Study Centre 42
Yarnton Manor 44
Yavneh Synagogue 80
Year, The Jewish 324
Yeshiva Etz Chaim 93
Yeshiva Gedola 93
Yeshiva Horomoh Beth
 Hamedrash 82
Yeshuath Chaim
 Synagogue 82
Yeshurun Synagogue ...80
Yesodey Hatorah Schools..93
Yesodey Hatorah
 Synagogue 82
Yiddish, Friends of 37
Yiddish Studies:
 Oxford 45
 QMW 46
 SOAS 46
 UCL 44, 57
York 129
"You Don't Have to be
 Jewish" 7

Young Jewish
  National Fund 53
Young Mapam 53
Youth Aliyah, Children
  and 21
Youth & Hechalutz
  Department, World
  Zionist Organisation ...24
Youth, Organisations
  concerned with
  Jewish 46-53
Yugoslavia (Serbia) 189

Z

Zaire 189
Zagreb 145
Zambia 190
Zangwill (Israel)
  Fellowship 37
Zangwill (Israel)
  Memorial Fund 37
Zemel Choir 100
Zimbabwe 190
Zinman College of
  Physical Education ...165
Zionist Federation of
  Great Britain &
  Ireland 24
Zionist Organisation,
  World 167
Zionist Organisations ..20-24
Zionist Youth Groups
 50-53
Zionist Youth,
  Federation of 50
Zurich 183

BELSEN IN HISTORY AND MEMORY
Jo Reilly, David Cesarani,
Tony Kushner and Colin Richmond (Eds)
272 pages 1997
0 7146 4767 5   cloth   £35.00/$47.50
0 7146 4323 8   paper   £15.00/$22.50

IN THE SHADOW OF THE HOLOCAUST AND THE INQUISITION
Israel's Relations with Francoist Spain
Raanan Rein
288 pages 1997
0 7146 4796 9   cloth   £32.50/$42.50
0 7146 4351 3   paper   £14.50/$18.50

THE HOUSE ON GARIBALDI STREET
Isser Harel
Introduction by Shlomo Shpiro
328 pages 1997
0 7146 4754 3   cloth   £27.50/$37.50
0 7146 4315 7   paper   £14.95/$18.50

REUVEN SHILOAH – THE MAN BEHIND THE MOSSAD
Secret Diplomacy in the Creation of Israel
Haggai Eshed
Forewords by Shimon Peres and Haim Herzog
Afterword by Yoav Gelber
368 pages 1997
0 7146 4812 4   cloth   £39.50/$57.50
0 7146 4361 0   paper   £19.50/$27.50

FROM RABIN TO NETANYAHU
Israel's Troubled Agenda
Efraim Karsh (Ed)
328 pages 1997
0 7146 4831 0   cloth   £35.00/$49.50
0 7146 4383 1   paper   £18.00/$24.00

FABRICATING ISRAELI HISTORY
The 'New Historians'
Efraim Karsh
232 pages 1997
0 7146 4725 X   cloth   £25.00/$35.00
0 7146 4274 6   paper   £13.50/$17.50

ABBA HILLEL SILVER AND AMERICAN ZIONISM
Mark A Raider, Jonathan D Sarna and Ronald W Zweig (Eds)
136 pages 1997
0 7146 4824 8   cloth   £29.50/$37.50
0 7146 4377 7   paper   £14.50/$19.50

THE JEWISH EXODUS FROM IRAQ, 1948–51
Moshe Gat
224 pages 1997
0 7146 4689 X   cloth   £35.00/$47.50
0 7146 4223 1   paper   £16.00/$18.50

RUSSIAN JEWS ON THREE CONTINENTS
Migration and Resettlement
Noah Lewin-Epstein, Yaacov Ro'i and Paul Ritterband (Eds)
568 pages 1997
0 7146 4726 8   cloth   £47.50/$64.50
0 7146 4276 2   paper   £24.50/$29.50

JEWISH-TRANSJORDANIAN RELATIONS 1921–48
Yoav Gelber
336 pages 1997
0 7146 4675 X   cloth   £37.50/$49.50
0 7146 4206 1   paper   £19.50/$25.00

A CHINA DIARY
Towards the Establishment of China-Israel Diplomatic Relations
E Zev Sufott
168 pages 1997
0 7146 4721 7   cloth   £29.50/$39.50
0 7146 4271 1   paper   £14.50/$18.50

Frank Cass Publishers

Newbury House, 900 Eastern Avenue, Ilford, Essex, IG2 7HH
Tel: +44 (0)181 599 8866 Fax: +44 (0)181 599 0984
North America: c/o ISBS, 5804 NE Hassalo Street, Portland OR 97213 3644
Tel: 1 800 944 6190 Fax: 503 280 8832
Website: http://www.frankcass.com E-mail: sales@frankcass.com

An Avenue of Memories
The Story of 58 Avenue Road
HANA RAVIV
Introduced by ISRAEL FINESTEIN

Hana Raviv, wife of the departing Israeli Ambassador, tells the remarkable story of a house which belonged to one of the most influential Anglo-Jewish families of its times and which, over the last hundred years, has been an integral part of the history of the Anglo-Jewish community, Zionism and the State of Israel. The Bentwich family was instrumental in the popularization of Herzl's political thought and their house served as a hub of Zionist activity in the early part of this century.

The Story of the last fifty years is told through an engaging account of each Israeli Ambassador and his family, and some of the historic events which took place in the residence throughout the years. Mrs Raviv explores how each family brought their own personality to the house and ultimately left their mark on it.

100 pages illustrated March 1998
ISBN 0 85303 343 9 cloth £19.50 ❖ ISBN 0 85303 344 7 paper c £12.50

Surviving the Holocaust with the Russian Jewish Partisans
JACK KAGAN and DOV COHEN

Two cousins recall in vivid detail their participation with the all-Jewish partisan group and describe life in pre-war Novogrodek, in modern day Belarus.

192 pages 85 photographs
ISBN 0 85303 336 6 hardback £25.00 ❖ ISBN 0 85303 335 8 paperback £14.50

Tales of Old Sarajevo
ISAK SAMOKOVLIJA

Isak Samokovlija, the 'Sholom Aleichem' of Sephardic Jewry, is introduced to English readers for the first time in this edition.

192 pages 11 illustrations
ISBN 0 85303 332 3 hardback £24.00 ❖ ISBN 0 85303 331 5 paperback £13.50

Vallentine Mitchell
UK AND OVERSEAS ORDERS TO:
Vallentine Mitchell, Newbury House, 900 Eastern Avenue, London IG2 7HH, England
Tel: +44(0)181 599 8866 Fax: +44(0)181 599 0984 E-Mail: info@vmbooks.com
US AND NORTH AMERICA ORDERS:
c/o ISBS, 5804 NE Hassalo Street, Portland, OR 97213-3644, USA
Tel: (503) 287-3093, (800) 944 6190 Fax: (503) 280-8832 E-mail: orders@isbs.com

Athens in Jerusalem
Classical Antiquity and Hellenism in the Making of the Modern Secular Jew
Yaacov Shavit

A wide-ranging discussion of how 'Hellenistic' ideas have shaped Jews' attitudes to themselves and the world around them and have influenced the nature of modern Jewish secular-national culture.

576 pages 1–874774–25–0 £45.00

Jewish Hymnography
A Literary History
Leon J. Weinberger

'It is a blessing to have in English such a felicitous treatment of the fruits of modern Israeli scholarship on *Piyyut* or Jewish hymnography incorporated into the author's own prodigious research.... The work is the best introduction in English to the whole subject.... It is bound to encourage scholars of English-speaking universities to mount courses in this heretofore neglected area of Hebrew poetry. The lack of a good textbook can no longer serve as an excuse.'
Reuven Kimelman

492 pages 1–874774–30–7 £45.00

Paperbacks

Studies in East European Jewish Mysticism and Hasidism
Joseph Weiss
Edited by David Goldstein
With a new Introduction by Joseph Dan

A classic for all those interested in Jewish religious developments in Eastern Europe, this paperback has a new introduction locating Weiss's work in the context of contemporary scholarship and the current resurgence of hasidism.

296 pages, paperback 1–874774–32–3 £14.95

Hasidism Reappraised
Edited by Ada Rapoport-Albert

'An opportunity to encounter virtually all the most important trends in the study of hasidism and move beyond the approaches and theories that have until now constituted conventional wisdom... essential for anyone with a serious interest in hasidism and indeed for any Judaica collection.'
Miles Krassen, Journal of Jewish Studies

'Comprehensive indeed, and profound, articulate, often gripping, and frequently counter to conventional wisdom ... a reflection of major watersheds in the study of hasidism.' *Lewis Glinert, Le'ela*

528 pages, paperback 1–874774–35–8 £24.95

The Littman Library of Jewish Civilization

At last: we reveal the secret of our unparalleled care.

If you think they resemble ordinary people, look again. This handful of individuals represents the 4,000 glittering stars of Jewish Care, where committed professionals and volunteers combine to provide 16 residential homes, 5 community centres, 5 special day care centres for people with Alzheimer's Disease, 6 sheltered homes for people with mental health problems, a locally based social work service and 3 specialist centres catering for problems from acute mental distress to unemployment. And there are stroke clubs and home visiting services, a Holocaust Survivors' Centre and kosher meals on wheels. And more and more.

Anglo-Jewry's largest social services organisation is Anglo-Jewry's largest source of pride. For more information, please call 0181 922 2000 and find out why we can justifiably say, without any fear of contradiction, *nobody cares like Jewish Care.*

Nobody cares like Jewish Care.

JEWISH CARE REGISTERED OFFICE: STUART YOUNG HOUSE 221 GOLDERS GREEN ROAD LONDON NW11 9DQ. TELEPHONE: 0181 922 2000 FAX: 0181 922 1998. CHARITY REGISTRATION NUMBER 802559. JEWISH CARE - A COMPANY LIMITED BY GUARANTEE. REGISTERED IN ENGLAND NUMBER 2447900.